Genetics, environment and intelligence

Genetics, environment and intelligence

Edited by

A. Oliverio

Institute of Psychology, University of Rome
and Laboratory of Psychobiology and Psychopharmacology
Via Reno 1, Rome
Italy

1977

NORTH-HOLLAND PUBLISHING COMPANY
AMSTERDAM · NEW YORK · OXFORD

PUBLISHERS
Elsevier/North-Holland Biomedical Press
335 Jan van Galenstraat, P.O. Box 211
Amsterdam, The Netherlands

SOLE DISTRIBUTORS FOR THE U.S.A. AND CANADA
Elsevier/North-Holland, Inc.
52 Vanderbilt Avenue
New York, N.Y. 10017, U.S.A.

Library of Congress Cataloging in Publication Data
     Main entry under title:

Genetics, environment, and intelligence.

     Includes bibliographies and index.
     1. Nature and nurture.   2. Intellect.
I. Oliverio, Alberto. [DNLM: 1. Genetics, Behavioral.
2. Social environment.   3. Intelligence. QH457 G325]
BF341.G43   153.9′2   77-23083
ISBN 0-7204-0644-7

Printed in The Netherlands

Contents

PART I

THE MEANING OF A COMPARATIVE APPROACH: INTERSPECIFIC APPROACH

E. W. Caspari   Introduction   Nature and function of genetic material
The genic control of behavior   Applications of genetics
to behavioral studies

J. A. King   Introduction   An "adaptive" behavior: digging   The
optokinetic reflex in visual acuity   Learning: an abstraction   Feeding strategies   Discussion and conclusion

PART II

GENETIC ASPECTS OF LEARNING AND BEHAVIOR IN ANIMALS

Introduction

ALBERTO OLIVERIO

More than ten years ago Fuller and Thompson in "Behavior Genetics" (1960) provided a valuable introduction to behaviour genetics and an excellent coverage of a field which was just at its beginning. Interest in behavioural genetics has grown rapidly in recent years: this growth is connected partly to the use of powerful new techniques of analysis and of animal models, partly to a new burst of interest in the nature and nurture controversy, in the genetic and environmental aspects of different types of intelligent behaviours.

A number of reviews, chapters and books on this topic indicate that in the last ten years discussion on this topic has been very lively: it will suffice to indicate here the books by Hirsch (1967), Parsons (1967), Spuhler (1967), Glass (1968), Lerner (1968), Vandenberg (1968), Manosevitz et al. (1969), Lindzey and Thiessen (1970), Robinson (1970), Thiessen (1970), Rosenthal (1971), Larmat (1973), Reuchlin (1973), van Abeelen (1974), Fedorov and Ponomarenko (1975), Ehrman and Parson (1976).

The large number of contributions on this topic also shows that there are different approaches to this subject: behaviour genetics, born as a science which was mostly centred on animals (insects and rodents) became involved with a number of human problems ranging from chromosome or hereditary metabolic diseases to the "IQ controversy", or to racial differences in behaviour.

Despite many criticisms the rôle of behaviour genetics has been mostly positive: the psychogenetic approach has been a bridge between the biological and the psychological sciences in its underlining the importance of behaviour as a phenotype within an evolutionary framework.

A phenotype, and therefore any kind of behavioural activity such as intelligence, must be considered as the expression of a given genotype within a given environment. Similarly, one must remember that when a geneticist speaks of an inherited trait, he refers not to a characteristic of an individual but to the difference between individuals or populations: from this follows that a particular trait may have a different distribution in two populations.

Finally, we should remember that heritability must be considered in terms of the context in which a genetic system acts: the genotype, the population, the environment. These considerations may appear naïve to some readers but the real meaning of these concepts has not been taken into serious consideration by a number of people dealing with the problem of the genetics of intelligence and in particular with the IQ problem in relation to race: the theories proposed by Jensen (1969), Eysenck (1971) or Schockley (1972) are at best biased by an inappropriate consideration of the real mechanisms of inheritance, of population genetics, of the rôle determined by the ontogenetic environment in the phenotypic development of each genotype.

In this book, we consider intelligence from different points of view: from a comparative, evolutionary approach, from the point of view of animal behaviour, from an ontogenetic standpoint, from a sociocultural and socioeconomic angle. It is difficult to integrate the different aspects of a behavioural activity such as intelligence: this book does not give a definite answer but indicates quite clearly, I hope, the intricate genotype $\times$ environment interactions which result in this complex adaptive behaviour.

This book consists of five parts. (1) The meaning of a comparative approach: interspecific approach, (2) genetic aspects of learning and behaviour in animals, (3) environmental influences and learning in animals, (4) genetics and the study of intelligence in man, and (5) environmental differences and mental performance in man. Each section contains chapters of theoretical interest as well as chapters presenting experimental results, so that as a whole the material provides a fair representation of the major contemporary interests within that field.

It is appropriate that Caspari, King and Warren should introduce the problem by concentrating on a comparative approach within an evolutionary point of view. The rôle of behaviour in selection and speciation, the adaptive value of "intelligent" behaviours, the comparative study of similarities and dissimilarities in extant organisms and the value of a phylogenetic approach are discussed in this section.

Quantitative intraspecific differences may result later on in qualitative differences: thus a genetic analysis of the individual differences within a given species may represent a useful approach to the evolution of behaviour. In addition, if a multidisciplinary approach is concentrated on a single species, on its different lines and inbred strains, we may catalogue the reasons for which an animal does not learn, and attempt to make genetic correlations between different traits. The second section discusses the findings collected on invertebrates (Médioni) and, to a greater extent, on mammals. The laboratory mouse may be considered as a prototype for behaviour genetic analyses: its learning patterns (D. Bovet) are discussed in relation to the variation of the brain structures (Wahlsten), sleep (Valatx, Chouvet and

Kitahama) and postnatal ontogenesis (Oliverio and Castellano).

There are a number of environmental influences which affect learning and behaviour in mammals. Early differences in the ontogenetic environment may result in drastic modifications of the phenotype: Part III deals with the effects of the environment on animal learning by considering such factors as early experience (Denenberg), environmental enrichment or impoverishment (Rosenzweig and Bennett) the influence of nutrition (Smart) on the effects of early separation from the mother or the mates (Suomi and Harlow).

The section that follows, on the genetic and ethnic approaches to the intelligence of man, provides an overall view of the studies conducted on the learning abilities of infants (Papoušek) and of adults (Vandenberg). The findings obtained by using an approach based on the study of mental development in twins are discussed by Wilson. Finally a complex theoretical synthesis of the rôle of genetics and environment in relation to intelligence is proposed by Royce.

Part V complements Part III in its discussion of the rôle of environmental differences on the mental performance of man. The problem of early stimulation is analysed by White who presents a number of findings on infantile stimulation. In discussing cultural deprivation, Kagan analyses the different causes which result in differences in intellectual progress: the problem, as he states it, is to understand why the children of minority families suffering economic disadvantages attain lower IQ scores and master school tasks more slowly. The attention of Marjoribanks is also focused on this problem as he discusses the relations existing between socioeconomic status, family environment and cognitive performance of the children. "How much are human behaviour patterns common to all mankind?" is the question posed by de Lacey who discusses behavioural development in terms of ethnic differences.

In the last chapter, Magali Bovet and Voneche reformulate the question "Is child stimulation effective?" into "What are the effects of positive, planned experience upon children's cognitive growth?" Their analysis, which reflects the position of the Piagetian school, presents a thorough and systematic discussion of the interactions between the environment – the external argumentation – and the processes of internal regulation acting on cognitive behaviour.

From flies to man: the reader will find here a valid illustration of the problem. This book will not answer all his questions but will indicate the state of a problem which is at the very root of psychology and the social sciences.

Literature cited

Abeleen van, J. H. F. (1974) *The Genetics of Behaviour*, North-Holland, Amsterdam

Ehrman, L. and Parsons, P. A. (1976) *The Genetics of Behavior* Sinauer, New York

Eysenck, H. J. (1971) *The IQ argument. Race, Intelligence and Education*, Library Press, New York

Fedorov, V. K. and V. V. Ponomarenko (1975) *Actual Problems of Behavior Genetics*, Akademia Nauk CCCP, Nauka Leningrad

Fuller, J. L. and Thompson, W. R. (1960) *Behavior Genetics*, Wiley, New York

Glass, D. C. (1968) *Genetics*, Rockefeller University Press, New York

Hirsch, J. (1967) *Behavior-Genetic Analysis*, McGraw Hill, New York

Jensen, A. R. (1969) How much can we boost IQ and scholastic achievement? *Harv. Educ. Rev. 39*, 1–123

Larmat, J. (1973) *La génétique de l'Intelligence*, Presses Universitaires de France, Paris

Lerner, M. (1968) *Heredity, Evolution and Society*, Freeman, San Francisco

Lindzey, G. and Thiessen, D. D. (1970) *Contributions to Behavior-Genetic Analysis. The Mouse as a Prototype*, Appleton, Century, Crofts, New York

Manosevitz, M., Lindzey, G. and Thiessen, D. D. (1970) *Behavioral Genetics: Method and Theory*, Appleton, Century, Crofts, New York

Parsons, P. A. (1967) *The Genetic Analysis of Behavior*, Methuen, Suffolk

Reuchlin, M. (1973) *L'Hérédité des Conduites*, Presses Universitaires de France, Paris

Robinson, D. N. (1970) *Heredity and Achievement*, Oxford University Press, New York

Rosenthal, D. (1971) *Genetics of Psychopathology*, McGraw-Hill Co., New York

Shockley, W. (1972) A debate challenge, *Phi Delta Kappan*, 415–419

Spuhler, J. N. (1967) *Genetic Diversity and Human Behavior*, Aldine Publishing Co., Chicago

Thiessen, D. D. (1970) *Gene Organization and Behavior*, Random House, New York

Vandenberg, S. G. (1968) *Progress in Human Behavior Genetics*, John Hopkins University Press, Baltimore

List of contributors

Edward L. Bennett
Department of Psychology
University of California
Berkeley, Calif. 94720
U.S.A.

Daniel Bovet
Cattedra di Psicobiologia
Università di Roma, Rome
Italy

Magali Bovet
Université de Genève
Faculté de Psychologie
3, Place de l'Université
1211 Geneva
Switzerland

Ernst W. Caspari
Department of Biology
University of Rochester
Rochester, N. Y. 14627
U.S.A.

Claudio Castellano
Laboratorio di Psicobiologia e
Psicofarmacologia
Via Reno 1, Rome
Italy

Guy Chouvet
Département de Médecine
Expérimentale
Université Claude Bernard
8 Avenue Rockefeller
69373 Lyon Cedex 2
France

P. R. de Lacey
School of Education
The University of Wollongong
P.O. Box 1144
Wollongong, N.S.W.
Australia 2500

Victor H. Denenberg
Department of Behavioral Sciences
Box V-154
The University of Connecticut
Storrs, Conn. 06268
U.S.A.

Harry F. Harlow
Primate Laboratory
University of Wisconsin
22 N. Charter St.
Madison, Wisc. 53706
U.S.A.

Jerome Kagan
Department of Social Relations
Harvard University
Cambridge, Mass. 02138
U.S.A.

John A. King
Department of Zoology
Michigan State University
East Lansing, Mich. 48824
U.S.A.

Kunio Kitahama
Département de Médecine
Expérimentale
Université Claude Bernard
8 Avenue Rockefeller
69373 Lyon Cedex 2
France

Kevin Marjoribanks
Department of Education
The University of Adelaide
Adelaide 5001
Australia

Jean Médioni
Psychophysiologie
Université de Toulouse
Faculté des Sciences
118 Route de Narbonne
31 Toulouse 04
France

Alberto Oliverio
Facoltà di Magistero
Università di Roma e
Laboratorio di Psicobiologia e
Psicofarmacologia
Via Reno 1, Rome
Italy

Hanuš Papoušek
Max-Plank Institute for Psychiatry
23 Kraepelin Str. 10
8 Munich
G.F.R.

Mark R. Rosenzweig
Department of Psychology
University of California
Berkeley, Calif. 94720
U.S.A.

Joseph R. Royce
The Center for Advanced Study
for Theoretical Psychology
University of Alberta
Edmonton, Alberta
Canada 76G 2GP

James L. Smart
Department of Child Health
University of Manchester
Clinical Sciences Building
York Place
Manchester 13 O JJ
U.K.

Stephen J. Suomi
Primate Laboratory
University of Wisconsin
22 N. Charter St.
Madison, Wisc. 53706
U.S.A.

Jean Louis Valatx
Département de Médecine
Expérimentale
Université Claude Bernard
8 Avenue Rockefeller
69373 Lyon Cedex 2
France

Steven G. Vandenberg
Department of Psychology
University of Colorado
Boulder, Colo. 80302
U.S.A.

Jacques Vonèche
Université de Genève
Faculté de Psychologie
3 Place de l'Université
1211 Geneva
Switzerland

Douglas Wahlsten
Department of Psychology
University of Waterloo
Waterloo, Ontario
Canada N2L 3G1

J. M. Warren
Department of Psychology
417 Bruce Moore Bldg.
Pennsylvania State University
University Park, Pa. 16802
U.S.A.

Burton L. White
Roy E. Larsen Hall
Appian Way
Graduate School of Education
Harvard University
Cambridge, Mass. 02138
U.S.A.

Ronald S. Wilson
Child Development Unit
University of Louisville
511 South Floyd Street
Louisville, Ky. 40202
U.S.A.

The meaning of
a comparative approach

Interspecific approach

PART I

Genetics, environment and intelligence, edited by A. Oliverio
© *Elsevier/North-Holland Biomedical Press, 1977*

Genetic mechanisms and behavior   1

ERNST W. CASPARI

Introduction

Genetics has undergone a considerable change during the last 25 years, both in its own problems and its relation to other biological disciplines. In the first half of this century, genetics was primarily concerned with the nature and location of the genetic material and its transmission. These questions brought it in close relation to cytology, and cytogenetics was the only interdisciplinary area active in this period. The early period has ended because its problems have been essentially solved. We know now that the genetic material is DNA and that both its primary functions, identical reproduction and specific activities are consequences of the chemical structure of DNA; also, its location on the chromosomes accounts for the way it is transmitted in sexual processes. While there are still many problems to be solved at the level of the gene, such as the mechanisms of DNA replication, transcription, mutation, DNA repair and recombination, all problems are attacked within the framework given by the model of the structure of DNA.

In the earlier period, genetics was a special field of biology, somewhat outside the main stream which was represented by evolutionary, developmental and physiological studies. Relations to other fields, e.g. evolution and development, were recognized but were not central to scientific interests at that time. With the identification of the primary function of genes as the control of the primary structure of proteins and thus, enzymes, the close relation of genetics and biochemistry became firmly established. Since biochemical compounds and processes are becoming increasingly important in our understanding of other aspects of biology, genetics has moved into a central position within the biological sciences.

There have arisen a large number of subfields of genetics which deal with the genic control of particular phenotypic characters in cells and tissues. The following are examples of these fields: biochemical genetics, immunogenetics, developmental genetics, pharmacogenetics and behavior genetics. Some of them have become sufficiently established to have founded their own special journals and societies. It is characteristic for all these fields that they are concerned with the genetic basis of particular phenotypes: antigens, antibodies and immunological reactions in immunogenetics; reactions to drugs in pharmacogenetics. In this way, the techniques and problems of the subfield are largely derived from fields other than genetics.

Behavior genetics belongs to this type of field. Its problem is the study of the genetic basis of behavioral characters. Its methods and problems derive from a number of disciplines which have not been traditionally connected with genetics: psychology, ethology and evolutionary biology. The problems with which behavior genetics is concerned are to a large degree derived from these component disciplines (Caspari, 1975). More specifically, the "nature–nurture" problem which takes up considerable space in the behavior-genetic literature is a long-standing problem in psychology which, for non-behavioral characters, has not been taken as a particularly serious problem in classical genetics. From the point of view of ethology and evolution, behavior has particularly interesting features, since it plays a large rôle in the adaptation of species to their particular environments, and in the isolation of populations which is the final step in species formation (Mayr, 1974). The genetic basis of social and sexual behavior has turned out to be an important and fascinating problem with many evolutionary implications.

Behavior genetics did not exist as a special field until about 1960. Since that time it has grown considerably. The journal "Behavior Genetics" has appeared since 1970, numerous conferences and symposia have covered different aspects of the field, and several textbooks have appeared: Fuller and Thompson (1960), De Fries and McClearn (1973) and Ehrman and Parsons (1976).

This chapter will deal with the genetic basis of behavior. It will briefly discuss the presently accepted theory of genic action, and apply it to behavioral phenotypes. Finally, it will discuss genetic methods which are used in the analysis of behavior, and some evolutionary implications of behavior genetics.

Nature and function of genetic material

It is assumed in the following parts of this chapter that the reader is acquainted with the contemporary theory of gene structure and gene action. The theory was originally devised from experiments on microorganisms, particularly bacteria and viruses. The application of this model to the development of animals and plants requires a certain amount of modification. But the composition of DNA of two complementary strands of nucleotides and its activity of transcription, copying of one of the strands into an RNA strand which is released from the DNA strand, are common to all organisms. The transcribed RNA-strand can function directly as RNA (ribosomal RNA, rRNA and transfer RNA, tRNA) or it can be translated into polypeptide strands, the amino-acid sequence of which is coded in the sequence of nucleotides in the RNA-strand (messenger RNA, mRNA).

Genic control of metabolism and development

Since particular genes control the primary structure of particular polypeptides, changes in the amino acid composition may affect the function of the protein. Many proteins have enzymatic functions, i.e. they catalyze specific metabolic reactions, and thus a mutant DNA may induce an altered enzyme which may be unable to carry out its function. Such enzymatic blocks have two immediate consequences: the product of the enzymatic reaction will be reduced or missing, and the substrate of the reaction will be either stored or metabolized by an alternate pathway. For the observed phenotypic changes, either or both of these primary gene effects may be decisive. Thus, in the human genetic condition phenylketonuria (PKU), the enzyme phenylalanine hydroxylase which catalyzes the oxidation of phenylalanine to tyrosine is missing or inactive. The resulting lack of tyrosine has no further effect since tyrosine is supplied in the food. The substrate phenylalanine, however, appears at elevated levels in the blood, and is converted to other compounds such as phenylpyruvic acid which appear in the urine. These substances also circulate in the blood, may be taken up by tissues and affect the developing brain and the pigment in the hair. Thus, the mutant gene has secondary effects on the development of mental characters such as intelligence and temperament, and on hair pigmentation. The mechanism by which the toxic products accomplish their secondary effects is not known but it has been suggested that they interfere with the action of other enzymes necessary for the synthesis of transmitter substances in the brain and of melanine pigment in the hair follicles.

The point of interest is the fact that although the primary product of a gene is a specific polypeptide chain, the block of an enzymatic function results in two secondary effects, lack of the product and accumulation of the substrate. Because of the interactions of different biochemical processes in organisms and cells, these may lead to a complex pattern of tertiary and quaternary effects, so-called pleiotropic effects. A number of genetic conditions in man, in which the primary biochemical effect is known, have been summarized by Omenn (1976). The pleiotropic effects in many of these conditions are complex, and while some of them can be understood as consequences of the primary effect of the gene, in no case are all the pleiotropic effects of a single mutant gene completely understood in this way.

The existence of pleiotropic patterns of gene action is the basis for a distinction between phenotypic characters which are "close" to or "removed" from the genes. Some characters, particularly the primary structure of proteins, mirror exactly the nucleotide structure of a specific gene. Other characters, such as lack or reduction of products of enzymatic reactions, (e.g. pigments) or storage of substrates, are farther removed from the gene. Storage of such products in nerve cells is a frequent consequence of genetic blocks and leads to severe tertiary syndromes in many human conditions as seen in Tay–Sachs disease, Fabry's disease and other genetic disorders (see Omenn, 1976). Characters which are "far removed" from the genes will be characterized by the fact that they are influenced by a large number of genes, and that variation in many of these genes has only a minor effect on the expression of the character. Among the characters far removed from the genes are many quantitative characters, such as size, weight, fertility as expressed in egg production and many behavioral characters.

Different types of cells in a higher organism differ in their chemical constitution. Some proteins, for example, are restricted to certain types of cells: hemoglobin is present in red blood cells but is not found in any other type of cell in the vertebrate body. Since the genes involved in hemoglobin synthesis are present in all cells, it is concluded that they are inactive in all cells except the red blood cells. Cell differentiation is generally regarded as involving the activation of genes. Only part of the genome (it is estimated to be about 10 per cent of all genes) is active in individual cells. Development is presently regarded as the sequential activation and inactivation of genes, leading to the formation of biochemical and functional differences between different types of cells in the same organism.

In this way, development has come to be regarded as a problem in the regulation of gene action. In bacteria, this is well understood: the regulating elements consist of a number of short nucleotide sequences linked to the structural parts of the gene which control specific processes needed for the initiation of transcription (promoter, operator) and a further regulatory gene which may or may not be linked to the structural gene and the products of which react with the linked regulatory elements – turning transcription on or off. In higher organisms, regulation is assumed to be more complex, but the hypotheses used at present assume a regulatory mechanism similar in type but more complex than that found in microorganisms (Paigen, 1971; Davidson and Britten, 1973). They have in common the assumption that a genetic unit consists of a structural gene which encodes the amino acid structure of a protein and closely linked regulatory elements ("receptor genes" in the scheme of Davidson and Britten) which activate or inactivate the structural gene. These regulatory elements may in turn be controlled by "integrator genes" (Davidson and Britten) which are analogous to the regulatory genes in bacteria, but which are assumed to control a battery of "receptors" rather than a single one. This assumption appears to be necessary, since frequently, in the course of development, not a single gene, but a number of genetically and functionally independent genes become activated at the same time. Finally, Davidson and Britten assume the existence of sensor genes the products of which are presumably proteins, formed as a reaction to "signals" (such as hormones) from the cellular environment.

These schemes of the regulation of genes in development are on the whole completely theoretical, but evidence for their essential correspondence to actual events is gradually accumulating. The existence of "controlling elements" which are able to inactivate structural genes closely linked to them has been first demonstrated by McClintock (1956, 1965) in maize. In *Drosophila*, the enzyme xanthine dehydrogenase is encoded in the structural gene rosy *ry*. Chovnick et al. (1976) could show that closely linked to *ry*, but certainly outside the borders of the structural region of *ry*, there exists a regulatory element that determines the amount of enzyme formed, i.e. the level of transcription. This regulatory element, just as McClintock's controlling elements, acts only on the structural region to which it is linked, not on its allele on the homologous chromosome (action in *cis* position). The xanthine dehydrogenase system is complicated by the fact that there are additional gene loci known which affect the activity and presence of the enzyme, particularly the sex-linked gene maroon-like (*ma-l*). This must represent a type of regulatory gene different from the linked element which acts only in *cis*, and must be assumed to affect the level of xanthine dehydrogenase indirectly by means of a gene product. Differences in the activity of xanthine dehydrogenase can thus be induced by mutations at the structural locus, leading to reduced activity per molecule, mutations at the linked controlling element, leading to a reduction in the number of molecules produced and by mutations at independent loci the method of action of which is unknown.

The different kinds of controls of enzyme activity can also be seen from experiments by Ganschow and Schimke (1969) in the mouse. Three strains with different activity levels of the enzyme catalase were investigated. Two of these strains differ in the type of enzyme produced: they form equal amounts of catalase molecules but the catalytic activity of each enzyme molecule is reduced in the mutant form. In the other pair of strains, the number of enzyme molecules present is increased in the mutant strain. This is due to a gene locus separate from the (structural) locus affecting enzyme activity; it acts by slowing down the degradation of the enzyme protein. In some respects, the two genes act additively: animals homozygous for the gene controlling an enzyme of normal activity and the reduced degradation gene have twice the normal catalase activity. But the heterozygote for the gene affecting enzyme activity is intermediate (actually codominant) while the gene reducing degradation is recessive.

Paigen and his collaborators investigated three enzymes in the mouse which are contained in a common cytoplasmic structure, the lysosome. The structural gene for β-glucuronidase, *Gus*, is located on chromosome 5, and a regulatory element, *Gur*, is closely linked to it. This regulatory element determines the level of the enzyme which is induced in the kidney by the male sex hormone dihydrotestosterone (Swank et al., 1973). In normal animals, β-glucuronidase activity shows a characteristic pattern of changes in postnatal development which is different in various organs, such as brain, heart and liver. Similar patterns of tissue-specific development are found for two other lysosomal enzymes, β-galactosidase and α-galactosidase, so that the development of these three enzymes is coordinate. The structural genes controlling these enzymes are on different chromosomes. Genetic variants altering the developmental patterns have been found for all three enzymes, each one affecting one enzyme only and in one tissue. These variants are under genetic control, and in each case, the gene inducing the developmental variation maps close to the structural locus for the enzyme (Lusis and Paigen, 1975). Such genes controlling the pattern of formation of a protein in development have been called "temporal genes" by Paigen (1971).

Nebert and his collaborators (1975) have studied the induction of a variety of enzyme activities, and of an identifiable protein, cytochrome P_1-450, by certain aromatic hydrocarbons in the mouse. They found that there are inducible and non-inducible strains, and that the difference in at least some of the strains is due to two alleles at a single locus *Ah* ("aromatic hydrocarbon responsiveness"). The pattern of response is highly pleiotropic at the level of enzyme induction, and the effects appear strongly coordinated (Atlas et al., 1976). Poland et al. (1976) have suggested that the primary effect of *Ah* may be control of the structure of a receptor protein which combines with the inducer drug and carries it inside the cell.

These four examples of the control of proteins in development and under the influence of environmental factors show how gene action can be controlled at the level of transcription. Further control is possible at other levels. In this connection, evidence should be cited showing that the processing of transcribed RNA may be more complex in animals than it is in bacteria.

In bacteria, the transcribed RNA molecules serve immediately as mRNA in the synthesis of proteins. In eucaryote cells, transcription takes place in the nucleus, but most proteins are synthesized in the cytoplasm, so that transport of the transcribed RNA molecules must take place. In addition, there is good evidence that the transcriptional RNA is processed before it functions in protein synthesis. The nuclear RNA contains very large molecules, up to ten times larger than those of the cytoplasmic mRNA, and it has been suggested that the high-molecular RNA (hnRNA) is not only transported out of the nucleus but also trimmed down before and during the process (cf. Lewin, 1975). The evidence on this process is still unclear and ambiguous, but such a processing of transcribed RNA has been clearly demonstrated for ribosomal RNA. For our present purposes, it is sufficient to realize that the action of genes can also be modified at post-transcriptional stages, in transport, processing and in the activity of translation.

Genotype and phenotype

In the first place, genes are recognized by their phenotypic effects. It is, for many experimental purposes, convenient to use mutant genes which have a constant effect on the phenotype. This is, however, by no means a general occurrence; genes with variable effects are very frequent. One example may suffice: the mutant gene Blind (*Bld*) in the mouse is lethal in homozygous condition, and in heterozygous condition affects the development of the eyelids so that the mice are born with open eyes. These open eyes do not develop normally (Watson, 1968). Not all organisms carrying the gene *Bld* have open eyes at birth and after birth their eyes may develop normally. The gene is said to have incomplete penetrance. Further, the effect on the eyelids is variable, ranging from completely open eyes to small scars over the eyes at birth and from complete lack of the eye to cataracts and slight microphthalmia in the adult. The gene has variable expressivity. Finally, sometimes only one eye of an animal is affected, the left eye more frequently than the right. This is designated as the specificity or pattern of action of the gene. The terms penetrance, expressivity and specificity were introduced by Timoféef-Ressovsky in 1934 and are widely used in the description of genes with variable expression.

In mutant genes with variable expression, the actual penetrance and expressivity are under the influence of the genetic background and of environmental factors. In the above-mentioned case of *Bld* in the mouse, penetrance can be raised to 100 per cent and expressivity and specificity strongly increased by a sex-linked gene (Teicher, unpublished results). So-called enhancer and suppressor genes are frequently found, and may affect a specific mutant gene or an array of genes. Environmental factors are less important for many characters in mammals since their early development proceeds in a sheltered and constant environment. But they can be easily observed in insects, such as *Drosophila*, and in plants.

In *Drosophila*, conditional mutant genes (i.e. mutant genes which express themselves only under certain environmental conditions) are widely used in developmental studies (cf. Suzuki et al., 1976). The most frequently used environmental variable is temperature, though nutritional conditions can also be used. The phenotypes range from conditional lethals to morphological characters, which appear mutant at one temperature but normal at another, to enzymatic characters. At the same gene locus, conditional and unconditional mutants may exist. In conditional genes, the phenotype produced depends on an interaction of a gene with a particular environment; neither one by itself is able to produce the mutant phenotype.

The genotype may thus be said to determine the developmental reaction of an organism on environmental variables. This can be seen in the molecular examples given in the previous section. The gene *Ah* in the mouse does not control the production of the enzymes concerned, but their inducibility by aromatic hydrocarbons. The regulatory gene *Gur* determines the level of β-glucuronidase activity on induction with male sex hormone. These relations between genotype and environment in the control of developmental processes, and thus phenotypic characters, have been described by early geneticists by the term "norm of reaction". The genotype determines not a particular character, but the norm of reaction of the organism on the environment, resulting in the character. This interaction of genotype and environment in the production of a phenotype is a fundamental concept of classical genetics. The frequent unconditional relation between genotype and phenotype is partly the result of low variability of the environment in early developmental stages in animals and partly the result of conscious selection of such genotypes by investigators.

The interaction of genes and environment is particularly impressive in plants. This is due to the fact that plants are developmentally open systems which contain embryonic cells throughout life. Plant geneticists have done much work on the interaction of genotype and environment on economically important characters such as height, yield and protein content. A general conclusion is that a particular genotype will give optimal results under particular environmental conditions, but no genotype is optimal under all environmental conditions. Furthermore, specific developmental processes such as the formation of flowers may be induced by environmental factors such as light conditions, and the norm of reaction is again dependent on the genotype. The interaction of genes and environmental factors has not been clarified at the molecular level in all cases. But in some cases at least, it has been shown that environmental factors are able to control the transcriptional activity of genes.

Mendelian and polygenic inheritance

All through genetics there runs a deep split between Mendelian and quantitative genetics. This is a remnant of the violent fight between two schools which dominated research in genetics in the first two decades of the 20th century, the Mendelians and the biometricians. The history of this fight has been described by Provine (1971) who concludes that it was ended by the theory of R. A. Fisher: the laws of biometrical genetics can be understood as the effects of a large number of Mendelian genes with small additive effects. While this is correct in principle, in practice the two areas of genetics have remained separated, both in technique and in the questions they ask. This division has become even sharper due to the merger of Mendelian genetics with molecular biology.

Quantitative genetics deals with characters which show variation in a measurable quantity, such as height, weight and the production of substances of economic importance, such as total protein, fat, milk and eggs. Many behavioral characters, such as IQ, belong to this class of characters. They are in general characters which have been described in the section *Genic control of metabolism and development* (p. 6) as characters "far removed" from the gene. Genes affecting quantitative characters are usually designated as polygenes, and the question has been raised whether the polygenes are a qualitatively different class from the Mendelian genes. The original hypothesis that polygenes are located in heterochromatin has been abandoned, but the hypothesis is being resurrected at intervals; the latest being the idea that polygenes correspond to the regulatory gene systems discussed earlier. But the more widespread assumption is that polygenes are in reality the usual Mendelian genes and that, in polygenic systems, we are dealing with remote pleiotropic effects of these same genes. It is well established that many single-gene mutations have larger or smaller pleiotropic effects on quantitative characters, such as viability, fertility and time of development, and since there are many genes exerting this pleiotropic effect, it may be impossible to isolate the individual genes involved.

Quantitative traits are investigated by the techniques of selection and by crossing different strains. Occasionally in these crosses, a separation into sharp classes is found, and this is interpreted as indicating the involvement of a single Mendelian gene. However, caution is necessary even in this case, since, as Fuller and Thompson (1960) have pointed out, a polygenic system with a developmental threshold may also produce segregation into sharply different classes.

In most cases, crosses affecting a quantitative trait result in variable progeny which is more or less intermediate between the parents and a second hybrid generation which may or may not be more variable than the first generation. The results of such crosses cannot give us much information about the individual genes involved (a rough estimate of the number of genes is probably as far as we can go) but it gives us some information on the genetic basis of the character involved. It should be realized that the same phenotypic effect can be achieved by different genotypic combinations; therefore it is not legitimate to draw conclusions on the mechanism of the biochemistry and development of a character from the analysis of a polygenic system. The knowledge obtained from quantitative genetics is valuable because we can draw conclusions on the changes a genetic system may undergo under the influence of artificial and natural selection.

It is a general rule that quantitative characters are affected by environmental variables. It is generally assumed that the rules discussed in the section *Genotype and phenotype* (p. 9) on genotype–environment interaction apply to polygenic systems. It is thus of importance to analyze the action of genes and of environment in the production of a polygenic character. These problems are of great importance to behavior genetics, and will therefore be briefly described here. Many discussions of this problem appear in the literature. I found the papers by De Fries (1971) and by Feldman and Lewontin (1975) particularly clear and instructive.

The analysis of the influence of genes and environment on quantitative characters has been most thoroughly developed in applied animal and plant breeding. By the method of variance analysis, it separates the observed variance of a population into a genetic and an environmental component, plus an interaction variance which can be experimentally investigated in domestic animals and plants. The term heritability has been introduced as a measure of the relative amount of genetic variance. Practically, this is an important concept, since its value predicts the possibility of improving a strain by selective breeding, and suggests the most effective breeding procedure. From a theoretical point of view, it must be realized that this is a tricky concept which contains a large number of assumptions. For practical reasons, heritability in the "broad" sense, using all genetic variability, has been distinguished from "narrow" heritability (Lush, 1949) which is based only on the additive component of variability. The narrow heritability is of interest since it constitutes the basis of selection, both in the improvement of domestic animals and plants, and of the increase in fitness in natural selection. In our discussion of gene action we have found that codominance – which is expressed as additivity for quantitative characters –is the rule for the direct products of structural genes, enzymes and antigens, but that regulatory genes as well as the effects further removed from the gene usually show dominance. It is thus hard to explain the fact that among the most general characters, i.e. those far removed from the genotype, a considerable additive genetic component is found. On the other hand, a dominance component is also frequently found. In addition to dominance, which constitutes the result of interaction between alleles, there exist also interactions between different loci, so-called epistasis. Examples are the collaboration of *ry* and *ma-l* in *Drosophila* in the production of xanthine dehydrogenase, and the two loci controlling the level of catalase in the mouse (see the section *Genic control of metabolism and development*, p. 7). Epistatic interactions make the statistical analysis of quantitative traits difficult, and their frequent occurrence has been occasionally denied. But the general theory of control of gene action presented in the section *Genic control of metabolism and development* (p. 6) would lead us to expect them to occur frequently. Actually, epistatic interactions in quantitative characters occur, for instance for pupal weight in the beetle *Tribolium*

(Goodwill, 1975). Milton and Koehn (1973) when discussing epistasis in populations of marine clams, state: "Although epistasis has been demonstrated . . . methodological restrictions have severely limited the number and scope of studies concerning this important concept of gene action." This difficulty may explain the apparently rare occurrence of epistatic effects in polygenic systems.

Interaction between genes and environment has been discussed in the section *Genotype and phenotype* (p. 7). For quantitative systems it has been studied extensively for nutrition in domestic animals, and for fertilizers, temperature, day length etc. in agricultural plants. In human populations, the interaction is harder to analyze, but comparison of monozygotic and dizygotic twins can be used for this purpose. A more difficult problem is constituted by the so-called heredity–environment correlation, i.e. the possibility that different genotypes may be unevenly distributed to the environment. This is particularly true for wild populations of animals where individuals can to a certain degree actively choose their environments.

These various possibilities of interaction of genes with other genes and with the environment make a simple-minded additive model rather unlikely, even though it is frequently convenient and sufficient for certain practical purposes. A great amount of statistical work has gone into attempts to take non-additive effects into account, and a great amount of ingenuity has been shown in attempts to devise mathematical models to correct for them. It appears doubtful to me whether the great variety of interactions can be meaningfully expressed in a single number, such as heritability.

The genic control of behavior

For the present purposes, behavior will be defined as active movements in response to stimuli. This definition includes locomotion by means of contractile organels such as muscles, cilia and flagella, but not the light reactions of plants which are essentially movements due to growth. Our definition may be regarded as unsatisfactory since for many individual processes it leaves some doubt as to whether or not they should be regarded as "behavior". It has, however, the value of pointing out that a behavioral character has three physiological components: a receptor for stimuli, a mediator structure (the nervous system in animals) and a locomotor component. Genes affecting sensory organs are frequent in multicellular organisms, and that mutations of these genes may affect some behavioral activities is trivial. The same applies to mutations affecting the locomotor apparatus. The main interest of behavior genetics concerns the mediator system, the brain and the central nervous system. However, in practice it not always easy to distinguish these three components. Thus it took many years until it was recognized that the body-color gene ebony in *Drosophila* has a pleiotropic effect on eye function and that the inbred mouse strain C3H is blind. The following section will try to show that genic action in the determination of behavior does not differ from that determining biochemical and physical characters. As Parsons (1976) stated: "No unique genetic principles are required when we consider the mechanism of the inheritance of behavioral traits."

Genes affecting behavioral characters

In many organisms, there are quite a number of gene mutations which are primarily recognized by their effects on a behavioral character. In the most recent list of mutations of the mouse (Mouse Newsletter 54, 1976) 62 out of a total of over 500 mutations are classified as "neurological and neuromuscular". This category does not include mutations affecting the eye and the inner ear, even though the latter are frequently recognized by circling and shaking movements. On the other hand, muscular ailments such as muscular dystrophy (*myd*) are included in this category, as well as degenerative diseases of brain cells. Others, however, affect characters which must be regarded as behavioral under any definition. To these belong *asp* (audiogenic seizure-prone) one of the genes which affect the occurrence of seizures after auditory stimulation (Collins and Fuller, 1968). This character is of interest because the most thorough analysis of gene–environment interactions concerns this character. Other clearly behavioral genes in the mouse include *Aal* (active avoidance learning) and *Exa* (exploratory activity) described by Oliverio et al. (1973, a and b). The last three are clearly single-gene differences, since the genes could be localized on the chromosome map in the mouse.

In human beings, a large number of monogenic conditions has been described which produce behavioral and neurological disorders affecting mostly intelligence and temperament. Some of these conditions, the biochemical basis of which is known, are summarized by Omenn (1971). Many of the conditions discussed deal with enzymes concerned with the metabolism of amino acids and carbohydrates; phenylketonuria described in the section *Genic control of metabolism and development* (p. 5) is an example. Other conditions involve storage of mucopolysaccharides and sphingolipids in neurons. The latter are substances which are normally found in the brain, particularly in the myelin sheath of the nerve fibers. Abnormal products of sphingolipid metabolism are apparently deposited in nerve cells and inhibit their function. It should be added that all chromosomal rearrangements known in man are accompanied by more or less severe disturbances of behavioral characters.

In *Drosophila*, the discovery of mutations with specific behavioral or neurological phenotypes occurred relatively late, due to technical problems. But a certain number have been described more recently (Kaplan and Trout, 1969; Hotta and Benzer, 1972). Mutations with behavioral effects have also been described in organisms as simple as *Paramecium* (Kung, 1971).

In reviewing the earlier literature on the genetic control of behavior, it was found (Caspari, 1958) that most behavioral characters studied are inherited in a polygenic fashion. This conclusion has been confirmed by later observations, and methods suitable for the analysis of polygenic characters, such as selection experiments and diallel crosses between established strains in animals, and twin studies and parent–offspring correlation studies in humans, constitute the bulk of the literature in behavior genetics. Characters such as phototaxis, geotaxis and mating speed in *Drosophila*, and wheel-running, exploratory drive, climbing a pole and agressive behavior in the mouse behave as polygenic characters (e.g. Bruell, 1969).

It is in agreement with this hypothesis that effects on behavioral characters are

pleiotropic effects of single genes first defined by morphological or bio-
characters. This fact was discovered early by Sturtevant (1915) in the case of
ehavior in *Drosophila*. It was also found that of 31 mutations occurring in the
mouse strain C57Bl/6, five differed from the original strain in wheel-running activity, and twelve in exploratory drive. Many behavioral characters are thus "far removed" from the genome, i.e. they can be affected by mutations at a large number of
loci with different primary effects (Oliverio and Messeri, 1973).

The question may be raised whether the frequent finding of polygenic inheritance
in behavioral characters may not be due to the technique: for any quantitative
character subjected to selection or studied by crosses of inbred strains, it is highly
likely that differences will turn out to be polygenic. If, on the other hand, methods
are used which are appropriate to the study of single loci, such as mutations and
crosses to recombinant inbred strains, individual loci affecting the character will
usually be found. This is true for the biochemical mutations affecting intelligence
in man, such as phenylketonuria and the gene affecting exploratory behavior in the
mouse recovered by analysis with recombinant inbred strains (Oliverio et al., 1973a).
It appears best to regard most behavioral characters as characters which are usually
remote from the genes and thus potentially affected by the pleiotropic effects of a
large number of loci.

It has been frequently suggested that behavioral characters differ from morphological polygenic characters by a greater prevalence of dominance and even
heterosis. This has been emphasized by Bruell (1964) for exploratory behavior and
wheel-running in the mouse and has also been found by Fulker (1966) with respect
to mating speed of *Drosophila* males. This is however not general for all behavioral
characters: Broadhurst (1960) found a low dominance component in the inheritance
of ambulatory scores in the rat. Bruell suggests, in agreement with Fulker (1966),
Mayr (1963) and other authors that the existence of dominant or heterotic inheritance of a character indicates strong selective pressures acting on the character in
question.

Closed behavioral programs

There are a number of behavioral characters in the performance of which the environment and previous experience plays little or no role. Environmental stimuli may
initiate the movements, but have no further effects on their execution. These types
of behavior have been called "innate" by psychologists and are opposed to
"acquired" behaviors. Mayr (1974) pointed out that every behavior pattern constitutes fundamentally a genetic program, and distinguished closed programs which do
not require input from the environment to "open" programs which can be modified
as a result of stimuli and experiences.

Closed behavioral programs are wide-spread in lower animals, particularly insects,
but also in vertebrates, fishes as well as birds. Both Mayr and Parsons point out that
closed behavior programs will be prevalent in organisms with a short life span. Open
systems will be favored in animals with prolonged care by the parents. A good ex-

ample of a closed behavioral system is the mating preferences in *Drosophila* which has been thoroughly discussed by Parsons (1976). Males display preferably to females of their own species, and females usually prefer males of their own species. The genetic basis of mating preference in *Drosophila* is polygenic and has been shown to be altered by selection. Since mating preferences form the basis of sexual isolation, they constitute an important component of the fitness of a species. But even for this character which at first sight appeared to be a completely closed program, an experiential component could be demonstrated (Pruzan and Ehrman, 1974).

To the class of closed behavioral programs belong the complex behavior sequences which are known as "fixed action patterns". Many cases have been described in insects, fishes and birds. They frequently are concerned with communication between members of the same species – recognition of species and sex in mating is one example – and for this purpose, stable, reliable signals and responses are important (Mayr, 1974). Nevertheless, little genetic evidence for the basis of these fixed reaction patterns is available. This is in part due to the fact that differences in these behavior patterns occur mostly in different species while there is little variation within one and the same species. Thus, there is a large literature on the behavior of F_1 in species crosses, but little on successive generations in which segregation could be observed.

The best investigated case remains the "hygienic" behavior in the honey bee (Rothenbuhler, 1964). This consists of the fact that in the strains "immune" against the bacterial disease foulbrood, the diseased larvae are taken out of their cells and ejected from the hive by the worker bees. This behavior is due to two genes. The first one controls the opening of cells in which diseased larvae are lying. The second one enables the bees to take larvae out of open cells and remove them from the hive. The whole complex behavior is thus made up of two units, each one controlled by one locus. The complex behavior is put together by the fact that the result of the first activity (open cell) acts as the releaser stimulus for the second activity. It should be added that hygienic behavior is modified by environmental factors such as humidity and availability of food, but apparently not by experience.

The origin of a closed behavior program does not differ from that of other developmental programs in animals. It is probably dependent on the proper differentiation of sensory, nervous and effector cells, and their proper location with respect to each other. While the genetic program of the differentiation of the brain has not been as thoroughly studied as that of other organs, there is no reason to assume that it differs in principle.

Open behavioral systems

In early psychology, innate behavior was sharply differentiated from acquired behavior. It was believed that innate behavior, if it existed at all, was restricted to lower functions controlled at the reflex level, and to lower animals. The nomenclature of Mayr implies that there is no difference in principle in the expression of closed and open programs of behavior. A character which is primarily determined by a closed program, such as sexual isolation in *Drosophila*, may have

l component. And while many of the activities of insects are cont-
ed programs, learning to collect food on certain colors has been
s for a long time, and training on olfactory cues has been demons-
osophila (Quinn et al., 1974). As Mayr (1974) points out, a closed
its stereotyped behavior is advantageous for communication, while
an open program is more flexible and thus offers advantages in the utilization of
the environment.

Nevertheless, it remains an established fact that open programs are more prominent in the higher vertebrates, mammals and birds, and are particularly important
in the behavior of human beings. It is thus legitimate that classical psychology, being
primarily concerned with the behavior of man, has placed emphasis on the learned
aspects of behavior.

It is well established in animal experiments that the ability to learn is itself under
the influence of the genotype. This was first suggested by Tryon's (1940) classical
experiment in which he produced by artificial selection maze-bright and maze-dull
strains of rats. The best material on the genetic basis of learning is available for
avoidance training in the mouse. Strain differences in avoidance learning were repeatedly demonstrated, first by Royce and Covington (1960) (see Bovet et al., 1969).
Diallel crosses of different strains (Collins (1964) and others) demonstrated a polygenic type of inheritance with dominance or heterosis for the superior strains, as
would be suspected if selection for positive avoidance learning was taking place in the
mouse. In agreement with the finding of polygenic transmission, Oliverio and Messeri
(1973) found that seven of 31 monogenic morphological mutations on a C57Bl background scored higher than the original strain on an avoidance learning test, indicating pleiotropic effects of the mutations on learning ability. Finally, Oliverio et al.
(1973) were able to identify, by means of crosses to recombinant inbred strains, a
single major gene, on chromosome 9, *Aal*, which controls the difference between
strains BALB and C57Bl/6 in their performance in avoidance learning. Similar results, though not as extensive, have been obtained for maze learning.

These results show that, from the genetic point of view, differences in learning
ability behave the same way as differences in unconditional behavioral characters
such as wheel-running and exploratory drive. It suggests that open and closed programs of behavior are differences in degree rather than a fundamental dichotomy.

The same conclusion is suggested by biochemical findings concerning the process
of learning. It has been suggested earlier (Caspari, 1971) that the development of
behavior is not in principle different from other developmental processes, since the
differentiation and pattern formation depend on a preestablished genetic program.
Furthermore, development of behavior by learning depends on the interaction of
environmental stimuli on the preestablished pattern of the nervous system. Learning
is thus a developmental process occurring later in life, as is well known to occur in
many processes in the open developmental system of plants. This view has become
much more concrete in the last five years, due to the extensive work of Hydén and his
collaborators on the biochemical correlates of learning. They found that when an animal which learns a complex task, such as reversal of the preferred hand or maze running, a small number of specific proteins is synthesized, among these a protein S-100

which is mostly or exclusively produced in the glia cells, combines with Ca
under change of conformation and is found associated with the membrane of n
(Hydén et al., 1973). S-100 and possibly some other proteins are first synthes.... m
the hippocampus, an area of the brain necessary for the establishment of a new behavior. Later on, the synthesis of specific proteins occurs in the cerebral cortex, in
specific areas for each learning task. Learning is also accompanied by RNA synthesis,
first in the hippocampus and later in specific areas of the cortex. The RNA synthesized in the hippocampus during learning includes hnRNA and probably new
messenger RNA (Cupello and Hydén, 1976). Thus, the changes going on in the
hippocampus and in other parts of the brain are exactly the same ones as those
which occur in the activation of genes in development: individual genes are turned
on, produce mRNA and thus induce the synthesis of a new species of protein. The
only new feature in this case is that at least one of the proteins is synthesized in
the glia cells, becomes modified by Ca^{2+} in the intercellular space, and after modification becomes a component of the neuronal membrane. The parallel to development is even closer, since S-100 is produced in the normal differentiation of the
nervous system: S-100 is not found in 4 day-old rabbits, but is synthesized in the
second and third week of life, i.e. during the time when the young rabbit starts to
explore the environment (Hydén, 1974). Strains of rats differing in performance in
a learning task also differ in specific protein synthesis in the hippocampus and other
parts of the brain: the low scoring strain did not produce new proteins in the active
fractions. Since the proteins are formed in normal development, the genes inhibiting
formation of these proteins probably are not mutations of the structural genes but
involve regulatory genes which apparently do not react on the stimulus inducing the
learning process (Hydén, Lange and Seyfried, 1973).

The results suggest that learning involves the activation of a low number of genes
in cells of the hippocampus and secondly of some other regions of the brain. It is thus
comparable to the model of gene action in development presented in the section
Genic control of metabolism and development (p. 6). Under this model, learning would
be in principle a developmental process which occurs in later periods of life. Mayr's
term "open program" is thus justified on the basis of biochemical knowledge.

Applications of genetics to behavioral studies

It has been stated in the introduction that the main interest in behavior genetics centers around the analysis of questions concerned with behavior by genetic means.
The original question of behavior genetics was whether behavior is inherited or
acquired. We have seen that this question has to be rephrased concerning the nature
of the program, i.e. whether it is open or closed. Even then, it cannot be answered
for behavior in general, but at most for a specific behavioral character in a defined
species. Even then, we frequently have interactions between genetic and environmental factors in the production of a behavioral character. The great social and
political implications of this question have made analysis difficult. A great part of
the behavior–genetic literature continues to be concerned with the analysis of

questions of this type, and a large part of this book will be concerned with it. For this reason I shall not discuss this problem any further, but shall call attention to two other problems which have been approached by genetic means.

The mechanism of behavior

Genetic methods can be used to analyze a phenotypic character. One method widely used in the study of behavior is the method of quantitative genetics. Experimentally, it is based on the statistical evaluation of selection experiments and diallel crosses. These methods have been discussed in the sections *Mendelian and polygenic inheritance* (p. 10–12) and *Genes affecting behavioral characters* (p. 13). The results are limited to statistical statements about the character since the genes are treated as acting additively on the same character rather than as individual units each with its own specificity.

Another method of analyzing behavior uses the specificity of individual mutations. It consists in collecting mutants affecting the character in question, identifying the loci involved by complementation tests, and establishing the function of each locus. In this way, the complex interlocking reactions constituting the synthetic metabolism of *Neurospora* and of some bacteria have been clarified. This method has been successfully applied to the chemotactic behavior of the bacterium *Escherichia coli* by Adler and his collaborators (cf. Adler, 1976). Many mutants were isolated which affect chemotactic behavior. A few of the loci involved affect the motor component, the differentiation and structure of the flagella and the mode of its movement. There is a great number of loci which affect attraction or repulsion by specific chemicals. These genes control specific chemoreceptors, proteins located on the surface of the cell which specifically bind the chemical. Attraction and repulsion are controlled by separate chemoreceptors, and thus probably by separate genes. There are at least two receptors for attraction to various amino acids, and at least nine for attraction to carbohydrates. Thus a rather complex pattern of sensory components has been found and to a large degree analyzed. In addition to these chemoreceptor genes controlling specific chemotaxis, there exist also mutants which inhibit all chemotaxis, general chemotactic mutations. These gene loci are believed to be concerned with a general pathway common to all chemotactic reactions, possibly transmission of the excitation of the chemoreceptors to the flagella. Complementation tests have shown that in these mutants few gene loci are involved – three in 38 mutants tested – and that thus the common pathway should be simple compared to the sensory component (Armstrong and Adler, 1969).

A method with a similar aim has been devised by Benzer and collaborators for *Drosophila* (Hotta and Benzer, 1972; Benzer, 1973). In this method, the expression of the mutation is studied in genetic mosaics which are produced early in development. Since the development of parts in *Drosophila* is laid down in very early stages, the pattern of mosaicism obtained in the adult can be related to the pattern of the early embryo. In this way, a developmental map for adult structures has been determined for the early embryo. For a behavioral mutant, the location of the structure responsible for the abnormal behavior can be determined from observations of the behavior pattern of genetic mosaics. Thus it was possible to identify the damaged structure for different behavioral mutants in the eye, the brain, the thoracic ganglia and the thoracic muscles (Hotta and Benzer, 1972). The localization has then been confirmed by neurophysiological and biochemical methods.

It is unlikely that Benzer's method may be applied directly to the mouse, because in the early development of the mouse, no cells can be ascribed to adult structures. But mosaicism may be a good means to analyze behavioral mutants in the mouse. It was thus possible to study mosaics for the ear mutant shaker-2 by means of mosaicism induced by the inactivity of one X-chromosome in females (Eicher, 1967; Deol and Green, 1969). The efficiency of the use of mosaics in the analysis of the effects of behavioral mutants points again to the close connection between developmental and behavioral genetics.

Evolutionary implications

The importance of behavior for evolution has been repeatedly mentioned in this article, and has been emphasized by Mayr (1963, 1974) and by Parsons (1976). First of all, behavior is itself a group of characters which are changing in evolution, and since changes in evolution are by definition genetic (for the changes in behavior due to cultural transmission, another term should be used), the genetic basis of behavior is of great importance for the interpretation of the data provided by ethologists.

In addition, behavioral changes belong to the most important components in evolutionary processes. Parsons (1976) reviews material which deals with the genetic basis of assortative mating, mating barriers and sexual isolation in Drosophila. Sexual isolation results in speciation, the breaking up of a species into two or more. Thus behavioral changes leading to sexual isolation precede, in evolution, morphological changes.

Mayr (1963) emphasizes that the same is true for aspects of behavior not concerned with mating. In the opening up of a new ecological niche a change in behavior will always be the first step, and morphological changes will follow which improve adaptedness of the population to the new environment. Thus the whole problem of the adaptedness of species to their environments, the fundamental observation explained by Darwin's theory of evolution, is to a large degree a problem of the genetic basis of behavior. The same is true for behavioral signals which produce communication within the species and between species, and are thus necessary for social organization and interspecies relations.

An important problem which has hardly been attacked is the evolution of open behavioral programs. As was mentioned earlier, some instances of conditioning and changing of behavior by experience are known from Drosophila and bees and probably occur in other insects. Nevertheless, in insects as well as in lower vertebrates, the more complex activities are controlled by fixed action patterns. Only in birds and mammals have open behavioral programs become frequent, and even essential. And in humans, open programs have reached such a prevalence that psychologists have seriously challenged the existence of closed programs. There is no doubt that this has been an evolutionary process, which has proceeded slowly at first, and apparently quite rapidly in human evolution. The analysis of this process needs a closer understanding of the genetic basis of open behavior programs and of learning. We have seen that some starts in this direction have been made, but that it has not yet proceeded far. The problem of the evolution of the plasticity of behavior in mammals and human beings appears to be one of the most attractive problems in the realm of behavior genetics.

Literature cited

Adler, J. (1976) The sensing of chemicals by bacteria, *Sci. Am. 234*, 40–47

Armstrong, J. B. and Adler, J. (1969) Complementation of non-chemotactic mutants in Escherichia coli, *Genetics 61*, 61–66

Atlas, S. A., Taylor, B. A., Diwan, B. A. and Nebert, D. W. (1976) Inducible monooxygenase activities and 3-methycholanthrene-induced tumorigenesis in mouse recombinant inbred sublines, *Genetics 83*, 537–550

Benzer, S. (1973) Genetic dissection of behavior, *Sci. Am. 229*, 24–37

Bovet, D., Bovet-Nitti, F. and Oliverio, A. (1969) Genetic aspects of learning and memory in mice, *Science 163*, 139–149

Broadhurst, P. L. (1960) Experiments in psychogenetics. Application of biometrical genetics to the inheritance of behavior. In: *Experiments in Personality. I. Psychogenetics and Psychopharmacology* (H. J. Eysenck, ed.) pp. 1–102, Routledge and Kegan Paul, London

Bruell, J. H. (1964) Inheritance of behavioral and physiological characters of mice and the problem of heterosis, *Am. Zool. 4*, 125–138

Caspari, E. (1958) The genetic basis of behavior. In: *Evolution and Behavior* (A. Roe and G. G. Simpson, eds.) pp. 103–127, Yale University Press, New Haven

Caspari, E. (1971) Differentiation and pattern formation in the development of behavior. In: *The Biopsychology of Development* (E. Tolbach, L. R. Aronson and E. Shaw, eds.) Academic Press, New York

Caspari, E. (1975) Probleme der modernen Verhaltensgenetik, *Verh. Dtsch. Zool. Ges. 68*, 13–17

Chovnick, A., Gelbart, W., McCarron, M., Osmond, B., Candido, E. P. M. and Baillie, D. L. (1976) Organization of the rosy locus in Drosophila melanogaster. Evidence for a control element adjacent to the xanthine dehydrogenase structural element, *Genetics 84*, 233–255

Collins, R. L. (1964) Inheritance of avoidance conditioning in mice. A diallel study, *Science 143*, 1188–1190

Collins, R. L. and Fuller, J. L. (1968) Audiogenic seizure prone (asp). A gene affecting behavior in linkage group VIII of the mouse, *Science 162*, 1137–1139

Cupello, A. and Hydén, H. (1976) Alterations of the pattern of hippocampal nerve cell RNA labelling during training in rats, *Brain Res. 114*, 453–460.

Davidson, E. H. and Britten, R. J. (1973) Organization, transcription and regulation in the animal genome, *Quart. Rev. Biol. 48*, 565–613

De Fries, J. C. (1972) Quantitative aspects of genetics and environment in the determination of behavior. In: *Genetics, Environment and Behavior* (L. Ehrman, G. S. Omenn and E. Caspari, eds.) pp. 5–21, Academic Press, New York

De Fries, J. C. and McClearn, J. (1973) *Introduction to Behavioral Genetics*, Freeman, San Francisco

Deol, M. S. and Green, M. C. (1969) Cattanach's translocation as a tool for studying the action of the shaker-l gene in the mouse, *J. Exptl. Zool. 170*, 301–310

Ehrman, L. and Parsons, P. A. (1976) *The Genetics of Behavior*, Sinauer Associates, Stanford

Eicher, E. M. (1967) The genetic extent of the insertion involved in the flecked translocation in the mouse, *Genetics 55*, 203–212

Feldman, M. W. and Lewontin, R. C. (1975) The heritability hang-up, *Science 193*, 848–856

Fulker, D. W. (1966) Mating speed in male Drosophila melanogaster. A psychogenetic analysis, *Science 153*, 203–305

Fuller, J. L. and Thompson, W. R. (1960) *Behavior Genetics*, Wiley, New York

Ganschow, R. E. and Schimke, R. T. (1960) Independent genetic control of the catalytic activity and the rate of degradation of catalase in mice, *J. Biol. Chem. 244*, 4649–4658

Goodwill, R. (1975) An analysis of the mode of gene action affecting pupa weight in Tribolium castaneum, *Genetics 79*, 219–229

Haglid, K., Hamberger, A. Hansson, M.-A., Hydén, H., Persson, P. and Rönnbäck, L. (1974) S-100 protein in synapses of the central nervous system, *Nature 251*, 532–534

Hotta, Y. and Benzer S. (1972) Mapping of behavior in Drosophila mosaics, *Nature 240*, 527–535

Hydén, H. (1974) A calcium-dependent mechanism for synapse and nerve cell membrane modulation, *Proc. Natl. Acad. Sci. U.S. 71*, 2965–2968

Hydén, H. and Lange, P. W. (1972) Protein synthesis in hippocampal nerve cells during re-reversal of handedness, *Brain Res. 45*, 314–317

Hydén, H., Lange, P. W. and Seyfried, C. (1973) Biochemical brain protein changes produced by selective breeding for learning in rats, *Brain Res. 61*, 446–451

Kaplan, W. D. and Trout, W. E. III (1969) The behavior of four neurological mutants of Drosophila, *Genetics 61*, 399–409

Kung, Ch. (1971) Genic mutants with altered system of excitation in Paramecium aurelia. II. Mutagenesis, screening and genetic analysis of the mutants, *Genetics 69*, 29–45

Lewin, B. (1975) Units of transcription and translation. The relationship between heterogeneous nuclear RNA and messenger RNA, *Cell 4*, 11–20, 77–93

Lush, J. L. (1949) Heritability of quantitative characters in farm animals, *Hereditas, Suppl. Vol. 356–375*

Lusis, A. J. and Paigen, K. (1975) Genetic determination of the α-galactosidase developmental program in mice, *Cell 6*, 371–378

Mayr, E. (1963) *Animal Species and Evolution*, Harvard University Press, Cambridge

Mayr, E. (1974) Behavior programs and evolutionary strategies, *Am. Sci. 62*, 650–659

McClintock, B. (1956) Controlling elements and the gene, *Cold Spring Harbor Symp. Quant. Biol. 21*, 197–216

McClintock, B. (1965) The control of gene action in maize, *Brookhaven Symp. Biol. 18*, 162–184

Mitton, J. and Koehn, R. (1973) Population genetics of marine pelecypods. III. Epistasis between functionally related isoenzymes of Mytilus edulis, *Genetics 73*, 487–496

Nebert, D. W., Felton, J. S. and Robinson, J. R. (1975) Developmental and genetic aspects of drug and environmental toxicity, *Proc. Eur. Soc. Toxicol. 16*, 82–95, Elsevier, Amsterdam

Oliverio, A., Eleftheriou, B. E. and Bailey, D. W. (1973a) Exploratory activity. Genetic analysis of its modifications by scopolamine and amphetamine, *Physiol. Behav. 10*, 893–899

Oliverio, A., Eleftheriou, B. E. and Bailey, D. W. (1973b) A gene influencing active avoidance performance in mice, *Physiol. Behav. 11*, 497–501

Oliverio, A. and Messeri, P. (1973) An analysis of single gene effects on avoidance, maze, wheel running and exploratory behavior in the mouse, *Behav. Biol. 8*, 771–783

Omenn, G. S. (1976) Inborn errors of metabolism. Clues to understanding human behavioral disorders, *Behav. Gen. 6*, 263–284

Paigen, K. (1971) The genetics of enzyme realization. In: *Enzyme Synthesis and Degradation in Mammalian Systems* (M. Recheigl, ed.) pp. 1–46, Karger, Basel

Parsons, P. A. (1977) Genes, behavior and evolutionary processes. The genus Drosophila, *Adv. Genet. 19*, 1–32

Poland, A., Glover, E. and Kende, A. S. (1976) Stereospecific high-affinity binding of 2, 3, 7,

8,-tetrachlorodibenzo-p-dioxin by hepatic cytosol, *J. Biol. Chem. 251*, 4936–4946

Provine, W. B. (1971) *The Origins of Theoretical Population Genetics*, University of Chicago Press, Chicago.

Pruzan, A. and Ehrman, L. (1974) Age, experience and rare-male mating advantages in Drosophila pseudoobscura, *Behav. Genet. 4*, 159–164

Quinn, W. G., Harris, W. A. and Benzer, S. (1974) Conditioned behavior in Drosophila melanogaster, *Proc. Natl. Acad. Sci. U.S. 71*, 708–712

Rothenbuhler, W. C. (1964) Behavior genetics of nest cleaning in honey bees. IV. Responses of F_1 and backcross generations to disease-killed brood, *Am. Zool. 4*, 111–123

Royce, J. R. and Covington, M. (1960) Genetic differences in avoidance conditioning of mice, *J. Comp. Physiol. Psychol. 53*, 197–200

Sturtevant, A. H. (1915) Experiments on sex recognition and the problem of sexual selection in Drosophila, *J. Anim. Behav. 5*, 351–366

Suzuki, D. T., Kaufman, T., Falk, D. and the U.B.C. Drosophila Research Group (1976) Conditionally expressed mutations in Drosophila melanogaster. In: *The Genetics and Biology of Drosophila*. (M. Ashburner and E. Novitski, eds.) Vol. 1a, pp. 201–263

Swank, R. T., Paigen, K. and Ganschow, R. E. (1973) Genetic control of glucuronidase induction in mice. *J. Mol. Biol. 81*, 225–243

Timoféeff-Ressovsky, N. W. (1934) Ueber den Einfluss des genotypischen Milieus und der Aussenbedingungen auf die Realisation des Genotyps, *Nachr. Ges. Wiss. Göttingen, Math. -Phys. Kl VI. Biol. N.F. 1*, 53–106

Tryon, R. C. (1940) Genetic differences in maze-learning ability in rats, *Yearb. Natl. Soc. Study Educ. 39*, 111–119

Watson, M. L. (1968) Blind, a dominant mutation in mice, *J. Hered. 59*, 60–64

Genetics, environment and intelligence, edited by A. Oliverio
© *Elsevier/North-Holland Biomedical Press, 1977*

Behavioral comparisons and evolution   2

JOHN A. KING

Introduction

The process of evolution is natural selection, which preserves the genes of successfully reproducing individuals in their progeny. The process is logically sound, simple to comprehend, readily observed and artificially duplicated, but foreever devious and mysterious. It is devious because there is no absolute, direct path to the preservation of genes in succeeding generations. Indeed, it operates through a series of compromises made possible by the abundance of genetic material packaged in an endless variety of cytoplasm. One of the most mysterious compromises natural selection produces in organisms is that between two basic concepts clothed with many close synonyms: rigidity and flexibility, stereotypy and plasticity, predictability and randomness, uniformity and diversity, stability and variability, hardwired and soft-wired, conservatism and radicalism. The compromise is a dilemma faced by mankind as well as nature: when to waver and when to stand firm on a course of action. Like each human being, each organism has developed a strategy that

Acknowledgement for support of many of the studies reported in this chapter is given to the National Institutes of Health, United States Public Health Service and the College of Osteopathic Medicine, Michigan State University. Martin Balaban and Lincoln Gray critically read the manuscript.

propells it down the diverging paths through an environment of selective forces. This chapter will examine how the compromise between rigidity and flexibility is made in a group of mice of the genus *Peromyscus*.

One goal of comparative studies is to understand the process of natural selection well enough to predict how a given individual, geographical race or species will behave. Material for this prediction has usually come from knowing either an animal's phylogenetic relationships or its ecology. Predictions based on these materials are often wrong because we have been examining inappropriate aspects of behavior. This chapter will take us through a search for predictability by examining four general and overlapping categories of behavior: adaptive, reflexive, abstractive, and strategic. The adaptive behavior will be sand digging; the reflexive behavior will be the optokinetic reflex used in studying visual acuity; the abstractive behavior will be learning; and the strategic behavior will be that employed in feeding. From each of these general categories of behavior, we will examine how the compromise between rigidity and flexibility can be made. The compromise can be made by diversity among individuals or local populations, by individuals during their development, by each individual's response to a new situation, or by the strategy individuals employ in solving problems. The illustrations of how natural selection could achieve these compromises are drawn from comparisons of animals of known genetic differences: geographic races or species. Such comparisons can serve as models for individual differences in most genetically diverse populations like those of human beings.

The subjects of this quest for predictability are mice of the genus *Peromyscus*, which is in the family Cricitidae. Although they bear a superficial resemblence to house or laboratory mice of the genus *Mus*, in the family Muridae, they are phylogenetically remote. *Peromyscus* is restricted in distribution to North America, unlike the cosmopolitan *Mus*. In Eurasia, their ecological and morphological counterparts are mice of the genus *Apodemus*, which are murids. Most species range in weight from 15 to 30 grams. They have larger eyes than house mice, and are primarily restricted to nocturnal activity. Their diet is primarily insects, seeds, and nuts, some of which they store because they are active throughout the year. The genus contains over 50 species, which are classified into seven subgenera, seven species groups, and over 200 subspecies or geographical races (Hooper, 1968). Representatives of the genus are found in most habitats on the continent; deserts, grasslands, forests, jungles, mountains, beaches (Baker, 1968). They have developed behavioral habits appropriate for the habitat: fossorial, scansorial, arboreal, terrestrial. As the most common North American rodent, they have been the subject of many studies (King, 1968b), including those of my students reported here.

An "adaptive" behavior: digging

Everyone expects differences among species. They have different phylogenies and they are adapted to different environments. The same expectation prevails with surgical interventions, pharmacological injections, or experiential treatments. The question is, can these differences be predicted? Do we know enough about the phylogeny of a species or its adaptations to a specific environment to predict a given behavior? Probably not until we have examined the behavior of a sufficient number of species from diverse habitats, so that we know what kinds of behavior can be exhibited. From these baseline data, predictable patterns may emerge. The first task, then, is to discover differences in as many different types of behavior and in as many different species as possible. Some investigators argue that adaptive behavior should be examined when making species comparisons. Adaptive behavior insures reproductive success under natural conditions. This argument assumes that the animals can readily be observed in the field, or that field-like tests can be created in the laboratory, and that the investigator can identify adaptive behavior. An alternative argument is that the behaviors to be sought are basic sensory-motor patterns that might be applicable to a variety of field situations. Pragmatists familiar with the vicissitudes of animal testing argue in favor of any test that produces differences, which eventually must fit a pattern or otherwise be explained. Some investigators apparently conjure the pattern first and then collect the most applicable data.

"Adaptive" behavior is used because it suggests behavior that the animal may be expected to use in the process of surviving or reproducing. If the animal repeatedly exhibits certain behavior patterns in the field, they are considered adaptive because animals are on a tight energy budget. According to this optimality theory, animals cannot afford the luxury of inefficient or non-adaptive behavior, which is selected out in the course of their evolution. Perhaps over the long run, that is, an entire life-time or over several generations, the energy budget is balanced and optimality theory can successfully predict behavior in general, but not in particular. Thus, the term adaptive behavior merely implies that the behavior would probably not be present without some adaptive function. There are ways to test whether a behavior is adaptive or not within a given generation or two, but this is rarely done because of the difficulty in modifying behavior in free-ranging animals. The tests require at least two free-ranging groups of animals: one group that exhibits the behavior and the other group that does not exhibit it, or that exhibits it to a measurably less degree. Then the survivorship, reproductive output, or some intermediate behavior is measured to find the effect of the presence or absence of a given behavior. Parent gulls remove the shells of hatched eggs from their nests. Tinbergen et al. (1962) showed this to be adaptive when they found that artificial nests with the shells left in were preyed upon by crows more than nests without shells. Here the experimenter mimicked the gulls' behavior in order to make the test. Another example of an adaptation test is the effect of the song-spread display in red-winged blackbirds on territoriality. This vocal and visual display of the red epaulets is considered adaptive in that it enables the male red-wing to establish and maintain a territory, which is necessary for successful breeding. The display was altered by the investigators, who devocalized the birds and/or painted the red epaulets black (Smith, 1972; Peek, 1972). The display was found to be more adaptive in establishing the territory than in keeping it after the females had nested. In the absence of such tests, our use of the term adaptive behavior is purely conjectural, but it does serve to distinguish a group of naturally occurring behaviors from those one would not expect to observe in the field.

One other comment about adaptive behaviors before we examine them in *Peromyscus*. The concept is prone to circular reasoning. If a behavior pattern is repeatedly exhibited by most individuals of a species, we assume it is adaptive. Then, after thorough study and careful measures of the assumed adaptive behavior, we evaluate an animal's adaptation to a particular environment by the amount of the behavior exhibited. For example, woodpeckers peck away wood in order to obtain food. Thus, pecking wood is adaptive, and those birds that peck the most wood are best adapted to wood pecking. The behavior is there because it is adaptive and it is adaptive because it is there.

Some of the adaptive behaviors that have been studied in *Peromyscus* are: gnawing, swimming, climbing, digging, nest building, hoarding, feeding, and vocalizing of the young. In each behavior, some species, subspecies, or population differences have been found. Digging sand can be examined in detail because several independent measures are available.

One would predict that terrestrial species of mice living on sandy or readily excavated sandy soils would be better at digging than semi-arboreal species living amid an abundance of refuges under fallen logs, in holes of trees and between roots. Some species have to excavate their own burrows and refuges, whereas other species can use existing refuges. Foraging mice may also dig sand away from food buried beneath. Two phylogenetically remote species have been compared in three independent tests. One species, *P. leucopus*, is a semi-arboreal species that primarily inhabits the mixed deciduous forests of northeastern United States. This widely distributed species might be expected to exhibit a variety of adaptive behaviors, but digging should not be among them because it rarely encounters sand in its native habitat, which has an abudance of refuges. In contrast, the other species, *P. floridanus*, is limited in distribution to peninsular Florida, where it lives on exposed sandy soils and has subterranean burrows in the sand. Although some field observers report (Blair and Kilby, 1936; Layne, 1969) that *P. floridanus* usually takes over the burrows of other animals rather than digging them for itself, the hypothesis is that the sand dwelling *P. floridanus* should dig in sand more than the semi-arboreal *P. leucopus*.

The results of one experiment (King et al., 1968) support this hypothesis because only 14% of the *P. leucopus* individuals tested dug any sand at all, whereas 87% of the *P. floridanus* did dig. The mice in this experiment were given five minutes to remove sand from a tunnel that blocked a passage between compartments of their cage. On the basis of this experiment, the initial conclusion is that the Florida mice were adapted to dig by the different selection pressures operating in their sandy environment. However, in another test where the mice were again free to remove sand from a tunnel (King and Weisman, 1964) the percentage of mice that dug did not differ significantly (*P. leucopus*, 75%; *P. floridanus*, 82%), but this time they were allowed 23 hours. Perhaps if the mice were given a longer period, all of them would dig and the test was not valid. On the other hand, similarity between the two species was also shown in the quantity of sand removed during the 23 hours: the maximum amount of sand dug by both *P. leucopus* and *P. floridanus* was approximately 86 pounds. Either the adaptive hypothesis must be discarded or it must be modified to include some other variable, such as the duration of the test. In still another test (Layne and Ehrhart, 1970), the observers recorded the latency, duration, and frequency of digging in a sand substratum for five minutes rather than the percentage of individuals digging. The performance of the two species was reversed, with *P. leucopus* doing more digging than *P. floridanus*. Now the adaptation hypothesis is in jeopardy; the ease of following the circular reasoning is broken, and we thrash about grasping for other explanations. The usual explanation is that the tests were not valid and better tests must be devised. Similar grasps have been observed among those searching for cross-cultural intelligence tests. Rather than attempting to confirm the hypothesis that one species is better adapted for digging than the other, these tests suggest another adaptive strategy that is often obscured by average performance scores. That strategy calls for genetic heterogeneity among individuals and between populations of the same species (Dobzhansky, 1971). The proportion of individuals that dig, for instance, may change throughout time, thus insuring the success of some members of the population, should digging be necessary for survival. Note that these experiments did not demonstrate this strategy; they only suggest that such polymorphism in behavior could exist and further experiments would be necessary to test for it. It is also important to remember that such polymorphism would result from changing selection pressures from time to time or from place to place and not from an individual's readiness to sacrifice its reproductive potential. The compromise in many regularly observed behaviors in the field is between diversity and uniformity among the individuals of the population. Some populations, races or species exhibit more diversity among the individual members than others.

The optokinetic reflex in visual acuity

If the problems with adaptive responses, such as digging, are guessing what behaviors are adaptive and the circularity of the reasoning, then a basic sensory-motor response like the optokinetic reflex for studying visual acuity may enable us to predict the behavior of a species. Visual acuity depends upon the optical physics of the eye, the neuroanatomy of the receptors and transmitting neurons, and the differentiation of the visual cortex. When visual acuity is measured by discrimination tests (Rahmann et al., 1968), motivation and learning ability intervene and obscure basic sensory-motor properties of each species. At the other extreme, neuro-electrical potentials from the receptor, transmittor, or associative cells reveal sensation, but not perception. A reflex provides the compromise. The optokinetic response in deermice is reliable, detectable and functional at the age of eyelid separation (Vestal and King, 1968). Species differences in visual acuity can be measured before the young mice are weaned and before they usually encounter modifying experiences outside the nest.

If species are to differ, they should certainly do so in a simple visual-motor reflex at its ontogenetic onset. Predictions of what happens later in life may be difficult to make.

Two sympatric species occur over much of eastern North America. In southern Michigan, the local *P. maniculatus* inhabit open, cultivated fields or grasslands, whereas the local *P. leucopus* inhabit woods, brush land, and overgrown fence rows. *P. maniculatus* is terrestrial and *P. leucopus* is scansorial and semi-arboreal. The species belong to different species groups, but to the same subgenus, which means that their phylogenetic relationships have progressed far enough for them to be reproductively isolated, even when caged together. (According to Dice (1968), laboratory pairings within species groups usually produce viable offspring.) Both species open their eyes at approximately the same age and grow at approximately the same rate (Vestal, 1973; King and Eleftheriou, 1960; King, 1965). In an optokinetic drum consisting of vertical black and white stripes of various widths, located at a radius of 40 cm from the mice, they exhibit a slow head movement in pursuit of the rotating stripes or an ocular nystagmus, when the stripes are broad enough to be perceptible.

At the age when the mice can first see, *P. maniculatus* has more acute vision than *P. leucopus* (Vestal, 1973). With maturation, the visual acuity of both species significantly improves, so that by six days after the onset of vision, both have almost reached the limits of the testing apparatus (a visual angle of 14 minutes of arc). However, *P. maniculatus* maintains its visual superiority for five days, before *P. leucopus* catches up. The initial species difference in visual acuity is lost and the species have similar acuity as adults, with visual angles of approximately four minutes of arc (King and Vestal, 1974). Although these two species ultimately have the same visual acuity, the differences in the rate of development illustrates another possible place for a compromise. Rapidly maturing individuals may be more rigid in their behavior than those whose maturation has a longer time to be shaped by intervening stimuli (Waber, 1976). This is suggested by the variance, which is three times larger in *P. leucopus* than in *P. maniculatus*. That even visual acuity can be altered by intervening stimuli in the rapidly maturing *P. maniculatus* is evident from a comparison between longitudinally and cross-sectionally tested groups, i.e., individuals tested repeatedly throughout development versus different individuals tested only once at each age (Vestal and King, 1971). Visual acuity was enhanced significantly for those individuals who had been exposed to the rotating visual stripes (and to handling) for three days after the onset of vision. The acuity of the longitudinally tested mice remained better for three days before both groups reached the limits of the apparatus. If these species differences in the rate of development of visual acuity are attributed to genetic differences, and if the rate of development influences the duration of exposure to modifying stimuli, the opportunities for either rigidity or flexibility are compounded. For example, a slowly developing mouse with little exposure to modifying visual stimuli may have the same acuity as a fast developing mouse with abundant stimuli. Or, as we shall see in the discussion on learning, the visual experiences could coincide with the rate of development (e.g. much stimulation and slow development) to enhance the acuity of one species and diminish it in the other.

From the analysis of an adaptive behavior like digging, we learned that genetic polymorphism of a behavioral trait may be the adaptive strategy. This brief analysis of the development of a visual-motor reflex suggests other sources of diversity among individuals (King, 1968a). First, the age that a behavior or perceptual capability first appears or its level of development when it occurs may differ genetically between species (Vestal and King, 1968; Vestal, 1973). Second, the rate of development of the response may differ among species as Vestal (1973) found in the development of visual acuity. Third, diversity can be added even to fundamental neurosensory processes like vision through differential visual exposures, which can affect acuity during development (Vestal and King, 1971) or even adult neurophysiology and performance (Blakemore, 1973). The evolutionary process of natural selection can stabilize or disrupt the expression of behavior patterns by acting upon these sources of variation among individuals (King, 1967).

Learning: an abstraction

Species comparison in behavior, whether at the instinctive or sensory-motor level, fail to provide compelling phylogenetic or ecologic patterns in mammalian evolution. If one cannot reliably predict that terrestrial mice dwelling on a sand substrate are sand diggers, nor predict that the visual acuity of two closely related species will be similar, then perhaps we should examine mental attributes, like learning or emotion, which are conceptually abstracted from the observed responses. One might expect that learning is an attribute that works in a variety of situations and is modifiable by definition. Natural selection should have produced some systematic pattern of learning ability among phylogenetically related mice or those inhabiting similar habitats (see Warren, this volume).

Experimental investigations of learning in *Peromyscus* have admittedly been superficial. Perhaps some time an investigator will carefully explore learning over a wide phyletic array of *Peromyscus* with a broad variety of learning tasks. In the meantime, let us examine what compromise between rigidity and flexibility natural selection has produced in two geographic races (subspecies) of *P. maniculatus* in two types of learning situations: passive avoidance and Sidman avoidance (1953).

Peromyscus maniculatus is widely distributed over most of the United States and Canada. Throughout this range, it has diversified into over sixty recognizable geographic races that can roughly be put into two categories of races or subspecies: sylvan and pastoral. The sylvan subspecies are generally boreal, forest inhabitants with dark pelages, large ears, and long tails. The pastoral races are usually southern inhabitants of grasslands, open fields, and deserts. Their pelage is paler than sylvan races and their ears are smaller and their tails shorter. Numerous intergrading populations exist, but morphological characteristics are distinguishable. In some regions, the two forms occur in proximity: when sylvan forms in alpine forests are surrounded by lowland, desert-dwelling pastoral races, or when pockets of prairie interdigitate with deciduous forests. Among the Great Lakes, agricultural practices have cleared away much of the original forests and the pastoral races have dispersed into the cultivated fields from prairie pockets and open beaches, so that both races occasionally inhabit adjacent fields and forests. The pastoral race is designated *P. m. bairdi* and the sylvan race is *P. m. gracilis*. They are interfertile in laboratory matings, but probably they are reproductively isolated in the field because of their strict habitat preferences (Harris, 1952; Wecker, 1963; Fitch, 1975). Natural hybrids are difficult to distinguish and they could even resemble the sympatric species *P. leucopus*. In addition to their morphological differences and habitat preferences, the two races differ in the growth rates and in many behavioral characteristics, including learning (King and Eleftheriou, 1960; King, 1961).

In a passive avoidance situation, where the mice could escape shocks to the feet by running across an electrified grid to a safe platform, the races performed differently (King, 1961). Once *P. m. bairdi* distinguished between the electric grid and the safe platform, it terminated further activity and sat quietly on the platform until the end of the minute-long test. In contrast, duration scores on the safe platform for *P. m. gracilis* suggested that they never learned to make the distinction between grid and platform because they repeatedly went back onto the grid after finding the safe platform. If the performance of both races had been recorded automatically, like so many passive avoidance tests for pharmacological effects on learning, the conclusion would be obvious: *P. m. bairdi* were better learners than *P. m. gracilis*. However, the behavior of these mice was carefully watched during the test and it soon became apparent that other factors in the behavior of these two races were operating. *P. m. bairdi* hopped about on the "hot" grid until it found the platform and then remained almost motionless, sometimes freezing in a position. On the other hand, when *P. m. gracilis* reached the platform, they groomed, stood up on their hind legs and sniffed the sides of the test chamber, and most revealing of all, some mice reached out onto the grid with a single paw, felt the shock, and jumped back onto the grid. This behavior resembled a bather testing how cold the water is before diving in. *P. m. gracilis* recognized the difference, but was either too excited by the shock to sit still or it continued to search for a better solution than merely sitting on the exposed platform. In this test the stereotypic freezing behavior of *P. m. bairdi* made it a far better "learner" than the plastic, exploratory behavior of *P. m. gracilis*.

A learning test that reverses the advantages of stereotypic freezing and plastic exploration is the Sidman avoidance test (King and Eleftheriou, 1959). In this test, an animal is confined to a chamber with a wire grid floor that is electrified for a brief pulse every 20 seconds or so. The timer that delivers the shock pulse every 20 seconds can be reset at any time during the 20 second interval by pressing a bar or performing some other operant behavior. To avoid being shocked, then, a mouse must press the bar and reset the timer at least once every 20 seconds. A mouse that freezes or remains motionless upon getting shocked, is unlikely to press the bar and will continue to get shocked every 20 seconds. In contrast, an active, exploratory mouse is likely to press the bar accidently, delay shock, and soon associate either increased general activity or specific bar pressing with avoidance of shock. Obviously, the learning scores of the two races were reversed in this test. *P. m. gracilis* maintained its activity by jumping about and pressing the bar that delayed the shock, whereas the passive sitting of *P. m. bairdi* caused it to receive repeated shocks, thus reversing the learning performance of the two races.

If these were human races rather than races of mice, one might postulate that the learning performance could be improved by training or some early treatment known to affect later learning ability. Among rodents, one such treatment is early handling (Levine, 1956; Whimby and Denenberg, 1967). When both races of mice were given a simulated handling experience during their first 25 days of life, their learning was altered, but not in the predicted direction. The good learner in the Sidman avoidance test (*P. m. gracilis*) became better and the poor learner (*P. m. bairdi*) became worse (King and Eleftheriou, 1959). Handling had strengthened the initial responsiveness to shock in both races, resulting in the active *P. m. gracilis* becoming more active and the inactive *P. m. bairdi* becoming less mobile. In terms of learning, the treatment made the race of good learners better and the race of poor learners worse. Equal treatments yielded opposite results.

Probably learning was of minor consequence in both test situations. Learning is an abstract concept derived from some motor activity like locomotion, pushing open doors, or bar pressing. In these tests, we were observing racial differences in response to electric shock (Foster, 1959) and learning was a consequence of these responses. These tests again emphasize that concepts like learning, intelligence, motivation, and emotion are abstractions derived from some concrete motor activities, which are better used for species comparisons than the abstractions from them.

Instead of studying the learning ability of these two races, we discovered that their approach or strategy upon encountering a new situation was different. In one race (*P. m. bairdi*), the behavior was rigid immobility, whereas in the other race (*P. m. gracilis*), the behavior was plastic and flexible, as if the mice were constantly seeking for new solutions to the problem of avoiding shock. The strategies differed along the rigidity-flexibility coninuum, but both strategies were apparently genetically fixed; *P. m. bairdi* was consistently rigid and *P. m. gracilis* was consistently flexible. However, the basic strategy of each race was vulnerable to modification by previous experience in the form of handling the infantile mice. The same experiences further polarized the strategies of the two races. If the strategies were genetically different and the difference could be enhanced by early experience, then natural selection could be operating on the epigenetic canalization of a behavioral strategy (Waddington, 1957). That is, the genotypic propensity to be modified by environmental factors was being selected for. Furthermore, it was not only the behavior pattern itself that was being selected, but also the strategy of solving the day to day problems of eating, mating, avoiding predators, etc. Natural selection was working on the process of ontogeny and the process of solving problems rather than operating on specific genetic traits that affected specific behavior patterns. No wonder we had failed to predict the behavior of a race or species of these complicated small mammals from our knowledge of their phylogenetic and ecologic relationships. We had been looking at the product rather than the process.

Feeding strategies

Most animals devote the major amount of their active time and energy in the location, pursuit and handling of food. The energy budget of optimality theory is most apparent in feeding because no animal can survive long without at least balancing the amount of energy consumed with the amount of energy expended. If the energy budget is positive, the animal can build up energy reserves in food caches or body fat, or it can use the excess energy to reproduce. A negative budget forces the animal to find food, to become dormant, or to starve, which probably causes most mortality. If starvation is just around the corner for animals, natural selection is readily apparent in how an animal finds its food. The strategy of finding food not only includes the problem of locating sufficient quantities of suitable nutrients, but also the risks of being injured by the prey or being poisoned by toxic plant substances as well as the risks of being killed by a predator while searching and eating (Schoener, 1971).

Among the sixty or more geographic races of *Peromyscus maniculatus*, two occupy ranges separated latitudinally by most of continental United States. One race, *P. m. blandus*, occurs in the southwest and the particular population discussed here is from the New Mexican desert about 50 miles north of the Mexican border. The other race, *P. m. borealis*, is from the Canadian province of Alberta, in the prairies near Calgary. The climates of both regions are dry, but precipitation is more efficiently used by vegetation in the north where evaporation is less than in the hot southern deserts. Climatic extremes with wide temperature fluctuations are also common to both regions, with extremely hot temperatures in the south and extremely cold temperatures in the north. Day-length fluctuations throughout the seasons are greater in the north than the south. Fauna and flora in the desert are more diverse than that of the northern prairies. Thus, *P. m. blandus* can select a wider variety of food than *P. m. borealis*, but *P. m. blandus* also has more species of competitors for the food because of the presence of other rodent species, seed-eating birds, and harvester ants (Brown et al., 1975; Whitford, 1976; Reichman, 1975; Merserve, 1976). The southern race should be more rigid in its feeding habits because it has more competitors than the northern race (Klopfer, 1973).

When the two races were offered a variety of four types of food, Gray (1977) expected that southern *P. m. blandus* would select fewer of the food items than the northern *P. m. borealis*. The four types of food offered were peanuts, wheat germ, sunflower seeds and millet. The foods differed in size, texture, nutrients, and probably taste and odor. Ten mice of each race were tested over six days, which enabled calculations of the diversity of foods taken by each mouse for each day, the diversity taken by each mouse over the six days, and the diversity shown by all ten mice of each race. The diversity was obtained from Shannon's index, $H' = -\sum_i p_i \log_e p_i$, where H' is the measure of diversity, p_i is the proportion of food taken in each of the four types, and $\log_e$ the natural log of p_i. H' has the important property that any change toward equalizing the set of p_i values will increase H'. Thus, a mouse that took 25% of the four foods each day would have the highest possible diversity in this situation or an

$H' = 1.39$, the natural log of four; whereas a mouse that ate 100% of one food and none of the other three foods would have a zero diversity and $H' = 0$. The results showed that the prediction was correct: *P. m. borealis* was significantly more diverse in selecting foods (mean $H' = 0.93$) than *P. m. blandus* (mean $H' = 0.65$). The direction of this difference was true if the calculations were done for the entire race, or for each individual within and over days. The foraging strategy of *P. m. borealis* is that of a generalist, which takes small amounts of various types of food each day; whereas *P. m. blandus* is a specialist, which selects primarily one suitable food type and stays with it day after day. The difference between this analysis and those of the preceding tests is that the critical measure of preference did not depend on which type of food was selected. Although racial preferences were apparent, the consistent measure was not upon the food item the mice preferred, but rather on how the mice made the selection. In the learning tests, we fallaciously attempted to find out which race was the best learner, instead of attempting to measure how they went about learning. Differences in learning to avoid shock were observed, but these differences were not measured.

The results of one test can be misleading because other factors could have entered into the selection of foods, which might have resembled or differed from food items in the natural environment of each race. What if the food was identical, but the mice had to perform different search and pursuit patterns to obtain it? Different individuals of the same two races were put into an elaborate apparatus consisting of a central living chamber with four radial chambers, each with a similar piece of food, positioned in such a way that the mouse had to climb, jump, swim or walk a narrow, elevated path to obtain the food (Gray, 1977). Here again a mouse could engage in one type of activity to get its daily ration of food or it could vary its activity, taking some food after climbing, swimming, jumping, or walking. It could also alter its pattern of foraging from day to day.

The results confirmed the food selection test in that the northern generalist, *P. m. borealis*, was much more diverse ($H' = 0.66$) than the southern specialist, *P. m. blandus*, ($H' = 0.19$). These different strategies were apparent within days and over days for each race. Other tests with the same races and with other species of mice (Drickamer, 1972) reveal that the diversity of foraging strategies is consistent and predictable, but predictions about the type of behavior or the particular item that will be maximally preferred are often wrong.

The compromise mice make between rigidity and flexibility in feeding strategies is no more fixed at birth than a sustained diet of milk. Dietary specialists develop from a flexible diet at weaning. When Gray offered four different foods to weanling mice of both races, the young *P. m. blandus*, which are specialists as adults, had diversity indices similar to that of both young and adult *P. m. borealis*. Sometime during development, young *P. m. blandus* change to a specialized strategy. When and how this ontogenetic change in feeding strategy occurs and what factors may influence it have yet to be investigated. But if rigidity develops with age in some genotypes, it certainly is worthwhile to investigate how such incapacitation can be prevented.

Discussion and conclusion

Predicting the behavior of a specific genotype correctly, whether it be a species, a geographical race, or an individual, is the type of scientific evidence that indicates we probably have isolated the factors responsible. Our predictions, however, can be influenced by many variables that are not always readily apparent. Although a knowledge of a species' phylogenetic relationships, its ecology, and the past experience of the sampled individuals are necessary, the predictions often go astray because we use the wrong dependent variable, that is, we measure the wrong behavior. Natural selection may act less upon the mean performance of an individual or a population, whether it is the mean amount of sand dug, the mean visual acuity, or the mean learning scores, than it acts upon the rigidity or flexibility of that performance – its diversity.

Within the genus *Peromyscus*, phylogenetic diversity is masked by a morphological resemblance that induces most casual observers to unite over fifty distinct species into a single category: mice. This broad category includes hundreds of other species of small rodents throughout the world. Most individuals of these numerous species have the capacity to perform "typical rodent-like" behavior: gnaw, dig, climb, swim, run, jump, groom, store food, build nests, retrieve young, fight, mate, vocalize, learn. Although some species are likely to perform some of these activities more than other species, the principle distinction between them is how they exhibit these activities in the variety of new situations they encounter in their search for food, mates and refuges. Among some populations, individuals will exhibit marked differences, so that a few individuals will survive any alteration or fluctuation of selection pressures. This behavioral polymorphism results from genetic-environmental interactions during ontogeny. The age when a behavior first appears, its rate of development, its canalization by different types of reinforcing stimuli contribute to the behavioral differences individuals exhibit from time to time, to the differences among individuals and among species. As a result, certain individuals become specialists, rigid in much of their behavior, perhaps because the selective forces in their environment were constant or predictable. Certain other individuals, as members of a race or a species, retain their juvenile, generalist patterns and constantly seek out different foods, new ways to avoid noxious stimuli, and strange habitats to invade. This variable strategy of life may be attributed to a relatively unpredictable environment. Since environments and their associated selection pressures are neither entirely predictable nor entirely unpredictable, mouse and man compromise their behavior between those pressures that reinforce rigidity and those that facilitate flexibility. Our task is to measure that compromise and discover what factors are necessary to change it.

Literature cited

Baker, R. H. (1968) Habitats and distribution. In: Biology of Peromyscus (Rodentia) (J. A. King, ed.) *Am. Soc. Mammal.* 2, 98–126

Blair, W. F. and Kilby, J. D. (1936) The gopher mouse, Peromyscus floridanus, *J. Mammal. 17*, 421–422

Blakemore, C. (1973) Environmental constraints on development. In: *Constraints on Learning* (R. A. Hinde and J. S. Hinde, eds.) Academic Press, London

Brown, J. H., Grover, J. J., Davidson, D. W. and Lieberman, G. A. (1975) A preliminary study of seed predation in desert and montane habitats, *Ecology 56*, 987–992

Dice, L. R. (1968) Speciation. In: Biology of Peromyscus (Rodentia). (J. A. King, ed.) *Am. Soc. Mammal. 2*, 75–97

Dobzhansky, T. (1971) *Genetics of the Evolutionary Process*, Columbia Univerisity Press, New York

Drickamer, L. C. (1972) Experience and selection behavior in the food habits of Peromyscus. Use of olfaction, *Behavior 41*, 269–287

Fitch, J. H. (1975) Behavioral habitat selection as a factor in the distribution of woodland deermice, Peromyscus maniculatus gracilis, in the Kingston Plains of Northern Michigan. Ph.D. dissertation, Michigan State University, unpublished

Foster, D. D. (1959) Differences in behavior and temperament between two races of the deermouse, *J. Mammal. 40*, 496–513

Gray, L. (1977) Diversity of foraging strategies of Peromyscus maniculatus is consistent and predictable. Ph.D. dissertation, Michigan State University, unpublished

Harris, V. T. (1952) An experimental study of habitat selection by prairie and forest races of the deermouse, Peromyscus maniculatus, *Contr. Lab. Vert. Biol., Univ. Mich. 56*, 1–53

Hooper, E. T. (1968) Classification. In: Biology of Peromyscus (Rodentia), (J. A. King, ed.) *Am. Soc. Mammal 2*, 27–69

King, J. A. (1961) Swimming and reaction to electric shock in two subspecies of deermice (Peromyscus maniculatus) during development, *Anim. Behav. 9*, 142–150

King, J. A. (1965) Body, brain, and lens weights of Peromyscus, *Zool. Jahrb. Anat. 82*, 177–188

King, J. A. (1967) Behavioral modification of the gene pool. In: *Behavior-Genetic Analysis* (J. Hirsch, ed.) pp. 22–43, McGraw-Hill, New York

King, J. A. (1968a) Species specificity and early experience. In: *Early Experience and Behavior* (G. Newton and S. Levine, eds.) pp. 42–64, Thomas, Springfield

King, J. A. (1968b) Biology of Peromyscus (Rodentia), *Am. Soc. Mammal. 2*, 593

King, J. A. and Eleftheriou, B. E. (1959) Effects of early handling upon adult behavior in two subspecies of deermice, Peromyscus maniculatus, *J. Comp. Physiol. Psych. 52*, 82–88

King, J. A. and Eleftheriou, B. E. (1960) Differential growth in the skulls of two subspecies of deermice, *Growth 24*, 179–192

King, J. A., Price, E. O. and Weber, P. L. (1968) Behavioral comparisons within the genus Peromyscus, *Pap. Mich. Acad. Sci. Arts Lett. 53*, 113–136

King, J. A. and Vestal, B. M. (1974) Visual acuity of Peromyscus. *J. Mammal 55*, 238–243

King, J. A. and Weisman, R. G. (1964) Sand digging contingent upon bar pressing in deermice (Peromyscus), *Anim. Behav. 12*, 446–450

Klopfer, P. H. (1973) *Behavioral Aspects of Ecology*, pp. 1–200, Prentice-Hall, Englewood Cliff

Layne, J. N. (1969) Nest building behavior in three species of deermice, Peromyscus, *Behavior 35*, 288–303

Layne, J. N. and Ehrhart, L. M. (1970) Digging behavior of four species of deermice (Peromyscus), *Am. Mus. Novitates 2429*, 1–16

Levine, S. (1956) A further study of infantile handling and adult avoidance learning, *J. Pers. 25*, 70–80

Merserve, P. L. (1976) Food relationships of a rodent fauna in a California coastal sage scrub community, *J. Mammal. 57*, 300–319

Peek, F. W. (1972) An experimental study of the territorial function of vocal and visual display in the male red-winged blackbird (Agelaius phoeniceus), *Anim. Behav. 20*, 112–118

Rahmann, H., Rahmann, M., and King, J. A. (1968) Comparative visual acuity (minimum separable) in five species and subspecies of deermice (Peromyscus), *Physiol. Zool. 41*, 298–312

Reichman, O. J. (1975) Relation of desert rodent diets to available resources, *J. Mammal. 56*, 731–751

Schoener, T. W. (1971) Theory of feeding strategies. In: *Annual Review of Ecology and Systematics* (R. F. Johnston, P. W. Frank and C. D. Michener, eds.) Vol. 2, pp. 369–404, Annual Reviews, Palo Alto

Sidman, M. (1953) Two temporal parameters of the maintenance of avoidance behavior, *J. Comp. Physiol. Psychol. 46*, 253–261

Smith, D. G. (1972) The role of the epaulets in the red-winged blackbird (Agelaius phoeniceus) social system, *Behaviour 41*, 251–268

Tinbergen, N., Broekhuysen, G. J., Feekes, F., Haughton, J. C. W., Kruuk, H. and Szulc, E. (1962) Egg shell removal by the black-headed gull, Larus ridibundus L. A behavior component of camouflage, *Behavior 19*, 74–117

Vestal, B. M. (1973) Ontogeny of visual acuity in two species of deermice (Peromyscus), *Anim. Behav. 21*, 711–719

Vestal, B. M. and King, J. A. (1968) Relationship of age at eye opening to first optokinetic response in deermice (Peromyscus), *Dev. Psychobiol. 1*, 30–34

Vestal, B. M. and King, J. A (1971) Effect of repeated testing on development of visual acuity in prairie deermice (Peromyscus maniculatus bairdii), *Psychon. Sci. 25*, 297–298

Waber, D. P. (1976) Sex differences in cognition. A function of maturation rate? *Science 192*, 572–574

Waddington, C. H. (1957) *The Strategy of the Genes*, Allen and Unwin, London

Wecker, S. C. (1963) The role of early experience in habitat selection by the prairie deermouse, Peromyscus maniculatus bairdii, *Ecol. Monogr. 33*, 307–325

Whimby, A. E. and Denenberg, V. H. (1967) Experimental programming of life histories. The factor structure underlying experimentally created individual differences, *Behaviour 29*, 296–314

Whitford, W. G. (1976) Temporal fluctuations in density and diversity of desert rodent populations, *J. Mammal. 57*, 351–369

Genetics, environment and intelligence, edited by A. Oliverio
© *Elsevier/North-Holland Biomedical Press, 1977*

A phylogenetic approach to learning and intelligence

3

J. M. WARREN

Introduction

Words like "phylogenetic" and "comparative" in a title are inevitably ambiguous. The reader cannot tell if they are to be taken in the evolutionary or functional sense. To the evolutionary biologist, "phylogenetic" means the study of similarities and dissimilarities in the homologous characters of related species, to determine the historical origins of the traits and to define the phyletic relationships among the species studied (Lorenz, 1950). To the functional biologist, "phylogenetic" and "comparative" convey no suggestion of historicity nor concentration on a single line of descent. The functional biologist works with convenient species chosen because they represent different degrees of development in a particular characteristic, like relative brain size or differentiation. Since the species investigated are usually only distantly related, one cannot learn anything about evolution, but one can learn much about the functional significance of differences in the organ system studied in different species.

These abstract definitions should be expressed in more concrete terms. A distinguished student of evolution wrote "some such sequence as dogfish-frog-cat-man is frequently taught as 'evolutionary,' i.e. historical. In fact, the anatomical differences among these organisms are in large part ecologically and behaviorally determined, are divergent and not sequential, and do not in any sense form a historical series" (Simpson, 1958, p. 11). Simpson is unquestionably correct from the evolutionary point of view. And yet it has been widely held, since the time of Harvey, that medical students gain a better understanding of the human circulatory system by studying the cardiovascular system in sharks, frogs and cats. It is unnecessary to describe more recent insights regarding the functions of biological systems that resulted from research on unrelated species, since no one denies valuable information is often gained by comparing species chosen for special adaptations, docility, convenience and economy rather than their phyletic affinities.

There have been very few evolutionary studies of learning by species within a single line of descent and they have had little theoretical influence. The theoretically influential research deals with functional differences in learning between unrelated taxa, and not with evolution. This is as it should be, given the current state of research on comparative intelligence. A primary problem in this area of investigation is the validation of suitable means for comparing learning in different species. Until reliable techniques are available for differentiating intelligence in fish and mammals, and in birds and reptiles, it is probably unrewarding to look for differences in learning among the anseriformes or psittaciformes.

Since the search for sensible methods of comparing intelligence in animals has been a major problem, my selective survey of differences in learning and intelligence will be organized in terms of the investigative techniques used in the past and today.

The intelligence test approach

Between species comparisons

For many years comparative psychologists accepted the seductively simple notion that the techniques used to measure intelligence in humans provided a good model for research on intelligence in animals. All that was presumed necessary was to set different kinds of animals a common problem in a standard environment and count the errors made, and trials and time taken to master the task. The species could then be ranked in intelligence on the quantitative performance measures.

For many years I have suppressed the results I obtained in an extensive program of research based on this intelligence test model. This youthful indiscretion provides a good example of the unavoidable defects of the mental test method, and is worth telling now for that reason.

The test used was the McGill "closed field" test of animal intelligence (Rabinovitch and Rosvold, 1951), which has several features that appeared to make it a good instrument for measuring intelligence in different species. Subjects are trained for several days to go from a fixed starting point to the goal box in the opposite corner of the apparatus, where they are fed. This training familiarizes each animal with the topography of the testing area, and also eliminates fear and timidity because habituation training continues until the subject consistently approaches the goal quickly and eats without hesitation. The intelligence test is a series of 12 detour problems, created by interposing barriers in various patterns between start and goal. Each problem is presented for eight trials; errors are recorded whenever the subject deviates from the direct path to the goal, and enters a defined error zone. The test was intentionally designed to simulate a human intelligence test, in that its 12 constituent problems were supposed to be analogous to the items in an intelligence test for humans.

The McGill test had also been extensively validated in experiments with members of the same species. Performance was reliably affected by genetic selection (Cooper and Zubek, 1958), early rearing conditions (Cooper and Zubek, 1958; Wilson et al., 1965) and brain damage (Warren, 1961b).

Mean scores for samples of Paradise fish (*Macropodus opercularis*), chickens, inbred mice, and cats are presented in Table I, which reveals a rather wide variation among the mouse strains, and, except for the cats, little variation between species. No coherent story about differences in intelligence among different grades of vertebrates is apparent in these data.

A further complication in regard to comparisons based on numerical scores is that there is no way to know if experimental conditions were optimal for any of the species sampled. It is known, however, that the performance of a group of animals often varies widely under different experimental conditions.

Accurate guidance by visual cues is probably essential for efficient performance on the McGill intelligence test, since each problem is presented for only eight trials before a different problem is set. We tested this hypothesis with mice, with different groups tested under conditions reckoned to enhance or to reduce the salience of the relevant visual cues. Substitution of transparent for opaque barriers should make them harder to see and increase errors. Vision is not a dominant sensory modality in nocturnal mice compared to contact sensitivity and olfaction. Deprivation of the latter two senses might improve performance by eliminating salient but irrelevant sensory input.

Table II shows that these expectations were realized with C57Bl mice; scores on each of the three experimental conditions are significantly ($P < 0.01$) different from the standard. The results from the C57Bl mice thus illustrate the more general point that most animal populations vary greatly in performance on the "same" task depending upon the precise conditions of testing. The extreme importance of sensory factors is emphasized by the fact that deprivation of receptor inputs that are not relevant to the task in hand improves performance. Indeed the rather good ($\overline{x} = 179$) performance of the C57Bl mice in the presence of a masking odor allows me to add

Table I Species differences in performance on the McGill intelligence test

Subjects	N	Mean errors
Paradise fish	18	361
Whigte Leghorn chickens	13	347
Mice		
C57Bl/Crgl	18	258
BalbC/Crgl	15	286
C3H/Crgl	16	488
Cats	21	67

Table II   "Intelligence" test errors under four experimental conditions

Condition	Strain			
	C57Bl/Crgl		C3H/Crgl	
	Mean	% change	Mean	% change
Standard	258		488	
Transparent barriers	343	+33	447	−8
Vibrissae removed	223	−14	469	−4
Masking odor	179	−31	439	−10

a wry footnote to Table I, which gives the mean score for a group of trapped wild cats. Cats reared in the laboratory often make scores of 179 or more on the McGill intelligence test (Coutant, 1974; Hara et al., 1974). Thus, under some conditions the scores for each species approximate those for another species.

The results from the C3H mice differ substantially from those for the C57Bl strain, in that they show little change in response to altered conditions. There is no obvious explanation of this discrepancy.

The findings in other simple learning situations, such as classical and operant conditioning, discrimination and maze learning are similar to those on the McGill test. The variation within species in learning rates under various experimental conditions is so great relative to the variation between species that no conclusions are justified concerning differences in learning capacity in different grades of vertebrates (Brookshire, 1970; Warren, 1973).

However, it is important to point out that the wide variance in learning proficiency observed in animals of the same species tested in different circumstances is quite lawful, and reflects interspecies differences in ecological adaptations in an orderly fashion. Animals generally learn responses that are compatible with demands imposed by their normal environment very quickly, but they learn responses that are incompatible with established species-typical adjustments very slowly, if at all (Hinde and Stevenson-Hinde, 1973; Seligman, 1970; Shettleworth, 1972; Warren, 1973). The absence of any systematic pattern of differences among vertebrate species in the rate of associative learning surely means that all contemporary vertebrates must learn some critical associations very quickly (as the toad that learns to avoid eating bumble bees), and that the capacity for simple associative learning is a primitive vertebrate trait.

Within species comparisons

It is impossible to interpret unambiguously "mental test" comparisons between species as informative about interspecific differences in learning ability, because one cannot assess the influence of species differences in response biases, predilections to attend to particular sensory cues, preparedness to associate specific stimuli and responses, etc. These factors are unimportant, or at least have no systematic effect in studies with animals of the same species. To be sure, one creates behaviorally deviant animals by inbreeding or by the imposition of lesions in the central nervous system, but the aberrant animals remain enough like their normal conspecifics to permit experimental analysis of the abnormal behavior, as in the studies of photophobia (DeFries, 1966) and neurotransmitter defects (Thiessen et al., 1970) in relation to hypoactivity in albino mice.

The purpose of this section is to consider the question of whether the concept of intelligence applies in any useful way to animals of the same species. Operationally, the problem is "Do individuals or groups of animals consistently surpass their conspecifics on learning and problem-solving tasks under a variety of conditions?" Two different methods have been used to determine the existence or nonexistence of intelligence in rodents and carnivores.

Between strain comparisons

Researchers who work with mice and rats seldom use the same individual in multiple learning tasks. The data from experiments with rodents that are relevant to the question of general intelligence come mostly from tests of the hypothesis: "Strain X is consistently superior to strain Y on learning tasks A, B, C . . ." The experimental evidence provides little or no support for the idea that one strain is generally superior to another in learning ability. Rather small changes in test conditions frequently reverse the ranking of mouse strains in relative performance on learning tasks, as for example the substitution of an auditory for a visual warning signal in avoidance learning by mice (Ehrman and Parsons, 1976), or by changes in the temporal distribution of training trials on active avoidance (Bovet et al., 1969). Tests in situations other than the maze that served as the basis for selection showed that Tryon's (1942) maze "bright" strain was inferior to his "dull" strain on three of five measures of learning and that the bright and dull strains differed substantially in motivation and emotional reactivity (Searle, 1949). When tested in a simpler maze than Tryon's, dull rats made twice as many errors as bright rats if the interval between trials was short (30 seconds), but if the intertrial intervals were several minutes long, the performance of the bright and dull groups were identical (McGaugh et al., 1962).

Results like those from experiments with mice and rats were also obtained with purebred breeds of dogs (Scott and Fuller, 1965). Scott and Fuller deride the idea of general intelligence in dogs as a "mistaken notion," on the grounds that a given breed may rate very high on one test but very low on another, with little overall consistency.

Individual differences

In other experiments, the same subjects are trained on a series of different tests and the consistency of individual differences in learning performance (intelligence) assessed by the magnitude of the correlations between tasks. The results from dogs (Anastasi et al., 1955) rats (Tryon, 1942), and cats (Warren, 1961a) are entirely consonant with the data from strain and breed comparisons; the correlations are typically low and non-significant, unless they are redundant measures of the same process, e.g., time and errors to learn a given task.

The inevitable inference from these data is that one cannot speak of intelligence within species of animals. No one has found evidence in support of a general level of capacity that results in an animal, strain or breed consistently performing above or below the level attained by other members of the species on several different learning tasks.

Our review of "mental test" experiments that compared groups of animals in respect to quantitative indices of performance on simple association learning tasks indicates that (a) comparisons of species in terms of the rate with which they learn are uninformative, and (b) there is no evidence of general intelligence within species; individuals and groups are not consistently superior to their conspecifics on a variety of different learning problems.

Here ends the nihilistic part of this essay. The remainder is an optimistic, perhaps overly optimistic, account of what comparative psychologists have learned about the evolution of intelligence, using other research methods.

Functional differences

Practitioners of the mental test method asked "How fast do animals learn?" and discovered little of lasting value about the evolution of intelligence. Comparative psychologists today endeavor to answer "What?" and "How?" questions instead, i.e. "What differences in the quality of their performance characterize learning by different species of animals?" and "How are these differences produced? What differential processes account for the species differences in learning?" Considering the small number of active workers in the field, a fair amount of progress has been made on the "What?" question, enough to hint at a skeleton of an outline for the evolution of intelligence among some vertebrate groups. Less has been accomplished with the "How?" question.

Before surveying this material, however, I shall illustrate one variant of contemporary approach that has supplanted the mental test method with an unpublished experiment from my laboratory. It was designed to determine if the most favorable conditions for retention of training are the same in Paradise fish, White Leghorn chickens and cats. The animals were tested in the McGill maze which has already been described. Subjects within each species were divided into three groups that received eight trails per day on different individual problems, represented by letters in Table III, which summarizes the experimental design. Somewhat naive predictions, based on the usual principles of learning for humans, would be: the retention groups, trained on problem A and retrained on A after four days without intervening training should be best on the retest, since they have not been exposed to interfering learning experiences. The retroaction groups that are trained on problem A, and tested on problems B, C, D, and E before the retest on A, should be inferior to the retention groups because the interpolated training should disrupt the retention and interfere with the retrieval of memories about A. The proaction groups were trained on four other problems before being confronted with the critical test problem (A) for

Table III   Sequences for presenting problems in retention.
Experiment in the McGill maze

Group	Days					
	1	2	3	4	5	6
Retention	A	—*	—	—	—	A
Retroaction	A	B	C	D	E	A
Proaction	—	B	C	D	E	A

* no training.

the first time. The proaction groups were controls for nonspecific habituation to the experimental situation as a heavy influence on critical test scores: they were expected to make fewer errors than the inexperienced retention and retroaction groups did on day 1, but more errors than the retention groups made in their retest on day 6.

The results are presented in Table IV, which shows errors on problem A on days 1 and 6, and percent savings on the retest on day 6.

$$\frac{(\text{Errors on day 1}) - (\text{Errors on day 6})}{(\text{Errors on day 1})} \times 100$$

(The "savings" scores for the proaction groups are figured by using the average for the other two groups as an estimate of their hypothetical scores on day 1.) The last column in Table IV shows the significant values of P from U-tests between the experimental groups within species.

All three groups of fish made significantly fewer errors on day 6 than the untrained fish did on day 1, but nothing more can be said since there were no significant differences among the groups of fish on the criterion task.

The behavior of the chickens on day 6 conforms perfectly to my extrapolation

Table IV   Median performance on criterion problem (A) in McGill maze

Species	Group	N	Errors		% savings	P*
			Day 1	Day 6		
Fish	Retention	12	47	29	38	
	Retroaction	10	42	26	38	
	Proaction	11	—	33	26	
Chickens	Retention	10	27	8	70	
	Retroaction	10	27	12	56	0.02
	Proaction	10	—	20	26	0.01
Cats	Retention	9	26	6	77	
	Retroaction	9	25	2	92	0.05
	Proaction	9	—	6	76	

* Versus retention group.

from studies of verbal learning by humans. The retention group has the highest savings score; interpolated training on the other problems significantly impaired retention by the retroaction group, and general familiarity with the learning situation did little to improve performance in the proaction group.

Cats are different. The proaction group performed as well as the retention group, and the retroaction group of cats was significantly superior to the retention group on day 6. Learning in the McGill maze by chickens thus appears to be highly specific and very vulnerable to interference from interpolated learning. More general, nonspecific learning is prominent in cats. The equivalent performance of the retention and proaction groups on day 6 presumably reflects the joint effects of specific (A) and general (B–E) experiences in the test situation.

The indication that mammals learn more about the general relationships among intra- and extra-maze cues during the same training experience as nonmammalian animals is strongly reminiscent of a classic comparison of maze learning by rats and ants (Schneirla, 1946) which showed that rats developed a wider representation of the maze than the ants. Schneirla's evidence included observations that rats eliminate entries into blind alleys abruptly while ants do so very gradually, and that rats learn the reversed pattern of the practiced maze with considerable savings, while ants learn the reversed pattern as a wholly new problem.

The persons who look for functional differences in learning among species are a hetereogeneous lot, but a few traits tend to distinguish them from the relict population of adherents to the mental test approach, and from the animal psychologists who deny significant differences in learning by different species. Productive students of comparative learning try to differentiate taxa by identifying learning phenomena that are always or almost always present in some species, and never or almost never present in other species. The better research on functional differences in learning is guided by theoretical models that are more sophisticated than that implicit in the scala naturae. Good modern work entails multiple complementary experiments instead of a single mental test. This is so because several converging operations are necessary to win belief for a comprehensive theory – and a very large amount of work is needed to identify and to analyze the processes that produce differences in learning performance by different species.

The following survey provides a sample of some of the research strategies used in comparative learning studies, and reviews some of the major findings on the evolution of intelligence in vertebrates.

Rats and non-mammalian vertebrates

Two important and extensive programs of comparative research have concentrated on differences in learning among rats, birds and fish, those of Bitterman (1975) and of Mackintosh and Sutherland (Mackintosh, 1974; Sutherland and Mackintosh, 1971). I shall describe each in turn.

Bitterman has not developed a comprehensive theory to explain or predict interspecies differences in learning. He has, however, been guided in his search for differences among vertebrates by the following principle: if rats show a learning phenomenon that contradicts the predictions of traditional stimulus-response association learning (S-R) theory (Hull, 1943), it is worth looking among non-mammalian vertebrates for animals that do behave in conformity with simple S-R theory, and thereby differ qualitatively from rats. This approach has yielded some provocative results.

The depression effect

If rats are trained to run down a straight alley with large or small amounts of food, they attain stable asymptotes of running speed, the group which receives the large reward running faster. If the rats that got the large reward are then shifted to the smaller, their speed decreases and they run, in fact, more slowly than the rats that got the small reinforcement all the time. Substitution of a small for a large reinforcement has, however, no effect on the speed with which goldfish or painted turtles approach food in similar experiments.

Magnitude of reinforcement and resistance to extinction

If goldfish or turtles are trained to make an instrumental response, and different groups receive varying amounts of food for each response, the number of responses in extinction (after reinforcements are terminated) is greater in the groups that received more food in training. The relation between amount of reinforcement and resistance to extinction is direct for the fish and turtles. For rats and pigeons, the relationship is inverse rather than direct; the more reinforcement in acquisition, the fewer responses in extinction.

The partial reinforcement effect

Rats reinforced on only some trials in training to do an instrumental act, respond more frequently in extinction than rats rewarded on every trial during training. The same is true of pigeons, but not always of turtles and fish. Turtles and fish do not show exaggerated resistance to extinction after partial reinforcement when the intervals between trials in training are long, but only when the intertrial intervals are short.

The results of experiments on these three phenomena may be viewed as indicating that rats and pigeons on the one hand, and turtles and fish on the other, differ in having or not having the capacity to generate expectations or anticipations concerning patterns of reinforcement. The behavior of the rats in respect to the depression effect and the inverse relation between amount of reward and resistance to extinction is consonant with the idea that the expectations of the more generously reinforced rats are more severely frustrated when the reward is reduced or eliminated so they are the first to stop responding. Partially reinforced rats, in contrast, come to expect occasional nonreinforced trials. They expect less and are less disturbed when reinforcements are completely shut off in extinction than rats consistently reinforced in acquisition, so they persist longer in responding during extinction.

Probability learning

In most discrimination learning tasks one stimulus is always, and the other never rewarded. A probability learning problem, however, is one in which both alternatives are rewarded part of the time, the respective frequencies being specified by a re-inforcement ratio, like 70:30. Animals respond to the task in three ways. They may maximize the number of rewards won by always choosing the more frequently re-warded alternative. They may match systematically by repeating or alternating responses after each reinforced trial, or by consistently choosing the same irrelevant stimulus. Thirdly, subjects may match randomly, by choosing the stimuli with frequencies equal to the likelihood of reward, with no systematic sequential pattern of choice responses over trials.

No one has ever observed random matching behavior in mammals; even when they match, mammals do so systematically, manifesting a clear temporal organiza-tion in their suboptimally profitable response patterns. Random matching is some-times, but not always, observed in pigeons, painted turtles, goldfish and African mouthbreeder fish. The conditions that are sufficient to produce random matching consistently have not been specified, but the occurrence of this phenomenon in non-mammalian forms and its non-occurrence in mammals suggests a gap between the species in their capacity to integrate behavior in terms of multiple recent events, in learning to respond adaptively to cues that are only partially correlated with re-inforcement.

Reversal learning

This task is essentially a series of reversed discriminations between a single pair of stimuli, for example Black (B) and White (W). The animal is first trained with W correct. When it reaches criterion B becomes correct until the criterion is satisfied again, when the reward value of the stimuli is reversed once more. The pattern of alternately rewarding and not rewarding W and B in regular rotation may be con-tinued indefinitely.

Many species of mammals have been trained on repeated reversals under a variety of experimental conditions. I know of no competent experiment in which mammals did not learn to solve reversals with progressively greater efficiency, to make substantially fewer errors on later reversals than on early ones. Much the same is true for birds, although the number of species studied is fewer than for mammals. Early experiments briefly suggested that turtles improve in reversal learn-ing only when tested with spatial, and not with visual cues; later work showed that turtles improve on both sorts of reversal tasks. For many years it seemed that fish were totally bereft of capacity for reversal learning, but it has now been shown that, under special conditions which enhance the salience of the correct cue (e.g., per-sistence of the correct stimulus until reward is delivered), goldfish do learn to learn reversals with fewer errors (Englehardt et al., 1973).

It is no longer possible to assert that mammals, birds and reptiles are capable of reversal learning, but fish are not. Yet the fact that improvement in reversal learning occurs only under limited and special conditions in goldfish, conditions which need not be met to demonstrate reversal learning in the other vertebrate classes studied, suggests very strongly a major, if not all-or-none, difference between fish and the other vertebrate animals.

Intuitively, the repeated reversal task seems to measure the plasticity of learned behavior in animals, the facility of extinguishing old habits and acquiring new ones. The restricted range of conditions conducive to reversal learning in goldfish implies relatively limited lability of learning processes in this species.

Work with different species may simultaneously contribute to the solution of problems of comparative intelligence and learning theory. If, for example, two phenomena are found in rats and attributed to the same basic process, and it is later observed that one but not the other occurs in fish, it is hard to maintain that both depend upon the same mechanism in rats. My example is not, of course, hypothetical. It concerns attention in rats and fish.

Dimensional transfer

The basic problem is whether animals learn to look for cues of a specific sort as a result of reinforced training, and learn to attend selectively to a particular stimulus dimension. The procedure involves two stages. Subjects are first trained to choose a circle rather than a cross; on half the trials each shape is white, and on half black. In this discrimination shape is relevant (consistently correlated with reward), and brightness is irrelevant (uncorrelated with reward). In the second phase, half the animals are trained on an intradimensional transfer task, to discriminate two new shapes, a square and a triangle perhaps. The remaining subjects are trained on an extradimensional shift, white versus black. More rapid learning of the intradimensional shift is taken as evidence that in initial learning, the animals learn to attend to the relevant dimension (shape) as well as to select the reinforced stimulus (circle).

Monkeys and rats learn intradimensional shifts more rapidly than extradimensional shifts. Carp and goldfish learn the two types of problems at the same rate. The evidence thus shows that learning to attend to a specific stimulus dimension in one discrimination problem facilitates learning a second discrimination with that dimension relevant by mammals but not by fish.

Overshadowing

The usual paradigm for demonstrating overshadowing is to train animals with a compound stimulus AB, and then to test for responses to the elements A and B presented singly. A large number of experiments with rats and pigeons show that learning about one cue is suppressed in the presence of the second, even though it is quite adequate for learning when presented on its own. It was once thought that overshadowing might reflect selective attention to the more salient cue in the compound, which resulted in no attention to and, therefore, no learning about the less conspicuous cue. This view is no longer tenable since carp are vulnerable to overshadowing in apparently the same way as rats and pigeons. The occurrence of overshadowing, but not of dimensional transfer, in fish suggests that the two effects need not depend upon the same process in species like rats and pigeons which show both.

Attention theory

The attention theory of discrimination learning (Sutherland and Mackintosh, 1971; Mackintosh, 1974) is an ambitious attempt to provide a systematic theoretical account of interspecies differences in learning. A key assumption of attention theory is that animals are limited in their capacity to process sensory information. In situations that require differentiation of two stimuli, they cannot respond to all of the cues present at one time. Discrimination learning, therefore, depends upon two independent processes: (1) learning the specific stimuli associated with reward and non-reward (the formation of response attachments); and (2) learning to attend to the relevant stimulus dimension – brightness, form, size, etc. (learning to switch in the correct analyzer). The two processes have different growth rates and are characterized by differences in other parameters.

The hypothesis that rats suffer from limited attention and from restricted ability to process information in visual discrimination learning is based on observations such as the following. Rats trained on visual discrimination problems with irrelevant cues learn more slowly than controls trained without irrelevant cues, as would be expected if irrelevant cues distract attention from the relevant cues. There is also a version of the overshadowing experiment, called multiple-cue discrimination. Rats are trained to differentiate visual stimuli that afford relevant cues in two dimensions. Subsequent tests with cues in the two dimensions presented alone typically show that the more a rat learned about one dimension, the less he had learned about the other. This inverse relation between the amount learned about the two sorts of cues follows directly from attention theory. If two cues for reinforcement are perfectly redundant, a rat with limited channel capacity should simplify its task by attending to only one signal.

For comparative learning, the most important derivation from attention theory is the overtraining reversal effect (ORE). This effect, observed under conditions specified by Mackintosh (1969a), refers to the fact that overtrained rats, given about 100 trials after criterion on an initial discrimination problem, learn to reverse the discrimination habit more quickly than non-overtrained rats, reversed immediately after they reached criterion in original learning.

This phenomenon strikes one as a paradox. We assume that extra training should strengthen the original habit and render it more, not less, recalcitrant to reversal. Attention theory accounts for the paradox by assuming the response attachments achieve their asymptotic strength sooner than stimulus analyzers. Overtraining increases the rats' attention to the relevant stimulus dimension without greatly increasing the strength of response attachments. On the reversal, overtrained rats choose the formerly correct stimulus for a considerable number of trials, and then abruptly switch to the stimulus that is now correct in the reversal task. Control rats make fewer consecutive choices of the previously correct alternative after reversal, respond to the relevant stimuli at a chance level of discrimination, and, finally, gradually develop a preference for the reinforced stimulus. The difference between the groups' performances in reversal learning reflects a differential in the strength of their stimulus analyzers. Overtrained rats respond to the relevant stimulus dimension, and quickly go from making all wrong to all right responses.

Analyzer strength is lower in the non-overtrained rats so both analyzer and response attachments are extinguished at the start of reversal training. Then, for a time, the non-overtrained rats are controlled by irrelevant analyzers, resulting in chance performance. Eventually, the non-overtrained rats relearn which is the relevant dimension and solve the reversal problem. In short, overtraining facilitates reversal learning by increasing the strength and persistence of attention to the relevant stimulus dimension.

The idea that a learned selective attentional process is independently affected by various experimental parameters is supported by studies of the influence of overtraining on extradimensional shift learning. In extradimensional transfer experiments, subjects learn a discrimination with cues in dimension A relevant and cues in dimension B irrelevant, followed by a shift problem in which dimension B becomes relevant. Overtrained rats are seriously disadvantaged compared to non-overtrained rats in extradimensional transfer. This follows neatly from attention theory. Overtrained rats are slower to attend to the newly relevant dimension on the transfer problem because overtraining on the original task induced a stronger and more persistent disposition in them to attend to the initially relevant dimension.

It is hard to find an ORE in birds and apparently impossible in fish. If the explanation of the ORE in rats is correct, the attenuation or absence of the ORE in birds and fish implies that attentional mechanisms are weaker in birds, and much weaker in fish, than in rats. If this is so, birds, rats and fish should differ in their ability to learn problems that require attention to cues which are inconsistently correlated with reinforcement. Mackintosh (1969b) tested this hypothesis with comparative studies of reversal and probability learning, tasks which involve, respectively, sequential or concurrent inconsistency of reinforcement. He found that performance in probability and reversal learning was closely related to the magnitude of the ORE in a given species. Fish were inferior to birds that were in turn inferior to rats on both reversal and probability learning.

Rats and cats

The most extensive tests of the generality of attention theory in mammals other than rats have been made with cats. In this section, experiments with cats will be reviewed that attempted to obtain several learning effects of importance in attention theory which are observed in rats (Sutherland and Mackintosh, 1971).

The overtraining reversal effect

Cats overtrained after reaching criterion on a black-white discrimination learn subsequently to reverse the discrimination at the same rate, and generate a learning curve that is almost the same as non-overtrained cats. No ORE is observed in cats even when particular pains are taken to duplicate the conditions most favorable for the effect in rats (Hirayoshi and Warren, 1967; Warren, 1975).

Table V   Previous training and mean errors in extradimensional transfer
learning by cats

Prior training	N	Relevant dimension	
		Size	Brightness
None	12	191	57
Criterion only	6	179	49
Criterion and overtraining	6	155	43

Overtraining and extradimensional shift learning

In an unpublished experiment, my colleagues and I recently trained 24 cats on a
discrimination with stimuli that presented independent differences in visual size
and brightness; for 12 cats, brightness was the relevant dimension and size was
irrelevant, and for 12 cats, size was relevant, and brightness irrelevant. These
groups were divided into matched subgroups given no training past criterion or
144 overtraining trials. All of the animals then learned an extradimensional shift
with the same stimuli, but with the previously irrelevant dimension now relevant.

The results are presented in Table V which shows mean errors to criterion by
naive cats which learned the tasks with no prior training, and by cats trained only
to criterion or overtrained on the other dimension. None of the intergroup
differences in error scores are statistically reliable. It is clear that overtraining
does not impair extradimensional transfer in cats, as it does in rats.

Overshadowing

If cats are trained to discriminate visual stimuli that differ in two dimensions, such
as rectangles that differ in brightness and in their horizontal or vertical orientation,
later tests show unequivocally that cats, unlike rats, learn the reinforcement value
of cues in both dimensions (Mumma and Warren, 1968). This finding contradicts
the predictions from the attention theory based on rats.

The results we obtained in a study of cats trained with auditory and visual stimuli
are even more difficult to reconcile with findings from rats. The cats are trained to
approach the one of two feeders which is signalled by a flashing light and a noise,
until they reach a stable criterion level of performance on this two-cue problem.
They are then given a set of test trials on which only the light or only the noise is
presented, to see if they learned about both stimuli in initial training or if one
stimulus had overshadowed the other. The performance of 37 intact cats and 8 with
cortical lesions that destroyed the auditory projection cortex is compared in Table
VI. The normal cats were more successful on trials with noise alone than light
alone. The animals subjected to decortication of the auditory areas made more
correct responses to light than to noise. Yet although the groups learned more
about one cue than the other, both groups showed learning on both cues; all of the
proportions in Table VI are significantly different from chance ($P < 0.01$).

This failure to find suppression of learning about the weaker element in a compound stimulus even in cats lacking the auditory cortex indicates that it may be

Table VI   Mean percent approach responses to light and to
noise on tests with single stimuli

Group	Light	Noise
Intact cats	69	84
Lesions in auditory cortex	76	68

difficult indeed to demonstrate in cats the kind of overshadowing effect frequently observed in rats and predicted by Sutherland and Mackintosh (1971).

Irrelevant cues and discrimination learning

In two recent experiments (Warren, 1976), it was found that when cats are trained to discriminate a circle and triangle, animals tested with the stimuli that varied irrelevantly in brightness and in size learned just as quickly as cats trained under constant conditions, with no irrelevant cues.

These discrepancies between rats and cats, especially in respect to the effects of overtraining on reversal learning and extradimensional transfer imply that in cats, as in birds and fish, selective attention is less well developed than in rats. According to attention theory, it follows that, since attentional mechanisms are feeble in cats, cats should, like non-mammalian species, be inferior to rats in their performance on reversal and probability learning problems. There is no empirical support for this notion. Even though cats show neither the overtraining reversal nor dimensional transfer effect, their performance on reversal and probability learning is completely typical of the mammals (Schweikert and Treichler, 1969; Warren, 1966).

The fact that attention theory is a poor predictor of the results of experiments with cats does not invalidate the theory for rats, birds and fish, but it does suggest that processes not encompassed by the theory are at work in cats. Most of the discrepancies between rats and cats can be interpreted as the consequence of a greater capacity for handling visual information in cats than in rats. If cats learn much more quickly than rats to identify relevant dimensions in visual discrimination learning, overtraining can add little to the strength of stimulus analyzers and will not, therefore, have an effect on reversal or dimensional transfer learning. The idea of an important difference in channel capacity for visual information in cats and rats is supported by the observations that cats, but not rats, learn the significance of multiple relevant cues, and that rats, but not cats, are impaired in discrimination learning when irrelevant cues are present.

Primates and other mammals

On tasks designed to demonstrate critical effects predicted by attention theory in rats, monkeys behave more like cats than rats. There has been no convincing demonstration of the overtraining reversal effect in monkeys; there is in fact a contrary trend for errors in reversal learning to increase as a function of prereversal overtraining trials (Warren and McGonigle, 1969). Monkeys learn the significance of both redundant cues on two-cue discrimination problems (Warren and Warren, 1969). In contrast to Sutherland and Mackintosh's rats, monkeys trained to attend to cues in one stimulus dimension show marked facilitation rather than retardation in extradimensional transfer (Schrier, 1971).

Although their behavior is similar on the tasks just mentioned, cats and monkeys can be differentiated qualitatively on more demanding tasks like the following. Groups of cats and of monkeys were trained on 60 discrimination reversals, half with visual cues relevant and spatial cues irrelevant, and the remainder with spatial cues relevant, and visual cues relevant. Then they learned a series of new visual discrimination problems, together with control animals that had no prior training. Attention theory and perhaps common sense suggests that training with visual cues might facilitate performance on the second stage, since this would be an intra-dimensional shift; training on spatial cues ought not to facilitate later visual discrimination learning since this is an extradimensional shift.

The results from neither species conformed with these expectations. The cats showed no transfer from the reversals to the discrimination problems. But both the groups of monkeys, trained on the reversals with either visual or spatial cues relevant, made significantly fewer errors than the naive controls on the set of visual discrimination problems. Analyses of the data showed that it did not matter if they were trained on the reversals with visual or spatial cues; the experienced monkeys formed a non-specific response rule, transferable across stimulus dimensions, a "win-stay, lose-shift" strategy of repeating rewarded, and not repeating unrewarded, responses. The cats and monkeys differed little in performance on the reversal task, but only the monkeys developed a general response rule. Experiments in other learning situations yield additional support for the conclusion that cats and other non-primates lack the capacity for learning response strategies found in monkeys and apes (Warren, 1974).

Monkeys and apes

There is an extensive literature on learning by primates which reveals essentially no qualitative differences between species because they were compared with the un-informative mental test method (Warren, 1973, 1974).

If we broaden our idea of intelligence to include observations of innovative and adaptively plastic behavior in situations other than formal learning experiments, however, there is good evidence that chimpanzees do, as common experience suggests, differ qualitatively from monkeys in intellectual capacity.

Rhesus monkeys reared in social isolation during infancy and early childhood are severely deficient in sexual behavior as adults. None of the male monkeys deprived of early social interactions ever succeeded in copulation, in spite of high levels of arousal and encouragement from sexually proficient females (Harlow, 1965; Mason, 1960). Rogers and Davenport (1969) observed the adult sexual behavior of 12 chim-panzees reared in strict social isolation to age three years. On their release from solitary confinement the chimpanzees were, like rhesus monkeys, fearful, withdrawn and grossly disturbed in their commerce with other chimpanzees. Yet as adults, most of the deprived chimpanzees copulated, although not with the grace of wild born chimpanzees; some unions resulted in pregnancies. Rogers and Davenport attribute the greater degree of recovery of sexual ability in chimpanzees compared to monkeys to differences in the rigidity and stereotypy of patterns of sexual behavior in the two species. The chimpanzees' repertoire of sex behavior is broader and more amenable to change by experience.

When first confronted with a mirror both chimpanzees and macaque monkeys respond as if their mirror image were another animal. Monkeys continue to do so, but chimpanzees within a few days stop making social responses to the mirror image, and use the mirror more and more as an aid to self-grooming. When the animals are anesthetized and colored dye is applied to the face, the chimpanzees make an extremely large number of responses to the regions marked by the dye, but this effect is not seen in monkeys. These observations support the idea that the chimpanzees see themselves and the monkeys see another monkey in the mirror (Gallup, 1970). From both a philosophic and a scientific point of view, it is hard to imagine a more provocative and significant functional difference between species than the observation that chimpanzees recognize their self-image and monkeys do not.

Wild monkeys and chimpanzees make and use tools, but no species of monkeys approaches the chimpanzee in regard to either frequency or variety of tool-using responses (Beck, 1974; Warren, 1976). Indeed, recent observations indicate that adult chimpanzees sometimes use tools in such delicate and sophisticated ways that it is impossible for a man to learn quickly to duplicate their performance (McGrew, 1974; Teleki, 1974).

It is now well known that chimpanzees and the other great apes can be taught language-like behavior by humans using three different training procedures (Fouts, 1974; Gardner and Gardner, 1969; Premack, 1971; Rumbaugh et al., 1973). A direct comparison of the findings from chimpanzees and monkeys on this subject is impossible. There is no published report of any attempt to teach language skills to monkeys. There may never be. Observations of monkeys reveal no traces of the abilities necessary for language-like behavior to primatologists experienced in this field (Premack, personal communication). It appears that the great apes are unique among non-human primates in their capacity to use linguistic signs in innovative and structured ways.

The experiments on interspecies differences in learning just reviewed reveal a series of functional differences among vertebrate groups which differ in the size and complexity of their brains, differences which correspond rather closely to our ideas of what might be important dimensions of animal intelligence.

Summary and conclusions

The concept of intelligence is of little use in dealing with learning by animals of the same species. Quantitative measures of performance on different learning tasks reveal a pattern of uncorrelated individual differences. There seems to be no evidence of qualitative differences in cognitive learning by members of the same species.

There are no significant differences among vertebrate species in simple associative learning. Capacity for efficient associative learning is probably essential for survival in all or almost all vertebrates.

The concept of intelligence is helpful in describing the set of qualitative differences observed between species of vertebrates in characteristics like: breadth of spatial learning, expectancy, lability of choice behavior, attention, capacity for processing sensory information, rule learning, language-like behavior, and self-recognition. The evolution of intelligence consists of the development of new and more sophisticated skills for learning and solving problems in the more progressive levels. This view of the evolution of intelligence in animals as the cumulative addition of particulate problem solving capacities is consonant with the current trend in genetic studies of human intelligence to concentrate on specific mental abilities rather than global IQ scores (Ehrman and Parsons, 1976; McClearn and De Fries, 1973).

Literature cited

Anastasi, A., Fuller, J. L., Scott, J. P. and Schmitt, J. R. (1955) A factor analysis of the performance of dogs on certain learning tests, *Zoologica 40*, 33–46

Beck, B. B. (1974) Baboons, chimpanzees and tools, *J. Hum. Evol. 3*, 509–516

Bitterman, M. E. (1975) The comparative analysis of behavior, *Science 188*, 699–709

Bovet, D., Bovet-Nitti, F. and Oliverio, A. (1969) Genetic aspects of learning and memory in mice, *Science 163*, 139–149

Brookshire, K. H. (1970) Comparative psychology of learning. In: *Learning: Interactions* (M. H. Marx, ed.) pp. 289–364, Macmillan, New York

Cooper, R. M. and Zubek, J. P. (1958) Effects of enriched and restricted early environments on the learning ability of bright and dull rats, *Can. J. Psychol. 12*, 159–164

Countant, L. W. (1974) Association cortex lesions and umweg behavior in cats, *J. Comp. Physiol. Psychol. 86*, 1083–1089

DeFries, J. C., Hegmann, J. P. and Weir, M. W. (1966) Open-field behavior in mice. Evidence for a major gene effect mediated by the visual system, *Science 154*, 1577–1579

Ehrman, L. and Parsons, P. A. (1976) *The Genetics of Behavior,* Sinauer, Sunderland, Mass.

Engelhardt, F., Woodard, W. T. and Bitterman, M. E. (1973) Discrimination reversal in the goldfish as a function of training conditions, *J. Comp. Physiol. Psychol. 85*, 144–150

Fouts, R. S. (1974) Language. Origins, definitions and chimpanzees, *J. Hum. Evol. 3*, 475–482

Gallup, G. G. (1970) Chimpanzees. Self-recognition, *Science 167*, 86–87

Gardner, R. A. and Gardner, B. T. (1969) Teaching sign language to a chimpanzee, *Science 165*, 664–672

Hara, K., Cornwell, P. R., Warren, J. M. and Webster, I. H. (1974) Posterior extramarginal cortex and visual learning by cats, *J. Comp. Physiol. Psychol. 87*, 884–904

Harlow, H. F. (1965) Sexual behavior in the rhesus monkey. In: *Sex and Behavior* (F. A. Beach, ed.) Wiley, New York

Hinde, R. A. and Stevenson-Hinde, J. (1973) *Constraints on Learning*, Academic Press, London

Hirayoshi, I. and Warren, J. M. (1967) Overtraining and reversal learning by experimentally naive kittens, *J. Comp. Physiol. Psychol. 64*, 507–510

Hull, C. L. (1943) *Principles of Behavior*, Appleton, New York

Lorenz, K. (1950) The comparative method in studying innate behaviour patterns, *Symp. Soc. Exp. Biol. 4*, 221–268

Mackintosh, N. J. (1969a) Further analysis of the overtraining reversal effect, *J. Comp. Physiol. Psychol. Monogr. Suppl. 67*, 1–18

Mackintosh, N. J. (1969b) Comparative psychology of serial reversal and probability learning: Rats, birds and fish. In: *Animal Discrimination Learning* (R. Gilbert and N. S. Sutherland, eds.) pp. 137–167, Academic Press, London

Mackintosh, N. J. (1974) *The Psychology of Animal Learning*, Academic Press, London

Mason, W. A. (1960) The effects of social restriction on the behavior of rhesus monkeys. I. Free social behavior, *J. Comp. Physiol. Psychol. 53*, 582–589

McClearn, G. D. and DeFries, J. C. (1973) *Introduction to Behavioral Genetics*, Freeman, San Francisco

McGaugh, J. L., Jennings, R. D. and Thompson, C. W. (1962) Effect of distribution of practice on the maze learning of descendants of the Tryon maze bright and maze dull strains, *Psychol. Rep. 10*, 147–150

McGrew, W. C. (1974) Tool use by wild chimpanzees in feeding upon driver ants, *J. Hum. Evol. 3*, 501–508

Mumma, R. and Warren, J. M. (1968) Two-cue discrimination learning by cats, *J. Comp. Physiol. Psychol. 66*, 116–121

Premack, D. (1971) On the assessment of language competence in the chimpanzee. In: *Behavior of Nonhuman Primates* (A. M. Schrier and F. Stollnitz, eds.) Vol. 4, pp. 168–228, Academic Press, New York

Rabinovitch, M. S. and Rosvold, H. E. (1951) A closed-field intelligence test for rats, *Can. J. Psychol. 5*, 122–128

Rogers, C. M. and Davenport, R. K. (1969) Effects of restricted rearing on sexual behavior of chimpanzees, *Develop. Psychol. 1*, 200–204

Rumbaugh, D. M., Gill, T. V. and von Glaserfeld, E. C. (1973) Reading and sentence completion by a chimpanzee (Pan), *Science 192*, 731–733

Schneirla, T. C. (1946) Ant learning as a problem in comparative psychology. In: *Twentieth Century Psychology* (P. L. Harriman, ed.) pp. 276–305, Philosophical Library, New York

Schrier, A. M. (1971) Extra-dimensional transfer of learning-set formation in stumptailed monkeys, *Learn. Motiv. 2*, 173–181

Schweikert, G. E. and Treichler, F. R. (1969) Visual probability learning and reversal in the cat, *J. Comp. Physiol. Psychol. 67*, 269–272

Scott, J. P. and Fuller, J. L. (1965) *Genetics and the Social Behavior of the Dog*, University of Chicago Press, Chicago

Searle, L. V. (1949) The organization of hereditary maze-brightness and maze-dullness, *Genet. Psychol. Monogr. 39*, 279–325

Seligman, M. E. P. (1970) On the generality of the laws of learning, *Psychol. Rev. 77*, 406–418

Shettleworth, S. A. (1972) Constraints on learning, *Adv. Study Behav. 4*, 1–68

Simpson, G. G. (1958) The study of evolution. Methods and present status of theory. In: *Behavior and Evolution* (A. Roe and G. G. Simpson, eds.) pp. 7–26, Yale University Press, New Haven

Sutherland, N. S. and Mackintosh, N. J. (1971) *Mechanisms of Animal Discrimination Learning*, Academic Press, New York

Teleki, G. (1974) Chimpanzee subsistence technology. Materials and skills, *J. Hum. Evol. 3*, 575–594

Thiessen, D. D., Owen, K. and Whitsett, M. (1970) Chromosome mapping of behavioral activities. In: *Contributions to Behavior Genetic Analysis. The Mouse as a Prototype* (G. Lindzey and D. D. Thiessen, eds.) pp. 161–204, Appleton, New York

Tryon, R. C. (1942) Individual differences. In: *Comparative Psychology* (F. A. Moss, ed.) 2nd ed., pp. 330–365, Prentice-Hall, Englewood Cliffs

Warren, J. M. (1961a) Individual differences in discrimation learning by cats, *J. Genet. Psychol. 98*, 89–93

Warren, J. M. (1961b) The effect of telencephobic injuries on learning by paradise fish (Macropodus opercularis), *J. Comp. Physiol. Psychol. 54*, 130–132

Warren, J. M. (1966) Reversal learning and the formation of learning sets by cats and rhesus monkeys, *J. Comp. Physiol. Psychol. 61*, 421–428

Warren, J. M. (1973) Learning in vertebrates. In: *Comparative Psychology* (D. A. Dewsbury and D. A. Rethlingshafer, eds.) pp. 471–509, McGraw-Hill, New York

Warren, J. M. (1974) Possibly unique characteristics of learning by primates, *J. Hum. Evol. 3*, 445–454

Warren, J. M. (1975) Overtraining, extinction and reversal learning by kittens, *Anim. Learn. Behav. 3*, 340–342

Warren, J. M. (1976a) Irrelevant cues and shape discrimination learning by cats, *Anim. Learn. Behav. 4*, 22–24

Warren, J. M. (1976b) Tool-use in mammals. In: *Evolution of Brain and Behavior in Vertebrates* (R. B. Masterton, M. E. Bitterman, C. B. G. Campbell, and N. Hotten, eds.) pp. 407–424, Erlbaum, Hillsdale

Warren, J. M. and McGonigle, B. (1969) Attention theory and discrimination learning. In: *Animal Discrimination Learning* (R. M. Gilbert and N. S. Sutherland eds.) pp. 113–136, Academic Press, London

Warren, J. M. and Warren, H. B. (1969) Two-cue discrimination learning by rhesus monkeys, *J. Comp. Physiol. Psychol. 69*, 688–691

Wilson, M. L., Warren, J. M. and Abbott, L. (1965) Infantile stimulation, activity and learning by cats, *Child Dev. 36*, 843–853

Genetic aspects of learning and behavior in animals

PART II

Genetics, environment and intelligence, edited by A. Oliverio
© *Elsevier/North-Holland Biomedical Press, 1977*

Towards a genetic analysis of learning and memory in invertebrates

4

JEAN MÉDIONI*

Introduction

The interest shown towards the forms and mechanisms of learning in the inverte-
brates is demonstrated by different reviews (e.g. Applewhite and Morowitz, 1967;
Eisenstein, 1967; Médioni and Robert, 1969 a and b; Alloway, 1972; and above all by
Corning et al., 1973).

The field of genetic analysis of behaviour has however not been overlooked, as
shown by several synthetic books, where a large part refers to at least a small number
of specifically chosen species, if not to the general group of invertebrates (Hirsch,
1967; Parsons, 1967; McClearn and De Fries, 1973; Roubertoux and Carlier, 1976).

Nevertheless, contrary to the vertebrates (notably the mammals), the genetics ×
learning intersection has been left almost untouched. This prompted us to present –at
times simply prospectively – selected works that could be useful in understanding
the behaviour of the invertebrates. We have limited ourselves to zoological groups
and to situations that are relevant to the genetics × learning intersection. Thus ex-
emplary cases of learning among invertebrates have been left out, in spite of their

---

*Equipe de Recherche Associée au Centre National de la Recherche Scientifique (E.R.A.
No. 700: "La préparation à l'action dans le comportement animal").

neurobiological interest, as we thought it improbable that their analysis lead to any genetic conclusions (e.g. the Horridge preparation, 1962; the octopus memory system according to Young, 1966, etc.).

Learning in invertebrates (with the exception of insects)

Considering strictly the genetic control of learning mechanisms and possibilities, there are only two zoological groups, insects apart, that can be taken into account, and even then only prospectively: infusorian ciliates and nematode worms.

The infusorian ciliates

Since the work carried out by Jennings (1906) and by Smith (1908) at the turn of the century, numerous publications have appeared on the learning possibilities of unicellular organisms, and above all on the ciliates. Following an outline of the less controversial results, we will try to link them to the recent attempts at a "genetic dissection of behaviour" (Kung et al., 1975).

Habituation

At present, it is a well established fact that certain ciliates can undergo a gradual decay of cell body contractions (*Spirostomum*) or of certain organelles (*Stentor, Vorticella*) in response to repetitive alarm stimuli that are not followed by an aggression or other damage (see Corning and Von Burg, 1973, for a detailed review of these studies).

Let us use as an example the main results of Wood (1970 a, b and c) on *Stentor coeruleus*: (a) regularly repeated mechanical shocks given to the substrate lead to a progressive decrease in the level of contractions of the cell body; (b) this is not a motor fatigue effect as the responses are immediately reinitiated upon the application of a stronger stimulus (transitory dehabituation); (c) some savings in the relearning process are shown in the 6 h following the initial habituation; (d) electrophysiological correlates of habituation can be recorded in an immobilized *S. coeruleus* using an intracellular microelectrode. In response to a mechanical shock, a slow "prepotential" is first recorded, the amplitude of which is proportional to the intensity of the stimulus; 10 msec later a spike appears, which is the precursor of the contraction. During habituation to a stimulus of constant intensity, the amplitude of the prepotential decreases progressively, whereas its latency increases; the spike parameters however remain unchanged. The habituation process in *Stentor* thus appears to result from a decrement in a correlate of the sensory reception and not of the response.

Associative learning

Since the first (negative) experiments carried out by Smith (1908), there have been numerous attempts to evidence associative learning in ciliates. As stressed by Corning and Von Burg (1973), the difficulties involved in trial-and-error learning, as well as in positively or negatively reinforced conditioning, are not insignificant: very strict controls suggest that the observed behavioral changes do not result from a memorization process but from diverse artifacts due to localized modifications in the aqueous medium; these could be brought about by thermal or radiant stimuli, or by the accumulation of metabolites around critical points of the experimental apparatus.

The more recent work of the Rucker team on paramecia (*Paramecium caudatum*) would seem to be exempt of these criticisms. The authors (Hanzel and Rucker, 1971, 1972; Huber et al., 1974) successfully repeated an experiment carried out by French (1940) but in more satisfactory conditions: paramecia individually sucked into a capillary pipette, learn to escape out of it more and more rapidly during 20 consecutive trials. Any progress made is achieved after the fifth trial by gradual elimination of haphazard movements. This is retained and can be still seen after 150 min. This performance however does not seem to develop in a very specific way, as it is accompanied by a parallel increase in the locomotor activity.

The most recent publications of the same team (Rucker and Hennessey, 1976; Hennessey and Rucker, 1976) describe a classical conditioning technique, applicable to paramecia. Repeated stimulations by a vibration (conditioned stimulus, C.S.) followed by a nociceptive electric shock (unconditioned stimulus, U.S.) eventually leads to the conditioning of a response that looks like a typical effect of the shock. This procedure can give rise to an experimental extinction, reconditioning and differentiation of two vibrational frequencies of which only one is reinforced. Control experiments show that pseudo-conditioning also plays a part but that sensitization, in its true sense, does not. Finally, the retention of this conditioning can reach 24 h.

Feasability of a "genetic dissection of behaviour" in paramecia

Paramecia show peculiarities in their sexuality and reproduction that make them especially convenient for a genetic analysis of behavioural, or other, traits. These diploid organisms possess, apart from an asexual means of reproduction, two distinct methods of genic rearrangement: conjugation, i.e. the exchange of nuclear material between a pair of organisms; and autogamy, during which a lone organism can, in the space of a few hours, pass into a completely homozygous state, thus expressing phenotypically its whole genotype including the recessive genes.

In *Paramecium aurelia*, these different processes can be controlled by modifying the culture conditions and, for example, by synchronizing the autogamy of a whole clone.

When a population of paramecia undergoing asexual reproduction is exposed to a potent mutagen agent, a large range of variants is obtained, some of which are behavioural. Controlled autogamy then allows the rapid stabilization of isogenic mutant strains.

Using ingenious screening techniques, Kung et al. (1975) were able to isolate nearly 300 mutant strains showing erroneous locomotion and/or orientation. Thus, "pawn" mutants are incapable of swimming backward to accomplish the avoiding reactions (Jennings, 1906) that characterize the locomotion of paramecia in a heterogeneous medium and that are the only means of progressive reorientation towards the more favourable environmental zones. Other mutants displace themselves very slowly and inefficiently; many display during every avoiding reaction a retreat that is much too long.

These perturbations all seem to be linked to different degrees of reduction of permeability of the cell membrane to Ca^{2+} ions, thus to its excitability level which determines the reversal of the ciliary beats and so the retreat movements. In certain mutants, there is absolutely no depolarization of the membrane; in other it does occur, but does not bring about the spikes necessary for the reversal of the ciliary beating; in other cases again, the membrane repolarization is too slow, etc.

These mutations are a potent tool in the analysis of electrogenesis, in an exceptionally large cell. Moreover, one could imagine that experimental mutagenesis can lead to the genetic control of more elaborate behavioural functions and notably memory on a cellular level. The difficulties inherent to this line of research must however not be underestimated: (a) apart from habituation, until now studied in other ciliates, demonstrations of the learning capacities of unicellular organisms are still rare and somewhat delicate; (b) the species most widely studied (except by Gelber, 1965) is *Paramecium caudatum* and not *P. aurelia*; (c) above all, the scarcity of the obtained mutants (1.10^{-4} on an average) makes it difficult to screen for characteristics more subtle than the gross anomalies of the action system.

The nematodes

The research group of Sidney Brenner (1973) undertook a "genetic dissection", comparable to those of Benzer (1973) on drosophila and of Kung et al. (1975) on paramecia. The subject for this study was a small round worm (1 mm long) *Caenorhabditis elegans* which has only 600 somatic cells, about 250 of which are neurons. The complete life cycle lasts just 3.5 days at 20°C. The large majority of these animals are self-fertilizing hermaphrodites; this facilitates the isolation of isogenic clones: starting with one adult, 100 000 F_2 decendants are obtained in one week. Cross-fertilization is nevertheless possible with "strict males" (about 0.1% of the population) allowing a genetic analysis, up to the establishing of factorial maps.

When treated with ethyl-methyl-sulphonate, an appreciable number of mutants were obtained, some of which show motor deficiencies to a greater or lesser extent. In 1973, 77 distinct genes, which are responsible for these deficiencies, were listed as well as other genes controlling the body size and shape. The exact target of the neurological mutations has only been identified in exceptional cases, following an ultrastructural study of the whole nervous system. In some cases, a genovariation can bring about an elective impairment in a highly circumscribed neuronal subset.

Using this biological material, it is thus possible to relate a certain gene to a certain neurological locality. However, taking into consideration the total lack of knowledge at this moment concerning nematode behaviour and its degree of flexibility, any work in the near future on the genetic determinants of memory would seem to pose many problems.

Learning and memory in insects

The behaviour of insects has been a particularly well developed study for economic and historical reasons. The behavioural stereotypy of these animals has long been stressed, as contrasting with vertebrates in this respect (Fabre, 1894; Bergson, 1907; Maier and Schneirla, 1935). As stated by Wells (1973) this opposition has been over-simplified: in fact insects are often capable of adjusting their behaviour in accordance with individual experience.

In view of a genetic analysis of memory, we will limit our critical evaluation of recent work to two orders of insects: Hymenoptera (mainly bees) and Diptera (mainly drosophilae). There is a striking difference between these two groups (Manning, 1972): although, in both cases, the central nervous system is able to reach a high degree of cephalization and condensation, the learning capacities seem to be very unequal. Bees are easily conditionable in all sorts of situations (Von Frisch, 1914 and 1919) whereas the diptera have a much more uncertain learning ability (Nelson, 1971).

Learning and memory in bees

Von Frisch and co-workers used the conditionability of bees, mainly in the exploration of the Umwelt of these insects (e.g. Daumer, 1956, for colour vision). More recently the bee has been used in investigations specifically aimed at the learning capacities: it has moreover been shown to be outstanding animal material for the physiological study of memory.

Classical conditioning

This was attained for the proboscis extension reflex, using either light (Kuwabara, 1957; Voskresenskaja, 1957; Masuhr and Menzel, 1972; Menzel et al., 1973) or an odour as a C.S. (Takeda, 1957; Vareschi and Kaissling, 1970; Vareschi, 1971; Menzel et al., 1973). With particularly prominent odours only one training trial can be enough (Menzel et al., 1973). Pavlovian conditioning is possible, not only in workers but also in drones, in spite of the lesser differentiation of their behaviour patterns (Vareschi and Kaissling, 1970).

Instrumental approach conditioning

In the bee, the flying approach can be conditioned on the basis of a social feeding reinforcement. The importance of each reinforcement (sugar water) does not play a major role (Menzel and Erber, 1972), but their number and duration is critical (Menzel et al., 1973). A fixed ratio reinforcement programme is effective up to 1:30 and a fixed interval programme up to $90 \sec^{-1}$. The experimental extinction is slower with intermittent than with constant reinforcement, as in the vertebrates (Grossman, 1973).

In photic conditioning, the speed of acquisition depends on the coloured light used as a C.S., but it does not result in a simple way from the spectral sensitivity of the photoreceptors (Menzel et al., 1973). The integration properties of the visual analyser are thus not to be confused with its purely sensory capacities: processing of the memorized visual information is already initiated at the level of the optic lobes. Time and duration of presentation of the light C.S. are decisive (Opfinger, 1931; Menzel, 1967): the associative link cannot develop if the bee does not perceive the C.S. during the two or three seconds before its arrival at the reinforcement place as well as during the first second of sugar water sucking.

It is however in the olfactory conditioning that the bee shows the most significant peculiarities. First of all, as in pavlovian conditioning, one-trial learning proved to be possible: it can withstand extinction for several dozen unreinforced test trials. Kriston (1971) showed however that the number of training trials needed varies with the smell used as C.S.: one trial is enough for floral scents, whereas as many as 10 or 20 are needed for fatty acid smells, although they are not repellent for the bee. Koltermann (1971, 1973) shows the importance of certain time-linked conditions for the recall of an instrumental approach conditioning, formed on an olfactory base: the use of the engram is much more efficient exactly 24 h (or 48, 72 etc.) after the training than for example after 20 h (or 44, 68 etc., respectively). The bee thus retains, at the same time as certain critical signals in its environment, the time at which they were recognized as such. This capacity represents a valuable evolutionary adaptation to make full use of certain sources of nectar and pollen that are only available at well-defined moments during the day.

The physiology of memory in bees

Menzel et al. (1973) undertook a detailed study of the mechanisms of memorization in bees. They used notably experimental retrograde amnesia: electroconvulsive shock (devoid of aversive effects for the bees) and various other disruptive treatments having an amnestic effect, within the limits of 5 to 7 min after the information input, above which the engram seems to be entirely consolidated.

Using one-trial olfactory conditioning of the proboscidian reflex on an immobilized insect, the authors carried out a localized chilling (1 °C) of different cerebral structures. Using a bilateral chilling of the α-lobe of the mushroom bodies, the time gradient of retrograde amnesia established with an electro-convulsive shock is exactly reproduced. On the other hand, if the chilling is carried out on the antennal lobes (integration of olfactory inputs), the amnestic effect is limited to 2 min. These facts would seem to be in agreement with the hypothesis of a two-stage memorization: the mushroom bodies would be involved in the long-term memory storage, the antennal lobes, however, only intervene in the first moments of the consolidation. Other aspects of this work (e.g. uni- or bilateral engrammation) cannot be considered in this text, but they combine to show us the wide possibilities offered by the bee in the study of the fundamental mechanisms of memory.

Classical conditioning of the proboscis reflex in flies

Frings (1941) carried out the first experiment in classical conditioning on a fly, *Cynomyia cadaverina*: the smell of coumarin (C.S.) coupled with the presentation of a sugar solution (U.S.) gradually became effective as a releaser for the proboscis extension reflex. These experiments however did not include any control groups for eventual sensitization and/or pseudo-conditioning effects.

The experiments carried out by Nelson (1971) on the blowfly *Phormia regina* are the first to take these objection into consideration, while at the same time outlining the difficulties involved in studies on associative learning in diptera. In these experiments, the C.S. is complex: it comprises two successive stimulations, $C.S._1$ and $C.S._2$, of the taste receptors on the foretarsii. In the princeps experiment, $C.S._1$ is a solution of NaCl and $C.S._2$ is pure water for half of the subjects and for the other half, the order is reversed. The U.S. is a drop of sugar water placed on the mouthparts at the end of $C.S._2$: in hungry flies, this regularly initiates the proboscis extension. During the 15 training trials the percentage of anticipatory responses regularly increases. Very careful control experiments show that a detectable percentage of these responses are due to pseudo-conditioning and to sensitization; they are dependent upon an increase of the "central excitatory state", which partially results from the reiteration of the C.S., as well as of the U.S. and some extrinsic stimulations. Nevertheless, the large majority of the observed responses before the U.S. originates in a "true" conditioning process, as proved by the positive results of a discrimination experiment between the two C.S. used.

Comparable experiments have since been carried out by Fukushi, on the responses of the housefly *Musca domestica* towards olfactory (1973) and visual (1976) stimuli. On the whole, his results are clearer than those of Nelson; sensitization is negligible and pseudo-conditioning only accounts for at most 15% of the responses to the C.S. It is difficult to say whether the difference results from the species studied, or from a specific difficulty when using tarsal taste stimuli as C.S.

Learning in Drosophila

Since the work carried out by the T. H. Morgan school, taking into consideration the accumulated knowledge of the genetics of *Drosophila melanogaster*, many authors attempted to study learning in this insect. As we will see, some of these studies are not very convincing.

The role of early experience: habituation or associative learning?
According to Thorpe (1939) the smell of peppermint is strongly repellent for drosophilae placed in an olfactometer; however, after a prolonged exposure to the odour, adults can loose their aversion towards it and even become significantly attracted. As peppermint essence is not a pure substance, the author explains these results by an olfactory habituation that allows another substance in the mixture to display its latent attractiveness. If, however, the flies are reared in their larval life with peppermint in the culture medium, they are immediately attracted, as adults, to the smell of peppermint. Firstly taken as "pre-imaginal conditioning", this process was reinterpreted as "latent learning" (Thorpe, 1956).

Hershberger and Smith (1967) confirmed these results but did not agree with the interpretation. According to them, an associative link develops between the smell and the reinforcing agent consisting of the nutritive larval medium. The experimental arguments supporting this proposition are neither complete nor coherent, as stated by Yeatman and Hirsch (1971). Manning (1967) also found "pre-imaginal conditioning" using a pure repellent substance, geraniol. He separated those adult drosophilae that, in the olfactometer, went towards the odourless side (about 50%) from those that "chose" the scented side. The latter then underwent a second olfactometric test. If during their larval life they had developed a conditioning based on the food-odour link, this conditioning should be expressed in the olfactometer by the orientation of a large majority towards the geraniol. However these animals show, on the second test, the same distribution (apparently random) between the two sides as the whole group showed in the first test. Thus Manning rejects the associative learning hypothesis in favour of a process related to habituation: the flies do not go towards the geraniol, they simply no longer find the odour offensive.

Cushing (1941) pointed out that the "Thorpe effect" is observed in the egg-laying behaviour of *Drosophila guttifera*, a species that in nature lives on mushrooms. The preference of females for a laying substrate supplemented with a mushroom extract is increased when the female larvae are reared on a similar nutritive medium. This result confirms a certain habituation towards the laying and rearing standard medium.

Tarsal reflex conditioning in Drosophila

Vaysse and Médioni (1973) developed a technique for studying the unconditioned proboscis extension reflex in response to a general stimulation of the taste receptors found at the extremity of the forelegs (tarsii) using sugary substances. The insect is fastened by the notum (dorsal part of the thorax) to a needle support; it "walks on the spot" by means of a conveyer belt which bears at intervals a rectangle of filter-paper soaked in a sugar solution of known concentration. The insect can come into contact with the sugar by its tarsii, but not by its proboscis. Using this technique it has been possible to study the stimulatory effectiveness of different sugars (Vaysse, Médioni, Thon and Laffont, unpublished) as well as the variations of the response threshold to sucrose induced by various factors: sex, duration, starvation, degree of inbreeding (Vaysse and Médioni, 1973; Médioni, 1976).

Attempts to bring about a classical conditioning of the tarsal reflex (with C.S. consisting of photic, vibratory, tactile stimulus) have to date been totally unsuccessful, even when reinforcing anticipatory proboscis extrusions by allowing the insect to take up a droplet of sugar. Médioni and Vaysse (1975, a and b), however, were able to devise a negatively reinforced conditioning procedure, based on the same technique of tarsal taste stimulation. This procedure is closely linked to passive avoidance conditioning, except that it involves the inhibition of a well-defined partial reaction (the tarsal reflex) and not of a global escape response. This conditioned inhibition is brought about when the proboscis extension, induced by an effective stimulation of the foretarsii, is immediately and regularly followed by a nociceptive electric shock applied to the middle and hind-legs, devoid of taste receptors. This punishment is omitted every time the reflex is not released. On an average, this procedure gives about a 50% suppression of the tarsal response, between the 20th and 30th training trial. Appropriate control groups show that there is a fairly significant level of pseudo-conditioning which accounts for about 20% of the observed suppressions. Similarly, the "desensitization", due to sensory adaptation and/or habituation, is also at the root of one out of five suppressions of the tarsal reflex. So that, on an average, three out of five results from a "true" conditioning, i.e. from an associative link between the proprioceptive feed-back of the tarsal reflex and the nociceptive stimulation. Complementary experiments show the possibility of an experimental extinction, i.e. of a restitution of the reflex, when the nociceptive reinforcement is withdrawn: this extinction develops approximately twice as slowly as the acquisition. More recently, Vaysse and Médioni (1976) have shown that using very mild electric shocks, the number of suppressions decreases whereas the relative contribution of pseudo-conditioning does not.

The main interest of this technique is that the study of the individual differences is made possible in *Drosophila* conditionability. An obvious complementary limitation is inherent in the slowness of the procedure (about 1 h per insect). To study the genetic factors involved, it will be necessary to work out experimental conditions allowing a faster acquisition. Some data (as yet unpublished) show that with more intense shocks, a result is obtained after 10 or 15 trials without any increase in pseudo-conditioning.

Attempts at spatial learning in Drosophila

Let us refer to the work of Hay (1975): introduced in batches of 200 in a "phototaxis maze," modified from Hadler (1964), the flies pass once only. Those taking the path to the left at the first choice point have to turn to the left 5 times while making their way towards the light, before coming across the second choice point, and vice-versa for the drosophilae that initially turned to the right. Under these conditions, the second choice is not random, but is biased towards the direction of the forced turns. There are no factors involved that are linked to the instantaneous situation, nor a contagion draining effect, nor tracks of smell left by the leading animals, nor a trend to follow the outer walls of the maze. This situation would seem to involve learning by association between the positive phototactic tendency and the repeated forced left or right turns. Bicker and Spatz (1976) found the same behavioural trend in a similar maze, even in total darkness and so challenge Hay's interpretation.

In the 1967, Murphey published a group of data suggesting that *Drosophila* can learn a position habit in a T-maze. The reinforcement used was rather unexpected: flies previously selected for an extreme expression of ascending geotaxis (Erlenmeyer-Kimling et al., 1962) had the opportunity of leaving the maze by an ascending vertical tube after a correct choice and by a descending tube after an error. After 50 training trials without correction as well as 50 trials of reversal learning, the results are statistically significant, even though they only show slight performance development. A training procedure with correction seems to be more effective, whether or not it is accompanied by a negative reinforcement (electric shock) in case of error.

This work was taken up by Yeatman and Hirsch (1971) who severely criticized several aspects of the original research. Using more satisfactory conditions, they completely failed to repeat Murphey's second experiment.

Following some more recently published work, Murphey finally gave up hope of developing a spatial learning procedure based on geotactic reinforcement (1969). The T-maze task would only allow a "spatial discrimination performance" founded on the use of momentaneous, but not memorized, cues: notably olfactory tracks (1973).

Learning of sensory discriminations in Drosophila

Quinn et al. (1974) convincingly established that it is possible to form a discrimination learning between different colours or odours. The experimental paradigm is the following: batches of 40 flies are confronted, either successively (odours) or simultaneously (colours), with pairs of sensory signals, one of which, S^-, is associated with a negative reinforcement (a nociceptive electric shock or a bitter taste stimulation) for 3 training trials at 60 sec intervals. The test trials (unreinforced) take place in an enclosure that the flies had not entered during the training, hence devoid of olfactory cues, e.g. alarm pheromones. Each of these experiments was complemented with another where the reinforced stimulus is the alternative one; for each signal pair, this was carried out 10 times.

The clearest results were obtained with olfactory discriminations. Table I shows the results obtained with the test trial, using 3-octanol, 4-methylcyclohexanol and stearic acid which were used in rotation as stimulus: (a) negatively reinforced, (b) unreinforced, (c) new, i.e. presented for the first time at the test trial. A comparison of the results relative to these latter categories of stimulus shows that the percentage of cases where a non-reinforced stimulus is avoided is not influenced by sensory adaption and/or habituation. The experimental extinction of an acquired discrimination can be carried out in 7 test trials and the reversal learning performed immediately afterwards.

In light wave-length discrimination tasks (450 against 610 and 350 against 470 nm), the results are not nearly as clear, although still significant: this may be due to the low level of divergence between the limbs of the Y-maze (< 30°) used in this experimental situation.

There is one aspect of these noteworthy experiments that must be pointed out, in as far as the genetic analysis of memory capacities is concerned: under the conditions described above, all the flies of the population under study have an equal probability

Table I   (After Quinn et al., 1974)

Odours used as	Percentage of insects avoiding the stimulus
Reinforced stimulus	40 ± 4
Familar, unreinforced stimulus	15 ± 2 ⎫ N.S.
New stimulus	12 ± 2 ⎭

of developing a conditioned avoidance of an olfactory stimulus. In other words, there would be no behavioural heterogeneity such as was observed by Tryon (1929) between "dull" and "bright" rats or by Nelson (1971) between "good learners" and "poor learners" in *Phormia*. Thus, during a new learning task carried out 24 h after the first one, the same proportion of "avoiders" (about one third) is found among the "avoiders" and the "non-avoiders" of the day before. This apparent homogeneity at the population level could, in our opinion, come from: (a) the preliminary, comparatively unstable character of this type of learning, carried out on a large number of insects at once, with a minimal amount of training; (b) the low inter-individual differentiation possibilities that may thus arise.

Studies carried out along comparable lines were more successful, in as far as discrimination between two monochromatic light sources is concerned: Spatz et al. (1974) placed batches of 300 flies in the starting-box of a T-maze. In order to arrive at the choice point, the insects had to cross two very constricted funnels. These passages were lit axially and from the front with optical fibers: one with blue light, and the other with yellow light. The crossing of one or other of these constrictions could be linked to the administration of an electric shock. Entry to the lateral branches of the T-maze was by two other funnels, one lit with blue and the other with yellow light. To detect the formation of any light-shock association, the performance of an experimental group (e.g. shock coupled with blue light) is compared with that of a control, never shocked, group. A significant avoidance was observed in 44 out of 46 experiments of this type. On the other hand there was never any significant divergence recorded: (a) when the maze was in total darkness, (b) when the electric shock was given without an associated light.

Menne et Spatz (personal communication, 1976) have developed another conditioning technique with visual signals, associating them with strong mechanical vibrations. By varying, over several orders of magnitude, the luminance of the monochromatic stimulus during the training period, they conclusively show that the discrimination is primarily based on the hue and that *Drosophila* have a discriminative colour vision.

The genetics × learning intersection: insect data

The genetic predisposition towards memorizing certain cues

Let us come back to the data of Kriston (1971) already cited in the section on olfactory learning in bees (p. 64). These insects are able to instantaneously memorize certain flower scents, whereas other (non-repellent) odours need 10–20 training trials. This difference in the processing of olfactory information according to its properties strongly suggests that the worker bees have a genetic predisposition towards a better retention of floral scents. This interpretation is all the more probable, as the difference remains in workers brought up ab ovo in the total absence of any floral scents. This could doubtlessly be considered as one manifestation of the co-evolution of plants and their pollinators.

Interspecific and interracial differences in learning performances

At the present time, geneticists and a growing number of ethologists are realizing that the importance of hereditary determinants in the individual variation of a characteristic cannot be estimated by simply observing that the members of closely related races, species, or strains differ in their "typical expression" of this trait. First of all, this approach does not teach us anything about the genetic mechanisms involved. Secondly but of importance, it does not take into consideration the existence of multiple interactions among the genes as well as between the genotype and the environment. In short, the phenotypic expression of a genetic system cannot come down to a group of strictly additive effects that, however, make up the underlying implicit postulate to inter-population comparisons. The observation of a difference between two genotypically distinct groups can only have a preliminary indicative value.

In the field of insect learning, one observation of this kind is due to Schneirla (1933, quoted by Lauer and Lindauer, 1973): ants sp. *Formica incerta* show performances superior to those of *F. subsericea* in maze learning.

In the bee, the hierarchy of the cues used in an instrumental approach conditioning varies with the race: *Apis mellifera ligustica* workers guide themselves above all on the patterning of a critical visual stimulus; *carnica* makes better use of nearby landmarks provided that they are sufficiently striking, e.g. a tree trunk, a path etc. (Lauer and Lindauer, 1973). When over flat bare ground these two races show an equal level of performance, which perfectly illustrates the importance of the above mentioned (genotype–environment) interactions. In similar learning tasks, the use of artificial auxiliary visual cues is more effective in *Apis mellifera carnica* than in *ligustica* (Hoefer and Lindauer, 1975).

Menzel, Freudel and Ruhl (1973) continued with similar comparisons on the Egyptian race *fasciata* and on the Indian bee *Apis cerana*: the two European races have a very high rate of visiting the experimental set-up (owing to a strong foraging motivation) which causes, during the first stages of a discriminative visual learning a larger number of errors, giving a faster development of acquisition in *fasciata* and *Apis cerana*. Other differences are revealed, notably in the "strategy of learning" (transition between the approach and the coming-into-contact with the discriminative cue). This study is however above all of methodological interest: it points out the difficulties met with in the identification of the behavioural factors that differentiate these populations of bee: the memory is doubtlessly relatively unimportant.

Hay (1975), in a previously quoted work (cf. p. 67), showed the existence of systematic differences between 10 inbred strains of *Drosophila* while in a maze. It was seen however that the intervention of learning was improbable in this situation.

Selective breeding experiments

Even though it makes up a particularly powerful analytical tool in genetics, selective breeding has only been very rarely used in the study of memory in invertebrates.

In the so-called instrumental learning situation of Murphey (1967, cf. p. 67), Yeatman and Hirsch (1971) tried to select drosophilae showing extreme performances in the T-maze. Even after 10 generations, there was no response to the divergent selection.

In another work already quoted (p. 66), Manning (1967) tries to select drosophilae reared in a food medium impregnated with the odour of geraniol, for a higher degree of aversive reactions to this odour, i.e. for the lowest possible degree of habituation: here again no response to the selective pressure is stated (6 generations).

After confirming Nelson's results (1971, cf. p. 65) on the conditioning of the proboscidian reflex in *Phormia*, McCauley and Hirsch (1977) undertook a bidirectional selection based on the performance of the flies in the 8 last training trials, the insects being classed as "good", "fair" and "poor" learners, according to the criteria set down by Nelson herself. The good learners were interbred, as well as the poor learners; at the same time, an unselected control strain is maintained and tested in a parallel way. There is a rapid divergence between the two experimental strains: after 7 generations they both significantly differ from the control strain. No sex-linked difference is observed. Taking into consideration the speed of the response to the selection, the additive genetic variation must be very large; it follows that the selected character is almost certainly not a component of fitness. Should one conclude then that memory in Diptera gives no evolutionary advantage, or, more cautiously, as the authors suggest, that the population used, reared under laboratory conditions for 20 years, is hardly comparable to a natural population of *Phormia*?

Taking into account the interference observed in this species, between classical conditioning and sensitization "noise" effects, it would be useful to develop a detailed analysis of the "good" and "poor" learners behaviour, in experimental situations allowing to assess the part played in the performance by the "central excitatory state" (Dethier et al., 1965).

McGuire and Hirsch (1976) describe in a preliminary communication how they successfully replicated the experiments of McCauley and Hirsch, using other strains and continued the divergent selection to 24 generations. As in the previous work, the heritability is high for the two strains "good" and "poor". Crosses carried out after the 14th generation of selection show: (a) that the genetic determination of the studied behaviour is polygenic; (b) that the genes under consideration are mostly autosomic; (c) that the "good learner" characteristic is partially dominant over the poor learner one. The in extenso publication of these results and the continuation of this research are eagerly awaited.

"Genetic dissection" of learning in Drosophila

In the well known studies of Benzer and his colleagues, experimental mutagenesis and screening were used to isolate mutant strains, showing serious behavioural deviations, in *D. melanogaster*: loss of flying abilities, even with full developed wings; suppression of phototaxis; disruption or transformation of the circadian rhythm of activity, etc. In a few especially propitious cases, ingenious procedures allowing the precise identification of the anatomo-physiological target of a behavioural mutation could be applied (Benzer, 1973).

In a recent work by the same research group (Dudai et al., 1976.), the discovery of a mutation that specifically alters the learning capabilities, in the situation of successive discrimination between two odours as described above (cf. p. 68) has been pointed out. This mutation was discovered after screening about 500 strains subjected to a mutagen agent, 20 out of which showed performance deficiencies when in a learning situation. However these deficiencies could be related to learning processes (as opposed to e.g. a drop in the olfactory sensitivity) in one case only. The mutant "*dunce*" (*dnc*) shows an external morphology as well as a viability comparable to that of the wild type. Flight and walking are in no way affected; neither are phototaxis, geotaxis or courtship displays; the same goes for the electroretinogram and synaptic transmission at the neuromuscular junction. The unconditioned reactivity to 7 different odours is also unchanged; but in spite of this, any discriminative learning is impossible using any of them. Finally, the sensitivity to a reinforcing electric shock is not involved either: the acquisition of an olfactory discrimination remains impossible even with the use of another negative reinforcement that is effective in the wild type (stimulation of the tarsal taste receptors with a bitter solution). The *dunce* mutation is incompletely recessive and sex-linked. The gene involved is found in the immediate proximity of the *yellow* locus, near one of the ends of the X chromosome.

This noteworthy discovery raises several questions: (a) how general are the effects of the mutation? Is it closely linked to the central functioning of the olfactory analyser? Or does it also suppress the learning capacity for other signals or other tasks? The use of *dunce* in other situations of associative learning (cf. p. 66 and p. 68) would probably give access to some information on this point; (b) another problem is that of the mode of action of the *dnc* gene: the Benzer team is well prepared to solve it rapidly, using elaborate phenogenetic techniques (Benzer, 1973); (c) finally we can ask, more speculatively, whether mutant flies "better endowed" for memorization than the wild type could be obtained. This question might seem nonsensical, if the investigations were limited to the role of learning in the natural conditions of life of *Drosophila*: for it is probable that natural selection has already carried out its normal optimization function. Yet as pointed out by Dobzhansky (1956) there are no intrinsically adaptive traits: the wild phenotype is a compromise between adaptive demands that are often contradictory. Moreover, it is still possible to imagine, in an experimental context, an increase by mutation of the learning capacities, even though it would be at the expense of the global fitness in the studied populations.

Early experience and evolutionary genetics

In *Drosophila*, panmixia is strongly biased by sexual selection (Petit, 1958; Boesiger, 1962; Ehrman et al., 1965). Is individual experience somehow able to account for this distortion? Such is the problem studied by the D. Mainardi team at Parma University.

On an infraspecific level, M. Mainardi (1967) has shown, on *D. melanogaster*, that the males of the *Oregon* wild type, reared in isolation and when mature, confronted with a female of the same strain and a *yellow* mutant female, showed no significant preference in their courtship for either phenotype. On the other hand, wild type males, reared with flies of the same strain, have a perfectly clear homogamic behaviour (D. Mainardi and M. Mainardi, 1966). This trend can be eliminated by raising a wild type male in a colony of *yellow* mutants.

In the case of interspecific sexual competition (between the sibling species *D. melanogaster* and *D. simulans*) there is no noticeable difference in the degree of homogamy displayed by *D. melanogaster* males raised in isolation or among conspecific insects (M. Mainardi and Le Moli, 1969).

These results confirm the generally accepted idea (David, 1976) that behavioural factors (and in particular early experience) only intervene in speciation as secondary isolating mechanisms that reinforce the breeding barriers established on another basis. As for the nature of the acquisition process brought into action during the isolation experiment on the infraspecific level (habituation? imprinting? associative learning?), it remains a complete unknown.

Conclusion

At the end of this review, which only looks into the research opening the way for a genetic analysis of learning and memory in the invertebrates, it may seem as though we were at the very start of an unending path. However, decisive progress has been made with the attempts at a genetic dissection of behaviour in diverse zoological groups (ciliates, nematodes, insects) and also with the device of conditioning techniques in animals especially convenient to genetic analyses, but also particularly rebellious in as far as conventional learning procedures are concerned. However, the peculiar suitability of some of these species, as compared with mammals, lies in their very short life cycles, which must inspire the researchers with great confidence during this "long walk".

Literature cited

Alloway, T. M. (1972) Learning and memory in insects. *Annu. Rev. Entomol. 17*, 43–56
Applewhite, P. H. and Morowitz, H. J. (1967) Memory and the microinvertebrates. In: *Chemistry of Learning: Invertebrate Research* (W. C. Corning and S. C. Ratner, eds.) pp. 329–340, Plenum Press, New York
Benzer, S. (1973) Genetic dissection of behavior, *Sci. Am. 229*, 24–37
Bergson, H. (1907) *L'évolution créatrice*, Alcan, Paris
Bicker, G. and Spatz, H.-C. (1976) Maze-learning ability of Drosophila melanogaster, *Nature 260*, 371
Boesiger, E. (1962) Sur le degré d'hétérozygotie des populations naturelles de Drosophila melanogaster et son maintien par la sélection sexuelle, *Bull. Biol. Fr. Belg. 96*, 3–121

Brenner, S. (1973) The genetics of behaviour, *Br. Med. Bull. 29*, 269–271

Corning, W. C., Dyal, J. A. and Willows, A.O.D. (1973) Invertebrate Learning, Plenum Press, New York

Corning, W. C. and Von Burg, R. (1973) Protozoa. In: *Invertebrate Learning* (W. C. Corning, J. A. Dyal and A. O. D. Willows, eds.) Vol. 1, pp. 49–122, Plenum Press, New York

Cushing, J. E., Jr. (1941) An experiment on olfactory conditioning in Drosophila guttifera, *Proc. Natl. Acad. Sci. N.Y. 27*, 496–499

Daumer, K. (1956) Reizmetrische Untersuchung des Farbensehens der Bienen, *Z. Vgl. Physiol. 38*, 413–478

David, J. (1977) Importance évolutive du comportement alimentaire et dú comportement de ponte chez les insectes. In: *Les Mécanismes Ethologiques de l'Evolution* (J. Médioni and E. Boesiger, eds.) pp. 34–46, Masson, Paris

Dethier, V. G., Solomon, R. L. and Turner, L. H. (1965) Sensory input and central excitation and inhibition in the blowfly, *J. Comp. Physiol. Psychol. 60*, 303–313

Dobzhansky, T. (1956) What is an adaptive trait? *Am. Nat.* 90, 337–347

Dudai, Y., Jan, Y. -N., Byers, D., Quinn, W. G. and Benzer, S. (1976) dunce, a mutant of Drosophila deficient in learning, *Proc. Natl. Acad. Sci. U.S.A.* 73, 1684–1688

Ehrman, L., Spassky, B., Pavlovsky, O. and Dobzhansky, T. (1965) Sexual selection, geotaxis and chromosomal polymorphism in experimental populations of Drosophila pseudoobscura, *Evolution 19*, 337–346

Eisenstein, E. M. (1967) The use of invertebrate systems for studies on the basis of learning and memory. In: *The Neurosciences: A Study Program* (G. C. Quarton, T. Melnechuck and F. O. Schmitt, eds.) pp. 653–665, Rockefeller University Press, New York

Erlenmeyer-Kimling, L., Hirsch, J. and Weiss, J. (1962) Studies in experimental behavior genetics. III. Selection and hybridization analyses of individual differences in the sign of geotaxis, *J. Comp. Physiol. Psychol. 55*, 722–731

Fabre, J. H. (1894) *Souvenirs Entomologiques*, lère Série, 3rd edn., Delagrave, Paris

French, J. W. (1940) Trial and error learning in Paramecium, *J. Exp. Psychol. 26*, 609–613

Frings, H. (1941) The loci of olfactory end-organs in the blowfly, Cynomyia cadaverina Desvoidy, *J. Exp. Zool. 88*, 65–93

Von Frisch, K. (1914) Der Farbensinn und Formensinn der Biene, *Zool. Jahrb. (Abt. Physiol.)* 35, 1–188

Von Frisch, K. (1919) Uber den Geruschsinn der Bienen und seine blütenbiologische Bedeutung, *Zool. Jahrb. 37*, 1–238

Fukushi, T. (1973) Olfactory conditioning in the housefly Musca domestica, *Annot. Zool. Jap. 46*, 135–143

Fukushi, T. (1976) Classical conditioning to visual stimuli in the housefly, Musca domestica, *J. Insect Physiol. 22*, 361–364

Gelber, B. (1965) Studies of the behaviour of Paramecium aurelia, *Anim. Behav. 13, Suppl. 1*, 21–29

Grossmann, K. E. (1973) Continuous, fixed-ratio and fixed-interval reinforcement in honey-bees, *J. Exp. Anal. Behav. 20*, 105–109

Hadler, N. M. (1964) Heritability and phototaxis in Drosophila melanogaster, *Genetics 50*, 1269–1277

Hanzel, T. E. and Rucker, W. B. (1971) Escape training in Paramecium, *J. Biol. Psychol. 13*, 24–28

Hanzel, T. E. and Rucker, W. B. (1972) Trial and error learning in Paramecium: a replication, *Behav. Biol. 7*, 873–880

Hay, D. A. (1975) Strain differences in maze-learning ability of Drosophila melanogaster, *Nature 257*, 44–46

Hennessey, T. M. and Rucker, W. B. (1976) Classical conditioning in paramecia: grade-B certified learning, in the press

Hershberger, W. A. and Smith, M. P. (1967) Conditioning in Drosophila melanogaster, *Anim. Behav. 15*, 259–262

Hirsch, J. (ed.) (1967) *Behavior-Genetic Analysis*, McGraw-Hill, New York

Hoefer, I. and Lindauer, M. (1975) Das Lernverhalten zweier Bienenrassen unter veränderten Orientierungsbedingungen, *J. Comp. Physiol. 99*, 119–138

Horridge, G. A. (1962) Learning of leg position by the ventral nerve cord in headless insects, *Proc. Soc. Lond. B 157*, 33–52

Huber, J. C., Rucker, W. B. and Mc Diarmid, C. G. (1974) Retention of escape training and activity changes in single paramecia, *J. Comp. Physiol. Psychol. 86*, 258–266

Jennings, H. S. (1906) *The Behavior of Lower Organisms*, Columbia University Press, New York

Koltermann, R. (1971) 24-Std-Periodik in der Langzeiterinnerung an Duft- und Farbsignale bei der Honigbiene, *Z. Vergl. Physiol. 75*, 49–68

Koltermann, R. (1973) Periodicity in the activity and learning performance of the honeybee. In: *Experimental Analysis of Insect Behaviour* (L. Barton Browne, ed.) pp. 218–227, SpringerVerlag, Berlin

Kriston, I. (1971) Zum Problem des Lernverhaltens von Apis mellifica L. gegenüber verschiedenen Duftstoffen, *Z. Vergl. Phsyiol. 74*, 169–189

Kung, C., Chang, S. Y., Satow, Y., Van Houten, J. and Hansma, H. (1975) Genetic dissection of behavior in Paramecium, *Science 188*, 898–904

Kuwabara, M. (1957) Bildung des bedingten Reflexes von Pavlovs Typus bei der Honigbiene (Apis mellifica), *J. Fac. Sci. Hokkaido Univ. Zool.*) *13*, 458–467

Lauer, J. and Lindauer, M. (1973) Die Beteiligung von Lernprozessen bei der Orientierung, *Fortschr. Zool. 21*, 349–370

Maier, N. R. F. and Schneirla, T. C. (1935) *Principles of Animal Psychology*, McGraw-Hill, New York

Mainardi, D. and Mainardi, M. (1966) Selezione sessuale in Drosophila melanogaster: l' apprendimento come determinante delle preferenze, *Ist. Lomb. Accad. Sci. Lett. Rend. Sci. Biol. Med. B 100*, 117–122

Mainardi, M. (1967) Scomparsa delle preferenze sessuali intraspecifiche nel maschio di Drosophila melanogaster allevato in isolamento, *Rend. Cl. Sci. Fis. Matem. Natur., Acad. Nazion. Lincei 43*, 107–108

Mainardi, M. and Le Moli, F. (1969) Assenza di fattori di apprendimento nell'isolamento riproduttivo tra Drosophila melanogaster e D. simulans, *Ist. Accad. Lomb. Sci. Lett. Rend. Sci. Biol. Med B 103*, 22–26

Manning, A. (1967) "Pre-imaginal conditioning" in Drosophila, *Nature 216*, 338–340

Manning, A. (1972) *An Introduction to Animal Behaviour*, 2nd edn., p. 18, Edward Arnold, London

Masuhr, T. and Menzel, R. (1972) Learning experiments on the use of side-specific information in the olfactory and visual system in the honeybee (Apis mellifica). In: *Information Processing in the Visual System of Arthropods*, (R. Wehner, ed.) pp. 315–321, Springer-Verlag, Berlin

McCauley, L. A. and Hirsch, J. (1977) Successful replication of, and selective breeding for, classical conditioning in the blowfly, Phormia regina, *Anim. Behav.*, in the press

McClearn, G. E. and De Fries, J. C. (1973) *Introduction to Behavioral Genetics*, Freeman, San Francisco

McGuire, T. R. and Hirsch, J. (1976) Selection for, and hybridization analysis of, classical conditioning in the blowfly, Phormia regina, Abstract of communication at the *6th Annual Meeting of the Behavior Genetics Association*

Médioni, J. (1976) Hétérosis et influence dépressive de la consanguinité dans le domaine des traits éthologiques: implications évolutives éventuelles. In: *Les Mécanismes Ethologiques de l'Evolution* (J. Médioni and E. Boesiger, eds.) pp. 115–131, Masson, Paris

Médioni, J. and Robert, M. C. (1969a) L'apprentissage chez les invertébrés, *Annee Psychol. 69*, 161–208

Médioni, J. and Robert, M. C. (1969b) L'apprentissage chez les invertébrés, *Annee Psychol. 69*, 491–530

Médioni, J. and Vaysse, G. (1975a) Suppression conditionnelle d'un réflexe chez la Drosophile (Drosophila melanogaster): acquisition et extinction, *C.R. Soc. Biol. 169*, 1386–1391

Médioni, J. and Vaysse, G. (1975b) Suppression of the tarsal reflex by associative conditioning in Drosophila melanogaster. Abstract of a communication at the *XIVth International Ethological Conference in Parma*

Menzel, R. (1967) Untersuchungen zum Erlernen von Spektralfarben durch die Honigbiene (Apis mellifica), *Z. Vergl. Physiol. 56*, 22–62

Menzel, R. and Erber, J. (1972) The influence of the quantity of reward on the learning performance in honeybees, *Behaviour 41*, 27–42

Menzel, R., Erber, J. and Masuhr, T. (1973) Learning and memory in the honey-bee. In: *Experimental Analysis of Insect Behaviour* (L. Barton Browne, ed.) pp. 195–217, Springer-Verlag, Berlin

Menzel, R., Freudel, H. and Rühl, U. (1973) Rassenspezifische Unterschiede im Lernverhalten der Honigbiene (Apis mellifica L.), *Apidologie 4*, 1–24

Murphey, R. M. (1967) Instrumental conditioning of the fruit fly, Drosophila melanogaster, *Anim. Behav. 15*, 153–161

Murphey, R. M. (1969) Spatial discrimination performance of Drosophila melanogaster: some controlled and uncontrolled correlates, *Anim. Behav. 17*, 43–46

Murphey, R. M. (1973) Spatial discrimination performance of Drosophila melanogaster: test-retest assessments and a reinterpretation, *Anim. Behav. 21*, 687–690

Nelson, M. C. (1971) Classical conditioning in the blowfly (Phormia regina). Associative and excitatory factors, *J. Comp. Physiol. Psychol. 77*, 353–368

Opfinger, E. (1931) Uber die Orientierung der Biene an der Futterstelle, *Z. Vergl. Physiol, 15*, 431–487

Parsons, P. A. (1967) *The Genetic Analysis of Behaviour*, Methuen, London

Petit, C. (1958) Le déterminisme génétique et psycho-physiologique de la compétition sexuelle chez Drosophila melanogaster, *Bull. Biol. Fr. Belg. 93*, 248–329

Quinn, W. G., Harris, W. A. and Benzer, S. (1974) Conditioned behavior in Drosophila melanogaster, *Proc. Natl. Acad. Sci. U.S. 71*, 708–712

Roubertoux, P. and Carlier, M. (1976) *Génétique et Comportements*, Masson, Paris

Rucker, W. B. and Hennessey, T. M. (1976) Truly random pseudoconditioning for classical conditioning in paramecia (abstract), *Cent. Cult. Behav. Educ. 507*, 389

Schneirla, T. C. (1933) Some important features of ant learning, *Z. Vergl. Physiol. 19*, 439–452

Smith, S. (1908) Limits of educability in Paramecium, *J. Comp. Neurol. Psychol. 18*, 499–510

Spatz, H.-C., Emanns, A. and Reichert, H. (1974) Associative learning of Drosophila melanogaster, *Nature 248*, 359–361

Takeda, K. (1961) Classical conditioned response in the honey bee, *J. Insect Physiol. 6*, 168–179

Thorpe, W. H. (1939) Further studies on pre-imaginal olfactory conditioning in insects, *Proc. Roy. Soc. B 127*, 424–433

Thorpe, W. H. (1956) *Learning and Instinct in Animals*, 1st edn., Methuen, London

Tryon, R. C. (1929) The genetics of learning ability in rats, *Univ. Calif. Publ. Psychol. 4*, 71–89

Vareschi, E. (1971) Duftunterscheidung bei der Honigbiene – Einzelzell-Ableitungen und Verhaltensreaktionen, *Z. Vergl. Physiol. 75*, 143–173

Vareschi, E. and Kaissling, K. E. (1970) Dressur von Bienenarbeiterinnen und Drohnen auf Pheromone und andere Duftstösse, *Z. Vergl. Physiol. 66*, 22–26

Vaysse, G. and Médioni, J. (1973) Premières expériences sur la gustation tarsale chez Drosophila melanogaster. Stimulation par le saccharose, *C. R. Soc. Biol. 167*, 560–564

Vaysse, G. and Médioni, J. (1977) Nouvelles expériences sur le conditionnement et le pseudoconditionnement du réflexe tarsal chez la Drosophile (Drosophila melanogaster). Effets de chocs électriques de faible intensité, *C. R. Soc. Biol.*, in the press

Voskresenskaja, A. D. (1957) Role of the "mushroom bodies" of the epipharyngeal ganglion in the conditioned reflexes of the bee (Russian), *Dokl. Akad. Nauk S.S.S.R. 112*, 964–967

Wells, P. H. (1973) Honey bees. In: *Invertebrate Learning* (W. C. Corning, J. A. Dyal and A. O. D. Willows, eds.), pp. 173–185, Vol. 2, Plenum Press, New York

Wood, D. C. (1970a) Parametric studies of the response decrement produced by mechanical stimuli in the protozoan, Stentor coeruleus, *J. Neurobiol. 1*, 345–360

Wood, D.C. (1970b) Electrophysiological studies of the protozoan, Stentor coeruleus, *J. Neurobiol. 1*, 363–377

Wood, D. C. (1970c) Electrophysiological correlates of the response decrement produced by mechanical stimuli, in the protozoan, Stentor coeruleus, *J. Neurobiol. 2*, 1–11

Yeatman, F. R. and Hirsch, J. (1971) Attempted replication of, and selective breeding for, instrumental conditioning of Drosophila melanogaster. *Anim. Behav. 19*, 454–462

Young, J. Z. (1966) *The Memory System of the Brain*, Univ. Calif. Press, Berkeley, Los Angeles

Genetics, environment and intelligence, edited by A. Oliverio
© *Elsevier/North-Holland Biomedical Press, 1977*

Strain differences and learning in the mouse   5

DANIEL BOVET

Introduction

Since the publication of the classic book by Fuller and Thompson in 1960, the field of behavior genetics has been developing in different areas: a number of experimental psychologists has been puzzled by the complexity of behavioral phenotypes existing in animals and men and has tried to define them in relation to their evolutionary meaning, to their biological substrates and to the complex genotype-environment interactions. A number of genetic approaches was devoted to learning and this book indicates the different strategies employed in this field: to the exception of a relatively small number of studies dealing with clearly defined behavioral phenotypes or with chromosomal or gene defects, the studies of the genetic determinants of behavior are still at a phenomenological level in human psychology. On the other hand, detailed psychogenetic quantitative analyses of different behavioral traits have been conducted in laboratory animals.

A research on the genetic determinants of the individual differences based on a comparative approach is justified by the similarities existing between many neurophysiological processes within mammals. In particular many learning mechanisms such as short- or long-term memory, consolidation processes and different learning abilities present many interspecific similarities: it is therefore possible that a comparative behavioral genetic study might be a fruitful approach to the organic foundations of behavioral individuality, to individual learning abilities and to a number of conditions resulting in mental retardation.

Within the comparative approach, the laboratory mouse has gained an outstanding place: Lindzey and Thiessen (1970) suggested a few years ago that the mouse might represent a prototype in behavior-genetic analyses. A large number of experiments have been conducted in the most recent years by using different lines, strains and mutations of mice in order to determine their aptitudes in a number of learning tasks ranging from active and passive avoidance to maze learning and lever-press instrumental learning: the reviews on this topic (Van Abeelen, 1974; Oliverio, 1974) indicate that much useful information has been collected in this area during the most recent years.

Random-bred mice

One of the major difficulties in the study of animal learning is the presence of large individual variability and of disturbing behavioral fluctuations evident from day to day. A number of factors contribute to this variability such as various sensory motivations and emotional reactions which play a role in what has been called "spontaneous or locomotor activity", "exploratory activity" or "curiosity": these behavioral patterns may be assessed through the use of the open-field or of the revolving wheels. In these tests the performance is extremely variable and fluctuates from day to day when a random-bred strain is considered (Table I).

If we consider active avoidance learning in a shuttle-box, the results indicate that the constancy of the motivation adopted results in a reduction of daily behavioral fluctuations: however, random-bred mice are still very variable in their individual performance levels. On the contrary, if we consider inbred mice, for example the strain SEC/1 ReJ, it is evident that their behavior is still rather fluctuating from day to day when we consider their open-field performance, while their levels of shuttle-box avoidance responding are very stable and their variability very low.

As an example of the individual behavioral variability evident in a group of genetically heterogeneous mice, Fig. 1 shows the shuttle-box avoidance performance of a group of mice belonging to an eight-way cross. The eight-way cross was derived by intercrossing eight different strains (A/J, A/HeJ, BALB/cJ, C57BL/6J, C57BL/10, C57BR/cdJ, DBA/2J, SEC/1 ReJ). F_1 animals from different parental strains were mated to obtain four-way cross offspring. Four-way cross animals with no parent strains in common were then mated to form eight-way crosses. The behavioral heterogeneity of these mice is clearly evident: the animals were given five 100-trail sessions during five consecutive days. When the mean percent avoidance is plotted according to frequency classes, it appears that a rectangular distribution characterizes this population since equal number of mice present low, high or intermediate performance levels. These findings indicate clear intrapopulation polymorphism and the presence of a variety of genotypes (Fig. 1).

A possibility to alter artificially the genetic homeostasis of a random-bred population and to shift the behavioral modality from the distribution previously observed

Table I Behavior of mice belonging to an eight-cross random-bred stock and to the SEC/1ReJ strain in the open field and shuttle-box avoidance test during five consecutive days (11th–15th from the beginning of training). The numbers represent the mean responses ± S.E. in two groups of 10 mice

Strain	Test	Days of testing				
		11	12	13	14	15
Random-bred mice	Open field	17.4 ± 6.8	22.6 ± 5.2	15.7 ± 6.1	23.2 ± 5.6	27.0 ± 8.1
	Shuttle-box	49.6 ± 4.1	50.1 ± 5.0	47.8 ± 4.8	48.7 ± 4.5	49.1 ± 5.0
SEC/1Re inbred mice	Open field	22.6 ± 3.0	27.5 ± 2.6	16.4 ± 2.0	15.6 ± 2.8	24.8 ± 3.2
	Shuttle-box	87.1 ± 0.7	88.0 ± 0.6	87.2 ± 1.0	87.9 ± 1.0	88.1 ± 0.6

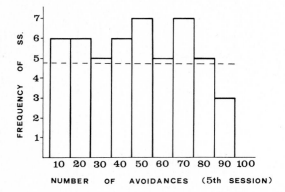

Fig. 1 Frequency distribution of avoidance responses in a group of 100 eight-way cross mice. The rectangular distribution indicates that individuals characterized by low, intermediate, or high avoidance levels are represented with similar frequencies (Messeri and Oliverio, 1972).

is to breed mice selectively for avoidance behavior. In a selection experiment carried out in a random-bred population of mice, it was in fact possible to select within four generations a line of mice which passed from the initial level of about 20% avoidance to a level of 80% (Bovet et al., 1969). This result seems to be indicative of the genetic plasticity of this species in relation to this trait; in addition, these findings are in agreement with other results suggesting that other behavioral traits that have a high adaptive value are characterized by genetic polymorphisms and by developmental flexibility. Examples in this line are the selection experiments for avoidance learning in rats (Bignami and Bovet, 1965; Fulker et al., 1972).

By using full sib-half sib correlations to the intrasire progenies of mice and dam-offspring regressions, rather high estimates of heritability were obtained in a measure of avoidance behavior (Oliverio, 1971). Estimates of heritability were calculated showing that nearly 50% of the variance among intrasire offspring was attributable to additively genetic causes. Comparable estimates were obtained by using the regression method (intrasire regression of the offspring on dams). In fact, the slope of the regression line indicated that heritability had the value of $h^2 = 0.52$, since the progenies of high avoiding dams was also characterized by high avoidance levels and that of low-avoiding dams by a low performance (Fig. 2). Thus, this experiment also shows that differences among mice for this measure of learning ability are conditioned by the genetic traits of the individuals, and that intrasire mating results in a decreased organismic diversity because of an arrangement of the population on a narrower range.

Inbred strains

Another versatile approach to assess to what extent different types of learning abilities are modulated by the genetic factors relies on the use of inbred strains of mice (Table II). The variability among these strains is at least as great as in any single feral population, a large group of inbred strains with unique alleles and no overlapping pedigrees being available as the best group to screen for a hoped-for variant (Roderick et al., 1971). Within strains, behavioral homogeneity is clearly evident from analyses of avoidance behavior of different inbred strains of mice trained in a shuttle-box with the same procedure described for random-bred animals (Fig. 3). The genetic differences characterizing different inbred strains of mice also result in clear behavioral differences in that various strains attain various avoidance levels. By comparing the overall performance levels reached by six strains of mice, it was evident that there are strains which are characterized by very high levels (such as A/J or SEC/1ReJ mice) strains which perform very poorly as C57BL/6 mice and strains which attain intermediate levels. Fig. 4, showing the different performances of these strains, also indicates that the learning patterns of these strains are generally much more homogeneous than those of mice belonging to a random-bred Swiss stock. These differences were also evident when an auditory, rather than a visual conditioned stimulus was employed, though the between-strains range was reduced, since the use of a tone or of a buzzer may represent a primary aversive unconditioned stimulus in avoidance learning of rodents.

The results of other learning tasks show that there is a positive correlation between active avoidance, maze learning and lever-press discriminated avoidance (and a negative correlation with passive avoidance), the high avoiding strains (such as DBA/2, BALB/c and SEC/1Re) being also characterized by high learning abilities in the other tasks quoted above, while low avoiding strains such as C57BL/6 mice exhibit a low performance also in the other learning tasks (Bovet et al., 1969; Destrade et al., 1976; Elias, 1970; Jaffard et al., 1976; Krivanek and McGaugh, 1968; Oliverio et al., 1972).

By crossing in a diallel design two strains characterized by high levels of avoidance and maze learning but by low levels of running activity (SEC/1Re and DBA/2) and C57BL/6 mice which attain poor avoidance and maze levels but are very active, it was shown that: (1) the mode of inheritance in a given behavioral measure depends on the crosses considered (Fig. 5). Crossing the C57 strain with the high avoiding-low running SEC mice resulted in SEC-like progeny, while crossing with the high avoiding-low running DBA mice yielded an offspring similar to the C57 phenotype. A similar dominance pattern was evident for maze learning. (2) Matherian analyses for F_2 segregation showed that the total F_2 variance contained, in addition to an environmental component, a significant genetic component (Oliverio et al., 1972).

These three inbred strains of mice and their F_1 hybrids seem to be a very useful model for a genetic approach to the biological aspects of learning. The results of different biochemical estimates suggest in part that these lines and their crosses not only differ in behavior but also in some critical brain chemicals. Mandel and his group (Ebel et al., 1973; Kempf et al., 1974) found large regional differences between these strains when their cholinergic and adrenergic levels and turnover were measured. These findings will be referred to in another chapter of this book. Also the brain levels of dopamine and of cyclic 3'5'-adenosine monophosphate (cyclic AMP) were found to be different in these strains (Trabucchi et al., 1976).

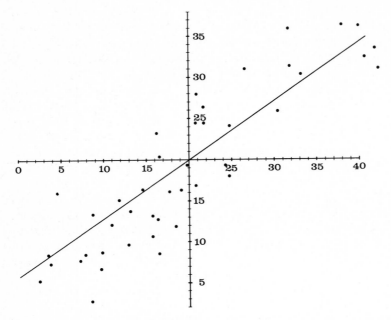

Fig. 2   Regression of offspring on dams. Dam values are shown along the horizontal axis, and mean values of offspring along the vertical axis. The axes intersect at the mean value of the performance of all dams and all offspring (Oliverio, 1971).

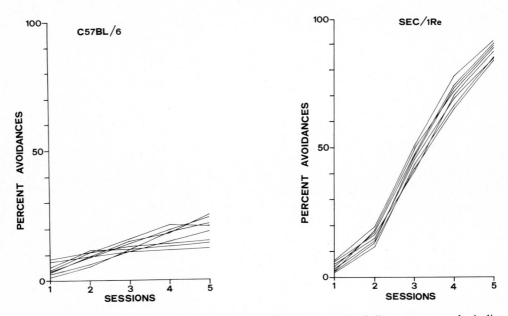

Fig. 3   Avoidance learning of C57BL/6 and SEC/1 Re mice. Each line represents the individual performance of a mouse during five 100-trial sessions (Bovet et al., 1969).

Table II Type of behavioral patterns studied in inbred strains of mice (three levels of reorganization of instinct)

Levels	Behavior patterns	Symptoms
General forms of organization*	Sensory processes Central nervous system Motor processes	Retinal degeneration Audiogenic seizures Myoclonies
Hereditary mechanisms**	Patterns of vigilance	Sleep-wakefulness "Spontaneous" locomotor behavior
	Alimentary behavior	Hunger, alimentary preferences Gustatory factors: saccharine, PTC, alcohol, thirst
	Sexual behavior	Copulatory behavior Female parental behavior Attachment
	Emotional behavior	Freezing Aggressivity
Individual adaptation to the environment and learning*** (role of an instinctive behavior in a given context)	Performance in a maze Visual discrimination Escape and avoidance behavior Perseverative behaviors	

* See Fuller and Thompson, 1960; Lindzey and Thiessen, 1970; Lindzey et al., 1971.
** See Lindzey et al., 1971; Valatx et al., 1972.
*** See Van Abeelen, 1974; Lindzey and Thiessen, 1970; Oliverio, 1974; Wahlsten, 1972.

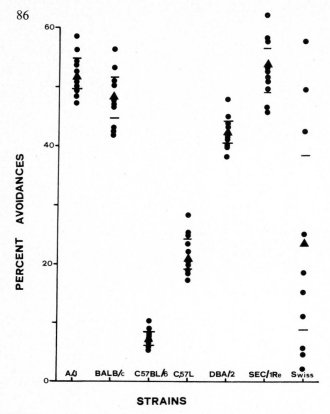

Fig. 4 Avoidance learning in six strains of inbred mice and in random-bred Swiss mice. Each point represents the mean performance of a mouse during five consecutive avoidance sessions. It is evident that the performances of the inbred strains are very homogeneous and that each strain reaches different levels of responding. The black triangles represent the mean percent avoidances of a 10-mice confidence limit of the mean (horizontal bars).

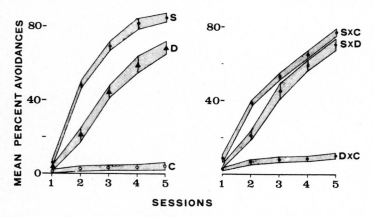

Fig. 5 Mean percent avoidances ($\pm 95\%$ confidence limits of the mean) during sessions 1–5 in three inbred stains of mice and their F_1 offspring. (C, C57BL/6; D, DBA/2; S, SEC/1 Re) (Oliverio et al., 1972).

Mutations and recombinant inbred strains

The importance of using mutant strains for tracing gene-behavior pathways and for studying "mechanism specific" behaviors has been stressed in recent reviews by Fuller (1965), and Lindzey et al. (1971). 27 coat-color alleles and four other mutations were therefore studied for their effects on avoidance, maze learning and activity (Oliverio and Messeri, 1973). All mutants were on C57BL/6J inbred background. Since this strain is characterized by high levels of activity and low levels of avoidance and maze learning, the possible depressant effects on activity or the stimulating effects on avoidance exerted by an allele on these behaviors should appear very clearly when analyzed on C57B/6J background (Fig. 6). Different single-gene mutations exhibited avoidance levels higher than that in the low-avoiding C57BL/6J normal strain (Albino, Jackson shaker, Jackson valtzer, Lustrous, Mocha, Ruby eyes, and Underwhite). These differences were evident when either a visual or an auditory conditional stimulus were used. While in three of these strains the higher performance levels were related to the increased number of intertrial responses (Shaker, Valtzer and Mocha mice), the higher performance of the other mutations seems to be due to a specific effect on behavior since maze solving ability was also enhanced in Albino, Underwhite and Lustrous mice. The fact that maze learning and avoidance were positively correlated may be due to a pleiotropic effect or may suggest that these two behavioral traits are determined by similar psycho-physiological mechanisms. Thus, also if these behaviors are influenced by genes at many loci, a single gene may substantially contribute to their genetic variance (De Fries and Hegman, 1970).

Recently, a powerful method of genetic analysis based on the strain distribution pattern (SDP) in a set of recombinant inbred strains (RI) (Bailey, 1971) has permitted the analysis of different behavioral patterns in the mouse. This type of genetic

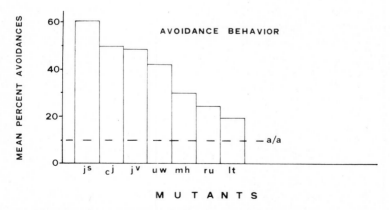

Fig. 6   Effects of different single-gene mutants on avoidance behavior. Only those mutants whose behavior is significantly different from that of normal C57Bl/6J mice (a/a, broken line) are represented (Oliverio and Messeri, 1973).

analysis was developed so that one could determine quickly the probable location of a new gene by matching its patterns of distribution (SDP) among a set of inbred strains. Used for this analysis were seven recombinant inbred strains derived from an initial cross of BALB/cBy strain with C57BL/6By (Bailey, 1971). RI strains are derived from a cross of two unrelated, but highly inbred progenitor strains having then been maintained independently from the F_2 generation with strict inbreeding. This procedure fixed genetically the chance recombination of the genes that occurred, although in ever-decreasing amounts in each succeeding generation after the F_1. The resulting battery of strains can be looked upon, in a sense, as a replicable recombinant population. The SDPs of distinctive loci (histocompatibility, isozymes, etc.) have been determined in the seven RI strains. The SDP method, therefore, is useful in searching for gene identity, since identical or similar SDPs of any pair of traits indicate possible pleiotropism or linkage of controlling genes.

By using this procedure, it has been possible to ascribe to a single gene a major gene effect on a complex behavior trait such as active avoidance learning. In fact, RI strains exhibited high or low levels of active avoidance learning, the two groups being similar to each of the progenitor strains, BALB/c and C57BL/6 respectively. The SDP of the strains permitted to link the gene responsible for a major effect on active avoidance learning (*Aal*) to H (w56) on chromosome 9 (Oliverio et al., 1973). This study shows that the methods employed in formal genetics can be applied with success to complex behavioral phenotypes. The identification of "major" genes covering part of the behavioral variability is a useful step for assessing possible correlation between brain biochemistry and behavioral traits.

Environmental effects

The findings reported in this chapter indicate that the genetic make-up modulates the learning abilities of mice and that it accounts for a large portion of their behavioral variability. It is important to stress another point and to indicate that differences in genotype may result in phenotypic differences through a different effect of early environmental differences on behavioral development. The results of any genetic experiment must in fact be regarded as specific to the environmental conditions under which the experiment is carried out. A number of handling experiences have been shown to alter brain postnatal development and to affect the behavior as measured in the adult age (Rosenzweig, 1966). Early handling experiences may also alter the mode of inheritance of different behavioral abilities: the relative restriction of small laboratory cages has been shown to reduce both additive genetic effects and directional dominance (Henderson, 1970). Other findings indicate that early environmental enrichment may affect the amount of normal genetic variation and lead to genotype × environment interactions (Henderson, 1972). In this view it seemed useful to assess the effects of early environmental differences upon the learning abilities of two strains (C57BL/6 and SEC/1Re) which are characterized, as mentioned above, by opposite learning abilities. In addition, C57 mice present a more precocious postnatal development of the brain in relation to SEC mice (Oliverio et al., 1975).

Litters deriving from C57 or SEC dams were assigned to three different laboratory conditions: (a) standard laboratory rearing in 14 × 20 × 9 cm laboratory cages; (b) enriched cages (55 × 25 × 9 cm) containing a hollow log, small maze, steel tube, rocks and wire-mesh ramps as described by Henderson (1972); (c) impoverished cages (14 × 20 × 9 cm) kept in a sound-insulated cabin. The light cycle consisted of 11 h of light and 13 h of darkness for the three conditions. All mice were kept until testing (6 weeks) in the three different conditions and then subjected to shuttle-box learning (100 trials per day during five consecutive days) and Lashley III maze (three trials per day during five consecutive days) as in Oliverio et al., 1972.

The results indicate that early environmental differences may be able to modify the learning abilities as measured in the adults. Fig. 7 indicates that impoverished and enriched mice belonging to the SEC strain respectively attained in the two tasks a lower and higher learning performance. On the contrary, the effects connected with an impoverished or enriched environment were less evident in the C57 strain which is more mature at birth and therefore is probably less sensitive to drastic environmental differences: in fact only impoverished C57 mice were different in their performance from the other groups belonging to the same strain.

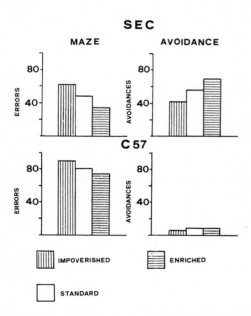

Fig. 7   Performances of C57BL/6 and SEC/1 Re mice raised in a standard, enriched or impoverished environment from birth to testing. Each group consisted of 24 mice. The numbers refer to mean percent avoidances or to mean maze errors. Differences between impoverished and enriched environments were at the 1% level in SEC mice, while in C57 mice the differences were evident only for the impoverished group tested in the maze (Oliverio, 1977, unpublished results).

To sum up there are complex genotype × environment interactions which must be taken into consideration when a given phenotype is considered.

It is clear that heredity plays a highly important role in the formation of different adaptive repertoires. However, different rearing and environmental factors also play an important role in the modulation of the learning abilities of either mice (Denenberg, 1969), rats (Rosenzweig, 1966), or men (White, 1971). The importance of these environmental effects is obviously more relevant in man since much of his behavior is molded by learning and by cultural evolution. However, the study of individual differences in learning and of their genetic determination may represent an important step for assessing the biological roots of behavior and for the understanding, as we have pointed out, of the type of interaction occurring between given environmental situations and genotypes.

Literature cited

Bailey, D. W. (1971) Recombinant-inbred strain, *Transplantation 11*, 325–327

Bignami, G. and Bovet, D. (1965) Expérience de sélection par rapport à une réaction conditionnée d'évitement chez le rat, *C.R. Hebd. Séances Acad. Sci. Paris 260*, 1239–1244

Bovet, D., Bovet-Nitti, F. and Oliverio, A. (1969) Genetic aspects of learning and memory in mice, *Science 163*, 139–149

De Fries, J. D. and Hegman, J. P. (1970) Genetic analysis of open-field behavior. In: *Contributions to Behavior-Genetic Analysis: The Mouse as a Prototype* (G. Lindzey and D. D. Thiessen, eds.), Appleton-Century-Crofts, New York

Denenberg, V. H. (1969) The effects of early experience. In: *The Behavior of Domestic Animals* (E. S. E. Hafez, ed.) pp. 95–130, Williams & Wilkins, Baltimore

Destrade, C., Jaffard, R., Deminiere, J. M. and Cardo, B. (1976) Effets de la stimulation de l'hippocampe sur la réminiscence chez deux lignées de souris, *Physiol. Behav. 16*, 237–243

Ebel, A., Hermetet, J. C. and Mandel, P. (1973) Comparison of acetylcholinesterase and choline acetyltransferase in temporal cortex of DBA and C57 mice, *Nature 242*, 56–58

Elias, M. F. (1970) Differences in reversal learning between two inbred mouse strains, *Psychon. Sci. 20*, 179–180

Fulker, D. W., Wilcock, J. and Broadhurst, P. L. (1972) Studies in the genotype-environment interaction: I, Methodology and preliminary multivariate analysis of a diallele cross of eight strains of rat, *Behav. Genet. 2*, 261–287

Fuller, J. L. (1965) Suggestions from animal studies for human behavior genetics. In: *Methods and Goals in Human Behavior Genetics* (S. G. Vandenberg, ed.) pp. 245–254, Academic Press, New York

Fuller, J. L. and Thompson, W. R. (1960) *Behavior Genetics*, Wiley, New York

Henderson, N. D. (1970) Genetic influences on the behavior of mice can be obscured by laboratory rearing, *J. Comp. Physiol. Psychol. 73*, 505–511

Henderson, N. D. (1972) Relative effects of early rearing environment and genotype on discrimination learning in house mice, *J. Comp. Physiol. Psychol. 79*, 243–253

Jaffard, R., Destrade, C. and Cardo, B. (1976) Effets de la stimulation de l'hippocampe sur l'évitement passif chez deux lignées de souris, *Physiol. Behav. 16*, 233–236

Kempf, E., Greilsamer, J., Mack, G. and Mandel, P. (1974) Correlation of behavioral differences in three strains of mice with differences in brain amines, *Nature 247*, 483–485

Krivaneck, J. and McGaugh, J. L. (1968) Effects of pentylenetetrazol on memory storage of mice, *Psychopharmacologia 12*, 303–321

Lindzey, G., Lohelin, J., Manosevitz, M. and Thiessen, D. D. (1971) Behavioral genetics, *Annu. Rev. Psychol. 22*, 39–94

Lindzey, G. and Thiessen, D. D. (1970) *Contributions to Behavior-Genetic Analysis. The Mouse as a Prototype*, Appleton-Century-Crofts, New York

Messeri, P. and Oliverio, A. (1972) L'Uso di ceppi puri e di ceppi eterogenei di topi nello studio del comportamento, *Boll. Zool. 39*, 639–640

Oliverio, A. (1971) Genetic variations and heritability in a measure of avoidance learning in mice, *J. Comp. Physiol. Psychol. 74*, 390–397

Oliverio, A. (1974) Genetic and biochemical analysis of behavior in mice, *Progress Neurobiol. 3*, 191–215

Oliverio, A. and Messeri, P. (1973) An analysis of single-gene effects on avoidance, maze, wheel-running and exploratory behavior in the mouse, *Behav. Biol. 8*, 771–783

Oliverio, A., Castellano, C. and Messeri, P. (1972) A genetic analysis of avoidance, maze and wheel-running behaviors in the mouse, *J. Comp. Physiol. Psychol. 79*, 459–473

Oliverio, A., Castellano, C. and Renzi, P. (1975) Genotype on prenatal drug experience affect brain maturation in the mouse, *Brain Res. 90*, 357–370

Oliverio, A., Eleftheriou, B. E. and Bailey, D. W. (1973a) Exploratory activity; genetic analysis of its modification by scopolamine and amphetamine, *Physiol. Behav. 10*, 893–899

Oliverio, A., Eleftheriou, B. E. and Bailey, D. W. (1973b) A gene controlling active avoidance learning in mice, *Physiol. Behav. 11*, 497–501

Renzi, P. and Sansone, M. (1971) Discriminated lever-press avoidance in mice, *Commun. Behav. Biol. 6*, 315–321

Roderick, T. H., Ruddle, F. H., Chapman, V. M. and Shows, T. B. (1971) Biochemical polymorphisms in feral and inbred mice, Mus musculus, *Biochem. Genet. 5*, 457–466

Rosenzweig, M. R. (1966) Environmental complexity, cerebral change and behavior, *Am. Psychol. 21*, 321–332

Trabucchi, M., Spano, P. F., Racagni, G. and Oliverio, A. (1976) Genotype-dependent sensitivity to morphine: dopamine involvement in morphine-induced running in the mouse, *Brain Res. 114*, 536–540

Valatx, J. L., Bugat, R. and Jouvet, M. (1972) Genetic studies of sleep in mice, *Nature 238*, 226–227

Van Abeelen, J. H. F. (ed.) (1974) *The Genetics of Behaviour*, North-Holland, Amsterdam

Wahlsten, D. (1972) Genetic experiments with animal learning: a critical review, *Behav. Biol. 7*, 143–182

White, B. L. (1971) *Human infants. Experience and Psychological Development*, Harvard University Press

Genetics, environment and intelligence, edited by A. Oliverio
© *Elsevier/North-Holland Biomedical Press, 1977*

Heredity and brain structure 6

DOUGLAS WAHLSTEN

Introduction

The brains of individuals belonging to a single species are remarkably similar, to the extent that an atlas of neuroanatomy is generally useful even though it describes the brain of a single individual. Nonetheless, significant within-species or even within-strain variation exists in brain structure. This variability may serve as a useful tool in research, or it may lead to serious confounding of an otherwise well-designed experiment. Because hereditary variation exists to some extent in virtually every laboratory animal population, it warrants the attention of all investigators in the neural and behavioral sciences.

The nervous system is the instrument of behavior and thinking. Differences in behavior, whether they result from differences in heredity or experience, necessarily reflect differences at some level of the nervous system. If the physical bases for hereditary differences in behavior can be identified, they may contribute greatly to our knowledge of the relations between brain and behavior.

Laboratory research has repeatedly demonstrated hereditary variation in many behaviors (see Van Abeelen, 1974; Broadhurst et al., 1974). When strains of mice, for example, are inbred or selectively bred for many generations under identical conditions in the lab, the only basis for a behavioral difference between the strains is their different ancestries. Mammalian offspring inherit from their parents (a) the physical substance of heredity contained in the ovum and sperm, (b) the post-fertilization environment of the mother, and (c) the post-partum environment provided by the parents. Although these various contributions can be manipulated experimentally, many of the studies considered in this review treat all three components as "heredity" in practice. This hereditary variation provides a rich source of material for the investigation of brain structure.

Structural versus neurochemical manifestations of heredity

This chapter is about structural variation, whereas other chapters treat biochemical variation in the brain. Structure and biochemistry are distinct features of the brain but are also closely related.

Distinctions between structure and neurochemistry

Some characteristics of the brain can clearly be labelled structural or neurochemical. The location of fibre tracts or nuclei in space is a structural measure, whereas the activity or concentration of acetylcholinesterase and the turnover rate of dopamine are neurochemical measures.

Other characteristics are less easily classified. For example, the myelin sheath enclosing the axon can be viewed in its structural aspect with electron microscopy. It exhibits distinct layers or lamellae, and defects of these lamellae and other myelin structures are known in certain neurological mutants (Samorajski et al., 1970; Suzuki and Zagoren, 1976). Myelin also has its chemical aspect. Certain lipid fractions of the total myelin are known to be deficient in the same neurological mutants which show fine structural abnormalities (Costantino-Ceccarini and Morell, 1971; Hogan et al., 1970).

In general, structure and chemistry appear as two aspects of the same thing. There may be a crude distinction in many cases according to the rate at which the molecules of the thing are lost and replaced. Structural characters are relatively permanent, whereas neurochemical characters may show rapid turnover and great lability. Nonetheless, all structures are composed of biochemical building blocks, and all labile neurochemical processes take place in an edifice of structure.

In practice, our only recourse is to operational definitions. A structural character is one which can be fixed relatively permanently in a microscope preparation or in a specimen bottle and which preserves the spatial relationships among its parts, whereas a neurochemical character is assayed by homogenizing tissue and destroying structure. Of course, it is also possible to combine these two methods in the same experiment. By dissecting the brain into its parts and then assaying the activity or concentration of neurotransmitters in each one, structure and neurochemistry can be studied simultaneously (e.g., Mandel et al., 1974; Wimer et al., 1973).

Interrelations between hereditary defects of structure and neurochemistry

Because all structure has a chemical basis, it is easy to see how a chemical defect in the brain can have structural consequences.

There are several mutations in mice which cause deficient myelin, including quaking (*qk*), jimpy (*jp*), dilute-lethal (*d^l*) and wabbler-lethal (*w^l*). Two of them (*qk*, *jp*) result in arrested formation of myelin, and the other two are characterized by degeneration of myelin a few days after it is formed. When brain tissue from newborn mouse cerebellum is removed and cultured in vitro, myelination still fails in *qk* and *jp*, but is extensive for the other two mutants (Hamburgh and Bornstein, 1970). This demonstrates that some biochemical factor external to the myelin proper is responsible for degeneration of myelin structure in the mutants *d^l* and *w^l*.

Manganese deficiency in mice causes defective otoliths in the inner ear, as a result of either a manganese deficiency in the diet or a hereditary mutation (pallid) which has the same effect (Erway et al., 1966). Supplementing the normal lab diet of pallid mice with extra manganese prevents the defects of inner ear structure.

Conversely, a structural defect may have neurochemical consequences. For example, the mutation weaver (*wv*) in mice is characterized by failure of migration and massive degeneration of the cerebellar granule cells (Rakic and Sidman, 1973; Sotelo and Changeux, 1974). Recently, Black (1976) observed that the locus coeruleus neurons, which normally innervate the cerebellum, showed an elevated level of an enzyme (tyrosine hydroxylase) involved in neurotransmitter synthesis in weaver mice. Results suggested that the structural defect in the cerebellum caused retrograde neurochemical changes in the locus coeruleus, although direct effects of the weaver mutation could not be ruled out entirely.

In general, a major structural change in one part of the brain may have significant consequences for the neurochemical function of relatively remote neurons. Simply observing a hereditary defect of neurotransmitter metabolism does not rule out the possibility of causation by a structural defect, and vice versa.

Problems of spatial and temporal order of effects

A primary defect of localized action may be greatly magnified through its trophic relations with other structures or because of the spread of effects resulting from its defective functioning. On the other hand, plastic changes in the nervous system may compensate for the original defect, making it difficult to detect and study.

Trophic interactions between neurons and between neurons and their target effector cells are well documented. Absence of target muscles sometimes leads to degeneration of spinal neurons, and absence of spinal neurons may cause atrophy of muscles (Hamburger, 1975). Many other examples of interactions of this nature are given in a recent review by Smith and Kreutzberg (1976).

Neurological mutations illustrate the same phenomena. Retinal degeneration in the mouse first appears as a defect of the rods themselves, becoming severe two weeks after birth (Tansley, 1954), and this defect is closely accompanied by disruption of triad synapses with horizontal and bipolar retinal cells (Blanks et al., 1974). By 30 days after birth, the cell nuclei in visual cortex are abnormally small (Gyllensten and Lindberg, 1964). Similarly, one type of hereditary deafness in cats begins with degeneration of the organ of Corti and spiral ganglion cells, and eventually leads to reduced cell size (atrophy) in the medullary auditory nuclei (West and Harrison, 1973).

It is well known that early visual experience, the primary effects of which must begin at the photoreceptors, can have a substantial influence on synapse formation and the organisation of visual cortex in mammals (Blakemore, 1974).

All these examples demonstrate that a particular tissue, be it nerve or muscle, may show a defect as a consequence of a primary defect which is remote from the tissue in space and time.

Just as there is spread of defect, there is also the opposite phenomenon, compensation for defect. Plasticity of early development can lead to remarkable recovery of function in some cases. For example, destruction of the corpus callosum in adult humans severely disrupts the transfer of visual information from one visual hemifield to the ipsilateral cerebral hemisphere, and this deficit seems to be permanent. However, failure of formation of corpus callosum in the fetus leads to a nearly normal ability to transfer visual information between the hemispheres (Sperry, 1968), although recent evidence indicates a deficit in tactile discrimination transfer in some cases of agenesis (Dennis, 1976). Many known cases of callosal agenesis were discovered at autopsy of patients showing no unusual symptoms.

Seemingly severe hereditary defects of brain structure may have relatively minor effects on function. Authors of a recent study of the reeler mutation in mice concluded: "Despite the cellular disarray in the hippocampus of the homozygous reeler, the resultant synaptic organization as revealed by electrophysiological techniques is essentially normal" (Bliss and Chung, 1974). However, compensatory growth does not always occur, as in the case of the weaver mouse cerebellum (Rakic, 1976). Many instances of structural and functional recovery following experimentally-produced brain damage (Eidelberg and Stein, 1974) substantiate the remarkable plasticity of synaptic organization, even in the adult animal.

Biochemical compensation for a hereditary defect is also possible. In the brain tissue of brindled mice, norepinephrine synthesis is 88% below normal, but synthesis of its precursor dopamine is 76% above normal (Hunt and Johnson, 1972), showing that the enzyme dopamine-β-hydroxylase is defective. However, the level of the rate-limiting enzyme in norepinephrine synthesis, tyrosine hydroxylase, is elevated by about 50% in mutants, suggesting that a deficiency in norepinephrine leads to elevation of tyrosine hydroxylase through a feedback loop. This raises the possibility that a functional deficit need not necessarily follow from a less active enzyme.

This phenomenon is evident in the Peru strain of mouse which has an amino acid substitution in the hormone vasopressin. They show lysine at position 8 instead of arginine. In other species, this defect generally leads to vasopressin which is less effective. Nonetheless, Peru mice have normal concentrating ability after water deprivation (Stewart, 1971). The relative amount of vasopressin compared to oxytocin in the pituitary, however, is elevated in Peru mice (Stewart, 1972), suggesting that a control mechanism may compensate for the less effective hormone.

All of these phenomena must be kept in mind when searching for hereditary defects in the brain. Relatively small defects may become magnified through trophic influences, and relatively large defects may be nullified through compensatory growth or biochemical adjustment. It is also possible that neither occurs. The actual situation can be assessed only by comprehensive investigation of each case.

Problems of pleiotropy and epistasis

Pleiotropy is a phenomenon in which a major Mendelian gene has multiple effects on different characteristics of the organism. For example, albinism causes lack of pigmentation in both the eyes and coat of mice, and it affects several behaviors as well (Henry and Schlesinger, 1967). Presumably, the common cause of these multiple effects is a defect in the enzyme tyrosinase.

The precise pathway from defective enzyme to modification of brain or behavior may be direct or indirect. Albinism may reduce visual discrimination learning ability (a) indirectly by reducing visual acuity, (b) directly by disrupting central mechanisms of associative learning, or (c) both. The pathway from gene to behavior must be dissected and analysed for each mutation.

The simple observation that a single mutation affects two traits does not prove that they have a direct physiological relation. In the case of the brindled mouse, low motor activity, dilute pigment and curly whiskers are consequences of a defect, not of the embryonic ectoderm, but rather of the endoderm. Three different enzymes are responsible for the three different defects. Low motor activity is a consequence of reduced norepinephrine in the brain, which in turn is a result of the reduced activity of the enzyme dopamine-β-hydroxylase (Hunt and Johnson, 1972). Dilute pigment follows from deficient tyrosinase, whereas curly whiskers appear to be caused by defective lysyl oxidase. All three enzymes are copper-dependent, and the brindled mouse suffers from defective copper transport in the intestine (Hunt, 1974). Thus, unusual behavior or brain may be genetically correlated with a trait such as coat color or whisker curling because of some remote event in the intestine. In this case there is no direct relation betweeen brain and hair, and knowing the status of one tells very little about the other.

Epistasis also presents problems for analysis. When the expression of one gene substantially modifies the expression of others, epistatic interaction exists. For example, the A/J strain of mice carries the gene for brown coat color, but this character is not expressed because A/J mice are albino, and albinism blocks the formation of pigment, irrespective of its potential color. Albinism and brown coat are traits controlled by two separate mutant genes, but they share a common physiological pathway, melanin synthesis.

These facts mean that two characteristics of the brain which show hereditary correlation may result from different types of relations. They may be genetically correlated but physiologically independent, physiologically related but genetically independent, or a mixture by degrees of both mechanisms. Only detailed investigation can determine the basis for the observed relationship. This generally is not an easy task. Whether the mutation reeler in the mouse directly affects both cerebellar granule cell degeneration and tyrosine hydroxylase expression in locus coeruleus, or whether the latter is purely the consequence of the former is not readily determined. Many relations of this kind are established early in neurogenesis, at a time when direct manipulation of specific regions of the brain is very difficult.

A technique which may be of great help in analysing these relations is the chimeric mouse. 8-cell stage embryos from two different strains can be merged into a single giant blastocyst which, when transplanted into a pseudopregnant female, develops into a viable adult mouse, half of whose cells are of each parental type (Mintz, 1971). Because the two cell types are well intermixed, certain relations between cells can be analysed. Applying this technique to hereditary muscular dystrophy in mice has shown that the primary defect is of nervous, not muscular, origin. Chimeras were produced between dystrophic and normal embryos, and adult muscles were assessed for the presence of a peculiar genetic marker, malic enzyme. It was found that many genetically dystrophic muslces were morphologically normal, whereas genetically normal muscles were often dystrophic in morphology (see Smith and Kreutzberg, 1976).

Similar techniques have been employed to study the locus of gene action for retinal degeneration in mice (Mullen and LaVail, 1976) and for numerous mutations in the fruit fly (Hotta and Benzer, 1973). Detailed analysis of heredity of single cells has been done using somatic cell hybrids and cloning (Minna et al., 1972). Sophisticated dissection and analysis are necessary in order to understand more fully the complex relations between heredity, brain and behavior.

The remainder of this chapter considers a number of reports of hereditary variation in brain structure in inbred strains and selected lines of laboratory animals. In the main, the physiological bases for the differences and their behavioral correlates have not been investigated extensively. Nonetheless, the studies are important because they use as subjects animals which also find frequent application in many areas of biopsychological research. They also stress that, unlike rare mutants which most researchers never encounter, common laboratory strains exhibit ubiquitous differences in brain structure that are relevant to virtually every study done in the area of behavioral genetics.

The experiments are considered according to the level of difference, beginning with a gross measure such as whole brain size and proceeding to the finer level of the topographical distribution of synapses within a brain region. At every level scrutinized to date, substantial variation between strains and lines has been detected.

Whole brain size

Whole brain size is a gross measure which bears no known direct relation to variation in brain function within a species. However, its ease of measurement and large individual variability have made it the focus of numerous studies, all of which demonstrated a high degree of hereditary variation in brain weight or volume.

Inbred strains

After many generations of brother-by-sister inbreeding in a controlled laboratory environment, members of the same strain possess nearly identical heredity, which makes the remaining variability within an inbred strain non-hereditary. Given that the animals are reared for many generations in identical laboratory environments, between-strain differences are necessarily the result of differences in heredity.

All the published studies of brain weight have reported large and significant differences among inbred strains of mice, the remarkable consistency of which is illustrated in Fig. 1 for three independent studies of the same strains. Although there is some indication that strains with greater body weight tend to have larger brains (Henderson, 1973), two large studies found no significant correlation between brain and body weights, one using 18 inbred strains (Storer, 1967) and the other using

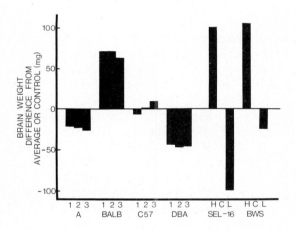

Fig. 1   Relative adult brain weights for inbred mouse strains and lines of mice selected for high and low brain weight. The same four inbred strains A/J, BALB/cJ, C57BL/6J and DBA/2J were measured using slightly different techniques in three studies (1: Storer, 1967; 2: Roderick et al., 1973; 3: Wahlsten et al., 1975). The average brain weight was determined for the four strains in each study (455.6, 479.2 and 426.0 mg for studies 1, 2 and 3, respectively), and the deviation of each strain from the mean was plotted on the graph, thereby eliminating the effects of different techniques across studies. For example, brain weight of A/J mice was 435, 455 and 399 mg for the three studies, but the deviations of A/J from the four-strain average in each study ranged narrowly from 20.6 to 27.0 mg below the mean. For the two selection experiments (Sel-16: Roderick et al., 1976; BWS, Jones, 1975), deviations of high (H) and low (L) selected lines from the control (C: Sel-16, 485 mg; BWS, 493 mg) line are given in the graph. Sel-16 data are from generation 16 of selection, and BWS are from generation 13.

20 strains (Roderick et al., 1973). Furthermore, sex differences in body weight are very large, but sex differences in brain weight are small (5 to 10 mg) and generally not significant. Thus, large hereditary variation in brain weight is not simply a consequence of whole body growth.

Henderson (1970, 1973) extended these findings by studying six inbred mouse strains as well as their 10 F_1 hybrids which were reared in either a standard lab cage or an enriched environment. Although hybrid brains were consistently heavier than the average of their inbred parents, the hybrid – inbred difference was much smaller than the variation between inbred strains. The effects of enrichment on hybrid brain weight (about 25 mg) were also greater than the average hybrid –inbred difference in the standard cages, showing that a relatively mild environmental manipulation such as enrichment can have a larger effect than the profound difference between inbred and hybrid heredities. Most important, the results demonstrated that the effect of enrichment depended strongly upon heredity. Enrichment increased brain weight 5% for the inbred strain DBA/1J, decreased it 5% for RF/J, and had no detectable effect on A/J and C57BL/10J brain weights; whereas enrichment consistently increased the brain weight of hybrids by about 5%.

Selected lines

In a non-inbred population, individual differences in brain size may reflect differences in heredity. If so, then mating males and females with large brains will result in offspring whose brain size exceeds the population mean. Several programs of selection for high and low brain weight have been undertaken, and all obtained large differences between selected lines.

Roderick et al. (1976) carried out replicated selection (Sel-6 and Sel-7) for brain weight using a foundation population from an eight-way cross of inbred strains. Parental brain weight was assessed after the pair had produced two litters. The breeding pairs with extremes of mean brain weight were identified, and their offspring were selected to become the parents of the next generation of the high and low lines. A randomly-mated control line was also employed. A very substantial divergence of brain weight occurred among the lines, yielding a realized heritability (ratio of additive hereditary variation to total variance in brain weight) of about 0.6. Because of a serious decline in fertility, the high lines of Sel-6 and Sel-7 were crossed in generation 11 to form Sel-16; low and control lines were similarly crossed. High fertility was restored, and brain weight differences remained large. By generation 16 (from the start of Sel-6 and 7) selection appeared to have reached a limit, with the difference between high and low lines being about 200 mg and symmetrical about their control score of 490 mg (see Fig. 1). Because of a high frequency of inherited retinal degeneration (*rd*) in both the foundation stock and the resulting selected lines, the utility of the lines was limited. Consequently, another selection program was carried out using a foundation stock free from *rd*, and this new program (Sel-17) yielded very similar results.

Roderick et al. (1976) also selected for the ratio of brain weight to spinal cord weight in another experiment (Sel-18). A modest separation of high and low lines was achieved, but fluctuations resulting from common environmental influences were much larger than line differences, showing that the ratio character had much less additive variation than simple brain weight and that brain and spinal cord weights must be highly correlated genetically. In the original selection studies (Sel-6 and Sel-7) body weight changed substantially as a correlated response to selection for brain weight. At generation 16, the mean body weight was 47.5 g for the high line, 40.4 g for controls and 29.0 g for the low line.

Fuller dealt with the problem of brain weight – body weight correlation by selecting for brain weight relative to body weight within each line. Beginning with the foundation stock, an eight-way cross of inbred strains which Roderick et al. used for Sel-17, lines were selected for high (BWS-H), medium (BWS-M) and low (BWS-L) brain weights relative to the average linear relation between brain and body weights for each line (Fuller and Herman, 1974). A large divergence of BWS lines was obtained, such that after 11 generations of selection, brain weights at 22 days after birth were 509 mg, 443 mg and 411 mg for H, M and L, respectively (Chen and Fuller, 1975). The adult brain weights in generation 13 differed by more than 100 mg, with the selection response being asymmetrical (Jones, 1975), as shown in Fig. 1.

Chen and Fuller (1975) further demonstrated that the reduction in brain weight produced by 2 μg of L-thyroxine given postnatally was roughly equivalent (40 mg) to the effects of 11 generations of selection for low relative brain weight, although the effect was less than the difference between BWS-H and M. In this study, thyroxine had an approximately equal effect on all three lines. Thus, in four separate experiments (Sel-6, Sel-7, Sel-17 and BWS) a large and rapid change in mouse brain weight resulted from selection for either high or low brain weight.

These studies of inbred mouse strains and selected lines have demonstrated three things. First, mouse brain size differs greatly in animals having different heredities but reared in the same environments (Fig. 1). Second, mouse brain weight is easily modified by changes in the environment. A relatively minor degree of environmental enrichment can lead to an average increase of about 25 mg in the brain weight of hybrid mice, whereas neonatal administration of thyroxine can cause a substantial 40 mg decrease in brain growth. Third, the extent of the change in brain weight wrought by environmental manipulations depends upon the heredity of the subject.

The significance of brain size

Although some people still talk about a larger brain as though it indicates higher intelligence, the animal data fail to confirm this notion. A review of hereditary variation in learning ability in animals revealed no consistent correlation with brain weight (Wahlsten, 1972), and a more recent review extended this notion by challenging the concept of general learning ability itself (Wahlsten, 1977). Strains with large brains do well on certain tasks but poorly on others, whereas those with small brains are quite good on many tests of learning and show no evidence of mental "retardation." These results do not imply that severe malnutrition will not retard both brain weight and learning ability. They simply show that there is no relation within the normal range of variation.

There is some evidence that larger brain size is correlated with higher activity levels in mice (Jensen, 1974; Padeh and Soller, 1976), but it is also apparent that the relation depends upon the situation in which the activity is measured and is not consistent when control lines are considered.

Human brain weight also varies widely, with brains of people regarded as highly intelligent ranging from 1 kg to over 2 kg. However, there has never been a significant relation demonstrated between brain size and heredity, racial or otherwise, or between brain size and "intelligence" (Tobias, 1970). Concerning the contentions of racists about brain size and learning ability, Tobias (1970, p. 3) concluded "that vast claims have been based on insubstantial evidence." The possibility of a relation between brain size and intelligence has not been rejected (Van Valen, 1974), but it is clear that any relation must be very small.

Major brain structures

Whole brain size is a very gross measure which undoubtedly obscures some important variation in the brain. Two strains of mice with similar brain weights may nonetheless differ greatly in the relative sizes, shapes or locations of structures within the brain.

Regional volume

Using a tracing technique on stained sections, Wimer et al. (1969) measured the volumes of neocortex, hippocampus and total forebrain of nine inbred strains of male mice, and they found significant differences on all measures. Comparing volumes of the regions to each other, the authors determined that the rank—order correlation between volumes of neocortex and hippocampus relative to total forebrain was −0.83. Thus, all structures of a large brain were not expanded equally. On the contrary, the tendency was for one region to be enlarged at the expense of another.

A preliminary report of regional volume in the brains of Sel-6 and 7 selected lines revealed no changes in the relative sizes of various structures, even though the whole brain size differed greatly among selected and control lines (Roderick et al., 1976). The same authors also attempted to breed selectively for high and low relative regional volumes, beginning with the same foundation stock as was used for Sel-17. No consistent selection response occurred. Thus, it is conceivable that the large variability and negative correlation of relative regional volumes in the mouse brain occur only among inbred strains.

Spatial locations of structures

Given the substantial individual differences known to exist in brain size, it is highly likely that the precise positions of structures with respect to each other will also differ across individuals and strains. Nevertheless, the great majority of studies which have placed electrodes into the same brain region of two or more strains or lines have employed identical stereotaxic coordinates for all groups. These studies are summarized in Table I according to the type of subject, brain region and physiological technique employed.

Only in the work by Cazala and Cardo (1972, 1974) have strain-specific electrode placements been used. These authors first did a preliminary study to determine the precise coordinates for each inbred strain which placed the electrode in the homologous structure. Having observed large strain differences in the frequency and current threshold for seizures evoked by stimulation of dorsal and ventral hypothalamus, they also examined their histology carefully and published diagrams of actual electrode tip placements (Cazala et al., 1974), thereby assuring that the experimental treatment had closely comparable direct effects for all three strains.

Unfortunately, the other studies may have been confounded by strain-specific

Table I   Summary of studies in which electrodes were placed in the brains of animals differing in heredity

Study	Subjects	Brain region	Physiological technique
Same coordinates for all groups:			
Leech (1972)	6 inbred mouse strains	Amygdala	Stimulation
Oliverio et al. (1973)	3 inbred mouse strains	Septum	Large lesion
Oliverio (1975)	2 inbred mouse strains	Septum	Large lesion
Gonsiorek et al. (1974)	BWS-H, BWS-L mice	Septum	Large lesion
Deagle and Lubar (1971)	2 rat stocks	Septum	Large lesion
Latham and Thorne (1974)	2 rat stocks	Septum	Large lesion
Lucas et al. (1974)	Normal and nervous pointer dogs	Hippocampus	EEG recording
Strain-specific coordinates:			
Cazala and Cardo (1972)	2 inbred mouse strains	Hypothalamus	Stimulation
Cazala et al. (1974)	3 inbred mouse strains	Hypothalamus	Stimulation
Coordinates not specified:			
Elias et al. (1973)	2 inbred mouse strains	Amygdala	Small lesion
Zaide (1974)	Tryon bright and dull rat lines	Amygdala	Stimulation

electrode placements. They could not ascertain with confidence whether group differences in effects of lesions reflected genuine hereditary differences in the function of a structure or, on the other hand, were caused by destruction of anatomically and functionally different tissue. This problem poses special difficulties for studies using large lesions, because many structures outside of the target region may also be damaged. When small lesions are employed, e.g. Elias et al. (1973), it is possible to eliminate confounding to a large extent by careful inspection of the actual electrode placement, even though the same coordinates may have been used for all strains.

The magnitude of the potential artifacts as well as possible methods of compensation were studied with great precision by Wahlsten et al. (1975). A standard series of eight small lesions was placed with respect to intra-aural zero to an accuracy of 0.01 mm through the forebrain and midbrain of seven commonly used inbred, hybrid and outbred mouse strains, and the lambda and bregma skull landmarks were measured. Results revealed substantial strain differences in (a) the positions of bregma and lambda points with respect to intra-aural zero and each other, (b) the position of fibre tracts with respect to bregma, and (c) the spatial locations of certain major fibre tracts with respect to each other. Concerning the practice of stereotaxic surgery, the authors concluded that coordinates needed to be determined specifically for each strain; there was no transformation which could make an atlas for one strain serve adequately for another. The existence of irreducible individual variability within a strain in the location of structures with respect to the bregma skull landmark was also demonstrated, as has recently been done by Slotnick and Leonard (1975).

These findings were extended by Jones (1975), who used a more refined stereotaxic technique to place a standard series of small lesions in the cortex, septum, amygdala and hippocampus of three inbred mouse strains and Fuller's BWS-H and L lines. After observing significant group differences in the location of homologous points in each structure with respect to the lesion centre, Jones derived coordinates for each group to yield homologous placements in each structure. The magnitude of group differences is apparent from the strain-specific coordinates for a septal lesion, given in Table II.

Table II Strain-specific coordinates for a lateral septal lesion

Group	Distance from bregma (mm)		
	Anterior	Lateral	Ventral
A/J	1.2	±0.5	3.2
C57BL/6J	1.2	±0.5	3.5
DBA/2J	0.7	±0.5	3.1
BWS-H	0.7	±0.5	3.8
HET	0.4	±0.5	3.6
BWS-L	0.7	±0.5	3.6

Data adapted from Table X of Jones (1975).

It is interesting that the problem of individual variability in human brain structure has been largely overcome by the use of X-ray visualization of structures during the course of neurosurgery (e.g., Dawson et al., 1968–1969).

Fibre tract anomalies

In all the research reviewed so far, the structures have had a normal appearance, although their sizes and/or locations have differed quantitatively. There have been several observations, however, of truly anomalous structures in certain inbred mouse strains. These include unusual routes of the columns of the fornix, unusual longitudinal fibres in the septal region, and absence or severe deficiency of the corpus callosum.

The anomalies of the columns of the fornix (F) were originally observed in the inbred strains A/J, BALB/cJ and their crosses (Wahlsten, 1974), and they have also been detected in two other sublines of BALB (Wahlsten, unpublished, 1976). There are two main types of defect.

In the most common one, occurring in 80% of A/J brains and 25 % of BALB/cJ, the columns proceed ventrally from the medial septal area, come into contact with the anterior commissure (CAA), and then, instead of travelling posterior to CAA and on to the mammillary bodies, a bundle of F loops around the anterior portion of CAA and then rejoins the main bundle of F just before it terminates in the mammillary region. By careful measurement of spatial locations of these fibre tracts, it was demonstrated that the problem was partly one of relative spatial location. The fornix was located more anterior with respect to the CAA in A/J mice than in C57BL/6J, a strain which never showed a defect. This spatial difference between the inbred parent strains showed intermediate inheritance in hybrid and backcross groups, and the frequency and degree of fornix anomalies were also intermediate in hybrids and backcrosses. The additional observation that the anterior commissure grows across midline in the developing mouse brain about one day before the fornix reaches the CAA at midline reveals why F loops around CAA and not vice versa (Wahlsten, 1975).

Another anomaly occurs when the fornix contacts CAA and then grows dorsally to arborize and terminate in lateral septum, a very aberrant condition. It appears in 70% of A/J mice and 30% of BALB/cJ as well as in their crosses, and it too is a consequence of the relative spatio-temporal growth of the fibre tracts.

Why the columns of the fornix sometimes loop around CAA and in other, instances, even in the same brain, deflect upward to lateral septum is not known. Both of these phenomena, however, illustrate vividly the remarkable plasticity of neurogenesis in the mouse brain. Large bundles travelling from the fornix to lateral septum have been observed in about 90% of BALB/cJ mice (Wahlsten, 1974) as well as in four other BALB sublines (Wahlsten, unpublished, 1976). Preliminary evidence suggested Mendelian inheritance, but the interpretation of hybrid and backcross results was rendered ambiguous because some of the inbred parents showed no trace of the defect.

Surely the most spectacular of all anomalies is absent corpus callosum. This defect was originally described in good anatomical detail by King (1936), but the data on inheritance proved inconclusive, and the mouse stock became extinct. Absence of corpus callosum was rediscovered in BALB/cJ and 129/J mice in 1965 by R. E. Wimer (personal communication), and its anatomy and mode of inheritance were explored further in BALB/cJ by Wahlsten (1974).

In 5 to 20% of BALB/cJ mice, depending on the shipment from the supplier, there are no callosal fibres crossing midline, and a few individuals have been observed wherein even the hippocampal commissure is missing, leaving a greatly enlarged longitudinal cerebral fissure extending into the third ventricle (see also Fig. 2 of Elias et al., 1973). The mode of inheritance of the defect has so far evaded specification, mainly because more than half of the mice in the same inbred strain are quite normal. Further study of the deficiency has detected partial and total absence in three other sublines of BALB, as shown in Fig. 2. Using much larger sample sizes, Jones (unpublished, 1977) obtained the data shown in Table III. The appearance of deficient corpus callosum in several other BALB sublines which have been inbred many

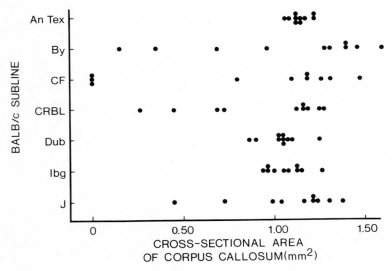

Fig. 2   Individual values of the cross-sectional area (mm²) of the corpus callosum at midline for seven sublines of BALB/c inbred mice. The area for each brain was determined from a tracing of the mid-sagittal section stained with Sudan black-B for myelin. The sublines are: AnTex from the Texas Inbred Mice Co., Houston; By, the Bailey subline from the Jackson Labs, courtesy of Dr. Robert L. Collins; CF from Carworth Farms but now available only from Charles River Mouse Farms, Wilmington, Mass.; CRBL from Charles River Mouse Farms; Dub from Flow Labs, Dublin, Virginia; Ibg from the Institute for Behavioral Genetics, University of Colorado, courtesy of Dr. John C. De Fries; J from the Jackson Laboratory, Bar Harbor, Maine. Information on the origin and generations of inbreeding is not available for all the sublines.

Table III   Frequency of deficient corpus callosum in several BALB sublines

Sublines	Number of mice			
	Total	Normal	Partial agenesis[a]	Complete agenesis
BALB/cDub[b]	43	42	1	0
BALB/cCRBL[b]	123	106	15	2
BALB/cCF[b]	140	112	19	9
BALB/cJ[c]	61	39	14	8

[a]Partial agenesis indicates a corpus callosum at midline which was less than half the normal size but where the structure was plainly evident, in contrast to complete agenesis where no transcortical fibres could be identified reliably that were definitely not part of the dorsal commissure of the fornix.
[b]Unpublished data from Wahlsten (1976) and Jones (1977).
[c]Pooled data from Wahlsten (1974) and unpublished data from Wahlsten (1976). Frequency of defect varies widely from one shipment to the next.

generations by different suppliers makes it highly unlikely that the variability within all four sublines is caused by segregation at one or more loci.

By lesioning the cerebral cortex of these sublines and then using a silver stain for degenerating fibres and terminals, Jones (unpublished, 1977) has also studied the topographical distribution of connections in defective and normal BALB brains. The aberrant connections have proven to be diffusely distributed in cortex. There appears to be no major structural reorganization of cortical fibres, except for the absence of contralateral projections when corpus callosum is absent entirely.

Study of the ontogeny of the corpus callosum in the prenatal mouse brain (Wahlsten, 1975) established that cases of total absence always resemble an early stage of growth of the structure, implying that the defect is a case of arrested development. It was also found that the longitudinal cerebral fissure formed a wider gap in BALB/cJ fetuses than in other inbred strains, and that some of the BALB fetuses were very retarded in overall growth compared to litter mates. These preliminary findings suggest that the variability of expression of corpus callosum in the adult may reflect a variable phenomenon, retardation of development, superimposed upon a regular event, wide cerebral fissure in fetal BALB mice.

It is interesting that various degrees of absence of corpus callosum and other midline commissures are observed in human brains, and that arrested development of the fibre tracts appears to be the rule as well (Loeser and Alvord, 1968). The authors state: "We believe that agenesis of the corpus callosum is one manifestation of dorsal midline dysgenesis ... Partial agenesis of the corpus callosum represents the mildest degree of this continuum of malformations" (p. 567). Hereditary factors have not yet been demonstrated in human callosal deficiency, although there have been reports of agenesis in more than one member of a family (e.g., Shapira and Cohen, 1973).

Topographical organization of connections

Hereditary variation in measures such as whole brain size, regional volume and spatial location of structures is ubiquitous and substantial. It clearly is of great importance for the methodology of brain research, but its relation to brain function is not at all apparent. Two brains could differ greatly in these gross measures but have nearly identical patterns of interconnections. Likewise, brains with comparable gross morphology could be organized in radically different ways. The topographical organization of connections between brain regions and the distribution of synapses on the neuron itself must have profound functional consequences (see Edds et al., 1972). Hereditary variation in these characters may have important implications for behavioral variation.

Studies of inbred strains

Barber et al. (1974) examined the distribution of dentate granule cell terminals (mossy fibre boutons) on pyramidal cells of the hippocampus using a stain for metallic zinc which has a high concentration in mossy fibre terminals. Among the eight inbred mouse strains which were studied, BALB/cJ and SM/J exhibited markedly different patterns of zinc staining. All strains had intense staining of zinc in the suprapyramidal layer. However, BALB/cJ possessed an unusually high concentration of mossy fibre terminals in the intrapyramidal region but a virtual absence of staining infrapyramidally. SM/J revealed the opposite pattern: low concentration of zinc in the intrapyramidal layer and high concentration in the infrapyramidal region. Across all eight strains, the correlation between the amount of area stained in the two layers was -0.80 ($P < 0.05$). The authors pointed out that the pattern might reflect variation in the spatial and temporal coordination of pyramidal cell formation and mossy fibre growth in the fetal or neonatal mouse. Neither the mode of inheritance nor the functional significance of this syndrome have yet been elucidated.

Another study from the same laboratory examined the ontogeny of spinal reflexes and synapses in five inbred mouse strains (Vaughn et al., 1975). C57BL/6J fetuses were greatly advanced in motor response to stimulation and in synapse formation, and LP/J fetuses were generally retarded in both measures compared with other inbreds. Painstaking analysis of electron micrographs of spinal cord revealed that "the basic sequence in which the neurons of the cutaneous reflex arc develop their synaptic connections" was essentially the same for all strains. Thus, there was strain variation in the overall timing of synaptogenesis but not in its detailed sequence or topography.

A recent report by Wahlsten and Wainwright (1977) suggests that the effect probably reflected variation in the overall rate of development of the whole fetus, not just the spinal cord. C57BL/6J fetuses were observed to be about half a day advanced compared to three other inbred strains in the development of external morphological features, body weight and crown-rump length, although they were not as advanced as hybrid fetuses with hybrid mothers. These findings demonstrate the necessity to study the development of a single character in relation to the overall maturity of the individual mouse. Processes which are unusually advanced or retarded relative to the ontogeny of the whole system are more likely to result in adult variation in the distribution of synapses and in behavior.

These sparse investigations of hereditary variation in brain organization indicate the rich diversity of structure which can be seen when sophisticated techniques are employed. This entire area of research is in its infancy, but it promises to yield important information about the mechanisms underlying hereditary variation in behavior among common laboratory strains.

Albinism and the visual system

Interest in the brains of albino animals was aroused when Sheridan (1965) first reported that the interocular transfer of visual information was deficient in albino compared to pigmented rats.

Subsequent anatomical investigation has shown that albino animals with lack of pigmentation in the retina have deficient ipsilateral projections to the lateral geniculate nucleus (Guillery and Kaas, 1971; Lund et al., 1974), the anterior colliculus (Giolli and Creel, 1973; Kalil et al., 1971) and the visual cortex (Dräger, 1974; Kaas and Guillery, 1973). The ipsilateral deficiency appears as a characteristic absence of terminals in certain layers of the lateral geniculate nucleus, showing that the defect is one of topographical distribution of terminals and not merely quantitative diminution. Electrophysiological recording has verified that the deficiency possesses functional consequences (Creel, 1971; Creel et al., 1974).

Extensive research has demonstrated that virtually any hereditary syndrome which causes lack of pigment in the retinal pigment epithelium will lead to deficiency of ipsilateral projections. The defect appears in albino animals of numerous mammalian species (Creel and Giolli, 1976). It also appears in rabbits with other alleles at the albinism locus which eliminate retinal pigmentation (Sanderson, 1975) and in non-albino ocular hypopigmentation syndromes in rats (Creel and Giolli, 1976). Wise and Lund (1976) employed rats with one red eye (no pigment at all) and one dark ruby eye (pigment in the iris and choroid) to demonstrate that the pigment epithelium deficiency is decisive for the ipsilateral projection deficiency.

The physiological mechanisms of ipsilateral deficiency are not entirely clear yet. Pigment appears very early in the mouse retina, about 12 days after conception (Theiler, 1972), and the optic axons reach the lateral geniculate nucleus 16 days after conception (Lund and Bunt, 1975), which suggests that the deficit may occur early in development. On the other hand, the retina of adult albino animals is known to degenerate under bright light (Chernenko and West, 1976), so it may also be a degenerative phenomenon. Research combining manipulations of heredity and illumination at different ages has not yet been reported. Hence, the physiological causes cannot be specified at this time.

Neurological mutants

Over 100 mutations have been identified in the laboratory mouse which cause gross aberrations in motor coordination or brain structure (Sidman et al., 1965; Searle, 1976), and many of these have been studied in great detail. A review of this vast literature is beyond the scope of the present chapter. Suffice it to say that much has been learned about the developmental mechanisms which form the basis for hereditary variation in brain structure. Some examples have already been presented in the section *Structural versus neurochemical manifestations of heredity* of this chapter, and several research problems have been demonstrated.

Mutants have advantages over inbred strains as research subjects because of the discrete nature of the variation in heredity and the fact that mutants and normal littermates share a common maternal environment. However, in most cases the viability of the affected individuals is greatly reduced, and the behavioral syndromes are clearly outside the normal range of behavior. Neurological mutants, inbred strains and selected lines all have an important place in brain research. This chapter has focussed on inbred strains and selected lines because so much is already known about their behaviors and their use in the laboratory is so widespread.

Discussion

From even a brief review it is apparent that hereditary variation in brain structure is ubiquitous and substantial. There is good cause to conclude that virtually every attribute of the brain will exhibit at least quantitative variation among strains and selected lines of lab animals, extending from the molar level of whole brain size to the microscopic level of synaptic distribution or possibly even synaptic morphology. For some characters differences can be identified at a glance, whereas others may require precise measurement of large samples from each population in order to detect a difference.

Does this imply that genes "determine" brain structure or specify a blueprint for the organization of the brain? No, it does not. The very same characters which show hereditary variation are also modifiable by experience. Brain growth is changed substantially by environmental enrichment or neonatal thyroxine administration. Dietary manganese deficiency produces a defect in the inner ear which is identical to a hereditary defect. Internal factors also provide evidence against a rigid conception of hereditary effects. There is an extreme degree of variation in major fibre tracts such as the corpus callosum within an inbred strain or within a single inbred litter, even though the animals share a common heredity. Furthermore, when the normal developmental pathway is blocked, the brain can be organized in a new way, which in the case of callosal agenesis in humans can largely compensate for the disruption.

These findings are relevant to the question of nature and nurture. It is apparent that both factors are absolutely necessary for the development of any organism.

"Nature" refers to factors internal to the organism, beginning with the substance of heredity contained in the reproductive cells. These internal factors constitute the basis for development of an organism. Given the proper external conditions, organisms with different heredities will develop differently. "Nurture," on the other hand, refers to factors external to the organism, including nutrition, temperature, etc. These factors constitute the conditions for development of an organism. Given suitable internal bases or heredity, an organism will develop in a definite way only under the proper conditions. Nature and nurture are opposites, and yet they comprise an indissoluble unity.

Posing the narrow question of which one is most important is fruitless. "Heritability" represents the relative importance of hereditary variation for the total measurable variation of a character in a particular population. However, heritability can change if the same population is reared in a different environment (Henderson, 1970b, 1973). Hence, the heritability ratio tells as much about the environment as it does about heredity. Because the vast majority of laboratory research on brain structure is conducted under careful environmental control using animal strains which have been bred under identical conditions for many generations, measures of heritability tell nothing about the broader question of nature and nurture. To determine the extent to which a particular character is plastic in response to external factors, the environment must be modified. Knowing the magnitude of the heritability ratio measured under carefully controlled and uniform lab conditions tells nothing about the modifiability of brain structure when those conditions are changed.

The most important conclusion from the research reviewed here is that the response of the developing organism to its external conditions depends upon its heredity. Modifiability is hereditary. Heritability is modifiable. Our task is to explore the manifold ways in which the brain and behavior of different organisms change in response to their conditions of living, and then, on this firm foundation of facts, come to understand the laws of development.

Acknowledgements

The author is grateful to G. Brian Jones for his helpful criticisms of the manuscript as well as the use of some of his preliminary data on absent corpus callosum. Preparation of this paper was supported in part by grant A0398 from the National Research Council of Canada.

Literature cited

Barber, R. P., Vaughn, J. E., Wimer, R. E. and Wimer, C. C. (1974) Genetically-associated variations in the distribution of dentate granule cell synapses upon the pyramidal cell dendrites in mouse hippocampus, *J. Comp. Neurol. 156*, 417–434

Black, I. R. (1976) Abnormal catecholamine enzymes in Weaver mutant mice, *Brain Res.* *105*, 602–605

Blakemore, C. (1974) Development of functional connexions in the mammalian visual system, *Br. Med. Bull. 30*, 152–156

Blanks, J. C., Adinolfi, A. M. and Lolley, R. N. (1974) Photoreceptor degeneration and synaptogenesis in retinal-degenerative (rd) mice, *J. Comp. Neurol. 156*, 95–106

Bliss, T. V. P. and Chung, S. H. (1974) An electrophysiological study of the hippocampus of the 'reeler' mutant mouse, *Nature 252*, 153–155

Broadhurst, P. L., Fulker, D. W. and Wilcock, J. (1974) Behavioral genetics, *Annu. Rev. Psychol. 25*, 389–415

Cazala, P. and Cardo, B. (1972) Etude préliminaire du comportement d'autostimulation chez la souris, *Physiol. Behav. 9*, 255–257

Cazala, P., Cazals, Y. and Cardo, B. (1974) Hypothalamic self-stimulation in three inbred strains of mice, *Brain Res. 81*, 159–167

Chen, C.-S. and Fuller, J. L. (1975) Neonatal thyroxine administration, behavioral maturation, and brain growth in mice of different brain weight, *Dev. Psychobiol. 8*, 355–361

Chernenko, G. A. and West, R. W. (1976) A re-examination of anatomical plasticity in the rat retina, *J. Comp. Neurol. 167*, 49–62

Costantino-Ceccarini, E. and Morell, P. (1971) Quaking mouse: in vitro studies of brain sphingolipid biosynthesis, *Brain Res. 29*, 75–84

Creel, D. J. (1971) Visual system anomaly associated with albinism in the cat, *Nature 231*, 465–466

Creel, D. and Giolli, R. A. (1976) Retinogeniculate projections in albino and ocularly hypo-pigmented rats, *J. Comp. Neurol. 166*, 445–456

Creel, D., Witkop, C. J. and King, R. A. (1974) Asymmetric visually evoked potentials in human albinos. Evidence for visual system anomalies, *Invest. Ophthalmol. 13*, 430–440

Dawson, B. H., Dervin, E. and Heywood, O. B. (1968–1969) Bio-engineering approach to stereotaxic surgery of the brain, *Proc. Inst. Mech. Eng. 183*, 281–297

Deagle, J. H. and Lubar, J. F. (1971) Effect of septal lesions in two strains of rats on one-way and shuttle avoidance acquisition, *J. Comp. Physiol. Psychol. 77*, 277–281

Dennis, M. (1976) Impaired sensory and motor differentiation with corpus callosum agenesis. A lack of callosal inhibition during ontogeny? *Neuropsychologia 14*, 455–469

Dräger, U. C. (1974) Autoradiography of tritiated proline and fucose transported trans-neuronally from the eye to the visual cortex in pigmented and albino mice, *Brain Res. 82*, 284–292

Edds, M. V., Barkley, D. S. and Fambrough, D. M. (1972) Genesis of neuronal patterns, *Neurosci. Res. Program Bull. 10*, 253–367

Eidelberg, E. and Stein, D. G. (1974) Functional recovery after lesions of the nervous system, *Neurosci. Res. Program Bull. 12*, 190–303

Elias, M. F., Dupree, M. and Eleftheriou, B. E. (1973) Differences in spatial discrimination reversal learning between two inbred mouse strains following specific amygdaloid lesions, *J. Comp. Physiol. Psychol. 83*, 149–156

Erway, L., Hurley, L. S. and Fraser, A. (1966) Neurological defect. Manganese in phenocopy and prevention of a genetic abnormality of inner ear, *Science 152*, 1766–1768

Fuller, J. L. and Herman, B. H. (1974) Effect of genotype and practice upon behavioral development in mice, *Dev. Psychobiol. 7*, 21–30

Giolli, R. A. and Creel, D. J. (1973) The primary optic projections in pigmented and albino guinea pigs. An experimental degeneration study, *Brain Res. 55*, 25–39

Gonsiorek, J. C., Donovick, P. J., Burright, R. G. and Fuller, J. L. (1974) Aggression in low and high brainweight mice following septal lesions, *Physiol. Behav. 12*, 813–818

Guillery, R. W. and Kaas, J. H. (1971) A study of normal and congenitally abnormal retino-geniculate projections in cats, *J. Comp. Neurol. 143*, 73–100

Gyllensten, L. and Lindberg, J. (1964) Development of the visual cortex in mice with inherited retinal dystrophy, *J. Comp. Neurol. 122*, 79–90

Hamburger, V. (1975) Changing concepts in developmental neurobiology, *Persp. Biol. Med.* *18*, 162–178

Hamburgh, M. and Bornstein, M. K. (1970) Myelin synthesis in two demyelinating mutations in mice, *Exp. Neurol. 28*, 471–476

Henderson, N. D. (1970a) Brain weight increases resulting from environmental enrichment. A directional dominance in mice, *Science 169*, 776–778

Henderson, N. D. (1970b) Genetic influences on the behavior of mice can be obscured by laboratory rearing, *J. Comp. Physiol. Psychol. 72*, 505–511

Henderson, N. D. (1973) Brain weight changes resulting from enriched rearing conditions. A diallel analysis, *Dev. Psychobiol. 6*, 367–376

Henry, K. R. and Schlesinger, K. (1967) Effects of the albino and dilute loci on mouse behavior, *J. Comp. Physiol. Psychol. 63*, 320–323

Hogan, E. L., Joseph, K. C. and Schmidt, G. (1970) Composition of cerebral lipids in murine sudanophilic leucodystrophy. The jimpy mutant, *J. Neurochem. 17*, 75–83

Hotta, Y. and Benzer, S. (1973) Mapping of behavior in Drosophila mosaics. In: *Genetic Mechanisms of Development* (F. H. Ruddle, ed.) pp. 129–168, Academic Press, New York

Hunt, D. M. (1974) Primary defect in copper transport underlies mottled mutants in the mouse, *Nature 249*, 852–854

Hunt, D. M. and Johnson, D. R. (1972) An inherited deficiency in noradrenaline biosynthesis in the brindled mouse, *J. Neurochem. 19*, 2811–2819

Jensen, C. (1974) Active avoidance learning and activity level. Paper presented to the *Fourth Annual Meeting of the Behavior Genetics Association*, June 6–8, Minneapolis, Minnesota

Jones, G. B. (1975) *Spatial organization of Mouse Forebrain. Six Strains Compared by a New Stereotaxic Technique*, unpublished M.A. thesis, University of Waterloo, Ontario, Canada

Kaas, J. H. and Guillery, R. W. (1973) The transfer of abnormal visual field representations from the dorsal lateral geniculate nucleus to the visual cortex in Siamese cats, *Brain Res. 59*, 61–95

Kalil, R. E., Jhaveri, S. R. and Richards, W. (1971) Anomalous retinal pathways in the Siamese cat. An inadequate substrate for normal binocular vision, *Science 174*, 302–305

King, L. S. (1936) Hereditary defects of the corpus callosum in the mouse, Mus musculus, *J. Comp. Neurol. 64*, 337–363

Latham, E. E. and Thorne, B. M. (1974) Septal damage and muricide. Effects of strain and handling, *Physiol. Behav. 12*, 521–526

Loeser, J. D. and Alvord, E. C. (1968) Agenesis of the corpus callosum, *Brain 91*, 553–570

Lucas, E. A., Powell, E. W. and Murphree, O. D. (1974) Hippocampal theta in nervous pointer dogs, *Physiol. Behav. 12*, 609–613

Lund, R. D. and Bunt, A. H. (1975) Prenatal development of central optic pathways in albino rats, *J. Comp. Neurol. 165*, 247–264

Lund, R. D., Lund, J. S. and Wise, R. P. (1974) The organization of the retinal projection of the dorsal lateral geniculate nucleus in pigmented and albino rats, *J. Comp. Neurol. 158*, 383–404

Mandel, P., Ayad, G., Hermetet, J. C. and Ebel, A. (1974) Correlation between choline acetyltransferase activity and learning ability in different mice strains and their offspring, *Brain Res. 72*, 65–70

Minna, J., Glazer, D. and Nirenberg, M. (1972) Genetic dissection of neural properties using somatic cell hybrids, *Nature New Biol. 235*, 225–231

Mintz, B. (1971) Allophenic mice of multi-embryo origin. In: *Methods in Mammalian Embryology* (J. C. Daniel, Jr., ed.) pp. 186–214, Freeman, San Francisco

Mullen, R. J. and LaVail, M. M. (1976) Inherited retinal dystrophy. Primary defect in pigment epithelium determined with experimental rat chimeras, *Science 192*, 799–801

Oliverio, A. (1975) Genotype-dependent electroencephalographic, behavioral and analgesic correlates of morphine. An analysis in normal mice and in mice with septal lesions, *Brain Res. 83*, 135–141

Oliverio, A., Castellano, C. and Messeri, P. (1973) Genotype-dependent effects of septal lesions on different types of learning in the mouse, *J. Comp. Physiol. Psychol. 82*, 240–246

Padeh, B. and Soller, M. (1976) Genetic and environmental correlations between brain weight maze learning in inbred strains of mice and their F$_1$ hybrids, *Behav. Genet. 6*, 31–42

Rakic, P. (1976) Synaptic specificity in the cerebellar cortex. Study of anomalous circuits induced by single gene mutations in mice, *Cold Spring Harbor Symp. Quant. Biol. 40*, 333–346

Rakic, P. and Sidman, R. L. (1973) Weaver mutant mouse cerebellum. Defective neuronal migration secondary to abnormality of Bergmann glia, *Proc. Natl. Acad. Sci. U.S. 70*, 240–244

Roderick, T. H., Wimer, R. E., Wimer, C. C. and Schwartzkroin, P. A. (1973) Genetic and phenotypic variation in weight of brain and spinal cord between inbred strains of mice, *Brain Res. 64*, 345–353

Roderick, T. H., Wimer, R. E. and Wimer, C. C. (1976) Genetic manipulation of neuro-anatomical traits. In: *Knowing, Thinking and Believing* (L. Petrinovich and J. L. McGaugh, eds.) pp. 143–178, Pergamon Press, New York

Sanderson, K. J. (1975) Retinogeniculate projections in the rabbits of the albino allelo-morphic series, *J. Comp. Neurol. 159*, 15–28

Samorajski, T., Friede, R. L. and Reimer, P. R. (1970) Hypomyelination in the quaking mouse, *J. Neuropath. Exp. Neurol. 29*, 507–523

Searle, A. G. (ed.) (1976) *Mouse Newslett. 54*, 6–22

Shapira, Y. and Cohen, T. (1973) Agenesis of the corpus callosum in two sisters, *J. Med. Genet. 10*, 266–269

Sheridan, C. S. (1965) Interocular transfer of brightness and pattern discriminations in normal and corpus callosum sectioned rats, *J. Comp. Physiol. Psychol. 59*, 292–294

Sidman, R. L., Green, M. C. and Appel, S. H. (1965) *Catalog of the Neurological Mutants of the Mouse*, Harvard University Press, Cambridge

Slotnick, B. M. and Leonard, C. M. (1975) *A Stereotaxic Atlas of the Albino Mouse Forebrain*, U.S. Department of Health, Education and Welfare, Rockville, Maryland

Smith, B. H. and Kreutzberg, G. W. (1976) Neuron-target cell interactions, *Neurosci. Res. Program Bull. 14*, 210–453

Sotelo, C. and Changeux, J. P. (1974) Bergmann fibers and granular cell migration in the cerebellum of homozygous weaver mutant mouse, *Brain Res. 77*, 484–491

Sperry, R. W. (1968) Plasticity of neural maturation, *Devel. Biol. Suppl. 2*, 306–327

Stewart, A. D. (1971) Genetic variation in the neurohypophysial hormones of the mouse, Mus musculus, *J. Endocrinol. 51*, 191–201

Stewart, A. D. (1972) Genetic determination of the storage of vasopressin and oxytocin in the neural lobes of mice, *J. Physiol. 222*, 157–158P

Storer, J. B. (1967) Relation of lifespan to brain weight, body weight, and metabolic rate among inbred mouse strains, *Exp. Gerontol. 2*, 173–182

Suzuki, K. and Zagoren, J. C. (1976) Variations of Schmidt-Lenterman incisures in quaking mouse, *Brain Res. 106*, 146–151

Tansley, K. (1954) An inherited retinal degeneration in the mouse, *J. Hered. 45*, 123–127

Theiler, K. (1972) *The House Mouse. Development and Normal Stages from Fertilization to 4 Weeks of Age*, Springer-Verlag, Berlin

Tobias, P. V. (1970) Brain-size, grey matter and race – fact or fiction? *Am. J. Phys. Anthrop. 32*, 3–26

Van Abeelen, J. H. F. (ed.) (1974) *The Genetics of Behaviour*, North-Holland, Amsterdam

Van Valen, L. (1974) Brain size and intelligence in man, *Am. J. Phys. Anthrop. 40*, 417–424

Vaughn, J. E., Henrikson, C. K., Chernow, C. R., Grieshaber, J. A. and Wimer, C. C. (1975) Genetically-associated variations in the development of reflex movements and synaptic junctions within an early reflex pathway of mouse spinal cord, *J. Comp. Neurol. 161*, 541–554

Wahlsten, D. (1972) Genetic experiments with animal learning. A critical review, *Behav. Biol. 7*, 143–182

Wahlsten, D. (1974) Heritable aspects of anomalous myelinated fibre tracts in the forebrain of the laboratory mouse, *Brain Res. 68*, 1–18

Wahlsten, D. (1975) Prenatal development of the brain in several mouse strains, *Behav. Genet. 5*, 109–110

Wahlsten, D. (1977) Behavioral genetics and animal learning. In: *Psychopharmacology of Aversively Motivated Behaviors* (H. Anisman and G. Bignami, eds.) Plenum Press, New York, in the press

Wahlsten, D., Hudspeth, W. J. and Bernhardt, K. (1975) Implications of genetic variation in mouse brain structure for electrode placement by stereotaxic surgery, *J. Comp. Neurol. 162*, 519–532

Wahlsten, D. and Wainwright, P. (1977) Application of a morphological time scale to hereditary differences in prenatal mouse development, *J. Embryol. Exp. Morphol.*, in the press

West, C. D. and Harrison, J. M. (1973) Transneuronal cell atrophy in the congenitally deaf white cat, *J. Comp. Neurol. 151*, 377–398

Wimer, R. E., Wimer, C. C. and Roderick, T. H. (1969) Genetic variability in forebrain structures between inbred strains of mice, *Brain Res. 16*, 257–264

Wimer, R. E., Norman, R. and Eleftheriou, B. E. (1973) Serotonin levels in hippocampus: striking variations associated with mouse strain and treatment, *Brain Res. 63*, 397–401

Wise, R. P. and Lund, R. D. (1976) The retina and central projections of heterochromic rats, *Exp. Neurol. 51*, 68–77

Zaide, J. (1974) Differences between Tryon bright and dull rats in seizure activity evoked by amygdala stimulation, *Physiol. Behav. 12*, 527–534

Genetics, environment and intelligence, edited by A. Oliverio
© *Elsevier/North-Holland Biomedical Press, 1977*

Postnatal brain maturation and learning in the mouse 7

ALBERTO OLIVERIO and CLAUDIO CASTELLANO

The mouse as a model for behavioural research

Each human infant presents a unique pattern of smiling, crying, suckling, vocalizing, sleeping or looking at strangers, a pattern which depends on the interaction between a given genotype and a variable environment. The uniqueness of these activities and their variation in relation to different environmental events is a subject which is gaining the attention of the developmental psychologists since it has been shown that changes in the surrounding internal or external milieu may permanently modify behavioural ontogenesis.

The importance of gestational and early postnatal environment has been stressed by Soviet psychologists, chiefly by Luria (1972), which suggests that a heterogeneous number of gestational and perinatal factors may result in mental retardation. Similarly, the interest for the early determinants of behaviour is increased following a number of studies which indicate that infants are reactive to environmental differences since the first days or weeks of life (Papoušek, 1967; White, 1971; Kagan, 1971; Scarr-Salapatek and Williams, 1973). This approach, which is discussed in different sections of this book, has raised an interest for a number of scales, measures and physiological tests which may be applied since the first days of life. While Soviet psychologists are more inclined towards a number of electrophysiological measures, which may be assessed in the newborn, the trend in the United States is more oriented towards the use of different scales in which a number of reflex activities and of behavioural postures are quantified (Bailey, 1969; Brazelton, 1973; Broman et al., 1975; Yarrow et al., 1975).

In this chapter we would like to stress that the experiments conducted on animal models may represent a useful step towards a better knowledge of the role of the environment on behavioural ontogenesis. Similarly we would like to show that a number of pharmacological, nutritional and environmental factors may affect the postnatal development of behaviour and interact with the genetic make-up of the individual.

In the recent years, many experiments have underlined the role of the mouse in a genetic approach to the study of animal behaviour. Many lines of inbred strains (Staats, 1972), are in fact available and a large body of information has been obtained on the neurological and behavioural maturation of this animal species, and on the biochemical correlates of these measures. One basic step in behavioural experiments was to demonstrate that while individual mice belonging to random-bred populations attain disparate learning levels, inbred strains are characterized by homogeneous performances within each strain. In a large number of learning situations ranging from positively rewarded maze learning to negatively rewarded active avoidance, different strains of mice were ranked for their high, intermediate and low learning patterns (Bovet et al., 1969). For example, by comparing the over-all performance attained by 9 strains of mice, Bovet et al. (1969) were able to show that their strains were very poor in avoidance performance in shuttle box; and in Lashley III maze situations, two other strains (DBA/2J and C57Br/cdJ) attained a very high level of performance while other strains showed intermediate values. These behavioural differences were demonstrated to be also qualitative, since the study of distributed versus massed pratice in avoidance and maze learning showed that under the same training conditions, some strains were characterized by good short-term performance, while other strains were characterized by more efficient memory storage mechanisms. A number of behavioural measures have been assessed in some of these strains which have been used in diallel studies and have been intercrossed until the F_2 and F_3 generation in order to assess genetic correlations (Oliverio et al., 1972). For example the high avoiding strains SEC 1/ReJ and DBA/2J mice, which are also good maze learners, are characterized by low levels of exploratory behaviour and running activity while the C57BL/6J strain presents poor avoidance and maze levels but is very active (Oliverio et al., 1972). By using these strains it has also been shown that the mode of inheritance of a given behavioural measure depends on the crosses considered: crossing the C57 strain with SEC mice resulted, in fact, in SEC-like progeny, while crossing DBA with C57 yielded an offspring similar to the C57 genotype. A similar behavioural pattern was evident for avoidance and maze learning.

As is mentioned in another chapter of this book, a number of studies are concentrated on the biochemical differences which characterize the various inbred strains of mice. The rationale for these investigations is to try to correlate the observed behavioural differences to given biochemical mechanisms at the brain level. Pryor et al. (1966) have measured, for example, acetylcholinesterase activity in five strains of mice, and observed that the high avoiding strains, A and DBA/2 also showed a higher acetylcholinesterase activity than the two low-avoiding strains C3H/He and C57BL/6. Mice belonging to the DBA/2 and C57BL/6 strains were subjected to detailed analyses by Ebel et al. (1973), and Mandel et al. (1973). The data indicate that DBA/2 are characterized by higher acetylcholinesterase and choline-acetyltransferase activities in the frontal and temporal lobe than C57BL/6 mice. These findings were interpreted by suggesting that they possibly reflect a more active acetylcholine metabolism in this strain.

As for the adrenergic system, Kempf et al. (1974), in experiments carried out on C57BL/6J, DBA/2J and SEC/ReJ mice, have demonstrated that the two high avoiding strains (SEC and DBA) present a higher noradrenaline turnover in their hypothalamus in comparison to C57BL/6 mice. On the contrary a lower noradrenaline turnover is evident in the first two strains when the pons and the medulla oblongata are considered. In line with these findings, Eleftheriou (1971) has demonstrated that DBA/2 mice exhibit the highest turnover rate of NE while C57BL/6 (and C3H) mice display a lower activity in all brain regions examined.

A number of experiments show the existence of wide differences between various inbred strains of mice when brain weight and brain size are considered. The variance between strains, which exceeds that within individual strains, indicates in these researches the existence of phenotypic differences attributable to hereditary factors. Both comparative studies and genetic analyses may bring interesting results in this field. Wimer et al. (1969) for example, have demonstrated behavioural differences associated with relative size of the hippocampus in mice, showing that the ratio of hippocampal to total forebrain volume was negatively correlated to open-field activity and positively correlated to passive-avoidance conditioning performance. A negative correlation was found in the same research between open-field and relative volume of neocortex.

More recently, Roderick et al. (1973) analyzed male and female mice from 25 inbred strains for their adult brain weight, spinal cord weight, ratio of brain weight to spinal cord weight, and ratio of brain weight to body weight. Strain differences in the size of these structures were evident for all the traits considered, and a similar ranking for each trait was found within the strains which are characterized by common ancestry (for example CBA/J and C3HeB/FeJ, C57BL/6J and C57Br/cdJ, and C57L/J).

In general, the results indicate that, as concerns the inbred strains, the two ratios, brain weight to spinal cord weight and brain weight to body weight, were different in different strains. A high correlation was found between brain and spinal cord weights, a fact which suggests that the weights of the various structures of the nervous tissue should be influenced in part by the same genes.

Behavioural ontogenesis and brain maturation in mammals

The maturity at birth of mammals, rather than the duration of gestation, represents an important evolutionary mechanism since in precocious mammals (such as ruminants) sensory and motor maturation at birth allows immediate identification with the mother to occur and the establishment of social and mother-offspring relationships resembling imprinting in birds (Scott, 1958; Sluckin, 1965). On the contrary, in non-precocious mammals, which form a heterogeneous group ranging from rodents to carnivores, primates and man, the immediate postnatal period is characterized by great maternal dependency, by a later onset of primary and social relationship and by immaturity of sensory and motor abilities. In man, carnivores and rodents, there is a sequence of neurologic and behavioural maturation which is quite similar (Fox, 1964; Scott, 1953). In newborn mice, reflex responses such as rooting, head orientation, labial suckling, and positive and negative thermotaxis may be considered as behavioural mechanisms that ensure the survival of mice, dogs and humans. The disappearance of these reflexes and the maturation of other neuromuscular reflex activities connected to myelination have similar developmental patterns in these species, the relative age of a 1–2 week-old mouse being equivalent to a 3–4 week-old dog or to 3 months in man for some behavioural features (Fox, 1964).

A number of studies conducted in cats, dogs, mice or rats have been devoted to an analysis of the development of different measures of postnatal behaviour ranging from the electrocortical activity to motor reflexes, sleep patterns, locomotor behaviour and mother–offspring relationships (Fox, 1964; Scott, 1953; Altman and Sundarshan, 1975; Van Abeelen, 1968; Verlay et al., 1969). These studies indicate, in the most general terms, that in non-precocious mammals the postnatal maturation of the cortex and of myelinized structures is paralleled by a maturation of a number of behavioural activities which are the necessary background for more complex adaptative behaviours. The existence of this period of postnatal brain maturation is important in relation to the different environmental factors which may positively or negatively affect this critical period and act on the development of behaviour.

The phylogenetic evolution of the nervous system, e.g. the passage from stereotyped subcortical mechanisms to more refined and adaptative cortical functions, is connected to the existence of expanded cortical structures which are still immature at birth (Altman, 1966). Experiments relying on a number of correlations between brain structure and behaviour indicate that the nervous system is modified by experience and that such modifications are involved in learning (Rosenzweig, 1966; Volkmar and Greenough, 1972; Horn et al., 1973; Campbell and Spear, 1972). Since many biological events and periodicities seem to be endogenous to the organism and are sensitive indicators of changes in the surrounding environment, the age of first identification of such periodicities in life has been of prime concern in developmental psychology. In particular, in addition to measures of reflex activities, the measurement of the electrocortical activity and of the sleep states is of particular interest as an index of neurological integration. The ontogenesis of the EEG in rats or mice (Math et al., 1974; Oliverio et al., 1975) is therefore a useful parameter in the study of postnatal brain maturation.

Finally, a point which is worth underlining in this introduction is related to the relationship existing between the genetic make-up of the individual and his postnatal behavioural developmental patterns. This point, which has been emphasized in a number of studies (Henderson, 1970, 1972; Blizard and Randt, 1974; Fuller and Herman, 1974; Werboff et al., 1968), indicates that within the same species there are individuals which will be more (or less) sensitive to the effects of a given environmental situation.

The findings, which have been summarized above, indicate two main points: (1) the mouse represents a useful approach to the study of the effects of the environment upon brain and behavioural ontogenesis since much information is being collected on this species and disparate inbred strains and lines are available; (2) a number of behavioural measures, such as reflex activities or the electrocorticographic activity, seem to be reliable tests for detecting altered behavioural patterns deriving from gestational or postnatal treatments which may result in a behavioural modification of adult behaviour. The examples discussed in the following section clarify these points.

A developmental approach to the behaviour of mice

On the ground of the findings previously reported, showing clear differences in behavioural, biochemical and neurological patterns between different strains of mice, a number of studies were focussed on the different factors (environmental, nutritional, pharmacological) which may result in early postnatal differences in these strains. These experiments aimed to assess if the patterns of behavioural and neurological postnatal development were different in those strains which are characterized by differences in the adult age. In this regard, the electrocorticographic (ECoG) activity of the mouse seems to be an important measure since it parallels the different stages of maturation of the cortex. Kobayashi (1963) has in fact indicated a clear parallelism between the ECoG activity and the postnatal maturation of the different cortical layers in the mouse. In an experiment by Oliverio et al. (1975), the maturation of the ECoG activity and the effects of in utero treatments with central nervous system-stimulating drugs were assessed in C57 and SEC mice which, as it has previously been noted, are characterized by opposite levels of activity, learning abilities, and brain chemistry.

C57BL/6J and SEC/1ReJ female and male mice were mated and the offspring was subdivided in litters of 6 to ensure an adequate supply of the mother's milk.

For each strain the electrocorticograms (ECoG) were recorded from freely moving animals at 2, 4, 6, 8, 12 and 80 days. From the ECoG analysis in both strains a progressive postnatal maturation of the electrical patterns was clearly evident which reached the adult level from the 12th day after birth (Fig. 1). It must be underlined that, at this age, the dendrites and the axons of the mouse cortex have completed their morphological development (Kobayashi et al., 1963). When the patterns corresponding to the first days of age were considered, clear differences were evident between the two strains. In fact, while in the C57 mice a regular rhythmic electrical activity was recorded from the first day of age and was characterized at four days of age by a regular activity, at a higher voltage (6–10 cycles/sec), the SEC strain showed a barely detectable electrical activity until the 8th day after birth. Thus, it was evident that slower patterns of postnatal cortical maturation characterize the SEC strain, which shows high levels of avoidance and maze learning as compared with the C57 strains. These present slower learning patterns and higher levels of exploratory and wheel-running activity. It is important to underline that no significant difference was evident between brain and body weights in the two strains considered.

In a second set of experiments, a group of pregnant SEC mice were injected sub-cutaneously with 15 mg/kg of amphetamine each day during the last 11 days of pregnancy. When the ECoG of the offspring was recorded, at 2, 4, 6, 8, 12 and 80 days of age, it was characterized by regular, rhythmic and high voltage waves at earlier ages than the offspring of saline injected mothers, a fact which suggests that a prenatal treatment with amphetamine accelerated the ECoG maturation of this strain (Fig. 2). This effect was not ascribable to the fact that amphetamine was still

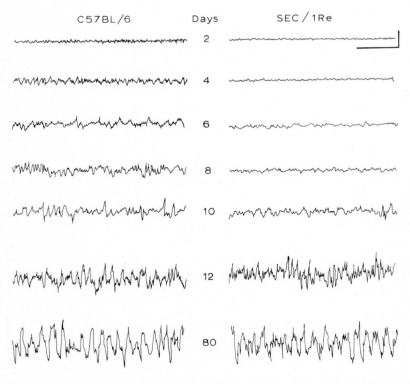

Fig. 1   Electrocorticograms in C57BL/6 and SEC/1 Re mice at different ages after birth. Samples of polygraphic recordings during waking indicate that the development of ECoG activity occurs at earlier stages in the C57BL/6 strain. The tracings are almost identical at age 12 days. Scale, 1 sec/200 μV.

Days   SEC/1Re   (AMPH.)

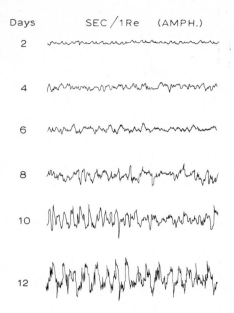

Fig. 2   Effects of in utero administration of amphetamine during the last 11 days of pregnancy on the development of electrocorticographic activity in SEC/1 Re mice. A comparison between the tracings of control SEC/1 Re mice (shown in Fig. 1) and those shown in this figure indicates that the ECoG maturation occurs earlier in the animals exposed to the drug in utero. Scale, 1 sec/200 μV.

active in the pups after birth, since no difference was evident if pregnant females were injected with drug during the last two days of pregnancy. These findings seem to underline the importance of the role that various environmental factors may play in the modulation of brain development and in the postnatal outset of a number of behavioural patterns.

A growing number of experimental and clinical findings suggests that malnutrition during pregnancy may affect brain growth and exert negative effects on postnatal behavioural development.

A number of studies (Altman et al., 1971; Dobbing and Sands, 1971; Smart et al., 1973) have shown that dietary deprivation during lactation, obtained by varying the litter size, is followed by clear reduction in brain and body weight. High vulnerability to environmental insults during suckling period, when brain grows fastest, has been demonstrated by Dobbing (1968). There is now a number of data (Fuller and Geils, 1973; Leathwood et al., 1974; Oliverio et al., 1975) which indicate a negative relationship between malnutrition on the one side, and brain development and learning ability in the adult on the other side. In this regard, the study of the ECoG activity on a number of reflex measures seems to be a useful method for assessing the effects of malnutrition on brain growth and behaviour.

The use of inbred strains of mice seems to be a fruitful tool in the study of the

effects of early malnutrition on the electrophysiological and behavioural development (Oliverio et al., 1975; Castellano and Oliverio, 1976). In a recent study, mice
from a random-bred stock and from the inbred strains SEC 1/ReJ and C57BL/6J
were mated and each pregnant female was placed into a clear plastic pen at least 1 day
before birth. The pups were cross-fostered within 8 h after birth in order to form litters
of 4 (small), 8 (intermediate), or 16 (large) pups per mother. The mice were weaned at
21 days, housed 4 per cage, and were allowed unlimited access to the food until the
end of the experiments. During this period they were maintained on a 12-h light –
12-h dark schedule.

Data on brain weight development were obtained by killing by decapitation entire
litters at 4, 8, 16, 24, 30 and 60 days of age. A number of reflex and developmental
measures were also assessed for each litter from 12 h of age to 17 days, by using the
method described by Fox (1965) and by Wahlsten (1974).

The study of ECoG activity was based on tracings recorded in mice belonging
to the different age groups within each litter size condition. The young mice were
implanted with 4 cortical electrodes in the front parietal area, according to the
method described by Oliverio et al. (1975) and Valatx and Bugat (1974). This
study also involved a measure of exploratory activity and of shuttle-box
avoidance learning in 60 day-old mice following dietary rehabilitation.

An analysis of the effects of early malnutrition on brain and body weight showed
that clear deficits were evident from the first weeks after birth. Mice from the
large litters were characterized at 16 and 24 days of age by body and brain weights
which were respectively 50% and 30% lower than those evident in mice belonging to
the small litters. This deficit was still evident in adult 60-day old mice.

When the development of a number of reflex activities is considered, it is evident
that in well nourished mice, reflexes such as the rooting reflex were mature since the
first day in all strains, other reflexes such as cliff aversion or righting appearing on the
third day, while other reflexes appeared at a later age. Early malnutrition exerted a
negative effect on the development of some of these reflexes: while the rooting reflex
was unaffected, cliff aversion, righting, placing and grasping appeared at a later
age in the large litters. Some differences were evident between C57BL/6 and
SEC/1Re mice: reflexes such as righting and placing, for example, were more affected
in C57 mice than in the SEC strain.

The measures of ECoG activity showed that the postnatal maturation of the ECoG
activity was delayed by malnutrition in all strains. For example, random-bred mice
belonging to well-nourished litters showed a rhythmic pattern (6–10 cycles/sec) from
the fourth day of age, and the tracing increased in voltage at 16 days and reached the
highest amplitude by the 24th day. On the contrary, the electrical activity was
extremely reduced at 4 or 8 days in the large litters, which showed only at 16 days of
age a pattern similar to that evident at 4 days in well nourished mice. When inbred
mice were considered, it was evident that ECoG maturation was more precocious in
well nourished C57 mice than in SEC mice (Fig. 3); thus a delay in the ECoG maturation was evident at an earlier stage (day 4–8) in the C57 strain, since small litters
from the SEC strain showed barely detectable ECoG activity at this stage. However,
the ECoG maturation of the mice belonging to the intermediate and to the large

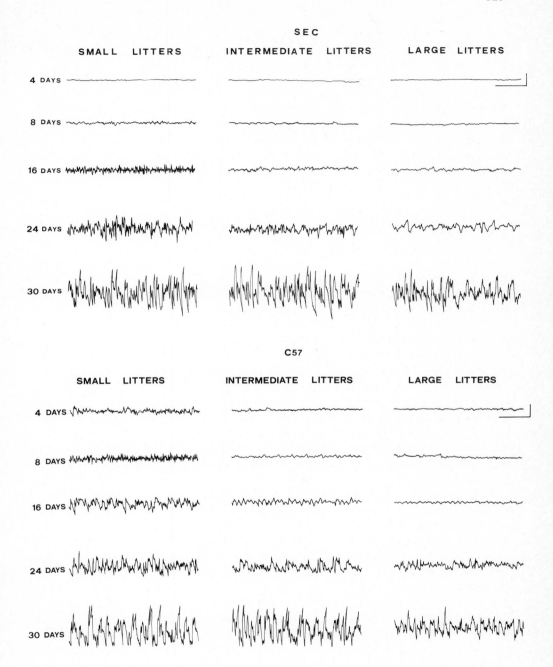

Fig. 3 Electrocorticograms at each chronological age in the SEC/1 Re (A) and C57BL/6 (B) mice. Samples of polygraphic recordings during waking indicate that the development of ECoG activity occurs at earlier stages in small litters than in intermediate or large litters. The tracings are almost identical at age 30 days. Scale, 1 sec/200μV.

litters of both strains reached an adult level only at 24–30 days of age, without showing those intermediate patterns which were evident in the small litters at 8 (C57BL/6) or 16 days (SEC/1Re).

The detrimental effects of malnutrition on brain development were evident when locomotor activity and avoidance learning were assessed in adult mice which were malnourished during the suckling period. These measures were taken in 60-day old mice following dietary rehabilitation. As concerns the locomotor activity, the C57BL/6 mice belonging to small litters were more active than SEC/1Re mice, as previously demonstrated (Oliverio et al., 1972); a general trend towards an increased exploratory activity, independently of the strain considered, was observed as litter size increased. On the contrary, avoidance learning of Swiss and SEC mice was greatly impaired in early malnourished mice. No effect following dietary deprivation was obviously detectable in the C57BL/6 mice, which were already characterized by poor avoidance levels even when reared in small litters.

To sum up, three main points emerged from this research:

(1) Maturation of a number of reflexes and of ECoG activity was delayed, but not stunted, following early malnutrition.

(2) Brain and body growth, avoidance learning and activity were permanently affected by reduced dietary intake in early life.

(3) The effects of early malnutrition on the different behavioural measures described were related to the genetic make-up of the individuals.

Some of these findings, particularly those concerning the delay of ECoG maturation following undernutrition, support some clinical data (Karyadi, 1974; Scrimshaw and Gordon, 1968; Stoch and Smythe, 1967).

In a further research, the effects of malnutrition on the ontogeny of reflexes and of ECoG activity were studied in the progeny of random-bred mice, fed with diets deficient in essential fatty acids (EFA-deprived) during the last week of pregnancy. It must be emphasized that the advantage of this method is that the use of EFA malnutrition during pregnancy avoids the possible pitfalls connected with an altered mother-offspring ratio, as in experiments in which malnutrition is obtained by varying the litter size.

The results showed that brain and body growth patterns were only slightly affected in mice deriving from females fed EFA-deprived diets during pregnancy. However a number of reflexes, for example placing reflex, appeared later in the EFA group than in control mice; similarly, grasping and bar-holding were also delayed by 2–3 days, as in mice malnourished during the suckling period (Oliverio et al., 1975; Castellano and Oliverio, 1976).

The reflexes which were delayed in their maturation (righting, placing, grasping and bar-holding reflexes) were those involving motor abilities which are normally evident during the first two weeks after birth: this fact suggested that the administration of an EFA-deprived diet affects the myelinization of the nervous motor system tracts.

The ECoG recordings also showed a clear delay in the maturation of the brain electrical activity of EFA-deprived mice, as compared with the controls. However the ECoG of control and EFA-deprived animals was similar starting from the third week of age. By using this type of malnutrition, it was also possible to show that the avoidance-learning ability was impaired following two months of rehabilitation in mice fed by females which were EFA-deprived during pregnancy. The selective deprivation of fatty acids seems therefore to affect permanently the patterns of brain development (Galli et al., 1975; D'Udine and Oliverio, 1977).

Recent findings seem to indicate that the effects of early malnutrition may be antagonized by a treatment in utero with anabolizers.

Genetic differences and postnatal development in mice

The experiments reported in the previous sections show that the genetic make-up of the individual modulates the exploratory or wheel-running activity, the learning abilities in different tasks and the total amount of sleep stages during the day or night. It has also been shown that the genotype may affect postnatal brain maturation in the mouse, a fact which suggests that the individual genetic make-up sets the limits within which the environment is able to affect the patterns of postnatal maturation. In an analysis of the wheel-running activity of different strains of mice it was found that there are strains which are more (or less) sensitive to synchronizing effects of the level of illumination (Malorni et al., 1975; Oliverio et al., 1977). Under conditions of 12 h light followed by 12 h darkness, it was shown that the external synchronizer induced higher levels of wheel-running activity during the dark hours and lower levels during the hours of light in all the strains considered. However, when the activity of different strains was assessed during the condition of continuous light (or darkness) it was found that there are strains, (for example C57BL/6) which conserve a pronounced circadian rhythm also in the absence of external synchronizers while other strains, (for example SEC/1Re) do not show clear circadian rhythms (Fig. 4).

It was suggested that the strains which show a clear-cut rhythmic activity independently of the environment reflected a more pronounced genetic determination. In fact, the strains which exhibited less pronounced rhythmic activity were those in which the ECoG and reflex activities were less mature at birth. Thus, there are strains which seem to be more "rigidly" conditioned by their genetic make-up such as C57BL/6 mice (more mature at birth, with circadian rhythm present also in absence of external synchronizer, clear-cut differences between the circadian patterns of sleep (Valatx et al., 1972), high locomotor activity and poor avoidance levels) and strains which are less "rigidly" determined and exhibit a longer postnatal period, in which their central nervous system is still not mature, such as the SEC/1Re strain (less mature at birth with circadian rhythm absent in absence of external synchronizer, no sharp differences between the circadian patterns of sleep, low locomotor activity and higher learning abilities). These strains, as mentioned by Mandel et al. (1973), are also characterized by clear biochemical differences in

128

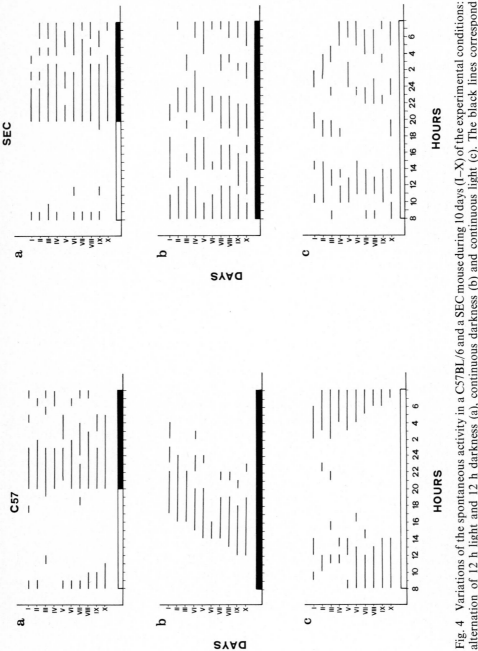

Fig. 4 Variations of the spontaneous activity in a C57BL/6 and a SEC mouse during 10 days (I–X) of the experimental conditions: alternation of 12 h light and 12 h darkness (a), continuous darkness (b) and continuous light (c). The black lines correspond to the waking periods during which the locomotor activity of the animal reaches a level higher than the average time activity of the animal recorded during 24 h. The black lines correspond to the waking periods during which the locomotor activity of the animal reaches a level higher than the average activity of the animal as recorded during 24 h.

some brain structures which exert an important role in the processes of arousal and of adaptation.

In conclusion, the mouse represents a good model for an analysis of the genetic, gestational or postnatal factors which result in a number of complex patterns of "instinctive" or adaptative behaviours. The findings summarized in this chapter indicate that postnatal brain maturation, in mice as in human infants, represents a critical period during which many environmental factors may exert a permanent effect at the brain level and result in a behavioural modification during the adult age.

Literature cited

Altman, J. (1966) *Organic Foundations of Animal Behavior*, Holt, Rinehart and Winston, New York

Altman, J., Das, D. G., Sundarshan, K. and Anderson, J. B. (1971) The influence of nutrition on neural and behavioral development. II. Growth of body and brain in infant rats using different techniques of undernutrition, *Dev. Psychobiol. 4*, 55–70

Altman, J. and Sundarshan, K. (1975) Postnatal development of locomotion in the laboratory rat, *Anim. Behav. 23*, 896–920

Bailey, N. (1969) *Manual for the Bailey Scales of Infant Development*, Psychological Corporation, New York

Bailey, D. W. (1971) Recombinant inbred strains, *Transplantation 11*, 325–327

Blizard, D. A. and Randt, C. T. (1974) Genotype interaction with undernutrition and external environment in early life, *Nature London 25L*, 705–707

Bovet, D., Bovet -Nitti, F. and Oliverio, A. (1969) Genetic aspects of learning and memory in mice, *Science 163*, 139–149

Brazelton, T. B. (1973) *Neonatal Behavioral Assessment Scale*, W. Heinemann Medical Books, London

Broman, S. H., Nichols, P. L. and Kennedy, W. A. (1975) *Preschool IQ. Prenatal and Early Developmental Correlates*, Lawrence Earlbaum Associates, Hillsdale

Campbell, B. A. and Spear, N. E. (1972) Ontogeny of memory, *Psychol. Rev. 79*, 215–236

Castellano, C. and Oliverio, A. (1976) Early malnutrition and postnatal changes in brain and behavior in the mouse, *Brain Res. 101*, 317–325

Dobbing, J. (1968) Vulnerable periods in developing brain, In: *Applied Neurochemistry* (A. N. Davidson and J. Dobbing, eds.) pp. 287–316, Blackwell, Oxford

Dobbing, J. and Sands, J. (1971) Vulnerability of developing brain. IX. The effects of nutritional growth retardation on the timing of the brain growth spurt, *Biol. Neonate 19*, 363–378

D'Udine, B. and Oliverio, A. (1977) *Behav. Proc.*, in the press

Ebel, A., Hermetet, J. C. and Mandel, P. (1973) Comparative study of acetylcholinesterase and choline-acetyltransferase enzyme activity in brain of DBA and C57 mice, *Nature New Biol. 242*, 56–57

Eleftheriou, B. E. (1971) Regional brain norepinephrine turnover rates in four strains of mice, *Neuroendocrinology 7*, 329–336

Eleftheriou, B. E., Elias, M. F., Castellano, C. and Oliverio, A. (1975) Cortex weight: a genetic analysis in the mouse, *J. Hered. 66*, 207–212

Fox, M. W. (1965) Reflex ontogeny and behavioral development of the mouse, *Anim. Behav. 13*, 234–241

Fuller, J. L. and Geils, H. D. (1973) Brain growth in mice selected for high and low brain weight, *Dev. Psychobiol. 5*, 307–318

Fuller, J. L. and Herman, B. H. (1974) Effect genotype and practice upon behavioral development in mice, *Dev. Psychobiol. 7*, 21–30

Galli, G., Messeri, P., Oliverio, A. and Pàoletti, R. (1975) Deficiency of essential fatty acids during pregnancy and avoidance learning in the progeny, *Pharmacol. Res. Commun. 7*, 71–80

Henderson, N. D. (1970) Genetic influences on the behavior of mice can be observed by laboratory rearing, *Comp. Physiol. Psychol. 72*, 505–511

Henderson, N. D. (1972) Relative effects of early rearing environment and genotype on discrimination learning in house mice, *J. Comp. Physiol. Psychol. 79*, 243–253

Horn, G., Rose, S.P.R. and Bateson, P.P.G. (1973) Experience and plasticity in the central nervous system, *Science 181*, 506–514

Kagan, J. (1971) *Change and Continuity in Infancy*, Whiley, New York

Karyadi, D. (1974) Electroencephalograms, learning and malnutrition: In: *Protein Calorie Malnutrition* (R. E. Olson, ed.) pp. 103–105, Academic Press, New York

Kempf, E., Graeilshamer, J., Mack, G. and Mandel, P. (1974) Correlation of behavioral differences in three strains of mice with differences in brain amines, *Nature London, 247* 483–485

Kobayashi, T., Inman, O., Buno, W. and Himwich, H. E. (1936) A multidisciplinary study of changes in mouse brain with age, *Recent Adv. Biol. Psychiat. 5*, 293–308

Leathwood, P., Bush, M., Berent, C. and Mauron, J. (1974) Effects of early malnutrition on Swiss white mice: avoidance learning after rearing in large litters, *Life Sci. 14*, 157–162

Luria, A. R. (1972) *L'Enfant Retardé Mental*, Privet, Paris

Malorni, W., Oliverio, A. and Bovet, D. (1975) Analyse génétique d'activité circadienne chez la souris, *C. R. Acad. Sci. Paris 281*, 1479–1484

Mandel, P., Ebel, A., Hermetet, J. C., Bovet, D. and Oliverio, A. (1973) Etudes des enzymes du système cholinergique chez les hybrides F_1 de souris se distinguant par leur aptitude au conditionnement, *C.R. Acad. Sci. Paris 276*, 395–398

Math, F., Desor, D. and Krafft, B. (1974) Ontogenèse de l'EEG chez le rat en semi-liberté, *Rev. Comp. Anim. 8*, 312–319

Oliverio, A., Castellano, C. and Messeri, P. (1972) A genetic analysis of avoidance, maze and wheel running behavior in the mouse, *J. Comp. Physiol. Psychol. 79*, 459–473

Oliverio, A., Castellano, C. and Renzi, P. (1975) Genotype or prenatal drug experience affect brain maturation in the mouse, *Brain Res. 90*, 357–360

Oliverio, A., Castellano, C. and Puglisi-Allegra, S. (1975) Effects of genetic and nutritional factors on post-natal reflex and behavioral development in the mouse, *Exp. Ag. Res. 1*, 41–56

Oliverio, A., Chouvet, G. and Valatx, J. L. Brain Res., in press

Papoušek, H. (1967) Conditioning during early postnatal development. In: *Behavior in Infancy and Early Childhood* (Y. Brackbill and J. Thompson, eds.) The Free Press, New York

Pryor, G. T., Schlesinger, K. and Calhoun, W. H. (1966) Differences in brain enzymes among five inbred strains of mice, *Life Sci. 5*, 2105–2111

Roderick, T., Wimer, R. E., Wimer, C. C. and Schwartzkrain, P. A. (1973) Genetic and phenotypic variations in weight of brain and spinal cord between inbred strains of mice, *Brain Res. 64*, 343–353

Rosenzweig, M. R. (1966) Environmental complexity, cerebral change and behavior, *Am. Psychol. 21*, 321–332

Scarr-Samapatek, S. and Williams, M. L. (1973) The effect of early stimulation on low-birth-weight infants, *Child Dev. 44*, 94–101

Scott, J. P. (1953) The process of primary socialization in canine and human infants, *Sociol. Res. Child Dev. Monogr. 28*, 1–34

Scott, J. P. (1958) *Animal Behavior*, University of Chicago Press, Chicago

Scrimshaw, N. W. and Gordon, J. E. (eds.) (1968) *Malnutrition, Learning and Behavior*, M.I.T. Press, Cambridge, Mass.

Sluckin, W. (1965) *Imprinting and Early Learning*, Aldine, Chicago

Smart, J. L., Dobbing, J., Adlard, B. P. F., Lynch, A. and Sands, J. (1973) Vulnerability of developing brain: relative effects of growth restriction during the fetal and suckling periods on behavior and brain composition of adult rats, *J. Nutr. 103*, 1327–1338

Staats, J. L. (1972) Standard nomenclature for inbred strains of mice, Fifth listing, *Cancer Res. 32*, 1609–1611

Stoch, M. B. and Smithe, P. M. (1967) The effect of undernutrition during infancy on subsequent brain growth and intellectual development. *S. Afr. Med. J. 41*, 1027–1029

Valatx, J. L., Bugat, R. and Jouvet, M. (1972) Genetic studies of sleep in mice, *Nature London 238*, 226–227

Valatx, J. L. and Bugat, R. (1974) Facteurs génétiques dans le déterminisme du cycle veille-sommeil chez la souris, *Brain Res. 69*, 315–330

Van Abeelen, J. H. F. (1966) Effects of genotype on mouse behavior, *Anim. Behav. 14*, 218–225

Verlay, R., Garma, L. and Scherrer, J. (1969) Aspects ontogénétiques des états de veille et de sommeil chez les mammifères, *Bord. Méd. 4*, 877–885

Volkmar, F. R. and Greenough, W. T. (1972) Rearing complexity effects branching of dendrites in the visual cortex of the rat, *Science 176*, 1445–1447

Wahlsten, D. (1974) A developmental time scale for postnatal changes in brain and behavior of mice, *Brain Res. 72*, 251–264

Werboff, J., Anderson, A. and Hagget, B. N. (1968) Handling of pregnant mice: gestational and postnatal behavioral effects, *Physiol. Behav. 3*, 35–39

White, B. L. (1971) *Human Infants. Experience and Psychological Development*, Harvard University Press, Harvard

Wimer, R. E., Wimer, C. C. and Roderick, T. H. (1969) Genetic variability in forebrain structures between inbred strains of mice, *Brain Res. 16*, 257–264

Yarrow, L. J., Rubenstein, J. L. and Pedersen, F. A. (1975) *Infant and Environment: Early Cognitive and Motivational Development*, Halsted Press, New York

Genetics, environment and intelligence, edited by A. Oliverio
© *Elsevier/North-Holland Biomedical Press, 1977*

Genetics of sleep and learning processes
Possible relationships

8

JEAN-LOUIS VALATX, GUY CHOUVET and
KUNIO KITAHAMA

Introduction

During the last twenty years, the phenomenology and the biochemical mechanisms of the sleep-waking cycle have been described in the majority of mammals (Allison and Van Twyver, 1974; Allison and Cicchetti, 1976; Zepelin and Rechtschaffen, 1974). In each species, results have been obtained in randomly selected individuals representing an average of a non-homogenous population. In spite of intra-species variability, significant changes have been shown between different species (Allison and Van Twyver, 1974; Allison et al., 1972; Allison and Cicchetti, 1976; Zepelin and Rechtschafeen, 1974). Are these differences due to environmental factors (Borbely et al., 1975; Fishman and Roffwarg, 1972; Mouret and Bobillier, 1971) or the result of alterations in the functioning of the central nervous system? What are the functions of sleep and specially the functions of paradoxical sleep (PS) during which the body is completely paralyzed and the brain very active?

To answer these questions, a genetic approach can be a good model. We have chosen the mouse (*Mus musculus*) because it is the best adapted species for this study. For fifty years, numerous pure inbred strains of mice have been isolated by selecting somatic traits such as coat color, plasmatic enzyme level, various neurological mutations, etc. (Green, 1966; Sidman et al., 1965). Now, the laboratory mouse can be used as a prototype in behavioral genetics to separate the different components of a given behavior and determine the respective influence of environmental and hereditary behavior (Bovet et al., 1969; Lindzey and Thiessen, 1970; Malorni et al., 1975; Oliverio, 1974; Thompson, 1956).

The observation of low intra-strain variability and a high inter-strain variability in sleep patterns allows a "genetic dissection" of the sleep-waking cycle in order to attempt to understand the neurophysiological mechanisms of the observed variations (Friedman, 1974; Valatx and Bugat, 1974; Valatx et al., 1972). The results we present here indicate that the origin of the sleep variations between strains might be located in utero at the moment of the formation of the nervous system.

For the role of sleep, numerous hypotheses have been reported (see Greenberg and Pearlman, 1974; Hartmann, 1973; Hennevin et Leconte, 1972; Jouvet, 1975). For several years, many experiments have been carried out to demonstrate the role of paradoxical sleep in memory processes; however, results are still contradictory (Kitahama et al., 1976; Leconte et al., 1973; Lucero, 1970; Smith et al., 1974; Vogel, 1975). Again, a genetic approach might answer this question. In other chapters of this book, evidence is brought showing that each strain of mice has its proper learning characteristics and differences between strains have a genetic support (Bovet et al., 1969; Kitahama and Valatx, 1976; Oliverio, 1974; Royce and Covington, 1960; Thompson, 1956). To study relationships between sleep and memory, we have chosen two strains which presented the same sleep cycle and different acquisition of an active avoidance conditioning (Kitahama and Valatx, 1976; Kitahama et al., 1976; Valatx and Bugat, 1974). The results we present here indicate that the basic mechanisms of memory storage are not related to sleep, but the so-called "reminiscence" (Bovet et al., 1969; Destrade et al., 1976) might be related to paradoxical sleep. Mechanisms underlying this phenomenon are still unknown.

Methodology

Animals

All the subjects were male, 12 week-old mice. For sleep study, four inbred strains (C57BR/cd/Orl (BR), C57BL/6/Orl (B6), BALB/c/Orl (C) and CBA/Orl: F_1 hybrids: BR.CBA and BR.C) were used. Then, to study the eventual linkage with the histocompatibility genes (H-loci) used as markers, recombinant inbred (RI) strains of Bailey were studied. Production of these strains is described by Bailey (1975): "The RI strains were derived from the cross of two unrelated and highly inbred progenitor strains, C and B6, and then maintained independently from the F_2 generation under full-sib mating regimen. This procedure progressively fixed the chance recombination of alleles as inbreeding proceeded and as full homozygoty was approached. The resulting battery of strains can be looked upon as a finite but replicable recombinant population". For each H-locus, a characteristic strain distribution pattern (SDP) is established by determining what allele (B6 or C) is present in these RI strains. Thus, we have studied parental strains: C57BL/6By, BALB/cBy, F_1 hybrids and seven RI strains: CXBD, CXBE, CXBG, CXBH, CXBL, CXBJ and CXBK. For the study, two inbred strains: C57BRcd/Orl (BR) and

C57BL/6/Orl, F_1 hybrids (BR × B6 and B6 × BR) and backcrosses (F_1 × BR and F_1 × B6) were used.

Sleep recordings

Under nembutal anesthesia, at least 8 mice from each strain were chronically implanted with cortical and muscular electrodes. Each mouse was put on synthetic litter in a glass jar with standard food and tap water ad libitum. Environmental conditions were constant as far as possible: ambient temperature was 24 ±1 °C, lighting schedule consisted of 12 h light (7.00–19.00) and 12 h darkness (19.00–7.00). After a 10-day period of adaptation to recording conditions, continuous recording (24 h per day) for a week was carried out. By visual analysis, all the recordings were scored by 30-sec epochs. Statistical analysis of RI data, variance and Student–Newman–Keuls multiple range test, was performed at the Jackson Laboratory, Bar Harbor, Maine, U.S.A. A statistical analysis described elsewhere (Kan et al., 1976; Valatx and Chouvet, 1975) was performed on sleep data from five consecutive days after the adaptation period in order to give an estimation of rhythmicity using sine wave harmonic decomposition.

Learning procedure

Apparatus: A Y-maze constructed from black plexiglas was used. After habituation to the apparatus, mice were trained to avoid an electric shock delivered through the grid floor of the maze by entering the correct lighted alley (see details in Kitahama and Valatx, 1976). Experimental procedure consisted of 5 or 10 sessions of 15 trials with a 30-sec inter-trial interval. Different intervals between sessions (0–24 h) were used to study the influence of sleep on the acquisition of this active avoidance response. In massed conditions (sessions without intervals) 4 or 8 consecutive sessions were scheduled.

Results

Sleep duration

Sleep-waking cycle in inbred strains and F_1 hybrids

Results are shown in Table I and can be summarized as follows: in inbred strains, (1) total, night and day sleep durations significantly differed from strain to strain; (2) slow-wave sleep (SWS) duration varied independently from paradoxical sleep (PS) duration; (3) strains could be classified in three groups according to their PS duration: the two C57 strains had the highest amount of PS, BALB/c the lowest and CBA the intermediate one. Considering slow-wave sleep duration, it was possible to do another classification. (4) Day-night variations were another parameter to separate strains. C57 strains had the greatest difference while BALB/c had no significant

Table I Sleep patterns in three inbred strains CBA, C57BR (BR) and BALB/C (C), F_1 hybrids between CBA and BR (CBA × BR and BR × CBA) and between BR and C (BR × C and C × BR) (duration in min. ±S. E. M.)

	Slow-wave sleep duration			Paradoxical sleep duration			PS/SWS		
	24 h	Night	Day	24 h	Night	Day	24 h	Night	Day
CBA	746 ± 7.10	322 ± 5.14	424 ± 3.75	66.5 ± 1.62	24.0 ± 0.77	42.5 ± 1.24	8.91	7.47	10.03
CBA × BR F_1	741 ± 10.7	331 ± 2.25	410 ± 6.97	65.0 ± 2.10	26.5 ± 1.40	38.5 ± 1.84	8.77	8.00	9.39
BR × CBA F_1	754 ± 11.9	316 ± 9.76	438 ± 6.76	65.5 ± 2.26	23.0 ± 1.56	42.5 ± 2.01	8.68	7.27	9.70
BR	639 ± 7.70	180 ± 8.72	459 ± 3.20	73.0 ± 2.50	19.0 ± 1.35	54.0 ± 1.49	11.42	10.55	11.76
BR × C F_1	692 ± 8.65	277 ± 3.50	415 ± 3.60	67.0 ± 2.00	20.0 ± 1.20	47.0 ± 1.40	9.68	7.22	11.32
C × BR F_1	735 ± 7.42	342 ± 4.34	393 ± 3.32	80.0 ± 2.50	36.0 ± 1.30	44.0 ± 1.20	10.88	10.52	11.19
C	723 ± 9.34	318 ± 6.49	405 ± 8.74	54.0 ±1.80	31.0 ± 1.50	23.0 ± 1.15	7.46	9.74	5.67

Note that the sleep patterns of the reciprocal hybrids between BR and CBA are identical and not different from CBA strain. In hybrids between C and BR mice, 24-h slow wave sleep (SWS) duration is not different from that of C mice and 24 h paradoxical sleep (PS) duration is not different from that of BR mice. For day-night differences, maternal effects are evident in hybrids between BR and C mice.

difference between day and night sleep duration.

In F_1 hybrids, results differed according to crossings. In CBA $\times$ BR hybrids, animals from reciprocal crosses (CBA $\times$ BR and BR $\times$ CBA) are identical for all the sleep parameters and not significantly different from CBA strain. In C $\times$ BR hybrids, reciprocal crosses (C $\times$ BR and BR $\times$ C) were not statistically different for total PS and SWS durations. However, PS duration was not different from BR strain while SWS duration was not different from C strain. For day-night differences, maternal effects seemed to be important in C $\times$ BR hybrids while in CBA $\times$ BR hybrids they were not apparent (see Table I, Fig. 1).

Sleep waking cycle in recombinant inbred strains

Statistical analysis allowed to rank order the RI strains with regard to parental strains and F_1 hybrids. We observed the most reliable differences for PS durations. This analysis allowed us to classify each RI strain as not different from one or another parental strain. Thus, a strain distribution pattern (SDP) could be established for total and night paradoxical sleep durations. Comparison with H-loci SDP indicated that total and night paradoxical sleep durations were probably linked to H-2 locus and non H-2 locus (H-37, H-38) respectively (Table II).

Circadian rhythm of sleep

Sleep rhythmicity of mice from two very different strains (C57BR and BALB/c) and their F_1 hybrids has been studied.

Slow-wave sleep. In both strains, the best fitting sine wave had a 24-h period but the maximum of sleep was earlier in C mice (8.70 a.m.) than in BR mice (11.80 a.m.). The daily mean level of hourly duration was slightly lower in BR strain (28 min) than in C strain (31 min). The amplitude of the variations around the mean level was higher in BR mice ($\pm$ 15.50 min) than in C mice ($\pm$ 9.00 min). In the C strain, the small difference between day and night durations can be explained by the fact that SWS duration progressively increased through the night until 8.70 a.m. then decreased during the light period while in BR strain, the sleep duration dramatically increased at the end of the night and decreased only at the end of the light period.

F_1 hybrids. In both reciprocal crosses, the amplitude of the variations around the mean level looked like to that of C mice. In BR $\times$ C hybrids, the maximum of sleep was not different from BR parental mice while in C $\times$ BR hybrids it was not different from C parental mice (Fig. 1).

Paradoxical sleep. Results are quite similar to those of SWS: the amplitude of the variations around the mean level was twice as high in the BR strain than in the C strain, but in the latter the maximum of PS duration was during the darkness period (4.54 a.m.) (Fig. 2).

Relationship between sleep and learning

The effects of sleep on the acquisition of an active avoidance response have been studied with or without intervals between conditioning sessions.

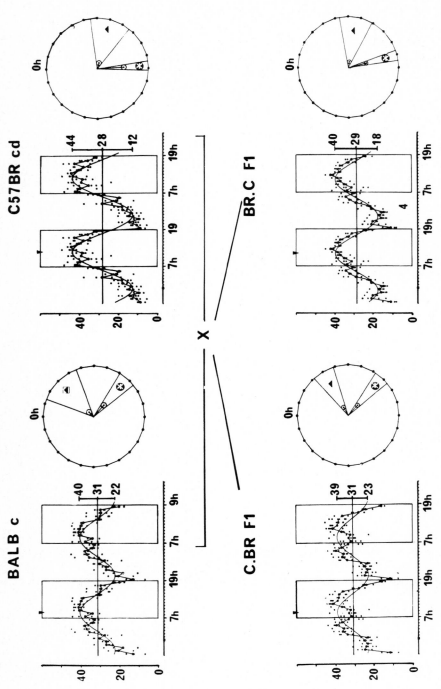

Fig. 1 Daily variations of the slow wave sleep (SWS) duration in BALB/c and C57BRcd mice and their F₁ hybrids. For each strain:
(1) the orthogonal plot (left) shows the time course of the hourly mean duration computed from 40 days of continuous recordings
(8 mice × 5 days). The best fitting sine curve (only the fundamental component $T = 24$ h) is superimposed on experimental data.
The daily mean level of hourly SWS duration (min) is indicated on the right with the extreme values of the variations around the mean
level. (2) the polar plot (right) indicates for each significant harmonic component the amplitude (A) in min, the phase (P) in h and
their confidence intervals ($P = 0.95$) (see technical details in Kan et al., 1977). White stars indicate fundamental ($T = 24$ h) component and black triangles the first harmonic ($T = 12$ h) component. Light periods are indicated by rectangles (07.00–19.00).

Table II   Strain Distribution Pattern (S.D.P.) of 24-h paradoxical sleep (PS) duration and night PS duration in seven recombinant inbred (RI) strains of mice compared to the SDP of histocompatibility genes (H–2, H–37, H–38)

RI strains	CXBD	CXBE	CXBG	CXBH	CXBI	CXBJ	CXBK
24-h PS duration (min ± S.E.M.)	66.8 ± 1.7	70.6 ± 1.7	70.3 ± 1.3	50.7 ± 1.4	77.2 ± 1.8	74.7 ± 2.5	87.0 ± 1.9
SDP	( )	B6	B6	C	B6	B6	B6
H–2	B6	B6	B6	C	B6	B6	B6
Night PS duration (min ± S.E.M.)	22.0 ± 1.0	30.0 ± 0.09	37.0 ± 1.4	19.2 ± 1.2	39.3 ± 1.3	12.3 ± 1.5	37.4 ± 1.7
SDP	B6	C	C	B6	C	B6	C
H–37	B6	C	C	B6	C	B6	C
H–38	B6	C	C	C	C	B6	C

Brackets indicate intermediate values between B6 and C duration. For night PS duration, there are two possibilities of linkage (H–37 and H–38). The study of specific congenic lines will allow determination of the right linkage.

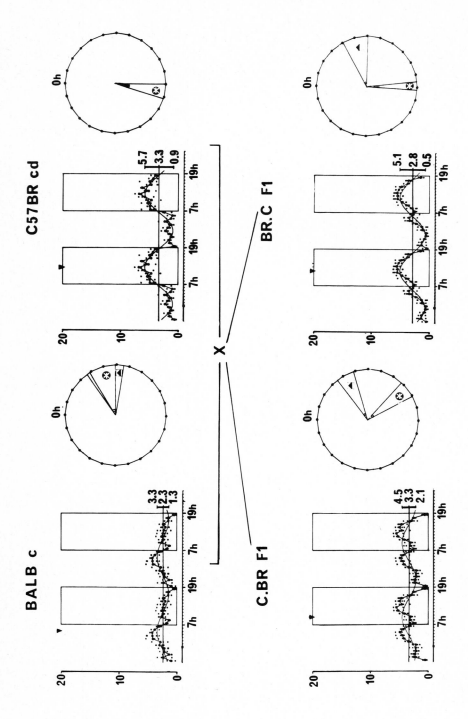

Fig 2 Daily variations of the paradoxical sleep (PS) duration in BALB/c and C57BR/cd mice and their F₁ hybrids. Same legend as in Fig. 1.

24-h intervals

In this condition, the acquisition was quite different in BR and B6 mice: at the beginning of the second and third sessions, BR performance was respectively 30 and 20% higher than in the previous session while B6 performance was the same (2nd session) or slightly higher (3rd session: 5–10%) (Fig. 3).

Without intervals

In these conditions (eight consecutive sessions) BR and B6 mice presented approximately the same acquisition pattern: a slow increase in performance.

Mixed conditions (4 consecutive sessions plus 23-h interval)

The acquisition in mixed conditions in BR and B6 mice was quite different: B6 mice exhibited the same low learning pattern as in the two previous conditions, and BR mice presented a slow learning during the four consecutive sessions on the first day, while at the beginning of the second day, session performance was 35% higher than on the first day (Fig. 3).

Discussion

Two points will be discussed, (i) origin of inter-strain sleep differences, (ii) relationships between sleep and learning processes.

Origin of inter-strain sleep differences

These results from inbred and recombinant strains give a new insight into sleep physiology. The first finding is the existence and stability of the differences in sleep

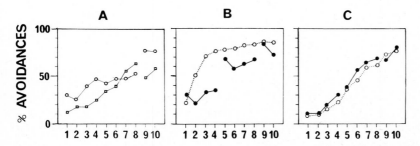

Fig. 3 Schematic representation of the acquisition of an active avoidance response in C57BR and C57BL/6 mice. (A) massed sessions (8 consecutive sessions without intervals) in C57BR and C57BL/6; (B) in C57BR and (C) in C57BL/6, one-daily session (24-h intervals, O----O) and mixed conditions (●—●) four daily sessions without intervals associated with 24-h intervals. On the ordinate, percentage of conditioned responses. Note in C57BR mice the jump in performance (≥25%) between the two first sessions in the 24-h interval conditions (B) and the slow increase in performance in massed conditions (A). Note in C57BL/6 mice the same learning curve whatever the experimental conditions, with or without sleep.

duration between strains of mice. The second one is that these differences are transmissible according to the Mendelian laws of heredity. Thus, sleep behavior can be considered as a complex somatic trait which may be subdivided into several units: duration of each stage of sleep, circadian rhythms and also phasic activity of paradoxical sleep. Indeed, Cespuglio et al. (1975) showed that the total number of eye movements per min of PS and their patterns of occurrence were different from strain to strain and had a hereditary component. For circadian rhythms in BR mice, they seem to be fixed whatever the external conditions (continuous light or darkness) while in C mice, they disappear under these conditions (Malorni et al., 1975).

The strain distribution pattern of recombinant inbred strains indicated that the total PS duration might be linked to H-2 locus, the major histocompatibility complex of the mouse (Bach and Van Rood, 1976). Further studies with specific congenic lines will allow us to confirm or not this linkage. That is an important point because H-2 locus has been located on chromosome 17 next to the T-locus region, the genes of which specify cell surface structure on embryos. Several recessive mutations at the T-locus are known to provoke selective defects in the neural tube during embryonic development (Bennett, 1975). The observed differences in sleep patterns could be the consequence of some discrete alterations of some parts of the brain (Ross et al., 1976). Knowing nervous structures supposed to be related to sleep mechanisms and using mice bearing mutations at the T–H2 complex, it will be possible to refine genetic dissection and go further into the understanding of biological mechanisms controlling this complex behavior.

Relationships between sleep and learning

Several authors have shown that the paradoxical sleep duration increased with or without delay after the first learning sessions (Fishbein et al., 1974; Leconte et al., 1973; Lucero, 1970; Smith et al., 1974). After sleep deprivation, animals presented a decay in their performance (Greenberg and Pearlman, 1974; Kitahama et al., 1976; Leconte et al., 1973; Vogel, 1975). With our genetic model, it has been possible to refine the genetic dissection of the active avoidance learning. The two C57 (BR and B6) mice present the same sleep patterns (Valatx and Bugat, 1974), the same locomotor and exploratory activity (Kitahama et al., 1976; Malorni et al., 1975) and the same final performance but differ in their speed of acquisition of this conditioning.

The first finding is that without sleep (massed sessions) both strains are able to learn and reach their final performance. Thus, basic storage processes characterized by a slow continuous integration of information are not disturbed by the absence of sleep. This finding confirms the inefficiency of sleep deprivation on acquisition and retention claimed by several authors (see references in Vogel, 1975).

However, in BR mice performance was improved in the 24-h interval conditions. This jump in performance out of any training is called "reminiscence" (Bovet et al., 1969; Destrade et al., 1976). By using a 3-h interval procedure, we have been able to show that reminiscence appeared between 6 and 9 h after the first session (Kitahama and Valatx, 1976). It is interesting to note that this delay is similar to that observed in the delayed augmentation of PS duration after the two first sessions (Fishbein et al., 1974; Smith et al., 1974). After specific PS deprivation by swimming pool technique or pharmacological agents, the reminiscence disappeared proportionally to the sleep deprivation duration (Kitahama et al., 1976). This finding is in agreement with results from many authors who showed the efficiency of PS deprivation on the acquisition of a conditioned response (see references in Greenberg and Pearlman, 1974 and Vogel, 1975).

Thus, our findings allow separate memory storage processing in two parts: a slow one which does not require sleep and a fast one (reminiscence) representing a fast integration of the already encoded information which would take place during the paradoxical sleep. Moreover, this reminiscence observed in BR mice for an active avoidance conditioning has been noted in C mice and not in BR mice for a food–reward conditioning (Destrade et al., 1976; Jaffard et al., 1976). Therefore, each type of learning might have a specific fast integration process.

Considering the phylogeny of the paradoxical sleep (appearance in birds and full development in mammals) (Allison and Van Twiver, 1974), it is interesting to generalize this concept of its role in the fast integration of information. This state of sleep appeared and developed at the same time as the development of the neocortex which allows integration of a great amount of information. Each type of learning necessitates the acquisition and the integration of different motor automatisms which have different and specific neuronal supports. The paradoxical sleep would represent the best moment to integrate the already encoded information in the neuronal circuitry involved in its long term storage. Why and what would be the functional linkage between PS and hippocampus supposedly involved in the processing of new information? (Destrade et al., 1976; Jaffard et al., 1976; Zornetzer et al., 1976).

Firstly, by electrical stimulation of the dorsal pontine region, some authors have shown that it was possible to elicit specific complex behaviors such as eating, drinking, fear, attack as by hypothalamic stimulation (Micco, 1974; Panksepp, 1971; Waldbillig, 1975). Secondly, the nervous structures involved in the PS regulation have been located in this pontine region (Jouvet, 1972; Moruzzi, 1972) and finally direct connections between the hippocampus and the dorsal pons have recently been demonstrated (Pickel et al., 1974; Segal and Landis, 1974; Bobillier, personal communication).

Thus, during PS, brain can activate the specific neuronal circuit of a given motor automatism without disturbing the subject which is completely paralyzed by an active inhibition from the locus coeruleus upon the spinal motoneurons (see references in Moruzzi, 1972). The integration of new information processed in the hippocampus would be quickly done during the paradoxical sleep by its distribution to the entire circuit at the same time. The lack of this fast integration in some strains of mice for a given learning task might be due to some discrete alterations in the connections between the pontine region and the hippocampus. For instance, B6 mice would not have all the connections between the hippocampus and the pontine neurons triggering the motor automatisms for an avoidance behavior, while in BR mice they would be fully functional. These connections might also have a role in the regulation of the sleep duration, which would explain the increase of the PS duration after learning sessions in BR mice presenting a fast acquisition while B6 mice have no PS variations and are insensitive to sleep deprivation. These eventual connective alterations might have their origin in utero at the moment of the formation of the central nervous system. The linkages of the paradoxical sleep and learning abilities to the histocompatibility systems (Oliverio, 1974) would be in favour of this hypothesis.

Conclusion

The inbred strains of mice provide good models to study sleep and learning behavior. The results we have presented indicate that inter-strain differences for sleep duration and learning processes have a genetically determined support. Secondly, the role of the paradoxical sleep in memory processing is reevaluated: PS seems not to be related to basic storage processing of new information, but rather necessary for a fast integration, i.e. a fast modification of motor automatisms underlying a given behavior to allow better adaptation to the environment. In the adult, paradoxical sleep would have an adaptative role as proposed by Greenberg and Pearlman (1974).

Literature cited

Allison, T. and Van Twiver, H. (1974) The evolution of sleep, *Nat. Hist. 79*, 169

Allison, T., Van Twiver, H. and Goff, W. R. (1972) Electrophysiological studies of the echidna, tachyglossus aculeatus. I. Waking and sleep, *Arch. Ital. Biol. 110*, 145

Allison, T. and Cicchetti, D. V. (1976) Sleep in mammals: ecological and constitutional correlates, *Science 194*, 732

Bach, F. H. and Van Rood, J. J. (1976) The major histocompatibility complex. Genetics and biology, *N. Engl. J. Med., 295*, 806

Bailey, D. W. (1975) Genetics of histocompatibility in mice. I. New loci and congenic lines, *Immunogenetics 2*, 249

Bennett, D. (1975) The T-locus of the mouse, *Cell 6*, 441

Borbely, A. A., Huston, J. P. and Waser, P. T. (1975) Control of sleep states in the rat by short light dark cycles, *Brain Res. 95*, 89

Bovet, D. Bovet-Nitti, F. and Oliverio, A. (1969) Genetics aspects of learning and memory in mice, *Science 163*, 139

Cespuglio, R., Musolino, R., Debilly, G., Jouvet, M. et Valatx J. L. (1975) Organisation différente des mouvements oculaires rapides du sommeil paradoxal chez deux souches de souris, *C.R. Acad. Sci. Paris 280*, 2681

Destrade, C., Jaffard, R., Deminière, J. M. et Cardo, B. (1976) Effets de la stimulation de l'hippocampe sur la réminiscence chez deux lignées de souris, *Physiol. Behav. 16*, 237

Fishbein, W., Kastaniotis, C. and Chattman, D. (1974) Paradoxical sleep prolonged augmentation following learning, *Brain Res. 79*, 61

Fishman, R. and Roffwarg, H. P. (1972) REM sleep inhibition in the albino rat, *Exp. Neurol. 36*, 106

Friedman, J. K. (1974) A diallel analysis of the genetic underpinnings of mouse sleep, *Physiol. Behav. 12*, 169

Green, E. L. (1966) *Biology of the Laboratory Mouse*, 2nd edn., McGraw-Hill, New York

Greenberg, R. and Pearlman, C. (1974) Cutting the REM nerve: an approach to the adaptative role of REM sleep, *Perspect. Biol. Med. 17*, 513

Hartman, E. L. (1973) *The Function of Sleep*, Yale University Press, New Haven, Connecticut

Hennevin, E. and Leconte, P. (1972) La fonction du sommeil paradoxal: faits et hypothèses, *Année Psychol. 2*, 489

Jaffard, R. Ebel, A., Destrade, C., Durkin, T., Mandel, P. and Cardo, B. (1976) Effects of hippocampal electrical stimulation on long term memory and on cholinergic mechanisms in three inbred strains of mice, *Brain Res.*, in the press

Jouvet, M., (1972) The role of monoamine and acetylcholine containing neurons in the regulation of the sleep-waking cycle, *Ergebn. Physiol. 64*, 165

Jouvet, M., (1975) The function of dreaming: a neurophysiological point of view. In: *Handbook of Psychobiology*, p. 499, Academic Press, New York

Kan, J. P., Chouvet, G., Hery, F., Debilly, G., Mermet, A. and Pujol, J. F. (1977) Daily variations of tryptophan-5-hydroxylase in the raphe nuclei and the striatum of the rat brain, *Brain Res. 123*, 125

Kitahama, K. and Valatx, J. L. (1976) Modalités d'apprentissage d'un labyrinthe chez les souris C57BR, C57BL/6 et BALB/c, *Physiol. Behav. 16*, 9

Kitahama, K., Valatx, J. L. and Jouvet, M. (1976) Apprentissage d'un labyrinthe en Y chez deux souches de souris. Effets de la privation instrumentale et pharmacologique du sommeil, *Brain Res. 108*, 75

Leconte, P., Hennevin, E. and Bloch, V. (1973) Analyse des effets d'un apprentissage et de son niveau d'acquisition sur le sommeil paradoxal consécutif, *Brain Res. 49*, 367

Lindzey, G. and Thiessen, D. D. (1970) Contributions to behavior-genetic analysis. The mouse as a prototype, Appleton-Century-Crofts, New York

Lucero, M. (1970) Lengthening of REM sleep duration consecutive to learning in the rat, *Brain Res. 20*, 319

Malorni, W., Oliverio, A. et Bovet, D. (1975) Analyse génétique du rythme d'activité circadien chez la souris, *C.R. Acad. Sci. Paris 281*, 1479

Micco, D. J. (1974) Complex behaviors elicited by stimulation of the dorsal pontine tegmentum in rats, *Brain Res. 75*, 172

Moruzzi, G. (1972) The sleep-waking cycle, *Ergebn. Physiol. 64*, 2

Mouret, J. and Bobillier, P. (1971) Diurnal rhythms of sleep in the rat: augmentation of paradoxical sleep following alterations of the feeding schedule, *Int. J. Neurosci. 2*, 265

Oliverio, A. (1974) Genetic and biochemical analysis of behavior in mice. In: *Progress in Neurobiology* (G. A. Kerkut and J. W. Phyllis, eds.) p. 193, Vol. 3, Pergamon Press, Oxford

Panksepp, J. (1971) Aggression elicited by electrical stimulation of the hypothalamus in albino rats, *Physiol. Behav. 6*, 321

Pickel, V., Segal, M. and Bloom, F. E. (1974) A radioautographic study of the efferent pathways of the nucleus locus coeruleus, *J. Comp. Neurol. 155*, 15

Ross, R. A. Judd, A. B., Pickel, V. M., Joh, T. H. and Reis, D. J. (1976) Strain-dependent variations in number of midbrain dopaminergic neurons, *Nature 264*, 654

Royce, J. R. and Covington, M. (1960) Genetic differences in the avoidance conditioning in mice, *J. Comp. Physiol. Psychol. 53*, 197

Segal, M. and Landis, S. (1974) Afferents to the hippocampus of the rat studied with the method of retrograde transport of horseradish peroxidase, *Brain Res. 78*, 1

Sidman, R. L., Green, M. C. and Appel, S. M. (1965) Catalog of the neurological mutants of the mouse, Harvard University Press

Smith, C. T., Kitahama, K., Valatx, J. L. and Jouvet, M., (1974) Increased paradoxical sleep in mice during acquisition of a shock avoidance task, *Brain Res. 77*, 221

Thompson, W. R. (1956) The inheritance of behavior activity differences in five inbred mouse strains, *J. Hered. 47*, 147

Valatx, J. L. and Bugat, R. (1974) Facteurs génétiques dans le déterminisme du cycle veille-sommeil chez la souris, *Brain Res. 69*, 315

Valatx, J. L., Bugat, R. and Jouvet, M. (1972) Genetic study of sleep in mice, *Nature 238*, 226

Valatx, J. L. and Chouvet, G., (1975) Genetics of the sleep-waking cycle, In: *Sleep, 1974*, 2nd European Congress Sleep Research, Rome 1974, p. 19, Karger, Basel

Vogel, G., (1975) A review of REM sleep deprivation, *Arch. Gen. Psychiat. 32*, 749

Waldbillig, R. J. (1975) Attack, eating, drinking and gnawing elicited by electrical stimulation of rat mesencephalon and pons, *J. Comp. Physiol. Psychol. 89*, 200

Zepelin, H. and Rechtshaffen, A. (1974) Mammalian sleep, longevity and energy metabolism, *Brain Behav. Evol. 10*, 425

Zornetzer, S. F., Boast, C. and Hamrick, M. (1973) Neuroanatomic localization and memory processing in mice: the role of the dentate gyrus of the hippocampus, *Physiol. Behav. 8*, 507

Environmental influences and learning in animals

PART III

Genetics, environment and intelligence, edited by A. Oliverio
© *Elsevier/North-Holland Biomedical Press, 1977*

Interactional effects in early experience research*   9

VICTOR H. DENENBERG

Introduction

The development of a new research area within the scientific disciplines of biology or behavior usually follows a certain predictable pattern. Generally this starts with the report of some exciting new finding that expands our fund of scientific knowledge and which suggest a new direction for research. Then there will be a series of empirical research studies which confirm and extend the original findings, and which incorporate new variables into the investigation. This research is primarily at the empirical level with only a very general theoretical basis for guidance. Eventually, however, sufficient information is gathered to permit the integration of the information into a more specific theoretical formulation which works for a while. However, as researchers get to know more about the phenomena they are studying and the variables which influence them, they increase the complexity of their research designs, and incorporate procedures and information from related fields. When this happens, it is generally found that the theoretical formulations developed previously are not sufficient to account for the new data. Furthermore, it may also be found that certain

*The preparation of this paper was supported, in part, by Research Grant HD-08195 from the National Insitute of Child Health and Human Development, NIH.

fundamental assumptions which are inherent in one's thinking and interpretations of research findings no longer seem to be valid. This leads to an intellectual plateau and a period of confusion as researchers try to find ways of incorporating the new information into current theoretical interpretations. The first attempt is usually to try to expand the original theoretical formulation to include the new findings. If that fails, however, then it is necessary to develop a different form of theoretical system. An outstanding example of this is the shift from a Newtonian mechanics view of the world to an Einsteinian relativistic view of the universe.

We can ask where the research field of early experience is with respect to the developmental landmarks noted above. The field is approximately 25 years old if measured in terms of the density of publications in the literature, although one can point to several important research papers which were published much earlier than that (Denenberg, 1972). The field has generated an extensive set of research findings (see reviews in Denenberg, 1969; Newton and Levine, 1968; and in many of the chapters of this book). There have also been a number of theoretical papers concerning possible mechanisms involved in early experience research, including the concepts of critical periods in development, the effects of stimulus intensity during early life upon emotionality, the organizational effects of neonatal hormones upon sexual and emotional behavior, and the role of maternal characteristics (Denenberg, 1964; Denenberg and Zarrow, 1971; Levine, 1969; Levine and Mullins, 1966; Russell, 1971; Scott, 1962).

Each of these theoretical papers focused upon a rather narrow segment of the early experience field and each was able to account for a certain set of the findings. However, as new empirical information was added to the literature, we found that even within their limited scopes none of the theoretical formulations was able to account for the growing body of research data. And certainly there was no theoretical formulation which was able to integrate the many diverse findings within this rather broad field.

I think that we are now at that plateau referred to earlier where we have more replicable findings than we can incorporate within our current theoretical notions, but we have not been able to advance to another theoretical level which will permit us to incorporate the diverse findings within some meaningful organizational framework. I think a major reason for the current state of affairs is that a simplifying assumption which we made has not held up. This assumption is that the experimental variables that we manipulated during the early life histories of the animals would have direct consequences upon their later behavioral and biological activities. In essence, this is an assumption of direct causation as a function of our intervention, and is a conventional kind of assumption which any researcher in any field makes when starting work*. The assumption seemed to be valid during the initial research years because we had found two very robust variables which gave us predictable results under a

---

* For those familiar with the statistical procedure of the analysis of variance, this assumption translates itself into a significant main effect.

wide variety of circumstances. These variables involved handling and free environment experience. These variables will be discussed in more detail later in this chapter. For now it is only important to note that the experimental manipulation of these variables in early life led to consistent behavioral and biological differences in adulthood. However, as we have moved forward in our research studies, we found that other variables did not behave in this straightforward manner and, indeed, both handling and free environment experience could also show complex rather than simple and direct effects.

What we have found in more than two decades of research is that many of the manipulations that we use in early experience research have effects which are dependent, in part, upon other variables and parameters in our research design. Thus, for example, whether the presence or absence of variable A in early life has a measurable effect upon some criterion score in adulthood is partially dependent upon the levels of variables B and C in the experimental design, as well as upon the parameters held constant for experimental convenience. When we say that the effects of a particular variable are partially dependent upon levels of other variables in the experiment as well as upon the values of parameters held constant, this means that the variables interact among themselves, and this interaction may mask or eliminate any evidence of a direct effect of an experimental variable. When the major variables that one works with are found not to have a direct impact upon some later end-point, but instead, the impact is modified (including being reversed) as a function of other variables in the experiment, it becomes very difficult, if not impossible, to use simple concepts of cause and effect to account for one's data and to develop theoretical formulations. Instead, one has to go to a complex theoretical system, such as general systems theory, in order to find an appropriate model for integrating the information available (Bertalanffy, 1969; Weiss, 1969). In studying behavioral development, I believe we need to use a general systems theory approach rather than causation theory, and I have discussed this at greater length in another paper (Denenberg, 1977).

Even though we do not have an adequate theoretical framework, we do have an exceptionally firm foundation of empirical findings in the field of early experience, and from those empirical findings have emerged a number of principles which will have to be incorporated within any theoretical system. The most basic of these principles is that many of the effects of early experience variables will express themselves in an interactive rather than a direct linear manner when a variety of behavioral and biological processes are measured in adulthood. There are a considerable number of very important ramifications which derive from this principle, and the remainder of this chapter will be devoted to this topic. I shall first discuss and illustrate the interactional principle with data involving differing genetic strains in combination with differing experiential variables in early life. I shall then give some illustrations based upon differing programs of life history (or differing schedules of experience). The objective is to show that the interactional principle is true both at the level of genetics and early experience as well as within an ontogenetic framework. I shall then conclude with some comments on the implications of the interactional principle for theoretical formulations concerning the effects of early experience and on some applied implications.

Since the purpose of this discussion is to illustrate a principle I will not review the literature but, instead, will select a few examples which are typical of the findings obtained in the literature.

The interactive effects of genetic variables with early experience variables

Problem-solving in the rat

A number of years ago, Tryon (1940) found that one could selectively breed for maze-bright and maze-dull rats. Since then, other researchers have confirmed this finding and have shown that rats which perform better in maze units will also perform better in several other kinds of learning apparatus. Cooper and Zubek (1958) used this knowledge of the genetic difference in maze performance as the basis for a very important question. They set up an experiment to determine whether the nature of the environment within which rats were reared after weaning would have any effect upon their ability to solve maze problems, and they also wanted to find out whether the environmental conditions would equally affect the two genetic strains. The subjects were rats from the bright and dull strains kept at McGill University. At the time of weaning the animals were placed into one of three environments. Control animals were placed into a normal laboratory environment. Restricted animals were placed singly into a bare cage except for a food box and water pan. Enriched animals were placed into a complex environment (called a free environment) which contained ramps, mirrors, swings, polished balls, marbles, barriers, slides, tunnels, bells, teeter-totters, and spring boards, in addition to food boxes and water pans. Previous research had shown that the procedures for restricting or enriching the early experiences of rats were sufficient to lower or improve their performance on a problem-solving task, but no one had asked the question as to what effect these experiences would have upon animals specifically selected for good and poor performance in maze learning. The animals were kept in the environments from weaning at 25 days until they were 65 days old, when they were given a series of tests on an apparatus called the Hebb-Williams problem-solving maze. Performance is scored in terms of the number of errors that an animal makes on a maze problem, and each animal is tested on 12 different problems. The results of the study are shown in Table I.

The first thing to note is that when the genetically different groups are reared under standard laboratory conditions (i.e., the normal environment) the expected difference in maze performance was obtained: the maze-dull animals made an average of 164 errors over the 12 problems while the maze-bright animals made 117 errors. However, note what happens when the two different strains of rats are reared in either

Table I   Mean number of errors on the Hebb-Williams maze of genetically maze-bright and maze-dull rats reared in normal, enriched, or restricted environments after weaning (from Cooper and Zubek, 1958)

Genetics	Normal environment	Enriched environment	Restricted environment
Maze-bright	117.0	111.2	169.7
Maze-dull	164.0	119.7	169.5

enriched or restricted environments. When reared in the enriched environment, both groups make essentially the same number of errors, and these are not different from the number of errors which the genetically maze-bright rats made when reared in the normal environment. The opposite side of the coin is seen with the animals in the restricted environment: the two groups here made almost identical errors, and their scores are equally as poor as those of the genetically maze-dull rats reared in the normal environment.

The animals used in this study had gone through 13 generations of genetic selection for maze-brightness and maze-dullness. We see, however, that whether this genetic difference expresses itself is a function of the environment within which the animals are reared. Under normal rearing conditions the difference is found; under enriched conditions the genetically poor animals do as well as any group in the experiment; and under the restricted conditions the genetically bright animals do as poorly as any group in the experiment. Therefore, we conclude from this experiment that the genetic backgrounds of the animals interact with the environmental conditions of rearing to jointly determine their problem-solving performance.

Activity and aggression in the mouse

A very different approach to the study of interaction between genetic variables and early experience conditions was that developed by Denenberg, Hudgens, and Zarrow (1964). They fostered newborn mice to lactating rat mothers who had pups approximately the same age as the mice. Even though the rat is a different species than the mouse, they are both rodents, and there is sufficient similarity between the two so that the rat mother can successfully rear mouse young. The importance of this procedure was that it enabled the researchers to separate experimentally the usual confounding between genetic, prenatal and postnatal environments which is present in all naturalistic situations and in the great majority of laboratory studies as well. Denenberg and his associates have done a lengthy number of experiments using this basic preparation. In a number of studies, mice had been reared by lactating rat mothers, in some instances with rat peers present and in other instances only with mouse peers present. In other studies, experimental mice have been reared by a mouse mother; but in the same cage was a non-lactating adult rat who acted maternally and took over the majority of the maternal caretaking activities of the mouse pups, while the lactating mouse mother was the source of food for her young. (See Denenberg (1970b) for a review of this series of experiments.) In the following summary, the data of all the studies are combined. All the experimental conditions are pooled and designated as an "experimental group" of mice which were either reared by a rat mother or else by a mouse mother in the presence of a non-lactating but maternal female rat. The "control group" refers to mice reared by a mouse mother in the presence of mouse peers both preweaning and postweaning.

For purposes of this discussion we shall only refer to two of the endpoints measured: activity and fighting. Activity was measured by placing the mouse into an open field and recording the number of squares entered in a 3 min trial. Fighting was measured by taking two adult male mice from their home cages and placing them into separate halves of a box divided by a removable guillotine door. Wood shavings were on the floor and each compartment was covered by a top containing food and water supplies. The mice remained in their separate compartments for several days. After this, a test was begun by removing the partition between the compartments, thus allowing the animals to interact with each other. The test continued for 6 min unless a fight occurred, in which case the session was terminated. This procedure was continued for seven days, and the presence or absence of fighting was recorded for each daily session.

Two strains of mice were used in this series of experiments. One strain was the C57BL/10J inbreed strain obtained from the Jackson Laboratory, and the other was the Purdue Rockland Swiss-Albino mouse. The latter animals had been randomly bred within our closed colony for many generations, but we deliberately avoided brother-sister breeding.

The results of these experiments, in a very compact form, are summarized in Table II. The activity measure is based upon number of squares entered, while the fighting measure is the percentage of each pair of animals which fought at least once in our fighting box test situation.

We found, overall, that being reared by a rat mother or in the presence of a non-lactating but maternal adult female rat, decreased the activity scores in the open-field equally for both mouse strains (in both strains the reduction in activity

Table II Effects upon two mouse strains of being reared by a rat mother or in the presence of a non-lactating but maternal female rat upon open-field activity and fighting (summarized from Denenberg, 1970b)

Endpoint	Strain of mouse	Control group*	Experimental group**
Activity in open-field	C57BL/10J	180.10 squares	139.23 squares
	Swiss-Albino	161.80 squares	125.07 squares
Incidence of fighting	C57BL/10J	44.8%	8.5%
	Swiss-Albino	80.0%	83.3%

 * Reared by mouse mother in the presence of mouse peers pre- and postweaning.
** Reared by rat mother or by mouse mother in the presence of a non-lactating but maternal female rat.

was 22.7%). This kind of invariance was not found when we look at the fighting data. Here the incidence of fighting for the C57BL/10J dropped from a control value of 44.8% to 8.5% for experimental animals, while the equivalent values for the Swiss-Albino mouse was 80.0% and 83.3%. Thus, the experimental treatment was not able to influence the fighting scores of the Swiss Albino, though they markedly reduced the scores of the C57BL/10J. In another study, Denenberg, Paschke, and Zarrow (1973) obtained the F_1 reciprocal crosses between these two strains, and reared one group with mice mothers under control conditions while experimental animals were reared by rat mothers. Fighting percentages between 50–59% were obtained among the four groups. These differences were not significant, thus suggesting that dominant genes strongly influence this behavior.

The results from the fighting data compel us to conclude that the expression of aggression is an interactive combination of an animal's genotype acting in conjunction with characteristics of the environment within which it is reared. This is a more limited conclusion than we are able to draw from the information on open-field activity, since those results yielded the same pattern for both genotypes. As I had indicated earlier, there are experimental data which seem to show direct effects upon later performance, and the activity data fall within this category, but there are also many sets of data, such as that of the fighting performance, which require that one discuss them in interactive terms rather than with respect to direct effects.

The interactive effects of life history experiences

Programming life histories

It is reasonable to assume that an organisms' behavior at any point in time is determined, to a large extent, by its total accumulated experience. In order to study this matter experimentally, we systematically manipulated the experiences which rats received throughout their early life. We chose to expose animals to different forms of social and/or stress experiences during different ages throughout their development. Each group of rats had a different program of life history experiences, arranged in factorial designs so that the additive and interaction effects of each independent variable could be separately assessed. We will be concerned here only with part of the data reported in the first experiment in this series (Denenberg, Karas, Rosenberg and Schell, 1968). For reviews of the complete series of experiments, see Denenberg (1969a, 1970a).

In the Denenberg et al. experiment, the independent variables consisted of free environment experience and handling. We have already discussed the nature of the free environment in the description of the Cooper and Zubek study, but we have not talked about handling as yet.

Handling is an experimental technique which is introduced at birth. In the colony, the cages of pregnant animals are inspected daily, and when a litter is found the pups are removed, culled to 8 animals, and then, by random assignment, the litter is either assigned to the control or handling condition. If the litter is a control, then the pups are returned to their home cage and are not disturbed until weaning at 21 days. Food and water are supplied by means of external sources, so that it is not even necessary to open the cage door until weaning. If the litter has been designated to be handled, the 8 pups are each placed singly into one gallon tin cans containing shavings where they are left for 3 min. After this, the litter is returned to its home cage. This procedure is continued for the first 20 days of life in most of our experiments. Research over a number of years has shown that this seemingly innocuous procedure has many profound effects. Handled rats have been found to be sexually precocious, to weigh more in adulthood, to be less emotional, to explore novel and social objects more, generally to learn better when noxious stimuli are used as reinforcers, and to have a lesser adrenal corticosterone response when exposed to novel stimuli but a greater response when exposed to distinctly noxious stimuli (Denenberg, 1969b).

The variables of handling and free environment experience were combined in the following fashion. The mothers used to generate the subjects for this experiment had themselves either received handling experience in infancy or were non-handled controls. When these females conceived, they were placed either into a standard maternity cage or else they were placed into a free environment where they gave birth. Within each of the four groups generated by the combination of the two prior variables, half of the litters received handling experience while the other half were non-handled controls. Finally, at the time of weaning, half of the litters were placed into standard laboratory cages while the other half were placed into the free environment where they remained until 42 days of age. At that time, the rats in the free environment were removed and placed into standard laboratory cages. The experimental design is shown in Table III. Starting at 70 days of age, the animals were tested for three successive days in the open field. Starting on day 73, these same animals were given 10 trials a day for 5 days in an avoidance learning shuttle-box. Table III also presents the mean activity scores in the open field and the mean number of avoidance responses for the 16 groups in the experiment.

The analysis of variance was used to evaluate these data statistically. For the variable of open-field activity, we found that those handled in infancy were significantly more active than non-handled controls. In addition, we found that the interaction of Mother Handling × Preweaning Housing and the interaction involving Mother Handling × Offspring Handling × Preweaning Housing were both significant. Fig. 1 shows the profile of means for the triple interaction.

In Fig. 1, the means in the right hand panel are higher than the four means in the left hand panel; this reflects the main effect of handling. In each panel, the two sets of curves cross; pups born of a mother who was not handled in her infancy were more active if reared in a free environment during the first 21 days of life, while pups born of a mother handled during her infancy were more active if they had been reared in a maternity cage during the preweaning interval. In addition, the wider spread of scores in the right hand panel indicates that the procedure of handling accentuated the differences brought about by the combination of the Maternal Handling variable and the Preweaning Housing variable.

Table III Experimental design for study investigating programmed life histories, and 70-day data for open-field activity and avoidance learning (from Denenberg, Karas, Rosenberg and Schell, 1968)

Mothers' experience in infancy	Pups' experience in infancy	Preweaning housing	Postweaning housing	Open-field activity	Avoidance learning
C	C	MC	LC	39.60	32.00
C	C	MC	FE	24.41	34.58
C	C	FE	LC	40.20	23.20
C	C	FE	FE	31.88	31.83
C	H	MC	LC	50.55	32.30
C	H	MC	FE	28.20	35.30
C	H	FE	LC	62.12	33.50
C	H	FE	FE	91.00	31.20
H	C	MC	LC	41.00	27.00
H	C	MC	FE	42.75	29.38
H	C	FE	LC	28.30	30.80
H	C	FE	FE	22.50	35.25
H	H	MC	LC	59.70	26.10
H	H	MC	FE	72.50	30.90
H	H	FE	LC	15.88	31.88
H	H	FE	FE	40.62	32.88

Symbols: C, non-handled control; H, handled; MC, maternity cage; LC, laboratory cage; FE, free environment.

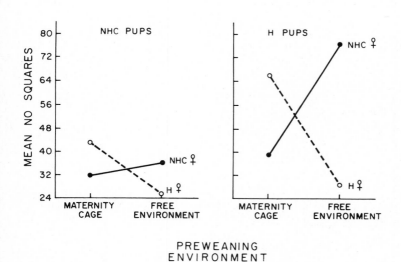

Fig. 1 Profile of means for the triple interaction involving Mother Handling (presence or absence) × Offspring Handling (presence or absence) × Preweaning Housing (maternity cage or free environment) upon open field activity.

158

The analysis of the number of avoidance responses made in the shuttle-box found no significant main effect, but did find that the interaction of Mother Handling × Preweaning Housing was significant. The profile of this interaction is shown in Fig 2. Here we see that pups born of mothers that received no handling experience in infancy learned best if they had been reared in a maternity cage between birth and weaning, while pups born of a handled mother had the higher learning scores if they had been reared in a free environment between birth and weaning.

Both sets of data, then, show that it is the interaction of different independent variables working in joint combination which brings about significant changes in adult performance. In addition, the independent variable of handling the pups was found to have a direct effect upon the open-field activity of the rats.

These data have another very important implication which is a derivative of the finding that the major impact is by means of significant interactions rather than by means of significant main effects. This implication has to do with another method that could have been used to evaluate the data, namely the use of correlational methodology. The experimental design in Table III shows that there are 4 independent variables, each at two levels. It is possible to calculate the correlation coefficients between each of the independent variables and the two criterion tests of open-field activity and avoidance learning. If one calculates the Pearson product–moment correlation coefficient between each of the four dichotomized independent variables and the two criteria (this is the same as calculating the point biserial correlation coefficient), the only correlation which is found to be significant is that relating the handling experience which the pups received to their open-field activity. Thus, if one had used a correlational approach to these data, the conclusions which would have been derived would have been enormously different from the conclusions der-

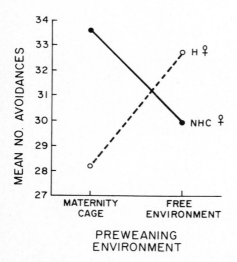

Fig. 2   Profile of means for the interaction of Mother Handling × Preweaning Housing for avoidance learning.

ived from the analysis of variance. Specifically, we would have concluded that handling experience in infancy is correlated with later activity in the open field, and we would have concluded that no other variable is related to open-field performance; furthermore we would have concluded that none of the variables studied in infancy had any relationship to subsequent shuttle-box learning. It needs to be emphasized that these are the only conclusions that can be derived from the usual correlational analysis, because the curves in Figs. 1 and 2 cross over. However, we know from the findings of significant interactions via the analysis of variance, as depicted in the figures, that three of the independent variables in the study are significantly related to subsequent performance measures, albeit not in a simple linear fashion. Putting this another way, correlational procedures are generally insufficient statistics to isolate a significant interactional pattern like those depicted in Figs. 1 and 2.

The reader may wonder why this point is being emphasized, since the analysis of variance does allow one to pick out the significant interactions. The reason for the emphasis is that many researchers who study developmental processes with humans only use correlational procedures to evaluate their data, and we have just demonstrated that the usual correlational procedures employed are not sensitive to interactional effects in which curves cross each other (for a more extended discussion on this topic, see Denenberg, 1977). The consequence of this analysis is as follows: conclusions based upon any statistical procedure which does not take into account the possibility of interactions (these include such procedures as simple order correlations, partial correlations, multiple correlations, and the t-test), must be regarded as highly tentative since there has been ample research to show that interactions across different time intervals as well as within a time span are quite commonly found in developmental research.

Malnutrition and life histories

I shall conclude this section with the description of a study involving humans. The effects of severe malnutrition upon the behavior of a population of Jamaican children has been reported in a series of papers by Richardson and his associates. In one of these studies, Richardson (1976) investigated life history factors influencing the IQ scores of boys 6 to 10 years of age. One group consisted of boys who had been treated in a hospital for severe malnutrition during their first two years of life. To evaluate the effects of the malnutrition statistically, a comparison group was formed by selecting male classmates of neighbors of a similar age who had not been hospitalized for severe malnutrition. For each boy in the study an index of social background was obtained by averaging the data of three scales which measured characteristics of each child's guardian, the economic conditions of the household, and the kinds of social experiences of the child. Finally, when each child was given the WISC intelligence test, his height was also measured as an index of his lifetime nutritional history. The major results of the study are summarized in Fig. 3.

Whether malnutrition during the first two years has an effect upon later IQ was dependent upon the level of social background to which the child had been exposed

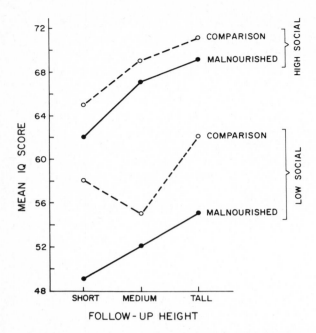

Fig. 3   Effects upon IQ of the presence or absence of severe malnutrition during the first two years of life, social background, and height at the time of IQ testing (from Richardson, 1976; low social background includes those in the lowest 4 deciles and high social background includes those in the 7th, 8th, and 9th deciles).

and his later height. If the child had a favorable social background and an overall history of good physical growth (as indexed by follow-up height), then severe malnutrition during the first 2 years of life only had a minor effect in depressing IQ scores. However, if the child was from a low social background and was relatively short for his age group, then early malnutrition had a significant impact upon the IQ score*. Richardson concludes, "The results suggest that the explanation that severe malnutrition in infancy causes central nervous system damage which then in turn causes mental retardation or impairment is too simple. A more complex conceptualization is needed which takes into account biologic and social variables that may influence the child's intellectual functioning and development over his lifespan.... It will also require the use of multivariate forms of analysis which take into account the interaction between variables" (Richardson, 1976, p. 61).

---

* Richardson used a multiple correlation procedure to evaluate the three variables of early malnutrition, social background, and follow-up height upon IQ. The multiple correlation procedure is valid here because the curves in Fig. 3 did not cross each other, unlike the situations in Figs. 1 and 2.

Conclusions and implications

We see from this brief review that differing biological backgrounds in combination with different patterns of experience during development will often act in an interactive rather than an additive (or causal) manner to affect later behavioral and biological processes. Because of this interactional characteristic, it is possible to draw false conclusions about the effects of a particular early experience variable as a function of other variables and parameters in a study. For example, if Cooper and Zubek had only reared their rats in free environments, they would have concluded that the genetic background did not influence problem-solving behavior; or if Richardson had not examined the effects of social background and follow-up height of his Jamaican boys, he would have concluded that severe malnutrition in early life had an overall constant effect of significantly depressing IQ scores.

Thus, one important implication that follows from this interactional principle is that it is necessary to be quite cautious in drawing conclusions about data. This is especially important if one has negative fiindings. As was discussed above, when one fails to get a significant effect by means of correlational statistics or the t-test, this failure may be due to the presence of interactive effects, rather than to the absence of any effect. As a general rule, if there has not been a test for interactional effects, one should be very sceptical of any conclusion to the effect that a variable does not influence developmental processes.

Another consequence of the interactional principle is that we have to give up the hope that we can make simple statements relating early experience variables to later events. For example, at one time, we thought we could flatly state that malnutrition in early life would depress later learning and intelligence; Richardson's data show that this is not so. There was also a time when we thought that one's intelligence (or problem-solving ability) was determined by one's genes; Cooper and Zubek's data refute this. And we also used to think that animals who were genetically aggressive would continue to be aggressive; the data of Denenberg et al. reject that conclusion.

To return full circle to the comments made at the beginning of this paper, it is because of the presence of interactional effects that we have not been able to formulate theories to integrate our many diverse findings. This means that the study of behavioral development is more complicated than we first thought (or hoped), and it will be necessary to extend our empirical data base in order to describe more fully developmental characteristics. Even though the lack of adequate theory is disappointing and frustrating, there is also a positive feature to keep in mind: the interactional principle suggests that there are combinations of experience which can yield beneficial outcomes despite initial handicaps. Thus the maze-dull rats and the severely malnourished Jamaican children could both function at intellectually competent levels if reared in the proper kind of environmental setting. Thus, in a real sense, the presence of interactions widens the scope of research potential. That more than compensates for the lack of theoretical neatness.

Literature cited

Bertalanffy, L. V. (1969) Chance or law. In: *Beyond Reductionism*. (A. Koestler and J. R. Symthies, eds.) pp. 56–76, Beacon Press, Boston

Cooper, R. M. and Zubek, J. P. (1958) Effects of enriched and restricted early environments on the learning ability to bright and dull rats, *Can. J. Psychol. 12*, 159–164

Denenberg, V. H. (1964) Critical periods, stimulus input, and emotional reactivity: A theory of infantile stimulation, *Psychol. Rev. 71*, 335–351

Denenberg, V. H. (1969a) Experimental programming of life histories in the rat. In: *Stimulation in Early Infancy* (A. Ambrose, ed.) pp. 21–34, Academic Press, London

Denenberg, V. H. (1969b) The effects of early experience. In: *The Behaviour of Domestic Animals* (E. S. E. Hafez, ed.) pp. 95–130, Bailliere, Trindall and Cassell, London

Denenberg, V. H. (1970a) Experimental programming of life histories and the creation of individual differences. A review. In: *Miami Symposium on the Prediction of Behavior, 1968, Effects of Early Experience* (M. R. Jones, ed.) pp. 61–91, University of Miami Press, Coral Gables, Fla.

Denenberg, V. H. (1970b) The mother as a motivator. In: *Nebraska Symposium on Motivation, 1970* (W. J. Arnold and M. M. Page, eds.) pp. 60–93, University of Nebraska Press, Lincoln, Nebraska

Denenberg, V. H. (1972) *Readings in the Development of Behavior*, Sinauer Assoc., Stamford, Conn.

Denenberg, V. H. (1977) Paradigms and paradoxes in the study of behavioral development. In: *The Origins of the Infant's Social Responsiveness* (E. B. Thoman, ed.) Lawrence Erlbaum Assoc., Hillsdale, N. J., in the press

Denenberg, V. H., Hudgens, G. A. and Zarrow, M. X. (1964) Mice reared with rats. Modification of behavior by early experience with another species, *Science 143*, 380–381

Denenberg, V. H., Karas, G. G., Rosenberg, K. R. and Schell, S. F. (1968) Programming life histories. An experimental design and initial results, *Dev. Psychobiol. 1*, 1–9

Denenberg, V. H., Paschke, R. E. and Zarrow, M. X. (1973) Mice reared with rats. Effects of prenatal and postnatal maternal environments upon hybrid offspring of C57BL/10J and Swiss-Albino mice, *Dev. Psychobiol. 6*, 21–31

Denenberg, V. H. and Zarrow, M. X. (1971) Effects of handling in infancy upon adult behavior and adrenocortical activity. Suggestions for a neuroendocrine mechanism. In: *Early Childhood. The Development of Self Regulatory Mechanisms* (D. N. Walcher and D. L. Peters, eds.) pp. 39–64, Academic Press, New York

Levine, S. (1969) An endocrine theory of infantile stimulation. In: *Stimulation in Early Infancy* (A. Ambrose, ed.) pp. 45–55, Academic Press, London

Levine, S. and Mullins, R. F., Jr. (1966) Hormonal influence on brain organization in infant rats, *Science 152*, 1585–1592

Newton, G., and Levine, S. (eds.) (1968) *Early Experience and Behavior*, Thomas, Springfield, Ill.

Richardson, S. A. (1976) The relation of severe malnutrition in infancy to the intelligence of school children with differing life histories, *Pediat. Res. 10*, 57–61

Russell, P. A. (1971) "Infantile stimulation" in rodents: A consideration of possible mechanisms, *Psychol. Bull. 73*, 192–202

Scott, J. P. (1962) Critical periods in behavioral development, *Science 138*, 949–958

Tryon, R. C. (1940) Genetic differences in maze-learning ability in rats, *39th Year-book, National Society for the Study of Education*, Pt. I, pp. 111–119

Weiss, P. (1969) The living system: Determinism stratefied. In: *Beyond Reductionism* (A. Koestler and J. R. Symthies, eds.) pp. 3–42, Beacon Press, Boston

Genetics, environment and intelligence, edited by A. Oliverio
© *Elsevier/North-Holland Biomedical Press, 1977*

Effects of environmental enrichment or impoverishment on learning and on brain values in rodents

10

MARK R. ROSENZWEIG and
EDWARD L. BENNETT

Introduction

This chapter is concerned with several interrelated questions concerning effects of experience in differential environments on subsequent behavior and on brain measures. It will draw chiefly on experimental results obtained with laboratory rats, although some work with other species and other orders will be mentioned. The three main questions to be considered in the chapter are the following:

(1) What effects does experience in differential environments have on later behavior, especially on learning or problem-solving behavior?

(2) What effects does such differential experience have on measures of brain anatomy and brain chemistry?

(3) To what extent can results of differential experience on behavior be related to effects of differential experience on brain measures?

The main experimental manipulation in these studies has been to place animals for various periods of time in laboratory environments that are either more complex and enriched than standard housing cages or that are more restricted and impoverished than the standard laboratory condition. The enriched (or complex or "free") conditions have been defined rather differently by different investigators, and we will consider later several dimensions of enrichment that should be considered separately. Also, what one investigator calls "restricted" is what another terms "standard laboratory condition." We will recommend later certain dimensions of treatment that we believe should be stated explicitly in all reports in this field.

In this chapter we shall give a necessarily incomplete review of studies related to the three main questions, but we shall cite many of the relevant publications. At a few points we shall also present previously unpublished data. In order to facilitate comparisons between behavioral and cerebral effects, we shall use generally similar sequences of headings in the first and the second part of this chapter; Table V (p. 190) indicates these headings and some of the main findings.

Effects of differential environmental experience on learning or problem-solving behavior

In the years since Hebb (1949) reported that enriched or "free" experience enhanced the learning ability of laboratory rats, a large number of experiments have been done to test and extend this work. A number of questions related to this work have by now been pretty well settled, but still more questions have been raised that have not as yet been answered definitively. Let us review briefly some of the settled conclusions in this area and also some of the still open questions. This area has been previously reviewed by Rosenzweig (1971), Greenough (1976), and Davenport (1976).

Dimensions of differential experience

Typically the "enriched," "complex," or "free" environment consists of 10 or more animals living in a rather large cage in which there is a variety of stimulus objects; often there is also a variety of visual and auditory stimulation from the environment around the cage (e.g., Forgays and Forgays, 1952; Bennett et al., 1974; Brown, 1968; Greenough et al., 1972a). Thus this type of environment includes social stimulation, stimulation from inanimate objects with which the animals can have direct contact, and stimulation through the distance receptors with objects with which the animals have no direct contact. There is much variation, however, in what investigators call "enriched." For example, in the study of Yeterian and Wilson (1976) the "enriched" condition consisted of animals housed singly in 18 × 25 cm cages which did not include any stimulus objects; flashing lights and static were present outside the enriched cages. The impoverished condition consisted also of single animals living in the same size cages but included only diffuse light and with auditory stimulation masked by a continuously sounding buzzer. Thus the enriched animals in this study had neither social stimulation nor stimulation from direct contact with manipulable objects but only additional stimulation from sources outside the cage.

In the case of base-line or control groups, there is also considerable difference among conditions used by various investigators. The "standard colony condition" often includes two or three rats in small breeding or colony cages (e.g., Rosenzweig et al., 1972; Doty, 1972). However, animals have been referred to as being in "normal" conditions when 10 were placed in a 60 × 60 × 45 cm cage or in a "simple" environment when 25 lived in a 76 × 76 × 20 cm cage.

"Restricted" is also a term which has been used quite variously. Thus, Cooper and Zubeck (1958) referred to animals as restricted when they were living in a group of 12 in a cage that measured 102 × 64 × 33 cm. Brown (1968) referred to animals as restricted when they lived two or three in a cage measuring 25 × 28 × 20 cm. Hughes (1965) referred to animals as restricted when they were isolated in cages measuring 8 × 20 × 20 cm. Bingham and Griffiths (1952) restricted the experience of some rats by keeping them individually in very small "squeeze" cages, 13 × 10 × 5 cm. Some restricted animals have been allowed to see and hear the normal activity of the laboratory, while others have been shielded from such stimulation. Thus the living space and the possibilities for both social stimulation and extra-cage stimulation have varied enormously among rats that have been designated as having restricted or impoverished experience.

While it may be economical to use such terms as "enriched experience," "standard laboratory conditions," or "restricted" experience, they are obviously slippery and even dangerous if they convey quite different things to different investigators and readers. We would like to propose that every abstract as well as every research report make clear the dimensions along which enrichment or restriction of experience were varied. In particular, it should be made clear how many animals were together in a living space, the size and other features of the living space, whether the subjects had direct contact with manipulable objects, and whether there was particular stimulation available only through distance receptors.

Effects of social stimulation

A few experiments have tested effects of social stimulation on subsequent problem-solving or learning behavior. Thus Brown (1968) found that simple environment groups of 25 rats that had lived in a bare enclosure, 76 × 76 × 20 cm, performed significantly better on the Hebb-Williams maze than did the restricted environment groups that had lived in twos or threes in colony cages, 25 × 28 × 20 cm. Since the larger groups also had larger living spaces, it is not certain that it was the amount of social stimulation that improved the scores of the groups of 25. Gardner et al. (1975) kept rats singly or in groups of 22 or 23 in either simple or perceptually complex environments. They concluded that isolation had deleterious effects on both learning and retention of a passive avoidance response.

Effects of interaction with inanimate stimulus objects

Brown (1968) found that when groups of 25 rats were provided with either small manipulable objects or wooden barriers, their subsequent Hebb-Williams performance was significantly better than that of groups of 25 that had no contact with special objects. Forgays and Forgays (1952) had reported that a group of 11 rats that had experienced a "free environment with playthings" later performed significantly better on the Hebb-Williams maze than a group of 11 that had experienced a "free environment without playthings."

Effects of intra-cage versus extra-cage stimulation

A few studies have investigated the relative effects of stimuli within the cage and with which the animals could have direct commerce versus extra-cage stimuli that could affect only the distance receptors. From the relatively sparse results available, it appears that extra-cage stimuli have produced no measurable effect on the subsequent behavioral test.

Forgays and Forgays (1952) placed two mesh cages, each housing 3 rats, on a shelf that also contained 11 free-environment rats and playthings; two other mesh cages with 3 rats each were placed on an empty shelf. The mesh-cage rats that could see free-environment rats and varied objects when tested later on the Hebb-Williams maze had almost identical scores to the mesh-cage rats that did not have extra-cage stimulation. The free-environment rats, which had direct access to the varied objects, performed significantly better than the mesh-cage groups.

Meier and McGee (1959) gave some rats "visual-tactual experience" in which their cage contained seven geometric objects constructed from wooden blocks. The "visual experience-only" group could see such blocks behind glass panels on either side of their cage. The rats were in these conditions from birth until about 160 days of age. On subsequent tests of form discrimination, the visual-tactile group was significantly better than the visual-only group; the latter were no better than rats raised under standard colony conditions without any special stimulation. In a somewhat similar experiment, Bennett and Ellis (1968) placed a wooden circle and a triangle on the walls of cages of rats; in some cages the rats could see and touch these objects, but in other cages there was wire mesh around the objects so the rats could see but not touch them. On later tests, the animals allowed direct contact discriminated the circle from the triangle significantly better than controls, whereas the rats allowed only visual inspection were no better than controls.

Generality of effects over types of animals

Strains of rats

Animals from a number of rat strains have been tested and found to show significant beneficial effects of enriched experience on various tests of learning or problem-solving behavior. Among these strains are Long-Evans (Brown, 1968; Greenough et al., 1972a), Sprague-Dawley (Woods et al., 1961; Doty, 1972), Wistar (Bingham and Griffiths, 1952; Denenberg et al., 1968), Holtzman (Ough et al., 1972), and the Berkeley S_1 and S_3 strains (Rosenzweig, 1964). In most of the reports in this field, the subjects are identified clearly as being obtained from a known line and named commercial supplier or as coming from the colony of a stated psychology laboratory. (It is somewhat disheartening to see a report of 1971 which identifies the subjects only as "hooded rats obtained from a commercial dealer.")

Sex of rats

Most studies in this field have employed only male rats as subjects. A considerable number have used both male and females but have not reported any separate analyses by sex, so presumably there were no striking differences between the effects of environment on performance of the two sexes. An occasional study (e.g., Denenberg et al., 1968) has used only female subjects and has shown beneficial effects of enriched experience on subsequent problem-solving behavior.

Species of rodents.

Relatively little has been done on effects of experience on learning in rodent species other than rats, but Oliverio reports in this volume on research with strains of mice. Greenough et al. (1972b) reported that Swiss-Webster male mice placed for 30 days in an enriched environment subsequently made significantly fewer errors on both brightness discrimination and the Lashley III maze than did littermates kept under either standard colony or isolation conditions.

Orders of mammals.

Some work has been done to study effects of differential experience on problem-solving in carnivores (cats and dogs) and in primates.

The experiment of Wilson et al. (1965) is similar in design to some of the studies with rats. They used the following four conditions, raising 10 or 11 kittens in each: (a) Control (C). These kittens received only the minimum amount of handling compatible with survival during their first 90 days; they remained with their mothers and littermates in large cages and could view the busy colony room. (Since these animals were housed in groups, their treatment was similar to that of standard colony rats.) (b) Handled (H). From birth through day 45 these kittens were treated like the controls except that they were taken from their cage and petted for 5 min per day. They were treated exactly like the controls on days 46–90. (c) Playroom (P). These kittens were treated like controls from birth through day 45, then on days 46–90, they were placed for 5 h per day in a large playroom with kittens from other litters, toys, boxes, a scratching post, etc. (P treatment is like the enriched condition used in some rat experiments.) (d) Handled plus Playroom (HP). This group received both treatments: handling until day 45 and playroom on days 46–90.

From their fourth through seventh month, the kittens were observed in regard to open-field behavior, contact with objects and with human beings, and were tested on relearning tasks (the Hebb-Williams maze, avoidance conditioning, and visual reversal training). The two treatments of handling and playroom experience produced different effects, with no significant interaction between the two treatments. H kittens made significantly more contact with novel objects and with human beings, and they required more trials to reach criterion on avoidance conditioning than did non-handled kittens; apparently, handling before weaning made kittens less fearful. Both groups that had playroom experience were significantly more active in the open field, and they made about 34% fewer errors on the Hebb-Williams maze than did kittens without playroom experience. Thus enriched experience with inanimate stimuli improved Hebb-Williams performance in cats as it does in rats.

Fuller (1966) reared 22 beagles in isolation cages from weaning (at 3 weeks of age) until 15 weeks of age. During the 3–15 week period, six dogs were taken out of their cages twice a day and allowed the run of the laboratory; during the time out of their cages they were treated as pets by the caretaker. Beginning at about 24 weeks of age, each dog was tested in a modified Wisconsin General Test Apparatus. They were trained, 16 trials/day, to select the food pan on one side. When the criterion was reached, the correct side was reversed the next day. Each dog was tested on 12 problems (11 reversals). On the first 5 problems, the pet-reared dogs made significantly fewer errors than the restricted dogs; thereafter the difference diminished and became non-significant. The isolation-reared dogs showed inappropriate emotional responses on the early reversals. Fuller suggested that the motivational factors could account for the difference between the groups and concluded: "At the moment it is premature to regard a decrement in performance following experiential restriction as equivalent to a general depression in learning ability" (p. 274). Other research on effects on differential experience on performance in dogs includes that of Melzack (1962) and Thompson and Heron (1954).

Harlow and his collaborators have carried out a number of studies on effects of isolation or varied social experience on later problem-solving ability of monkeys. Until recently they had concluded that while socially isolated monkeys were harder to train and showed emotional problems, their eventual performance was as good as that of animals with previous social experience. Commenting on their failure to find effects on learning ability, Griffin and Harlow (1966, p. 546) pointed out, "The apparent contradiction between rhesus monkeys and other species on learning after isolation may be an artifact of the types of tasks employed. Tasks that do not extensively adapt Ss or do not discard data indicating problems in adaptation will probably show performance deficits." But recently Gluck et al. (1973) found that monkeys reared in enriched environments were superior to monkeys that had lived in partial isolation on complex oddity tasks. Since all the animals had been thoroughly adapted to testing and had not shown differences on previous two-choice discrimination or delayed-response problems, the results with the oddity task caused Harlow and his associates to change their stance and conclude that the oddity task was reflecting differences in intellectual ability between the enriched and isolated animals and not simply motivational differences. It will be important to see whether replications or other complex tasks indicate intellectual differences in monkeys caused by differences in early experience.

Other evidence that impoverished early experience impairs cognitive abilities in primates came from a study on chimpanzees by Davenport et al. (1973). They compared wild-born animals with restricted subjects born in the laboratory and raised singly in enclosed cribs for their first two years. At approximately three years of age, all subjects were caged together in a large "relatively enriched laboratory environment of continual varied social contact." The chimpanzees had a common and extensive experience on a variety of learning and problem-solving tasks prior to the present study which began at the age of 12 to 14 years. In this experiment, animals learned two-choice object discrimination problems to a preset criterion. As soon as discrimination of a given pair of objects reached criterion, the previously correct object was made incorrect, and the previously incorrect object became correct. Although the early-restricted animals were almost as good as the wild-born chimpanzees in original learning of each problem, the restricted made significantly more errors on the reversal tests. The authors conclude that the severe early restriction caused persistent cognitive deficits that were not overcome by subsequent prolonged environmental enrichment.

Generality of effects over tests of learning or problem-solving behavior

The Hebb-Williams maze has been the most frequently used test for effects of differential environment, but a number of other tests have also been employed. Positive effects of prior enriched experience have been reported by a number of investigators for the Lashley III maze (Ray and Hochauser, 1969; Bennett et al., 1970; Greenough et al., 1972a; and Riege, 1971). Positive results have also been reported for passive avoidance (Doty, 1972; Freeman and Ray, 1972), DRL bar pressing (Ough et al., 1972), and brightness discrimination (Edwards et al., 1969; Bernstein, 1972 and 1973). Not all of the reports are positive, however. There have been occasional failures to find significant results even with the Hebb-Williams maze (Woods et al., 1961, in the case of high drive; Hughes, 1965; Reid et al., 1968; Davenport, 1976). More often the failures to find differences in performance between animals having experienced enriched versus impoverished environments have come for relatively simple tasks such as visual discrimination (Bingham and Griffiths, 1952; Woods et al., 1960; Krech et al., 1962; Gill et al., 1966), T-maze (Hymovitch, 1952), or Y-maze (Freeman and Ray, 1972).

Age at onset of differential experience.

In most cases the rats have been assigned to the differential environments at or about weaning (from 20 to 25 days of age). In a few experiments, animals have been assigned to the differential environments shortly after birth (Forgays and Read, 1962; Denenberg et al., 1968). In several experiments, rats have been assigned to the differential environments 30 days or more after weaning (Hymovitch, 1952; Woods, 1959; Forgays and Read, 1962; Nyman, 1967; Brown, 1968; Bennett, 1976; Rosenzweig, 1971); in two experiments, rats were not assigned to the differential environments until they were 300 days of age (Riege, 1971; Doty, 1972). In recent experiments we have placed rats with cortical lesions or sham-operated control rats in enriched or impoverished environments at 6 days of age (Will et al. 1976), at 30 days of age (Will et al., 1977), or at 100 days of age (Will and Rosenzweig, 1976). Positive results of differential experience have been reported in all of these experiments, whether the experience occurred preweaning, postweaning, or whether it started at 300 days of age.

Although it seems that there is not a "critical age" for induction of behavioral effects, a few investigators have asked whether there is a preferential period. Forgays and Read (1962) gave rats free environment experience at one of five ages:— 0–21, 22–43, 44–65, 66–87 and 88–109 days. A sixth group with no enriched experience served as controls. When the rats were about 123 days old they were pretrained and tested on the Hebb-Williams maze. The three groups whose enriched experience started at 22, 44, or 66 days of age showed quite similar scores, and all were significantly better than the group with no enriched experience. The group that received the enriched experience preweaning (0–21 days) also performed better than the control group. The 88–109 day enrichment group had scores only slightly worse than the 0–21 day group, but the 88–109 day group was not quite significantly different from the control group. Nyman (1967) gave only 10 days of enriched experience at 30–40, 50–60, or 70–80 days of age; at each of these periods, some animals received 8 h a day of enriched experience while other animals received only 1 h a day. When they were tested on an elevated version of the Hebb-Williams maze, all rats that had received 8 h per day of enriched experience were significantly better than the control group, while for the 1 h per day exposure, only the 50–60 day group was significantly better than the control group. In our own laboratory, we have tested animals after having given enriched experience starting at 5 days of age, at 25 days of age, or 85 or more days of age. The differences in Hebb-Williams performance between animals given enriched experience versus either standard colony or isolation treatment have been similar for all of these age ranges.

It should be pointed out that for at least one behavioral test, the age at which differential experience is given has an effect on the results. We have pointed out previously that some tests are more sensitive to enrichment of experience above the colony base line, whereas other tests are more sensitive to restriction of experience below that normally found in colony existence (Rosenzweig, 1971). We were puzzled some years ago when we found that we could produce clear differences between enriched-experience and impoverished-experience rats on the Visual Reversal Discrimination Task in the Krech hypothesis apparatus when differential experience started at 25 days of age, but that there were no differences when the differential experience started at 60 or 90 days of age. On the other hand, we found for the Lashley III maze just as large differences between enriched and impoverished experience groups when the period of differential treatment ran from 60 to 90 days of age as when it extended from 25 to 55 days of age (Rosenzweig, 1971, Tables IV and V). We were able to account for these effects when we tested not only enriched-experience and impoverished-experience animals but also those from the standard colony condition. On the Visual Reversal Task, run after 25–55 day differential experience, enriched-experience and colony control rats made similar numbers of errors, while the impoverished-experience group was inferior to both. Thus this test appears to be sensitive to restriction of experience from the colony level and not to enrichment. When restriction or isolation are begun only at 60 days of age, the rats cannot then be affected because they have already had colony experience and the effects of this experience appear to persist. But on the Lashley III maze, colony control and isolated rats made similar numbers of errors, while enriched-experience rats made significantly less. Thus this test is sensitive to enrichment of experience above the colony level. Further enrichment can be given and can take effect not only immediately after weaning but also at 60 days of age and even later. Our tests on Hebb-Williams performance with enriched-experience, colony controls, and isolated rats show that this test, like the Lashley III maze, is sensitive to effects of enrichment. Consistent with the effects obtained in the Lashley maze, Hebb-Williams performance can be improved by enriched experience which begins long after the age of weaning.

Duration of differential experience

Rats have been tested on the Hebb-Williams maze after as little as 10 days of differential experience (Nyman, 1967), 20 days (Forgays and Read, 1962), or as much as 130 days of differential experience (Woods et al., 1961). A large number of studies have used periods intermediate between these extremes. Positive effects of prior differential experience have been reported for all of these durations from 10 to 130 days, so apparently the effects can be induced rather rapidly.

We noted in the previous section (*Age at onset of differential experience*, p. 169) that Nyman (1967) found that whereas 8 h/day of enriched experience at any of the three 10–day periods produced significant improvement, 1h/day was less effective and caused significant reduction of errors only when given at 50–60 days of age. Thus, although a small amount of differential experience can produce measurable behavioral effects, the effects may increase with longer experience. Little has yet been done to determine relations between the duration of differential experience and magnitude of behavioral effects.

Permanence and persistence of behavioral effects

Investigators have asked several different questions under this heading: (a) will the behavioral effects remain if the animals are kept in the differential environments for prolonged periods or, as the animals habituate to the environments, will the effects disappear? (b) Will the behavioral effects persist if the animals are removed from one environment and placed in another for a period that precedes the behavioral test (e.g., if the enrichment period is followed by a period in standard colony or isolation conditions)? (c) Will the effects of prior differential experience persist during a lengthy program of behavioral testing? Let us note some findings concerning each of these questions.

Permanence of effects during prolonged differential experience

The small number of findings on this question suggest that behavioral differences are found after prolonged differential experience and that there is no loss of effect caused by habituation of animals to the differential environments. As noted above, Woods et al. (1961) found rats with 130 days in the enriched condition (EC) to perform significantly better on the Hebb-Williams maze than rats that were in the impoverished condition (IC) during the same period. Cummins et al. (1973) placed Wistar albino rats in EC or in IC at weaning and kept them there for 509 days. At the end of this period, they were tested on the Hebb-Williams maze, and the EC rats made significantly fewer errors than the IC rats.

Persistence of effects after animals are moved from one condition to another

In most reports, the animals have been tested immediately or shortly after the conclusion of their period of differential experience. In some cases, however, rats have been removed from the enriched condition and placed for a considerable period in the standard colony (SC) environment before being tested. Thus, Forgays and Read (1962) placed their enriched-experience rats into SC for 2 months, and Denenberg et al. (1968) placed their EC rats into SC for an entire year before testing. In both cases, the EC rats were significantly better than the controls on the Hebb-Williams maze, so effects of a brief early period of enriched experience appear to persist during an ensuing period of existence in standard laboratory cages.

There do not seem to be reports of behavioral testing after other sequences, such as from EC to IC or from IC to EC. Of course, when the start of EC or IC experience is delayed until well after weaning, the experiment does involve a change from the usual colony environment to EC or IC. We saw previously in the section *Age at onset of differential experience* that positive effects of differential experience can be obtained at any part of the life cycle. This is further evidence that early experience does not fix behavioral capacities once and for all.

Persistence of effects during testing

Do the effects of prior differential experience persist during a lengthy program of behavioral testing? There is considerable divergence of results concerning this question. Hebb (1949) in the first report on this subject reported that the enriched-experience rats improved their relative standing in the last 10 days of a total of 21 days of testing. He interpreted this to mean that the richer experience of this group during development made them better able to profit by new experiences at maturity. Woods (1959) found the difference between free environment and isolated rats to remain relatively constant when tested on six problems at 63–65 days of age, six other problems at 95–97 days, and six final problems at 156–158 days of age. On the other hand, we found that when three different tests were given successively in a battery (Dashiell checkerboard test, Lashley III maze, and reversal discrimination) whichever test was given first showed a significant difference between EC and IC littermates, whereas the later tests did not. Sturgeon and Reid (1971) gave rats a first battery of Hebb-Williams test patterns starting at 110 days of age. After the first 24 tests, which showed a large difference related to enriched or impoverished environments, tests 1–12 were presented in rotated form and they no longer showed much difference. Then the same battery was presented again, starting at 190 days of age, and at this time there were only slight and non-significant differences between groups.

It should be recalled that Fuller (1966) found restricted-experience beagles to be inferior to pet beagles when the animals were tested for reversal learning, but a significant difference lasted only through the first five reversals.

The later studies on this question therefore indicate that the differences in problem-solving ability brought about by differential experience can be overcome during the course of prolonged testing. The testing itself provides considerable experience, and this may cause further changes. It may be, however, that prolonged differential experience may bring about intellectual differences that will persist or at least that will show up when rather difficult tests are given. This is the indication of the report by Gluck et al. (1973). They found that monkeys reared in enriched environments did not differ from monkeys living in partial isolation on two-choice discrimination or delayed-response problems, but after this lengthy testing, when complex oddity tasks were given, the enriched-experience animals were significantly superior to the restricted-experience monkeys.

Effects of differential experience on brain anatomy and chemistry

Since the early 1960's, a series of papers has reported changes in brain chemistry and brain anatomy brought about by placing animals in environments of differential complexity. Among recent reviews of this field are those of Bennett (1976), Greenough (1976), and Rosenzweig and Bennett (in the press). It has been demonstrated that rats given experience in enriched environments show, in comparison with littermate animals raised in standard colony conditions or under even more restricted conditions, greater weight of cerebral cortex, greater thickness of cerebral cortex, greater branching of dendrites of cortical neurons, greater density of synaptic spines on cortical neurons, lesser activity of acetylcholinesterase but greater activity of cholinesterase in cerebral cortex, and greater RNA/DNA in cortical tissue. In the next paragraphs, some of the questions that we shall take up are similar to those raised with regard to the behavioral effects: how different dimensions of experience influence the magnitude of the effects, generality of the cerebral effects over strains of rats and over the two sexes, effects of age of onset and duration of the differential experience on magnitude of the cerebral changes, and permanence and persistence of the effects.

Stimulus dimensions in production of cerebral effects

As was true in regard to experiments on behavioral effects of differential experience, the stimulus situation has been varied along at least three dimensions in experiments on cerebral effects: (a) social stimulation, the number of rats caged together, (b) number and variety of objects with which direct contact is permitted (manipulanda), and (c) extra-cage stimulation, usually visual or auditory stimulation from outside the cage.

Social stimulation.
Stimulation by cagemates is effective in altering brain weights and various aspects of brain chemistry (Rosenzweig et al., 1972; Welch et al. 1974). Indeed, Welch et al.

imply that social stimulation alone may account for the effects of enriched experience on brain measures. We have shown, however, that even among rats caged in groups of 12, the inanimate environment causes significant differences in brain measures, as the next paragraph demonstrates.

Stimulation from interaction with objects in the environment

Rats placed for 30 days in a group of 12 in a semi-natural outdoor environment develop significantly greater brain weight measures (especially in occipital cortex) than do 12 littermate rats in the usual Berkeley EC environments (Bennett, 1976, Table 17.4). And rats in EC develop significantly greater brain weight measures than do littermate Group Condition (GC) rats placed in groups of 12 in cages of the same sort but without inanimate stimulus objects (Bennett, 1976, Table 17.6). The brain weights of rats in GC also differed significantly from those of rats in IC. Thus both social and inanimate stimulations are effective in causing changes in brain weight measures; significant effects of both variables have also been found for some measures of brain chemistry.

As well as the experiments just described, another way to show the importance of inanimate stimulation in producing brain effects comes from experiments in which the social factor was excluded. In a series of experiments begun in 1967, we found that rats that received a daily injection of methamphetamine before being put in the enriched condition for two hours per day developed larger than usual brain weight effects. In her doctoral thesis, Su-Yu Chang (1969) reported that the rats given methamphetamine showed less social interaction than rats given saline injections, whereas the methamphetamine rats showed a greater than usual interaction with the stimulus objects. In further research along this line (Rosenzweig and Bennett, 1972), we found that placing rats individually in EC for 2 h per day resulted in significant differences in brain measures from IC, if the animals were given small injections of methamphetamine before the daily period in the enriched environment but not if they were given injections of saline. Some facilitating treatment is necessary if isolated rats are to show much interaction with inanimate stimulus objects. We concluded that the anatomical and chemical changes characteristic of enriched experience will develop in the rat brain whenever the animal interacts with a relatively complex environment for at least a minimum daily period over at least a minimum duration of days. "Social stimulation, which heretofore has always been included in the enriched condition, is now found not to be necessary" (p. 304).

Granted that inanimate stimulation produces cerebral effects, is a considerable amount and variety of such stimulation required? To investigate this question we carried out three successive experiments, in each of which littermates were assigned to the following four groups: (a) EC with variable toys in variable positions; 12 animals in a standard EC cage were given six "toys" per day from our usual pool of stimulus objects. (b) Fixed EC, with six toys in the EC cage, but each toy was attached in a fixed position throughout the 30-day duration of the experiment. (c) Fixed toys but variable positions; this group had the same six toys as group b, but the positions and the arrangements of the toys were changed daily according to a schedule set in advance. (d) The usual IC environment with animals housed individually in small cages. The cages for groups a, b, and c were placed side by side in a small room. Each day, the animals from each of these groups were taken out and put in a holding cage, separately for a, b, and c. At that time, the toys in cage a were changed in the usual way, the toys in cage b were not moved but might be cleaned somewhat if they were dirty, and the toys in cage c were rearranged according to the schedule.

In all but one of the three replications of this experiment, each of the enriched-condition groups showed brain weight values that differed significantly from those of the littermate IC group. (In the third replication, the group with fixed toys in fixed positions did not develop significant differences from the IC group.). Only occasionally did one of the EC groups differ significantly from the other two (see Table I). Even when results from all three replications were combined, only one significant difference was found among the brain values of two EC groups; this was for weight of ventral cortex, between groups a and c. Thus it appears that it does not require a considerable degree of novelty in order to induce cerebral effects. In two of the three experiments, even fixed toys in fixed positions were enough to cause significant effects. It should be noted that were we now to replicate these experiments (which were conducted in 1972), we would also have included a group with no objects in the cage in order to be able to eliminate clearly the social factor, as was done in the experiment mentioned under the previous heading.

Ineffectiveness of extra-cage stimuli

We have reviewed elsewhere possible effects of extra-cage stimulation on brain measures (Rosenzweig et al., 1972; Rosenzweig and Bennett, 1976), and we have concluded that it is difficult, if not impossible, to alter the brain values measured, by extra-cage stimulation within the range of most experiments. Let us review here some of the observations on which this conclusion is based.

Experiments conducted in our laboratory in 1965 and 1966 showed that the usual extra-cage environment did not modify the cerebral results obtained with either EC or IC animals. That is, IC animals kept in the EC room had brain weights virtually identical to those of the IC animals housed at the same time in the IC room, and animals kept in an EC cage in the quiet IC room developed brain values closely similar to those of the EC rats housed in the busy, active EC room.

Although rats raised in IC conditions in the main laboratory or in the isolation room did not differ in cerebral measures, rats isolated in an extremely impoverished environment did have cerebral values that differed even more from those of the EC group than did the values of the usual IC group (Krech et al., 1966). To obtain this extreme condition, cages were suspended individually in fiberglass boxes, and these boxes were placed in an audiometric test chamber.

Singh et al. (1967, 1970) reported that rats that could observe vertical stripes on the wall outside their cage developed both behavioral and cerebral differences from rats whose cages faced a blank wall. Particularly large differences were reported in acetylcholinesterase activity; the group that could see the stripes were stated to develop twice as much acetylcholinesterase activity in posterior cerebral cortex as

Table I   Effects of three degrees of environmental enrichment on brain weight measures

	Varied objects vs. IC	Fixed objects, varied positions vs. IC	Fixed objects, fixed positions vs. IC	Varied objects vs. fixed objects, fixed positions	Varied objects vs. fixed objects, varied positions
A. S_1 males, 25–55 day, N = 11 per group					
Occipital Cortex	6.9**	11.7***	4.6*	2.1	−4.3*
Total cortex	4.2***	1.5	0.4	3.7**	2.6*
Rest of brain	0.4	−1.8	−3.3**	3.8**	2.2
Cortex/rest of brain	3.8**	3.4*	3.9**	−0.1	0.4
B. Fischer males, 40–70 day, N = 12 per group					
Occipital cortex	6.8**	8.3***	9.4***	−2.4	−1.4
Total cortex	2.8	2.3	4.6**	−1.7	0.4
Rest of brain	−1.0	0.6	2.5	−3.4*	−1.6
Cortex/rest of brain	3.8***	1.7	2.0*	1.7	2.0*
C. S_1 males, 85–115 day, N = 12 per group					
Occipital cortex	1.3	3.2	0.3	1.0	−1.8
Total cortex	3.2**	2.8*	1.9	1.3	0.3
Rest of brain	−0.4	−0.6	−0.1	−0.3	0.2
Cortex/rest of brain	3.6**	3.5**	2.0	1.6	0.1
A–C combined, N = 35 per group					
Cortex					
Occipital	4.8***	7.3***	4.8***	0.0	−2.4
Somesthetic	3.4	4.0***	3.0**	0.5	−0.6
Rem. dorsal	2.4*	2.8	2.3*	0.1	−0.3
Ventral	3.9**	0.1	2.0	1.9	3.8**
Total	3.3***	2.3**	2.4***	0.8	1.0
Rest of brain	−0.4	−0.5	−0.1	−0.2	0.2
Total brain	1.2	0.7	1.0	0.2	0.5
Cortex/rest of brain	3.7***	2.8***	2.6***	1.1	0.9

*$P < 0.05$; **$P < 0.01$; ***$P < 0.001$.
Entries represent percentage differences, first group minus second group.

did the controls (1967). The acetylcholinesterase measures not only showed large effects but the values were highly variable for controls as well as for experimentals. An attempt to replicate this experiment in our laboratory by Maki (1971) showed no cerebral differences as a consequence of the extra-cage stimuli.

Two further experiments gave clear evidence that direct interaction of the rats with the stimulus objects is necessary to obtain the usual EC–IC cerebral effects (Ferchmin et al., 1975). These "observer" experiments included three groups of animals: the usual EC rats, the IC rats, and the Observer Condition (OC) rats. The OC rats were placed in small wire-mesh cages inside the EC cage; thus they were exposed to all of the general noises, sights, and smells of the laboratory. In addition, the OC group had a small amount of contact with the EC rats through the wire mesh of the OC cages. The literature of "observational learning" suggested that the mere act of watching the EC animals at close hand might make the OC group more like EC rats than like IC rats in both brain weight and behavior. The results were clearly just the opposite. The brain weights of the OC rats were essentially identical to those of the IC rats. When tested for exploratory behavior in a Greek cross apparatus, the observer rats, like the IC rats, showed a significantly lower level of exploration than the EC rats. For some measures, the scores were even more extreme than those of the ICs.

To date we find no compelling evidence that extra-cage stimuli above the levels available in IC contribute independently to the EC–IC differences in brain measures.

Generality of effects over types of animals

Strains of rats

Initial work on brain acetylcholinesterase activity and on brain weights showed similar effects in several lines of rats tested. These were the Berkeley S_1 and S_3 lines (descendants, respectively, of a Tryon maze-bright and Tryon maze-dull line), the K-line (derived from a cross between the S_1 and the S_3 lines), and RDH, RDL, and RCH lines (lines selectively bred by Roderick (1960) for high and low brain cholinesterase) (Krech, et al., 1960; Rosenzweig et al., 1962). Later we obtained similar effects with rats of the inbred Fischer line and with Long-Evans rats. Other investigators reported similar EC–IC cerebral differences using still other lines or stocks of rats: Sprague-Dawley (Geller, 1971), Wistar (Walsh et al., 1971), and Long-Evans (Greenough, 1976).

Effects in hybrids and foundation stocks

Henderson (1970) compared the responses of hybrid mice and foundation stocks to differential experience. He kept mice in enriched environment cages or standard colony cages from birth until about six weeks of age. The subjects included inbred mice from six strains, the 30 possible crosses among the six strains, and mice from 10 four-way crosses. Among the inbred mice, the enriched-environment mice showed 1.1% greater total brain weight than did mice from standard cages; among the hybrids the corresponding difference was 5.1% and among the four-way crosses, 4.2%. Henderson argued that the presence of the brain weight differences and the fact that it is largely unidirectional indicates that there is selective advantage in the ability of the mouse to respond with increased brain size to an enriched environment. We have attempted to follow up Henderson's work by performing experiments with hybrid rats, as will be reported below.

As samples of the many possible rat hybrids that could have been used, we decided to breed males of the Fischer inbred strain to females of the Berkeley S_1 line and of the Berkeley S_3 line. We have described the selection of the Berkeley lines and have given information about their behavioral and physiological differences (Rosenzweig, 1964). The S_1 and S_3 stocks are now maintained by a random breeding procedure. Rats of the inbred Fischer line, developed at the National Institutes of Health, were obtained from the Simonsen Laboratory, Gilroy, California. Male Fischer rats were bred to female S_1 and female S_3 rats in our colony. Pups of the three foundation lines and of the two sorts of hybrids were assigned at weaning (about 25 days of age) to either the enriched condition (EC), the standard colony condition (SC), or to the impoverished condition (IC), and were maintained there for either 30 or 80 days until sacrifice.

Rather similar patterns of EC–IC effects in brain weight and brain cholinesterase–acetylcholinesterase ratio were seen for the three foundation lines and the two kinds of hybrids (Table II). In order to compare the patterns of effects, it is necessary to examine the results in some detail at this point. For brain weights, our usual finding has been clear effects in the various regions of the cerebral cortex and only small effects in the rest of the brain; among the cortical regions, the occipital cortex usually shows the largest EC–IC effects. A particularly stable value is the ratio of cortex to the rest of the brain, since this measure tends to eliminate differences related to changes in body weight. (Typically EC rats tend to grow less in body weight than do IC animals, although the EC brain and especially the EC cortex are somewhat heavier than are those of IC littermates.)

The S_1 × Fischer hybrids at the 30-day duration of differential experience were the only group to depart from the overall pattern of effects in Table II. This group showed only small EC–IC differences in the cortex, perhaps because they showed the largest EC–IC loss in body weight which tends to pull down both cortical and subcortical weights. The cortical/subcortical weight ratio for the S_1 × Fischer hybrids is quite comparable with that of the other groups with which it is compared.

The cholinesterase/acetylcholinesterase ratio gives a purely chemical measure which eliminates effects of tissue weight. With this measure, all the lines and hybrids show rather large increases in all cortical regions with enriched experience; there is little effect in the rest of the brain. The patterns of effects are rather similar among the groups.

Thus our data do not support the conclusion of Henderson, which was based on mice, that hybrids show larger effects of differential environmental experience than do inbred animals. Our results testify to the generality of cerebral effects of differential experience across lines of rats.

Table II Percentage differences, EC minus IC, in cerebral weights and enzymatic activities, for male rats of the S_1, S_3, and Fischer strains and for S_1 × Fischer and S_3 × Fischer hybrids

	30-day				80-day			
	S_1	S_1 × Fischer	Fischer	S_3 × Fischer	S_1	S_1 × Fischer	S_3	S_3 × Fischer
N (pairs)	167	11	36	10	195	12	44	10
A. Brain Weights								
Cortex								
Occipital	10.9***	2.5	7.0***	6.8*	7.1***	6.9**	5.0***	10.6**
Somesthetic	4.9***	1.8	−0.2	3.9*	2.4***	4.2*	0.4	0.0
Rem. dorsal	6.1***	5.1*	2.7**	6.0*	4.9***	5.0**	3.1***	8.8***
Ventral	4.8***	0.6	2.5*	6.8	3.1***	3.7	0.8	3.2
Total	6.0***	2.8*	2.8***	6.2***	4.2***	4.6***	2.1**	5.9***
Rest of brain	0.7*	−2.6*	−1.9**	1.8*	1.1**	−0.7	−1.5*	0.7
Total brain	3.0***	−0.2	0.1	3.7***	1.1***	1.5	0.0	2.9*
Cortex/rest of brain	5.2***	5.6**	4.9***	4.3*	5.3***	5.3***	3.6***	5.2**
Terminal body weight	−10.0***	−17.3***	−15.3***	−7.7**	−8.4***	−14.2***	−11.0***	−5.5
B. Cholinesterase/acetylcholinesterase ratio								
N (pairs)	85	11	36	10	132	12	35	10
Cortex								
Occipital	8.7***	11.0**	7.4***	8.1*	8.7***	5.3*	10.6***	11.4***
Somesthetic	3.7***	7.3*	1.9	8.8*	4.9***	1.6	4.0**	5.2
Rem. dorsal	5.5***	6.7*	2.9***	12.0***	5.8***	0.5	3.0*	5.7
Ventral	5.0***	4.8*	2.4**	7.1**	5.5***	0.6	4.2**	6.9*
Total	5.5***	6.7**	3.1***	9.2***	6.0***	1.0	4.6***	7.4**
Rest of brain	−1.2*	−0.9	−1.7*	0.8	−1.0*	−2.3*	−1.7	1.5
Total brain	0.8	1.3	0.0	3.5**	1.0**	1.4	0.2	3.5
Cortex/rest of brain	6.8***	7.6***	4.9**	8.3***	7.0***	3.5*	6.7***	5.8**

* $P < 0.05$; ** $P < 0.01$; *** $P < 0.001$.

Sex differences in effects of differential experience

With the hybrids, we put female pups into EC, SC, and IC groups separately from the males. Table III presents EC–IC brain weight and brain chemistry effects for the females which can be compared with those of the male hybrids in Table II. When we compare female and male groups of the same heredity and same duration of experience for the stable cortical/subcortical weight ratio, all four comparisons are in favor of the males. Overall, percentage EC–IC difference in the weight ratio is 5.2 ($P < 0.001$) for the males and 3.1 for the females ($P < 0.001$). In the case of the cortical/subcortical ratio for the enzymes, the males show the larger effect in three of four comparisons. Overall, the percentage EC–IC difference in cholinesterase–acetylcholinesterase ratio is 6.6 ($P < 0.001$) for the males and 4.6 ($P < 0.001$) for the females.

On other brain measures, however, the females appear to show larger EC–IC brain weight differences than the males; this is true for weight of total cortex, weight of the rest of the brain, and weight of total brain. These differences in absolute weights of brain regions are probably related to differences in body weights; we

Table III   Percentage differences, EC minus IC, in cerebral weights and enzymatic activities, for hybrid female rats

	30-day		80-day	
	$S_1 \times$ Fischer	$S_3 \times$ Fischer	$S_1 \times$ Fischer	$S_3 \times$ Fischer
A. Brain and body weights				
N (pairs)	12	12	12	12
Cortex				
Occipital	4.7*	2.6	4.8**	5.0
Somesthetic	4.4*	4.3	6.0*	−1.4
Rem. dorsal	6.2**	4.1**	8.0***	4.3*
Ventral	4.0	5.1*	6.0*	7.8**
Total	5.0**	4.4***	6.7***	5.4***
Rest of brain	1.6	3.1***	2.5	1.3
Total brain	3.1**	3.6***	4.3**	3.0*
Cortex/rest of brain	3.3**	1.3	4.1***	4.2**
Terminal body weight	2.9	3.0	7.4*	10.0**
B. Cholinesterase/acetylcholinesterase ratio				
Cortex				
Occipital	11.2**	−1.0	9.5***	5.9*
Somesthetic	2.8	0.8	2.4*	2.2
Rem. dorsal	5.9**	5.2*	6.0**	8.9***
Ventral	2.8*	4.1	6.3*	6.2*
Total	4.9***	3.6*	6.4***	6.8***
Rest of brain	1.3	0.3	0.4	1.5
Total brain	2.5**	1.4	2.3	3.2*
Cortex/rest of brain	3.5*	3.3	6.1***	5.2**

*$P < 0.05$; **$P < 0.01$; ***$P < 0.001$.

have shown previously for S_1 male rats that brain weight measures are in part determined by body weights (Rosenzweig et al., 1972). In the present experiments with hybrids, among the four groups of males, the EC rats developed significantly lower body weights than their IC littermates (-11.0%, $P < 0.001$); in the four groups of females, EC rats developed heavier body weights than their littermates in IC (5.9%, $P < 0.001$). Since both cortical and subcortical weights are affected by body weights, the cortical/subcortical weight ratio is relatively immune to changes in the body weight, and this stability helps to explain the reproducibility of this weight ratio measure from one experiment to another. The ratio of activity of cholinesterase to acetylcholinesterase is independent of both body and brain weights. Both the cortical/subcortical weight ratio and the cholinesterase/acetylcholinesterase ratio measures show larger differences between EC and IC rats in the case of males than in the case of females.

Among the cortical areas, the pattern of brain weight effects appears to differ somewhat between males and females. For three of the four types of hybrids, the difference between EC and IC rats is greater for males than for females in the occipital cortex, whereas in the somesthetic cortex, the difference is larger for females in three out of four comparisons. Diamond (1976) has described a similar sex difference in effects of differential experience on thickness of cortex in Long-Evans rats; that is, the EC–IC differences were greater for males in the occipital area but were greater for females in the somesthetic area.

Sex differences and the standard colony base line

Further insight into the origin and significance of the sex differences in cerebral effects and in the overall interpretation of environmental effects can be gained by examining the EC and IC values in relation to those of the SC littermates. Each hybrid experiment included SC as well as EC and IC animals. Certain main comparisons of EC to SC and of SC to IC values as well as EC to IC values are given in Table IV. We have asked previously whether our EC–IC effects are due principally to enrichment of experience above the colony level (EC minus SC) or due principally to impoverishment of experience below that of the colony (SC minus IC), and we have shown that both enrichment and impoverishment contribute to the overall effect (Rosenzweig et al., 1972). In the present data, we can find both kinds of effect, with some measures responding more to enrichment and others more influenced by restriction of experience.

The overall EC-IC effect in weight of occipital cortex (the largest percentage effect in most experiments) can be seen in Table IV to be principally due to enrichment in these experiments; that is, the mean EC–SC occipital weight effect for all eight groups is 5.2% ($P < 0.001$), whereas the comparable mean SC–IC effect is 0.0%. The difference between enrichment and impoverishment effects in occipital cortex is particularly striking in the case of the females. Whereas the males show a positive enrichment effect (EC minus SC, 4.1%) and a positive impoverishment effect (SC minus IC, 2.0%), the females show a rather large positive enrichment effect (EC minus SC, 6.1%) but a negative impoverishment effect, with SC females actually showing somewhat lesser occipital cortex weights than IC females (SC

Table IV   Percentage differences among EC, SC and IC conditions in cerebral weights and enzymatic activities for hybrid male and female rats

Group	Duration (days)	N	EC minus SC		Cortex rest	Terminal body weight
			Occip. cortex			
A. Brain weights						
Males						
$S_3 \times F$	30	10	4.3	3.5**	1.6	−1.2
$S_3 \times F$	80	10	7.3*	4.3**	1.7	6.1**
$S_1 \times F$	30	8	0.4	2.2	3.4*	−9.4**
$S_1 \times F$	80	9	3.8	1.0	2.7**	5.6
Total males:		37	$\overline{X}$: 4.3**	2.8***	2.3***	3.3
Females						
$S_3 \times F$	30	12	4.4	2.2*	0.9	−0.6
$S_3 \times F$	80	12	4.3	3.5**	3.3*	3.3
$S_1 \times F$	30	10	8.8**	3.9**	0.9	2.8
$S_1 \times F$	80	11	7.3***	3.1*	4.1***	−1.4
Total females:		45	$\overline{X}$: 6.0***	3.2***	2.3***	1.0
Both sexes combined:		82	$\overline{X}$: 5.2***	3.0***	2.3***	2.2*
B. Cholinesterase/acetylcholinesterase ratio						
Males						
$S_3 \times F$	30	10	0.5	3.3*	4.1*	
$S_3 \times F$	80	10	8.4***	2.8	2.9	
$S_1 \times F$	30	8	4.2	1.6	2.9*	
$S_1 \times F$	80	9	3.3	0.5	0.2	
All males:		37	$\overline{X}$: 3.4*	2.1*	2.5**	
Females						
$S_3 \times F$	30	12	−0.6	0.0	−0.9	
$S_3 \times F$	80	12	4.1	2.9	2.6	
$S_1 \times F$	30	10	2.4	1.6	0.6	
$S_1 \times F$	80	11	1.9	0.2	2.1	
All females:		45	$\overline{X}$: 1.9	1.2	1.1	
Both sexes combined:		82	$\overline{X}$: 2.6**	1.6	1.7**	

$*P < 0.05;\ **P < 0.01;\ ***P < 0.001.$

SC minus IC				EC minus IC			
Occip. cortex	Total	Cortex rest	Terminal body weight	Occip. cortex	Total	Cortex rest	Terminal body weight
2.4	2.6*	2.6	− 6.6**	6.8*	6.2***	4.3**	−7.7**
3.0	1.6	3.5*	−10.9***	10.6**	5.9**	5.2**	−5.5
0.6	0.8	2.2	− 9.8**	1.0	2.9	5.7**	−18.3***
1.6	2.8*	2.8**	−19.1***	5.6*	3.8**	5.7***	−14.5***
2.0	2.0**	2.8***	−13.8***	6.4***	4.9***	5.2***	−11.0***
−1.7	2.1*	0.3	3.5	2.6	4.4***	1.3	3.0
0.7	0.8	0.8	6.5*	5.0	5.4***	4.2**	10.0**
−3.3	0.5	2.0*	− 1.8	5.2*	4.4**	2.9**	0.9
−2.8	3.1*	0.2	8.2**	4.2**	6.3***	4.3***	6.6*
−1.7	1.9***	0.8	4.8***	4.2***	5.2***	3.1***	5.9***
0.0	2.0***	1.7***	− 5.9***	5.2***	5.0***	4.0***	−3.8***
7.5*	5.7**	4.0*		8.1*	9.2***	8.3***	
2.8	4.5*	2.9		11.4***	7.4**	5.8**	
5.9	4.2	4.4*		10.4**	5.6*	7.4***	
3.0	0.3	3.3		6.5	0.8	3.5	
6.3***	3.8***	4.0***		9.9***	6.0***	6.6***	
−0.4	3.6*	4.2*		−1.0	3.6*	3.3	
1.7	3.8*	2.6		5.9*	6.8***	5.2**	
7.3*	3.3	2.9*		9.9**	5.0**	3.5*	
6.8**	5.9***	4.0**		8.8***	6.1***	6.2***	
3.5**	4.2***	3.4***		5.4***	5.4***	4.6***	
4.7***	4.0***	3.7***		7.4***	5.6***	5.5***	

minus IC, − 1.7%). For total cortex weight also, the EC–SC effect (3.0%, $P < 0.001$) is larger than the corresponding SC–IC effect (2.0%, $P < 0.001$). In the case of the cortical/subcortical weight ratio, the enrichment and impoverishment effects are similar in magnitude for the males (EC minus SC, 2.3%, vs. SC minus IC, 2.8%), whereas for the females, the enrichment effect on this measure is considerably larger than the impoverishment effect (EC minus SC, 2.3%, vs. SC minus IC, 0.8%).

In the case of the chemical measure, the cholinesterase/acetylcholinesterase ratio, a rather different pattern is found, but it is not as clear as that for brain weights. Here the impoverishment effects are somewhat larger overall than are the enrichment effects, and this is especially true for female subjects.

We might note that it is not only among rats that the males are more responsive to environment than the females. Sackett (1972) has reported that male monkeys are more responsive to the environment and are more affected by isolation than are female monkeys.

We can summarize in the following way the foregoing review of genetic and sex variables in production of cerebral responses to differential experience: whereas the sections *Generality of effects over types of animals* (p. 177) and *Strains of rats* (p. 177) showed that genetic differences between stocks or lines of rats do not account for clear differences in effects of environments on brain measures, the sections *Effects in hybrids and foundation stocks* (p. 177) and *Sex differences in effects of differential experience* (p. 181) demonstrate that the XX versus XY chromosomal patterns are associated with differences in magnitude of cerebral responses, especially to impoverishment of experience.

Species of rodents

Similar effects to those obtained with rats have also been shown with other species of rodents. La Torre (1968) used two inbred strains of mice and found brain weights, acetylcholinesterase and cholinesterase activities to show EC–IC differences similar to those reported for rats. Rosenzweig and Bennett (1969) assigned Mongolian gerbils at 30 days of age to the EC, SC, and IC environments and kept them there until 60 days of age. Measures of brain weights, acetylcholinesterase and cholinesterase showed EC–SC–IC differences rather similar to those obtained with rats. Feral deermice (*Peromyscus*) showed EC–SC–IC effects in brain weights, acetylcholinesterase and cholinesterase generally similar to those found with other species of rodents, although the *Peromyscus* values were more variable than those of the laboratory rodents (Rosenzweig and Bennett, unpublished).

Cerebral effects as function of age at onset of differential experience

How the magnitude of cerebral effects of differential experience varies with age at onset of the experience has not been a major focus of research, but much pertinent information has been obtained. The first EC − IC experiment in which animals were placed in conditions at an age greater than 25 days used the starting age of 105 days when the rats were young adults (Rosenzweig et al., 1964). The results for brain weights were not greatly different from those previously obtained with a 25-day starting age. Later, we varied both age at onset and duration of the EC – IC period. Most of the differences between EC rats and IC littermates in weights of standard brain sections decreased somewhat with age of onset of differential rearing, but even with experience beginning at 290 days, significant effects of differential experience were found; (see Table 5 of Rosenzweig and Bennett, in the press). We have found that the magnitude of EC – IC differences does not decrease greatly with age of onset of differential experience for acetylcholinesterase, cholinesterase, or cortical thickness (Rosenzweig et al., 1972) or for RNA/DNA (Bennett and Rosenzweig, unpublished).

An exception to the relative age-independence of effects of differential experience on brain measures is the report of Greenough et al. (1976). They stated that dendritic branching in occipital cortex was not affected significantly by placing rats in EC or IC for 90 days starting at 90 days of age, whereas significant effects were obtained with 30 days of EC versus IC experience starting at weaning.

Malkasian and Diamond (1971) studied effects of preweaning experience on a few brain measures. They placed nursing rat pups and their mothers in environments of various degrees of complexity and looked for cerebral effects of early differential experience. Groups were sacrificed at 14, 19 and 28 days of age, respectively, and brain sections were analyzed for thickness of cortex and for cross-sectional areas of neuronal nuclei and perikeria. We have shown some of the results and commented on them in detail elsewhere (Rosenzweig and Bennett, in the press). Here it will suffice to note that, although the number of measures allowing comparisons of preweaning and postweaning effects is rather small, they do indicate greater cerebral responsiveness in the preweaning period than after weaning. For example, effects on cortical thickness were reported to be about twice as large with a 22-day preweaning period of differential experience as with a 30-day postweaning period of differential experience.

Cerebral effects as a function of duration of differential experience

We have recently reported considerable data on differences between EC and IC rats in weights of standard brain regions and in RNA and DNA of occipital cortex as a function of the duration of differential experience. Bennett (1976) reported brain weight effects for durations ranging from 30 to 160 days and for several starting ages (Table 17.1); he also gave RNA/DNA effects for durations ranging from 4 to 125 days, all experiments starting at weaning (Table 17.2). Rosenzweig and Bennett (in the press) present more extensive brain weight data, with durations ranging from 1 to 160 days and starting ages ranging from 25 to 282 days (Tables 2 and 5); They also report EC–IC differences in RNA, DNA and RNA/DNA for durations ranging from 4 to 125 days and starting ages ranging from 27 to 303 days (Table 4).

Exposure to EC versus IC for 1 or 3 days beginning at weaning did not produce significant differences in brain weights, but by 4 days highly significant effects were found. After a slight dip at 8 days, the magnitude of effects rose again at 15 days and reached a plateau at 30 days duration; there were only small changes in the size of the EC–IC differences between the 30- and 160-day durations. With starting ages of 60 days or more, the 4-day duration was generally insufficient to produce significant EC–IC differences, but clear effects were found at the 15-day duration.

In the case of the nucleic acids, the 4-day duration produced significant EC–IC differences in occipital cortex, and not only among weanlings but also in animals put into the differential environments at 63, 102, 202 and even at 303 days of age. The difference observed between EC and IC rats in most 4-day experiments were these: a small drop in DNA/weight, in EC vs. IC; a rise in RNA/weight, and an increase of 6–8% in RNA/DNA. The negative EC–IC difference in DNA/weight increased to about −6% at 15-day duration and then remained relatively constant through the longest duration studied in these experiments, 125 days. The EC–IC difference in RNA/weight remained positive through the 30-day duration and thereafter showed only small and irregular differences. The EC–IC percentage difference in RNA/DNA rose more rapidly than the tissue weight effect in occipital cortex and remained larger than the weight effect through the 30-day duration; then it became somewhat smaller than the weight effect although remaining highly significant.

The development of differences in thickness of occipital cortex between EC and IC male rats as a function of duration of differential experience has been summarized by Diamond (1976). Four days sufficed to produce a significant 4% effect. With greater durations of experience, the magnitude of the EC–IC difference increased to 7–8% for durations of 15 to 80 days. After 160 days in EC or IC, however, the difference had fallen to only 3%.

While the time courses have been the most thoroughly studied for effects on brain weight, nucleic acids and cortical thickness, it should not be supposed that other cerebral measures necessarily show a similar time course. For example, we know that cortical cholinesterase activity does not regularly differ between EC and IC rats after 30 days of exposure, although by 60 days there is a clear effect (Rosenzweig et al., 1972); acetylcholinesterase activity, on the contrary, does show a clear EC–IC difference at 30 days. For other variables, such as dendritic branching and dendritic spines, no information is yet available about the course of development of differences as a consequence of differential experience.

Permanence and persistence of cerebral effects

Questions concerning permanence and persistence of cerebral effects have been raised paralleling those that we reviewed in relation to behavior in the sections *Permanence of effects during prolonged differential experience* (p. 171), *Persistence of effects after animals are moved from one condition to another* (p. 172) and *Persistence of effects during testing* (p. 172, 173).

Permanence of cerebral effects during prolonged differential experience

A good deal of evidence is available to show that the cerebral effects brought about by differential experience are relatively permanent; that is, they tend to last even when the animals remain in the differential environments for long periods of time. Some of these findings have already been presented in the section *Cerebral effects as a function of duration of differential experience.* When discussing this question several years ago, Rosenzweig (1968) suggested that there were both permanent and transitory components of these cerebral changes. Unfortunately, the term "transitory" was seized upon by a number of writers, and they concluded that the effects in general were not permanent. We have now presented extensive data that indicate that the brain weight changes last for as long as we have tested, 160 days (Rosenzweig and Bennett, in the press). Cummins et al. (1973) reported that differential cortical dimensions were apparent when the animals spent more than 500 days in differential conditions. We have recently shown the EC–IC effect on RNA/DNA ratio to last for as long as we have tested it, 125 days (Bennett, 1976, Table 17.2).

Persistence of cerebral effects after animals are moved from one condition to another

There is less consensus about how well the induced cerebral effects persist when animals are removed from one environment and placed in another. Brown (1971) reported surprisingly large (and variable) differences in acetylcholinesterase and cholinesterase activities produced by her version of an enriched environment. She claimed that these effects vanished within a few days after animals were removed from EC and placed in isolation. Under our conditions of EC, we have not found this to be the case; differences in cortical brain weight measures and in acetylcholinesterase activity decline after our EC rats are placed into IC but remain measurable for the longest period that we have tried, seven weeks. The decrease in EC–IC differences is slower when the EC period has lasted for 80 days than after only 30 days of EC experience (Bennett et al., 1974).

Little information is available about effects of changes in the opposite direction, from an impoverished to an enriched condition. We have reported that when rats had been in IC from 25 to 105 days of age and were then placed in EC from 105 to 155 days, the final weight of total cortex was as great as that of littermate rats that had remained in EC throughout (Rosenzweig et al., 1967, Fig. 3). In other words, it appears that the cerebral effects of impoverishment can be readily overcome by subsequent enrichment, whereas some of the effects of enriched experience tend to persist through a subsequent period of impoverished experience.

Persistence of cerebral effects during behavioral testing

We have consistently observed that cerebral differences are reduced or abolished during behavioral testing (Rosenzweig et al., 1967) although we have not published such results in detail. That is, in experiments in which cerebral measures have been obtained from some animals at the end of the period of enriched or impoverished experience whereas cerebral measures have been taken from other EC and IC animals only after an intervening period of behavioral testing, the tested animals always show diminished EC–IC differences. Using a similar experimental design, Cummins et al. (1973) found significant EC–IC differences in forebrain weight and in the product of cerebral length and width after 509 days of EC or IC experience. When some groups were then tested on the Hebb-Williams maze before sacrifice, the cerebral EC–IC differences were reduced because of increases in the values of the IC rats. Behavioral testing may provide a type of enriched experience to which animals that have been in IC now show a rapid cerebral response.

Relations between effects of experience on adaptive behavior and on cerebral measures

The studies we have reviewed to this point have demonstrated effects of experience on both behavior and on brain. We have examined several aspects of generality versus specificity of effects and also ways in which the production and persistence of effects are influenced by parameters of the experimental situations. Table V presents an overall view of the material that we have examined. It shows a high degree of comparability between effects of environment and experimental parameters on learning or problem solving, on the one hand, and on cerebral measures, on the other. For some of the headings of the table, no comparison can be made between behavioral and cerebral effects because one or the other sort of investigation does not seem to have been carried out. Thus, for example, as to generality of effects among orders of mammals, there exist several behavioral studies, but there do not appear to be any reports as yet of effects of differential experience on brain measures in carnivores or in primates, Obtaining cerebral measures on other orders of mammals would appear to be worthwhile in itself and to allow a more critical evaluation of the comparability of behavioral and cerebral measures.

The general similarity of effects of differential experience on adaptive behavior and on cerebral measures would support the hypothesis that the behavioral effects are mediated by cerebral effects of environment. To test this hypothesis critically, special attention should be paid to any apparent discrepancies between the behavioral and the cerebral effects. Let us consider one example: Gottlieb (1974) has suggested that there may be discrepancies between the behavioral and cerebral effects because "in contradistinction to behavior in the Hebb-Williams test, the brain changes can be induced in adult animals. Furthermore the brain changes are reversible; that is, the increases in weight and changes in neurochemicals brought about by enriched condition are then lost if the animal is returned to the impoverished condition" (p. 569). Let us examine more closely the bases for alledging the existence of this double discrepancy.

In support of the claim that behavioral effects can be caused only if animals are exposed to a complex environment early in life, Gottlieb cited Hymovitch (1952) who reported that exposure of rats to a free environment from 30 to 75 days of age aided later performance on the Hebb-Williams maze, whereas exposure from 85 to 130 days had no effect. It should be pointed out that Hymovitch's study was conducted with very small groups of rats (only 3 to 6 per condition) and that it has not been supported by later, larger experiments. Forgays and Read (1962) exposed groups of about 9 rats each to a complex environment for periods of three weeks beginning either at birth, at day 22 (weaning), or days 44, 66, 88. All groups were tested on the Hebb-Williams maze beginning on day 123. All groups except the 88–109 day group were significantly better on the Hebb-Williams maze than the group with no enriched experience. The 88–109 day group had scores only very slightly worse than those of the 0–21 day group and just missed differing significantly from the control group. Nyman (1967) exposed rats to an enriched environment at 30–40, 50–60 or 70–80 days of age. 8 h/day exposure at any of the three periods showed significant beneficial effects for later spatial learning, as compared with the control condition. In unpublished experiments, we have found effects of EC versus SC experience on Hebb-Williams maze scores when exposure to EC began after 80 days of age. In six experiments in which differential experience started at 85, 101 or 123 days of age, the ratio of total errors of SC to EC rats was 1.27 ($N = 45$ per group). In six experiments in which differential experience started at around 33 days of age, the ratio of errors of SC to EC rats was 1.18 ($N = 53$ per group).

Doty (1972) placed 18 Sprague-Dawley rats in an enriched environment at 300 days of age while keeping 18 littermates in standard laboratory cages. After 360 days of differential experience, the rats were tested on a light-dark active avoidance task, an avoidance reversal task, and a passive avoidance task. The EC group was only slightly better than the control rats on the first task, but was significantly better on the latter two tasks. The preponderance of evidence thus indicates that enriched experience that begins well after weaning can alter problem solving ability as well as cerebral value, so there does not seem to be a discrepancy here between the behavioral and cerebral effects.

The second discrepancy alleged by Gottlieb is that the brain changes induced by enriched experience are reversible whereas the behavioral effects are not. Here the behavioral effects are again taken from Experiment III of Hymovitch (1952). In this experiment, Group 1 received enriched experience between 30 and 75 days of age, and they spent the period from 85 to 130 days of age in isolation cages; group 2 rats were in isolation cages from 30 to 75 days of age, and they had enriched experience from 85 to 130 days of age; group 3 rats received enriched experience at both 30 to 75 days of age and 85 to 130 days; group 4 remained throughout in normal colony cages, the number of rats per cage not being stated. When the rats were tested on the Hebb-Williams maze, group 3, which had both early and late enriched experience, had the best performance (152.6 errors), and group 1 with only early enriched experience scored only slightly worse (161.3 errors); group 2 with only late enriched experience scored 248.8 errors. It may be that group 1 with early enriched experience and later isolation lost some of the beneficial effects of the early experience, since they did show a slightly larger error figure than group 3, but again it is impossible to be sure since the two groups included only 6 and 3 subjects, respectively. Gottlieb does not cite any source for his statement that the cerebral changes are reversible. As we have seen above, whereas Brown (1971) reported that the effects of enriched environment vanished within a few days after animals were removed from EC and placed in isola-

Table V   Comparison of effects of experience in differential environments on behavioral and cerebral measures

Effects of various aspects of differential environments	Effects on learning or problem-solving	Effects on cerebral measures
Social aspects	Social grouping versus isolation aids subsequent learning and retention (p. 165).	Social grouping versus isolation produces some cerebral effects (p. 173–174).
Interaction with objects in environment	Interaction with stimulus objects in environment aids subsequent performance, when social stimulation is equivalent (p. 165).	Interaction with stimulus objects in environment produces cerebral effects, independently of social effects (p. 173–174).
Intra-cage versus extra-cage stimulation	Extra-cage stimuli produce no effects in most cases (p. 166).	Extra-cage stimuli above the level of IC produce little or no effects on brain measures (p. 175, 177).
Generality of effects Among strains of rats	High generality: enriched-experience rats perform better than colony or impoverished-experience rats (p. 166).	High generality (p. 177).
Sex of rats	Similar effects in both sexes, but little explicit comparison between sexes (p. 166).	Effects of enrichment similar in both sexes; effects of impoverishment larger in males (p. 180–181, 184).
Species of rodents	A few studies show effects among mice; no studies on rodents other than rats and mice (p. 167).	Similar effects found for rats, mice, gerbils, and *Peromyscus* (p. 184).
Orders of mammals	Enriched experience aids solving of some problems in cats, dogs, and monkeys (p. 167–169).	(No reports on animals other than rodents.)

Effects as function of age at onset of differential experience	Positive effects obtained for all ages tested: preweaning, immediately postweaning, or adult (p. 169–171).	Positive effects obtained for all ages tested: preweaning, immediately postweaning, or adult (p. 184–185).
Effects as function of duration of differential experience	Many durations used in various studies, but little attempt to study how magnitude of effect varies with duration. Significant results obtained with as little as 1 h/day of EC over a 10-day period (p. 171).	As little as 4 days EC causes significant increases of cortical weight and RNA. Most effects rise to a plateau as duration of experience increases (p. 185–186).
Persistence of effects During prolonged differential experience	Effects persist (p. 171).	Effects persist. As experience is prolonged beyond 30 days, some measures show decreased differences, while others show increases (p. 186–187).
After animals are moved from one environment to another	Effects persist when rats moved from EC to SC; effects of other shifts not tested (p. 172).	Partial loss of differences when rats moved from EC to IC. Greater persistence with longer initial exposure (p. 187).
During prolonged behavioral testing	Discrepant results; some reports of persisting difference, some reports that groups converge during testing (p. 172–173).	Effects are diminished during testing; IC values move to approach those of EC rats (p. 187–188).

tion, we have found considerable persistence of both brain-weight and chemical effects; some of these have remained significant for the longest period that we have tested (7 weeks). It appears that more work is needed both on the behavioral side and with the cerebral measures to determine the persistence of the effects induced by differential experience. It seems premature to conclude on the basis of available evidence that there is a discrepancy between the behavioral and the cerebral effects.

The overall correspondence between behavioral and cerebral effects in Table V lends considerable support to the hypothesis that the behavioral effects are mediated by at least some of the cerebral effects. Since a number of cerebral effects have been described, and since they vary in their time courses and responsiveness to various parameters of the experimental treatments, more fine-grained analyses are necessary to yield searching tests of the hypothesis. In particular, it would seem highly desirable for the same investigators to work on both the behvioral and cerebral sides. This will ensure that truly comparable treatments are being used as the independent variables, so that the most critical analyses can be made of effects on the dependent variables.

Acknowledgements

This research received support from the National Institutes of Mental Health (Grants RO1-MH26704 and RO1-MH26327) as well as from the National Science Foundation (Grant GB-20268X) and Division of Biomedical and Environmental Research of the U.S. Energy Research and Development Administration through the Laboratory of Chemical Biodynamics, Lawrence Berkeley Laboratory. The authors wish to thank Marie Hebert for dissection of brains and Hiromi Morimoto for enzymatic analyses, Donald Dryden and Kenneth Chin for behavioral testing, Jessie Langford for secretarial work, and the many students who volunteered their assistance.

Literature cited

Bennett, E. L. (1976) Cerebral effects of differential experience and training. In: *Neural Mechanisms of Learning and Memory* (M. R. Rosenzweig and E. L. Bennett, eds.) pp. 279–287, MIT Press, Cambridge, Mass.

Bennett, E. L., Rosenzweig, M. R. and Diamond, M. C. (1970) Time courses of effects of differential experience on brain measures and behavior of rats. In: *Molecular Approaches to Learning and Memory* (W. L. Byrne, ed.) pp. 55–89, Academic Press, New York

Bennett, E. L., Rosenzweig, M. R., Diamond, M. C., Morimoto, H. and Hebert, M. (1974) Effects of successive environments on brain measures, *Physiol. Behav. 12*, 621–631

Bennett, T. L. and Ellis, H. C. (1968) Tactual-kinesthetic feedback from manipulation of visual forms and nondifferential reinforcement in transfer of perceptual learning, *J. Exper. Psychol. 77*, 495–500

Bernstein, L. (1972) The reversibility of learning deficits in early environmentally restricted rats as a function of amount of experience in later life, *J. Psychosom. Res. 16*, 71–73

Bernstein, L. (1973) A study of some enriching variables in a free-environment for rats, *J. Psychosom. Res. 17*, 85–88

Bingham, W. E. and Griffiths, W. J. (1952) The effect of differential environments during infancy on adult behavior in the rat, *J. Comp. Physiol. Psychol. 45*, 307–312

Brown, C. P. (1971) Cholinergic activity in rats following enriched stimulation and training: Direction and duration of effects, *J. Comp. Physiol. Psychol. 75*, 408–416

Brown, R. T. (1968) Early experience and problem-solving ability, *J. Comp. Physiol. Psychol. 65*, 433–440

Chang, S. -Y. (1969) *Changes Produced in Rat Brain by Environmental Complexity and Drug Injection*, Doctoral dissertation, University of California

Cooper, R. M. and Zubek, J. P. (1958) Effects of enriched and restricted early environments on the learning ability of bright and dull rats, *Can. J. Psychol. 12*, 159–164

Cummins, R. A., Walsh, R. N., Budtz-Olsen, O. E., Konstantinos, T. and Horsfall, C. R. (1973) Environmentally-induced changes in the brain of elderly rats, *Nature 243*, 516–518

Davenport, J. W. (1976) Environment as therapy for brain effects of endocrine dysfunction. In: *Environments as Therapeutic Agents for Brain Disorders* (R. Walsh and W. R. Greenough, eds,) Plenum Press, New York

Davenport, R. K., Rogers, C. M. and Rumbaugh, D. M. (1973) Long-term cognitive deficits in chimpanzees associated with early impoverished rearing, *Devel. Psychol. 9*, 343–347

Denenberg, V. H., Woodcock, J. M. and Rosenberg, K. M. (1968) Long-term effects of pre-weaning and postweaning free-environment experience on rats' problem-solving behavior, *J. Comp. Physiol. Psychol. 66*, 533–535

Diamond, M. C. (1976) Anatomical brain changes induced by environment. In: *Knowing, Thinking, and Believing*, pp. 215–239, (L. Petrinovich and J. L. McGaugh, eds.) Plenum Press, New York

Doty, B. A. (1972) The effects of cage environment upon avoidance responding of aged rats, *J. Gerontol. 27*, 358–360

Edwards, H. P., Barry, W. F. and Wyspianski, J. O. (1969) Effect of differential rearing on photic evoked potentials and brightness discrimination in the albino rat, *Devel. Psychobiol. 2*, 133–138

Ferchmin, P., Bennett, E. L. and Rosenzweig, M. R. (1975) Direct contact with enriched environment is required to alter cerebral weight in rats, *J. Comp. Physiol. Psychol. 88*, 360–367

Forgays, D. G. and Forgays, J. W. (1952) The nature of the effect of free-environmental experience on the rat, *J. Comp. Physiol. Psychol. 45*, 322–328

Forgays, D. G. and Read, J. M. (1962) Crucial periods for free-environmental experience in the rat, *J. Comp. Physiol. Psychol. 55*, 816–818

Freeman, B. J. and Ray, O. W. (1972) Strain, sex, and environmental effects on appetitively and aversively motivated learning tasks, *Devel. Psycholobiol. 5*, 101–109

Fuller, J. L. (1966) Transitory effects of experiential deprivation upon reversal learning in dogs, *Psychonom. Sci. 4*, 273–274

Gardner, E. B., Boitano, J. J., Mancino, N. S., D'Amico, D. P. and Gardner, E. L. (1975) Environmental enrichment and deprivation. Effects on learning, memory and exploration, *Physiol. Behav. 14*, 321–327

Geller, E. (1971) Some observations on the effects of environmental complexity and isolation on biochemical ontogeny. In: *Brain Development and Behavior* (M. B. Sterman, D. J. McGinty and A. M. Adinolfi, eds.) pp. 277–296, Academic Press, New York

Gill, J. H., Reid, L. D. and Porter, P. B. (1966) Effects of restricted rearing on Lashley stand performance, *Psychol. Rep. 19*, 239–242

Gluck, J. P., Harlow, H. F. and Schiltz, K. A. (1973) Differential effect of early enrichment and deprivation on learning in the rhesus monkey (Macaca mulatta), *J. Comp. Physiol. Psychol. 84*, 598–604

Gottlieb, G. (1974) Die Entwicklung des Verhaltens, In: *Grzimeks Tierleben* (K. Immelmann, ed.) pp. 551–570, Kindler Verlag, Zurich

Greenough, W. T. (1976) Enduring brain effects of differential experience and training. In: *Neural Mechanisms of Learning and Memory* (M. R. Rosenzweig and E. L. Bennett, eds.), pp. 255–277, MIT Press, Cambridge, Mass.

Greenough, W. T., Snow, F. M. and Fiala, B. A. (1976) Environmental complexity versus isolation. A sensitive period for effects on cortical and hippocampal dendritic branching in rats? *Neurosci. Abs. 2*, 824 (Abstract No. 1184)

Greenough, W. T., Madden, T. C. and Fleischmann, T. B. (1972a) Effects of isolation, daily handling, and enriched rearing on maze learning, *Psychonom. Sci. 27*, 279–280

Greenough, W. T., Wood, W. E. and Madden, T. C. (1972b) Possible memory storage differences among mice reared in environments varying in complexity, *Behav. Biol. 7*, 717–722

Griffin, G. A. and Harlow, H. F. (1966) Effects of three months of total social deprivation on social adjustment and learning in the Rhesus monkey, *Child Devel. 37*, 533–548

Hebb, D. O. (1949) *The Organization of Behavior*, Wiley, New York

Henderson, N. D. (1970) Genetic influences on the behavior of mice can be obscured by laboratory rearing, *J. Comp. Physiol. Psychol. 72*, 505–511

Hughes, K. R. (1965) Dorsal and ventral hippocampus lesions and maze learning: Influence of preoperative environment, *Can. J. Psychol. 19*, 325–332

Hymovitch, B. (1952) The effects of experimental variations on problem-solving in the rat, *J. Comp. Physiol. Psychol. 45*, 313–321

Krech, D., Rosenzweig, M. R. and Bennett, E. L. (1960) Effects of environmental complexity and training on brain chemistry, *J. Comp. Physiol. Psychol. 53*, 509–519

Krech, D., Rosenzweig, M. R. and Bennett, E. L. (1962) Relations between brain chemistry and problem-solving, among rats raised in enriched and impoverished environments, *J. Comp. Physiol. Psychol. 55*, 801–807

Krech, D., Rosenzweig, M. R. and Bennett, E. L. (1966) Environmental impoverishment, social isolation and changes in brain chemistry and anatomy, *Physiol. Behav. 1*, 99–104

La Torre, J. C. (1968) Effect of differential environmental enrichment on brain weight and on acetylcholinesterase and cholinesterase activities in mice, *Exp. Neurol 22*, 493–503

Maki, W. S., Jr. (1971) Failure to replicate effect of visual pattern restriction on brain and behaviour, *Nature New Biol., 233*, 63–64

Malkasian, D. R. and Diamond, M. C. (1971) The effects of environmental manipulation on the morphology of the neonate rat brain, *Intl. J. Neurosci. 2*, 161–170

Meier, G. W. and McGee, R. K. (1959) A re-evaluation of the effect of early perceptual experience on discrimination performance during adulthood, *J. Comp. Physiol. Psychol. 52*, 390–395

Melzack, R. (1962) Effects of early perceptual restriction on simple visual discrimination, *Science 137*, 978–979

Nyman, A. J. (1967) Problem solving in rats as a function of experience at different ages, *J. Genet. Psychol. 110*, 31–39

Ough, B. R., Beatty, W. W. and Khalili, J. (1972) Effects of isolated and enriched rearing on response inhibition, *Psychonom. Sci. 27*, 293–294

Ray, O. S. and Hochhauser, S. (1969) Growth hormone and environmental complexity effects on behavior in the rat, *Devel. Psychol. 1*, 311–317

Reid, L. D., Gill, J. H. and Porter, P. B. (1968) Isolated rearing and Hebb-Williams maze performance, *Psychol. Rep. 22*, 1073–1077

Riege, W. H. (1971) Environmental influences on brain and behavior of year-old rats, *Devel. Psychobiol. 4*, 157–167

Roderick, T. H. (1960) Selection for cholinesterase activity in the cerebral cortex of the rat, *Genetics 45*, 1123–1140

Rosenzweig, M. R. (1964) Effects of heredity and environment on brain chemistry, brain anatomy, and learning ability in the rat, *Kans. Stud. Educ. 14*, 3–34

Rosenzweig, M. R. (1968) Effects of experience on brain chemistry and brain anatomy, *Atti Accad. Naz. Lincei 109*, 43–63

Rosenzweig, M. R. (1971) Effects of environment on development of brain and of behavior.

In: *The Biopsychology of Development* (E. Tobach, L. R. Aronson and E. Shaw, eds.) pp. 303–342, Academic Press, New York

Rosenzweig, M. R. and Bennett, E. L. (1969) Effects of differential environments on brain weights and enzyme activities in gerbils, rats and mice, *Devel. Psychobiol. 2*, 87–95

Rosenzweig, M. R. and Bennett, E. L. (1972) Cerebral changes in rats exposed individually to an enriched environment, *J. Comp. Physiol. Psychol. 80*, 304–313

Rosenzweig, M. R. and Bennett, E, L. (eds.) (1976) *Neural Mechanisms of Learning and Memory*, MIT Press, Cambridge, Mass.

Rosenzweig, M. R., and Bennett, E. L. (1977) Experiential influences on brain anatomy and brain chemistry in rodents. In: *Studies on the Development of Behavior and the Nervous System* (G. Gottlieb, ed.) Academic Press, New York, in the press

Rosenzweig, M. R., Bennett, E. L. and Diamond, M. C. (1967) Effects of differential environments on brain anatomy and brain chemistry. In: *Psychopathology of Mental Development* (J. Zubin and G. Jervis, eds.) pp. 45–56, Grune & Stratton, New York

Rosenzweig, M. R., Bennett, E. L. and Diamond, M. C. (1972) Chemical and anatomical plasticity of brain: Replications and extensions, 1970. In: *Macromolecules and Behavior* (J. Gaits, ed.) 2nd edn., pp. 205–277, Appleton-Century-Crofts, New York

Rosenzweig, M. R., Bennett, E. L. and Krech, D. (1964) Cerebral effects of environmental complexity and training among adult rats, *J. Comp. Physiol. Psychol. 57*, 438–439

Rosenzweig, M. R., Krech, D., Bennett, E. L. and Diamond, M. C. (1962) Effects of environmental complexity and training on brain chemistry and anatomy. A replication and extension, *J. Comp. Physiol. Psychol. 55*, 429–437

Sackett, G. P. (1972) Exploratory behavior of rhesus monkeys as a function of rearing experiences and sex, *Devel. Psychol. 6*, 260–270

Singh, D., Johnston, R. J. and Klosterman, H. J. (1967) Effect on brain enzyme and behavior in the rat of visual pattern restriction in early life, *Nature 216*, 1337–1338

Singh, D., Maki, W. S., Jr., Johnston, R. J. and Klosterman, H. J. (1970) Affect of visual pattern restriction in early life on brain enzyme, body weight and learning in the rat, *Nature 228*, 471–472

Sturgeon, R. D. and Reid, L. D. (1971) Rearing variations and Hebb-Williams maze performance, *Psychol. Rep. 29*, 571–580

Thompson, W. R. and Heron, W. (1954) The effects of restricting early experience on the problem-solving capacity of dogs, *Can. J. Psychol. 8*, 17–31

Walsh, R. N., Budtz-Olsen, O. E., Torok, A. and Cummins, R. A. (1971) Environmental complexity induced changes in the dimensions of the rat cerebrum, *Devel. Psychobiol. 4*, 115–122

Welch, B. L., Brown, D. G., Welch, A. S. and Lin, D. C. (1974) Isolation, restrictive confinement or crowding of rats for one year. I. Weight, nucleic acids and protein of brain regions, *Brain Res. 75*, 71–84

Will, B. E. and Rosenzweig, M. R. (1976) Effets de l'environnement sur la récupération fonctionnelle après lésions cérébrales chez des rats adultes, *Biol. Behav. 1*, 5–16

Will, B. E., Rosenzweig, M. R. and Bennett, E. L. (1976) Effects of differential environments on recovery from neonatal brain lesions, measured by problem-solving scores, *Physiol. Behav 16*, 603–611

Will, B. E., Rosenzweig, M. R., Bennett, E. L., Hebert, M. and Morimoto, H. (1977) Relatively brief environmental enrichment aids recovery of learning capacity and alters brain measures after postweaning brain lesions in rats, *J. Comp. Physiol. Psychol. 91*, 33–50

Wilson, M., Warren, J. M. and Abbott, L. (1965) Infantile stimulation, activity, and learning by cats, *Child Devel. 36*, 843–853

Woods, P. J. (1959) The effects of free and restricted environmental experience on problem-solving behavior in the rat, *J. Comp. Physiol. Psychol. 52*, 399–402

Woods, P. J., Fiske, A. S. and Ruckelshaus, S. I. (1961) The effects of drives conflicting with exploration on the problem-solving behavior of rats reared in free and restricted environments, *J. Comp. Physiol. Psychol. 54*, 167–169

Woods, P. J., Ruckelshaus, S. I. and Bowling, D. M. (1960) Some effects of "free" and "restricted" environment rearing conditions upon adult behavior in the rat, *Psychol. Rep. 6*, 191–200

Yeterian, E. H. and Wilson, W. A. (1976) Cross-model transfer in rats following different early environments, *Bull. Psychonom. Sci. 7*, 551–553

Genetics, environment and intelligence, edited by A. Oliverio
© *Elsevier/North-Holland Biomedical Press, 1977*

Early separation and behavioral maturation

11

STEPHEN J. SUOMI and HARRY F. HARLOW

Introduction

In past years, a considerable body of research in the area of social development was primarily geared toward resolution of the nature–nurture conflict. Vigorous arguments raged between those who viewed social development as a sequence of maturing systems genetically preprogrammed and only modestly influenced by environmental extremes, as opposed to those who considered social development basically to be a product of the social environment of the organism, with unlearned response systems regarded as unimportant and uninteresting. These conflicts are now largely past history, for today the predominant view is that development is best understood as an interaction between heredity and environment, between nature and nurture (Lehrman, 1970; Hinde, 1974).

Acknowledging the existence and also the importance of an interaction between these two spheres is one matter; specifying the details of the interaction is quite another. The current consensus of opinion regarding the former is not shared in respect to the latter. There exist several differing theories as to how genes and environment interact in determining the course of social maturation. Some emphasize learning factors. Others stress motivational interpretations. Alternative viewpoints exist as well.

We feel that none of the above positions is either totally correct or totally incorrect. Rather, it is our view that social maturation encompasses such a complex series of phenomena that no single approach can do it explanatory justice. Some phenomena are best understood from a learning level of analysis, while some phenomena are best subsumed under motivational explanations. Other phenomena are better addressed from different points of view. The problem involves knowing when to take what point.

In this chapter we will present an account of social maturation in the rhesus monkey (*Macaca mulatta*). We will describe normative patterns of social development in the species and then show how such patterns can be influenced and altered by various environmental contingencies. In the process, we propose to argue that separate theoretical approaches are necessary to account for the specific phenomena associated with two different classes of heredity—environment interactions: those that are associated with denying a monkey access to certain classes of social stimuli and those that are associated with the interruption of previously established social relationships.

Rhesus monkey social development in feral environments

A rhesus monkey infant born into a feral environment is hardly able to survive on its own, let alone assume a contributory role within its social group. Indeed it is relatively helpless, highly dependent on the mother for both physical and social needs during the first weeks of life. The infant constantly remains in or within her arms reach. Unlike adult females in some other macaque species, the rhesus mother is quite possessive and does not permit other female group members to take the infant away from her.

Within a few weeks, however, the infant begins to venture out on its own, leaving the mother's reach for short periods of time. While she usually permits it to come and go as it pleases, the mother constantly monitors her infant's activities and never allows it to enter into potentially dangerous situations. The infant uses its mother as a security base for these initial forays, returning to her side or ventrum every few seconds. The distances and durations of these early excursions increase dramatically as the infant grows older, but the mother continues to serve as its home base.

On these trips, the infant encounters new stimuli, both inanimate and animate, and it begins to interact increasingly with other monkeys in its social unit. These may be other adult females, adolescents of both sexes, and occasionally adult males, but most often the infant's interactions involve other infants like itself. Play with age-mates emerges as the infant's predominant social activity during the second quarter of its first year of life. Interactions with its mother decrease both in frequency and in duration.

By the end of its first year, the young rhesus is largely independent of its mother, although it may still spend considerable time in relative physical proximity to her. However, virtually all of its social interactions are now with other monkeys. Increasingly, the interactions involve like-sexed partners, particularly in the case of males. Moreover, the sexes are differentiated by the nature of their predominant behaviors as well as by the nature of their partners. Males play and fight more than do females; females groom more and are more likely to interact with neonates than are males. These differences increase as the monkeys approach sexual maturity.

Adolescent monkeys differ by sex in another important respect, location within the social unit. In general, female adolescents tend to stay close physically to their mothers; they also usually share their mothers' social status. In contrast, most male adolescents drift toward the periphery of the social unit, often forming smaller sub-groups. Only a few males remain in the proximity of their mothers, usually only those whose mothers are either very high or very low in social status within the social unit.

With sexual maturity, most rhesus monkeys largely maintain the repertoire of be-haviors and confraternity with partners developed during adolescence. This is not to say that postpubescent changes in pattern of social behavior do not occur, for adult rhesus monkey interactions tend to be highly dynamic, rather than basically static or stereotyped. But general trends evident prior to puberty clearly carry over to adult activities. Females largely repeat the life-styles of their mothers. Males may work their way back into the center of the group, move to a different social unit, or remain on the periphery of the rhesus social community.

These patterns of social development have been repeatedly reported by field in-vestigators (e.g., Southwick et al., 1965; Lindburg, 1973; Kaufmann, 1966). Most pro-bably they represent patterns of social development that have evolved over countless generations of rhesus monkeys. They are patterns that probably will continue to evolve, assuming that feral environments will continue to exist for rhesus monkeys.

Social development in "adequate" laboratory environments

The patterns of social development in rhesus monkeys observed by field investigators have been basically replicated by rhesus monkeys living in certain laboratory en-vironments. Such environments always contain at least mothers and peers (Hansen, 1966); most also contain one or more adult males and adolescents of both sexes (Hinde and White, 1974; Ruppenthal et al., 1974). Detailed longitudinal study of infants reared in these environments have not only verified the patterns exhibited by feral-born and reared rhesus, but also have yielded important details of develop-ment that would be difficult to discern in the field.

For example, as a result of laboratory study we now understand many of the vari-ables that initially tie mother and infant to one another and lead to the development of their complex social relationship. Several studies have clearly demonstrated that infants are predisposed to exhibit certain behavior patterns almost reflexively shortly after birth. Among the more important of these patterns appear to be sucking and clinging. Sucking clearly is necessary for the infant to obtain nutrition, while clinging enables the infant to obtain and maintain contact comfort with its mother. Harlow's classic (1958) work with surrogates established the predominance of the latter over the former in contributing to the development of an attachment relationship with the mother.

Other work (Sackett, 1970; Suomi et al., 1970) has shown that neonatal rhesus monkeys have definite social preferences for members of their own species over those of closely related species within the same genus, as well as preferences for adult female over adult male rhesus monkeys. These preferences appear to be unlearned. It does not take much imagination to see how such preferences might help tie the infant to its mother early in life.

For her part, the mother is clearly strongly motivated to keep her infant in intimate physical contact. While those variables that influence a mother's attraction to her infant presently are all not well understood, it is likely that hormonal factors play major roles. Also, it appears that contact stimulation by the infant may itself be highly reinforcing for the mother – a lactating female will readily adopt an infant that is not her own, unless the infant fails to cling to her, in which case it is usually abandoned by the female (Harlow and Harlow, 1965).

Laboratory research has also underscored the importance of a mother for development of the infant's exploratory activities. Demonstrations by Harlow and colleagues (e.g., Harlow and Zimmermann, 1958) have verified field observations that the infant uses its mother as a security base for its exploratory forays. Recent work by Simpson (1976) has suggested that the mother serves an additional function: that of providing a standard by which the infant can practice and master physical feats. Simpson has observed that during the second and third months of life the infant returns to or looks at its mother on a very regular schedule when it is exploring or playing away from her. He hypothesizes that infants use these contacts with the mother as standard time units through which to gauge achievement of specific physical feats, e.g. mastering the art of climbing up a certain branch. Simpson's analysis is intriguing; if true, it could tie the infant to its mother even closer psychologically than previously suspected by most investigators.

Another factor tying infant to mother, one that has long been recognized by field workers, laboratory investigators, and theoreticians alike, is the emergence of social fear in the infant. Elegant laboratory research by Sackett (1966) has demonstrated that neonatal monkeys do not exhibit social fear, but that between 60 and 80 days of age fear responses to certain social stimuli appear in each infant's repertoire, independent of rearing environment. Routine developmental data collected by several different laboratories have documented that rhesus infants that had previously explored virtually everything within reach all became considerably more wary of most novel social stimuli during this chronological period. Infants most often displayed this wariness by seeking proximity and/or physical contact with their mothers. The similarity of these findings to the emergence of "stronger anxiety" and related phenomena in human children is striking; the mother monkey appears to provide her infant with all the security and trust that has been ascribed to human mothers for their infants (Bowlby, 1973). A mother that abates her infants' fears effectively most likely will rear an infant that is not reluctant to enter into interactions with other monkeys and thus expose itself to socialization by the rest of the social unit (Suomi and Harlow, 1976).

Longitudinal laboratory researches have also verified field observations that during the second half of year 1, infants become increasingly independent of their mothers, interacting more and more with other monkeys, particularly peers. The mechanisms underlying the development of such independence have been the subject of considerable debate over the past decade. Some investigators have claimed that the mother is primarily responsible for the infant's growing independence, actively rejecting her infant's attempts to obtain and maintain contact more frequently and vigorously as it matures (Hansen, 1966). Others have argued that maternal rejection serves only to strengthen the infant's tendency to seek contact when distressed. They maintain that the primary factors responsible for the infant's burgeoning independence are its own curiosity and the intrinsic attractiveness of its social environment (Rosenblum, 1971). Actually, recent data suggest that all the above arguments are partially correct and that no argument is totally correct. Specifically, both the mother and the infant most probably contribute to the waning of their mutual affectional relationship, only at different points chronologically (Hinde and White, 1974). Moreover, there appear to be individual differences among mother–infant pairs with respect to both the frequency and the effectiveness of maternal rejection in developing infant independence. Finally, the attractiveness of the social environment for the infant depends in large part on who is a part of it. Infants exposed to many different age–sex classes of conspecifics leave their mothers earlier chronologically than those that have few potential playmates (Suomi, 1976). These data all indicate that the dynamics of the mother–infant relationship in rhesus monkeys are highly complex and subject to influence from a number of sources.

Whatever the underlying reasons, rhesus monkeys do spend increasing amounts of time interacting with other conspecifics as they mature. Recent work has indicated that the form and frequency of such interactions are highly dependent on both the age and sex of the subject and the age and sex of available social partners besides the mother. For example, both male and female youngsters spend most of their second year of life in play interactions with similar-aged peers, if the peers are available. If a female is playing with a female peer, the play will most likely be of a chasing, non-contact form; if a male is playing with another male, the play will most likely be contact-oriented (often termed "rough-and-tumble play"). If the participants in a play bout are of both sexes, the type of play may take either form, often depending on who initiated the bout (Harlow and Lauersdorf, 1974). To further complicate the issue, males are more likely to reciprocate the play initiation of another male than that of a female peer, whereas females are equally likely to reciprocate the play initiate of both male and female peers. As a result, males generally exhibit higher overall levels of play than do females, at least within sex-mixed groups of peers (Ruppenthal et al., 1974).

Other sex differences in form and frequency of social behaviors appear as rhesus infants mature to adolescence. Although females may play less than males in terms of absolute frequency, they exhibit higher levels of affiliative behaviors such as grooming and non-ventral contact than males, particularly with their own mothers. They appear to be more interested in neonates than the males are. The males, in contrast, exhibit higher levels of aggressive activity, tend to associate with other males, and appear to be very interested in adult males. Thus, the social interests and relationships likely to be shown in adulthood are clearly developing in adolescent male and female rhesus monkeys (Suomi, 1977).

When does social development asymptote in a maturing rhesus monkey? When is the monkey considered to be an adult socially? Recent data from our laboratory suggest that a monkey's relative stage of social maturation can be readily determined by the manner in which it interacts with members of various age–sex classes (adult females, neonatal males, juvenile females, etc.) as well as the way in which members of each age–sex class respond to its interactions.

For example, an adolescent female usually interacts with an adolescent male in a manner considerably different from the manner that an adult female would interact with the same male. Correspondingly, the adolescent male's reactions to the female will in large part depend on whether it perceives the female to be an adolescent or an adult. Prior knowledge of the forms of such interaction patterns can enable an investigator to determine a given subject's social maturational status simply by observing its interactions with other monkeys.

Thus, it is possible to define adulthood operationally for the rhesus monkey on the basis of social behavior, and it is possible to determine the chronological point at which any subject achieves such a status. To date, the best available evidence indicates that rhesus monkeys reared in socially complex laboratory environments exhibit rates of social maturation and achieve degrees of social sophistication comparable to ferally-reared rhesus monkeys. It is thus tempting to presume that the various factors found to influence development in such laboratory environments generalize to the species' natural habitat. However, in the current absence of totally definitive field data, the generalization of many such factors to feral environments remains to be demonstrated empirically.

Maturation of social behavior in socially impoverished environments

The normative pattern of social development shown by monkeys reared under the conditions described above is hardly typical of that seen in other laboratory environments that are considerably more sterile socially. Many researches performed over the past 15 years have clearly demonstrated that monkeys reared in environments that do not provide appropriate social stimulation are unlikely to exhibit species-normative social development. Indeed, in most cases the degree of social abnormality displayed by such subjects can be traced almost directly to the specific inadequacies of their particular rearing environment.

Perhaps the most clear-cut case exists for rhesus monkeys that are reared under conditions of total social isolation initiated at birth and maintained for at least the first 6 months of life. When these monkeys are removed from isolation and first exposed to conspecifics, they do not exhibit normal patterns of social interactive behaviors. Rather, they fail to initiate any social activity. When other monkeys try to interact with them, they vigorously attempt to withdraw, and when that is impossible, they become immobilized. Their primary behavior patterns are those that were developed during the isolation period, and they take the form of self-directed activities not commonly exhibited by monkeys reared in complex social environments (Suomi and Harlow, 1972).

Among the behaviors exhibited by monkeys when they emerge from isolation are self-mouthing, self-clasping, and stereotypic rocking. It can be argued that such patterns represent ethologically logical consequences of unlearned response systems maturing in an isolation environment. For example, instead of directing non-nutritive sucking toward a maternal nipple, an infant reared in isolation learns to suck its own digits. Instead of clinging to a mother, an infant reared in isolation learns to clasp its own body. Mason and Berkson (1975) and Sackett (1966) have suggested similar mechanisms when describing the maturation of stereotypic rocking and social fear in isolation-reared monkeys. Thus, many of the apparent behavioral abnormalities exhibited by isolates can be traced to the learning of behavior patterns derived from unlearned response systems that mature in ethologically barren environments. However, this learning is probably appropriate for the isolation environment.

Recent successful efforts to rehabilitate isolate-reared monkeys using conspecific "therapists" have added weight to a learning interpretation of isolation-induced behavioral deficits (Suomi et al, 1974). When exposed to social stimulation specifically geared to promoting basic positive social behaviors incompatible with self-directed stereotypies, the isolates' behavior drops out and is replaced by activities largely appropriate for the social situation (Suomi and Harlow, 1972; Novak and Harlow, 1975). In contrast, when isolates are exposed to social stimuli that are appropriate for the socially sophisticated age-mates, they fail to develop appropriate social repertoires and instead continue to exhibit their well-developed self-directed stereotypic behavior (Mitchell et al., 1966).

Study of monkeys reared in single cages where they can see and hear but not touch other monkeys ("partial social isolation") provide more evidence in support of a learning deficit interpretation of isolation effects. Results of several studies indicate that monkeys so reared develop behavioral repertoires generally similar to those of total social isolates, although absolute levels of disturbance behaviors are usually not as high in partial social isolates (Cross and Harlow, 1963). Nevertheless, as adults, these monkeys exhibit inappropriate aggression (Mitchell et al., 1966), incompetent sexual behavior (Senko, 1966), and gross abnormalities in maternal behavior among primiparous females (Ruppenthal et al., 1976). It can be argued that lack of opportunity for physical contact with conspecifics results in the failure to display appropriate physical contact-related behaviors when appropriate stimulation is presented.

Studies of monkeys reared in laboratory environments less barren socially than those described previously, but lacking certain age-sex classes of conspecifics, present additional data supportive of a learning-based hypothesis. For example, monkeys separated from their mothers at birth and reared in groups of same-aged peers exhibit excessive self-orality, just as the isolates. Like the isolates, peer-reared infants do not have access to a maternal nipple for non-nutritive sucking. However, they do not develop the patterns of self-clasping shown by isolates. Instead, they cling to each other. They also do not develop patterns of self-directed stereotypies shown by isolates. Their cage-mates apparently provide them with the necessary moving stimulation (Mears and Harlow, 1975). Peer-reared monkeys do not exhibit the extreme withdrawal upon exposure to fear-provoking stimuli typically shown by isolates. However, they are considerably more sensitive to such stimuli than are mother-reared infants of similar age. It is perhaps not coincidental that independent research has reported that infants are less effective than adult females in reducing fear among rhesus monkeys under a year of age (Meyer et al. 1975).

Perhaps the most interesting facet of peer-only rearing concerns the nature of the actual interactions among group members. We have known for some time that peer-reared infants persist in mutual clinging behavior far longer chronologically than do mother and infant in normal environments; correspondingly, peer-reared infants are retarded in development of play patterns with their partners (Harlow, 1969; Chamove et al., 1973; Suomi and Harlow, 1975). Recent data now suggest that peer-only reared monkeys respond to specific social initiations in a different fashion than infants reared by their mothers or than the mothers themselves. Thus, in a peer-only environment monkeys learn to interact in a manner that in many instances would be inappropriate within a feral-living social group.

When peer-only reared monkeys achieve sexual maturity they appear to be basically competent in most social and non-social activities. Two exceptions to this rule are clearly evident: male sexual behavior and female maternal behavior. The males often display incomplete mounting patterns, e.g., single foot-clasp mounts, instead of the standard double foot-clasp male form (Goy et al., 1974). Females are as likely to abuse their first-born infants as are isolate-reared females, although they never display the indifferent maternal care that is the norm among isolate mothers (Ruppenthal et al., 1976). Clearly, peer-only rearing is not without its long-term effects.

Infant monkeys reared by their mothers but denied access to age-mates present still another developmental picture. They display few anomalies in social maturation during the first 3 months of life. The infant learns to direct its non-nutritive sucking and clasping tendencies toward the mother, and she readily provides it with kinesthetic stimulation while serving as a security base as well. The problems begin when the infant reaches the age at which normally reared monkeys start to develop play repertoires with age-mates. Mother-only-reared infants have only their mothers to fill the role of playmate, and recent findings have established that in several different types of social groupings rhesus monkey mothers are less likely to play with infants than are virtually all other members of the social unit (Suomi, in the press; Redican, 1976). When these infants are finally exposed to peers later in life they have some difficulty forming normal social relationships with age-mates. Peer-deprived monkeys are generally contact-shy. They usually do not initiate play interactions with other monkeys, and when drawn into social interactions, they are often hyper-aggressive.

Existing evidence suggests that the long-term prognosis for mother-only reared infants deteriorates the longer the offspring are denied access to peers, with serious impairments apparent after as little as 8 months of peer isolation. (Alexander and Harlow, 1965). Detailed longitudinal data on these animals' social maturation through physiological adulthood are scarce; as such, they suggest that male monkeys peer-deprived in infancy are capable of adequate sexual behavior as adolescents and adults, but tend to be hyper-aggressive, while similarly deprived females are generally adequate primiparous mothers, but are deficient in grooming. These results are consistent with a learning interpretation of environmentally altered social maturation.

Final support for such a position can be found within the range of social environments that promote feral-like social maturation, as described earlier in the chapter. Work by Hinde's group has demonstrated that numerous variables, including social status of mother, age and sex of siblings, and age and sex of available playmates can influence the mother–infant relationship in significant fashion, most probably contributing to individual differences displayed in adulthood. In a similar vein, recent reports by Redican (in the press) and by Suomi (in the press) suggest that the behavior of some adult males can have considerable influence on the development of specific behavior patterns in both male and female infants. If such patterns persist through adulthood (no relevant data have yet been analyzed), then further evidence of an environmental basis for individual differences in social ontogeny can be claimed.

The preceding review provides more than ample evidence that a monkey's pattern of social maturation is highly dependent on the social composition of its environment throughout infancy and pre-adolescence. The position we advocate is that variations in social maturation that can be traced to a lack of certain social stimuli (e.g., a maternal nipple) are best understood in a learning context. Monkeys denied access to certain age–sex classes of conspecifics during periods of social maturation do not have the opportunity to learn interaction patterns specific to that type of social relationship. When faced with a similar social relationship as adolescents or adults, they often fail to exhibit appropriate behavior patterns for the situation. Instead, they demonstrate coping behavior because they have not learned the appropriate patterns and must continually adjust until they have had ample exposure to the relevant stimuli.

By and large, the monkey rearing-condition data are consistent with this theoretical interpretation. For example, peer-only-reared females generally exhibit species-appropriate behavior as adults until they have their first offspring, at which time they are far more likely to exhibit abusive maternal behavior than are females who were reared by their mothers. However, when they have second infants, their maternal behavior is usually quite acceptable. It can be argued plausibly that the peer-reared females have not been denied opportunities to form most social relationships, only that between a mother and infant. Hence, they appear to be socially competent until they find themselves in a mother–infant relationship; whereupon they must "learn on the job," and mistakes are not uncommon. By the time a second infant is born, they have had ample opportunity to learn appropriate behavior, and subsequent maternal activities approach the normal. In another example, monkeys that spend the first 6 or more months of life in total social isolation almost always exhibit hopeless social incompetence. The one exception is those instances in which isolates are provided with social stimuli appropriate for the learning of basic social skills such as contact acceptability (Suomi et al., 1974).

These examples provide evidence of a general rule regarding social environments and social development. When an organism is denied the opportunity to interact with certain types of social stimuli during periods of social development, its social maturation will be incomplete in the sense that when first exposed to similar classes of stimuli later in life it may exhibit inappropriate behavior. If exposure to such stimuli is continued, under favorable conditions the inappropriate behavior will drop out and a species-normative relationship may develop. If exposure is not continued under such circumstances, the inappropriate behavior will continue to be exhibited each time the subject is subsequently exposed to such stimuli.

Social isolation effects on social development have been analyzed from other theoretical perspectives, e.g., critical periods, (Scott, 1962), emergence trauma (Fuller and Clark, 1966), and motivational deficits (Seligman, 1975). We believe that such effects are best interpreted from a learning perspective, while expressly not maintaining that the other views are necessarily incorrect or wholly incompatible with our interpretations.

Effects of social separations on social maturation

The preceding discussion has been directed toward demonstrating the efficacy of a learning interpretation of isolation-induced social deficits. In this section we will argue that not all instances of environmental influence on species-normative social maturation can be readily explained by a learning approach. Rather, there are some cases in which motivational interpretations prove to be far more useful in understanding the phenomena. Many of these instances involve social separation, the breaking of a previously established social relationship. It is our position that phenomena associated with social separation and phenomena associated with social isolation initiated at birth are very different in nature, and are each best served by different explanations.

The distinction between separation and isolation is not new. For example, Gewirtz (1961) differentiated privation, in which the opportunity to form a social relationship does not exist for the subject, from deprivation, in which an existing social relationship for the subject is terminated or at least interrupted. Harlow and Novak (1973) made a similar distinction using the same terminology: "The main difference between the effect of privation as opposed to deprivation in monkeys is clearly related to the development of social bonds. The absence of social bonds before privation results in the production of later individual, self-oriented repetitive behaviors, while the presence of social bonds before deprivation leads to the development of social affectional disorders .... Thus, the evidence indicates that privation and deprivation produce qualitatively different syndromes, privation producing intense behavioral anomalies and deprivation producing disorders in affect associated with increases in aggression and fear. Most of the effects of privation can be successfully ameliorated through patient adaptation procedures and social imitation, while the effects of deprivation appear to eventually disappear with renewed social contact." (Harlow and Novak, 1973, pp. 466 and 470).

During the past decade we at Wisconsin, as well as a number of other investigators working at different laboratories, have carried out numerous deprivation studies in monkeys using social separation as the principal manipulation. These studies have fallen into two general categories. The first is mother–infant separation, in which a mother and her infant are reared together in the same environment for a specified period of time, one member of the pair is removed and housed in a different environment for a specified period of time, and then the pair is reunited in the original environment. The second form, repetitive peer separation, involves rearing groups of peers together for a period sufficient for them to develop strong mutual social attachments, then separating them from one another for short-term periods on a regular schedule, e.g., 4 days separated and 3 days together, over a period of several months.

While a comprehensive review of the monkey separation literature is beyond the scope of this chapter, the findings from these studies do follow a general pattern. Virtually all subjects in all social separations respond immediately to the loss of access to their attachment object with vigorous protest. Typically, their activity levels show sharp increases coincidental with the onset of separation; extreme levels of vocalization are also common. For some subjects, if the separation is continued for more than a few days these behavior patterns change considerably and are replaced by depressive-like behaviors: severe reductions in activity levels, social withdrawal, and a lack of interest in novel stimuli. Some investigators have used such phenomena as the basis for developing an animal model of human depression (Kaufman and Rosenblum, 1967; McKinney and Bunney, 1969; Harlow and Suomi, 1974).

While the immediate consequences of social separation have been the focus of attention in most studies of this sort, our concern in this chapter is instead on long-term effects of the separation after the participants have been reunited. Evidence is accumulating that suggests that even brief separations have measurable effects on a subject's social behavior months and even years after reunion has occurred, while more severe forms of separation may considerably alter the pattern of social maturation displayed by the subject.

For example, Mitchell et al. (1967) reared mothers and infants together for the infants' first 8 months of life, except for 2 h of separation every 2 weeks, during which mother and infant were housed in separate holding cages. When the infants were tested with stimulus animals during their second year of life, they exhibited significantly higher levels of fear, submission, social withdrawal, disturbance, and screech and coo vocalizations, and lower levels of threat than did non-separated control subjects otherwise similar in age and rearing history. Thus, it appears that even brief mother–infant separations can result in measurable effects when subjects are exposed to novel social stimuli later in life.

More extensive work by Hinde and his colleagues has focused on long-term consequences of maternal separation in monkeys reared in complex social groups containing their mothers, other adult females and their offspring, adolescents, and single adult males. When the subjects were approximately 6 months of age, their mothers were removed from the group for a 6-day period and then returned. When tested at 1 year of age, and again at $2\frac{1}{2}$ years of age, clear-cut differences from non-separated control subjects were evident. Separated subjects were less active, less likely to play, and more reluctant to explore novel stimuli, both social and non-social, than were control subjects. These differences were most pronounced when the animals were confronted with strange objects in a strange cage. (Hinde and Spencer-Booth, 1971).

Other long-term differences between monkeys separated from, then reunited with their mothers during the first year of life, and non-separated controls become apparent when both groups of animals are subjected to brief peer separations when they are adolescents. Young et al. (1973) reported that monkeys separated from their mothers for a 30-day period during the first year of life exhibited much more severe reactions to short-term peer separations during the third year of life than did control monkeys who had not experienced maternal separation during year one. Differences between the two adolescent groups were most pronounced for self-directed behaviors and passive social contact (separated monkeys higher) and for social approach and play (control monkeys higher).

The above findings all indicate that maternal separations early in life may yield long-term behavioral effects among monkeys that otherwise display relatively normal behavioral repertoires. The effects appear to be most pronounced when the monkeys are placed in potentially stressful situations, such as exposure to novel stimuli or additional social separations involving other conspecifics. It is difficult to argue that such differences between the two groups reflect learning deficits, because in all other respects the previously separated subjects exhibit species-appropriate behavioral repertoires in interactions with members of their social group. Clearly, these subjects are not incompetent socially, as are monkeys isolated from birth from certain age–sex classes of conspecifics. Yet, they are not totally normal, either.

Considerably more powerful long-term consequences of separation are displayed by monkeys reared only with peers from birth and subsequently subjected to repetitive peer separations. As mentioned earlier, most subjects in these studies exhibited biphasic reactions of a depressive nature to each peer separation. More central to the present discussion, however, are the cumulative effects, effects that can be described as maturational arrest, produced by such separations.

For example, Suomi et al. (1970) reared monkeys from birth in peer groups, then repetitively separated the peers from each other for 4-day periods, beginning when the subjects were 3 months of age. Between the ages of 3 and 9 months, each monkey was separated for a total of twenty 4-day periods. Levels of their behaviors at 3 months (prior to separation) at 6 months (midway through the separation sequence), and at 9 months (after the 20th separation) were compared with levels of the same behaviors exhibited by non-separated control monkeys during the same age periods. Control groups showed considerable change in levels of most behaviors between 3 and 9 months of age, including decreases in infantile behavior patterns of ventral cling and self-clasp, and increases in the more advanced behaviors of play and locomotion. In sharp contrast, repetitively separated monkeys continued to exhibit essentially the same levels of behavior at 9 months of age that they displayed when they were only 3' months old. It was as if their social maturation had ceased for a 6-month period.

Other studies differing slightly in experimental procedures have reported essentially the same type of results. For example, Seaman (1975) reared monkeys in groups of four from birth without mothers for the first 4 months of life, then subjected them to three 19-day separations, during which each monkey was individually housed. At the end of the third separation, when subjects were almost a year of age, they demonstrated behavioral repertoires more similar to those of 120-day-old monkeys than those of socially normal monkeys their own chronological age. Clearly, maturational arrest had occurred.

Phenomena associated with maturational arrest, like the previously described long-term effects of mother–infant separations, provide clear-cut cases of environmental influence on social maturation, yet such phenomena are not easily accounted for by learning deficit interpretations. This is due to the fact that monkeys exposed to repetitive separations have had essentially the same prior social history as their non-separated control counterparts, and at least during reunion periods have been exposed to the same classes of social stimuli as the controls. Hence, the argument that aberrations in their social behavior can be traced to a lack of exposure to relevant social stimuli simply does not hold much weight. Rather, alternative explanations must be considered.

A closer examination of behaviors exhibited by subjects immediately after reunion gives a clue as to the possible basis for the above-reported long-term effects attributable to social separation. Infants just reunited with their mothers almost always direct much more behavior toward their mother than they did immediately prior to separation. A considerable proportion of such activity involves clinging, passive contact, and proximity-maintaining behaviors. These are basically infantile forms of interaction that some investigators have viewed as representing behavioral regression (Harlow and Suomi, 1974). Partly because the infant is now spending more time with its mother than it did before separation, exploration and play with peers drop well below pre-separation levels. Even after the subject's overall behavioral levels have begun to return to pre-separation baselines, it reinstates reunion-like behavior with its mother at the slightest sign of environmental stress. Thus, it can be argued that the monkey that has experienced maternal separation is clearly capable of exhibiting species-normative patterns of behavior, but under certain stimulus conditions it chooses to display forms of behavior directed toward objects of attachment not usually exhibited by monkeys its age.

With respect to the more severe maturational arrest demonstrated by monkeys subjected to repetitive peer separations, the same principle seems to hold: behavior patterns displayed during reunion offer evidence as to the basis of the resulting maturational arrest. During reunion periods repetitively peer-separated infants spend virtually all of their time in mutual ventral contact and thus have little time to engage in exploratory and/or play activity. Over successive separations and reunions, they continue to cling voluntarily to one another; during comparable chrono-logical periods their control counterparts are busy developing normal play reper-toires. Thus, maturational arrest results, not because the repetitively separated monkeys have been denied access to appropriate social partners, but rather because of the manner in which they choose to interact with such partners.

Such data bode ill for a learning deficit interpretation of long-term separation effects on social maturation. Instead, we believe, they are best understood from a motivational point of view. Reunited monkeys have the capability to display many forms of behavioral reactions, but those they choose to exhibit are disproportionately directed toward their recently lost social partner and take a form previously dis-played prior to the separation. At present, there exist at least three attractive motiva-tional theories that can account convincingly for the bulk of the monkey separation literature: Bowlby's theory of anxious attachment (Bowlby, 1973), Seligman's learned helplessness formulations (Seligman, 1975), and Solomon's opponent-process approach (Solomon and Corbit, 1974).

Bowlby's approach emphasizes social motivational factors as the basis for the infant's renewed interest in its previously lost attachment object. Seligman's theory has cognitive components tied to motivational changes that accompany certain forms of social separation. Solomon has applied his opponent – process notions to a wide variety of situations (including social separations) that are characterized by extremes in hedonic or aversive states and are thought to have similar physiological concomitants. At present, we do not know which theoretical approach is most effica-cious (they are not necessarily inconsistent or incompatible with one another), but we do know that all three of these motivational explanations are quite plausible in the face of current separation data (Suomi, et al., in the press).

Summary and conclusions

In this chapter, we have discussed social maturation exhibited by rhesus monkey subjects. A large body of data has consistently shown that within a relatively wide range of "normal" environments, including both those in the field and some within laboratory settings, rhesus monkeys exhibit regular and predictable sequences of social maturation. While certain aspects of such maturation are undoubtedly specific to the rhesus species, the general pattern is probably shared by most higher primates, including man (Harlow et al., 1972). In this respect, the pattern most probably reflects millions of years of evolution. Yet within the range of "normal" environments, individual differences in social maturation can be detected. Undoubtedly, some of these differences can be traced to variation in the subjects' social environments. They further remind us that social maturation is best understood as a product of inherited characteristics and propensities, and stimulation provided by the social environment.

This view of maturation is underscored by the data from studies of social matura-tion of monkeys reared in privation or deprivation environments. These data clearly demonstrate that species-characteristic social maturation does not follow the same course across all social environments. Monkeys isolated from certain classes of conspecifics during periods of social development at best attain incomplete maturation. If exposed as adults to social relationships denied during their development, they usually display incompetence. Monkeys subjected to social separation subsequently show episodes of behavioral regression; in extreme cases maturational arrest is the long-term consequence. Clearly, adverse social environments can influence to a great degree the expression of emerging social capabilities selected for by evolutionary pressures over countless generations.

The present data also clearly demonstrate that interactions between nature and nurture can be expressed in a number of ways and viewed from a variety of theoretical perspectives. It is unlikely that one single most appropriate explanation exists for understanding such interactions. The rhesus monkey social isolation data are perhaps best interpreted from a learning deficit perspective. In contrast, the monkey separation data suggest that the influence of separation experiences on social maturation patterns may be best understood in motivational terms. Such data should serve to caution us, preventing us from making simplistic assumptions regarding nature–nurture interactions. We must take care not to underestimate the potential complexity of such interactions in our search for underlying mechanisms and explanatory principles for social maturation.

Acknowledgments

This research was supported by USPHS grants MH-11894 and MH-28485 from the National Institute of Mental Health and RR-0167 from the National Institutes of Health.

The authors wish to thank Mrs. Helen LeRoy for her editorial assistance and Miss Theresa Schwoegler for her help in the preparation of the manuscript.

Literature cited

Alexander, B. K., and Harlow, H. F. (1965) Social behavior of juvenile rhesus monkeys subjected to different rearing conditions during the first 6 months of life, *Zoolog. Jahrb. Physiol. 60*, 167–174

Bowlby, J. (1973) *Separation. Anxiety and Anger*, Basic Books, New York.

Chamove, A. S., Rosenblum, L. A. and Harlow, H. F. (1973) Monkeys (Macaca mulatta) raised only with peers. A pilot study, *Anim. Behav. 21*, 316–325

Cross, H. A., and Harlow, H. F. (1965) Prolonged and progressive effects of partial isolation on the behavior of macaque monkeys. *J. Exp. Res. Pers. 1*, 39–40

Fuller, J. L. and Clark, L. D. (1966) Genetic and treatment factors modifying the postisolation syndrome in dogs, *J. Comp. Physiol. Psychol. 61*, 251–257

Gewirtz, J. L. (1961) A learning analysis of the effects of normal stimulation, privation, and deprivation on the acquisiton of social motivation and attachment. In: *Determinants of Infant Behaviour* (B. M. Foss, ed.), Methuen, London

Goy, R. W., Wallen, K. and Goldfoot, D. A. (1974) Social factors affecting the development of mounting behavior in male rhesus monkeys. In: *Reproductive Behavior* (W. Montagna and W. A. Sadler, eds.) Plenum Press, New York

Hansen, E. W. (1966) The development of maternal and infant behavior in the rhesus monkey, *Behavior 27*, 107–149

Harlow H. F. (1958) The nature of love, *Am. Psychol. 13*, 673–685

Harlow, H. F. (1969) Age-mate or peer affectional system. In: *Advances in the Study of Behavior*, (D. Lehrman, R. Hinde and E. Shaw, eds.) Vol. 2, Academic Press, New York

Harlow, H. F., Gluck, J. P. and Suomi, S. J. (1972) Generalization of behavioral data between non-human and human animals, *Am. Psychol. 27*, 709–716

Harlow, H. F. and Harlow, M. K. (1965) The affectional systems. In: *Behavior of Non-Human Primates* (A. M. Schrier, H. F. Harlow and F. Stollnitz, eds.) Vol. 2, Academic Press, New York

Harlow, H. F. and Lauersdorf, H. E. (1974) Sex differences in passion and play, *Perspect. Biol. Med. 17*, 348–360

Harlow, H. F. and Novak, M. A. (1973) Psychopathological perspectives, *Perspect. Biol. Med. 16*, 461–478.

Harlow, H. F. and Suomi, S. J. (1974) Induced depression in monkeys, *Behav. Biol. 12*, 273–296

Harlow, H. F. and Zimmermann, R. R. (1958) The development of affectional responses in infant monkeys, *Proc. Am. Philos. Soc. 102*, 501–509

Hinde, R. A. (1974) *Biological Bases of Human Social Behavior*, McGraw-Hill, New York

Hinde, R. A. and Spencer-Booth, Y. (1971) Effects of brief separations from mothers on rhesus monkeys, *Science 173*, 111–118

Hinde, R. A. and White, L. E. (1974) Dynamics of a relationship, *J. Comp. Physiol. Psychol. 86*, 8–23

Kaufmann, J. H. (1966) Behavior of infant rhesus monkeys and their mothers in a free ranging band, *Zool. 51*, 17–28

Kaufman, I. C. and Rosenblum, L. A. (1967) The reaction to separation in infant monkeys: Anaclitic depression and conservation-withdrawal, *Psychosom. Med. 29*, 648–675

Lehrman, D. S. (1970) Semantic and conceptual issues in the nature-nurture problem. In: *Development and Evolution of Behavior. Essays in Memory of T. C. Schneirla* (L. R. Aronson, ed.) W. H. Freeman, San Francisco

Lindburg, D. G. (1973) The rhesus monkey in North India. An ecological and behavioral study. In: *Primate Behavior* (L. A. Rosenblum, ed.) Vol. 2, Academic Press, New York

Mason, W. A. and Berkson, G. (1975) Effects of maternal mobility on the development of rocking and other behaviors in rhesus monkeys. A study with artificial mothers. *Dev. Psychobiol. 8*, 197–211

McKinney, W. T. and Bunney, W. E. (1969) Animal model of depression, *Arch. Gen. Psychiat. 21*, 240–248

Mears, C. E. and Harlow, H. F. (1975) Play: early and eternal, *Proc. Natl. Acad. Sci. 72*, 1878–1882

Meyer, J. S., Novak, M. A., Bowman, R. E. and Harlow, H. F. (1975) Behavioral and hormonal effects of attachment object separation in surrogate-peer-reared infant rhesus monkeys, *Dev. Psychobiol. 8*, 435–436

Mitchell, G. D., Harlow, H. F., Griffin, G. A. and Møller, G. W. (1967) Repeated maternal separation in the monkey, *Psychonom. Sci. 8*, 197–198

Mitchell, G. D., Raymond, E. J., Ruppenthal, G. C., and Harlow, H. F. (1966) Long-term effects of total social isolation upon behavior of rhesus monkeys, *Psychol. Rep. 18*, 567–580

Novak, M. A. and Harlow, H. F. (1975) Social recovery of monkeys isolated for the first year of life. I. Rehabilitation and therapy. *Dev. Psychol. 11*, 453–465

Redican, W. K. (1976) Adult male-infant interactions in nonhuman primates. In: *The Role of the Father in Child Development* (M. E. Lamb, ed.) Wiley, New York

Redican, W. K.· (1977) Adult male-infant interactions in captive rhesus monkeys. In: *Proceedings of the 6th Congress of the International Primatological Society* (D. Chivers, ed.) Academic Press, New York, in the press

Rosenblum, L. A. (1971) The ontogeny of mother-infant relations in macaques. In: *The Ontogeny of Vertebrate Behavior* (H. Moltz, ed.) Academic Press, New York

Ruppenthal, G. C., Arling, G. L., Harlow, H. F., Sackett, G. P. and Suomi, S. J. (1976) A 10-year perspective of motherless-mother monkey behavior, *J. Abnorm. Psychol. 85*, 341–349

Ruppenthal, G. C., Harlow, M. K., Eisele, C. D., Harlow, H. F., and Suomi, S. J. (1974) Development of peer interactions of monkeys reared in a nuclear-family environment, *Child Dev. 45*, 670–682

Sackett, G. P. (1966) Monkeys reared in isolation with pictures as visual input. Evidence for an innate releasing mechanism, *Science 154*, 1468–1472

Sackett, G. P. (1970) Unlearned responses, differential rearing experiences, and the development of social attachments by rhesus monkeys. In: *Primate Behavior* (L. A. Rosenblum, ed.) Vol. 1, Academic Press, New York

Scott, J. P. (1962) Critical periods in behavioral development, *Science 138*, 949–958

Seaman, S. F. (1975) *The Effects of Tofranil or Placebo on the Peer–Peer Separation Syndrome*, unpublished Undergraduate Honors Thesis, University of Wisconsin

Seligman, M. E. P. (1975) *Helplessness. On Depression, Development and Death*, W. H. Freeman, San Francisco

Senko, M. G. (1966) *The Effects of Early, Intermediate, and Late Experiences upon Adult Macaque Sexual Behavior*, unpublished M. A. thesis, University of Wisconsin

Simpson, M. J. A. (1976) The study of animal play. In: *Growing Points in Ethology* (P. P. G. Bateson and R. A. Hinde, eds.) Cambridge University Press, Cambridge

Solomon, R. L. and Corbit, J. D. (1974) An opponent-process theory of motivation. I. Temporal dynamics of affect, *Psychol. Rev. 81*, 119–145

Southwick, C. H., Beg, M. A. and Siddiqi, M. R. (1965) Rhesus monkeys in North India. In: *Primate Behavior. Field Studies of Monkeys and Apes* (I. DeVore, ed.) Holt, Rinehart and Winston, New York

Suomi, S. J. (1976) Mechanisms underlying social development. A re-examination of mother-infant interactions in monkeys. In: *Minnesota Symposium on Child Development* (A. Pick, ed.) Vol. 10, University of Minnesota Press, Minneapolis

Suomi, S. J. (1977) Development of attachment and other social behaviors in rhesus monkeys. In: *Attachment Behavior* (T. Alloway, P. Pliner, and L. Krames, eds.) Plenum, New York

Suomi, S. J. (1977) Adult male–infant interactions among monkeys living in nuclear families, *Child Dev.*, in the press

Suomi, S. J. and Harlow, H. F. (1972) Social rehabilitation of isolate-reared monkeys, *Dev. Psychol. 6*, 487–496

Suomi, S. J. and Harlow, H. F. (1975) The role and reason of peer friendships in rhesus monkeys. In: *Peer Relations and Friendship: ETS Symposium on the Origins of Behavior* (M. Lewis and L. A. Rosenblum, eds.) Wiley, New York

Suomi, S. J. and Harlow, H. F. (1976) The facts and functions of fear. In: *Emotions and Anxiety, New Concepts, Methods and Applications* (M. Zuckerman and C. D. Spielberger, eds.) Erlbaum, Hillsdale, N.J.

Suomi, S. J., Harlow, H. F. and Domek, C. J. (1970) Effect of repetitive infant–infant separation of young monkeys, *J. Abnorm. Psychol. 76*, 161–172

Suomi, S. J., Harlow, H. F. and Novak, M. A. (1974) Reversal of social deficits produced by isolation-rearing in monkeys, *J. Hum. Evol. 3*, 527–534

Suomi, S. J., Mineka, S. and Harlow, H. F. (1977) The motivations of the psychopathologies. In: *Handbook of Behavioral Neurobiology. Motivation* (E. Satinoff and P. Teitelbaum, eds.) Plenum, New York, in the press

Suomi, S. J., Sackett, G. P. and Harlow, H. F. (1970) Development of sex preferences in rhesus monkeys, *Dev. Psychol. 3*, 326–336

Young, L. D., Suomi, S. J., Harlow, H. F. and McKinney, W. T. (1973) Early stress and later response to separation, *Am. J. Psychiatr. 130*, 400–405

Genetics, environment and intelligence, edited by A. Oliverio
© *Elsevier/North-Holland Biomedical Press, 1977*

Early life malnutrition and later learning ability A critical analysis

12

JAMES L. SMART

Introduction

The possibility that nutrition might exert an influence on the development of behaviour has long been entertained, at least at the level of folklore and prejudice. In the 17th century, for instance, it was thought that personality characteristics might be transmitted in breast milk and, accordingly, much attention was given to the choice of a suitable wet-nurse to give suck to the offspring of the affluent. Thus Burton in 1651 advised parents

> "that they make choice of a sound woman of good complexion, honest, free from bodily diseases, if it be possible, and all passions and perturbations of the mind, as sorrow, fear, grief, folly, melancholy. For such passions corrupt the milk, and alter the temperature of the child, which now being moist and pliable clay, is easily seasoned and perverted." (quoted in Fomon, 1974).

However, scientific interest in nutrition as an environmental influence on behaviour development has been slow to kindle; perhaps because nutrition is such a sine qua non of development, and has been considered an essential contributor to the developing framework, but apparently without influence on the final facade. The fitful glow of interest was fanned into flame in the 1960's, not, as so often happens, by any technological or methodological advance, but by the growth of conscience among the privileged communities of the world for those who were less fortunate.

There was concern about nutrition or, more explicitly, about malnutrition. Quite apart from the misery of malnutrition, what were its long-term sequelae, and how might these most economically be ameliorated? It soon became clear that there were immense difficulties inherent in field studies with indigent human populations, because of the inevitable association of malnutrition with a host of other disadvantageous socioeconomic factors. Dissociating the effect of one from that of the others was a daunting task; hence the attractiveness of experimental animal studies with genetically homogeneous stocks housed in environmentally controlled conditions.

From the outset the questions were of an applied nature and, while this factor undoubtedly supplied impetus to the research, it may have resulted in a certain lack of sophistication especially among the early investigations. More recently the behavioural side of this research has passed from the hands of the nutritionists, who first posed the questions, to behavioural scientists: psychologists and ethologists. Thus the questions have become more pointed, the analyses finer-grained and the conclusions, paradoxically, less clear.

The time would appear to be ripe to take stock of the situation; to stand back and attempt to achieve a comprehensive overview of progress so far, and to ask where to go from here. The present review centres on the question of whether learning ability is impaired by a period of nutritional privation early in life. Because of its importance, the question has attracted a great deal of experimental effort, and no two studies have been identical. They differ, among other things, in strain of animal, timing, duration and severity of malnutrition, duration of recovery period, age of animal when tested, and type of test. I am asking at the outset whether there are effects which transcend this multiplicity of approaches?

This is an attempt at an exhaustive review of all published studies known to me, which meet the criteria laid down in the second section of the Introduction (*Limits of review*, p. 217). Many reviews represent the verification of an opinion: they are undertaken from some theoretical standpoint and the evidence assessed accordingly. The understandable tendency is to emphasise the confirmatory evidence and to play down or ignore the contradictory. I have tried to avoid this trap by accepting all the published evidence at its face value and, as far as possible, adopting only numerical or statistical reservations (see the section *Some problems of reviewing*, below). In a further attempt at objectivity the evidence has been translated into an algebraic sum of experiments for or against the hypothesis that early malnutrition impairs learning ability, with each experiment contributing one unit to the sum. A statistical analysis of the resulting figures is also presented.

Some problems of reviewing

A major difficulty with this formally numerical type of review lies in the fact that not all studies deserve equal weighting: some are undoubtedly better than others. It is possible to overcome this problem to some extent by adopting criteria of acceptability which allow the exclusion of certain studies. Thus I shall at some stages in the succeeding analysis exclude experiments on the grounds of insufficient information or inadequate numbers of animals. I shall attempt to keep prejudice in check with respect to the remainder, in spite of a lingering feeling that some of the findings are more substantial than others.

Another, entirely intractable problem is the possibility that some negative results remain unpublished. Human nature being what it is, negative results are probably less likely to be published than positive results. The researcher who has detected no effect of early treatment or who has obtained an opposite effect to that predicted may be reluctant to submit his results for publication. Even if he does so, he may meet with little sympathy from referees and editors. I very much hope that this is not so, both from the point of view of this review and of the subject. I take the firm attitude that the question of early nutrition in relation to later learning ability is sufficiently important that the results of all competently conducted investigations ought to be published, be they positive or negative.

On the grounds that any difference is better than no difference at all from the point of view of publication, instances of no significant difference are more likely to remain unpublished than significant effects which are contrary to expectations. This is fortunate with respect to the algebraic sum attempted in the review. No-difference results, though part of the overall picture, do not alter the algebraic sum, whereas opposite results do.

The policy throughout the review will be to accept the authors' statistical analyses of their results. This is obviously far short of the ideal, which would be to reanalyse each set of data in what is currently deemed to be the most appropriate way. For example, few, if any, of the studies reported below pass muster with respect to the important recommendations of Abbey and Howard (1973) that the unit for analysis should be the litter. Some have transgressed more than others, but most have used several animals per litter and have considered them to be independent for purposes of analysis. Regrettably there is often no mention at all of the number of source litters.

Limits of review

This review is confined to studies of mammalian species other than man, in which nutritional privation has been imposed early in life: in gestation, the suckling period, the early postweaning period or some combination of these. The privation has to have been of the protein–calorie malnutrition type; that is, the restriction has been of total intake or of protein intake, and not one of specific vitamins or minerals. One further condition is that at least one month of nutritional rehabilitation – ad libitum feeding on a good quality diet – should have elapsed between the end of malnutrition and the commencement of behavioural testing. Hence observations on currently undernourished animals (Baird et al., 1971; Stoffer and Zimmerman, 1973) or animals which have just begun nutritional rehabilitation (Smart and Dobbing, 1972) are not included.

There is always a problem with the interpretation of results from experiments which purport to test animal learning ability. Do the results truly reflect capacity to learn, or do they reflect some other aspect of behaviour? This is especially so of tests of passive avoidance behaviour, in which the animal is required to inhibit a particular response, usually on pain of electric shock. The resulting inhibition is more often interpreted as an emotional response than an indication of learning. At most it is a very rudimentary form of learning, and I have decided accordingly to exclude it from the review. It is in any case adequately reviewed by Levine and Wiener (1976).

Analysis

Empirical overview

This somewhat unconventional algebraic sum overview necessitates some further definitions at this point. The analysis is in terms of experiments for and against the hypothesis that early nutritional privation impairs later capacity to learn. Two quite different tests on the same animals (e.g. Lashley III maze and pole-jump avoidance) count as two experiments. However, two-part tests (e.g. initial learning followed by reversal learning or by extinction) count as one experiment. Slow extinction is taken to be maladaptive. Where there are more than two treatment groups simultaneously under study, the number of experiments is deemed to be the number of possible comparisons of control with experimental groups; that is, one less than the total number of groups. Thus, a study with four nutritional groups counts as three experiments. The criteria are necessarily arbitrary, but hopefully fairly sensible. Well nourished control animals are designated C and previously undernourished animals PU.

The vast majority of investigators have chosen to test male animals, for reasons discussed below, and hence the overview is confined as far as possible to males. Unfortunately in some reports it is not clear whether male or female animals were used and in others the results for males and females are combined. Unsatisfactory as these papers are in this respect, their results are included in the overview.

The creation of abnormally large foster-litters has been one of the most popular methods of undernutrition during the suckling period, though there has been little standardisation of litter size between studies and some of the so-called large litters can have experienced only mild undernutrition. Consequently, only experiments in which the large litters started off with at least 13 neonates are included in the review.

The analysis has been conducted on three levels, which differ markedly in severity of critical evaluation. (i) This least critical analysis accepts all results at their numerical face value, irrespective of statistical analysis. Thus a C error score of 15 compared with a PU score of 20 is taken as an instance of C superiority, even though the difference is not statistically significant. This level of analysis was undertaken to cover the possibility that the majority of non-significant results might have been in one rather than the other direction. (ii) An analysis conducted on the basis of the authors' statistical evaluation of their own results. Only effects of treatment or differences between groups significant at the 5% level of probability or less contribute numerically to this analysis. (iii) as (ii), but excluding studies in which any group of animals was known to number fewer than 8 individuals or to represent fewer than 4 litters. It is somewhat staggering to realise that this criterion results in the exclusion of almost exactly half of the experiments which have been carried out in this field of research (39 experiments remain out of 80).

The analysis draws upon 34 papers, the vast majority of which are on rats: 25 on rats, 6 on mice, 2 on pigs and 1 on cats.

The results of the overview are given in Table I, according to species of animal and level of analysis. These have been analysed statistically by the Sign Test (Siegel, 1956), assuming as null hypothesis the median finding that there should be as many instances of PU superiority as of C superiority. In fact, the observed frequencies deviate significantly from those indicated by the null hypothesis at all levels of analysis ($P < 0.01$ in each case, Table I). Instances of C superiority predominate.

Meaningful inter-species comparison is possible only between rat and mouse. Apparently the mouse is rather more consistently susceptible to early undernutrition, in that instances of C superiority predominate significantly in the mouse, even at the most critical level of analysis, but not in the rat. Also, reports of no significant difference are rare for mice but commonplace for rats. It must be pointed out, however, that 6 of the 13 experiments on mice were carried out in one laboratory (Leathwood et al., 1974; Leathwood et al., 1975; Bush and Leathwood, 1975) and that the figures for mice are thus heavily dependent on studies of two-way active avoidance in one strain of animals.

Table I Review of the effects of early undernutrition on performance in tests of learning ability in 4 species according to the direction of the differences obtained

Species	No. of expts.	Analysis I[†]			Analysis II			Analysis III		
		C[††]	PU	=	C	PU	NS	C	PU	NS
Rat	60	37	16**	7	18	5**	37	9	3	17
Mouse	13	11	2*	0	10	2*	1	8	0**	1
Pig	6	6	0*	0	5	0	1	0	0	0
Cat	1	1	0	0	1	0	0	1	0	0
Total	80	55	18***	7	34	7***	39	18	3**	18

The units are numbers of experiments indicating superior performance by C or PU animals or no difference.
†Criteria for analyses I, II and III: I, numerical values; II, significant differences; III, significant differences and adequate numbers of animals (see text for further details).
††C means instances of C superiority; PU, of PU superiority; and NS, no significant difference.
*$P < 0.05$;   **$P < 0.01$;   ***$P < 0.001$ (Sign test).
References to source papers are given with Tables II, III, and IV.

Sex differences?

Most investigators, as already mentioned, have tested male rather than female animals for lasting after-effects of early nutritional privation. The reasons for this are probably to be found in some of the early papers on this subject. Kennedy (1957) was the first to report the highly repeatable finding that growth-retarding rats in the suckling period results in a permanent stunting of body growth which is considerably more severe in male rats than in females. If this were so for the body, might not it also be so for the brain and even for behaviour? Nine years later Barnes et al. (1966) found visual discrimination performance in a water Y-maze to be impaired in male PU rats but not in females. They concluded that males are more behaviourally vulnerable to early malnutrition than females.

Since then studies of learning by PU females have been rare and comparisons with males in the same study even rarer. A few investigators have tested both males and females and then pooled their results without comment, from which it ought to be safe to conclude that the sexes did not differ significantly in their response to early undernutrition (Mysliveček et al., 1968; Guirintano, 1974; Morris, 1974). However, the numbers of animals were small in each case and the likelihood of a significant effect of sex, consequently, not great. The only study which affords any support to the suggestion of Barnes et al. (1966) is that of Howard and Granoff (1968) and even this is perplexing. Male PU mice display significantly enhanced delayed response visual discrimination in a water Y-maze compared to their controls, whereas corresponding females do not. No other paper reports significant effects on one sex but not the other, but in three papers in which results are quoted separately for males and females, the numerical difference in performance attributable to early nutrition is greater for females than for males (Ottinger and Tanabe, 1969; Slob, 1972; Randt and Derby, 1973). However, in no case were the effects of nutrition significant.

There would appear to be no good reason for excluding females from investigations of the influence on behaviour of early nutritional privation, except perhaps that their behaviour may be more variable than that of males due to their oestrous cycle. Statistically significant effects may therefore be more difficult to demonstrate in females. Presumably this factor is likely to be a considerable problem in the most popular experimental species, rats and mice, whose oestrous cycle is only 4 or 5 days long. One solution is to ovariectomise the females some weeks before testing. It is probably significant that in the two investigations employing this technique the ovariectomised PU rats were found to differ from appropriate controls in much the same way as males did, in long-term activity (Slob et al., 1973) and in social behaviour (Whatson et al., 1976).

Timing of malnutrition

It is generally agreed that the outcome of early malnutrition on brain development is a function of the timing, duration and severity of the privation (Dobbing, 1974). I shall attempt in the next two sections to relate timing and duration to ultimate behavioural effect. Severity will not be considered because of the very great difficulty involved in arriving at a satisfactory definition which would allow comparison of degree of severity between studies. Severity in terms of what, one might ask, and when?

The effects of early malnutrition are analysed in Tables II, III and IV according to species of animal and to the timing of the nutritional privation. The shorthand notation of Smart and Dobbing (1971) is adopted for convenience here. G, L and W refer respectively to Gestation, Lactation and the early post-Weaning period, and the superscript minus denotes nutritional privation. Thus $G^- L^-$ animals were malnourished during gestation and the suckling period, and well nourished thereafter.

Cross-species comparison with respect to the timing of nutritional insult is complicated by differences between species in maturity at birth, and Dobbing (1976) has recommended that stages of brain maturation should be used as reference points rather than birth. In fact, rats and mice, the major species in this review, are both predominantly postnatal brain developers (Dobbing and Sands, 1971; Uzman and Rumley, 1958) and the cat is likely to be the same. Hence birth can safely be used as a reference point for these three species as it indicates a similar stage of brain development in each case. Rather more caution is necessary with respect to the pig, which is a perinatal brain developer (Dickerson and Dobbing, 1967).

The first analysis is taken from the overview and compares the effects of undernutrition during one or another period of early life, gestation, the suckling period or

Table II Review of the effects of early undernutrition on performance in tests of learning ability in the rat according to the timing of nutritional privation

Treatment	No. of expts.	Analysis I[†]			Analysis II			Analysis III		
		C[††]	PU	=	C	PU	NS	C	PU	NS
G^-	7	4	3	0	3	0	4	3	0	0
$G^- L^-$	7	3	2	2	3	1	3	2	1	2
L^-	27	15	8	4	4	3	20	1	2	10
$L^- W^-$	15[×]	12	2[*]	1	8	1[*]	6	3	0	4
W^-	4	3	1	0	0	0	4	0	0	1

The units are numbers of experiments indicating superior performance by C or PU animals, or no difference. Superscripts, see Table I. See text for explanation of treatment nomenclature (G^- etc.).

[×]Includes 1 $G^- L^- W^-$ experiment.

References: Baird et al., 1971; Barnes et al., 1966; Caldwell and Churchill, 1967; Cowley and Griesel, 1966; Cravens, 1974; Eayrs and Lishman, 1955; Fraňková, 1970a, 1973; Fraňková and Barnes, 1968; Guirintano, 1974; Guthrie, 1968; Howard et al., 1976; Hsueh et al., 1974; Morris, 1974; Mysliveček et al., 1968; Mysliveček et al., 1969; Ottinger and Tanabe, 1969; Rajalakshmi et al., 1967; Simonson and Chow, 1970; Slob et al., 1973; Smart, 1976; Smart et al., 1973; Smart et al., 1977; Tikal et al., 1976; Zimmerman and Wells, 1971.

Table III Review of the effects of early undernutrition on performance in tests of learning ability in the mouse according to the timing of nutritional privation

Treatment	No. of expts.	Analysis I†			Analysis II			Analysis III		
		C††	PU	=	C	PU	NS	C	PU	NS
G⁻	1	1	0	0	1	0	0	1	0	0
G⁻L⁻	4	3	1	0	2	1	1	1	0	1
L⁻	8	7	1	0	7	1	0	7	0*	0

The units are numbers of experiments indicating superior performance by C or PU animals or no difference. Superscripts, see Table I. See text for explanation of treatment nomenclature (G⁻ etc.).

References: Bush and Leathwood, 1975; Castellano and Oliverio, 1976; Howard and Granoff, 1968; Leathwood et al., 1974; Leathwood et al., 1975; Randt and Derby, 1973.

the early postweaning period. It will be immediately obvious from Tables II and III that the suckling period has been by far the most popular time for imposing nutritional deprivation on rats and mice, probably because it is the most vulnerable period for brain development, at least in terms of cell multiplication and increase in weight (Dobbing and Smart, 1973). Unfortunately there has been comparatively little work on the other two periods, especially the early postweaning period which is investigated in its own right in rodents in only two papers (Barnes et al., 1966; Guirintano, 1974). Across the two species, the period which most consistently shows effects on later learning appears to be gestation. Cats too are adversely affected by gestational food restriction (Simonson, 1977). Whether or not the suckling period is a vulnerable one for the development of learning ability seems to depend on the species under consideration. In the rat it does not appear to be so, insofar as only 1 experiment (Barnes et al., 1966) out of 13 provides firm evidence of impaired performance in a learning test (Table II, Analysis III). But in the mouse, the evidence of vulnerability is virtually unequivocal (Table III).

Another type of analysis is to consider only those papers which report comparisons between differently timed nutritional privations within the same study. This may

Table IV Review of the effects of early undernutrition on performance in tests of learning ability in pig and cat according to the timing of nutritional privation. The units are numbers of experiments indicating superior performance by C or PU animals or no difference.

Species	Treatment	No. of expts.	Analysis I†			Analysis II			Analysis III		
			C††	PU	=	C	PU	NS	C	PU	NS
Pig	L⁻W⁻	1	1	0	0	1	0	0	0	0	0
	W⁻	5	5	0	0	4	0	1	0	0	0
Cat	G⁻	1	1	0	0	1	0	0	1	0	0

Superscripts, see Table I. See text for explanation of treatment nomenclature (G⁻ etc.). References: Barnes et al., 1970; Barnes et al., 1976; Simonson, 1977.

arguably be more meaningful than the empirical overview, in that the control of non-nutritional variables will have been better within any one study than between studies. Because such investigations are so demanding of time and animal resources, they have been few and are often open to criticism on the grounds that the numbers of animals are small. For instance, the most heroic of these embraced a three levels of protein (10, 20 or 30%) times three periods of nutritional treatment (G, L or W) experimental design, but had only three male and two female rats in each of the nine groups so generated (Guirintano, 1974). The low protein diet had a deleterious effect only when imposed during the suckling period and only on performance in one of the three multiple-T water mazes employed. Both Ottinger and Tanabe (1969) and Smart et al. (1973) compared the effects of G^- and L^- treatments on performance in the Hebb-Williams maze, but obtained conflicting results. In both studies, the G^- rats resembled their controls, but whereas Ottinger and Tanabe's L^- rats had significantly high error scores, those of Smart et al. tended to have low error scores. To complete the confusion, Hsueh et al. (1974) found performance in an elevated multiple T-maze to be impaired in G^- rats and relatively unaffected in L^- animals. In mice, both G^- and L^- treatments have been found to impair two-way active avoidance conditioning (Bush and Leathwood, 1975). Apart from Guirintano (1974) only Barnes et al. (1966) have compared the L^- and W^- treatments. In both investigations, there was evidence of impaired learning in the L^- but not the W^- rats.

In an investigation of learning in PU pigs, 8 week periods of nutritional privation were imposed at different times within the first 15 weeks of postnatal life, starting at 3 days, 3 weeks or 7 weeks (Barnes et al., 1970). One would expect the earliest period of privation to have the greatest effect on brain development, since the pig's brain growth spurt begins about 5 weeks before birth and continues for a similar period postnatally (Dickerson and Dobbing, 1967). However, this prediction correlates poorly with the observed effects on behaviour. Pigs fed a low protein diet from 3 to 11 weeks of age displayed the greatest impairment of active avoidance conditioning and the slowest extinction.

In summary, it would appear from the overview that the gestation period is a vulnerable one with respect to later performance on tests of learning. There is quite firm evidence of vulnerability in the suckling period for the mouse but not for the rat. Nutritional privation in the early postweaning period alone has little lasting effect in the rat, but may be harmful in the pig. Analysis of papers reporting comparisons between differently timed nutritional treatments within the same study did not prove illuminating, possibly because they are few in number.

There are many problems here for the student of changes in physical brain growth, the central one being our complete ignorance of the nature of the physical basis of the behavioural parameters which have been measured. For example, what is the likely effect of permanently reducing the number of neurons, which is a predictable consequence of late gestation undernutrition in the rat? Is the absolute number of neurons important; or the expected consequent reduction in dendritic trees; or a still later reduction in the quantity of their ultimate synaptic connections? There must be many examples like this in which restriction imposed at one early stage may produce results which are either due primarily to deficits produced at that stage, or secondarily to later, but dependent events of growth even though there may be no contemporaneous nutritional restriction at the later stage.

Duration of malnutrition

The greater the duration of malnutrition, the greater one would expect its ultimate effect to be, given that the timing of the privation was appropriate. Whether or not this is so for learning ought to become clear from comparison of the effects of two consecutive periods of malnutrition with those of one or the other period above. Certainly L^-W^- treatment appears to be more convincingly harmful than either L^- or W^- on their own (Table II). However, the effects of G^- and L^- treatment do not appear to be additive in that G^-L^- rats show, if anything, less evidence of impaired learning than G^- rats.

This is puzzling and extremely unsatisfactory with respect to any anatomical explanation of the behavioural effects that I know of. Any attempt at interpretation in our present state of knowledge would be little more than idle speculation. It is even not out of the question that the finding is an artifact of different laboratories concentrating on different periods of privation. Thus Smart and his colleagues account for 3 of the 7 experiments on G^-L^- rats, and Barnes and his colleagues and ex-colleagues for all but 3 of the 14 experiments on L^-W^- rats. Investigations of these nutritional categories are therefore not as representative as one would like to see with respect to such factors as strain of animal and methods and conditions of rearing.

Aspects of learning investigated

It would appear to be appropriate in this kind of review to ask which, if any, aspects of learning ability are more affected than others by early undernutrition. In fact, this deceptively simple question is not that easy to answer, principally because the measures which are taken in tests of learning are measures of performance rather than of learning ability or capacity (Levitsky and Barnes, 1973; and discussed below). However, some clue to the answer may emerge from an analysis of which tests have been most effective in revealing differences between C and PU animals. The results of such an analysis are given for rats in Table V for five types of primary test and two secondary types, reversal and extinction of already-learned responses.

This analysis fully bears out the conclusion that there are no consistent effects of early malnutrition on active avoidance performance in rats (Levine and Wiener, 1976). Yet this is in marked contrast to the findings from active avoidance studies in other species. C mice have performed significantly better than their PU counterparts in 8 out of 9 two-way active avoidance experiments and even in the 9th, the direction of the difference was the same (Randt and Derby, 1973; Leathwood et al., 1974; Leathwood et al., 1975; Bush and Leathwood, 1975; Castellano and Oliverio, 1976). It might be suggested that this apparent species difference was a by-product of differences in the test procedures adopted for rats and mice. Two-way active avoidance was used in all the mouse studies, whereas a diversity of avoidance conditioning techniques has been used for rats. As far as can be ascertained, however, this is not the case, since restricting the analysis to two-way active avoidance studies for both species does not alter the conclusion. Out of 8 such experiments on rats, one demonstrated PU superiority (Morris, 1974) and 7 no significant effect of early treatment (Guthrie, 1968; Tikal et al., 1976; Howard et al., 1976). Until some other interpretation is put forward there would appear to be no alternative but to suppose that there is a true species difference between rats and mice with respect to effects on avoidance conditioning. Furthermore, previously malnourished pigs, like corresponding mice, are slow to learn a conditioned avoidance response (Barnes et al., 1970).

Returning exclusively to the rat, neither spatial discrimination nor reversal learning show consistent adverse effects of early nutritional privation (Table V). Visual discrimination tests reveal evidence of impaired PU performance, but with the reservation that all three positive results are due to the same source (Barnes et al., 1966). More convincing evidence comes from what might be termed the multiple cul-de-sac tests of topographical learning, utilising the Hebb-Williams, Lashley III and multiple-T mazes. It has been argued that such tests, and in particular the Hebb-Williams maze, are better tests of learning capacity and less akin to rote learning than avoidance and discrimination tasks (Meyers, 1971). Certainly these topographical problems would appear to make demands on abilities which would stand the animal in good stead in its natural environment. The above findings are discussed later in a more theoretical way in relation to motivation and arousal.

Table V   Review of the effects of early undernutrition on performance in different tests of learning ability in the rat

Test	No. of expts.	Analysis II[†]		
		C[††]	PU	NS
Hebb-Williams maze	12	5	1	6
Multiple-T and Lashley III mazes	11	5	0	6
Active avoidance	24	4	4	16
Visual discrimination	9	3	0	6
Spatial discrimination	4	0	1	3
Reversal	7	1	0	6
Extinction	7	4	0	3

The units are numbers of experiments indicating superior performance by C or PU animals or no difference. Superscripts, see Table I. Certain experiments are represented twice above, in which initial learning was followed by reversal learning or extinction. Experiments with females are included.
References as in Table II, plus Di Benedetta and Cioffi, 1972; Cowley and Griesel, 1962; Tikal et al., 1972.

The other aspect of learning which appears to be reliably affected is extinction, which typically occurs more slowly in PU than in C rats (Fraňková and Barnes, 1968; Fraňková, 1973; Simonson and Chow, 1970). The same is true in pigs (Barnes et al., 1970; Barnes et al., 1976). Slower extinction would be expected to follow slower and less perfect acquisition of a learned response. However, the differences in rate of extinction referred to above were in most cases greater and more highly significant than any differences in the preceding acquisition. To some extent at least the extinction effect would appear to be a separate one. PU rats have in addition been observed to make more perseverative errors in a water T-maze than controls, which may be a related phenomenon to slower extinction (Smart et al., 1977). Repetition of the same wrong-turning would appear to be analogous to a failure to extinguish an unrewarded response.

Transgeneration effects?

Transgeneration effects are defined as effects of preceding generations of nutritional privation, detectable in a generation which has not itself experienced nutritional privation. These have not been included in the preceding analyses and are discussed separately from them because the situation is qualitatively a different one. It is that much more likely that any such transgeneration effects are mediated through non-nutritional alterations in mother–young relationships, prenatal and postnatal.

The most convincing evidence of a transgeneration effect on learning is provided by Cowley and Griesel (1966), who found that one generation of nutritional rehabilitation was not sufficient to offset two generations of malnutrition. They maintained a population of rats on a marginally low protein diet (14.5%) for two generations, and transferred some of the next generation of females to a more adequate diet (21% protein). Their male offspring were tested in the Hebb-Williams maze when adult and found to be inferior in performance to controls with an ancestry of adequate nutrition, though rather better than rats with an unbroken three-generation ancestry of low protein nutrition.

The other claim to have demonstrated a transgeneration effect is somewhat less substantial. Bresler et al. (1975) report learning deficits in the grandoffspring of female rats maintained on a low protein diet for one month prior to mating and throughout pregnancy. However, these are of marginal statistical significance and in one case depend on the control rats starting off worse but improving relatively more than the experimentals.

A major concern with respect to transgeneration studies, especially those covering several generations, is that there should not be genetical change within the populations as a result of selection or inbreeding. Both are distinct possibilities in a population in which mortality is high, as it might be in a malnourished laboratory colony. How trenchant such a criticism would be would depend on the nature of the findings. One would be strongly tempted to invoke genetical change as an explanation, if a behavioural deficit were to prove staunchly resistant to several generations of nutritional rehabilitation. A stepwise progression back to control levels of performance over successive generations would be largely immune from such criticism.

Some attitudes and recommendations for future research

Capacity to learn, performance and motivation

I have so far in this review accepted the results of the various tests which have been employed as true indications of ability to learn, with only the briefest of reservations expressed in the section *Aspects of learning investigated* (p. 224). My hope has been that some statement about the performance of PU animals would shine through the collation of these many differently conducted studies, and I am inclined to think that it does. In empirical overview, the PU animals were likely to perform less well than their controls. Nevertheless, it is only sensible to question what bearing this conclusion has on capacity to learn.

The relationship of performance on tests of learning and true capacity to learn has been thoughtfully reviewed by Levitsky and Barnes (1973). Basically the problem is that the process of learning is intrinsic to the nervous system and cannot, with our current knowledge and technology, be measured directly. It can only be inferred from observed changes in behaviour or, in some cases, changes in electrical activity of the nervous system. What we measure are changes in performance in response, usually, to repeated presentations of particular configurations of stimuli, which would be quite satisfactory if change in performance faithfully reflected capacity to learn. However, it seems quite likely that it often fails to do so. Fig. 1 illustrates some of the problems with respect to two hypothetical sets of results for control and experimental animals. In both cases (a) and (b) the rate of change in performance is slower in the experimental group, but in (a) they do eventually attain the same level of performance, whereas in (b) they never do so. I would be reasonably happy to interpret case (a) as evidence of slower learning in the experimental group, but reluctant to place that interpretation on case (b). Parallel final levels of performance, such as those reported by Simonson and Chow (1970) and Hsueh et al. (1974), are more likely to reflect factors, such as differences in distractibility or even the occurrence of "superstitious" behaviour in the experimental animals (Skinner, 1948). Hence it is desirable, though obviously not always practicable, that change in performance should be graphed such that judgements of this sort can be made.

As long ago as 1908, Yerkes and Dodson postulated that there is an optimum level of motivation for any given task and that this level is likely to be inversely related to the difficulty of the task. Conversely, performance on a particular task is likely to be influenced by level of motivation. Others have rephrased these tenets in terms of arousal and emotionality (e.g. Hebb, 1949; Bindra, 1959). Ideally, therefore, every comparison between groups of animals should have built into it the requirement that

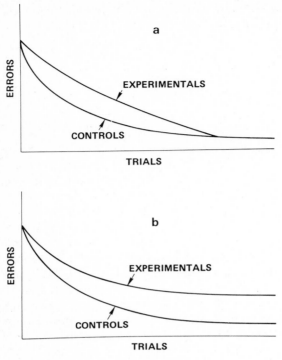

Fig. 1 Hypothetical learning curves for control and experimental animals (reproduced from Levitsky and Barnes, 1973).

their levels of motivation, arousal or whatever be equivalent, unless that is the variable under investigation. Regrettably this condition has been violated in early malnutrition studies, almost without exception. Levels of deprivation and of shock have undoubtedly been kept the same for C and PU animals, but there is now ample evidence that their effects are not equivalent. PU rats have been found to be more responsive in food-getting situations (e.g. Barnes et al., 1968; Smart et al., 1973) and water-getting situations (Smart and Dobbing, 1977) and to react more strongly to electric shock (Levitsky and Barnes, 1970; Smart et al., 1975; Lynch, 1976b). In fact they display heightened responsiveness with respect to every motivational system which has so far been thoroughly investigated. These findings have prompted the conclusions that PU rats over-react in unpleasant circumstances (Levitsky and Barnes, 1970) or, in more general terms, have a lowered threshold of arousal (Dobbing and Smart, 1974). They may even go some way towards explaining some of the contradictory results in the early malnutrition literature.

Certain predictions can be made about performance in tests of learning on the strength of these differences in responsiveness. Levitsky and Barnes (1973) have suggested that on these grounds alone PU animals ought to perform better than C animals on simple tasks, but should be less able on difficult problems. While this conjecture has not yet been put to the test experimentally, there is some qualified support for the idea in the general overview insofar as PU inferiority was more marked in fairly complicated tests of topographical learning than in tests more akin to rote learning (Table V).

Conversely it may be possible to obviate differences in performance by first equilibrating responsiveness in C and PU animals by some appropriate treatment. Thus Leathwood et al. (1975) treated PU mice with the minor tranquilliser Chlordiazepoxide to test the hypothesis that deficits in active avoidance performance were due to increased "emotionality". No effort was made to accurately equilibrate "emotionality", but performance was indeed shifted near to untreated control levels in drugged PU mice.

The above two predictions sidestep the issue of whether there are lasting effects of early malnutrition on true learning capacity: in fact, they largely assume that there is none. To properly investigate the question it would be necessary to adopt some such procedure as to run several groups of C and PU animals in the same experiment at different levels of motivation. Thus one might test 6 groups, comprising one C and one PU group at each of three levels of, say, food deprivation. An alternative would be to titrate degree of deprivation against a standard level of performance on some simple task before testing on some more complex problem. Barnes et al. (1976) have shown an awareness of this sort of approach by varying shock levels to suit individual pigs prior to avoidance conditioning. However, the matching was qualitative and the experimenters themselves express doubts about its effectiveness. Titration against some quantitative behavioural citerion is advisable.

Greater control of motivational and arousal factors would probably enable us to make more confident statements about the relationship of early malnutrition to true learning capacity. However, true learning capacity, whatever it may be, may prove to be like the holy grail –almost mythical and totally elusive. I most certainly baulk from any attempt to define it here. I can imagine arriving at a new level of doubt, having controlled for various motivational factors, and wondering whether differences in performance thus obtained related to differences in the formation of short term memory, "consolidation" into long term memory, decay or recall. The pragmatic argument may have a lot to recommend it that what matters in the end is indeed performance. Hence, the most useful and practicable course is probably to continue to collect information about performance in tests of learning, but under a variety of conditions.

Possible mechanisms

Which mechanism mediates the lasting effects of early malnutrition on behaviour is currently a highly controversial issue (see reviews by Levitsky and Barnes, 1973; Levine and Wiener, 1976; Crnic, 1976). The most straightforward idea is that early malnutrition exerts its influence directly through its retarding effect on the brain's structural development. There can be no doubt that nutritional insult at the time of the brain growth spurt causes lasting deficits and distortions of brain growth (Dobbing and Smart, 1974), but it has so far proved impossible to demonstrate conclusively that this matters for behavioural development. One feels intuitively, however, that any effect that this may have is more likely to be harmful than beneficial. The problems are two-fold. First, as has already been mentioned, we are largely ignorant of the physical basis of the behaviours which are being measured. Hence, we are neither in a position to make meaningful predictions about behavioural effects from a knowledge of differences in brain structure, nor vice versa. Bereft of such a theoretical framework, correlational analysis of brain–behaviour relationships is hazardous. Furthermore, any such relationship is much more likely to involve aspects of brain structure like synaptic connectivity, which are only now beginning to be quantified, than the structural measures that have been taken so far (Dobbing and Smart, 1974).

Secondly, there is the quite different problem that the experimental control of environmental conditions has probably been more illusory than real. Reservations about the direct effect hypothesis started to be voiced in the early 1970s, when it was pointed out that there were likely to be many non-nutritional side-effects of the various procedures adopted for restricting early growth (Plaut, 1970; Fraňková, 1971; Smart and Preece, 1973). Principally on the basis of the considerable early stimulation literature (see reviews by Daly, 1973; Russell, 1971) it was suggested that these indirect effects of nutritional privation might of themselves be responsible for any lasting effects on behaviour. The difficulty arises because, to cover the period of the brain growth spurt, these procedures have to be applied at a time when the young animal is still dependent on its mother, and therefore it is not altogether surprising that they have been found to influence several aspects of mother–infant interaction (Grota and Ader, 1969; Fraňková, 1971; Smart and Preece, 1973; Massaro et al., 1974). Serious attempts have been made to overcome this problem with respect to the mother–litter separation method of restricting growth (Slob et al., 1973; Lynch, 1976a). Litters to be undernourished are provided alternately with lactating and non-lactating foster-mothers for periods of 12 h at a time. Yet even in this instance, there are differences in maternal care: the foster mothers spend more time in the nest with undernourished than with well-fed young (Lynch, 1976a) in just the same way as low protein mothers do with their litters (Massaro et al., 1974). The finding that underfed young experience more maternal contact may well apply to all methods of early growth restriction except the large litter method (Grota and Ader, 1969) and separation techniques which deny the young access to any adult female conspecific.

The correspondence between the early malnutrition and early stimulation situations has, of course, to be an inverse one, because it is part of the early malnutrition ethic that its effects be harmful while early stimulation tends to be thought of as beneficial. Thus the notion has grown up that undernourished young are also understimulated. Perhaps the best evidence that this may be so comes from studies in which additional stimulation has been found to ameliorate the effects of early undernutrition (Fraňková, 1970b; Levitsky and Barnes, 1972). It is unlikely however, that an answer is to be found in a simple sum of stimulus inputs.

Explanation in terms of indirect effects of malnutrition offers not one but a group of alternative mechanisms: in fact, much the same group whose members have been invoked individually and in combination to account for the early stimulation effects. Additional stimulation, hypothermia, stress and altered maternal behaviour have all been plausibly postulated as mediators of the early "handling" phenomenon

(Russell, 1971). Of these, the last three might possibly operate in the early malnutrition situation.

Recently Levitsky and Barnes (1972, 1973) have proposed another possible mechanism, which would appear to owe its origins more to research on environmental impoverishment and enrichment than to that on early stimulation. It is more a cognitive mechanism. They suggest that the undernourished animal, by virtue of its nutritional condition, is in a state of functional isolation from its environment: that is, that it either cannot fully receive or cannot fully utilize information from its environment. Hence the latent or redundant learning which they propose would normally occur during this period would be lost to the underfed animal (Levitsky, 1977). This deficit would be detected later in the PU animal as impaired learning. The suggestion is intriguing and apparently open to experimental investigation with respect to specific environmental stimuli (Smart, 1977).

The possibility of endocrinological factors as mediators of early undernutrition effects should not be forgotten. There is already some evidence of lasting effects on the hypothalamic-hypophyseal-adrenocortical axis which may of themselves have implications for behaviour (Adlard and Smart, 1972). Such hormonal effects could result from the direct influence of undernutrition on the growth and development of endocrine glands or from the other alterations in the early environment discussed above.

Which, if any, or which combination of these proposed mechanisms mediates the effects of early malnutrition is still open to conjecture. None can yet be discounted. The importance of the controversy lies in the extrapolation from experimental animals to man. Extrapolation on the basis of effects of "altered brain structure" or of "functional isolation", if either proved true for experimental animals, would appear to be much safer than generalisations from the standpoint of effects of "altered maternal behaviour", which might differ markedly between species.

Conclusions

The results of 80 experiments were collated from 34 papers. PU animals performed less well in tests of learning ability than their controls in a significant majority of cases. The few studies of PU females lend little support to the suggestion that they are behaviourally less vulnerable to early malnutrition than males. Analysis of timing of nutritional insult revealed that gestation was the most consistently vulnerable period in rat, mouse and cat for later learning performance. The suckling period was susceptible to nutritional insult in the mouse but apparently not in the rat. Only the pig was affected by postweaning malnutrition. Duration of nutritional insult affected outcome, but not always in the expected way. Malnutrition throughout both the suckling and early postweaning periods was more harmful than malnutrition during only one or the other of these periods. On the other hand, malnutrition throughout both gestation and the suckling period apparently had, if anything, less effect than during gestation alone. Performance was more affected by early malnutrition on some tests than others. Spatial discrimination and reversal learning were un-affected. Active avoidance was unaffected in rats but consistently impaired in mice. Topographical learning of fairly complex mazes and, perhaps, visual discrimination were impaired, and extinction slowed. There is some evidence of transgeneration effects of malnutrition, though caution is expressed regarding the possibility of in-advertent genetic change. Differences in performance may reflect differences in other aspects of behaviour and not necessarily differences in capacity to learn. For example, PU animals are in general more responsive than controls. Strategies are re-commended for controlling this factor to make more effective comparisons of true learning capacities. Which, or which combination, of several proposed mechanisms mediates the lasting effects of early malnutrition on behaviour is still a matter for conjecture.

Acknowledgements

The Medical Research Council and the National Fund for Research into Crippling Diseases supported this work. I am also most grateful to my colleagues Professor J. Dobbing, Dr. P. G. Croskerry, Miss E. A. Byrne and Mr. J. Wearden for their con-structive comments on drafts of the review.

Literature cited

Adlard, B. P. F. and Smart, J. L. (1972) Adrenocortical function in rats subjected to nutri-tional deprivation in early life, *J. Endocr. 54*, 99

Abbey, H. and Howard, E. (1973) Statistical procedure in developmental studies on species with multiple offspring, *Dev. Psychobiol. 6*, 329

Baird, A., Widdowson, E. M. and Cowley, J. J. (1971) Effects of calorie and protein defi-ciencies early in life on the subsequent learning ability of rats, *Br. J. Nutr. 25*, 391

Barnes, R. H., Cunnold, S. R., Zimmermann, R. R., Simmons, H., MacLeod, R. B. and Krook, L. (1966) Influence of nutritional deprivations in early life on learning behavior of rats as measured by performance in a water maze, *J. Nutr. 89*, 399

Barnes, R. H., Levitsky, D. A., Pond, W. G. and Moore, U. (1976) Effects of postnatal dietary protein and energy restriction on exploratory behavior in young pigs, *Dev. Psychobiol. 9*, 425

Barnes, R. H., Moore, A. U. and Pond, W. G. (1970) Behavioral abnormalities in young adult pigs caused by malnutrition in early life, *J. Nutr. 100*, 149

Barnes, R. H., Neely, C. S., Kwong, E., Labadan, B. A. and Franková, S. (1968) Postnatal nutritional deprivations as determinants of adult rat behavior towards food, its consump-tion and utilization, *J. Nutr. 96*, 467

Bindra, D. (1959) *Motivation: A Systematic Reinterpretation*, Ronald, New York

Bresler, D. E., Ellison, G. and Zamenhof, S. (1975) Learning deficits in rats with malnourished grandmothers, *Dev. Psychobiol. 8*, 315

Bush, M. and Leathwood, P. D. (1975) Effect of different regimens of early malnutrition on behavioural development and adult avoidance learning in Swiss white mice, *Br. J. Nutr. 33*, 373

233

Caldwell, D. F. and Churchill, J. A. (1967) Learning ability in the progeny of rats administered a protein-deficient diet during the second half of gestation, *Neurology 17*, 95

Castellano, C. and Oliverio, A. (1976) Early malnutrition and postnatal changes in brain and behavior in the mouse, *Brain Res. 101*, 317

Cowley, J. J. and Griesel, R. D. (1962) Pre- and post-natal effects of a low protein diet on the behaviour of the white rat, *Psychol. Afr. 9*, 216

Cowley, J. J. and Griesel, R. D. (1966) The effect on growth and behaviour of rehabilitating first and second generation low protein rats, *Anim. Behav. 14*, 506

Cravens, R. W. (1974) Effects of maternal undernutrition on offspring behavior. Incentive value of a food reward and ability to escape from water, *Dev. Psychobiol. 7*, 61

Crnic, L. S. (1976) Effects of infantile undernutrition on adult learning in rats. Methodological and design problems, *Psychol. Bull. 83*, 715

Daly, M. (1973) Early stimulation of rodents. A critical review of present interpretations, *Br. J. Psychol. 64*, 435

Di Benedetta, C. and Cioffi, L. A. (1972) Early malnutrition, brain glycoproteins and behaviour in rats, *Bibl. Nutr. Diet. 17*, 69

Dickerson, J. W. T. and Dobbing, J. (1967) Prenatal and postnatal growth and development of the central nervous system of the pig, *Proc. R. Soc. B 166*, 384

Dobbing, J. (1974) The later development of the central nervous system and its vulnerability. In: *Scientific Foundations of Paediatrics* (J. A. Davis and J. Dobbing, eds.) pp. 565–577, Heinemann, London

Dobbing, J. (1976) Vulnerable periods in brain growth and somatic growth. In: *The Biology of Human Fetal Growth* (D. F. Roberts and A. M. Thomson, eds.) pp. 137–147, Taylor and Francis, London

Dobbing, J. and Sands, J. (1971) Vulnerability of developing brain. IX. The effect of nutritional growth retardation on the timing of the brain growth-spurt, *Biol. Neonat. 19*, 363

Dobbing, J. and Smart, J. L. (1973) Early undernutrition, brain development and behavior. In: *Ethology and Development. Clinics in Developmental Medicine, No. 47.* (S. A. Barnett, ed.) pp. 16–36, Spastics Society with Heinemann, London

Dobbing J. and Smart, J. L. (1974) Vulnerability of developing brain and behaviour, *Br. Med. Bull. 30*, 164

Eayrs, J. T. and Lishman, W. A. (1955) The maturation of behaviour in hypothyroidism and starvation, *Br. J. Anim. Behav. 3*, 17

Fomon, S. J. (1974) *Infant Nutrition.* 2nd edn., Saunders, Philadelphia

Fraňková, S. (1970a) Behavioural responses of rats to early overnutrition, *Nutr. Metab. 12*, 228

Fraňková, S. (1970b) Nutritional and environmental determinants of rat behaviour. *Proceedings of the VIIIth International Congress on Nutrition, Prague*, Exerpta Medica Int. Congr. Series No. 213, 236

Fraňková, S. (1971) Relationship between nutrition during lactation and maternal behaviour of rats, *Act. Nerv. Sup. Praha. 13*, 1

Fraňková, S. (1973) Influence of the familiarity with the environment and early malnutrition on the avoidance learning and behaviour in rats, *Act. Nerv. Sup. Praha. 15*, 207

Fraňková, S. and Barnes, R. H. (1968) Effect of malnutrition in early life on avoidance conditioning and behavior of adult rats, *J. Nutr. 96*, 485

Grota, L. J. and Ader, R. (1969) Continuous recording of maternal behaviour in Rattus norvegicus, *Anim. Behav. 17*, 722

Guirintano, S. L. (1974) Effects of protein-calorie deficiencies on the learning ability of the Wistar rat, *Physiol. Behav. 12*, 55

Guthrie, H. A. (1968) Severe undernutrition in early infancy and behavior in rehabilitated albino rats, *Physiol. Behav. 3*, 619

Hebb, D. O. (1949) *The Organization of Behavior*, Wiley, New York

Howard, E. and Granoff, D. M. (1968) Effect of neonatal food restriction in mice on brain growth, DNA and cholesterol, and on adult delayed response learning, *J. Nutr. 95*, 111

Howard, E., Olton, D. S. and Johnson, C. T. (1976) Active avoidance and brain DNA after postnatal food deprivation in rats, *Dev. Psychobiol. 9*, 217

Hsueh, A. M., Simonson, M., Chow, B. F. and Hanson, H. M. (1974) The importance of the period of dietary restriction of the dam on behavior and growth in the rat, *J. Nutr. 104*, 37

Kennedy, G. C. (1957) The development with age of hypothalamic restraint upon the appetite of the rat, *J. Endocr. 16*, 9

Leathwood, P., Bush, M., Berent, C. and Mauron, J. (1974) Effects of early malnutrition on Swiss white mice: avoidance learning after rearing in large litters, *Life Sci. 14*, 157

Leathwood, P. D., Bush, M. S. and Mauron, J. (1975) The effects of chlordiazepoxide on avoidance performance of mice subjected to undernutrition or handling stress in early life, *Psychopharmacologia 41*, 105

Levine, S. and Wiener, S. (1976) A critical analysis of data on malnutrition and behavioral deficits, *Adv. Pediat. 22*, 113

Levitsky, D. A. (1977) Malnutrition and the hunger to learn. In: *Malnutrition and Mental Retardation* (D. A. Levitsky, ed.) Cornell University Press, Ithaca, in the press

Levitsky, D. A. and Barnes, R. H. (1970) Effect of early malnutrition on the reaction of adult rats to aversive stimuli, *Nature Lond. 225*, 468

Levitsky, D. A. and Barnes, R. H. (1972) Nutritional and environmental interactions in the behavioral development of the rat: long-term effects, *Science N.Y. 176*, 68

Levitsky, D. A. and Barnes, R. H. (1973) Malnutrition and animal behavior. In: *Nutrition, Development and Social Behavior.* (D. J. Kallen, ed.) pp. 3–16, DHEW Publication No. (NIH) 73–242

Lynch, A. (1976a) Postnatal undernutrition: an alternative method, *Dev. Psychobiol. 9*, 39

Lynch, A. (1976b) Passive avoidance behavior and response thresholds in adult male rats after early postnatal undernutrition, *Physiol. Behav. 16*, 27

Massaro, T. F., Levitsky, D. A. and Barnes, R. H. (1974) Protein malnutrition in the rat: its effects on maternal behaviour and pup development, *Dev. Psychobiol. 7*, 551

Meyers. B. (1971) Early experience and problem-solving behavior. In: *The Ontogeny of Vertebrate Behavior* (H. Moltz, ed.) pp. 57–94, Academic Press, New York

Morris, C. J. (1974) The effects of early malnutrition on one-way and two-way avoidance behavior, *Physiol. Psychol. 2*, 148

Mysliveček, J., Chaloupka, J., Hassmannová, J., Rokyta, R., Semiginovsky, B., Sobotka, P., Springer, V., Vožeh, F., and Záhlava, J. (1968) Continued investigations on the brain development in animals with different nutrition levels. In: *Ontogenesis of the Brain* (L. Jilek and S. Trojan, eds.) pp. 401–411, Charles University, Prague

Mysliveček, J., Hassmanová, J. and Springer, V. (1969) Conditioning (avoidance reaction) in rats with different individual development, *Act. Nerv. Sup. Praha 11*, 280

Ottinger, D. R. and Tanabe, G. (1969) Maternal food restriction: effects on offspring behavior and development, *Dev. Psychobiol. 2*, 7

Plaut, S. M. (1970) Studies of undernutrition in the young rat: methodological considerations, *Dev. Psychobiol. 3*, 157

Rajalakshmi, R., Ali, S. Z. and Ramakrishnan, C. V. (1967) Effect of inanition during the neonatal period on discrimination learning and brain biochemistry in the albino rat, *J. Neurochem. 14*, 29

Randt, C. T. and Derby, B. M. (1973) Behavioral and brain correlations in early life nutritional deprivation, *Arch. Neurol. 28*, 167

Russell, P. A. (1971) "Infantile stimulation" in rodents: a consideration of possible mechanisms, *Psychol. Bull. 75*, 192

Siegel, S. (1956) *Nonparametric Statistics for the Behavioral Sciences*, McGraw-Hill, New York

Simonson, M. (1977) Effects of maternal malnourishment on development and behavior. In: *Malnutrition and Mental Retardation*, (D. A. Levitsky, ed.) Cornell University Press, Ithaca, in the press

Simonson, M. and Chow, B. F. (1970) Maze studies on progeny of underfed mother rats, *J. Nutr. 100*, 685

Skinner, B. F. (1948) "Superstition" in the pigeon, *J. Exp. Psychol. 38*, 168

Slob, A. K. (1972) *Perinatal Endocrine and Nutritional Factors Controlling Physical and Behavioural Development in the Rat*, Doctoral Thesis, University of Rotterdam

Slob, A. K., Snow, C. E. and De Natris-Mathot, E. (1973) Absence of behavioral deficits following neonatal undernutrition in the rat, *Dev. Psychobiol. 6*, 177

Smart, J. L. (1976) Reversal of spatial discrimination learning in a water maze by previously undernourished rats, *Anim. Learn. Behav. 4*, 313

Smart, J. L. (1977) Early undernutrition and the development of behavior: problems and pitfalls. In: *Malnutrition and Mental Retardation* (D. A. Levitsky, ed.) Cornell University Press, Ithaca, in the press

Smart, J. L. and Dobbing, J. (1971) Vulnerability of developing brain. II. Effects of early nutritional deprivation on reflex ontogeny and development of behaviour in the rat, *Brain Res. 28*, 85

Smart, J. L. and Dobbing, J. (1972) Vulnerability of developing brain. IV. Passive avoidance behavior in young rats following maternal undernutrition, *Dev. Psychobiol. 5*, 129

Smart, J. L. and Dobbing, J. (1977) Increased thirst and hunger in adult rats undernourished as infants: an alternative explanation, *Br. J. Nutr. 37*, 421

Smart, J. L., Dobbing, J., Adlard, B. P. F., Lynch, A. and Sands, J. (1973) Vulnerability of developing brain: relative effects of growth restriction during the fetal and suckling periods on behavior and brain composition of adult rats, *J. Nutr. 103*, 1327

Smart, J. L. and Preece, J. (1973) Maternal behaviour of undernourished mother rats, *Anim. Behav. 21*, 613

Smart, J. L., Whatson, T. S. and Dobbing, J. (1975) Thresholds of response to electric shock in previously undernourished rats, *Br. J. Nutr. 34*, 511

Smart, J. L., Whatson, T. S. and Dobbing, J. (1977) Perseverative behaviour by adult offspring of underfed mother rats, *Act. Nerv. Sup. Praha*, in the press

Stoffer, G. R. and Zimmermann, R. R. (1973) Air-blast avoidance learning sets in protein-malnourished monkeys, *Behav. Biol. 9*, 695

Tikal, K., Benešová, O. and Fraňková, S. (1972) The effect of pyrithioxine (Encephabol Merck) on behavior, learning and biochemical variables of brain in rats malnourished in early life. II. Active avoidance and discriminative learning, *Act. Nerv. Sup. Praha 14*, 174

Tikal, K., Benešová, O. and Fraňková, S. (1976) The effects of pyrithioxine and pyridoxine on individual behavior, social interactions, and learning in rats malnourished in early postnatal life, *Psychopharmacologia 46*, 325

Uzman, L. L. and Rumley, M. K. (1958) Changes in the composition of the developing mouse brain during early myelination, *J. Neurochem. 3*, 170

Whatson, T. S., Smart, J. L. and Dobbing, J. (1976) Undernutrition in early life: lasting effects on activity and social behavior of male and female rats, *Dev. Psychobiol. 9*, 529

Yerkes, R. M. and Dodson, J. D. (1908) The relation of strength of stimulus to rapidity of habit-formation, *J. Comp. Neurol. Psychol. 18*, 459

Zimmermann, R. R. and Wells, A. M. (1971) Performance of malnourished rats on the Hebb-Williams closed-field maze learning task, *Percept. Mot. Skills 33*, 1043

Genetics and the study of intelligence in man

Genetics, environment and intelligence, edited by A. Oliverio
© *Elsevier/North-Holland Biomedical Press, 1977*

Genetics, environment and intelligence
A theoretical synthesis

13

JOSEPH R. ROYCE

Historical introduction

The basic problem is to provide a viable explanation for the fact that there are individual differences in intelligence. This is one of the oldest problems in psychology, dating back to Galton in the 19th century. Although it was clear from the beginning that both nature and nurture were important sources for the observed variation in intellectual performance, this question has been bedeviled by a variety of prejudices and fads which have given us more heat than light. At the time of Galton the pendulum was focused on nature as the basis for variability. Subsequently the pendulum swung to nurture, particularly via the extremist views of John B. Watson and the behaviorists. And, although the contemporary synthesis of these antithetic views makes it clear that both nature and nurture are involved, the issues are still clouded by polemics.

There are similar conceptual difficulties concerning the nature of intelligence. The original conception, due primarily to Binet and the notion of the IQ, was that intelligence is a general ability to adapt to the environment. E. L. Thorndike, on the other hand, caught up in the behavioristic ethos of the 20s and 30s, was struck by the importance of S–R bonds. Thus, he viewed intelligence as a summation of many highly specific units. Subsequent developments in the psychological testing movement resulted in a veritable explosion of intelligence tests, accompanied by such conceptual chaos that the slogan of the times defined intelligence as "whatever intelligence tests measure". While this was originally merely a confusion of ignorance, it contained an element of truth, for subsequent correlational studies and sophistication in psychometric theory provided a variety of clues concerning the construct validity of these tests. However, it required the maturity of factor analysis, beginning around 1940, for answers to the question of test validity. In particular, it was Thurstone (1947), with his multiple factor theory and the mathematization of factor analysis, who provided the modern view of intelligence. The essence of this view is that intelligence is a complex which can best be understood by breaking it down into its many components.

The purpose of this brief historical perspective is to provide a backdrop for the currently available synthesis. The synthesis which has evolved is based on the following assumptions:

(1) Intelligence is a multi-dimensional complex.

(2) The factor model is the best available approach for identifying the components of individual differences.

(3) There is no question regarding either heredity or environment as the crucial source of observed variation. Rather, it is a question of determining exactly how both heredity and environment contribute to the observed differences.

We now move on to a consideration of how to put it all together. We begin with a brief exposition of the factor model.

The factor model

We take our point of departure from the basic factor equation, which states that any behavior, indicated as a standard score Z_{ji} (where $Z = X/\sigma$), is equal to the product of the loading (a_j) of the measurement j on factor one, times the amount of this factor possessed by individual i (F_{1i}), plus the product involving the loading of the variable on factor two ($A_{j2}F_{2i}$), plus the product involving the loading on factor three, etc., until all the common factor variance is accounted for. In simplified* mathematical terms this has been expressed as follows:

$$Z_{ji} = a_{j1}F_{1i} + A_{j2}F_{2i} + a_{j3}F_{3i} + \ldots + a_{jm}F_{mi} \tag{1}$$

If we now restate this in the more compact matrix form, we get

$$Z = AF \tag{2}$$

where Z is a matrix of standardized test scores, A is a matrix of factor loadings,

---

*The simplification occurs via omitting the uniqueness and correlational terms. It should be noted, however, that we will make reference to the correlations between factors in the context of qualitative change.

and F is a matrix of factor scores. However, since the focus of our attention is on the underlying components rather than the original observations, we solve for F and get

$$F = A^{-1}Z \tag{3}$$

But since this involves an impractical form of F because of the fact that there is no inverse for A, we turn to a variation of F, as follows:

$$F = A'R^{-1}Z \tag{4}$$

A major aspect of individual differences theory (or individuality theory) involves an elaboration of hereditary and environmental sources of variation. Thus, we must find a way to link heredity and environment to factors. One approach is to decompose the A matrix into its hereditary, environmental, and interaction components, as follows:

$$A = H + E + I \tag{5}$$

Substituting in Eqn. 4, we get

$$F = H'R^{-1}Z + E'R^{-1}Z + I'R^{-1}Z \tag{6}$$

Thus, the factor-gene model involves an elaboration of the first term

$$F_H = H'R^{-1}Z \tag{7}$$

The second term is the basis for the factor-learning model

$$F_E = E'R^{-1}Z \tag{8}$$

And the third term deals with heredity–environment interaction effects

$$F_I = I'R^{-1}Z \tag{9}$$

Conceptual elaborations of Eqns. 7, 8, and 9 will be presented in subsequent sections of this chapter.

Development of the factor model up to this point has been focused on structural aspects, factors as the components of behavioral complexes (see Eqns. 1 and 2.) The ultimate goal, however, involves going beyond structure to process or dynamics. The essence of process is change. Thus, we must develop a factor change model. This can be indicated as (where Δ = change)

$$F_\Delta = A'_\Delta R_\Delta^{-1} Z_\Delta \tag{10}$$

Factor change involves two general classes of phenomena, quantitative and qualitative. Quantitative refers to change in the performance level of any one factor. Qualitative refers to change in the relationship (e.g., the correlations) between two or more factors. Quantitative change involves the usual analysis of variables as a function of other variables, and requires no further comment at this juncture. Qualitative change, however, is a complex issue which has received relatively little attention. While its full complexity is still undergoing analysis (e.g., Royce, 1973; and in preparation), the recent statement by Buss and Royce (1976) will suffice for our purposes. They have dealt with the issue of qualitative change in terms of factor convergence and factor divergence. Factor convergence refers to the coalescence of two or more previously independent factors, and factor divergence involves the differentiation of a given dimension into two or more distinct factors. The analysis of change must also include how factor changes affect behavior. Thus, we need a change version of Eqn. 2, such as:

$$Z_\Delta = A_\Delta F_\Delta \tag{11}$$

The challenge here is to provide an understanding of temporality and factor change. This means we must be able to specify the performance level of any factor of the n-dimensional system at any moment in time. It also requires an elaboration of factor interactions and integrations at any point in time. Full elaboration of these multi-dimensional changes, which is beyond the scope of this paper, must include detailed specification of sequential, parallel, and recursive processing.*

The structure of intellect

Although the equations indicated above apply to all individual differences, the focus of this book is on variations in intelligence. Thus, if the standard score in equation one refers to performance on an intelligence test, then the factors on the right side of that equation constitute the underlying sources of the observed variation. The implication is that a relatively small number of factors or source traits (say around 100) will account for a very large number of observables or surface traits (i.e., hundreds, or even thousands of covarying behaviors). However, the number of intellectual components is not known. It is clear that the low number of Primary Mental Abilities identified by Thurstone was simply due to the early period (1940) in which he did his research. However, the subsequent decades have produced such a proliferation of cognitive factors that "acceptability" criteria had to be devised.

---

*Eqns. 10 and 11 are inadequate expressions of the factor change model. These equations, while not incorrect, are not sufficiently detailed. Our extended elaboration of individuality theory (e.g., see Royce, 1973; Royce and Buss, 1976; Royce, in preparation) will include further development of the factor change model.

This resulted in what is called invariance analysis. This is a potent and pragmatic strategy, involving both internal (i.e., within the factor model) and external analyses (i.e., experimental manipulation of factors), for determining the construct validity (Royce, 1973) or "thinghood" of factors (Royce, 1976).

In addition to factor proliferation and factor invariance, there is also the problem of factor intercorrelations. Factor intercorrelations lead directly to the possibility of higher order factors. There have, of course, been numerous claims for "g" at the second or higher order, but these claims have usually emerged from a priori solutions of one kind or another. Although there have been relatively few higher order factor analyses, the accumulated evidence, while it does not support a single "g" factor à la Spearman,* does support the existence of several second order factors, such as reasoning, memory, visualization, verbal, and fluency. Furthermore, the intercorrelations between second order factors are of sufficient magnitude to suggest that still higher order analyses are called for. Thus, the evidence for a multiplicity of levels is now convincing for the cognitive (intellectual) domain** but one can't be certain as to just how many levels there are. Furthermore, in spite of empirical weakness at the higher strata, the weight of the available evidence, combined with theoretical considerations, favors a hierarchical view as to the organization of intellectual factors. I will, therefore, provide further elaboration of the structure and function of intellectual factors in terms of a multi-dimensional multi-level hierarchy.

The current version of this hierarchy, called the cognitive hierarchy, is indicated in Fig. 1. As displayed, Fig. 1 is a static representation of the cognitive system. Its structure is designed to eventually incorporate all the dimensions necessary for the processing of cognitive information***. Thus, in principle, it applies to all persons, regardless of age and regardless of the task at hand. However, it is obvious that there are changes in cognitive structure over time, as well as differences in cognitive processing which are due to variations in task requirements. How shall we deal with the problem of stability and change in cognitive structure? We have introduced the concept of cognitive hierarchical template as an answer to this problem. The major characteristic of a template is that its form remains invariant. Thus, it says that the stability of cognitive structure lies in its hierarchical organization, whereas structural change occurs via shifts in the particular subset of dimensions, factor weights, and the

---

*Spearman's "g" would require that all primaries be intercorrelated. This has never been empirically demonstrated.

** I shall be using the terms intellect, intelligence and cognition as synonyms. Intelligence is the historically relevant term, but cognition is the appropriate current term. The cognitive system is one of six systems which comprise the total psychological system of individuality theory (see Royce, 1973; Royce and Buss, 1976; Royce, in preparation).

*** Factor invariance is the standard guide for adding more dimensions. However, a more adequate methodology for the quantitative assessment of factor invariance is needed. As this evolves, it is anticipated that some factors of Fig. 1 will be dropped and others will be added. However, it is my view that the overall hierarchical structure will remain intact, although I predict that the complete inventory of dimensions will increase significantly (e.g., at least double or triple the present number).

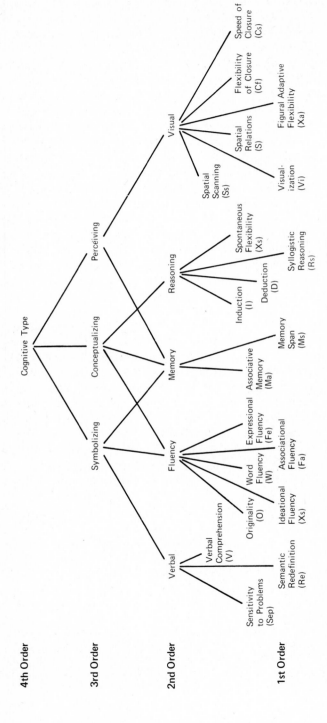

Fig. 1   The hierarchial structure of the cognitive system (revised version of Royce, 1973).

relationships composing the hierarchy. In individuality theory, the cognitive system is only one of 6 subsystems of the total psychological system, the latter being defined as a multi-dimensional, organized system of processes by means of which an organism produces mental and behavioral phenomena (Royce, 1973). Although each of the sub-systems is also a complex, multi-dimensional unit, and although there are important interactions and integrations between sub-systems which are explored elsewhere (e.g., see Royce, 1977b; Royce and Kearsley, 1977) such considerations will be ignored in this paper so that we may focus on intelligence (or cognition) per se. The cognitive system has been defined as a multi-dimensional, organized system of processes by means of which an organism produces cognitions (Royce, 1973), where the term cognition refers to both mental and behavioral phenomena of the perceptual, conceptual, and symbolizing sub-systems (Royce and Buss, 1976).

According to hierarchy–individuality theory, the construct at the apex of any psychological system is a system type (Royce and Buss, 1976). This is a modal construct which reflects the subject's profile on the entire sub-domain in question. Individuals sharing the same profile on a subset of cognitive dimensions thereby constitute a cognitive type, where such types may be identified by using profile and pattern analytic procedures as suggested by Bolz (1972), Cattell et al. (1966), DuMas (1949), Meehl (1950) and Zubin (1954). The third-order constructs of symbolizing, conceptualizing and perceiving are viewed as sub-system processors, the implication being that differences in the three sub-hierarchies reflect differences in cognitive integration as well as different dimensional profiles. Furthermore, according to the following postulate: "In general, the closer a higher-order theoretical construct is to the apex of a within-systems hierarchy, the greater its potential influence on that class of behavior and the greater its role as a personality integrator" (Royce and Buss, 1976), these sub-system processors should have extensive integrative effects on the appropriate subset of lower order factors. Thus, we would expect that a person whose cognitive system is dominated by the conceptualizing sub-system is primarily rationally oriented in interacting with the environment in contrast to the sensory orientation of the perceptual subtype or the metaphoric awareness of the symbolizing subtype.

What are the relationships between these higher order cognitive processors and their corresponding first order factors? We begin with conceptualizing. The theory is that the second order factors of fluency, memory and reasoning (and their respective first-order factors) are cognitive processors which focus on the formation, elaboration and functional significance of concepts. Thus, although both fluency and memory components are involved, it is clear that various reasoning dimensions are most critical in this sub-system of cognitive processing. While all kinds of reasoning are involved (e.g. induction), the primary focus is on the logical consequences (e.g. the deductive and syllogistic reasoning factors) of information currently available to the person.

The perceptual processing route, on the other hand, is linked primarily with the second order memory and visual factors and their respective first-order factors. These cognitive processes are focused on the transmission and transformation of sensory inputs. And, while it is true that such cognitive processing is primarily in terms of current stimuli impinging on the person via factors such as spatial scanning and speed of closure, there is a secondary involvement of memory components as well, as in the case of the flexibility of closure dimension (which involves holding the visual percept "in mind").

Symbolizing refers to those cognitive processes which focus on the formation and use of symbols and metaphors. Second-order linkages are via the verbal, fluency and memory factors and their first-order factors. In terms of processes, the focus is on analogical possibilities (i.e., "new-formation") rather than inductive or deductive consequences.

The dynamics of intellect

Complete understanding of the dynamics of intellectual (or cognitive) processing requires a detailed account of the interactions among the factor dimensions in terms of information flow as well as the temporal sequentiality of these interactions. Thus, factors are construed as organismic processors which transmit and transform information as it proceeds from S inputs to R outputs. This kind of analysis involves details of simultaneous, sequential and recursive processing for specified situations. For example, if the task at hand involves a highly complex visual display, such as a pilot is confronted with, the implication is that many of the perceptual dimensions will be processing simultaneously. On the other hand, the involvement of various conceptual and sensory-motor factors is dependent upon the psychobiological idiosyncrasies of that particular pilot (i.e., his multi-dimensional profile) and when these mediational processors are needed as the pilot proceeds through take-off, ascent, level flight, descent and landing. While the multi-dimensional model of factor analysis has been applied to a wide range of pure and applied problems, research to date has been essentially of a static nature. Thus, the typical investigation identifies the relative weights (i.e., factor loadings) to be assigned to a given predictor variable, but these beta weight equivalents do not shift with the changing requirements of the situation. The system–dynamics model of Royce and Kearsley (1976) attempts to deal with this problem via a comprehensive factorial description of cognitive dimensions as well as an outline of the functional interactions between different stages of cognitive processing as represented by factor dimensions. The Royce and Kearsley approach is based on the biological principle that function depends upon structure. Thus, whereas Fig. 1 (see p. 244) indicates the structural inter-relationships between the dimensions, Fig. 2 shows their functional interactions (omitting, for the sake of simplicity, the first order dimensions).

The cognitive type construct is primarily concerned with allocating processing control to one of the three sub-systems via an attention mechanism which brings into play the third-order P-processor (perceiving dimension), the C-processor (conceptualizing dimension), or the S-processor (symbolizing dimension). Modification in the duration or degree of processing control occurs via feedback cycles which exist between each of the major sub-system processors and cognitive type.

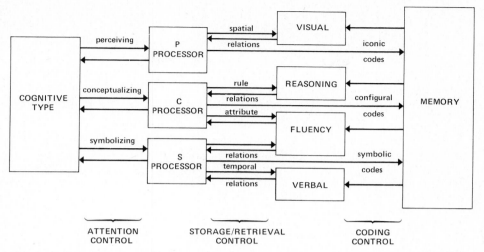

Fig. 2 Interactions among the second, third and fourth order dimensions (Royce and Kearsley, 1976).

The main function of the third-order processors with respect to the second-order dimensions is to determine when current processing requires memory storage or retrieval. For example, at some point in the processing of a visual input pattern, the visual dimension may "call" for a memory search for relevant spatial arrangements. The P-processor would then initiate a retrieval operation via the memory dimension. Feedback cycles between the memory dimension, the other second-order dimensions and the major processors of each sub-system allow varying degrees of interaction between current information and stored information.

The second-order dimensions have more specific functions. The verbal and visual dimensions are concerned with processing the temporal and spatial components of the input. The reasoning and fluency dimensions are concerned with specification of the transformation rules and identification of attributes of the input pattern respectively. The fluency dimension abstracts the relevant attributes (e.g. colors, words, numbers, size, etc.) and determines the nature of the processing required by the first-order dimensions. The reasoning dimension identifies relations in the input (e.g. bigger than, less than, equal to, above, etc.) and selects the appropriate first-order dimensions for further processing. The memory dimension controls the interaction between permanent (associative memory dimension) and temporary storage (memory span dimension). Although the second-order memory dimension is common to all three of the sub-systems (and hence provides the major source of interaction among them), each sub-system generates and uses different codes.

Fig. 3 illustrates the first-order component interactions of the perceiving sub-hierarchy. The speed of closure dimension, which determines the figure–ground aspects of the input pattern based on the knowledge of previously experienced patterns, is influenced by the associative memory dimension. The flexibility of closure dimension interprets the parts of the pattern as a complete unit and requires

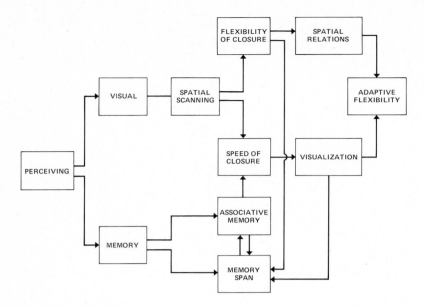

Fig. 3   Interactions among the dimensions of the perceiving subsystem (Royce and Kearsley, 1976).

keeping the units in temporary storage, hence the interaction with the memory span
dimension. The visualization dimension is linked to the memory span dimension to
allow a feedback cycle between the speed of closure, visualization and memory span
dimensions to operate. This feedback cycle indicates that pattern interpretation can
be affected by the contents of both temporary and permanent storage. This particular
circuit also provides a possible explanation for findings such as those reported by
Carmichael et al. (1932), and Franks and Bransford (1971), where preceding or concurrent labels alter the perceived shapes of visual stimuli.

The interactions between dimensions previously discussed are those which would
occur if there existed no interaction between the dimensions of the three different
sub-systems. However, it is to be expected that most cognitive tasks involve simultaneous processing in more than one sub-system and hence dimensional interactions.
Elaboration of these inter-relationships between the dimensions of different sub-
systems is best exemplified by considering a particular task in detail. I have chosen
one such task which has received some experimental attention and which also spans
the range of cognitive activities. It is my hope that such a detailed examination of
a specific task will serve to demonstrate the application of the theoretical framework*.

The cognitive task to be considered is the tachistoscopic recognition of words,
a task studied in detail by Sternberg (1969). The sequence of processing involves

---

*The reader who wants a more detailed analysis of cognitive dynamics is referred to the
paper by Royce and Kearsley (1976). Also, see Royce, Kearsley and Klare (1976) for a meta-
theoretic analysis of the relationships between factors and process.

mainly the perceiving and symbolizing sub-systems, as illustrated in Fig. 4. The square boxes indicate processing dimensions, the links between dimensions, the sequence of control and information flow, and the ovals indicate the type of memory code by means of which stored or retrieved information is represented. Most of the processing in the perceiving sub-system precedes the processing in the symbolizing sub-system, although there is simultaneous interaction between the two sub-systems via the memory dimensions. Iconic codes are used to represent the visual information which comprises the feedback loop between the speed of closure, memory and visualization dimensions (discussed previously). However, symbolic discursive codes are employed in the input to the verbal comprehension dimension from memory span and associative memory. The output of the adaptive flexibility dimension is the visually perceived word which must be further specified by the comprehension and fluency dimensions. The steps indicated in the right-hand column of the figure correspond to (but are more detailed than) the stages which Sternberg has suggested are involved in this task. As can be seen from the diagram, although this is one of the most elementary of cognitive tasks, the interactions between the first-order dimensions alone are quite complex and involve much more than the three general stages Sternberg proposed.

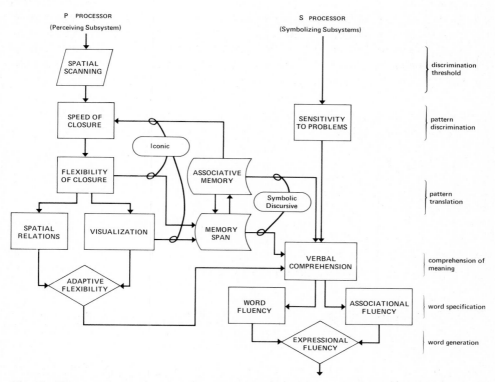

Fig. 4 The sequence of processing in the tachistoscopic recognition task (Royce and Kearsley, 1976).

While the recent contributions to cognitive dynamics represent a significant contribution beyond the usual structural research of factor analysis, the most obvious shortcoming is the lack of knowledge concerning temporality. The analyses summarized above show functional sequentiality, not temporal sequentiality. As in process descriptions anywhere in science, the explanatory power and practical applicability of the multi-factor approach will be enhanced to the extent it is eventually possible to provide exact temporal specifications.

The life-span development of factors of intelligence*

The prototypic, quantitative, life-span developmental curve for intellectual growth is shown in Fig. 5. The abscissa is chronological age and the ordinate is the scaled score on a given factor. There are three parameters of psychological interest: K_1, K_2, and K_3. On the age dimension, maturity (M), or maximum performance, is indicated by K_2 and, the onset of senility (S), or performance level before death, is indicated by K_3. The location of the y-intercept, K_1, indicates the extent of prenatal development, or the degree to which the factor is present at birth (B). Since this version of K_1 assumes a ratio scale with absolute zero as well as a means of getting measures of individual differences in cognitive processes before birth, and since neither of these conditions can be met given the present state of the (measurement) art, K_1 will be best conceived as originating at the origin, where such a y-value is the lowest scaled score of performance.

The value of the parameter K_2 indicates the maximum factor performance level (P) which occurs at maturity (M). If a factor does not reach optimal developmental level in the life-span of an individual (i.e., continues to either increase

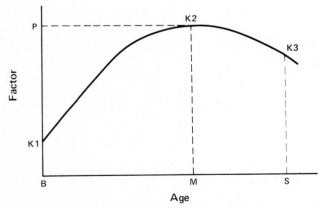

Fig. 5   The generalized life-span development curve (modified version, Royce, 1973).

---

*This section is a condensation of a more complete statement of the problem. For more details the reader is referred to Royce (1973) and Kearsley et al. (1976).

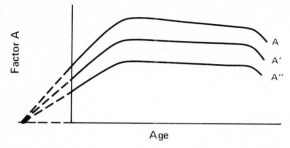

Fig. 6 Differential performance levels of the same factor as a function of age (Royce, 1973).

or decline over the entire life-span), the value of K_1 will take the value of the factor score at birth or death (for a decrease or increase, respectively). The curve segment K_1-K_2 indicates the rate of developmental change during childhood, adolescence, and early adulthood.

The parameter K_3 represents the factor score at the onset of senescence (S) (or death if there is no senescent period). It is to be expected that factor scores will always decline in any post-senescence measurement. The segment of development represented by the K_2-K_3 portion of the curve is, of course, factor change over the major part of the life-span of the individual.

In Fig. 5 we showed the protypic factor as a function of age. In Fig. 6 we show differential performance levels of the same factor, A, as a function of age. The implication is that the same factor can become manifest at a high level as in A, a middle level as in A', or a low level as in A''.

The relationship between actual performance level and performance level limit is brought out in Fig. 7. Here we see a difference between actual and potential performance level for a given factor, where actual performance level refers to the observed score on a given factor, and potential performance level refers to a heredity–environment determined theoretical upper limit.

A similar set of concepts is called for when we focus on age of maturity, the age at which maximum performance occurs. However, in this case (see Fig. 8) the difference between actual (M_a) and potential (M_t) performance is a matter of timing rather than level of performance per se. M_t denotes the heredity–environment determined earliest possible age of maturity.

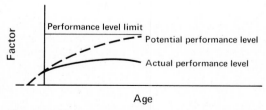

Fig. 7 The relationship between performance level and performance level limit (Royce, 1973).

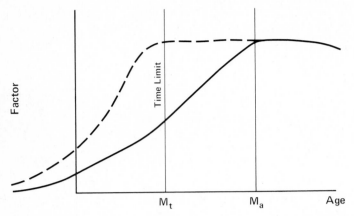

Fig. 8   The relationship between performance and age of maturity (Royce, 1973).

Heredity and environment

Developmental issues

Let us now take a closer look at the relationships between heredity, environment, and development. Note, for example, that the actual performances depicted so far are due to both heredity and environment. Hence, it will be necessary to tease out exactly how such effects are operating. Before proceeding further, however, let me offer several additional definitions. Henceforth I shall refer to the age of maturity performance limit as the time limit. This limit implies that the performance in question does not occur earlier for a given genotype and performance level regardless of amount of training or other environmental interventions. The performance level limit refers to the highest possible level of performance for a given genotype in interaction with the most optimal environment, independent of time (i.e., given infinite time)*. Further, by hereditary effect I shall mean any observed variance due to the

---

* The concept of limit is both interesting and debatable. And whether the reader sees value in it or not, it has received considerable attention in the scientific literature (e.g., the speed of light as an upper bound for rate of change and the mathematics of limits). In the present context, I view the matter quite pragmatically. If the concept helps us in developing a viable theory of individual differences, let us keep it. If it serves no useful purpose, it should be dropped. I found it to be of value in coming to grips with the hereditary and environmental sources of variation. I think it should be retained for the simple reason that all organisms, including man, are obviously finite. Thus, this concept is part of my set of underlying assumptions regarding the nature of man.

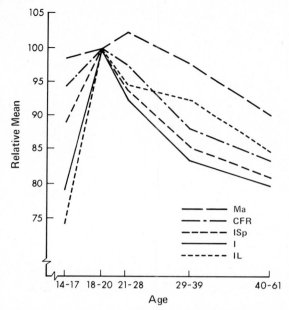

Fig. 13   Performance as function of age. Fluid abilities: Associative Memory (Ma), Figural Relations (CFR), Intellectual Speed (ISp), Induction (I), and Intellectual Level (IL) (adapted from Horn and Cattell, 1966).

order dimension which reflects a different class or sub-system of factors (see the cognitive hierarchy in Fig. 1). Although the curves indicated in Fig. 16 are consistent with the prototypic developmental curve (see Fig. 2), there are interesting parametric variations. The perceiving dimension, for example, reflects a high degree of prenatal initial development with a maximum performance limit around the age of 20, followed by a fairly constant but low rate of decline thereafter. The symbolizing dimension, on the other hand, is characterized by a less rapid development at birth, a negatively accelerating curve with age, and a maximal performance level prior to senescence or death. The conceptualizing sub-system has a lag period in early childhood before it begins development, followed by a rapid growth to a maximum performance level in middle adulthood (age 38), then a steady but low rate of decline.

Footnote (continued)

of more accurate estimates of higher order dimensions. However, it will be some time before these differential weights can be accurately established. It should be mentioned in passing that the procedure reflected in Fig. 16 is roughly comparable to the procedure in reports which plot IQ as a function of age, since IQ is also an average of performance on many tests or/and factors.

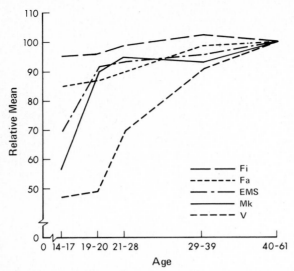

Fig. 14 Performance as a function of age. Crystallized abilities: Ideational Fluency (Fa), Experiential Evaluation (EMS), Mechanical Knowledge (Mk), and Verbal Comprehension (V) (Adapted from Horn and Cattell, 1966).

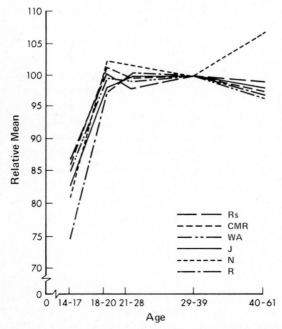

Fig. 15 Performance as a function of age. Mixed fluid-crystallized abilities: Logical Evaluation (Rs), Semantic Relations (CMR), Common Word Analogies (WA), Practical Judgment (J), Number Facility (N), and General Reasoning (R) (Adapted from Horn and Cattell, 1966).

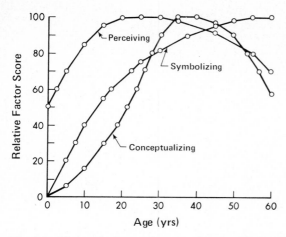

Fig. 16 Theoretical growth curves for the third-order dimensions (Kearsley et al., 1977).

Since the curves in Fig. 16 were derived from the Horn–Cattell data depicted in Figs. 13–15, it would not be surprising to see similarities. Thus, the third-order perceptual factor looks most like Fig. 13, the symbolizing dimension looks most like Fig. 14, and conceptualizing looks most like Fig. 15. A reasonable inference from the available evidence is that the perceptual curve is heredity-dominant, the symbolizing curve is environment-dominant, and conceptualizing is a more even mixture of the two sets of influences. Although there are no direct data available to test these inferences, they are consistent with the empirical findings at the first order (from which these theoretical curves were derived). These conclusions also make good theoretical sense. For example, it is difficult to account for the high performance level of the perceptual factor at birth on grounds other than genetic. Similarly, the continuous cumulative growth of the symbolizing dimension strongly suggests cultural-learning effects. While these heredity–environment inferences must be taken as speculative, they are sufficiently precise to serve as hypotheses which can be experimentally tested and eventually confirmed or refuted.

The factor-gene model

In Fig. 17, we have depicted my guess as to the most probable linkage between the multiple-factors of behavioral variation and the underlying multiplicity of genes, linked via a variety of unspecified, intervening biological mechanisms* (labeled psy-

---

*However, the reader who is interested in the neural correlates of cognitive factors is referred to Royce (1966, 1973), Royce et al. (1976) and Kearsley and Royce (1977).

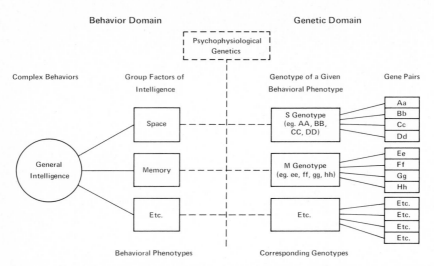

Fig. 17 Showing the most probable linkage between the multifactor theory of psychology and the multiple-factor theory of genetics (Royce, 1957a). The capital letter signifies the presence of the trait or phenotype; the small letter means the absence of the characteristic.

chophysiological genetics). Note that in both the behavioral and genetic domains many elemental factors account for a complex. On the behavioral side, many different factors or behavioral phenotypes account for the complex we call general intelligence. On the genetic side, various combinations of many genes account for a particular behavior phenotype such as S or M. Thus, a person may inherit all of the capital letter forms of the gene pairs of the space factor (i.e., AA, BB, CC, DD). Since this means that the individual has the maximum number (four chosen arbitrarily) or capital letter genes for this particular genotype, and assuming optimal environmental conditions, we would expect him to perform at the highest level in tasks involving the perception of spatial relationships. If another person inherited genes e, f, g, and h from the available gene pairs of the M factor, we would expect a minimal performance on pure memory tasks.

Such profile differences are brought out most dramatically when the element or component aspect of factor analysis is contrasted with the component obfuscating results of more traditional psychometric approaches. For example, if we average the two profiles depicted in Fig. 18, we get exactly the same value, 50, or an IQ of 100. If the IQ was the only information available, we would conclude that these two individuals are intellectually identical. It is obvious, however, that they are identical only in their performance on the perception factor. Otherwise, person A is essentially verbal in his intellectual strength whereas person B is essentially quantitative. These high and low peaks of mental ability profiles are, of course, well established in the psychological literature.

However, only a beginning has been made in providing genetic correlate evidence

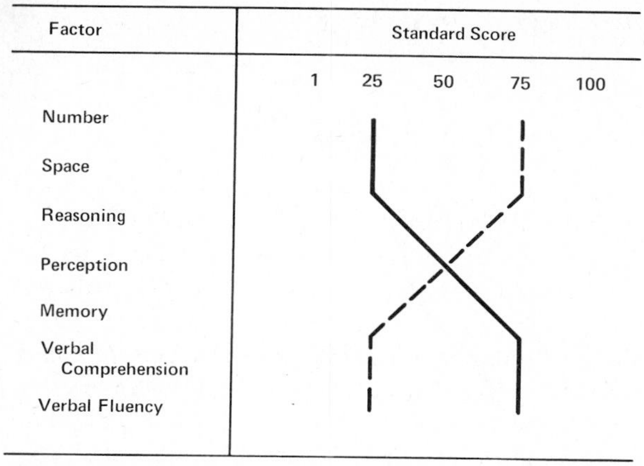

Factor	Standard Score				
	1	25	50	75	100

Number

Space

Reasoning

Perception

Memory

Verbal Comprehension

Verbal Fluency

Fig. 18   Showing two persons, A (solid line) and B (dotted line) with the same IQ but with opposite mental ability profiles (Royce, 1957b).

for such factorially determined components. In addition to the Horn–Cattell fluid factors, evidence on human intelligence comes from four studies (Thurstone et al., 1955; Blewett, 1954; and Vandenberg, 1962, 1967) involving monozygotic and dizygotic twins and the Primary Mental Abilities. These findings are briefly summarized in Table I. The interpretation is that the first four factors, word fluency, verbal, space and number, manifest a strong hereditary determination. The implication is that the performance of single-egg twins is more alike on these four factors (which reveal significant chi square values) than is the case for two-egg or fraternal twins; hence, the importance of the genotype. The trouble is that, in spite of the impressive convergence on these four factors, the available data on human populations are very

Table I   F-Ratios of DZ and MZ within-pair variance on 6 subtests of the Primary Mental Abilities test (From Vandenberg, 1967)

Name of PMA subtest		Blewett (1954)	Thurstone, et al. (1955)	Vandenberg (Michigan) (1966)	Vandenberg (Louisville) (1966)
Word fluency (3 parts)	W	2.78**	2.47**	2.57**	2.24**
Verbal (based on 31 parts)	V	3.13**	2.81**	2.65**	1.74*
Space (3 parts)	S	2.04*	4.19**	1.77*	3.51**
Number (3 parts)	N	1.07	1.52	2.58**	2.26**
Reasoning (3 parts)	R	2.78**	1.35	1.40	1.10
Memory (2 parts)	M	not used	1.62	1.26	not used
Number of DZ pairs		26	53	37	36
Number of MZ pairs		26	45	45	76

*$P < 0.05$;   **$P < 0.01$.

minimal, and furthermore, they are, in general, contradictory*.

The factor-learning model

The key to how learning affects factors lies in how we conceive of learning. Traditional treatments of learning will not be adequate since they were not developed in the context of factor analysis. Thus, I will define learning as any change in psychological structure (i.e., factors and their relationships) due to experience (e.g., practice effects).

This conception of learning puts the focus on the psychological structure which underlies change in performance per se and it applies to all structural levels and facets, such as cognitive structure and affective structure, and all of their individual components. Thus, changes at the higher order levels of psychological structure would represent shifts in style or/and world view (see Royce, 1975, and Wardell and Royce, 1976) changes in cognitive structure relate to the usual school learning or general fund of knowledge an individual has acquired, and changes in affective structure refer to temperament and value shifts. All are manifestations of acculturation, shifts in psychological structure due to cultural learning. The implication is that different cultures and/or environments will maximize different combinations of structural components. For example, the environmental-cultural forces of relatively "primitive" societies will reinforce those cognitive and affective components which are consistent with such activities as hunting, fishing, agriculture and other basic survival behaviour. Similarly, so-called "developed" cultures will require that their participants learn a great deal about numbers and words, in some cases to the extent of developing "experts" in one of the knowledge specialties such as the arts or the sciences. In short, differential reinforcement is probably the learning mechanism which can best account for the acculturation process. But note one important difference between the present account and the traditional socialization account. The standard view reinforces responses; in this view, it is the change in underlying psychological structure which is important. Thus, all the findings on schedules of reinforce-

---

*The most convincing experimental confirmation of the factor–gene model is the research on mouse emotionality. The research in question involved 42 measures, 6 inbred mouse strains and their F_1 offspring, and a total of 775 subjects (Royce et al., 1973; Poley and Royce, 1973; Royce et al., 1975). A diallel analysis (Mather and Jinks, 1971) was carried out on each of 15 factors. The most pervasive finding is that the genetic correlate for each factor is polygenic, and, in general, in the direction of complete dominance effects. However, a major point of this investigation is that mode of inheritance depends on the factor in question. For example, autonomic balance showed no dominance effects, whereas the breakdown of dominance effects for the other factors was as follows: partial dominance – motor discharge, food motivation, a tunneling factor and activity level (males); complete dominance – audiogenic reactivity, underwater swimming (males), and activity level (females); and overdominance – acrophobia, territorial marking (males). Furthermore, directional dominance was demonstrated for underwater swimming and audiogenic reactivity.

ment and the other principles of learning, such as primacy–recency, spaced versus massed trials, the effects of varying C.S.–U.S. interval and inter-trial intervals, the effects of interpolated activity on acquisition and forgetting, the goal gradient principle, the effects of latent and unconscious learning, habit, family hierarchy, etc. are relevant, but they must be reviewed in terms of how they affect structure rather than responses.

The factor-learning model is focused on changes in the dimensions of the total psychological system which are due to experience. The essence of what is involved can be captured by reference to Fig. 19, where we see a progressive change in the contributions of various factors to total variance in a task involving the acquisition of a complex motor skill. Fleishman reports a systematic decrease in the contribution of non-motor factors, with an attendant systematic increase in the contribution of motor factors. Thus, we are dealing with a special case of Eqn. 10, a case where the change in factor score is due to practice effects. What requires elaboration, therefore, are the conceptual relationships between learning principles and factors.

While the elaboration of these relationships has just begun, the flavor of what is involved can be captured from the examples cited below (Buss, 1973):

"A reinforcement is any stimulus event that will increase or maintain the score of an ability factor. If reinforcement occurs on a continuous schedule, the maximum possible change in the ability factor score is quickly reached. If, however, the same maximum change in the ability factor score is brought about more slowly by a schedule of partial reinforcement, the effect of the latter will result in more permanent change over time.

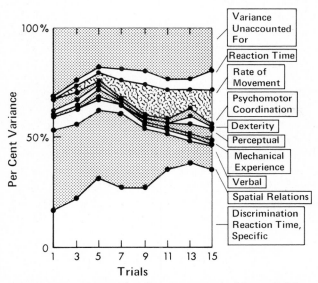

Fig. 19   Percentage of variance represented by each factor at different stages of practice on the Discrimination Reaction Time Task (percentage of variance is represented by the area shaded in for each factor) (After Fleishman and Hempel, 1955) (Royce, 1973).

Extinction occurs when there is a decrease of an ability factor score caused by failure of reinforcement. Extinction is more rapid when acquisition occurs under a schedule of continuous reinforcement as opposed to a schedule of partial reinforcement.

The involvement of an ability factor under stimulus conditions somewhat different from original learning is called stimulus generalization.

Discrimination is achieved when an ability factor is operative in one stimulus situation but not in another.

Drives provide the impetus for action as well as defining the direction of behavior (goals). In human ability learning, perhaps the most important drive or motive is achieving cognitive proficiency which facilitates adaptation to the environment.

The score of an ability factor is enhanced by an intermediate drive level (inverted U function). However, the more complex the task, the lower is the optimal drive level (Yerkes–Dodson law).

Increases in the score of an ability factor is facilitated more by distributed practice as opposed to massed practice.

Transfer occurs when practice on task x has an effect on performance on task y (positive vs. negative transfer). Transfer effects have their basis, in part, in changes in underlying factor scores brought about by practice on task x.

Overlearning enhances the stability of the level of an ability factor since skills can be evoked at a low threshold.

Further growth of an ability factor is moderated in the organism by a physiological and psychological readiness variable, by which is meant that the individual must be ready for the conditions of the task in the sense that appropriate behavior is in the individual's repertoire."

What is important here is that these learning principles, originally developed in the context of behavior change, have been reinterpreted in the context of structural change (i.e. in terms of how learning affects change in factors). If reinforcement, for example, elevates the score on factor α, this is an example of a quantitative change due to learning. If it also modifies the correlation between factors α and β (e.g. the appropriate positive reinforcement of two previously uncorrelated factors), it constitutes an example of a qualitative change due to learning*.

Cognitive factors and interaction effects

According to the factor model (see section two) factor–gene relationships can be represented via Eqn. 7, factor–learning relationships can be accommodated via Eqn. 8, and Eqn. 9 refers to interaction effects. However, behavior geneticists have been so focused on demonstrating gene effects that they have neglected interaction effects. The consequence is that we are presently unable to assign proportions of the total variance to heredity, environment and interaction effects. However, we do have one example of the importance of interaction effects in the cognitive domain, but it goes

---

*The reader is referred to Buss (1973) for an elaboration of linkages of the factor-learning model to cognitive development, and to Cattell for both a formalization of multivariate structural learning (Cattell, 1971) and for linkages to affect (Cattell, 1977).

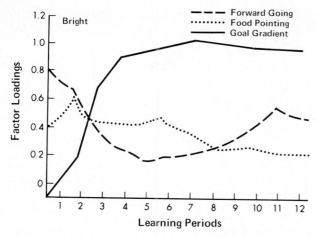

Fig. 20   Factors obtained from Tryon's Maze Data: bright (Royce, 1966).

back to the early work of Tryon on the inheritance of maze learning. Wherry (1941) generated "learning trials" correlation matrices for Tryon's "bright" and "dull" rats and factored them. He found the same three factors – forward going, food pointing, and goal gradient – for each strain. But he also found that dull animals made greater use of the food pointing (or visual) factor and low use of the forward-going factor, whereas the "bright" animals clearly outclass the "dull" ones in the extent to which the goal gradient (or insight) factor is involved in maze learning. These striking results (e.g. $N = 550$ for each strain) are brought out in Figs. 20 and 21. Although Wherry's analysis does not allow for a direct assessment of gene–environment effects on factored dimensions, it is relevant to the interactional issue

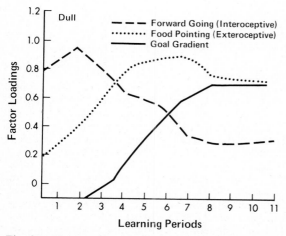

Fig. 21   Factors obtained from Tryon's Maze Data: dull (Royce, 1966).

because it constitutes a clear demonstration that different factors were differentially involved at different phases of learning and that factors were differentially invoked by "bright" and "dull" strains of rats*.

Concluding remarks

This chapter has been confined to intelligence per se. However, it is obvious that there are important interactions between intellectual and other functions of the organism. Although these interactions are not well understood, important inroads have been initiated, in the domain of cognitive styles for example (Wardell and Royce, 1976). We are pursuing such system interactions (e.g., cognitive–affective, cognitive–styles, cognitive–values) as part of a general theory of individual differences (Royce, 1973; and book in preparation). The combination of systems-information theory and factor theory (Royce and Buss, 1976) provides conceptual leverage on the difficult problems of functional dynamics (Royce and Kearsley, 1976, Royce and McDermott, 1977) and personality integration (e.g., see Royce, 1975, 1976, 1977a,b; Meehan and Royce, 1977; Royce and Kearsley, 1977).

---

*Although there are scattered bits of evidence in the behavior genetics literature on interaction effects, this issue has not been subjected to a sustained attack. Furthermore, since most of the factor-hereditary research has been conducted on humans, it has been impossible to tease out hereditary and environmental effects because of weaknesses of experimental control when dealing with human subjects. The obvious answer, therefore, is to combine animal research, factor methodology and quantitative methods of genetic analysis. See Thompson (1966) for a summary of multivariate experiments in behavior genetics, Royce (1950, 1966a) for reviews of the factor approach in animal behavior, and Royce and his associates (Royce et al., 1973; Poley and Royce, 1973; Royce et al., 1975) for the only existing research program which combines factor analysis, diallel analysis and animal behavior. The latter, which is briefly summarized in the footnote on p. 262 is not elaborated in detail in this chapter because it is in the affective domain. Finally, for an example of non-factor analytic interaction effects, see the author's research (Royce and Covington, 1960; Royce, 1966b, 1972; Royce et al., 1971; Holmes et al., 1974) on avoidance learning. This research indicates that specifiable departures from optimal stimulus parameters (e.g., C.S.–U.S. interval, 3 sec; intertrial interval, 120 sec; shock level, 400 V) can completely obliterate highly replicable strain differences in the rate of avoidance conditioning.

Literature cited

Blewett, D. B. (1954) An experimental study of the inheritance of intelligence, *J. Ment. Sci.* *100*, 922–923

Bolz, C. R. (1972) Types of personality. In: *Multivariate Personality Research* (R. M. Dreger, ed.) Claitor's Publishing Division, Baton Rouge

Buss, A. R. (1973) A conceptual framework for learning affecting the development of ability factors, *Hum. Dev. 16*, 273–292

Carmichael, L. C., Hogan, H. and Walters, A. A. (1932) An experimental study of the effect of language on the reproduction of visually perceived form, *J. Exp. Psychol. 15*, 73–86

Cattell, R. B., Coulter, M. A. and Tsujioka, B. (1966) The taxonomic recognition of types and functional emergents. In: *Handbook of Multivariate Experimental Psychology* (R. B. Cattell, ed.) pp. 288–329, Rand McNally, Chicago, Ill.

Cattell, R. B. (1971) *Abilities. Their Structure, Growth, and Action*, Houghton Mifflin, Boston

Cattell, R. B. (1977) *Personality and Learning Theory*, in the press.

DuMas, F. M. (1949) The coefficient of profile similarity, *J. Clin. Psychol. 5*, 123–131

Franks, J. J. and Bransford, J. D. (1971) Abstraction of visual patterns, *J. Exp. Psychol. 90*, 65–74

Holmes, T. M., Aksel, R. and Royce, J. R. (1974) Inheritance of avoidance behavior in Mus musculus, *Behav. Genet. 4*, 357–371

Horn, J. L. and Cattell, R. B. (1966) Age differences in primary mental ability factors, *J. Gerontol. 21*, 210–220

Kearsley, G. P. and Royce, J. R. (1977) Neuropsychological aspects of individual differences in cognition, *Center Paper in Progress.*

Kearsley, G. P., Buss, A. R. and Royce, J. R. (1977) Developmental change and the multi-dimensional cognitive system, *Intelligence*, in the press

Mather, K. and Jinks, J. L. (1971) *Biometrical Genetics. The Study of Continuous Variation*, Chapman and Hall, London

Meehan, K. and Royce, J. R. (1977) A multi-factor theory of values, *Center Paper in Progress*

Meehl, P. (1950) Configural scoring, *J. Consult. Psychol. 14*, 165–171

Poley, W. and Royce, J. R. (1973) Behavior genetic analysis of mouse emotionality. II. Stability of factors across genotypes, *Anim. Learn. Behav. 1*, 116–120

Royce, J. R. (1950) The factorial analysis of animal behavior, *Psychol. Bull. 47*, 235–259

Royce, J. R. (1957a) Factor theory and genetics, *Educ, Psychol. Meas. 17*, 361–376

Royce, J. R. (1957b) Psychology in mid-20th century, *Am. Sci. 45*, 53–57

Royce, J. R. (1966a) Concepts generated from comparative and physiological psychological observations. In: *Handbook of Multivariate Experimental Psychology* (R. B. Cattell, ed.) pp. 642–683, Rand McNally, Chicago

Royce, J. R. (1966b) Optimal stimulus parameters in the avoidance conditioning of inbred strains of mice, *Multivariate Behavioral Research 1*, 209–217

Royce, J. R. (1972) Avoidance conditioning in nine strains of inbred mice using optimal stimulus parameters, *Behavior Genetics 2*, 107–110

Royce, J. R. (1973) The conceptual framework for a multi-factor theory of individuality. In: *Multivariate Analysis and Psychological Theory* (J. R. Royce, ed.) pp. 305–407, Academic Press, London

Royce, J. R. (1975) Epistemic styles, individuality, and world-view. In: *Perspectives in Information Science* (A. Debons and W. J. Cameron, eds.) NATO Advanced Study Institutes Series, International Publishing, Leyden

Royce, J. R. (1976) Toward a theoretical synthesis of personality factors, *Center Paper in Progress*

Royce, J. R. (1977a) Meaning, value and personality. In: *The Search for Absolute Values. Harmony Among the Sciences*, The 5th International Conference for the Unity of Sciences, International Cultural Foundation, New York

Royce, J. R. (1977b) Personality integration. A synthesis of the parts and wholes of individuality theory, *Center Paper in Progress*

Royce, J. R., A Multi-factor Theory of Individuality, in preparation

Royce, J. R. and Buss, A. R. (1976) The role of general systems and information theory in multi-factor individuality theory, *Can. Psychol. Rev. 17*, 1–21

Royce, J. R. and Covington, M. (1960) Genetic differences in the avoidance conditioning of mice, *J. Comp. Physiol. Psychol. 53*, 197–200

Royce, J. R. and Kearsley, G. P. (1976) A multi-dimensional system dynamics model of cognitive processing, *Center Paper in Progress*

Royce, J. R. and Kearsley, G. P. (1977) System interactions and integration, *Center Paper in Progress*

Royce, J. R., Kearsley, G. P. and Klare, W. (1976) The relationship between factors and psychological processes, *Center Paper in Progress*

Royce, J. R. and McDermott, J. (1976) A multidimensional system dynamics model of affect, *Motiv. Emotion 1*

Royce, J. R., Holmes, T. M. and Poley, W. (1975) Behavior genetic analysis of mouse emotionality. III. The diallel analysis, *Behav. Genet. 5*, 351–372

Royce, J. R., Poley, W. and Yeudall, L. T. (1973) Behavior-genetic analysis of mouse emotionality. I. First and second order factors and their brain correlates, *J. Comp. Physiol. Psychol. 83*, 36–47

Royce, J. R., Yeudall, L. T. and Bock, C. (1976) Factor analytic studies of human brain damage: I. The factor analysis, *Multivar. Behav. Res.* in the press

Royce, J. R., Yeudall, L. T. and Poley, W. (1971) Diallel analysis of avoidance conditioning in inbred strains of mice, *J. Comp. Physiol. Psychol. 27*, 5–7

Sternberg, S. (1969) Mental processes revealed by reaction time experiments, *Am. Sci. 57*, 421–457

Thompson, W. R. (1966) Multivariate experiment in behavior genetics. In: *Handbook of Multivariate Experimental Psychology* (R. B. Cattell, ed.) pp. 711–731, Rand McNally, Chicago

Thurstone, L. L. (1947) *Multiple Factor Analysis*, University of Chicago Press, Chicago

Thurstone, T. C., Thurstone, L. L. and Strandskov, H. H. (1953) *A Psychological Study of Twins*, No. 4, University of North Carolina Psychometric Laboratory, Chapel Hill

Vandenberg, S. C. (1962) The hereditary abilities study. Hereditary components in a psychological test battery. *Am. J. Hum. Genet. 14*, 220–237

Vandenberg, S. C. (1967) The primary mental abilities of South American students. A second comparative study of the generality of a cognitive factor structure, *Multivar. Behav. Res. 2*, 175–198

Wardell, D. and Royce, J. R. (1976) Toward a multi-factor theory of styles, *Center Paper in Progress*

Wherry, R. J. (1941) Determination of the specific components of maze ability for Tryon's bright and dull rats by factorial analysis, *J. Comp. Psychol. 32*, 237–252

Zubin, J. (1954) The measurement of personality, *J. Coun. Psychol. 1*, 159–164

Genetics, environment and intelligence, edited by A. Oliverio
© *Elsevier/North-Holland Biomedical Press, 1977*

Individual differences in adaptive processes of infants

14

HANUŠ PAPOUŠEK

Underlying theoretical concepts

Biological variation in populations

In their views on individual differences, developmental behaviorists have depended on theoretical positions in contemporary genetics more than they perhaps have been aware of. Therefore, it may be worth recapitulating the most relevant postwar change in genetic concepts, in which the typological interpretation of individual variability has been replaced by population concepts (Dobzhansky, 1951).

Typologically oriented biologists typically tried to detect essential types in the similarity of individuals and disregarded variation as the imperfect manifestation of an ideal type. This thinking brings to mind the philosophies of Plato and Aristotle. A parallel position in traditional psychology viewed individual differences as "margin of error" and developed sophisticated statistical methods in order to unveil essential characteristics and relations behind them (Anastasi, 1965).

Biology in general had to emancipate itself from essentialist views in order to form concepts reflecting the reality observed in nature. In these new concepts, a species consists of populations rather than of individuals. A species is a reproductive community, an ecological unit with a large intercommunicating gene pool, where an individual is merely a temporary vessel holding a small portion of the contents of the gene pool for a short period of time (Mayr, 1971). The individual's possibility of influencing the gene pool is negligible. It is in the population that the genes interact in numerous combinations. This interaction permits the population to function as a major unit of evolution. Evolution is sometimes defined as a change in the genetic composition of populations.

Different genetic sources constantly contribute to the variation in genotypes: particulate inheritance, mutation, gene flow from other populations and occurrence of new genotypes through recombination. The evolutionary advantage is evident: a large number of available genetic types within a population increases the survival probability and permits better utilization of the environment. However, since extreme genetic variability would be as undesirable as extreme uniformity, opposing forces, such as natural selection, chance and accident, erode variation. The genetic variability is thus maintained in a dynamic equilibrium. Even in a well-protected gene pool of a species, almost any morphological or behavioral feature of an individual may vary due to genetic variation. In sexually reproducing species, i.e. in man as well, not two individuals can be expected to be genetically identical, presumably not even most monozygotic twins (Mayr, 1971).

In addition to genetic sources, different non-genetic factors increase the variability of individuals, e.g., age, season of the year, or habitat factors. Social circumstances and cultural traditions are the most typical environmental factors of this kind in man. Broadly speaking, genetic variation serves to bring about adaptation in whole populations, whereas non-genetic variation adapts individuals.

Individual variation has long been a matter of interest to descriptive taxonomists. An evolutionist, on the other hand, is less interested in the mere existence of variation than in its significance. Phenotypic variability has often been analyzed from the viewpoint of the nature–nurture dilemma. However, as to the variability observed in nature, it is never possible to distinguish genetic variation from non-genetic modifications unless careful breeding experiments can be carried out, something which can hardly be expected in man.

Individual differences in the typology of the nervous system

The introduction of conditioning into the study of brain functions by I. P. Pavlov increased the hopes of those who were searching for unitary typological cues. Pavlov himself introduced the concept of "type of higher nervous activity" into science, assuming that "genotypes of certain basic properties of the nervous system" would explain differences even between the four classical human temperaments. Originally he described four corresponding combinations of three such basic properties detectable in conditioning procedures: strength of the nervous system, equilibrium of the excitation and inhibition processes, and mobility of these processes (Pavlov, 1927).

Pavlov himself soon became aware of the weakness of any simple typology. He had to change his criteria and add up to 24 other combinations to the original four "types" during his intensive studies of differences in dogs. However, he found the studies of individuals more productive than the studies of standard groups. Only a small amount of evidence, e.g. by Fedorov (1953) or Krasuskij (1953), supported a real genetic determination of "genotypic combinations". The formative influence of embryonic and early postnatal environmental impact could not be disproved. The relationship between the types of nervous activity and behavioral tendencies appeared problematic as well when accumulating evidence from Pavlov's laboratories showed that forms of behavior depend to a great degree on environmental factors (Teplov, 1972).

On the whole, Pavlov's concept of basic nervous processes represents a major contribution to the neurosciences, whereas the idea of typological classification led to difficulties and misunderstandings. Later at his laboratories, Krasuskij (1963) carefully analyzed data on 116 dogs and found 48 major variants in the properties of their nervous systems. For a student of human development it is of course very difficult to extrapolate from this research to human studies of individual differences at our present state of knowledge.

Individual differences in learning

Conditioning as a learning phenomenon certainly attracted more attention in psychology, particularly in behaviorism, than Pavlov's interest in individual differences in conditioning. Individual variability could play only a marginal role as long as essentialist or normative interests prevailed. Similarly, as in Pavlovian concepts, learning was considered as a potential unitary adaptive function closely related to behavioral or intellectual development according to most theories. Only later, in contemporary neo-behaviorism, has the attention to individual differences increased as a consequence of interactions between theories of learning, personality and cognitive development.

Eysenck's Postulate of Individual Differences (Eysenck, 1957) is probably the most important example. Analyzing correlations between the dichotomy in as complex personality dimensions as extraversion and introversion and conditionability, he finds the equilibrium in strength to be a constitutional factor of personality (Eyzenck, 1966). This standpoint brings him closer to the neo-pavlovian interpretation of the so-called "dynamism" of the nervous processes as the crucial property of the nervous system (Nebylitsyn, 1966). "Dynamism" is characterized by the ease and speed of formation of conditioned responses as well as of differentiation, and is believed to be responsible for Pavlov's original "equilibrium of the nervous processes".

An opposite approach is to disregard all typologies and to attempt to detect significant typological parameters with the help of multivariate factor analyses applied to broad sets of tests. Cattel (1972) as a typical representative of this trend recommends such an analysis of self-rating inventories, rated life behaviors, and experimental tests.

In addition to these two typological approaches, individual differences found in multiple learning tasks were analyzed from the viewpoint of the degree to which learning capacities depend on one unitary function and how far they are related to intelligence.

For instance, Stake (1961) tested 240 school children with twelve learning tasks including different contents (verbal vs. non-verbal), types (memory tests, relational learning), and modes of presentation (individual and group tests). He could find only a little evidence for a unitary capacity.

Stevenson et al. carried out several extensive studies with up to 600 pupils combining rote memory tests, discrimination learning, probability learning, incidental learning and problem-solving tasks including anagrams, probability concepts and conservation concepts (Stevenson, 1972). They found significant correlations only between different tests within categories of sets, but no convincing evidence for a unitary capacity common to more categories. Assuming that in younger children learning capacities are less differentiated and perhaps of one common type, they also investigated preschool children, however, without any particular success.

Stevenson (1972) concludes that a fine-grain analysis of any learning situation reveals a host of factors influencing performance, such as attention, perception, memory and motivation. In his view, learning is related to but not identical with intelligence. Both functions may be influenced in the same way by personality characteristics, such as anxiety. However, there is too little information available on other personality factors, and most of the evidence comes from statistical rather than causal analyses.

Stevenson's conclusion reflects one major difficulty in psychology, namely a lack of methods for the analysis of cases where a subject may respond with discontinuous structural shifts rather than with continuous changes in complex parameters. Perhaps newer mathematical models of discontinuous processes, such as Thom's (1975) attempts to project trajectories of behavioral trends upon uneven, four-dimensionally controlled planes, will help to fill that gap.

Individual differences in cognitive processes

Theoreticians of cognitive psychology have shown more respect for the impetus of individuality stressed by psychoanalysts. Being primarily interested in the final integration of many complex capacities in the adult human, they avoided perhaps more easily the temptation to search for unitary functions in animal studies. On the other hand, they have often tended to view different aspects of cognition, such as perception, coding, memory, mediation, formation of concepts and hypotheses, problem solving etc., as isolated independent phenomena. Only recently has more attention been paid to suggestions to conceptualize processes of thought, motivation, and behavior as interrelated complementary processes.

In terms of development, the integration of various functions subsumed in the process of cognition has mostly been regarded as a process of differentiation and hierarchic integration. Pointing out that differentiation leads not only to increasing complexity but also to decreasing interdependence of subsumed functions, Lewin (1951) in fact explained the necessary existence of hierarchic integration maintaining the unity of parts and raising them to a higher degree of order.

On broader grounds of comparative biology and organismic concepts of system theory, Werner (1948) more explicitly discussed three developmental stages in differentiation and integration in respect to both the part–whole and subject–object relations. The developmental trend proceeding from the stage of sensorimotor operations to the stage of perceptual operations and finally to the conceptual stage is universal according to Werner. However, the subject may operate on different levels in different cases depending on which cognitive operations a given task requires. Thus, even a shift to a lower developmental level may be an adaptive or even a creative step. Unlike the views that treated individual differences in the traditional normative ways, Werner's view has not made the approach to individual differences more operational, but has certainly showed a direction for further research in which new operational approaches are being sought. He suggests that new concepts should consider multilinear development of cognitive functions with pluridirectional interrelations.

Adding effectiveness as another aspect of integration, Witkin et al. (1962) pointed out a potential relation between the level of integration and pathology. Due to different effectiveness, integration may at one time lead to adequate adjustment and at another to a pathological disturbance. The degree of effectiveness does not depend on the degree of complexity of integration. This view is certainly interesting for those who study relations between personality features and behavioral disorders.

Individual differences in adaptive processes at the beginning of human life

The significance and constraints of studies

All of the above theoretical aspects related to the problem of individual differences brought out the significance of their earliest development. In spite of non-genetic factors influencing prenatal development, the proportion of genetically determined characteristics is larger in the newborn than in the adult. A lower degree of differentiation in the newborn offers a better chance to detect potential unitary learning functions. Above all, however, we can better understand how individual differences develop if we observe them from the very beginning.

Two additional practical aspects should be mentioned in this connection. First, the increasing frequency of behavioral disorders and maladjustment the treatment of which is difficult in older children and adolescents calls for a preventive approach and an attempt to correct whatever may threaten the early developmental stages. Second, we have to realize that politically individual variability, no matter how important for biological survival, represents a major obstacle to increasing prescriptive or normative tendencies dictated by the needs of administration, industrial production, etc. Having once seen babies wearing uniforms in day-care centers, one is struck by the danger that conformist trends might soon mold the earliest development of personality. But a lack of respect for individuality might simply reflect a lack of corresponding interest in science.

Perhaps the difficult access to newborns and infants will partly excuse the scientist. Methodological problems and ethical restraints can certainly be named as additional reasons. However, with regard to present human potential, no reason can excuse society for neglecting what may threaten its own further healthy development.

Circumstances of the reported studies

The data to be reported below can necessarily be only a small contribution to the solution of the problems already mentioned. On the other hand, they are a part of more systematic research in the earliest postnatal development of personality, and resulted from a rather unique chance to observe infants from birth up to six months under very advantageous research conditions.

In infants carefully selected as to the evidence of conceptional age and to the course of pregnancy and birth, a team of pediatricians and psychologists cooperated on parallel investigations of somatic and mental development, differentiation of behavioral states, the role of chronobiological factors, immunological resistance, development of social interaction and play activities. Mothers of these subjects were encouraged to stay at the unit and nurse, fathers to visit and participate in care. For details we refer to previous publications (Papoušek, 1967a; Papoušek, 1967b).

Thus, various experimental studies and parallel naturalistic observations could be carried out in the same subjects in order to obtain complex evidence of individual characteristics. At the same time, it was possible to maintain most environmental factors at a relatively high level of comparability. Only data on individual differences in learning abilities of infants will be discussed in this communication.

Age and individual differences in the studies by Janoš

The late Oldřich Janoš was the senior psychologist in our team and he was responsible for the theoretical concepts concerning individual differences. Unfortunately, his Czech monograph on "Age and individual differences in the higher nervous activity of infants" (Janoš, 1965) has not been translated into any other language and has not received due attention, although it resulted from an enormously elaborate and exact analysis.

Fundamental designs of associative conditioning reported by Janoš, i.e. acquisition and extinction of a conditioned response, differentiation between reinforced and non-reinforced stimuli and double reversal of such differentiation, have otherwise been used only for typological purposes. Janoš, however, stressed the significance of such a study for the interpretation of development: "Whether we are interested in the influence of different factors upon the higher nervous activity of the very young children or are looking for optimal conditions for their healthy development, solid evaluation, comparison and interpretation of these functions in individual children will always be necessary."

In regard to Stern's terminology (Stern, 1921), Janoš analyzed only inter-individual variability. As to the typological concepts, rather than looking for discontinuous criteria of classification in the sense of Aristotelian logic, he considered individual differences as continuous characteristics, as did Hempel and Oppenheim (1936): "The function of a continuous type is not to class the individual with some categories but to place him in a progression arising from the delineation of a certain basic (typological) progressive property." This view is similar to Cattel's concept (1950), as well. Consequently, Janoš preferred the term "individual differences" to the term "typological differences".

Investigations of early postnatal variability were recommended by some authors as crucially important (Troshikhin, 1952; Volokhov, 1951), whereas other authors held them for irrelevant (Krasuskij, 1953). Janoš saw a reason for it in the discrepancy between two typological tendencies: on one hand to detect a genotype before environment intervenes excessively, on the other to classify only definite phenotypes. He himself believed that reliable knowledge of the earliest ontogeny was necessary for understanding the development of a mature individual. He also refused to interpret observed parameters as fundamental properties of the nervous system, arguing that not enough was known on the essential processes responsible for conditioning.

In his monograph, Janoš concentrated his attention on the role of age upon interindividual variability. His study represented over 6000 experimental sessions in 69 infants between 2 and 28 weeks of age. Two modifications of the method of conditioned palpebral reflexes were used: in one, the unconditioned response was elicited with optic stimulation (flash of light), in the other one with trigeminal stimulation (puff of air). In both cases, a 1000 Hz tone served as a conditioning signal to be differentiated from a 250 Hz tone. Successful extinction and re-acquisition of a conditioned response were to disprove possible "pseudoconditioning".

Age was found to be a very important factor. With increasing age, the speed of conditioning increased significantly as well, i.e. the number of sessions necessary to reach given criteria decreased both in acquisition ($N = 63, r = 0.62, P < 0.001$) and differentiation ($N = 51, r = 0.43, P < 0.01$). The rate of the reversal of differentiation suggested a similar trend but the correlation was not significant ($N = 41, r = 0.17, P > 0.1$), probably due to an effect of negative selection since the older the infant was at the beginning of differentiation experiments, the slower he had been in the preceding tests. Such an interpretation was reinforced by Papoušek's data (1967b) from designs ruling out such negative selection and confirming an analogous significant influence of age even in the reversal of differentiation.

Since in many previous studies infants had been grouped within one class of age ranging from birth to 12 months, it was important to show that in conditioning, a mere difference of one month in age already caused a significant difference in speed. A similar effect of age was also found in other forms of conditioning and in the development of play activities (Janoš et al., 1963).

In both modifications of palpebral conditioning, Janoš (1965) demonstrated that the average acquisition curve of conditioning in the youngest group of full-term infants showed a break around the age of two months from where the rate of conditioning increased (Fig. 1). In contrast to a smoother and steeper curve of 2-month old infants, such a biphasic curve indicated a more general deflection in the course of postnatal development, particularly when qualitative changes in other behavioral and conditioning criteria were observed at the same age (Janoš et al., 1963).

A group of premature infants (Fig. 1), comparable to the older group as to chronological age but to the younger group as to conceptional age, interestingly showed the same biphasic course of conditioning as the younger group, as if the additional amount of extrauterine stimulation resulting from premature delivery had not influenced the maturational trend at all. In fact, no significant difference in the rates of conditioning between premature and full-term infants of equal conceptional age disproved such an interpretation (Janoš, 1965).

In most parameters reported by Janoš, the amount of inter-individual variability which was independent of age was remarkable. The slowest subjects in individual tests needed 4 to 6 times more sessions to reach given criteria than the fastest subjects. Some qualitative differences in the course of differentiation and reversal of differentiation deserve particular attention in regard to the question of fundamental properties of the nervous system. When a stable conditioned response to a 1000 Hz tone had been established, and then a non-reinforced 250 Hz tone introduced, different changes appeared in frequencies of responses to both signals. Typically, they had been classified as criteria for the evaluation of excitatory and inhibitory nervous processes as well as their equilibrium. Janoš showed that first it was necessary to exclude a "pseudo-differentiation", i.e., an instant correct discrimination in rather rare cases where it was not possible to speak of a process. Further on, he was able to detect characteristic types of differentiation curves which appeared repeatedly if tests were repeated. However, as mentioned above, he did not see enough evidence to interpret such characteristics as parameters of particular

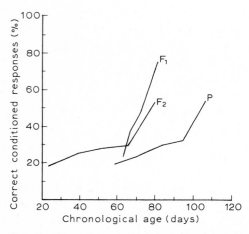

Fig. 1   Vincent curves (Hilgard and Campbell, 1937) of palpebral conditioning with trigeminal reinforcement in premature infants (P) and full-term infants of corresponding chronological (F_1) or conceptional (F_2) ages (acc. to Janoš, 1965)

fundamental properties of the nervous system.

It is impossible to outline Janoš's outstanding contribution thoroughly here. Therefore, a few more aspects will be discussed in the next section concerning a parallel study carried out in the same experimental population and under the same conditions.

Individual differences in conditioned head movements

The main functions of the palpebral response at the beginning of life are to prevent injury to the eyes and excessive optic stimulation. It can hardly become instrumental for other purposes. Another response used in our studies, i.e. conditioned head movement reinforced with milk, belongs to the category of pyramidal movements that can function very early as instrumental acts of different types, e.g. nutritional, protective, communicative etc. Therefore, it was relevant to ask whether two so different methods would produce comparable information on age and individual differences in the same infants.

In our design of head-turn conditioning (Papoušek, 1959; Papoušek, 1961a; Papoušek, 1967b), we used conditioning signals as is done in associative designs, but also made reinforcement contingent on the subject's responses as in operant designs. Typically, whenever an electric bell sounded from the middle line the infant could obtain milk as soon as he turned his head at least 30° to the left. Thus we were able to analyze adaptive changes in the latency and intensity of conditioned response in addition to the speed of conditioning or the type of acquisition curve.

In the studies to be reported here we investigated three distinctly different age groups (3 days, 3 months, 5 months), but each group was itself homogeneous as to age at the beginning of conditioning. Therefore, we could analyze all conditioning procedures in relation to the initial grouping and avoid the effect of negative selection mentioned in connection with Janoš's study.

We recorded head movements polygraphically and in addition respiration, heart rate and general motility. In protocols, we coded types of movement and of vocal and facial responses. Thus we obtained complex records which included changes in behavioral state and autonomic and emotional changes.

We were able to confirm Janoš's findings on the significant influence of age upon the speed of conditioning, reconditioning, and differentiation, and extended the validity of this influence of age to the first reversal of differentiation as well as to conditioning in newborns. We concluded that the capacity for conditioning is functional from birth, its speed increasing significantly with every month of age until the first peak is reached between 5 and 6 months of age. Analogous developmental trends were found in latency and intensity of conditioned responses. No significant age difference was found in the speed of extinction of conditioned responses.

Additional developmental changes were found in the shapes of acquisition curves and in the infant's capacity to group consecutive correct responses. A relatively smooth increase in percentage of correct responses was least frequent in newborns and most frequent in 5-month-old infants, whereas curves with several gross waves showed an opposite distribution. Biphasic curves with a delayed onset of acquisition were found only in 2 of 14 newborns and in none of the older infants. An analysis of the first 10 correct responses revealed that 60.7% were isolated and only 6.4% were immediately followed by two or more consecutive correct responses in newborns as compared with 18.7% single correct responses ($P < 0.001$) and 60.6% correct responses occurring in groups of 3 or more in 5-month-old infants ($P < 0.001$).

In contrast to Janoš (1965), who found no difference between full-term infants and prematures of equal conceptional age, premature infants were significantly slower in head-turn conditioning in our study (Table I). Biphasic acquisition curves appeared most frequently in this age group as well.

Almost ideal comparability of environmental circumstances gave us a rare opportunity to find out to what extent two different methods of conditioning can reveal the same features in the same individual at least at the earliest age. The few existing studies of this question have been concerned only with older children or adult human and animal subjects. At most there has been only a small amount of evidence indicating agreement between methods using different reinforcements (Ivanov-Smolenskij, 1933; Strelau, 1966). Ivanov-Smolenskij (1935) suggested that there is a partial type of higher nervous activity characteristic for the separate functions, such as alimentary, defense, orienting and sexual, as well as the general synthetic type of higher nervous activity. The question whether such a general synthetic type could be more evident before individual subsystems in the nervous system reach a higher degree of differentiation remained open (Strelaw, 1972). The fact that we did not primarily aim at typological properties of the nervous system did not lessen the importance of this question.

We were able to compare 26 infants (15 boys and 11 girls) whose age varied from 3 to 150 days and who were grouped into three relatively homogeneous groups. These subjects participated in both kinds of conditioning treatment and began the second treatment within 20 days of the first. An identical criterion of an established condi-

Table I Comparison of the rate of conditioning between premature and full-term infants according to chronological and corrected ages (head-turn conditioning with appetitional reinforcement)

		Age (days)				Trials to criterion	
		Chronological		Corrected			
	N	M	SD	M	SD	M	SD
(a) Prematures without perinatal distress	9	71.00	5.65	3.00	1.58	260.9	94.6
(b) Prematures with perinatal distress	8	71.00	4.40	3.13	0.99	259.6	75.9
(c) Full-term newborns	20	3.45	1.09			172.7	80.7
(d) Full-term 3-month-old	14	85.78	1.76			42.3	18.4

Significance of differences in trials to criterion: a − b, $P > 0.10$; a − c, $P < 0.02$; a − d, $P < 0.002$; b − c, $P < 0.05$; b − d, $P < 0.002$; c − d, $P < 0.002$ (non-parametric two-tail Man-Whitney U-test).

tioned response was used in both methods: 5 consecutive correct responses in a session immediately preceded by three sessions in which the average percentage of the conditioned response was 50% or higher.

The given criterion was reached significantly faster in head-turn conditioning (13.5 sessions) than in palpebral conditioning (19.0 sessions, $P < 0.001$). However, the relative rates of conditioning in the same infants correlated with a high level of significance ($r = 0.84$, $P < 0.001$) in spite of the difference between the methods. The difference in speed was partly determined by the difference in age between groups, but even within groups, the infants were either fast in both methods or slow in both of them (Janoš and Papoušek, 1966).

With the help of Vincent curves (Hilgard and Campbell, 1937), we also tried to analyze the course of conditioning. For this purpose, we selected the three homogeneous groups shown in Fig. 2: 5 premature infants (P), 6 full-term infants of the same chronological age (F_1), and 6 full-term infants of the same conceptional age (F_2) as the prematures.

The average acquisition curves were very similar for both methods. However, the curves for the 3-month-old infants were smooth and steep, whereas for the younger infants they were distinctly discrete, and for the premature babies biphasic. As to the speed of conditioning and the shape of the acquisition curve, premature infants were comparable to the younger full-term infants of equal conceptional age rather than to those of equal chronological age. Thus it was confirmed again that the excessive impact of premature extrauterine life had no detectable positive effect on the capacity of conditioning.

On the whole we can say that both methods disclosed identical information on age differences in conditioning as well as on those inter-individual differences that are independent of age. Such concordance gives more validity to the conclusions of

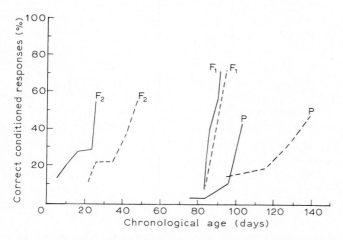

Fig. 2   Vincent curves (Hilgard and Campbell, 1937) of two conditioning methods in the same infants, premature (P) and full-term of corresponding chronological (F_1) and conceptional (F_2) ages. Head-turn conditioning, ——; palpebral conditioning with trigeminal reinforcement, – – –.

individual methods, even if this validity still remains restricted to the earliest postnatal development of human infants.

As to the age-independent inter-individual variability, we attempted to examine correlations between the main conditioning parameters and seasonal or sexual differences. No matter how justified our expectancies may have been, we could not prove any significant correlation (Papoušek, 1967c). Either it was too early to look for seasonal or sexual differences in the first 6 months of life in our subjects or the functions investigated were not suitable for this purpose. Similarly, we found no significant correlation with the main anthropometric indicators, such as birth weight and length, rapidity of increase in weight and length during the first three months after birth, head or chest circumference. The caloric quotient in food-intake showed a correlation with the speed of conditioning in newborns ($N = 14$, $r = 0.59$, $P < 0.05$) and 3-month-old infants ($N = 14$, $r = 0.63$, $P < 0.02$), indicating that infants with lower caloric intakes were faster in conditioning. A possible interpretation that hunger might increase motivation for learning was contradicted by another analysis (Papoušek, 1969) based on a larger amount of data on the average course of experimental sessions. During an average session of conditioning or conditioned differentiation, which in fact represented one of the usual feedings of a hungry infant, there was no significant change found in either the probability of a correct response or its latency as a function of the gradual satiation of hunger. This was true both for infants at the age of 0 to 3 months and infants between 3 and 6 months of age.

As to the intra-individual variation, we found that both the probability of a correct response and the latency of a correct response were significantly influenced by the infant's behavioral state immediately preceding the application of conditioning signals. Distinguishing four levels of waking, we showed a U-form dependence indicating the best conditioned performance in the state of lively, well coordinated movements and/or quiet vocalization. Passive, motionless wakefulness or fussy wakefulness with uncoordinated gross movements were obviously two parallel unfavourable deviations from the optimal waking state. Passive wakefulness was related to the poorest performance of all (Papoušek, 1969; Papoušek and Bernstein, 1969).

Another aspect deserving attention is the contingency of reinforcement on the infant's activity. Head-turn conditioning can hardly be conceptualized without admitting that some fundamental cognitive function on the perceptual side helps to detect the relation between the proprioceptive feedback information on the course of movements and the information related to milk reinforcement. Additional cognitive steps must be assumed for the resulting decision to repeat the movement in question and verify whether it would lead to the same consequence (Papoušek and Papoušek, 1975). Although it is the experimenter's decision that makes a reinforcement contingent, it is the subject's capacity to detect contingency which finally decides whether he will correspondingly adapt his behavior or not. Here is one of the factors which may be responsible for discontinuous changes in behavior, e.g. for a critical turning point known as an 'Aha'-phenomenon. Our discovery that the newborn is capable of responding adaptively to contingency pleased us because it opened new ways for studies of conceptual capacities (Papoušek, 1961b; Papoušek and Bernstein,

1969). However, this discovery also revealed that in man, from the very beginning of postnatal development, the individual variability in conditioning capacity may also be determined by factors that are discontinuous and difficult to control in experiments.

Concluding remarks

The rapid development of the infant and the lability of his behavioral state in the first months of life are enough to justify an attempt to find out how far these two variables influence individual adaptive capacities. No matter how simple such a task may seem, recent surveys (Horowitz, 1969; Leites, 1972) confirm that the amount of evidence for such an interaction is still very limited. The questions we have tried to answer in this communication can also be put in a different context. For us, the analysis of individual variation was crucial for a better understanding of a basic learning process, and this again was only a departure point for studies of more complex adaptive processes interacting during early development. We do not share the enthusiasm of those who see measurable parameters of one or several fundamental properties of the nervous system and beyond that, believe they can find omnipotent typological criteria in those parameters. Rather, we assume multivariate determination even in simple forms of conditioning and at the lowest level of postnatal differentiation. But for whatever reason one might be studying conditioning in infants, one should be aware of its dependence on age and behavioral state before analyzing other sources of variability.

Acknowledgements

The studies were carried out at the Research Institute of the Care for Mother and Child in Prague. The devoted help of the author's former collaborators is very much appreciated. He especially thanks Mrs. Hana Krulišová, M. D. and Miss Jarmila Melicharová for their research assistance. The preparation of this communication was kindly facilitated by grants from the "Deutsche Forschungsgemeinschaft" (Pa 208/1) and from the "Stifterverband für die Deutsche Wissenschaft" to the Max Planck Institute for Psychiatry in Munich.

Literature cited

Alekseyeva, M. S. (1953) A comparative assessment of type of nervous system by the motor and secretory alimentary methods, *Trudy Inst. Fiziol. I. P. Pavlova*, Vol. 2, Leningrad
Anastasi, A. (1965) *Individual Differences*, Wiley, New York

Cattel, R. B. (1950) *Personality. A Systematical, Theoretical, and Factual Study*, McGraw-Hill, New York

Cattel, R. B. (1972) The interpretation of Pavlov's typology, and the arousal concept, in replicated trait and state factors. In: *Biological Bases of Individual Behavior* (V. D. Nebylitsyn and J. A. Gray, eds.) pp. 141–164, Academic Press, New York

Dobzhansky, T. (1951) *Genetics and the Origin of Species*, 3rd edn., Columbia University Press, New York

Eysenck, H. J. (1957) *The Dynamics of Anxiety and Hysteria*, Routledge and Kegan Paul, London

Eysenck, H. J. (1966) Neurose, Konstitution und Persönlichkeit, *Z. Psychol. 172*, 145–179

Fedorov, V. K. (1953) Effects of parents' nervous system training upon lability of nervous processes in descendants (mice), *Trudy Inst. Fiziol. I. P. Pavlova*, Vol. 2, Leningrad

Hempel, C. G. and Oppenheim, P. (1936) *Der Typusbegriff im Lichte der neuen Logik*, Leiden

Hilgard, E. R. and Campbell, A. A. (1937) Vincent curves of conditioning, *J. Exp.Psychol. 21*, 310–319

Horowitz, F. D. (1969) Learning, developmental research, and individual differences. In: *Advances in Child Development and Behavior* (L. P. Lipsitt and H. W. Reese, eds.) pp. 83–126, Vol. 4, Academic Press, New York

Ivanov-Smolenskij, A. G. (1933) *Experimental Studies of the Child's Higher Nervous Activity*, Medgiz, Moscow

Ivanov-Smolenskij, A. G. (1935) The experimental investigation of higher nervous activity in children, *Fiziol. Zh. SSR 19*, 149–155

Janoš, O. (1965) *Age and Individual Differences in the Higher Nervous Activity of Infants*, (Czech) Státní zdravotnické nakladatelství, Prague.

Janoš, O., Papoušek, H. and Dittrichová, J. (1963) The influence of age on some higher nervous functions during the first months of life. (Czech) *Act. Nerv. Super. 5*, 407–410

Janoš, O. and Papoušek, H. (1966) Comparison of appetitional and aversive conditioning in the same infants, *Act.Nerv.Super. 8*, 203–204

Krasuskij, V. K. (1953) Methods of studying nervous system types in animals, *Trudy Inst. Fiziol.I.P.Pavlova*, Vol. 2, Leningrad

Krasuskij, V. K. (1963) Methods of evaluation of nervous processes in dogs, *J.Higher Nerv. Activ. 13*

Leites, N. S. (1972) Problems of interrelationship between typological features and age. In: *Biological Bases of Individual Behavior* (V. D. Nebylitsyn and J. A. Gray, eds.) pp. 74–85, Academic Press, New York

Lewin, K. (1951) *Field Theory in Social Sciences*, Harper and Row, New York

Mayr, E. (1971) *Population, Species and Evolution*, Belknap Press of Harvard University Press, Cambridge, Mass.

Nebylitsyn, V. D. (1966) Some questions relating to the theory of the properties of the nervous system, *XVIIIth Intern. Congr. Psychol., 9th Symposium*, pp. 23–32

Papoušek, H. (1959) Method of studying conditioned food reflexes in infants during the first six months of their life, *Zh. vyssh. nerv. deyat. 9*, 143–148

Papoušek, H. (1961a) Conditioned head rotation reflexes in infants in the first months of life, *Acta Paediatr. 50*, 565–576

Papoušek, H. (1961b) The physiological view of early ontogenesis of the so-called voluntary activity, *Plzeň.Lékař.Sbor.Suppl.3*, 195–198

Papoušek, H. (1967a) Conditioning during early postnatal development. In: *Behavior in Infancy and Early Childhood* (Y. Brackbill and G. G. Thompson, eds.) pp. 259–274, The Free Press, New York

Papoušek, H. (1967b) Experimental studies of appetitional behavior in human newborns and infants. In: *Early Behavior. Comparative and Developmental Approaches* (H. W. Stevenson, E. H. Hess and H. L. Rheingold, eds.) pp. 249–277, Wiley, New York

Papoušek, H. (1967c) Genetics and child development. In: *Genetic Diversity and Human Behavior* (J. N. Spuhler, ed.) pp. 171–186, Aldine Publishing Co., Chicago

Papoušek, H. (1969) *The Development of Learning Abilities in the First Months of Human Life*, (Czech) Doctor of Sciences Dissertation, Charles University, Prague

Papoušek, H. and Bernstein, P. (1969) The functions of conditioning stimulation in human neonates and infants. In: *Stimulation in Early Infancy* (A. Ambrose, ed.) pp. 229–252, Academic Press, London

Papoušek, H. and Papoušek, M. (1975) Cognitive aspects of preverbal social interaction between human infants and adults. In: *Parent – Infant Interaction* (M. O'Connor, ed.) pp. 241–269, Elsevier, Amsterdam

Pavlov, I. P. (1927) *Conditioned Reflexes*, Oxford University Press, London

Stake, R. (1961) *Learning Parameters, Aptitudes, and Achievements*, Psychometric Monographs, No. 9

Stevenson, H. W. (1972) *Children's Learning*, Appleton-Century-Crafts, New York

Stern, W. (1921) *Die Differentielle Psychologie*, Barth, Leipzig

Strelau, J. (1966) The problem of general and partial types in the light of diagnosis of types of the nervous system, *XVIIIth International Psychological Congress, Symposium 9*, Moscow

Strelau, J. (1972) The general and partial nervous system types: data and theory. In: *Biological Bases of Individual Behavior* (V. D. Nebylitsyn and J. A. Gray, eds.) pp. 62–73, Academic Press, New York

Teplov, B. M. (1972) The problem of types of human higher nervous activity and methods of determining them. In: *Biological Bases of Individual Behavior* (V. D. Nebylitsyn and J. A. Gray, eds.) pp. 1–10, Academic Press, New York

Thom, R. (1975) *Structural Stability and Morphogenesis*, Addison-Wesley, Reading

Troshikhin, V. A. (1952) Some tasks in the study of higher nervous activity during ontogenesis, *Zh. Higher Nerv. Activ. 2*, 561–571

Volokhov, A. A. (1951) Regularities in the ontogenesis of nervous activity in the views of evolutionary theories, Moscow

Werner, H. (1948) *Comparative Psychology of Mental Development*, Follett, Chicago

Witkin, H. A., Dyk, R. B., Faterson, H. F., Goodenough, D. R. and Karp, S. A. (1962) *Psychological Differentiation*, Wiley, New York

Genetics, environment and intelligence, edited by A. Oliverio
© *Elsevier/North-Holland Biomedical Press, 1977*

Hereditary abilities in man 15

STEVEN G. VANDENBERG

"I have no patience with the hypothesis occasionally expressed, and often implied, especially in tales written to teach children to be good, that babies are born pretty much alike, and that the sole agencies in creating differences between boy and boy, and man and man, are steady application and moral effort."

Francis Galton

Nature of intelligence

Research in behavior genetics is just about 100 years old (Galton, 1875) and during most of that time there has been a preoccupation with intellectual ability and specifically with the IQ. While intelligence may be the most socially relevant trait that genetics can study, it seems puzzling why this attribute has been seen in such a one-dimensional way. Actually, there are a number of theories concerning the nature of intelligence, but two major points of view can be distinguished. The first one regards intelligence as a general, unitary attribute, so that all individuals can be ranked along this one dimension. The other view is that intelligence consists of a number of separate abilities and that individuals vary within themselves, i.e., some will have more of ability A than of ability B or C, others will excell on C rather than on A or B, etc.

The concept of general intelligence largely owes its influential position to Alfred

Binet. The French Ministry of Public Instruction commissioned Binet in 1904 to look for a method of diagnosing children who would be unable to profit from the regular teaching in elementary school. Binet had earlier experimented with measures of separate functions, such as memory, motor skills, visual perception and verbal comprehension (Binet and Henry, 1896). However, now that Binet was trying to predict a single criterion, i.e. success in elementary school, he was automatically led to construct a single index which would predict educational achievement. The first attempt was merely a list of 30 tasks of increasing difficulty as judged by the frequency of successful completion by 50 children. This "scale" was published in 1905 (Binet and Simon, 1905). The 30 items selected are shown in Table I.

In 1908 an improved scale with many new items was published, in which groups of items were listed for ages 3 through 13. Even more important was the introduction

Table I The 1905 Binet Scale

 1 Visual co-ordination of head and eyes
 2 Grasp a cube placed on the palm
 3 Grasp a cube held in line of vision
 4 Make a choice between pieces of wood and chocolate
 5 Unwrap chocolate from paper
 6 Obey simple orders; imitate gestures
 7 Touch head, nose, ear, cap, key, and string
 8 Find objects which the experimenter names in a picture
 9 Name objects pointed out in a picture
10 Tell which of two lines is the longer
11 Immediate memory for three digits
12 Tell which of two weights is the heavier
13 Suggestibility:
      a. Find object which is not among those presented, as in No. 8
      b. Point to patapoum and mitchevo (nonsense words) in the picture No. 8
      c. Tell which of two equal lines is the longer
14 Give definitions of house, horse, fork, and mama
15 Immediate memory for sentences of fifteen words
16 Give differences between: paper and cardboard; fly and butterfly; wood and glass
17 Immediate memory for thirteen pictures of familiar objects
18 Immediate memory for two designs, exposed 10 sec
19 Immediate memory for list of digits, 3, 4, or 5 in the series
20 Give similarities between: blood and wild poppy; fly, butterfly, and flea; newspaper, label, and picture
21 Just noticeable differences in length of lines
22 Arrange 3, 6, 9, 12, and 15 g weights in order
23 Find which weight has been removed from No. 22
24 Find rhymes
25 Complete simple sentence by adding one word (after Ebbinghaus)
26 Construct sentence containing Paris, gutter, fortune
27 Knowledge of what is the best thing to do in 25 situations of graded difficulty
28 Reverse clock hands at 3:57, at 5:40, and tell the time it would be
29 Draw results of folding a piece of paper into quarters and cutting the once-folded edge
30 Distinguish between liking and respecting, between being sad and bored

of the concept of "mental age". A child's mental age was determined by adding up credits (in terms of fractions of a year) for each item passed beyond the age level at which every item was completed (the so-called basal age). Thus, if a 6-year-old child could do one fourth of the items for age 7 and every item for age 6, he would have a mental age of 6.25 years. Obviously Binet thought of mental development as something similar to physical growth.

The mental age of a child was sufficient information for the individuals responsible for decisions about the child's education. If the child's mental age was similar to his chronological age, then he was normal; if higher, then he was precocious; if lower, he was retarded. In 1916, Terman published a revision of the Binet scale which incorporated a suggestion of Stern (1911) that the ratio or quotient be reported between mental age and chronological age and to call this the intelligence quotient or IQ. This quotient was then multiplied by 100 to remove the decimals. This IQ was destined to be regarded as synonymous with intelligence and almost as real, constant and unitary as the height of the child under study. The success of the method in distinguishing various degrees of mental retardation in children insured its wide acceptance, first by psychologists and teachers and finally by the general public, especially after the refinements introduced by Terman, who used much larger samples of children to select the tasks for each age level.

The items which Binet had included in his first version, as well as those in later scales, were all selected according to the criterion of age progression, i.e. with increasing age an item was more likely to be completed successfully. Other than clarity of instruction this was the only criterion. As a result most items ought to correlate rather highly with one another. Binet thought that they all reflected "higher mental processes" and the items in Terman's version (the Stanford Binet) did indeed all correlate positively with one another. Further support for the unitary point of view came from England. In 1904 a professor at the University of London, Charles Spearman, published a paper entitled, "General intelligence objectively determined and measured" in which he proposed a method for determining to what extent different tests measured the same attribute which was to be called "general intelligence." He also proposed a symbol, "g" for this attribute. The method started from the matrix of correlations between each test with every one of the other tests. The portion of the variance of each test not accounted for by "g" he called specific ("s") and for that reason, this theory is usually called the two-factor theory of Spearman. It might have been better to call it the one-factor theory because Spearman did not attribute much importance to the various specific variances in each particular test. Gradually various investigators, including some students of Spearman, showed that some subset of the tests may have some common specific variance, beside the "g" that they share with all the tests. It is ironical that the method proposed by Spearman to support the idea of a monopoly for general intelligence ("g") began to demonstrate that there were other factors in intelligence which were common to at least several of the tests in a given study. An example of such findings is the study by Jones (1949) in which the inter-correlations between success ("passing") on items of the Stanford Binet at ages 7, 9, 11 and 13 were analyzed. The method used was Thurstone's multiple factor analysis which was a generalization of

Table II Percentage of variance at four ages contributed by 8 factors in the Stanford-Binet

Content	Ages			
	7	9	11	13
Verbal	21.1	15.0	25.2	19.4
Reasoning I	18.3	13.7	—	11.8
Reasoning II	—	—	—	6.4
Memory	9.4	9.6	11.5	8.3
Visualization	—	—	—	7.8
Spatial	—	8.9	12.2	7.0
Residual	—	3.1	2.8	—
Number	8.8	—	—	—

Table III Number of items at four ages measuring 8 kinds of factors

Content:	Ages			
	7	9	11	13
Verbal	11	15	14	13
Reasoning I	9	14	–	7
Reasoning II	–	–	–	4
Memory	7	7	9	6
Visualization	–	–	–	3
Spatial	–	10	11	4
Number	6	–	–	–

Spearman's method. Jones found different combinations of factors present at the four age levels, due to the fact that different types of content and different numbers of these types were included at the four age levels, as shown in Tables II and III. (This finding of different content at different ages may in part be responsible for some of the changes over time in IQ that have been reported for individual children.)

In spite of such growing evidence that there are a number of independent factors in intelligence, the idea of a unitary attribute, i.e. general intelligence remained attractive and the use of tests which give one score indicative of the IQ persisted. There are several reasons for this. First of all there is a very practical one: a single index is much easier to use especially by persons not trained in psychology, but charged with making decisions about admission to the public school or to an institution for the feeble-minded or about the proper assignment in various institutions.

Secondly, when faced with various degrees of retardation, it is much less obvious that there are differences within an individual in different abilities, because the generally low level of performance is so obvious, compared to that of a normal child. Nevertheless studies by Meyers et al. (1964) and by Kebon (1965) have shown that there are at least four independent factors in the test performance of children and adults at various levels of retardation.

There are several variants of the other view, that there are a number of independent factors in intelligence. The most important point in which these theories differ is with respect to the number of independent factors considered to be significant, with that number ranging from two to 120. For instance, the Scholastic Aptitude Test measures just two: verbal ability and quantitative ability.

At the other extreme, Guilford (1956) has proposed a model for the structure of intellect which classifies 120 independent abilities according to three types of categorization: the tests used to measure these abilities can be subdivided according to their content, the type of mental operations they call for and the types of products they use. Guilford distinguishes four types of content: semantic (or verbal), symbolic, pictorial, and behavioral. Vocabulary tests are the best known examples of tests of verbal content. A test consisting of items showing a series of numbers with a blank in which a number is to be inserted according to a rule to be discovered from the preceding numbers would be an example of symbolic content, although symbolic is not limited to conventional numbers, but could refer to a newly given set of symbols. Pictorial refers to the use of pictures, whether photographs or drawings, in the test items. Behavioral refers to test items in which human behavior is displayed either by movies, still photos or drawings or by live actors or possibly referred to in verbal descriptions.

The five kinds of operations distinguished by Guilford are memory, convergent production, divergent production, evaluation and cognition. Memory tests require no explanation. They generally deal with short term memory for things memorized a short time before. Tests of convergent production require the subject to produce an answer that is narrowly circumscribed by the question, so that ideally there is only one correct answer. The opposite of long is short, of black is white, etc. are examples. In contrast, tests of divergent production call for an answer that is not hemmed in by clear restrictions, allowing a great deal of individual expression. Most projective tests would fall in this category but some ability tests fall here as well. Many of such tests have been constructed by Guilford.

The products are divided into six categories: units, classes, relations, systems, transformations and implications. Most vocabulary tests call for single words. Those tests provide good examples of items consisting of units. An example of a test using classes is a vocabulary test in which one has to identify the one word which does not fit in with the others, such as apple, banana, celery, orange, pear. Here the word celery does not fit in with the class "fruits." An example of transformations would be a test with items in which a series of clocks is shown in which the subject has to figure out the position of the two hands in the last clock face on the basis of the successive changes in the position of the hands in the earlier clock faces. We will not discuss examples of the other products. To summarize these three sets of classification, Guilford has used the cube model shown in Fig. 1. Each test belongs in one of the 120 smaller cubes and is characterized by three letters indicating which category in each of the three classifications the test fits. For instance the vocabulary test item about the fruits would be NMC because its content is semantic (M), the mental operation required is convergent production (N) and its product is a class (C).

290

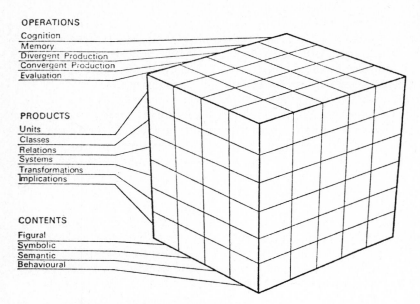

Fig. 1   Guilford's scheme of ability factors.

Most advocates of the multiple factor point of view hold a position in between the two extremes described. Thurstone (1938) obtained 13 factors in a study in which 57 tests were administered to University of Chicago students, but he apparently had more faith in six of these, because they were included in the Primary Mental Abilities tests batteries he developed for three age levels. These six abilities are: verbal, numerical, spatial, word fluency, reasoning and memory. Verbal ability calls for knowing what words mean as for instance shown by picking the correct synonym or opposite in a multiple choice question. Word fluency on the other hand calls for the production in a short time of as many words as possible that fit some restriction such as words that begin with "c" or words that end in "tion."

Spatial ability is measured by tests which require the subject to see whether an object such as an American flag is shown from the same side as the model on the left. A sample item is shown in Fig. 2. The spatial tests in the PMA battery use only two-dimensional designs. In other spatial tests the drawings may be of three-dimensional objects as shown in Fig. 3. Numerical ability refers to the ability to perform simple arithmetic under limited time conditions. Reasoning requires usually the discovery of some rule to apply in order to find the required answer and memory usually measures short term memory.

Fig. 2   Two-dimensional spatial test item.

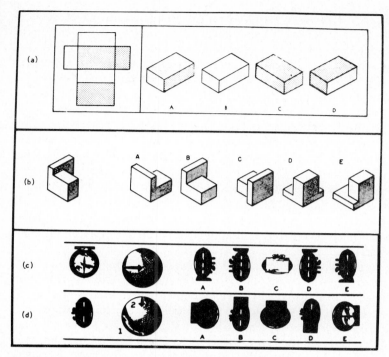

Fig. 3, a–d   Item from several dimensional spatial tests.

A compromise between the multiple factor and general factor theories was proposed by Burt (1949). It is called the hierarchical theory, in which general intelligence is a "higher order" ability factor which measures what the separate abilities have in common and the separate abilities are lower order factors which account for the rest of the explained variance. If a large enough number of tests are administered there may even be several levels in the hierarchy, as shown in Fig. 4. This is also the view of Philip Vernon (1950). Whether or not there will be a hierarchy of factors depends on whether or not the factors at the lowest level are correlated or not. This depends in part on the procedures used in the factor analysis. Guilford keeps the

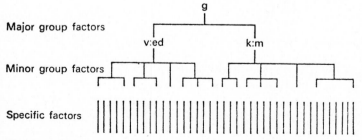

Fig. 4   Diagram illustrating hierarchical structure of human abilities. From Vernon (1950).

factors orthogonal, while Thurstone permitted factors to be oblique, i.e. correlated.

Cattell (1963) and Horn and Cattell (1966) suggested a variation of the hierarchical theory. They gave new names to Vernon's two higher order factors v:ed and k:m. The first factor they called crystallized intelligence and the second one fluid intelligence. These two may be somewhat correlated but a general factor shared by fluid and crystallized intelligence does not play a prominent role in the author's theory. Fluid intelligence begins to decline early in life while crystallized intelligence stays intact longer. Crystallized intelligence is found to predominate in tests based on earlier learning such as vocabulary or numerical skill, while fluid intelligence is required when the subject has to solve a problem without being able to retrieve the solution from memory.

It has been suggested that verbal skills are mainly controlled by the left hemisphere of the brain, and spatial and performance skills mainly by the left, with only minimal contact between the two parts through the corpus callosum which connects the two hemispheres. It is possible that fluid intelligence depends more on the right hemisphere and crystallized intelligence on the left hemisphere.

These alternate views of intelligence are all attempts to fit a model to the data. One should be careful not to take any model too seriously. We may want to keep several models in mind, especially when we remember that there is no such thing as intelligence, only intelligent behavior, which is sampled in the tests. Analysis of the correlations between tests can by itself not furnish an answer to the question which of these theories is to be preferred. Other criteria will have to be used, such as the relative success in differential prediction of various occupations or curricula; differential impairment of factors as a result of illness of age, etc. as discussed by Vandenberg (1968, 1973). In all the discussions of the results of factor analyses one should always keep in mind that only those aspects of intelligence will be found for which tests have been included. If no memory tests are included, there will be no memory factor. Guilford's cube model has the merit of calling attention to a number of new abilities which may have been overlooked before. Whether they are useful or not can only be discovered by trying them in various applied problems such as selection for school or occupation or in clinical situations.

Development of intelligence

Infant tests do not correlate well with adult intelligence but after the age of five years, the correlation increases steadily. Fig. 5 shows the correlations between scores on tests administered at different ages and the IQ at age 10 reported by Honzik (1973). Stanley and Hopkins (1972) have found that group tests predict later IQ somewhat poorer than do individual tests, especially if the group test is non-verbal. These results are shown in Fig. 6.

In contrast to the empirical approach to test construction discussed above, Piaget has developed a theoretical system based on very detailed observations of a

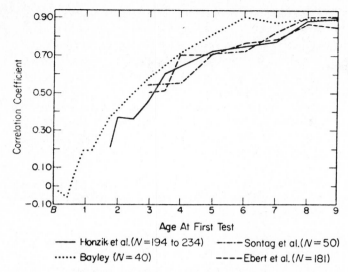

Fig. 5   Prediction of IQ at 10 years from scores at earlier ages. (Data from Honzik et al., 1948; Bayley, 1949; Sontag et al., 1958; Ebert et al., 1943).

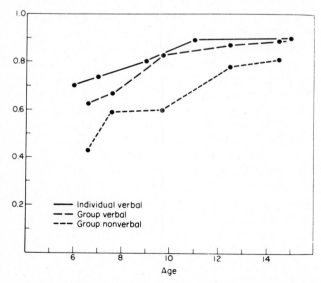

Fig. 6   Correlation coefficients between IQ scores at various ages and IQ scores at maturity (age 17, corrected to a common terminal variability) for individual verbal, group verbal, and group non-verbal intelligence tests.

small number of children. Piaget used what he called the clinical method, in which the goal is to observe carefully what the child does or says, regardless whether it is correct. Piaget felt that an analysis of incorrect responses can discover much more about the child's thinking than will the fact that the child passed a certain number of items. Piaget used many tasks of his own invention that are particularly revealing of certain aspects of the child's cognitive processes.

Piaget has emphasized the invariant order in which each child acquires various concepts. This order has been observed by and large in many Western and non-Western countries and is in part due to the fact that many "higher" concepts require mastery of "lower" concepts. A convenient summary of Piaget's theories is provided by Phillips (1969).

Nevertheless, there are differences between children in the age at which they acquire concepts. Up to now it has not been investigated whether there is an hereditary component in such age differences.

Research on hereditary factors in intelligence

After an interval of about a quarter of a century, there has been a return of interest in behavior genetic research (Thurstone, et al., 1953; Blewett, 1954; Cattell, 1960; Vandenberg, 1962; Gottesman, 1963; Nichols, 1965; Scarr, 1966). Hirsch (1963) has reviewed some of the reasons for the neglect of biological factors in the social sciences. Although the recent studies repeated to some extent the assertion made by the earlier studies that heredity counts, one can clearly see some new developments.

1. There has been an increasing sophistication about the statistical methodology and the diagnosis of zygosity. In fact the kind of circular reasoning in older twin studies which used judgments about similarity to classify twins as MZ or DZ is largely a thing of the past.

Cattell proposed a "multiple abstract variance analysis" in which a set of theoretical equations relate a number of unknowns to a variety of observations such as measurements of full sibs, of identical twins reared together and apart, of unrelated children reared in the same home, etc. Finding the more rare kinds of subjects necessary for this approach has proved to be very difficult. Elston and Gottesman (1968) showed how to estimate genetic variance from data not just on twins, but also on their siblings and parents. Up to now this method has not yet been applied to real data. Klein et al. (1973) showed that much larger samples will be necessary to establish that the genetic component in one trait is greater than in another one. Eaves and Jinks (1972) did the same thing for the comparison of heritabilities for two socioeconomic or ethnic groups. Kang et al. (1974) have calculated the sampling variance of the intra-class correlation in studies of twins, full-sibs, and especially half-sibs. This paper grew out of the Indiana group's interest in the children of MZ twins, who provide an interesting comparison with other half-sibs and an opportunity to get a different view of maternal or paternal effects. In the paper, it is shown that an increase of children within families is more efficient than an increase of families.

Because the authors are only concerned about one trait at a time the number of families required for an estimate of heritability is quite reasonable, i.e. about 100. The much more useful comparison of different traits would of course require much larger samples.

2. There has been a move away from an emphasis on general intelligence in favor of different specific abilities, coupled with a search for abilities that show particularly strong genetic components. Evidence that some abilities may be under stronger genetic control than are others, comes primarily from twin studies. Tables IV to VII summarize the F ratios between DZ and MZ within pair variances for the subtests of the PMA in four studies, for the DAT in two studies, for the individually administered Wechsler Intelligence test in one study and for a number of separate tests in one Swedish study. It seems clear that the most consistent and highest F ratios were obtained for (in that order): spatial, vocabulary, fluency of producing words fitting some category (perhaps partly a personality trait), speed in simple arithmetic and "reasoning." The latter category is a very broad one because the tests differ widely in choice of strategies and materials. Further evidence on differential

Table IV F ratios of dizygous and monozygous twin within-pair variance

Name of PMA subtest	Blewett 1954	Thurstone 1955	Vandenberg (Michigan) 1962	Vandenberg (Louisville) 1966
Verbal	3.13**	2.81**	2.65**	1.74*
Space	2.04*	4.19**	1.77*	3.51**
Number	1.07	1.52	2.58**	2.26**
Reasoning	2.78**	1.35	1.40	1.10
Word fluency	2.78**	2.47**	2.57**	2.24**
Memory	not used	1.62	1.26	not used
N_{DZ}	26	53	37	36
N_{MZ}	26	45	45	76

*$P < 0.05$;   **$P < 0.01$.

Table V   Two twin studies of the Differential Abilities Tests

	1961	1964
Verbal reasoning	2.29**	2.38
Numerical ability	1.39	1.37
Abstract reasoning	1.47	1.23
Space relations	1.67	2.19**
Mechanical reasoning	1.36	1.46
Clerical speed and accuracy	2.54**	3.13**
Language use I: spelling	3.64**	2.58**
Language use II: sentences	3.06**	2.00**
	25 DZ	86 DZ
	47 MZ	109 MZ

*$P < 0.05$;   **$P < 0.01$, (from Vandenberg, 1968).

Table VI *F* ratios between the within-pair variances of 60 fraternal (DZ) and 60 identical (MZ) twins for the scaled scores of 11 subtests of the WAIS

Subtest	*F*
1 Information	3.88***
2 Comprehension	2.25**
3 Arithmetic	2.78***
4 Similarities	1.81*
5 Digit span	1.53*
6 Vocabulary	3.14***
7 Digit symbol	2.06**
8 Picture completion	1.50
9 Block design	2.35**
10 Picture arrangement	1.74*
11 Object assembly	1.36
Verbal score	3.38***
Performance score	3.41***
Total score	3.47***

*$P < 0.05$ **$P < 0.01$ ***$P < 0.001$
(from Vandenberg, 1968).

Table VII *F* ratios between like-sexed fraternal twins (DZ) and identical twins (MZ) within-pair variances for 14 psychological tests, administered to Swedish twins of elementary and high school age (From Wictorin, 1952)

	Boys	Girls	All cases
Simplex, a general intelligence test	1.98**	2.84**	2.38**
C test, a general intelligence test	2.41**	4.35**	3.37**
Verbal analysis, a verbal comprehension test	1.14	0.96	1.12
Form perception, a paper formboard test	1.51*	1.23	1.34*
Picture perception, a perceptual speed test	1.17	1.54*	1.36*
Number perception, a clerical checking test	1.58*	1.91**	1.59**
Number series, a numerical reasoning test	2.37**	1.70*	2.01**
Number analysis, a numerical reasoning test	1.61*	1.68*	1.63**
Numerical classification, a numerical reasoning test	1.47	1.64*	1.57**
Numerical reasoning, verbal arithmetic problems	2.83**	1.96**	2.18**
Routine simple arithmetic	1.87**	1.51*	1.68**
Memory for 2-digit numbers (recall)	1.15	1.39	1.24
Memory for 3-digit numbers (recognition)	0.94	1.34	1.17
Paired associates word-number memory	1.32	1.00	1.16
N_{DZ}	66	75	141
N_{MZ}	66	62	128

*$P < 0.05$; **$P < 0.01$.

heritabilities can be found in Vandenberg (1968) from where these tables were taken. How much weight is given to the scanty evidence, (as contrasted with intuition) of greater environmental differences within each family for DZ than MZ twins may well prove to be a touchstone for assessing not only one's "hereditarian" or "environmentalist" leanings but also for an independent dimension running from respect for empirical evidence versus a preoccupation with preconceptions. Except in one monograph by Zazzo (1960), the only systematic treatment of this topic has been by Vandenberg (1976). After reviewing the evidence up to 1973, it was concluded there that biological differences between twins were the major influence producing within family and within peer group differences in reactions to twins. This supports the common practice of including genetic-heredity correlations and interactions with the genetic variances. Apart from this conclusion, it should be pointed out that studying the correlation and interaction of heredity and environment by detailed analyses of twins' interpersonal lives, perhaps even longitudinally, has been badly neglected. Special classes or even a summer camp for twins might provide an opportunity to do so.

3. Multivariate analyses of genetic components. Very little has been done so far with regard to the question whether there exist genetically independent abilities. The factor analytic studies by Thurstone, Guilford and others do not really address this question, because they only analyzed the correlations in the population which are produced by environmental as well as hereditary influences. A modest beginning has been made by Vandenberg (1965), Loehlin and Vandenberg (1968) and Bock and Vandenberg (1968) who compared covariances of pair differences on a number of tests for identical (MZ) and fraternal (DZ) twins. If we can assume that the environmental influences will produce the same degree of covariance for pair differences in the two types, one can subtract the MZ from the DZ covariances to obtain an estimate of the genetic covariances, (as in Loehlin and Vandenberg) or one can (as in Bock and Vandenberg) generalize the F test that is frequently used in univariate studies to determine whether the within pair variance is significantly greater in DZ than in MZ twins.

Instead of evaluating $F = \sigma^2_{w\,DZ} / \sigma^2_{w\,MZ}$ one asks in this case how many eigen values are significant in the characteristic equation

$$\left| \text{Cov}_{w\,DZ} - \lambda\, \text{Cov}_{w\,MZ} \right| = 0$$

In practice, this number is usually equal to the number of eigen values greater or equal to unity, although with increasing sample sizes more eigen values will acquire statistical significance. Using the first procedure Loehlin and Vandenberg concluded, on rather small samples, that the same ability factors appeared in the environmental and in the genetic covariation among 15 subtests of Thurstone's Primary Mental Abilities Test (PMA), but that in the environmental covariation there were three oblique higher order factors resembling number, space plus a general v:ed higher order factor, while only the one general factor appeared in the genetic covariance.

Applying the second method to twin pair differences on the Differential Aptitude Test, DAT (Bennett et al., 1959), Bock and Vandenberg found that three dimensions were significant in the genetic covariance for boys and two for girls. There was a general factor for both sexes and a factor contrasting verbal (educational) with spatial-mechanical tasks for boys only. An additional, less significant factor for both sexes was identified with the clerical speed test.

Earlier, Vandenberg (1965) had reported three significant X^2 values for the roots of the determinental equation based on a small sample, suggesting three independent hereditary components. In a large Finnish study of adult twins mainly concerned with alcoholism, a different set of tests but measuring abilities similar to the PMA was administered (Partanen et al., 1966). A multivariate generalization of the F test led to the conclusion that the genetic covariance in the six abilities measured (verbal, word fluency, space, number, memory and reasoning) had six significant roots, i.e. there were six independent genetic factors, which were however not identical to the original measures but showed some variance shared by different subsets in several of the vectors associated with these six eigen values.

Eaves and Gale (1974) reanalyzed the data of Loehlin and Vandenberg (1968) with a model in which the additive genetic and dominance components can be partitioned out of the observed covariance by removal of between and within family environmental components. They concluded that a single genetic component fits well enough to suggest an absence of strong major gene effects for the abilities tested by the Primary Mental Abilities test or as they phrased it, much pleiotropy at multiple loci. Similar studies will have to be repeated with larger samples (and more tests) to delineate more clearly the major processes determining genetic covariance.

Another way to throw light on these processes will be to correlate the score on test 1 in twin A with the score on test 2 in twin B, or to obtain similar off-diagonal covariances between mid-parent and mid-child. The lower these values are in comparison to the diagonal ones, the less the genetic components in the two tests share common variance. This method has not been used in human behavior genetics.

4. The method of path analysis (Wright, 1921, 1934) provides an opportunity to specify complex models including environmental influences for behavior genetic analyses. Long neglected, these are now becoming better known to psychologists, sociologists and others. Jencks (1972) and Rao et al. (1974) have used this method, but unfortunately had to use a collection of earlier reported studies in which a variety of different psychological tests had been administered at different ages to subjects from different backgrounds. Rao et al. (1974) found different proportions of

Table VIII   Estimates of components of variance for IQ corrected for attenuation* (Rao et al. 1974)

Source	Parents	Children
Genotype	0.121 ± 0.152	0.75 ± 0.058
Genotype–environmental covariance	0.117 ± 0.32	0.120 ± 0.054
Common environment	0.523 ± 0.178	0.091 ± 0.025
Random environment	0.239 ± 0.089	0.037 ± 0.032
Total	1	1

*Data from Jencks (1972) and Burks (1928).

genetic and environmental variance for parents and children, as did Burks (1928). The results of Rao et al. are shown in Table VIII. The percent genetic variance in IQ for children is 0.752 but for parents only 0.121, while for the environmental variances the situation is reversed. At least two possibilities, not mutually exclusive, come to mind, which can account for this discrepancy.

Children may perhaps be exposed to less varied environments than are adults. After all, going to school may provide much less variation than making a living in all kinds of occupations calling for a wide range of abilities: from primarily manual skills to highly abstract ones, and from very routine ones such as book-keeping to frequently novel ones. Because of the more uniform environment, children would express greater genetic variability.

In addition it may well be a consequence of the fact that the child's genotype is "predicted" from his parents' IQ scores and not vice versa. If measures were also available for the grandparents, the discrepancy might well decrease. Similarly the environmental indices which are due to parental choices may be poorer predictors of the child's IQ, than they are of parental attributes. In a recent doctoral dissertation, Spuhler (1976) used data from the Boulder family study to explore the Morton-Rao model. Because only data on parent–child and sib–sib resemblance were available, she had to make three assumptions: (a) no difference between parents and children for percent genotypic and environmental variance ($z = k = 1$), (b) no assortative mating ($m = 0$) and no genotype–environment interaction ($r = 0$). Under these assumptions two hypotheses were tested: (1) that there was no additive genetic variance ($h = 0$) when the common environmental effect c is not zero and (2) that the effect of common environment is zero ($c = 0$) when h is not zero. Individual estimates of c, h, and i (index of environmental level influences) for the four ability factors (spatial, verbal, memory and perceptual speed) are given in Table IX. A significant chi square value was found whenever the first hypothesis was tested, indicating more stable variation. It should be noted that the estimates for i, the index of environmental influences is unusually high because questionnaires concerning parental child-rearing attitudes were added to the usual socioeconomic and census type information. The basic assumption for the linear model underlying path analysis has been questioned by Lewontin (1974) but development of other models seems uncalled for, until one or more specific cognitive traits have been isolated that seem to be worthy of such efforts because of a repeated demonstration of a large genetic component or possibly even a major gene effect through a variety of techniques such as twin studies, parent–offspring resemblance and adoption studies.

5. Another assumption that has been questioned widely is that genetic–environment correlations are negligible (or that they can be grouped with heredity, or with environment, depending on the kind of data and type of analysis).

Meredith (1973) has proposed a model for multivariate data, which in principle is capable of testing this assumption, as well as several others, because it provides more observed terms than unknown parameters. The problem of moving from model to estimation procedures has not been solved yet, but possibly more serious is the fact that this method requires matrix operations such as inversion on matrices whose elements are themselves covariance matrices, a complication that can cause many

Table IX Analysis of genetic and environmental influences in cognitive ability dimensions (Spuhler, 1976)

Ability	Hypothesis tested	df	X^2	Parameter estimates
Spatial	$h = m = r = 0, k = z = 1$	2	7.945*	$\hat{c} = 0.612 \pm 0.041, \hat{t} = 0.622 \pm 0.084$
	$c = m = r = 0, k = z = i = 1$	3	68.324***	$\hat{h} = 0.863 \pm 0.059$
Memory	$h = m = r = 0, k = z = 1$	2	8.509*	$\hat{c} = 0.584 \pm 0.44, \hat{t} = 0.579 \pm 0.089$
	$c = m = r = 0, k = z = i = 1$	4	55.755***	$\hat{h} = 0.829 \pm 0.062$
Perceptual speed	$h = m = r = 0, k = z = 1$	2	9.875**	$\hat{c} = 0.551 \pm 0.048, \hat{t} = 0.592 \pm 0.098$
	$c = m = r = 0, k = z = i = 1$	3	53.214***	$\hat{h} = 0.780 \pm 0.68$
Verbal	$h = m = r = 0, k = z = 1$	2	22.230***	$\hat{c} = 0.549 \pm 0.049, \hat{i} = 0.950 \pm 0.108$
	$c = m = r = 0, k = z = i = 1$	3	148.684***	$\hat{h} = 0.77 \pm 0.069$

*$0.01 < P < 0.05$; **$0.001 < P < 0.01$; ***$P < 0.001$.

headaches in computing as for example when two roots are closely similar in size. Perhaps the latter problem could be minimized by analyzing only a few continuous traits at one time. Plomin et al. (1977) have recently proposed methods using adoption data to test for the presence of genetic-environmental correlations and interactions. Placing members of MZ twin pairs in separate classes with different curricula would be another way.

6. As some specific abilities are consistently found to have a higher genetic component than most, it may become worthwhile to search for linkage between a major gene affecting a continuous variable and known marker genes. Haseman and Elston (1972) have written a computer program for this purpose, which unfortunately will require extremely large samples of related individuals (Robertson, 1973), unless the linkage is very close and/or the major gene effect exceptionally large (Blackwelder and Elston, 1974). It may be more promising to apply more classical methods of segregation analysis, followed by Morton's sequential test of linkage.

In a recent doctoral dissertation, Fain (1976) derived relationships that will be obtained between sibship means and variances when a continuous variable is influenced by a major gene, separately for an autosomal additive locus or one with complete dominance, as well as for a sex-linked additive locus or a completely dominant one. Simulated data were used to confirm these patterns. Actual data on eight cognitive tests from the small number of informative families in the Boulder study were analyzed for a possible major gene effect, as shown by a better fit to the data of a mixture of normal distributions than of a single normal distribution (Bock and Kolakowski, 1973) as well as by visual inspection of scatterplots of within sibship means versus variances. The data for two cognitive measures, mental rotation and visual memory, were finally submitted to the sequential linkage test procedure of Morton (1956). While no conclusive evidence for linkage was found, the small number of informative sibships made any other finding unlikely. More data are needed to accept or reject the possibility of linkage of each cognitive test to each marker locus. It is hoped to continue this analysis by adding further sibships.

Literature cited

Bayley, N. (1949) Consistency and variability in the growth of intelligence from birth to eighteen years, *J. Genet. Psychol. 25*, 165–196

Bennett, G. K., Seashore, H. G., and Wesmann, A. G. (1959) *Differential Aptitude Tests*, 3rd edn. The Psychological Corporation, New York

Binet, A. and Henri, V. (1896) La psychologie individuelle, *Année Psychol. 2*, 411–465

Binet, A. and Simon, T. (1905) Méthodes nouvelles pour le diagnostic du niveau intellectuel des anormaux, *Année Psychol. 11*, 191–244 and 245–366

Blackwelder, W. C. and Elston, R. C. (1974) Comment on Dr. Robertson's communication, *Behav. Genet. 4*, 97–99

Blewett, D. B. (1954) An experimental study of the inheritance of intelligence, *J. Ment. Sci. 100*, 922–933

Bock, R. D. and Kolakowski, D. (1973) Further evidence of sex-linked major-gene influence on human spatial visualizing ability, *Am. J. Hum. Genet. 25*, 1–14

Bock, R. D. and Vandenberg, S. G. (1968) Components of heritable variation in mental test scores. In: *Progress in Human Behavior Genetics* (S. G. Vandenberg, ed.) pp. 232–260, The Johns Hopkins Press. Baltimore

Burks, B. S. (1928) The relative influence of nature and nurture upon mental development: a comparative study of foster parent-foster child resemblance and between parent-true child resemblance. *The 27th Yearbook of the National Society for the Study of Education*, Part 1, Public School Publishing Company, Bloomington, Ill.

Burt, C. (1949) The structure of the mind: a review of the results of factor analysis, *Br. J. Educ. Psychol. 19*, 100–114 and 176–199

Catell, R. B. (1960) The multiple abstract variance analysis equations and solutions for nature-nurture research on continuous variables, *Psychol. Rev. 67*, 353–372.

Catell, R. B. (1963) Theory of fluid and crystallized intelligence: a critical experiment, *J. Educ. Psychol. 54*, 1–22

Eaves, L. J. and Jinks, J. L. (1972) Insignificance of evidence for differences in heritability of IQ between races and social classes, *Nature 240*, 84–88

Eaves, L. J. and Gale, J. S. (1974) A method for analyzing the genetic basis of covariation, *Behav. Genet. 4*, 253–268

Ebert, E. and Simmons, K. (1943) The Brush Foundation study of child growth and development. I. Psychometric tests, *Monographs of the Society for Research in Child Development 8* (2, Whole No. 35).

Elston, R. C. and Gottesman, I. I. (1968) The analysis of quantitative inheritance simultaneously from twin and family data, *Am. J. Hum. Genet. 20*, 512–521

Fain, P. R. (1976) *Major Gene Analysis. An Alternate Approach to the Study of the Genetics of Human Behavior*, Unpublished doctoral dissertation, University of Colorado

Galton, F. (1875) The history of twins as a criterion of the relative powers of nature and nurture, *Fraser's Mag. 12*, 566

Gottesman, I. I. (1963) Heritability of personality: a demonstration, *Psychol. Monogr. 77* No. 9 (Whole number 572)

Guilford, J. P. (1956) The structure of intellect, *Psychol. Bull. 53*, 267–293

Haseman, J. K. and Elston, R. C. (1972) The investigation of linkage between a quantitative trait and a marker locus, *Behav. Genet. 2*, 3–20

Hirsch, J. (1963) Behavior genetics and individuality understood. Behaviorism's counterfactual dogma blinded the behavioral sciences to the significance of meiosis, *Science 142*, 1436–1442

Honzik, M. P., Macfarlane, J. W. and Allen, J. (1948) The stability of mental test performance between two and eighteen years, *J. Exp. Educ.*

Honzik, M. P. (1973) The development of intelligence. In: *Handbook of General Psychology* (B. B. Wolman, ed.) Prentice Hall, Englewood Cliffs, N.J.

Horn, J. L. and Cattell, R. B. (1966) Refinement and test of the theory of fluid and crystallized general intelligence, *J. Educ. Psychol. 57*, 253–270

Jencks, C. (1972) *Inequality. A Reassessment of the Effect of Family and Schooling in America* Basic Books, New York

Jones, L. V. (1949) A factor analysis of the Stanford Binet at four age levels, *Psychometrika 14*, 299–330

Kang, K. W., Lindemann, J. P., Christian, J. C., Nance, W. E. and Norton, J. A. (1974) Sampling variances in twin and sibling studies of man, *Hum. Hered. 24*, 363–372

Kebon, L. (1965) *The Structure of Abilities at Lower Levels of Intelligence*, Skandinaviska Test Forlaget. A.B, Stockholm

Klein, T. W., De Fries, J. C. and Finkbeiner, C. T. (1973) Heritability and genetic correlation. Standard errors of estimates and sample sizes, *Behav. Genet. 3*, 355–364

Lewontin, R. C. (1974) The analysis of variance and the analysis of causes. *Am. J. Hum. Genet. 26*, 400–411

Loehlin, J. C. and Vandenberg S. G. (1968) Genetic and environmental components in the covariation of cognitive abilities: an additive model. In: *Progress in Human Behavior Genetics*. (S. G. Vandenberg, ed.) pp. 261–285, The Johns Hopkins Press, Baltimore

Meredith, W. (1973) A model for analyzing heritability in the presence of correlated genetic and environmental effects, *Behav. Genet. 3*, 271–278

Meyers, C. E., Dingman, H. F., Orpet, R. E., Sitkei, E. G. and Watts, C. A. (1964) Four ability factor hypotheses at three preliterate levels in normal and retarded children, *Monogr. Soc. Res. Child Devel. 29.6* (Serial No. 96)

Morton, N. E. (1956) Sequential tests for the detection of linkage, *Am. J. Hum. Genet. 7*, 277–318

Nichols, R. C. (1965) The National Merit Twin Study. In: *Methods and Goals in Human Behavior Genetics* (S. G. Vandenberg, ed.) pp. 231–242, Academic Press, New York

Partanen, J., Bruun, K. and Markkanen, T. (1966) *Inheritance of Drinking Behavior*, Almqvist and Wiksell, Stockholm

Phillips, J. L. (1969) *The origins of Intellect*, W. H. Freeman, San Francisco

Plomin, R., De Fries, J. C. and Loehlin, J. C. (1977) Genotype–environment interaction and correlation in the analysis of human behavior, *Psychol. Bull. 84*, 309–322

Rao, D. C., Morton, N. E. and Yee, S. (1974) Analysis of family resemblance. II. A linear model for familial correlation, *Am. J. Hum. Genet. 26*, 331–359

Robertson, A. (1973) Linkage between marker loci and those affecting a quantitative trait, *Behav. Genet. 3*, 389–391

Scarr, S. (1966) Genetic factors in activity motivation, *Child Devel. 37*, 663–674

Sontag, L. W., Baker, C. T. and Nelson, V. L. (1958) Mental growth and personality development: A longitudinal study, *Monogr. Soc. Res. Child Devel. 23* (2 Whole No. 68)

Spearman, C. (1904) General intelligence, objectively determined and measured, *Am. J. Psychol. 15*, 201–293

Spuhler, K. P. (1976) *Family Resemblance for Cognitive Performance. An Assessment of Genetic and Environmental Contributions to Variation*, Unpublished doctoral dissertation, University of Colorado

Stanley, J. C. and Hopkins, K. D. (1972) *Educational and Psychological Measurement and Evaluation*, Prentice Hall, Englewood Cliffs, N.J.

Stern, W. (1911) *Die Differentielle Psychologie in Ihren Methodischen Grundlagen*, Barth, Leipzig

Terman, L. M. (1916) *The Measurement of Intelligence*, Houghton Mifflin, Boston

Thurstone, L. L. (1938) Primary mental abilities, *Psychom. Monog. No. 1*

Thurstone, T. G., Thurstone, L. L. and Stradskov, H. H. (1953) *A Psychological Study of Twins*, Report No. 4 of the Psychometric Laboratory, University of North Carolina, Chapel Hill

Vandenberg, S. G. (1962) The heriditary abilities study: hereditary components in a psychological test battery, *Am. J. Hum. Genet. 14*, 220–237

Vandenberg, S. G. (1965) Multivariate analysis of twin differences. In: *Methods and Goals in Human Behavior Genetics* (S. G. Vandenberg, ed.) pp. 29–43, Academic Press, New York

Vandenberg, S. G. (1966) Contributions of twin research to psychology, *Psychol-Bull. 66*, 327–352

Vandenberg, S. G. (1968) The nature and nurture of intelligence. In: *Genetics* (D. C. Glass, ed.) pp. 3–58 Russell Sage Foundation and Rockefeller University Press, New York

Vandenberg, S. G. (1976) Twin Studies. In: *Human Behavior Genetics* (A. R. Kaplan, ed.) pp. 90–150 C. C. Thomas, Springfield, Ill.

Vandenberg, S. G. (1973) Comparison studies of multiple factor ability measures In: *Multivariate Analysis and Psychological Theory* (J. Royce, ed.) Academic Press, New York

Vernon, P. E. (1950) *The Structure of Human Abilities*, Methuen, London

Wictorin, M. (1952) *Bidrag till Raknefardighetens Psykologi, en Tvillingundersökning*, Elanders, Götesborg

Wright, S. (1921) Correlation and causation: method of path coefficients, *J. Agr. Res. 20*, 557–585

Wright, S. (1934) The method of path coefficients, *Ann. Math. Stat. 5*, 161–215

Zazzo, R. (1960) *Les Jumeaux, le Couple et la Personne*, Presses Universitaires de France, Paris

Genetics, environment and intelligence, edited by A. Oliverio
© *Elsevier/North-Holland Biomedical Press, 1977*

Mental development in twins

RONALD S. WILSON

Introduction

The development of mental functions during childhood has been a topic of recurrent interest in psychology, and during recent years this topic has become the focus of heated controversy. Much of the controversy concerns the nature of intelligence, the manner in which intelligence evolves during childhood, and the dependence of intelligence upon genetic and environmental factors. One by-product of the controversy is an extensive amount of research in this area, often accompanied by strong opinions about the interpretation of the results.

The current wave of research, however, was preceded by some very careful work in infant mental development, notably by Bayley and Piaget. Bayley's research was chiefly in the psychometric tradition, extending the techniques of mental measurement into the early years of life, and looking for predictability between infant measures and later IQ. She noted a change in mental functions during the second year which oriented these functions away from the primitive sensory-motor coordinations of infancy, and more towards the basic rudiments of intelligence.

Bayley also noted episodes of acceleration and delay in mental development, and a gradual stabilization of individual differences by school age. Much present research is rooted in Bayley's work, and it is perhaps our most important legacy from a longitudinal program (Bayley 1949, 1955, 1965, 1969).

Piaget (1952) has furnished a detailed microanalysis of mental functions and their development which illuminates the complexity of these functions, even in infancy. The emphasis is upon successive stages of mental development which build upon cumulative experience and incorporate primitive cognitive structures into more advanced modes of operation. The stages are passed through in the same order by all infants, and some investigators believe that the transitions between stages are entirely dependent on the massive inflow of experience. An exposition of this view, along with a set of procedures for assessing the infant's sensory-motor development, may be found in Uzgiris and Hunt (1975). Piaget himself does not espouse this viewpoint, and in any event the issue is incidental to Piaget's extraordinary achievement in detailing how cognitive functions are elaborated.

The present chapter makes no effort to survey the voluminous literature in the area of mental development. Instead, data are reported from a longitudinal study of twins who have been tested periodically throughout childhood. Twins offer a unique opportunity to appraise the course of mental development for pairs of offspring that are matched on the major dimensions of genetic similarity, prenatal experience, and home environment. In so far as these factors make a differential contribution to mental development, it should be evident in the data for monozygotic and dizygotic twins.

In addition, the twin sample offers a powerful resource to investigate several other factors reputed to influence mental development, including prematurity, low birth weight, birth sequence and socioeconomic status of the home. One advantage of a longitudinal sample is that it can reveal whether some factors are important initially but then diminish, while others only become influential at later ages.

Background

The Louisville Twin Study was instituted in 1957, and at present there are 419 pairs of twins active in the longitudinal program, ranging in age from 3 months to 15 years. Recruiting is an ongoing process in which about 25 pairs are added each year. The twins make visits to the Twin Study every three months during the first year, every six months during the second and third years, and annually thereafter. At each visit, the twins are given a standard test of mental development, and the mother is interviewed about their characteristic patterns of behavior at home.

A special effort has been made to keep the sample as representative as possible. The twins are recruited from the complete Board of Health birth records for the metropolitan Louisville area, and particular emphasis is given to securing and maintaining families of low socioeconomic status. The distribution of twin families by socioeconomic status is shown in Table I, where the families are categorized by the rating of the father's occupation (Reiss, 1961).

Tests of mental development

The tests employed in this program have been selected from the best standardized and most carefully constructed psychometric tests available. In this regard, some new

Table I Classification of socioeconomic status for all families particip-
ating in the Louisville Twin Study

SES index	% of sample	Typical occupations
0–9	10.2%	Unskilled laborer, janitor, welfare case
10–19	17.9%	Truck driver, construction worker
20–29	11.1%	Shipping clerk, machine operator
30–39	10.0%	Gas station manager, retail sales, plumber
40–49	10.5%	Electrician, business machine operator
50–59	11.3%	Manager retail trade, technician
60–69	9.4%	Insurance agent, draftsman
70–79	8.5%	Public school teacher, credit manager
80–89	7.2%	College professor, banking management, engineer
90–99	3.9%	Dentist, physician, lawyer

and revised tests for preschool children have become available within the past few years which represent major advances in assessment. Bayley's life-time work in mental development culminated in the Bayley Scales of Infant Development (1969), and it is the first well-standardized instrument for infant appraisal. The Stanford–Binet Form L–M was restandardized on a fresh sample in 1972 (Thorndike, 1973), and these new norms corrected for many of the deficiencies in the original 1937 standardization sample.

The Wechsler Preschool and Primary Scale of Intelligence (WPPSI) was published in 1967 (Wechsler, 1967), and it represented a well-standardized downward extension of the Wechsler Intelligence Scale for Children. It yields measures of full scale IQ, verbal IQ, and performance IQ from 10 separate subtests. Finally, the McCarthy Scales of Children's Abilities (McCarthy, 1972) were recently published, and while the scales differed somewhat in focus from the Binet and WPPSI – particularly by avoiding any reference to IQ – nevertheless they sampled domains of cognitive abilities which were collectively metricized by a General Cognitive Index.

The importance of such standardized psychometric instruments can hardly be overestimated. They furnish a means of appraising mental development during a period of rapid growth, and of obtaining a reliable assessment of individual differences. A child is compared with a representative sample of his age peers, and his relative placement (whether advanced or delayed) is expressed in a standard-score format that remains constant across ages and tests. These crucial features of standardization and scoring have never been available in previous tests, and in a literal sense the new tests may be classified as landmarks of mental measurement. When employed with a longitudinal twin sample from birth to school age, the tests yield a detailed picture of each twin's mental development from infancy onward, and a measure of concordance among cotwins.

Tests and ages

The Bayley Mental Scale has been administered at 3, 6, 9, 12, 18 and 24 months of age; the Stanford-Binet at 2.5 and 3 years; and the WPPSI at 4, 5 and 6 years. Recently, the McCarthy has been substituted at the 4-year visit since it yields a broader sample of the child's capabilities at that age. As later data will show, over 300 twins have been tested at each age, and over 250 twins have data covering at least a 4-year block within this period.

The twins were tested by separate examiners who also alternated between the twins over successive visits. The tests were given within 2 weeks of the twins' birthday, and the test procedures were intensively rehearsed by the examiners to assure comparability among all twins. Additionally, the scoring was verified by an independent examiner before the data were finally recorded.

Zygosity determination

Zygosity was established for same-sex twins by blood-typing on 22 or more antigens; if the twins were discordant on any anti-serum test, they were classified as dizygotic (Wilson, 1970). For technical and psychological reasons, the blood-typing was deferred until the twins were 3 years old, so the data on infant development were gathered before zygosity was established. Opposite-sex twins were classified as dizygotic on the basis of the sex difference.

Infant mental development

Since the twins have been tested repeatedly during infancy, the data on the Bayley Mental Scale were surveyed at each age to see how the twins compared with the singleton standardization sample. Given the general prematurity of twins for size and

Table II   Raw scores for infant twins on Bayley's Mental Development Scale

Age (months)	n	Twin mean	Twin SD	5th and 95th Centile scores	Bayley mean
3	385	32.6	9.08	15–46	36.7
6	390	67.5	8.62	50–78	71.8
9	321	84.9	5.50	74–93	87.8
12	351	98.3	6.38	87–109	102.6
18	394	121.6	6.69	111–133	125.4
24	372	139.6	8.92	127–155	144.6

Bayley means taken from manual, p. 20; 9-month mean is interpolated.

gestational age, it might be anticipated that their early developmental status would lag.

The data are presented initially in raw score form in Table II, along with the corresponding means from Bayley (1969).

It will be seen that the twins were somewhat below the singleton norms at each age, which is suggestive of a continuing lag in developmental status. The extent of this lag and its dependence upon premature delivery and low birth weight are topics of later intensive analysis.

For the moment, however, attention is turned to the conversion of raw scores to Mental Development Index scores. The conversion tables in the Bayley manual display certain peculiarities*, and since the twin sample was nearly four times as large as the Bayley standardization sample, we have taken advantage of this data base to generate new conversion tables appropriate for twins. The twin–norm MDI scores were obtained from the conventional standard-score formula of $(X_i - \overline{X}_{Twin})/SD_{Twin}$, then converted to a scale with $\overline{X} = 100$ and $SD = 16$. This adjusts for the lower raw-score mean of the twins and also preserves any skew in the score distribution if present, an acknowledgement that developmental status is more often seriously delayed than advanced. Thus the bottom-end MDI scores fall further below the mean than the corresponding upper-level scores exceed it. The complete conversion tables are given in Appendix 1 for ages 3 through 24 months. They enable any investigator to assess other twins in reference to this large representative sample.

Returning to the twins' lag in development, it may be represented at each age by an MDI score showing the extent of their deviation below the singleton mean. The MDI scores for all ages are presented in Table III.

The MDI scores hover within a narrow band about 8–10 points below the singleton average. The range gives a clue as to the discrepancy: there are more low-scoring twins during infancy, and very few that would qualify as really precocious. This trend toward lower scores among the twins may be a reflection of premature delivery and lower gestational age – the average duration of pregnancy was 37.4 weeks for the entire sample. The twins are therefore being compared with term-birth singletons

---

*The tables make it evident that the raw score distribution in the standardization sample was skewed towards the low end at certain ages. However, the conversion tables were established by reference to the normal distribution, and in order to preserve a symmetrical spread of MDI scores above and below the mean, the conversion scale was stretched at the top. This had the unusual feature of making a one-point change in raw score yield a possible one-to-five point change in MDI score, the latter occurring at the upper end of the distribution. The conversion thus gave disproportionate weight to single-item passes near the ceiling of the test, and made some infants seem more precocious than their performance warranted. The nonlinear conversion also posed a special problem for comparing twins since it tended to magnify score differences within pairs, particularly if one twin obtained a high raw score.

In addition to the twin-norm conversion described in the text, a new set of singleton norms has been computed by the same standard-score formula, using Bayley's singleton mean. The norms yield equal increments between MDI scores at any point in the distribution, and correct for the top-end spread in the original norms. They are available from the author upon request.

Table III Bayley MDI scores for twins
          in relation to singleton norms

Age (months)	Mean	SD	Range
3	92.6	17.4	48–138
6	92.0	15.7	45–121
9	91.7	17.0	45–130
12	89.0	16.8	45–124
18	90.8	14.5	45–130
24	91.2	16.8	45–126

$N \geq 320$ at each age. Lower limit MDI of 45 set for very slow infants ($n < 5$).

that are about 2.5 weeks older from date of conception. Other studies have shown that first-year Bayley scores are depressed for premature infants (e.g. Tilford, 1976). Accordingly, the relationship between developmental status and gestational age was explored by separating the twins into three groups: term births (39 weeks or more), intermediate (37–38 weeks), and clearly premature (36 weeks or less). The Bayley scores were analyzed for each group, and the means are presented in Table IV. The MDI scores are in terms of singleton norms so that the degree of deficit may be related to the degree of prematurity.

The data show that the deficit was most pronounced for the clearly premature group, extending throughout the first year and gradually recovering during the second. By contrast, the term-birth twins were essentially comparable to singletons during infancy, making it evident that there was no initial lag in development for full-term twins. They did decline somewhat in the second year, in contrast to the gradual rise of the premature group, and by 24 months all three groups had converged within 5 points of each other.

These data make it clear that developmental status in the first year was significantly retarded for twins delivered at 29–36 weeks of gestational age. The primitive sensory–motor coordinations of infancy appear to be particularly susceptible to prematurity, and so separate norms have been prepared for evaluating the developmental status of premature twins. The norms are presented in Appendix 2, and they

Table IV Average MDI scores for twins of different gestational ages

Age at testing (months)	Gestational age		
	≤ 36 wks.	37–38 wks.	39–44 wks.
3	81	96	98
6	80	92	100
9	81	93	97
12	82	88	94
18	85	92	94
24	88	91	93

were computed from the distribution of scores for the twins in the clearly premature group ($n = 106$).

The norms are given through 18 months, the last age at which these twins were significantly below the other groups. Their scores at 24 months would be evaluated in relation to the overall twin norms given in Appendix 1, and of course the term-birth and intermediate twins would be evaluated by these norms at all ages. Term-birth twins will appear somewhat precocious by these norms during infancy, but the advantage recedes in the second year.

The trend toward convergence among all three groups at 24 months indicates that the Bayley Scale was no longer measuring the aspects of sensory-motor coordination that were susceptible to prematurity. What it measured at 24 months were functions more distinctly cognitive and concept-related. This change in functions measured is the subject of later discussion, but for the moment it may be suggested that the effects of prematurity are quite limited on those cognitive processes that ultimately develop as the foundation elements of intelligence.

Binet tests

At 2.5 and 3 years of age, the twins were tested on the Stanford–Binet Form L–M. While the Binet is the test of choice at these ages and flows logically from the Bayley, it does have an artificial lower limit. A child must pass at least six items to obtain a mental-age score of 2 years 0 months, the lowest score listed in the tables. Fewer than six passes means that a child cannot be evaluated on the Binet.

In such cases the Bayley has been given as a substitute test since it is still appropriate at 2.5 years. It covers those low-scoring cases that are excluded on the Binet and gives an estimate of their lag in development, which can also be related to their previous status at 24 months.

Again taking advantage of the large sample, and to extend the continuity of the norms to the new test, a conversion table has been prepared for transforming each twin's raw score to a twin–norm MDI or IQ score. Bayley raw scores are entered in the table up to the transition point at which a Binet basal score can be obtained; Binet mental-age scores are entered thereafter. The table may be found in Appendix 3.

Tests at ages 4, 5 and 6 years

As previously indicated, the WPPSI was administered at 4, 5 and 6 years of age, with the McCarthy recently substituted at 4 years. It has yielded comparable scores (WPPSI IQ, 92.4; McCarthy GCI, 91.8), and so the data have been combined for both tests*. The overall means for the twins at these ages have the intriguing feature of

---

* For investigators who may wish to evaluate 4-year old twins in reference to this sample, a twin-norm conversion table for 4-year WPPSI IQ scores is also included in Appendix 3. At ages 5 and 6, the twins matched the singleton distribution closely enough to make a separate conversion table unnecessary.

312

Table V   IQ scores for twins at 4, 5, and 6 years

Age (years)	n	Mean	SD	Range	True gain
4	338	92.0	15.2	45–131	
5	407	96.2	14.4	45–132	5.1
6	387	100.9	13.5	45–129	4.0

showing a genuine and significant gain. The results are displayed in Table V.

The gain figures in the final column are based solely on those cases that have been tested at two adjacent ages (e.g., 4 and 5 years, or 5 and 6 years), so the increment is a true reflection of gain over age. It appears to reflect a genuine upward shift in mental status for the entire twin sample that brings them into alignment with the singleton standardization group. The gain is larger than would be expected from 1-year retest effects, especially since no such gain was evident at earlier periods with shorter retest intervals.

The gain primarily reflects a recovery in the capabilities measured by the Verbal Scale of the WPPSI, since Verbal IQ was more depressed for twins at age 4 and showed a greater gain by age 6 (Wilson, 1975). Apparently the capabilities related to word knowledge, information, and comprehension are slower to consolidate for twins, and only reach full manifestation by school age. It is often suggested that the

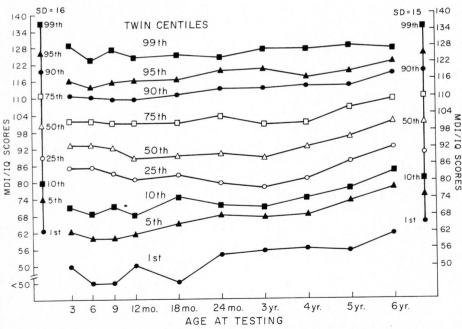

Fig. 1   Centile curves of MDI/IQ scores for the twin sample from 3 months to 6 years of age. See text for explanation.

twin situation is a deterrent to the development of language capabilities and other verbal skills (e.g. Record et al., 1970), and thus the lag is induced by the experience of being raised as twins. While the hypothesis sounds plausible, for a determinate test it will require a comparison of twins with siblings from the same families, so that the factors of home environment and parental heritage will be controlled.

The pattern of lag and recovery in mental development during the preschool years may be best visualized by plotting a set of reference values from the score distribution at each age. The twins' scores were expressed in terms of the singleton norms, then distributed by centile ranks. At each age the scores for the following centiles were plotted: 1st, 5th, 10th, 25th, 50th, 75th, 90th, 95th, and 99th. The values have been smoothed very slightly and the resulting curves are displayed in Fig. 1. For reference, the expected normal distribution of singleton scores is shown adjacent to each ordinate, so that the offset of the twin distribution may be perceived. The left distribution has $SD = 16$, appropriate for the Bayley and Binet scores; the right distribution has $SD = 15$, appropriate for the WPPSI scores.

The results show that the entire twin distribution was displaced downward at the early ages, and aside from minor fluctuations the centile values remained essentially constant through 3 years. There was some modest upward shift in the 1st and 5th centiles, indicating that some of the lowest-scoring twins were showing gains as they grew older.

At ages 4 through 6, however, there was a steady upward climb in the twins' scores that brought the distribution in parallel with the singleton distribution. By age 6, the IQ scores for twins and singletons coincided within 3 points throughout the range from the 5th to 95th centiles, so there was no significant difference in score dispersion within these broad limits.

The upper and lower extremes for the twins were somewhat more deviant, and they are of particular interest. The 99th centile curve showed no corresponding upshift beyond age 4, and indeed it was remarkably flat across all ages. It appears that if there was any limitation in mental development it was at the topmost extreme; fewer twins attained IQ scores beyond 125 than might be expected in a singleton population. The nature of this subtle upper-limit restraint is a matter of speculation, but it is worth noting that a similar phenomenon was observed in comparing the IQ of twins with their school-age siblings (Wilson, 1977c).

The lower extreme (1st centile) indicates that a larger proportion of twins qualified as developmentally retarded than singletons, especially during infancy. The retardation in infancy was principally a function of prematurity, but as its effects waned the 1st centile scores gradually moved upward. It reflected an upward trend among some twins who appeared retarded at the early ages but progressed into the normal range by school age. Two particularly interesting examples are shown in Fig. 2. Note that for one pair the upward trend continued in unison throughout the preschool years, suggesting that some inner programming was progressively actualizing mental development for these twins.

Even with such cases, however, the 1st centile curve was not pulled fully into line with the theoretical singleton distribution by age 6. Empirically, a few more twins scored in the retarded range than expected from a normal distribution. Unfortunately,

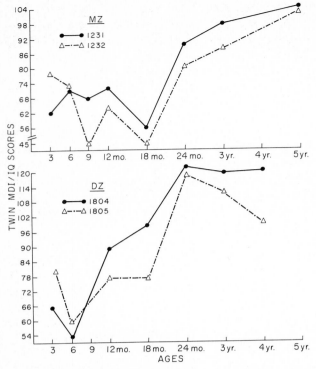

Fig. 2 Mental development trends for two pairs of twins showing marked gains from infancy to childhood.

the WPPSI manual does not include an empirical distribution of singleton scores, so it remains indefinite whether more 6-year twins actually qualified as retarded than singletons. We might speculate, however, that the low-end skew in the twin distribution comes closer to representing the real-world dispersion of scores than the artificial boundaries of the normal distribution.

Predictive correlations between ages

The next question concerned the ordering of individual differences and how stable these differences remained from age to age. It has often been observed that infants may show episodic spurts and lags in development during the first two years, then gradually stabilize as school age approaches. From a prediction standpoint, this would generate a set of low-order correlations among the early measures of mental status, but with a steady improvement at later ages. The age-to-age correlations were computed for the entire sample, and the correlation matrix is shown in Table VI.

The results display a simplex pattern: adjacent ages correlate more highly than distal ages, and the correlations become larger at later ages. Scanning down each

Table VI   Age-to-age correlations for twin MDI/IQ scores, 3 months to 6 years

Ages	6 mo.	9 mo.	12 mo.	18 mo.	24 mo.	30 mo.	3 yr.	4 yr.	5 yr.	6 yr.
3 mo.	0.53	0.42	0.38	0.39	0.24	0.32	0.17	0.25	0.35	0.29
6 mo.		0.59	0.54	0.48	0.27	0.25	0.28	0.30	0.31	0.27
9 mo.			0.61	0.47	0.35	0.35	0.34	0.41	0.42	0.31
12 mo.				0.53	0.45	0.32	0.33	0.35	0.45	0.39
18 mo.					0.66	0.55	0.60	0.60	0.58	0.53
24 mo.						0.70	0.75	0.70	0.63	0.64
30 mo.							0.81	0.81	0.67	0.69
3 yr.								0.83	0.72	0.73
4 yr.									0.80	0.80
5 yr.										0.86

N values for correlations range from 343 to 97; median $n = 225$.

column shows that the predictive correlations increased as the criterion age was approached. While the first-year scores had limited predictive power for the later ages, the prediction improved markedly by 24 months. For illustration, the between-age correlations are plotted for four reference ages: 6 months, 12 months, 24 months and 6 years. Each curve shows the vector of correlations between the reference age and all other ages. The curves are presented in Fig. 3.

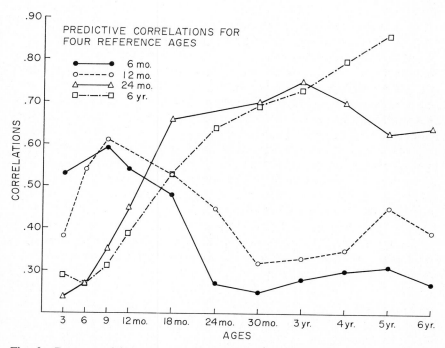

Fig. 3   Patterns of between-age correlations for mental development scores as exhibited at four reference ages.

The figure reveals two distinct sets of curves – the 6- and 12-month curves are quite similar, while the 24-month curve more closely matches the 6-year curve. From the standpoint of predictive power and the ordering of individual differences, there is clearly some major realignment within the second year that orients toward school-age intelligence. The pattern of correlations reaffirms the earlier observation of Bayley (1955) that some significant change takes place during the second year, and it represents the stage during which the foundation elements of intelligence are elaborated*.

What is the nature of these developing processes? For perspective, it might be useful to touch briefly on Piaget's formulations about the particular cognitive functions that are prominent during the 18 to 24 month period**.

Recall that the infant prior to this stage has begun to show evidence of object permanence and the representation of objects in memory; an awareness of causality; and the use of imitation in acquiring certain action patterns. All of these functions become more advanced and more widely employed during this period. In addition, the registration of experience in memory plays an increasingly important role in the child's construction of time and space, bringing to bear the recollection of past events with the anticipation of future ones. Such recollections gradually create a sense of what is constant and what is transient among the attributes of the physical world. It makes available an internal monitor for appraisal of current perceptions and prediction of likely outcomes.

This elaborate storage and retrieval mechanism enables the child to associate his experiences with certain signifiers, or symbols. Indeed, the representation of experience by symbols and the manipulation of such symbols are the primary features of this stage. Words become absorbed into the symbol system via imitation and practice, and while they are not essential to representational thought, they do reveal how socially mediated symbols become linked with memories of past experience. The development of this symbol system and its use in communication is a major milestone, since it makes the experience of others accessible in summary form as a guide to adaptive behavior.

Therefore, the functions that become prominent during this stage transform the infant from being sense-dominated to being symbol-oriented. The representation of experience by symbols and the manipulation of such symbols comprise the rudiments of later intelligence. In a developmental sense, it is the basic transition accomplished by most infants during this stage; and as the earlier correlations have shown, those infants who become precocious by 24 months are likely to remain above average in later years. The reordering of individual differences is broad-band rather than point-to-point, and remains subject to later episodes of advancement or lag, but the trend is towards a stabilization of ranking.

---

*A factor analysis was also performed which will be reported in more detail elsewhere. Briefly, it revealed a large general factor with loadings above 0.80 for all tests between 24 months and 6 years; and a second factor with loadings greater than −0.50 for the tests from 3 months to 12 months. The remaining factors had eigen values less than 1.0.
**The following discussion is drawn from Wilson (1977b).

Twin concordance for trends in mental development

If early mental development is determined by the joint contributions of genotype and environment, then dizygotic twins should display an intermediate degree of similarity in mental development, and monozygotic twins should be significantly more concordant. Some illustrative curves are presented in Fig. 4 for several sets of twins.

The monozygotic pairs represented in Figs. 4A–4D display quite different patterns of mental development, but there is high congruence within each pair. Note especially the twins in 4B, who follow a steady downward course after infancy, and contrast them with the pair in 4A or the pair in Fig. 2. Evidently the inner programming can dictate trends in either direction, and some infants who are entirely competent for sensory-motor coordination may drop back progressively as the processes of intelligence unfold.

Turning from these illustrative cases to the full sample, the question was whether monozygotic twins as a group were more concordant than dizygotic twins for the trends in mental development during the preschool years. The analysis was per-

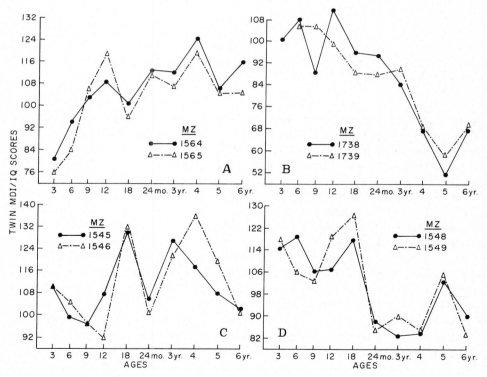

Fig. 4 For legend, see p. 318.

318

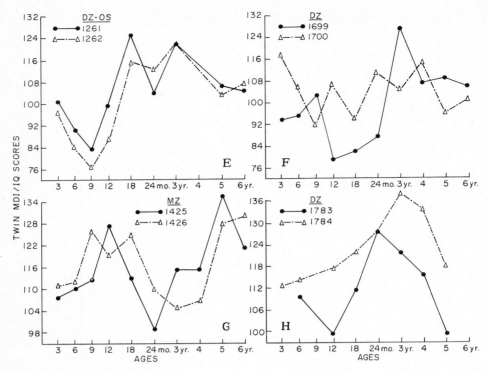

Fig. 4 Profiles of mental development scores during childhood for eight pairs of twins. See text for interpretation.

formed by a repeated-measures analysis of variance that was specifically adapted for twin data (Haggard, 1958; Wilson, 1972, 1977a). The analysis appraises both the overall elevation of the score profile and the age-to-age changes that determine the profile contour. It also provides within-pair correlations for each aspect of the score profile.

The test ages have been grouped into interlocking blocks so that the maximum sample size would be retained, and any shifts in developmental stability would be revealed. The within-pair correlations for overall level and profile contour are presented in Table VII.

The results show that the monozygotic correlations for overall level were very high, reaching the 0.90 values for age groupings after the second year. By combining several tests, the errors of measurement were reduced and a more precise estimate was obtained of each twin's average status during the age period. With measurement replication over ages and genetic replication within pairs, the correlations for monozygotic twins may be said to represent the best estimate of true-score reliability for mental development in the preschool years.

The results also revealed significant concordance for monozygotic twins in the profile of age-to-age changes. These correlations reflected a congruence in spurts and

Table VII Twin concordance for trends in mental development during preschool years

Ages	Zygosity	No. of pairs	Within-pair correlations for		Variance within pairs for trend
			Overall level	Age-to-age change	
3, 6, 9, 12 mo.	MZ	49	0.88*	0.49**	59.4**
	DZ	55	0.79	0.20	117.2
6, 12, 18, 24 mo.	MZ	58	0.84*	0.64*	45.6**
	DZ	56	0.73	0.53	96.7
18, 24, 30, 36 mo.	MZ	35	0.90**	0.47	40.0***
	DZ	44	0.72	0.35	107.0
3, 4, 5 yrs.	MZ	54	0.93***	0.47**	39.4***
	DZ	60	0.74	0.17	95.2
4, 5, 6 yrs.	MZ	55	0.90***	0.41*	37.2***
	DZ	58	0.66	0.11	110.3

$*P \leq 0.06$; $**P \leq 0.01$; $***P \leq 0.001$ for $R_{MZ} > R_{DZ}$, or for Var. DZ > Var. MZ.

lags during each time block, as illustrated by the curves in Fig. 4, and they are independent of the concordance for overall level. Thus the profile correlations represented additional systematic variance accounted for by pair membership.

The degree of similarity for both aspects jointly considered is expressed in the final column as the variance within pairs for developmental trend. The more closely the twins matched each other for the vector of scores over ages, the smaller would be the variance within pairs for trend. The results show that monozygotic twins were significantly more concordant for developmental trend in the first year, and the match became closer in each succeeding age period. By contrast, the trends for dizygotic twins were more divergent and showed no tendency towards closer consolidation with age. The dizygotic correlations also receded further below the monozygotic correlations over successive ages.

These results reinforce an earlier conclusion that on a sample-wide basis, the most powerful determinant of mental development was the genetic blueprint supplied for each twin by the parents (Wilson, 1974). Monozygotic twins sharing the same genotype manifested a high level of concordance for the trends in mental development throughout the preschool years; and while the trend for each pair may have included idiosyncratic spurts and lags, nevertheless both twins generated a similar profile.

Dizygotic twins also displayed a substantial degree of concordance, but significantly less so than monozygotic twins and in an age pattern that moved towards an intermediate level of concordance as the measures of intelligence stabilized. The dizygotic correlations reflect the joint contributions of a partially shared genotype, 50% on the average, although augmented by assortative mating, plus the cumulative experiences shared in common by both twins. It may be noted that dizygotic twins became less concordant during the preschool years while being continuously exposed to the same family environment. Thus the massive quantity of shared experiences did not push dizygotic twins closer and closer together. From the standpoint of mental development, there is a limited extent to which shared experiences can compress the variability within dizygotic pairs.

What contribution is made by the differential treatments that parents presumably apply to their dizygotic twins? It is now recognized that such differential treatments as may exist are frequently evoked by the demands of the child, and reflect the child as instigator rather than as the passive product of the parents' conditioning.

More to the point, however, is the fact that there is no demonstrated relationship between the presumed differential treatment variables and the measures of intelligence among dizygotic twins. The alleged potency of these variables is based on conjecture, not on empirical data, and as an explanation it is without substance. It remains to be established whether any parental treatment differences are causally related to score differences within dizygotic pairs. Indeed, the parental treatment is typically in the opposite direction – to minimize differences and attempt to bring both twins to a common level.

Factors related to early mental development in twins

Since twins constitute a distinctive sample with respect to prenatal and perinatal factors, a number of such factors are often reported to affect the mental development of twins – for example, birth size, birth sequence, differences in birth weight, and gestational age. Further, the role of home environment variables such as socioeconomic status and parental education should be as important for twins as for singletons. The contributions of these factors have been assessed in the present sample; and since the twins have been followed for several years, any age change in importance of each factor can be detected.

Socioeconomic variables

When recruited, each family in the study was assigned a score on the Reiss (1961) scale based on the father's occupational status (see Table I for a representative listing). Also, the education of the parents was recorded as the number of years of schooling completed. These variables were correlated with the mental development scores of the twins, and the results are presented in Table VIII.

The results show no relationship between socioeconomic status and the twins' mental development in the first year, then a substantial gain in the second year and a modest increase thereafter. Essentially the same pattern was evident for parents' education, with perhaps a slightly stronger relationship for the father. The interesting feature is that the correlations became significant at an age where mental functions oriented more clearly toward school-age intelligence.

It might be noted that father's education and mother's education were sub-

Table VIII   Correlation of twins' mental development scores with
socioeconomic status and parental education

Age	MDI/IQ and SES	MDI/IQ and father's education	MDI/IQ and mother's education
3 mo.	0.04	0.15	−0.01
6 mo.	0.08	0.22	0.09
12 mo.	0.02	0.12	0.09
24 mo.	0.29	0.27	0.27
3 yrs.	0.32	0.39	0.35
6 yrs.	0.33	0.38	0.33

$N \geq 350$ at each age.

stantially correlated ($r = 0.67$), so there was extensive assortative mating. The previously reported dizygotic correlations were boosted somewhat by assortative mating, since it increased the average degree of genetic similarity among zygotes above 50% for the trait in question.

Birth sequence

A question is often raised whether being first-born or second-born in the pair has any effect upon mental development. This possibility seems to arise from the fact that second-born twins are more often breech deliveries and are slightly more at risk for mortality or physiological defect.

Accordingly, the twins were ordered by first- and second-born in each pair and compared for mental development scores at 3 months of age, when any birth sequelae should be prominent; then later compared at 2 years and 6 years of age. The results are summarized in Table IX.

It is evident that in a large representative sample of twins, birth sequence had no systematic effect whatsoever on mental development. The means were equal, and while there was a wide range of differences evident within the pairs, the differences favored the second-born as often as the first. Thus if there are individual cases in which some anomaly of mental development appears to depend upon birth sequence, it is a matter of coincidence.

Table IX   Effect of within-pair birth sequence on mental development scores

Age	No. pairs	Twin MDI/IQ Scores		Range of differences
		1st born	2nd born	
3 mo.	189	100.0	100.3	−35 to +39
24 mo.	179	100.2	99.9	−42 to +47
6 yr.	193	99.4	100.6	−37 to +39

Prematurity and mental development

We return to the measures of birth size and gestational age which reflect the degree of prematurity for each infant. There were many studies asserting that low birth-weight was associated with a limitation in mental development (e.g. Drillien, 1964, 1969; Wiener, 1962), and often this was interpreted as a suppressive effect due to prenatal malnourishment. However, more recent studies have found the long-term effects of prematurity to be much diminished (Drillien, 1972; Francis-Williams and Davies, 1974), and it appears that the earlier negative effects may have been due in part to the postnatal care of the premature infant. To quote Francis-Williams and Davies (1974, p. 709): "During the past 10 years, many of the factors now known to be harmful to infants of low birthweight (such as excessive use of oxygen, prolonged starvation, hypothermia and the use of ototoxic drugs in too-large doses) have gradually been eliminated . . ."

Twins offer an unusually powerful resource to trace the relationship between prematurity and mental development. Aside from differences between pairs in gestational age, there are also differences within pairs in birth weight. Some of the largest differences in birth weight occur for monozygotic twins where a placental transfusion has taken place via interconnections in the vascular system. Since these infants are genetically alike but have experienced unequal prenatal nutrition, it is a matter of some interest to follow their course of development after birth.

The measures of birth weight and gestational age were correlated with the mental development scores obtained during infancy and childhood, and the results are sum-marized in Table X.

The results show that birth weight and gestational age were strongly related to developmental status during the first 6 months, and the relationship remained significant throughout the first year. Beyond that age, however, the correlation declined to a residual value between 0.10 and 0.15. From two years on, birth weight and gestational age accounted for only 2% of the variance in mental test scores, so the long-term effects of prematurity were extremely limited. This perspective from the correlational analysis further confirms the earlier results from the analysis of three

Table X Correlations between mental development scores and birth weight and gestational age

Age	MDI/IQ and birth weight	MDI/IQ and gestational age
3 mo.	0.50	0.48
6 mo.	0.48	0.58
12 mo.	0.30	0.37
24 mo.	0.14	0.12
3 yrs.	0.11	0.05
6 yrs.	0.15	0.11

$N \geq 350$ at each age.

gestational-age groups, where the large initial differences in developmental status were nearly equalized by 24 months.

Acknowledging that the relationship between prematurity and later childhood IQ was negligible for the full sample, it seemed desirable to analyze the smallest infants further since they are the cases typically hypothesized to suffer the consequences of restricted mental development. Also, the relative birth weight within each pair is often reputed to have some influence on mental development, with the heavier twin having an advantage (Willerman and Churchill, 1967). Therefore, a series of analyses were undertaken for low-weight twins and for those pairs in which there was a large difference in birth weight.

Examining the scatterplot of birth weight and 6-year IQ scores, no relationship was evident for birth weights above 1750 g. The twins weighing less than 1750 g, however, were more often below average in IQ at age 6. Of the 34 twins, 23 in this extreme group had IQ scores below 100.

These results raise an intriguing question about the dispersion of scores in pairs where both twins were very small, versus pairs where one twin was very small but the other was larger. In the former case, the gestational period was typically shorter, and aside from the increased risk this posed, it also suggested a possible embryological or intrauterine anomaly that may have precipitated early delivery. Where only one twin was low weight, however, it may have reflected some differential influence upon prenatal growth such as the transfusion syndrome which would not necessarily have shortened pregnancy. Was this low-weight twin as likely to be below average in intelligence as the members of the preceding pairs?

The question was addressed by sorting all pairs involving a twin below 1750 g into four general groups: (a) both twins below 1750 g; (b) one index twin paired with a cotwin up to 2050 gms; (c) one index twin paired with a cotwin up to 2500 g; and (d) one index twin paired with a cotwin up to 3250 g. The most recent IQ scores were plotted for the index twin and the heavier twin in each pair, and the results are displayed in Fig. 5. Most of the IQ scores were from the 6-year tests; the remainder were from tests at 4 or 5 years.

A preponderance of low scores was found for the two groups with both twins of low birth weight. The duration of pregnancy was substantially shorter for these groups, and 35 of the 44 twins obtained IQ scores below 100. It is noteworthy, however, that one monozygotic pair obtained very high scores, so the effects of low birth weight and prematurity did not automatically push the later measures of intelligence below average.

Turning to the groups where the low-weight index twin was paired with a substantially heavier cotwin, the IQ scores clustered around the mean, with as many scores above 100 as below. Most of the pairs were monozygotic twins, and there was notably high concordance for the IQ scores ($r = 0.87$) among these pairs, even though the weight differences were considerable.

For several monozygotic pairs the weight disparity was definitely attributable to the placental transfusion syndrome; in one such case the lighter twin weighed 1530 g, the heavier twin 3230 g, and a significant weight difference was still evident at 6 years. The IQ scores at age 6 were unrelated to these weight differences, however,

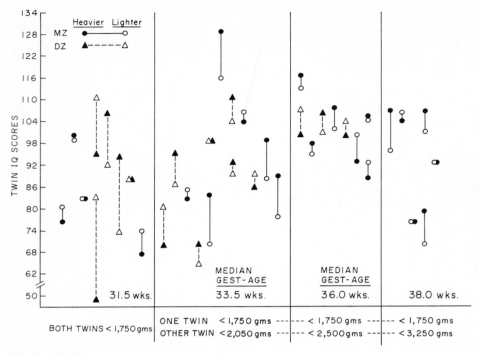

Fig. 5 Childhood IQ scores for twins below 1750 g in birthweight and their heavier cotwins.

being 106 and 104 respectively. Evidently the imbalance in prenatal nutrition had a more pronounced effect on physical size than mental development. If this pair is representative, it would suggest that human brain development is better buffered against such prenatal anomalies than the determinants of body mass and bone growth.

Performing a heavier-lighter comparison for all monozygotic twins in these groups, the mean IQ advantage for the heavier twin was 2.2 points, which was statistically nonsignificant ($P = 0.19$). These pairs did not show a systematic downward bias in IQ, as had been evident for the previous group, and perhaps the most impressive feature of these results was the absence of association between very low birth weight and later IQ in twin pairs of unequal birth size. For the monozygotic twins that made up the bulk of this group, the common genotype appeared to speak through the inequalities of prenatal growth and pull both twins toward a common level. Fujikura and Froelich (1974) have reported similar results.

Finally, the heavier-lighter comparison was extended to all monozygotic twins in Fig. 5, providing 22 pairs of matched genetic replicates. The mean deficit for the lighter twin was -2.7 points, which in this matched sample approached significance ($0.10 > P > 0.05$). However, the within-pair correlation was 0.89, so even with the most radical selection of low birth-weight twins, the concordance within monozygotic pairs remained very high. The deficit accruing to the twin below 1750 g accounted for less than 1 percent of the variance in the test scores. If the light-weight twin was compromised in any way relative to his heavier cotwin, it was a subtle effect indeed.

From this perspective, it is time to set aside birth weight differences as a ready explanation for differences in IQ; and to acknowledge further that very low birth weight has only a limited association with later IQ. It appears as a consequential factor when both twins are very small and the duration of pregnancy has been short. The question then becomes one of whether low birth weight is directly related to mental development via the mechanism of poor nutrition, or whether it is one symptom in a broader constellation of deficiencies.

The effects of prenatal malnutrition have been widely studied in recent years, and many of the results are surveyed in a volume edited by Lloyd-Still (1976). It appears that malnutrition interacts with other variables such as socioeconomic status and postnatal care, and it is difficult to weigh its contribution independently of these other factors. As the influence of malnutrition upon mental development becomes more definitely established, it should be possible to determine whether some infants are more susceptible to its effects than others, and whether there is an enduring deficit that is not compensated by school age. Such results should ultimately be reconciled with the data from low birth-weight singletons and twins, as briefly recapped in this chapter.

An auxiliary hypothesis which might be considered is a link between early initiation of labor (and thus premature delivery), and a higher risk potential in the fetus affecting many developmental processes. Premature delivery represents an intermediate point back towards spontaneous abortion, and it might be speculated that such premature infants make up a selective sample prejudiced in one of two possible ways: (a) a poor intrauterine environment which is inadequate to sustain full-term fetal growth; or (b) a fetus that is genetically at greater risk for inadequate development. In the latter case, if the elaborate mechanisms regulating prenatal growth are compromised by marginal instructions in the genetic programming, then the cases most at risk for premature birth may be susceptible to deficiencies in other areas of development. Thus the association between extreme prematurity and below-average intelligence may have a common root at the genotypic level, where the manifold coding of growth processes may have been biased towards higher risk potential.

Final comment

By way of final comment, we can remark that the present data reaffirm and broaden many of the conclusions from Bayley's work on the growth of intelligence. Indeed we can hardly improve on her summation, which is quoted below (Bayley, 1955, pp. 813–814).

"It becomes evident that the intellectual growth of any given child is a resultant of varied and complex factors. These will include his inherent capacities for growth, both in amount and in rate of progress. They will include the emotional climate ...

and the material environment in which he grows: the opportunities for experience and for learning, and the extent to which these opportunities are continuously geared to his capacity to respond and to make use of them. (In) individual growth curves, there may be plateaus, periods of no growth, and occasionally actual decrements. There may be rapid forging ahead. Each child appears to develop at a rate that is unique for him. I suspect that each child is a law unto himself . . . ."

In the final phrase we might substitute the term zygote for child, and add only that the twin data strongly implicate the genotype as the major determinant of these inherent capacities. Other influences are played out upon the foundation provided by the genotype.

Does this suggest that the quality of the home environment is unimportant? Not at all. The contribution of the parents is in potentiating the child's inherent capabilities, in creating an atmosphere of enthusiasm for learning, and in adapting their expectations to the child's capability. The wide diversity within families emphasizes the importance of giving each child full opportunity for development, and indeed of making sure that the opportunity is taken. The ultimate goal is the maximum realization of each child's intelligence, coupled with a sense of satisfaction and personal accomplishment in its use. There is no better way to foster such development than by a supportive and appropriately stimulating family environment.

Acknowledgment

This chapter is based on data collected by the Louisville Twin Study during the past eight years. I am particularly indebted to the psychometricians whose conscientious efforts have made this program possible; to Adam P. Matheny, Jr. and Anne B. Dolan for suggestions and critical readings of the manuscript; and to the twins and their families who have participated in the longitudinal study. This research was supported in part by grants from the National Institute of Child Health and Human Development, National Institute of Mental Health, National Science Foundation, and The Grant Foundation.

Literature cited

Bayley, N. (1949) Consistency and variability in the growth of intelligence from birth to eighteen years, *J. Genet. Psychol. 75*, 165–196
Bayley, N. (1955) On the growth of intelligence, *Am. Psychol. 10*, 805–818
Bayley, N. (1965) Comparisons of mental and motor test scores for ages 1–15 months by sex, birth order, race, geographical location, and education of parents, *Child Devel. 36*, 379–411
Bayley, N. (1969) *Bayley Scales of Infant Development*, Psychological Corp., New York
Drillien, C. M. (1964) *The Growth and Development of the Prematurely Born Infant*, E. and S. Livingstone, Edinburgh
Drillien, C. M. (1969) School disposal and performance for children of different birth-weight born 1953–1960, *Arch. Dis. Childh. 44*, 562–570

Drillien, C. M. (1972) Aetiology and outcome in low-birthweight infants. *Devel. Med. Child Neurol. 14*, 563–574

Francis-Williams, J. and Davies, P. A. (1974) Very low birthweight and later intelligence, *Devel. Med. Child Neurol. 16*, 709–728

Fujikura, T. and Froehlich, L. A. (1974) Mental and motor development in monozygotic twins with dissimilar birth weights, *Pediatrics 53*, 884–889

Haggard, E. A. (1958) *Intraclass Correlation and the Analysis of Variance*, Dryden Press, New York

Lloyd-Still, J. D. (1976) *Malnutrition and Intellectual Development*, Publishing Sciences Group, Littleton, Mass.

McCarthy, D. (1972) *McCarthy Scales of Children's Abilities*, Psychological Corp., New York

Piaget, J. (1952) *The Origins of Intelligence in Children*, International Universities Press, New York

Record, R. G., McKeown, T. and Edwards, J. H. (1970) An investigation of the difference in measured intelligence between twins and single births, *Ann. Hum. Genet. Lond. 34*, 11–20

Reiss, A. J., Jr. (1961) *Occupations and Social Status*, Free Press of Glencoe, New York

Thorndike, R. L. (1973) *Stanford-Binet Intelligence Scale (3rd. rev.): 1972 Norms Tables*, Houghton-Mifflin, Boston

Tilford, J. A. (1976) The relationship between gestational age and adaptive behavior, *Merrill-Palmer Q. 22*, 319–326

Uzgiris, I. C. and Hunt, J. McV. (1975) *Assessment in Infancy*, University Illinois Press, Urbana

Wechsler, D. (1967) *Wechsler Preschool and Primary Scale of Intelligence*, Psychological Corp., New York

Wiener, G. (1962) Psychologic correlates of premature birth. A review, *J. Nerv. Ment. Disorders 134*, 129–144

Willerman, L. and Churchill, J. A. (1967) Intelligence and birth weight in identical twins. *Child Devel. 38*, 623–629

Wilson, R. S. (1970) Bloodtyping and twin zygosity, *Hum. Hered. 20*, 30–56

Wilson, R. S. (1972) Twins: Early mental development, *Science 175*, 914–917

Wilson, R. S. (1974) Twins: Mental development in the preschool years, *Develop. Psychol., 10*, 580–588

Wilson, R. S. (1975) Twins: Patterns of cognitive development as measured on the Wechsler Preschool and Primary Scale of Intelligence, *Develop. Psychol. 11*, 126–134

Wilson, R. S. (1977a) Analysis of twin data and estimation of heritability effects, *Acta Genet. Med. Gemell.* in the press

Wilson, R. S. (1977b) Sensory-motor and cognitive development. In: *Communicative and Cognitive Abilities. Early Behavioral Assessment* (F. Minifie and L. Lloyd, eds.) University Park Press, Baltimore, in the press

Wilson, R. S. (1977c) Twins and siblings. Concordance for school-age mental development, *Child Devel. 48*, 211–216

Appendix 1

Conversion table for twins' scores on Bayley Mental Scale

Twin MDI score	Twin norms, raw scores						Twin MDI score
	3 mo.	6 mo.	9 mo.	12 mo.	18 mo.	·24 mo.	
45	2	38	66	76	98	109	45
46	—	—	—	—	—	—	46
47	3	39	—	77	99	110	47
48	—	—	67	—	—	111	48
49	4	40	—	78	100	—	49
50	—	—	—	—	—	112	50
51	5	41	68	—	101	—	51
52	—	—	—	79	—	113	52
53	6	42	—	—	102	—	53
54	—	—	69	—	—	114	54
55	7	43	—	80	—	—	55
56	—	44	—	—	103	115	56
57	8	—	70	81	—	—	57
58	9	45	—	—	104	116	58
59	—	—	—	82	—	—	59
60	10	46	71	—	105	117	60
61	—	—	—	—	—	118	61
62	11	47	72	83	—	—	62
63	—	—	—	—	106	119	63
64	12	48	—	84	—	—	64
65	13	—	73	—	107	120	65
66	—	49	—	—	—	—	66
67	14	—	—	85	108	121	67
68	—	50	74	—	—	—	68
69	15	51	—	86	—	122	69
70	—	—	—	—	109	123	70
71	16	52	75	—	—	—	71
72	—	—	—	87	110	124	72
73	17	53	—	—	—	—	73
74	18	—	76	88	111	125	74
75	—	54	—	—	—	—	75
76	19	—	—	—	—	126	76
77	—	55	77	89	112	127	77
78	20	—	—	—	—	—	78
79	—	56	—	90	113	128	79

Appendix 1 (*continued*)

Twin MDI score	Twin norms, raw scores						Twin MDI score
	3 mo.	6 mo.	9 mo.	12 mo.	18 mo.	24 mo.	
80	21	—	78	—	—	—	80
81	—	57	—	—	—	129	81
82	22	58	—	91	114	—	82
83	23	—	79	—	—	130	83
84	—	59	—	92	115	—	84
85	24	—	—	—	—	131	85
86	—	60	80	—	—	132	86
87	25	—	—	93	116	—	87
88	26	61	—	—	—	133	88
89	—	—	81	94	117	—	89
90	27	62	—	—	—	134	90
91	—	—	—	—	118	—	91
92	28	63	82	95	—	135	92
93	—	—	—	—	—	—	93
94	29	64	83	96	119	136	94
95	30	65	—	—	—	137	95
96	—	—	—	—	120	—	96
97	31	66	84	97	—	138	97
98	—	—	—	—	—	—	98
99	32	67	—	98	121	139	99
100	—	—	85	—	—	—	100
101	33	68	—	—	122	140	101
102	34	—	—	99	—	—	102
103	—	69	86	—	123	141	103
104	35	—	—	100	—	142	104
105	—	70	—	—	—	—	105
106	36	71	87	—	124	143	106
107	—	—	—	101	—	—	107
108	37	72	—	—	125	144	108
109	—	—	88	102	—	—	109
110	38	73	—	—	—	145	110
111	39	—	—	—	126	146	111
112	—	74	89	103	—	—	112
113	40	—	—	—	127	147	113
114	—	75	—	104	—	—	114

Appendix 1 (*continued*)

Twin MDI score	Twin norms, raw scores						Twin MDI score
	3 mo.	6 mo.	9 mo.	12 mo.	18 mo.	24 mo.	
115	41	—	90	—	128	148	115
116	—	76	—	—	—	—	116
117	42	—	—	105	—	149	117
118	43	77	91	—	129	150	118
119	—	78	—	106	—	—	119
120	44	—	—	—	130	151	120
121	—	79	92	—	—	—	121
122	45	—	—	107	131	152	122
123	—	80	—	—	—	—	123
124	46	—	93	108	—	153	124
125	47	81	—	—	132	—	125
126	—	—	94	—	—	154	126
127	48	82	—	109	133	—	127
128	—	—	—	—	—	155	128
129	49	83	95	110	—	156	129
130	—	—	—	—	134	—	130
131	50	84	—	—	—	157	131
132	51	—	96	111	135	—	132
133	—	85	—	—	—	158	133
134	52	—	—	112	136	—	134
135	—	86	97	—	—	159	135
136	53	—	—	—	—	—	136
137	54	87	—	113	137	160	137
138	—	—	98	—	—	—	138
139	55	88	—	114	138	161	139
140	56+	—	—	—	—	162	140

Appendix 2

Conversion table for premature twins (29–36 weeks gestational age) on Bayley Mental Scale

Twin MDI Score	Age at testing, raw scores				
	3 mo.	6 mo.	9 mo.	12 mo.	18 mo.
50	3	—	64	76	—
51	—	38	—	—	100
52	4	—	65	77	—
53	—	39	—	—	101
54	—	—	—	—	—
55	5	—	—	78	—
56	—	40	66	—	102
57	6	—	—	79	—
58	—	41	—	—	—
59	—	—	67	—	103
60	7	42	—	80	—
61	—	—	68	—	104
62	8	43	—	81	—
63	—	—	—	—	105
64	9	44	—	—	—
65	—	—	69	82	—
66	10	45	—	—	106
67	—	—	70	83	—
68	11	46	—	—	—
69	—	—	—	—	107
70	12	47	71	84	—
71	—	—	72	—	108
72	13	48	—	85	—
73	—	—	—	—	109
74	—	49	—	—	—

Twin MDI score	Age at testing, raw scores				
	3 mo.	6 mo.	9 mo.	12 mo.	18 mo.
75	14	50	73	86	—
76	—	—	—	—	110
77	15	51	74	87	—
78	—	—	—	—	111
79	16	52	—	—	—
80	—	—	—	88	—
81	17	53	75	—	112
82	—	—	—	89	—
83	18	54	—	—	—
84	—	—	76	—	113
85	19	55	—	90	—
86	—	—	77	—	114
87	20	56	—	91	—
88	—	—	—	—	115
89	21	57	—	—	—
90	—	—	78	92	—
91	22	58	79	—	116
92	—	—	—	93	—
93	23	59	—	—	—
94	—	—	—	—	117
95	24	60	80	94	—
96	—	—	81	—	118
97	25	—	—	95	—
98	—	61	—	—	—
99	26	—	—	—	—

Appendix 2 (*continued*)

Twin MDI score	Age at testing, raw scores				
	3 mo.	6 mo.	9 mo.	12 mo.	18 mo.
100	—	62	—	—	119
101	27	—	82	96	—
102	—	63	—	—	120
103	28	—	83	97	—
104	—	64	—	—	—
105	29	—	—	—	121
106	30	65	84	98	—
107	—	66	—	—	122
108	—	—	85	—	—
109	—	—	—	99	—
110	31	67	—	—	123
111	—	—	86	100	—
112	32	68	—	—	124
113	—	—	—	—	—
114	33	69	—	101	—
115	—	—	87	—	125
116	34	70	—	102	—
117	—	—	88	—	—
118	35	71	—	—	126
119	—	72	—	103	—
120	36	—	—	—	127
121	—	73	89	104	—
122	—	74	—	—	128
123	37	—	90	105	—
124	—	—	—	—	—
125	38	75	—	106	129
126	—	—	91	—	—
127	39	76	—	107	130
128	—	—	—	—	—
129	40	—	—	—	—
130	—	77	92	—	—
131	41	78	—	108	131
132	42	—	93	—	—
133	—	79	—	109	132
134	—	—	—	—	—
135	43	—	—	—	—

Appendix 3

Conversion table for twins' scores on tests at ages 2.5, 3, and 4 years.

Twin MDI/IQ score	2.5 years Bayley raw score	3 years Binet mental age score	4 years WPPSI IQ score	Twin MDI/IQ score	2.5 years Bayley or Binet	3 years Binet mental age score	4 years WPPSI IQ score
50	—	*	*	75	137	—	68
51	123	*	*	76	—	2–3	69
52	—	*	*	77	138	—	70
53	124	*	*	78	139	2–4	71
54	—	*	*	79	—	—	72
					****		
55	125	*	50	80	—	2–5	73
56	—	*	—	81	—	—	74
57	126	*	51	82	2–0	—	75
58	—	*	52	83	—	2–6	76
59	127	*	53	84	—	—	77
60	—	*	54	85	2–1	2–7	78
61	128	*	55	86	—	—	79
62	129	*	56	87	—	—	80
63	—	*	57	88	2–2	2–8	81
64	130	*	58	89	—	—	82
65	—	—	59	90	—	2–9	83
66	131	—	60	91	2–3	—	—
67	132	—	61	92	—	—	84
68	—	—	62	93	—	2–10	85
69	133	2–0	63	94	2–4	—	86
70	134	—	64	95	—	2–11	87
71	—	—	—	96	—	—	88
72	135	2–1	65	97	—	—	89
73	—	—	66	98	2–5	3–0	90
74	136	2–2	67	99	—	—	91

Bayley raw scores at age 2.5 yrs. for lower range MDI/IQ scores (< 80); Binet mental age scores thereafter. See text for explanation.

Appendix 3 (*continued*)

Twin MDI/IQ score	2.5 years Binet mental age score	3 years Binet mental age score	4 years WPPSI IQ score	Twin MDI/IQ score	2.5 years Binet mental age score	3 years Binet mental age score	4 years WPPSI IQ score
100	—	3–1	92	125	3–1	3–11	116
101	—	—	93	126	—	—	117
102	2–6	3–2	94	127	—	4–0	—
103	—	—	95	128	—	—	118
104	—	—	96	129	3–2	—	119
105	2–7	3–3	97	130	—	4–1	120
106	—	—	98	131	—	—	121
107	—	3–4	99	132	—	4–2	122
108	—	—	100	133	3–3	—	123
109	2–8	—	—	134	—	4–3	124
110	—	3–5	101	135	—	—	125
111	—	—	102	136	—	—	126
112	2–9	3–6	103	137	3–4	4–4	127
113	—	—	104	138	—	—	128
114	—	—	105	139	—	4–5	129
115	—	3–7	106	140	3–5	—	130
116	2–10	—	107	141	—	—	131
117	—	3–8	108	142	—	4–6	132
118	—	—	109	143	3–6	—	133
119	2–11	—	110	144	—	—	134
120	—	3–9	111				
121	—	—	112				
122	3–0	3–10	113				
123	—	—	114				
124	—	—	115				

Environmental differences and mental performance in man

Genetics, environment and intelligence, edited by A. Oliverio
© *Elsevier/North-Holland, Biomedical Press, 1977*

Early stimulation and behavioral development 17

BURTON L. WHITE

Background

The demand for knowledge about the psychological and educational development of the human infant is stronger today than ever before. The huge input (in the United States) of federal and foundation monies during the last decade has been both symptomatic and, of course, influential. Nevertheless, a good deal of elementary information about early human development simply is not yet available. To give but one example, the development of intrinsic interest in learning, or simple curiosity, is largely unexplored. We have neither a single established method for measuring it (in the infant) nor any substantial evidence on how external factors influence its growth. This condition prevails in respect to many other fundamental areas of early human development.

The reasons are not hard to find. Infants are less accessible for scientific research than college students and school-age children to say nothing of mice and pigeons. During the first four days of life, with effort, they are accessible in groups in hospitals. Predictably, we have a fair amount of research on such babies. Unfortunately, four days is a fairly small piece of life.

The special importance of infancy

Throughout recorded history, few professional efforts have focussed on the education of children less than 6 years of age. A handful of pioneers such as Comenius,

Froebel, and Pestalozzi sponsored education for 4- and 5-year-olds during the 17th and 18th centuries (Cole, 1959), but it was not until the work of Sigmund Freud (1905) that Western society was effectively urged to attend to the influence of experiences during infancy on life-long function. Subsequently, the work of J. B. Watson, Irwin, Gesell and others has added to the interest in this earliest period of life. Probably the most potent spur to the present-day renewed concern with infancy has been the early work of Piaget (1952, 1954). Piaget's remarkable studies of the intellectual development of his own three children during infancy have inspired a substantial number of modern workers. Perhaps the most vigorous proponents of Piaget's work on infancy have been Hunt (1961) and Flavell (1963). Hunt, especially, has claimed that the experiences of the first two years of life are of very great importance for all that follows. Not everyone in academic circles shares Hunt's position (although I must say that I do). Many respected professionals have serious doubts about this thesis based in part on the frequently found low predictive value of developmental standing in infancy (Furfey and Muhlerbein, 1932; Anderson, 1939; and N. Bayley, 1940)*. That is, infants who appear precocious during infancy are, if anything, likely to score slightly below average on intelligence tests as adults.

There seems to be an increasing confidence, however, that a study of the moment-to-moment experiences of the first years of life has much to teach us. This belief seems to be one consequence of a large number of studies of the mother–child relation (e.g. Ainsworth et al., 1967; Moss, 1967; Caldwell et al., 1969; David and Appel, 1961) including studies of maternal deprivation (Spitz, 1945; Bowlby, 1951) and studies of early experience in other species (Harlow, 1962; Levine, 1957; Denenberg, 1967).

Hunt (1961, 1965) has argued persuasively that intellectual capacity and intrinsic motivation are especially vulnerable during infancy. Hebb (1949) and Robert White (1959) have both written eloquently on this topic. In the closely related area of language development, which is broadly acknowledged to be of fundamental importance for intellectual growth, most research has concentrated on post-infancy periods. On the other hand, though elaborate productive language is rare during infancy, it has long been known (McCarthy, 1954) that receptive language functions are acquired rapidly during that time.

The current boom in educational programs for infants is testimony to the growing belief in the likelihood of the importance of infancy for such developmental processes. Spokesmen often address their remarks toward the prevention of serious harm to children. The more subtle but probably more common moderate deficiencies that large numbers of presumably "normal" children suffer are also worthy of our attention. It is quite conceivable that our current standards of "normalcy" for young children will some day come to be viewed as unacceptably low. It would genuinely surprise me if several decades from now we have not learned how to structure the experiences of infancy so as to assure a far more interesting, pleasurable and productive beginning for each child.

---

* For an exception to this view see Knobloch and Pasamanick, 1960.

The need for basic data on human development

In the U.S.A., the most widely utilized source of information on the behavior of the human infant is probably the work of Arnold Gesell (1949). His schedules of development are at once widely used yardsticks for normal development and also outlines of development. Other infant behavior scales, such as those of Cattell (1940); Buhler and Hetzer (1935) and Bayley (1965) characteristically offer about the same degree of detail. The Griffiths scale (1954) is a considerably sounder instrument in terms of test construction but it is not founded on a significantly better body of normative data. These instruments are designed primarily for screening purposes. They usually cover most major areas of behavior including intellectual or adaptive behavior, motor, social, and linguistic functions. Typically, an infant's status in all of these very large domains is assessed in less than one hour. The infant is tested on 20 to 30 items, and his mother is asked to supply information on habitual per- formances in language, etc. Considering the complexity of each of these areas, it is patently obvious that infant tests such as these do not more than make an arbitrary scratch on the surface of an extremely complex series of interwoven processes. A look at the work of modern linguists such as Brown and Bellugi (1964), or of cognitive theorists such as Piaget (1952, 1954) indicates the enormous difference between in-depth studies of infant capacity and screening practices. Furthermore, in-depth assessments of infant capacity have barely begun. An enormous amount of un- glamorous work still has to be done in charting the development during infancy of the many sensory capacities, motor abilities, interests, etc., of infants. Traditional topics such as individual and sex differences, rates and ranges of development, etc., have as yet been dealt with only in the most preliminary fashion.

Problems we face in studying the effects of early experience on development

It is only natural that the first focus of research in the growing field of infant develop- ment be on the various behaviors that infants exhibit. I have described in general terms the need for vast amounts of information on the rapidly changing abilities, interests, etc., of the human infant, but knowledge of how infants behave will not suffice. We cannot afford to assume that experience is only of minor importance for the course of development. As parents, psychologists, educators, child welfare professionals, etc., it is our responsibility to structure the environment of each child so as to maximize the likelihood of optimal development. In another publica- tion (White et al., 1964), we suggested that so-called "normative" data on develop- ment can only be assumed to be normative for subjects reared under the same general conditions as the standardization sample. In our report on the ontogenesis of visually-directed reaching, institutionally-reared infants exhibited mature reaching at about five months of age. In a series of subsequent experiments (White, 1967), in which groups of infants were reared in especially designed environments, they learned to reach by three months of age. For a species where the course of development is largely determined by genetic factors, perhaps the study of rearing conditions is of minor importance. For man, it is likely to be of profound importance.

To study rearing conditions means to study patterns of care-taking behavior, the physical surround, the social surround, the daily schedule, etc. Further, it means that these factors must be studied, as they change during the subject's development. The infant less than 6 months of age cannot move about by himself. The infant, 18 months old, lives in a radically different world. The older infant changes his locus of activity many times each day. The 6-month-old is considerably more a captive of a comparatively invariant set of physical conditions. Clearly, the study of the environment will be a much more complicated task than the study of child behavioral phenomena per se. This is not the end of the problem, however, for different environments may produce common experiences in children, whereas common environments may result in different experiences. As Thomas et al. (1964) and Escalona (1968) point out, experience is a function of both external conditions and the nature of the experiencing organism. We cannot rely on a study of static sets of rearing conditions if we seek understanding of patterns of early experience and their effects.

An enormous amount of work must be done analyzing the course of experience throughout infancy. Existing examples of this kind of study are the baby biographies of the past (Preyer, Shinn, cited in Wright, 1960), the recent work of Church (1966) and especially the work of Piaget. Such work is so time-consuming and so laborious that few undertake it, and one is inclined to despair. It is my contention (and I believe it undeniable) that to the extent that experience influences development, we must embark on many such studies*.

Even though we do not yet possess detailed knowledge about the fabric of infant experience, the topic of the effects of such experience has received attention from researchers for several decades. Indeed the hardiest perennial in the garden of psychological issues seems to be the nature–nurture or hereditary–environmental dispute. The topic is centuries old and has never been set aside for very long by either society or students of development. During this century we have seen the pendulum swing from an emphasis on what is inherited (Darwinianism, instinct theory) over to the mechanisms of learning (e.g. Pavlov, Thorndike, Watson, etc.) then back to the role of maturation (e.g. Gesell) then back to the plasticity of early development (e.g. Hunt, Project Headstart) etc. Currently, the issue seems characteristically alive and controversial, with rebutters to the environmentalists in the areas of education (e.g. Jensen, 1969) and ethology (e.g. E. K. Hess) and advocates in studies of learning (e.g. Gewirtz, Lipsitt), comparative studies (e.g. Denenberg) perceptual motor development (e.g. B. White) and social development (e.g. M. Ainsworth).

---

*Recently, three techniques for the quantitative analysis of ongoing experience have appeared (Caldwell, 1968; White, 1969c; Clarke-Stewart, 1973).

What do we actually know now about the early development of intelligence

The most valuable data about infant behavior are from direct studies of human infants. It has become traditional to supplement such direct evidence with the findings from studies of other animal species. Few would deny the utility for understanding human sensory function, for example, from studies of vision in other mammals; nor would anybody argue that valuable information about the developing central nervous system has not come from studies of creatures as far removed from man as the horsehoe crab (Hartline, 1949) or the frog (Lettvin, 1959). On the other hand, certain cautions are necessary. Clearly, some topics such as the acquisition of language are explorable for all intents and purposes only through human subjects. In addition, though mammals share many common characteristics, one is always risking when extrapolating across species. All such indirect evidence should therefore be treated as tentative until such time as direct confirmation on human infants is obtained. The same caveat is necessary when evaluating evidence attained in studies of humans older than infants. The classic example is, of course, the Freudian theory of infantile sexuality which has had enormous influence but was constructed out of studies of adults. It has never been extensively confirmed by direct studies of infants. This distinction between direct and indirect evidence is quite important for the consumer of knowledge about infant development. Except for Piaget's theory of the ontogenesis of intelligence (1952) and Gesell's concept of "reciprocal interweaving", none of the existent theories of infant development are rooted in studies of human infants. A case in point is learning theory as espoused by followers of Pavlov, Skinner and Spence, etc. Classical, operant and instrumental conditioning are commonly claimed to constitute the primary modes of learning in infancy, but this conception is based mainly on studies of adult humans, dogs, cats and pigeons. Very few learning theorists have made serious investments in an unprejudiced view of learning phenomena in infancy as a prelude to their expositions.

Studies of learning

Over the better part of this century, much research stemming from the work of Pavlov and Thorndike has been performed with human infants. The studies have been characterized by high precision, small sample size and restricted scope. Many investigators in this field believe that the only important kind of learning that infants are capable of is one or another form of conditioning. A major purpose of their efforts has been to demonstrate that infants can be conditioned at birth or soon after (Marquis, 1941; Lipsitt, 1963, 1966, 1967; Papoušek, 1961; Kaye, 1965; Siqueland, 1964; Lintz et al., 1967; Fitzgerald et al., 1967). Indeed, there have been attempts to condition infants in the womb (Spelt, 1938). Apparently, the goal is to prove that infants normally learn through conditioning.

Russian investigators have been at this effort longer than anyone else, probably because of the pervasive influence of Pavlov on their studies of human function. In general, they have had little success with newborns (Brackbill, 1962). It is not until the third month of life that they have been able to establish discriminative responses (i.e., positive responses to one previously neutral stimulus and in the same test situation, negative responses to a related neutral stimulus). The ability to establish such responses is potentially of great importance for the study of sensory capacities.

We now know (Gollin, 1967; Horowitz, 1968; Lipsitt, 1967) that with enormous care and effort, under rigidly controlled laboratory conditions, short-lived conditioned responses can be established in new-borns. This achievement is an important accomplishment from a technical point of view, but I doubt that it has taught us much about how infants learn. It is quite unlikely that the kinds of circumstances demanded by the conditioning paradigm occur often enough in the life of any child to account for more than a very small amount of what is mastered. It appears that research in this tradition has two other potential values for the field. As mentioned earlier, it has developed powerful tools for the study of sensory capacity in the pre-verbal child; and, second, it may prove useful in therapeutic situations where short-term modifications in behavior are necessary.

Studies of language

The acquisition of primary aspects of language such as the earliest spoken vocabulary has been thoroughly documented (McCarthy, 1954), although not on a wide variety of subcultural groups. More sophisticated studies of language, such as those of Brown and Bellugi (1964), have not dealt with the first 18 months of life.

Receptive language on the other hand has been much less investigated. That the child can hear well enough to discriminate words and inflections by the time he is 6 months old is highly probable, though not well documented (Friedlander et al., 1965). In fact, Eisenberg (1966) has described auditory research in infancy as "a vast wasteland." If we grant the likelihood that the infant is listening to and processing language with increasing facility from 6 months on and juxtapose the fact that shortly after 18 months they routinely reveal a surprisingly rapid acquisition of complicated expressive language skills, it strongly suggests an important learning period from 6 to 18 months.

Studies of the development of higher mental abilities (intelligence)

The development of intelligence (defined crudely as problem-solving capacity) and its many constituents such as object permanence, causality, means-ends behavior, perception of time etc., has been studied most extensively by Piaget (1952, 1954).

Piaget's work has had enormous influence on current thinking. In Piaget's view, the newborn is essentially non-intellectual, totally incapable of intelligent or purposeful (means–end) behavior, but he is designed to take in and be modified by experiences. At 6 months or so, the infant shows primitive intelligence in the form of means–end behavior but still does very little of what we call "thinking" or manipulation of ideas. By 18 months, true ideation or mental representation begins to supplement and replace immediate action as the primary mode of coping with problems. Support for this view has been provided by some recent studies of sorting behavior by Ricciuti (1964, 1965). Infants 12 to 24 months of age, when given the opportunity, reveal classificatory behavior in the sequences with which they handle small objects, indicating that some sort of mental organization is guiding their play. A similarly important metamorphosis is characteristic of other cognitive developments such as the conception of causality, time etc., during this comparatively brief period of infancy. Innumerable studies have given general support to Piaget's views sensorimotor intelligence. Indeed, it seems to be the only available coherent information on the topic in this author's view.

The development of curiosity

A topic of fundamental importance for intellectual development is the development of curiosity. A synonym for curiosity is "intrinsic interest in learning." When phrased this way, it is clear that an understanding of how this human attribute develops would be most desirable. Very little direct study of the process has been undertaken.

Infants normally first exhibit what may be labelled curiosity at about 2 months of age. Also about this time, the infant also becomes considerably more interested in his surroundings than in the first month of life (Gesell, 1949; White, 1967). In his interest in the nearby scene, in human faces, and most strikingly in his own hands, he first shows what looks like either curiosity or a clear precursor. Visual and tactual interest grows steadily from then on. At about 8 months of age, the infant exhibits a particular interest in tiny particles (Schwarting, 1954). Again, when it comes to the details of the development of curiosity, especially after the first half year of life, with the exception of some work on the 5 to 19 months old by Charlesworth (1963), there is virtually no evidence. Recent observations strongly suggest that there is no more interested creature alive than the 18 month old infant (White, 1969c). Perhaps if psychologists knew more about this period, we might be able to help more infants maintain this apparently normal enthusiasm for learning that is commonly diminished in many children by the time they reach school age. I doubt if a more important educational problem exists.

What do we know about the effects of experience on development

Natural experimental (correlational) studies

There are three major types of studies that might be labelled as "natural experimental studies of the effects of experience on development."

Screening studies

A huge investment of talent and funds has been made in long term longitudinal studies. Several such studies were begun in the U.S. during the 1920's and 1930's (Kagan, 1964). Generalizations about the benefits of accepting, democratic mothers, for example, are the kinds of information generated by such studies. An intensive analysis of these studies was reported in a provocative book by Bloom (1965) which claimed that early experience, especially during infancy, is of vital importance for development. In a widely quoted passage (p. 68), Bloom stated that 50% of intelligence, as commonly measured at age 17, is achieved by age 4. This simple statement captured the imagination of many readers. By and large, the thesis of this paper is sympathetic to this general position, but it must be noted that any implication that we are currently able to measure human intelligence with precision is unfortunate. To talk about 50% of something presupposes its accurate identification, which has not been done for the "intelligence" of infants and young children. Further, it assumes that the half of "intelligence" mastered by the 4 year old is equal to the half acquired throughout the rest of life. This assumption is clearly misleading.

In the same book, an attempt is cited (Wolf, p. 78) to characterize the major environmental factors in early development. 13 process variables are listed which presumably cover the topic of environmental influences on the development of intelligence. One such "variable" is the "availability of books"; another is the "emphasis on the use of language in a variety of situations", etc. Such analytical efforts require a great expenditure of energy in digesting the voluminous results of the longitudinal studies. They are not without merit, but they should not be taken as indications that we are generally knowledgable about early experience and developmental processes. The fact is that the longitudinal studies on which the analysis rests heavily were not designed to provide detailed information on the processes of development. The Fels study, for example, made the following investment in infancy: (i) Gesell tests at 6, 12, 18, and 24 months. (ii) Interviews with the mother, annually from birth. (iii) 2 to 4 observations of mother–child interactions every six months from birth. This data base is about average for the infancy period for the longitudinal studies. Contrast this investment of less than 30 h per infant for the first 2 years of life for all behavioral development with the several thousand hours of effort by Piaget in trying to understand intellectual development during infancy. Clearly, the longitudinal studies provide only the barest outlines of knowledge about environmental influences on infant development.

Deprivation studies

A large number of such studies evaluating the effects of the absence of the mother during the early years have been summarized by Bowlby (1951), Casler (1961), and Yarrow (1961, 1964). Although the scientific quality of the studies is highly variable and often open to serious criticism, the weight of the evidence overwhelmingly suggests that the absence of the mother for more than three months during infancy (beginning after the first six months) has serious negative consequences for most aspects of development. The question of the irreversibility of the effects is largely unexplored at this time.

What it is about the mother's absence that is important is a matter of some debate. Spitz, who wrote the pioneering article on the topic (1945) claimed that the cause of the problem was the serious disturbance of the developing mother–child libidinal bond. This position stemmed directly from Freudian notions about the development of the sexual instinct in infancy. If the two major motivational forces in infancy are the sexual and aggressive instincts, and if the mother is seen as a central link in the chain of discharge of sexual energy, then clearly her removal is catastrophic. Yarrow and Casler, on the other hand, impressed by the literature from studies of other species emphasize that maternal deprivation also usually means a drastic reduction in opportunities for learning and exposure to varied stimulation. Their view is more consistent with that of Hunt (1961), who points out that even if the mother is present throughout infancy, a child may be severely deprived if the opportunity to confront appropriate variations in circumstances is not provided. Somewhat in contradiction to the aforementioned point of view, are the findings of an early study by Dennis (1941). In an experiment which probably could not be performed today, the Dennises reared a pair of fraternal twins from the end of the first to the end of the 14th month of life under conditions of "restricted practice and minimum social stimulation." With very few exceptions the behavioral development of these infants was largely unaffected by what appeared to be a significant degree of long-term deprivation. The Dennises also reported (1940) that severe restrictions on motor practice in early infancy produced by the cradling practices of the Hopi did not seem to retard the onset of walking. Dennis and Sayegh and Dennis' more recent work (1957, 1965) with larger samples in an institution for infants in the Middle East has tended to provide more support, however, for the environmentalist's position.

Cross-cultural studies

The work of Erikson (1950), Mead (1951) and Whiting (1963) are examples of such research. In such work, various national characteristics have been attributed to patterns of child-rearing. At this point in history, very little in the way of useful detailed knowledge about experience in infancy has come from such studies. They do hold much promise for future work.

Experimental work on the effects of early experience

Studies of this kind fall into two distinct categories: those that manipulate infant experience over periods of less than an hour and those that cover longer periods of time. The former are far more common for several reasons: among which (a) they are less expensive to execute, (b) rigorous experimental control over human experience is feasible only for such brief periods, and (c) society is quite ambivalent about scientific "tampering" with human experience, especially that of helpless and possibly vulnerable infants. Unfortunately, though they are far more numerous than long-term experiments, it is highly questionable whether one can generalize extensively the findings from brief, laboratory-based sessions to the issue of the complex and cumulative effects of experience in real life.

Examples of short-term manipulations of experience are the studies of Rheingold (1956, 1961). She performed a series of conditioning studies which indicated that the sucking and head-turning behavior of neonates and various behaviors of older infants can be conditioned to previously neutral stimuli. Their studies feature very careful control over test circumstances to ensure that no extraneous stimulus is likely to interfere with the effect of the conditioned stimulus, e.g., a pure tone. With great technical skill they have demonstrated that this form of learning is within the infant's capacity. Unless reinforced trials continue, however, the effects are very short-lived. Furthermore, nothing very close to the experimental conditions is likely to occur with regularity in the ordinary life of an infant.

Experimental studies of the effects of early experiences that last longer than an hour or so have rarely been performed with human infants. Rheingold (1956) provided individual mothering (from 9–4, 5 days/week) for a group of eight, six-month-old institutionally-reared infants for an 8-week period. She found no evidence of significant improvement in postural, "adaptive" or "intellectual" behavior in post-test performance.

That some form of learning can occur during the first week of life has been demonstrated by the teaching experiments of Lipsitt et al. That some form of learning does occur was demonstrated by Marquis (1941). 18 neonates were put on a 4-h feeding schedule. 16 other infants were put on a 3-h schedule. At day 9 the 3-h group was changed to a 4-h schedule. Measures of motor activity showed that the 3-h group had adapted to the 3-h schedule. Casler (1965) provided small extra amounts of tactile stimulation to a group of 8 institutional infants (stroking the middle part of the body) for 20 min each day from week 22 to week 32 and found modest general developmental acceleration (according to Gesell test scores) to be a consequence. Casler performed a parallel study with the same design where the experimental treatment was a sober, continuous repetition of number recitation to the infant's midsection (i.e. one, two, three, four, five, one, two, etc.). 10 weeks of such "enrichment" produced no detectable effects. Fantz and Nevis (1967) suspended one of two small colored objects over each of the cribs of 10 home-reared and 10 institutionally-reared infants from 3 to 24 weeks of age. The familiar object was paired with a novel target and a 20-sec test of the infant's preference was made each week from 3 to 10 weeks and twice monthly from 16 to 24 weeks. No significant experiential effects were found.

My colleagues and I have performed a series of related enrichment studies over a period of 8 years (White, 1967, 1969b). This research, which included four experimental and two control groups (average number of subjects, 15) featured the special arrangement of physical circumstances and activities in which the infant lived, 24 h a day, from birth to 4.5 months of age. Enrichment procedures* included:

---

* The various experimental conditions or enrichment procedures in this series of studies were designed primarily on the basis of several years of observational work with similar infants, the results of each of the experiments and a general intent to provide environmental conditions that would mesh with the emerging interests and rapidly changing abilities of such infants.

extra handling, practices designed to increase head-rearing, swiping at appropriate objects, visual exploration and prehension, the provision of interesting and developmentally appropriate forms and objects in the infant's immediate surround, and the provision of red and white striped mitts designed to make the infant's hands more perceivable. The consequences of these various procedures have repeatedly supported the idea that experience can play an important role in early development. Primary sensorimotor developments such as visual exploration, hand regard, and visually-directed reaching, appeared to be very sensitive to such changes in rearing conditions. Even rudimentary cognitive foundations seem quite open to influence from such apparently innocuous environmental factors (White, 1969a).

Greenberg et al. (1968) following up on this work reports acceleration of the blink response to changes in visible stimulation as a consequence of continuous exposure to objects somewhat similar to those utilized in the work of White et al. 10 home-reared babies were provided with stabiles over their cribs from their 6th to their 14th week of life. The visually-based blink response subsequently came in at about 8 weeks as opposed to 11 weeks for controls.

Earlier it was noted that Dennis and Dennis had reported that minimal social nurturance and opportunities for practicing emerging skills seemed to produce surprisingly little retardation of infant development. Dennis et al., have subsequently reported two studies on infants reared in an institution in Lebanon. In the first of these studies (1957) various infants were tested throughout the 2 to 12 months age range with the Cattell scale. In addition, a group of 4.5 to 6 year old children who had been reared in apparently similar ways in the same institution were tested with the Goodenough draw-a-man, Knox cube and Porteus maze tests. Serious retardation was found increasingly throughout the first year but the older group was only slightly inferior to a comparison home-reared group. While not denying the likelihood of deficits in language-related areas in the other children, the writers point out that the fairly serious retardation of the first year apparently did not lead to parallel serious deficits four years later.

In a second study, Sayegh and Dennis (1965) tested the hypothesis that the deficits seen in the institutional population during the first year of life were attributable to inadequate learning opportunities. Five 7 to 12-month old infants, were given 1 h of supplementary practice to accustom them to the upright position, to encourage interest in objects and to develop manual skills for 15 days. Their rate of development (measured by scores on the Cattell test) was 4 times that of control although they were still severely retarded. Furthermore, when supplementary training ceased, so too did the developmental enhancement.

Two older studies of special interest are those of Irwin (1960) on the effects of reading stories to infants, and of Skeels (1966) on the rearing of institutional infants by retarded women.

Irwin (1960) had working-class mothers read stories to their infants (in their own homes) for 20 min a day from the time the infants were 13 until they were 30 months of age. These children showed significant increases in produced speech sounds, both tokens and types.

Skeels reported in 1938 on the later development of a group of 13 subjects who as young infants had undergone institutional rearing; and beginning at about 18 months of age (range 7.1 to 35.9 months), had spent an average of 18.9 months in an "enriched" atmosphere. The enrichment consisted of living as "house guests" in a home for retarded women rather than in the conventional orphanage. Most of the experimental group was placed into adoptive homes shortly after the experiment ended. Follow-up studies were conducted 2.5 and 21 years later. Though the age at first admission and length of stay at the orphanage in early infancy was quite variable, all experimental subjects appeared retarded ($\overline{X}_{IQ} = 64.3$). At the end of the enrichment period their development had accelerated dramatically ($\overline{X}_{IQ} = 91.8$) in contrast to controls ($\overline{X}_{IQ} = 60.5$). 2.5 years later their improvement had increased ($\overline{X}_{IQ} = 95.9$) and 21 years later the group was grossly normal, in sharp contrast to the control subjects. In the author's (Skeels) opinion, within the general enrichment situation, the intense one-to-one relationship which most of the experimental infants formed with the retarded women was the core factor underlying the positive results.

Recently, several sizeable experimental programs focussed on early intellectual development have been performed in the U.S.A. These newer projects attempt to preclude poor intellectual development by providing a broad heterogeneous pattern of enrichment experiences to home-reared low income infants. As such they are at once directly relevant to the concerns of families with young children and simultaneously less controllable and interpretable than more conventional experimental work. If they produce excellent results and if they record, in detail, how they did, society can reproduce their effots. On the other hand, since it is impossible to exercise a great deal of control over the many experiential factors involved, it is most difficult to determine the varying degrees of effectiveness of the numerous intended or unintended enrichment factors. The Skeels study is, in many respects, similarly constituted; and Skeels points out that his pinpointing of the personal relationship factor can only be considered a post hoc speculation.

Schaeffer (1969) trained 8 full-time college-educated women to tutor low-income Negro infants in their homes. For a 21 month period, beginning at 14 months of age, each of these tutors averaged just under 4, 1-h a day private sessions a week with each of 20 infants. They concentrated on verbal stimulation using books, toys and anything available to maintain the infant's interest. The experimental treatment was frankly opportunistic and evolutionary. The effects on development were striking. Average IQ gains (at 36 months) over controls were 17 points. Equally significant results were obtained on measures of linguistic and perceptual development. In spite of the expense, the results seemed well worth the effort. Two years later, however, after no additional training, the experimental children looked no different from the controls; the gains were lost.

Gordon (1967) has aimed at more than affecting infant development. His goal was to produce a plan for intervention that would be economically viable. He, therefore, trained low-income women with modest educational backgrounds to tutor mothers of infants who ordinarily would develop very poorly. The program featured a series of "learning games" for mothers to play with their infants beginning in the first months of life and continuing throughout infancy. These games were designed on the basis of whatever ideas seemed reasonable in the light of general modern psychological thinking. For example, Piaget's sensorimotor theory (1952, 1954) and its application in the work of Uzgiris and Hunt (1975) and Escalona and Corman (1968) was the basis for many of the games. General ideas about the virtue of extensive exposures to words as labels and as cues to physical differences among objects were the basis for other games. Finally, certain items from standard infant tests were utilized. These ideas plus any others (e.g. the pat-a-cake game) were used to provide the means whereby mothers would become more sensitive to infant development and would be encouraged to devote considerable time to training and presumably enjoying their infants. Scores on the Griffiths' infant scale indicate about a 6-point overall gain for girls and a non-significant 1.5 point gain for boys. Sub-scores in the areas of hearing and speech and eye–hand activity were the most substantial.

Gordon seems to trade impact on infant development for parent involvement and feasibility. As for experimental control, one cannot expect such an action-oriented program to resemble for example, the laboratory-based studies of vocalization rates.

Heber (1972) has reported on a unique and potentially very important intervention study. Children of retarded mothers were brought into a center daily throughout their preschool years (3 months–6 years) and reared for most of their waking hours by a trained staff with paraprofessionals. Had they been reared at home by their own mothers, the children would have very probably developed like their older siblings, into poor achievement patterns. Instead the children in the study have apparently developed levels of ability considerably above the national average ($\overline{X} = 127$ at 66 months of age). Two additional points should be noted as caveats: first, Heber had no more scientifically-based knowledge on how to rear a child than anyone else when he designed his program. He therefore cannot say much in detail about how his results were achieved, beyond describing the general procedures. Second, there is reason to believe that some of the impressive test results were due to extraneous factors such as test sophistication and differential testing schedules of experimentals versus controls. In spite of such difficulties, however, this study has powerful implications for the field of education. Replications by other researchers should be performed soon.

For a summary of intervention studies, between 1965 and 1974, see Bronfenbrenner's analysis recently published by the Federal Department of Health, Education and Welfare (1974).

The opportunity to perform long-term controlled interventions is quite rare. Further, such studies, of necessity, cannot be nearly as rigorously controlled as short-term studies. They are, however, obviously very valuable.

New information on the role of early experience in the development of intelligence

The preschool project

The Harvard Preschool Project began in 1965. Its task was to learn how to structure the experiences of the first 6 years of life so as to help each child make the most of whatever potential he had at birth. For 11 years, a group numbering between 10 and 20 has worked consistently on this problem. Our first few years led us to focus on that period of life between 6 and 24 months of age.

During the first 6 months of life the abilities that children acquire are modest in both number and complexity as compared with those they acquire in the next 18 months. Perhaps the most obvious ability is the capacity to use the hands as tools to reach for and grasp objects. In addition, children ordinarily acquire partial control of the rest of their bodies. By 6 months of age most children can hold their heads erect steadily, and have acquired reasonably complete basic visual and auditory capacities. They are still quite limited and helpless creatures, however. They cannot move their bodies through space more than a few inches or so, except by rolling. They cannot walk, run, climb or even pull themselves to a standing position. Most cannot even pull themselves to a sitting position without help. They do not talk, nor do they understand language. They have nearly no intellectual capacity at all. Compared to the 2-year-old, the 6-month-old is extremely inept.

Not only are the achievements of the first 6 months of life comparatively modest, but I believe the experiences required for their normal development are modest as well. The repeated finding that lasting intellectual deficits do not manifest themselves (for most children who will do poorly later in life) until sometime during the second year of life, is consistent with the notion that most children develop reasonably well during the first months of life. Then, too, our earlier research on institutionally-reared infants (1971) indicated that such children usually score adequately on standard tests of general development throughout the first year of life.

This is not to say that Spitz's "human wrecks" who were devastated by their first year of life in institutions 40 years ago (1945) didn't exist. Nor, is it to say (more generally) that children are not vulnerable during their first months of life. It is rather to say, that most families seem to love and care for their new infants and that the species requirements (from the environment) for the adequate development of primitive skills such as hand-eye coordination in reaching, ear-eye coordination in orienting to sounds, accurate visual convergence and focussing, etc., are most always met by even the poorest of families.

It should be noted that there are research results (White, 1971; Greenberg et al., 1968) that indicate that what passes currently for adequate or normal development is neither inevitable nor optimal. Through controlled modifications of environmental conditions, infants were provided with experiences that meshed with their emerging interests and developing abilities. Repeatedly, the acquisition of abilities was substantially altered. In some instances basic abilities were acquired much more rapidly than in the population as a whole. Babies are not usually reared under such custom-built conditions, however, so the current norms for development in the first 6 months of life remain appropriate. Future generations of children will very probably develop at somewhat more rapid rates as society as a whole becomes more sophisticated about child-rearing practices.

In summary, during the first 6 months of life, the achievements of infants are simple and modest in number. Except for an unfortunate few, most children do not incur any obvious lasting handicaps due to inadequate experiences. Children can rather easily be harmed during this period if subjected to extremely abusive experiences such as: constant darkness, total absence of human contact, physical beatings, and others too horrible to think about. But such extreme experiences are not common as far as anyone can tell. Finally, there is some reason to believe that the "average expectable environment" of today can be significantly improved upon and that children would develop better given the opportunity for more suitable early experiences.

Once the first 6 months end, however, the picture of development changes dramatically. Certain abilities that distinguish man as a species become available for development for the first time. Language learning, for example, becomes possible. So too, do the more complicated forms of social learning involving attachment to another person, perceptions of self and social skills such as the use of another person as a resource.

Not only do tremendously significant processes ordinarily begin to take shape, but for several identifiable and interesting reasons, it becomes much less assured that variations in the "average expectable environment" and resultant experiences will be inconsequential. At about this time, the infant begins to be able to move about either through crawling or scooting, etc. This new capacity enables the infant to do much more to satisfy its remarkably deep curiosity. Unfortunately, however, such infants cannot be allowed to go where and as they will. They would very likely hurt themselves for one thing. They would very likely do some damage for another. They might also create a good deal of extra work for their caretaker for another. Also in cases where slightly older siblings exist, they might get into all sorts of difficulty with them.

The 6 to 8 month old child is usually about to enter into a remarkable period for the formation of basic human qualities, and simultaneously he becomes much more difficult to care for. What seems to result is a rather wide variation in coping styles by generally untrained childrearers (parents and professionals) and a commensurately wide variation in histories of experience by infants. Along with such variations appears to be a gradual crystallization within each child in regard to: rate of language learning, rate of expansion of curiosity, rate of learning of problem-solving skills, and rate and type of social skill and attachment development. By 24 months of age, reasonably reliable indicators of future trends in these and other fundamental areas are usually present. Furthermore, recent evidence from experiments in remedial education suggest that those trends are difficult to modify significantly from 24 months on (Bronfenbrenner). What then are the experiences children undergo

Table I Demographic information: 1-year-old starters ($n = 19$)

Sub ID	Sex	Hollings-head-Redlich code	Family income	Mother education	Father education	Mother[a] occupation
03	F	I	$20 000 or over	College graduate	Post-col. graduate	Secretary
17	F	I	$20 000 or over	College graduate	Post-col. graduate	None
24	M	I	$20 000 or over	Post-col. graduate	Post-col. graduate	(Doctor)
19	F	I	$12 000–$20 000	Partial/jr. col.	Post-col. graduate	(Nurse)
31	M	II	$12 000–$20 000	Post-col. graduate	Post-col. graduate	Restaurant manager
08	M	II	less than $3000	Post-col. graduate	Post-col. graduate	Teacher
20	F	II	$12 000–$20 000	Post-col. graduate	Post-col. graduate	(Teacher)
11	F	II	$12 000–$20 000	College graduate	Post-col.	None
16	M	III	$7000–$12 000	Partial/jr. col.	Partial/jr. col.	None
32	M	III	$3000–$7000	High sch. graduate	Partial/high sch.	None
45	F	III	$7000–$12 000	Partial/high sch.	High sch. graduate	None
44	F	III	$7000–$12 000	Partial/jr. col.	College graduate	None
42	M	III	$7000–$12 000	High sch. graduate	High sch. graduate	(Book-keeper)
43	M	III	$7000–$12 000	High sch. graduate	Partial/voc. col.	None
34	M	IV	$7000–$12 000	Partial/High sch.	High sch. graduate	None
01	F	IV	$7000–$12 000	High sch. graduate	High sch. graduate	None
40	F	IV	$7000–$12 000	Partial/high sch.	Jr. high graduate	None
37	M	V	Under $3000	Partial jr. col.	—	None
41	F	V	Under $3000	Partial/high sch.	Elementary school	None

[a] Parentheses denote Mother's occupation prior to our study.
[b] Parentheses used when parents are divorced and mother is head of household.
[c] Caucasian used to mean of European background other than Irish, Italian, Jewish or Spanish.
[d] Parentheses denote the religious background where parents no longer profess a religious faith.

Father[b] occupation	Mother[c] ethnic	Father[c] ethnic	Mother[d] religion	Father[d] religion	Number of children in household
Chemist	Caucas.	Jewish	None (Prot.)	None	2
Physicist	Caucas.	Caucas.	None	None	2
Univ. professor	Italian	Jewish	Prot.	Jewish	4
Univ. professor	Caucas.	Caucas.	Prot.	Prot.	3
Restaurant owner	Italian	Italian	Catholic	Catholic	3
Ph.D. student	Caucas.	Caucas.	Prot.	Prot.	1
Architect	Jewish	Caucas.	Jewish	Jewish	4
Univ. professor	Italian	Caucas.	None	None	2
Physical ed. teacher	Caucas.	Caucas.	Catholic	Catholic	3
Small repair shop	Irish	Italian	Catholic	Catholic	8
Owner of small catering service	Caucas.	Caucas.	Catholic	Catholic	2
Bank treasurer	Caucas.	Irish	Catholic	Catholic	3
Route service canteen filler	Irish	Italian	Catholic	Catholic	3
Hair-dresser	Jewish	Jewish	Jewish	Jewish	3
Truck-driver	Caucas.	Caucas.	Catholic	Catholic	3
Mainten-ance man	Italian	Italian	Catholic	Catholic	13
Crane operator	Caucas.	Caucas.	Catholic	Prot.	3
(Prof. soldier)	Caucas.	Caucas.	Catholic	—	3
House-painter	—	—	None (Catholic)	None	4

Table I Demographic information: two-year-old starters ($n = 20$)

Sub ID	Sex	Hollings-head-Redlich Code	Family income	Mother education	Father education	Mother[a] occupation
12	M	I	$12 000–$20 000	Post-col. graduate	Post-col. graduate	Prenatal teacher
10	F	I	$20 000 or over	Post-col. graduate	Post-col. graduate	Lawyer
21	M	I	$12 000–$20 000	College graduate	Post-col. graduate	None
05	M	I	$20 000 or over	Partial/ jr. coll.	Post-col. graduate	Nurse
09	F	I	$7000–$12 000	Post-col. graduate	Post-col. graduate	Social worker
13	M	I	$20 000 or over	Post-col. graduate	Post-col. graduate	(Teacher-college)
33	M	I	$20 000 or over	Partial/ jr. coll.	Post-col. graduate	None
02	M	II	$3000–$7000	College graduate	Post-col. graduate	None
38	M	III	$3000–$7000	Partial/ jr. coll.	High sch. graduate	None
35	F	III	$7000–$12 000	Partial/ voc. col.	Partial/ voc. col.	(Lab. technician)
18	F	III	$7000–$12 000	Partial/ jr. col.	Partial/ jr. col.	None
22	F	III	$3000–$7000	Partial/ jr. col.	College graduate	Cocktail waitress
36	M	III	—	High sch. graduate	Partial/ voc. col.	None
39	M	III	$7000–$12 000	Partial jr. col.	High sch. graduate	None
28	F	III	$3000–$7000	Jr. high graduate	Partial/ voc. col.	None
27	M	III	$7000–$12 000	Partial/ jr. col.	College	None
30	F	III	$12 000–$20 000	Jr. high graduate	Partial/ High sch.	Maintenance ct. house
14	M	IV	$3000–$7000	Partial/ High sch.	Partial/ High sch.	(Hair-dresser)
25	M	IV	$3000–$7000	High sch. graduate	Partial/ High sch.	None
07	M	IV	$3000–$7000	Partial/ High sch.	Jr. high graduate	Waitress

[a] Parentheses denote Mother's occupation prior to our study.
[b] Parentheses used when parents are divorced and mother is head of household.
[c] Caucasian used to mean of European background other than Irish, Italian, Jewish, or Spanish.
[d] Parentheses denote the religious background where parents no longer profess a religious faith.

Father[b] occupation	Mother[c] ethnic	Father[c] ethnic	Mother[d] religion	Father[d] religion	Number of children in household
Physician	Jewish	Jewish	Jewish	Jewish	4
	Jewish	Jewish	Jewish	Jewish	3
Lawyer	Caucas.	Caucas.	Prot.	Prot.	2
Psycho-analyst	Caucas.	Caucas.	Catholic	Episcopal.	3
Univ. professor	Caucas.	Spanish	None (Unit.)	None (Catholic)	1
Physician	Caucas.	Jewish	Prot.	Jewish	3
Exec. Shoe Mfg.	Jewish	Jewish	Jewish	Jewish	3
Medical student	Caucas.	Caucas.	Prot.	Prot.	2
Travel agent	Latin America	Latin America	Catholic	Catholic	6
Sr. lab. technician	Caucas.	Caucas.	Catholic	Catholic	6
TV repair show owner	Italian	Italian	Catholic	Catholic	7
(City reg. planner)	Caucas.	Caucas.	None (Catholic)	None (Catholic)	3
Industrial tool salesman	Italian	Italian	Catholic	Catholic	2
Machinist	Irish	Irish	Catholic	Catholic	2
Accountant	Italian	Italian	Catholic	Catholic	2
(Antique dealer)	Greek	Irish	Greek Orthodox	None (Catholic)	3
Court officer	Irish	Irish	Catholic	Catholic	7
MBTA bus driver	Irish	Irish	Catholic	Catholic	2
Painter	Caucas.	Caucas.	None	None	2
Steel worker	Caucas.	Caucas.	Prot.	Prot.	6

between 6 and 24 months of age? How do they vary with the different patterns of developing abilities?

An instrument to measure experiences*

Until very recently we would find no quantitive instruments for use in characterizing the typical experiences of young children**. The followers of Kurt Lewin, Barker, Wright and the Schoggens had long advocated the development of such instruments but until recently, in vain. We have produced an instrument of this kind.

We constructed a coding scheme inductively from observations of many children (White and Watts, et al., 1973). It contains 35 individual and several combination classes, plus a category for those times when no purpose is discernible in the behavior of the subject.

The data to be presented was gathered in a sample of 39 children. They came from a variety of backgrounds, including Anglo-Saxon, Italian and Jewish ancestry. Their families can be grouped according to the widely used Index of Social Position developed by Hollingshead and Redlich (1958) which employs occupation, education, and residence as class criteria. For each child, we predicted either a high or a low level of competence at 3 years of age based upon the levels achieved by older siblings***. Table I portrays various important characteristics of our total sample of children.

Experiences of young children

Table II contains data on the experiences of all the subjects. Note the predominance of non-social tasks. Regardless of whether a child is developing very well or very poorly, he spends far more time oriented toward interactions with physical reality than he does trying to affect people during these age ranges. For 12–15 month old children the figures are 89.7% for non-social tasks versus 10.3% for social tasks. By 18–21 months the figures are 83.8% non-social and 16.2% social; at 24–27 months, 80.0% non-social and 20% social; and at 30 to 33 months they are 79.1% non-social and 20.9% social (see Table III). There is a doubling of social tasks between the first and second birthdays. (Later we will dwell on the rather striking fact that mothers apparently spend rather modest amounts of time in direct interactions with their' children during this period.)

A second rather striking feature of these data is that for the most part, our subjects

---

*The development of this instrument was the work of Kitty Riley Clark, Andrew Cohn, Cherry Wedgewood Collins, Barbara Kaban, and Burton L. White.
** Two other such instruments have since become available (Caldwell, Clarke-Stewart).
*** There was one only child in the study. It was predicted that he would develop very well, on the basis of the apparently high quality of his mother's child-rearing practices.

Table II Typical experiences of 1 and 2 year old children; median group values; percent of time awake

	12–15 mo. N = 19	18–21 mo. N = 19	24–27 mo. N = 20	30–33 mo. N = 20
Social tasks				
To please	0.1	0.0	0.2	0.1
To cooperate	2.8	4.6	3.9	3.5
To gain approval	0.0	0.0	0.0	0.0
To procure a service	1.0	1.0	2.3	1.8
To gain attention	2.2	2.0	2.6	2.8
To maintain social contact	2.2	2.8	5.0	2.7
To avoid unpleasant circumstances	0.0	0.0	0.1	0.0
To annoy	0.0	0.0	0.0	0.0
To direct	0.0	0.1	0.2	0.5
To assert self	0.5	1.5	1.3	1.4
To provide information	0.0	0.0	0.2	0.7
To compete	0.0	0.0	0.0	0.0
To reject overtures	0.0	0.0	0.0	0.0
To enjoy pets	0.0	0.0	0.0	0.0
To converse	0.0	0.0	0.1	0.7
To produce verbalization	0.0	0.0	0.0	0.0
Non-social tasks				
To eat	4.4	10.3	5.5	2.9
To gain information (visual)	16.0	10.6	13.7	7.7
To gain information (visual and auditory)	6.0	6.0	9.8	10.6
Live language directed to child	1.7	1.4	2.8	2.8
Overheard language	0.8	1.3	2.6	2.0
Mechanical language	0.2	0.0	0.0	1.7
Sesame Street	0.0	0.0	0.0	1.2
Non-task	12.2	11.8	9.5	6.8
To pass time	3.4	3.2	2.3	1.7
To find something to do	0.0	0.0	0.0	0.0
To prepare for activity	1.4	2.0	1.7	2.2
To construct a product	0.0	0.0	0.0	0.1
To choose	0.0	0.0	0.0	0.0
To procure an object	3.3	3.1	1.8	2.0
To engage in large muscle activity	0.0	0.0	0.4	0.0
To gain pleasure	0.0	0.0	0.7	0.1
To imitate	0.0	0.0	0.3	0.1
To pretend	0.0	1.5	0.5	1.8
To ease discomfort	0.6	0.4	0.5	0.2
To restore order	0.7	0.6	0.6	0.9
To relieve oneself	0.0	0.0	0.0	0.0
To dress	0.0	0.0	0.0	0.0
To operate a mechanism	0.0	0.2	0.2	0.2
To explore	12.8	6.6	4.6	2.3

Table II (*continued*)

	12–15 mo. N = 19	18–21 mo. N = 19	24–27 mo. N = 20	30–33 mo. N = 20
Mastery	8.7	11.4	8.9	12.7
gross	6.7	2.4	3.9	2.3
fine	2.4	3.9	2.0	6.5
verbal	0.0	0.1	0.0	0.1
To eat and gain information (visual)	4.2	1.9	1.4	0.7
To eat and gain information (visual and auditory, live direct)	0.1	0.0	0.3	0.0

Table III   Percent of time spent in social vs. non-social tasks

	Social tasks	Non-social tasks
12–15 mo. N = 19	10.3*	89.7
18–21 mo. N = 19	16.2	83.8
24–27 mo. N = 20	20.0	80.0
30–33 mo. N = 20	20.9	79.1

*All values are group median percent duration.

Table IV   All tasks: percentage self vs. other initiated

Group	Self initiated	Mother initiated	Other adult initiated
12–15 mo. N = 19	86.5*	13.0	0.0
18–21 mo. N = 19	87.7	9.9	0.0
24–27 mo. N = 20	89.7	8.4	0.3
30–33 mo. N = 20	90.9	7.0	0.2

*All values are group median percent duration.

initiated their own experiences. There is a remarkable consistency in the task-initiation data throughout the 12–33 month period with scores of 86.5, 87.7, 89.7 and 90.9% (See Table IV). The only other person to initiate any substantial fraction of a child's experiences during this age range was his mother*. Furthermore, where tasks are initiated by the child's mother, they are likely to be social tasks and, in particular, to cooperate experiences consisting of simple requests.

Another rather unexpected finding is that the most frequent experience of most children in this age range is what we call gain information – visual, which is staring steadily at one object or scene for at least 3 sec. (For 12–15 month olds, 16.0%; 18–21 months, 10.6%; 24–27 months, 13.7%; and 30–33 months, 7.7%**. Of the many child psychologists I have asked, only one guessed correctly that visual inquiry was the most frequent activity of this age range. Little wonder, however, when you realize how few professionals have studied the 1–3 year old child under natural circumstances.

Non-task behavior (desultory scanning or wandering about) is the second most common activity seen among our 1 and 2 year old children (12.2% at 12–15 months; 11.8% at 18–21 months; 9.5% at 24–27 months; and 6.8% at 30–33 months). During the period studied this experience seems to be declining gradually.

Experiences at 12 to 15 months and development at three years

The central purpose of our natural longitudinal experiment was to identify experiences that contribute maximally to the development of competence in children. We selected our sample of children in order to heighten the probability that we would be studying some children who were developing very well and others who would develop much lower levels of competence. Since groups of such children usually look similar in achievement at about 12 months of age and gradually diverge in achievement sometime late in the second year of life, data on their experiences before they turn 2 years of age interest us the most.

Table V provides socioeconomic status information on the children we observed from their first birthdays and who were most widely separated on measures of competence at three years of age. Our most competent 3 year olds were generally from higher SES levels than our least competent 3 year olds. We shall concentrate our discussion on experiential differences associated with the largest differences in achieved competence.

Although SES clearly influenced the development of competence in our study, the influence was not sufficient to overpower other factors, as seen in the following correlation (Table VI).

As might be expected, the influence of SES on the level of competence achieved at 3 years of age is greatest for intellectual and related skills. SES for these 39 subjects,

---

*A reminder is in order that our data cover only the hours between nine and six on weekdays. Unquestionably, fathers and others initiate some activities for such children on weekends at least.

**All figures are medians of percent of total duration.

Table V   SES characteristics of children with highest and lowest levels of competence at 3 years of age.

Achieved competence level	Hollingshead Redlich SES ratings* (No. of Ss in each category)					Group median
	I	II	III	IV	V	
Highest (n = 8)						
Female	2	2	0	1	0	II
Male	1	1	1	0	0	
Lowest (n = 5)						
Female	0	0	1	1	0	IV
Male	0	0	1	1	1	

*Classes I and II are upper to middle classes, Classes III, IV and V are middle to lower classes. A. B. Hollingshead and R. C. Redlich, *Social Class and Mental Illness* (John Wiley and Sons, New York, 1958).

Table VI   Relationships among major demographic variables and achieved levels of competence (n = 39)

	Overall rank	Social rank†	Non-social rank††
Hollingshead-Redlich SES rating	0.43**	0.00	0.55***
Income	0.16	−0.15	0.28
Mother's education	0.59***	0.27	0.77***
Father's education	0.46**	0.08	0.75***
Mother's occupation†††	0.11	−0.10	0.20
Father's occupation	0.44**	0.05	0.71***

*$P \leq 0.05$; **$P \leq 0.01$; ***$P \leq 0.001$.
Spearman rank correlation; †rank with respect to social skills; ††rank with respect to non-social skills, i.e. linguistic and intellectual skills; †††only 10 of the 39 mothers of the study were employed.

however, only accounted for about 30% of the variance in such achievements. It is to be remembered that we are not talking about a representative sample of children. For one thing we sought out children likely to develop either very well or poorer than average. For another, our selection process produced some lower SES children likely to develop either very well or poorly and higher SES children most of whom were likely to develop well. One cannot claim that results from studies of such children can be generalized to national populations. Nevertheless, in our sample some children from SES levels 3 and 4 held their own with subjects from SES levels 1 and 2 who at age 3 years, were functioning beyond the 95th percentile in basic academically-relevant areas.

Interestingly, SES had no apparent influence whatsoever on the development of social competence in our subjects.

Patterns of tasks during the second year of life that relate to competence at three and five years of age

Multiple regression analyses were performed on the relations among experiences at 12–15 months of age and achievement levels at 3 years of age. We selected those experiences that individually correlated most strongly with competence at 3 years and also occurred regularly in the lives of our children. We used sufficient numbers of experiences to make the analysis heuristically meaningful. Fewer experiences might have been needed for predictive purposes, but would have left us with too sparse a picture. On the other hand, we kept the numbers of experiences small enough to capture impressive predictive power (at least for our sample). The results may be seen in the 8 multiple regressions we ran.

Overall competence
Time spent in 8 experiences at 12–15 months of age predicts how each of our 19 one-year-old starters rank in overall competence at 3 years of age (multiple $r = +0.84$, $P = 0.049$). Procuring a service and gaining attention among the 6 common social experiences are apparently key indicators. High scores in such experience are associated with good overall development. Likewise, high scores in steady staring (gain information–visual) while eating, and eating and listening to live language addressed directly to the child are also associated with good development over the second and third years of life. Low scores in gross motor activity, passing time and procuring objects round out the pattern of tasks experienced at 12–15 months of age and linked to competence at 3 years.

Social competence
Our capacity to predict social competence at 3 years of age is not as impressive as is the case with overall competence (multiple $r = +0.77$, $P = 0.107$). There is substantial overlap in the predictive tasks (5 of 8 are the same). Maintaining social contact replaces seeking attention, gross motor activity drops out and exploring enters the picture. The meanings of the changes are not immediately apparent to us. The major finding is that most of the experiences that lead to general competence apparently also lead to social competence.

Non-social competence
The regression analysis is very strong in respect to the association between early tasks and later non-social competence (multiple $r = +0.92$, $P = 0.001$). 7 of the 8 tasks are the same as in the case of overall competence. Gross motor activity drops out, while preparing for activities enters. High scores in the latter experience are associated with high non-social competence.

Stanford-Binet performance
As might be expected, our data are also strong in regard to the prediction of performance on the Stanford-Binet test at 3 years of age (multiple $r = +0.89$, $P = 0.001$).

Table VII Task experiences (12–15 months) predicting outcome variables (36 months) regression analysis

Dependent variables	Multiple r	P^*	Regression equation
PSP abstract abilities test	0.8568	0.006	Predicted A.A. score = 6.5754 + % duration (0.1240) + % duration (0.1149) + Gain attention Eat and gain info. (v) % duration (0.0782) + % duration (0.1199) + % duration (−0.0367) + Gain info (v) Live language directed to S Pass time % duration (0.2776) Prepare for activity
PSP dissonance test	0.7578	0.068	Predicted dissonance score = 4.8930 + % duration (0.6075) + Procure a service % duration (0.0382) + % duration (0.0654) + % duration (−0.0644) + Gain attention Gain info. (v) Live language directed to S % duration (−0.0173) + % duration (0.5624) Pass time Prepare for activity
Non-social competence rank (1 = high, 39 = low)	0.9176	0.001	Predicted non-social rank = 37.7065 + % duration (−0.6243) + Procure a service % duration (−2.2283) + % duration (−0.3873) + % duration (−1.6.41) + Gain attention Gain info. (v) Live language directed to S % duration (0.0358) + % duration (−1.1897) + % duration (0.2713) Pass time Prepare for activity Procure an object
Stanford-Binet intelligence test	0.8920	0.001	Predicted Binet score = 67.0602 + % duration (1.5902) + % duration (6.5512) + Procure a service Gain attention % duration (0.6994) + % duration (2.9799) + % duration (−0.2671) + Gain info. (v) Live language directed to S Pass time % duration (3.1625) Prepare for activity

362

PSP language test	0.9274	0.001	Predicted language = 46.3204 + % duration (−1.4235) + Procure a service score + % duration (1.9750) + % duration (0.0715) + % duration (1.1439) + Gain attention Gain info. (v) Live language directed to S + % duration (−0.4920) + % duration (1.7519) + % duration (−2.1737) Pass time Prepare for activity Procure an object
Overall competence rank (1 = high, 39 = low)	0.8438	0.049	Predicted overall rank = 23.0248 + % duration (0.1882) + % duration (−2.9090) + Procure a service Gain attention + % duration (0.3765) + % duration (−1.2075) + % duration (0.3407) + Gross motor Eat and gain info. (v) Gain info. (v) mastery + % duration (−1.9713) + % duration (0.0414) + % duration (0.6750) Live language Pass time Procure an object directed to S
Social competence rank (1 = high, 39 = low)	0.7691	0.107	Predicted social rank = 54.0601 + % duration (−2.8875) + % duration (−1.1046) + Procure a service Maintain social contact + % duration (−1.6720) + % duration (−1.7093) + % duration (−0.3008) + Eat and gain info. (v) Live language Pass time directed to S + % duration (−0.7232) + % duration (−1.1852) Procure an object Explore

* Statistical probability.

Again the pattern overlaps with those for the previous analyses, especially for non-social and overall competence.

Language capacity
Once again we find our data predicting with impressive power (multiple $r = +0.93$, $P = 0.001$). And again, we found almost the same pattern of tasks involved.

Abstract thinking ability
As before the predictive power is high (multiple $r = +0.86$, $P = 0.006$) and there is much overlap in the tasks involved.

The ability to sense dissonance
Here we found somewhat lower predictive power (multiple $r = +0.76$, $P = 0.068$). Again, the same core tasks are involved.

What we seem to find surfacing repeatedly in our data is a strong relationship between 6 to 10 of the typical experiences of our children when they are 12–15 months old and their achievement of competence at 3 years of age. According to these analyses, for good general educational development, children at 12–15 months of life should have a good deal of social experience (as we define it) although it need not occupy more than 10–12% of their time. In particular, they should be encouraged in their attempts at seeking attention and assistance (after first determining they cannot handle a task themselves). A note of caution should be added in respect to the task of procuring a service. There is an important distinction to be made between procuring a service in order to maintain social contact on the one hand, versus procuring a service because you want to cope with a task, have tried it first and failed or have thought about it and concluded you could not handle it alone. It is the latter condition we are talking about rather than the former. By 13 months of age, we have found children using such overtures in a skillful manipulative manner. Between 7 or 8 and 13 months of age we have watched such behavioral trends surface in many infants.

Listening to language directed to the child by another person is centrally involved in all of our analyses. Restrictive practices such as lengthy playpen confinement (which lead to high pass time scores) are negatively associated with good development. Less easily understood are the negative correlations of gross motor activity and procuring objects.

In spite of a markedly increased pace of scientific research during the last decade, knowledge with respect to the role of experience in the development of intelligence is still in very short supply. The most powerful information we could have would be information gathered through the use of the experimental method where hypotheses about the influence of experience on intellectual development would undergo actual testing with children. Ideally such experimental procedures should cover long periods of time in a young child's life. The practice of experimentation that lasts a matter of minutes, or at most an hour or two, will not lead to a proper scientific understanding of the cumulative effects of experience on the development of the human mind.

Although our current knowledge is admittedly fragmentary, what we do have is sufficient for certain purposes. First, it appears that certain developmental acquisitions make considerably greater demands upon experience than others. We have learned, in recent years, that visual motor capacities in the first months of life apparently require only common experiences with patterned and variable light images seen under conditions of normal illumination. Apparently, no special tuition is necessary for the normal development of visual focussing ability, visual motor pursuit and the several other related capacities. Put another way, it would appear that the average expectable environment within a broad range of variation is sufficient to insure good development of such abilities. However, we have also learned that ordinary variations in average expectable environments make considerably greater difference in the rate and quality with which language achievement takes place. Certain processes, therefore, seem to be more environmentally sensitive than others. Such differences in sensitivity become extremely important when one tries to understand the role of experience in development.

From various sources, we know that relatively little language learning takes place in the first half year of life, but that a tremendous amount takes place from that point on to the second or third birthday. With respect to language development, we not only have learned that variations in environmental circumstances are highly significant for the acquisitional process, but we have also learned something about the timing of the developmental process.

Our most powerful view of the growth of intellectual ability is that view provided by Piaget. That view, also, points to the period from about 6 or 7 months of age on through the next year and a half or two as a particularly sensitive one with respect to intellectual curiosity and the building of intellectual substructures. Recent research suggests strongly that the natural inclination of adults to restrict locomobility in the newly crawling child is likely to interfere with both linguistic and intellectual development. The free-roaming infant has access to a variety of experiences that nourish linguistic and intellectual development. The child confined to a small area, out of consideration for possible accidents or damage to the house, etc., seems in contrast to be less able to profit from developmentally suitable experiences.

Given the many restrictions or obstacles in the way of the scientific study of the role of experience in human development, I would predict that the rounding out of our knowledge base will be a very slow process. This process is likely to stretch over several decades. There is then all the more reason for international cooperation in this particular endeavor. Researchers from the various countries involved in such work should make a special effort to pool their resources and their findings. Children appear to behave similarly in many fundamental areas regardless of nationality. Although one must not forget situational idiosyncracies nor ignore important cultural values, there seems to be a core of knowledge of human development which is linked more to the species than to any individual country, family or child.

Literature cited

Ainsworth, M. D. Salter and Bell, S. M. (1967) *Some Contemporary Patterns of Mother-Infant Interaction in the Feeding Situation*, Oral presentation at the inaugural meeting of the Center for Advanced Study in the Developmental Sciences and join study group with the Ciba Foundation, London, pp. 13–17

Anderson, L. D. (1939) The predictive value of infancy tests in relation to intelligence at five years, *Child Devel. 10*, 203–212

Bayley, N. (1940) Mental growth in young children, *Yearb. Nat. Soc. Stud. Educ. 39*, 11–47

Bayley, N. (1965) Comparisons of mental and motor test scores for ages 1–15 months by sex, birth order, race, geographical location, and education of parents, *Child Devel. 36*, 379–411

Bloom, B. S. (1965) *Stability and Change in Human Characteristics*, John Wiley and Sons, New York

Bowlby, J. (1951) *Maternal Care and Mental Health*, Monograph 2, World Health Organization, Geneva

Brackbill, Y. (1962) Research and clinical work with children. Some views on Soviet Psychology, Chapter V, *Am. Psychol. Ass.*

Bronfenbrenner, U. (1974) *Is Early Intervention Effective*? A report on Longitudinal Evaluations of Preschool Programs, pp. 74–25, DHEW Publication No. (OHD)

Brown, R. and Bellugi, U. (1964) Three processes in the child's acquisition of syntax, *Harv. Educ. Revi. 34*, 133–151

Buhler, C. and Hetzer, H. (1935) *Testing Children's Development from Birth to School Age*. Farrar and Reinhart, New York

Caldwell, B. M. (1968) A new "approach" to behavioral ecology. In: *Minnesota Symposia on Child Psychology, II* (J. P. Hill, ed.) University of Minnesota Press, Minn.

Caldwell, B. M., Wright, C. M., Honig, A. S. and Tannenbaum, J. (1969) *Infant Day Care and Attachment*, Paper read as part of a panel on Impact of Evolving Institutional Settings on Early Child Development: Issues and Research Findings at the 46th Annual Meeting of the American Orthopsychiatric Association

Casler, L. (1961) Maternal deprivation: a critical review of the literature, *Monogr. Soc. Res. Child Devel. 26*, No. 2, Serial No. 80

Casler, L. (1965) The effects of supplementary verbal stimulation on a group of institutionalized infants, *J. Child Psychol. Psychiat. 6*, 19–27

Cattell, P. (1940) *The Measurement of Intelligence of Infants and Young Children*, Psychological Corporation, New York

Charlesworth, W. R. (1963) *The Role of Surprise on Novelty in the Motivation of Curiosity Behavior*, Paper read at Society for Research in Child Development, Berkeley

Church, J. (1966) *Three Babies: Biographies of Cognitive Development*, Random House, New York

Clarke-Stewart, K. A. (1973) Interactions between mothers and their young children: characteristics and consequences, *Monogr. Soc. Res. Child Devel. 38*, Nos. 6–7, Serial No. 153

Cole, L. (1959) *A History of Education*, Rinehart and Company, New York

David, M. and Appel, G. (1961) A study of nursery care and nurse-infant interaction. In: *Determinants of Infant Behavior* (B. M. Foss, ed.) pp. 121–136, T. and A. Constable, London

Denenberg, V. H. (1967) Stimulation in infancy, emotional reactivity, and exploratory behavior. In: *Biology and Behavior. Neurophysiology and Emotion* (D. H. Glass, ed.) Russell Sage Foundation and Rockefeller University Press, New York

Dennis, W. and Dennis, S. G. (1941) Infant development under conditions of restricted practice and minimum social stimulations, *Genet. Psychol. Monogr. 23*, 147–155

Dennis, W. and Najarian, P. (1957) Infant development under environmental handicap, *Psychol. Monogr. Gen. Appl. 71*, No. 7, whole No. 436

Eisenberg, R. B. (1966) The development of hearing in man: an assessment of current status, *Rep. Natl. Adv. Neurol. Dis. Blind. Conc.*

Erikson, E. (1950) *Childhood and Society*, Norton, New York

Escalona, S. K. (1968) *The Roots of Individuality*, Aldine Publishing Company, Chicago

Fantz, R. L. and Nevis, S. (1967) The predictive value of changes in visual preferences in early infancy. In: *The Exceptional Infant* (J. Hellmuth, ed.) Vol. I, Special Child Publications, Seattle, Wash.

Fitzgerald, H. E., Lintz, L. N., Brackbill, Y. and Adams, G. (1967) Time perception and conditioning and autonomic response in human infants, *Percept. Mot. Skills 24*, 479–486

Flavell, J. (1963) *The Developmental Psychology of Jean Piaget*, Van Nostrand, Princeton, N. J.

Freud, S. (1957) Three essays on the theory of sexuality (1905). *Standard Edition of Complete Psycholological Works of Sigmund Freud 7*, pp. 1901–1905, Hogarth Press and Institute of Psychoanalysis, London

Friedlander, B. Z., McCarthy, J. J. and Soforenko, A. Z. (June 1965) *Automated Psychological Evaluation and Stimulus Enrichment With Severely Retarded Institutionalized Infants*, Oral presentation to the American Association on Mental Deficiency (Psychology Section)

Furfey, P. H. and Muehlenbein, J. (1932) The validity of infant intelligence tests, *J. Genet. Psychol. 40*, 219–223

Gesel, A. and Amatruda, C. S. (1949) *Developmental Diagnosis*, Paul B. Hoeber, New York

Gesell, A., Ilg, F. L. and Bullis, G. P. (1949) *Vision: Its Development in Infant and Child*, Hoeber

Gollin, E. S. (1967) Research trends in infant learning. In: *Exceptional Infant* (J. Hellmuth, ed.) Special Child Publications, Seattle, Wash.

Gordon, I. and Lally, F. R. (1967) *Intellectual Stimulation for Infants and Toddlers*, The Institute for the Development of Human Resources, University of Florida

Greenberg, D., Uzgiris, I. C., and Hunt, J. McV. (1968) Hastening the development of blink-response with looking, *J. Genet. Psychol. 113*, 167–176

Griffiths, R. (1954) *The Abilities of Babies*, University of London Press, London

Harlow, H. F. (1962) Development of affection in primates. In: *Roots of Behavior* (E. S. Bliss, ed.) Harper, New York

Hartline, H. K. (1949) Inhibition of activity of visual receptors by illuminating nearby retinal areas in the limulus eye, *Fed. Proc. 8*, 69

Hebb, D. (1949) *Organization of Behavior*, John Wiley and Sons, New York

Heber, R. (1972) *Rehabilitation of Families at Risk for Mental Retardation*, Progress Report to DHEW

Hollingshead, A. B. and Redlick, F. C. (1958) *Social Class and Mental Illness*, John Wiley and Sons, New York

Horowitz, F. D. (1968) Infant learning and development: retrospect and prospect, *Merrill-Palmer Q. Behav. Devel. 14*, 101–120

Hunt, J. McV. (1961) *Intelligence and Experience*, Ronald Press, New York

Hunt, J. McV. (1965) Intrinsic motivation and its role in psychological development. In: *Nebraska Symposium on Motivation*. (D. Levine, ed.) pp. 139–282, University of Nebraska Press, Lincoln, Nebraska

Irwin, O. C. (1960) Infant speech: effect of systematic reading of stories, *J. Speech Hear. Res. 3*, 187–190

Jensen, A. R. (1969) How much can we boost IQ and Scholastic Achievement? *Harvard Educ. Rev. 39*, 1

Kagan, J. (1964) American longitudinal research on psychological development, *Child Devel. 35*, 1–32

Kaye, H. (1965) The conditioned Babkin reflex in human newborns, *Psychon. Sci. 2*, 287–288

Knobloch, H. and Pasamanick, B. (1960) Environmental factors affecting human development, before and after births, *Pediatrics 26*, 2

Lettvin, J. Y., Maturana, H. R., McCulloch, W. S. and Pitts, W. H. (1959) What the frog's eye tells the frog's brain, *Proc. Instit. Radio Eng. 47*, 1940–1951

Levine, S. (1957) Infantile experience and resistance to physiological stress, *Science, 126*, 405

Lintz, L. M., Fitzgerald, H. E. and Brackbill, Y. (1967) Conditioning the eyeblink response to sound in infants, *Psychon Sci. 7*, 12

Lipsitt, L. P. (1967) Learning in the human infant. In: *Early Behavior Comparative and Developmental Approaches* (H. W. Stevenson, E. H. Hess and H. L. Rheingold, eds.) pp. 225–247, Wiley, New York

Lipsitt, L. P. (1963) Learning in the first year of life. In: *Advances in Child Development and Behavior* (L. P. Lipsitt and C. C. Spiker, eds.) pp. 147–195, Vol. I, Academic Press, New York

Lipsitt, L. P., Pederson, L. J. and Delucia, C. (1966) Conjugate reinforcement of operant responding in infants, *Psychon. Sci. 4*, 67–68

Marquis, D. P. (1941) Learning in the neonate: the modification of behavior under three feeding schedules, *J. Exp. Psychol. 29*, No. 4

McCarthy, D. (1954) Language development in children. In: *Manual of Child Psychology* (L. Carmichael, ed.) pp. 492–630, 2nd edn., John Wiley and Sons, New York

Mead, M. (1951) Two-Child Care in Samoa. In: *Readings in Child Psychology* (W. Dennis, ed.) Prentice Hall, New York

Moss, H. A. (1967) Sex, age and state as determinants of mother-infant interactions, *Merrill-Palmer Q. Behav. Devel. 13*, 19–36

Papoušek, H. (1961) Conditioned motor digestive reflexes in infants. II, A new experimental method for the investigation, *Cesk Pediat. 15*, 981–988

Piaget, J. (1952) *The Origins of Intelligence in Children*, International Universities Press, New York

Piaget, J. (1954) *The Construction of Reality in the Child*, Basic Books, New York

Rheingold, H. L. (1956) The modification of social responsiveness in institutional babies, *Monogr. Soc. Res. Child Devel. 21*, S. No. 63, No. 2

Rheingold, H. L. (1961) The effect of environmental stimulation upon social and exploratory behavior in the human infant. In: *Determinants of Infant Behavior* (B. M. Foss, ed.) pp. 143–171, Vol. I, Wiley, New York

Ricciuti, H. N. (1964) *Object Grouping and Selective Ordering Behavior in 12 to 24-month-old Infants*, Paper read at a Conference on Infancy Research at Merrill-Palmer Institute, Detroit, Mich.

Ricciuti, H. N., and Johnson, L. J. (1965) *Developmental Changes in Categorizing Behavior from Infancy to the Early Preschool Years*, Paper read at the Society for Research in Child Development Meeting, Minn.

Sayegh, and Dennis, W. (1965) The effect of supplementary experiences upon the behavioral development of infants in institutions, *Child Devel. 36*, No. 1.

Schaefer, Earl. (1969) *It Works*, Infant Education Research Project, U.S. Department of HEW

Schwarting, B. H. (1954) Testing infant's vision, *Am. J. Ophthal. 38*, 714–715

Siqueland, E. (1964) Operant conditioning of head-turning in four-month infants, *Psychon. Sci. 1*, 223–224

Skeels, H. M. (1966) Adult status of children with contrasting early life experience, *Monogr. Soc. Res. Child Devel. 31*, 3, Serial No. 105

Skeels, H. M., Vpdegroff, C., Willman, B. L. and William, H. M. (1938) *A Study of Environmental Stimulation. An Orphan Preschool Project*, University Iowa State Child Welfare, 15, No. 4

Spelt, D. K. (1938) Conditioned responses in the human fetus in utero, *Psychol. Bull. 35*, 712–713

Spitz, R. A. (1945) Hospitalism: an inquiry into the genesis of psychiatric conditions in early childhood, *The Psychoanalytic Study of the Child*, pp. 53–74, Vol. I, International Universities Press, New York

Thomas, A., Chess, S., Birch, H. G., Herzig, M. E. and Dorn, S. (1964) *Behavioral Individuality in Early Childhood*, New York University Press, New York

Uzgiris, I. C., and Hunt, J. McV. (1975) *Assessment in Infancy*, University of Illinois Press, Chicago, Ill.

White, B. L., Castle, P. and Held, R. (1964) Observations on the development of visually-directed reaching, *Child Devel. 35*, 349–364

White, B. L. (1967) An experimental approach to the effects of experience on early human behavior. In: *Minnesota Symposium on Child Psychology* (J. P. Hill, ed.) pp. 201–225, Vol. I, University of Minnesota Press, Minneapolis, Minn.

White, B. L. (1969a) The initial coordination of sensorimotor schemes in human infants. Piaget's ideas and the role of experience. In: *Studies in Cognitive Development. Essays in Honor of Jean Piaget* (J. H. Flavell and D. Elkind, eds.) pp. 237–256, Oxford University Press, New York

White, B. L. (1969b) Child development research. An edifice without a foundation, *Merrill-Palmer Q. Behav. Devel. 15*, 50–79

White, B. L. (1969c) *Moment-to-Moment Tasks of Young Children*, Paper read at a symposium presented at the Society for Research in Child Development, Santa Monica, Calif.

White, B. L. (1971) *Human Infants. Experience and Psychological Development*, Prentice Hall, Englewood Cliffs, N. J.

White, B. L., and Watts, J. C., et al. (1973) *Experience and Environment: Major Influences on the Development of the Young Child*, Vol. I, Prentice Hall, Englewood Cliffs, N. J.

White, R. W. (1959) Motivation reconsidered. The concept of competence, *Psychol. Rev. 66*, No. 5

Wright, H. F. (1960) Observational child study. In: *Handbook of Research Methods in Child Development* (P. Mussen, ed.) pp. 71–139, Wiley, New York

Yarrow, L. J. (1961) Maternal deprivation. Toward an empirical and conceptual re-evaluation, *Psychol. Bull. 58*, 459–490

Yarrow, L. J. (1964) Separation from parents during early childhood. In: *Child Development Research* (M. L. Hoffman and L. W. Hoffman, eds.) Vol. I, Russell Sage Foundation, New York

Genetics, environment and intelligence, edited by A. Oliverio
© *Elsevier/North-Holland Biomedical Press, 1977*

On cultural deprivation 18

JEROME KAGAN

Introduction

Every society presents its members with a set of psychological requirements and a calendar announcing the approximate age of expected appointments. The substance of the requirements is a function of the unstated, and often unconscious, presuppositions of the culture as well as the pragmatic skills and characterological traits most citizens recognize are necessary to maintain the society's functions. Most families in a given community are aware of these values and prepare their young children for their future evaluation during adolescence and early adulthood. The fifth century Athenians esteemed physical coordination, 18th century colonial Americans valued Christian piety and conformity, the Utku Eskimo of Hudson Bay, control of aggression. The families in these settings tried to socialize the locally sacred qualities in their young. But despite a consensual prototype toward which all move, there is always variation in the level of attainment or perfection of the profile of prized attributes. Indeed, if a characteristic was equally perfected in all adults it would not be among the cherished dimensions, for it would be of no value in differentiating among citizens. That is why an erect posture and a pleasing manner, though appreciated, are rarely high in the hierarchy of special qualities. They are too easy to obtain.

If modern families are a correct guide to the past, it was probably the case then, as it is now, that children from families with greater power, status and wealth were in firmer possession of the important characteristics than were the less privileged. This is the puzzle we seek to understand. Is this because the former had different genetic constitution, treated their children differently, were more confident that they could influence their children's future, were more effective role models, or is the difference due to a combination of these factors?

All societies invent categories that simultaneously describe and explain the 10–20% of children whose profile of behavioral accomplishment is least pleasing. In trying to understand this variation, the community can select from a limited number of interpretations: luck, super-natural power, diet, illness, heredity, family practices, peer experiences and institutional practices, each of which is seen as potentially influencing the abilities, skills, motivation, energy or emotions of the child. Since some of these forces will be either inconsistent with the society's cosmology or just plain absent, in practice, the adult community has only a few choices. In modern Mayan Indian villages in northwest Guatemala the valued traits include physical endurance, alertness to opportunity, and responsibility. A failure to obtain some semblence of these qualities by 10 years of age is usually blamed on date of birth, demons, or failure of the family to train the 7 and 8 year old properly. Rarely is luck, heredity, or peer experience called upon to account for success or failure. In North America and Western Europe, the valued traits form three competence-performance pairs – intelligence and academic success, an affection for people and effective habits of social interaction, and a desire for autonomy and behavioral independence. Although the latter two are prized, the community believes that the first pair, intellectual competence and school success, is most important for the attainment of economic security and status and, hence, award it a special salience.

Since there is such obvious diversity in the cognitive, attitudinal and motivational qualities of preadolescents who score in the lowest 20% of the norm referenced instruments we use to evaluate intellectual and academic skills, it is reasonable to invent nominal classifications that will simultaneously separate the heterogenous group into more homogenous subpopulations and imply the reason for the deviance of each population.

The organically mentally retarded are the smallest group. It is presumed that they have a defect in central nervous system function, due to a genetic or at least biological etiology, that leads to poor cognitive performance. A second group, called minimally brain damaged, is assumed to have a subtle central nervous system impairment, either cell damage, slower development of the central nervous system, or biochemical disturbance, that cannot be localized, but which impairs cognitive functioning. A third group, called the physically handicapped, has obvious sensory or physical impairments that can be expected to impede cognitive development because of the facilitating function that keen sight and hearing have for cognitive work. A fourth group, classified as emotionally disturbed, presumably has an intact biological system but is held to be anxious, hostile, or inattentive because of unknown psychological experiences encountered during the first half dozen years. After these four groups have been set aside, there is still a sizable group of children who still score in the lowest 20%, perhaps half of the original sample. They are not evenly distributed across the society and are more often found in urban than in rural areas and in families which are not only economically less secure than the majority but also hold a value system different from the majority, two characteristics that define the term ethnic minority.

In the United States and Western Europe, children from ethnic minorities always make up the majority of the group who fail in school and obtain low scores on tests of intellectual capacity. Given the cosmology of the modern West, only two reasonable interpretations are possible. One assumes that these children are biologically incapable of learning academic skills easily and effectively; the second is that experiences in the family and neighborhood did not establish a properly rich repertoire of language or an appropriate profile of motivation, standards, and styles of problem solving. The educated citizens in our contemporary society who are egalitarian in philosophy are reluctant to blame the child for his plight. Hence they invented a term that lifted the responsibility from the child and family and placed it in a nether world between the home and the national legislature, somewhere in the "culture." During the 1960s this child was called culturally deprived, meaning he was deprived of psychological stimulation as an infant, encouragement as a preschool child, and proper cultural experiences as a preadolescent. The unstated referent was a middle-class growth experience. But the term cultural deprivation, which was only invented 20 years ago, became obsolescent when ethnic minorities resented the implication that their children were deficient in anything. They insisted their children were merely different. Hence the term learning disabled or academically handicapped has increased in usage. But whatever the term, we should not continue to quarrel about the label to apply to these children, it always involves a reference to cognitive ability.

It is interesting to note that the current, presumably sophisticated, discussion of the different intellectual profiles of lower class black and middle class white children has a close analogue in the debates among Colonial Americans in the late 18th century. Thomas Jefferson believed, like Arthur Jensen, that the memory competence of Negroes was equal to that of the whites, but the black was deficient in reasoning and imagination.

> "Comparing them by their faculties of memory, reason and imagination it appears to me that in memory they (Negroes) are equal to whites; in reason much inferior, as I think one could scarcely be found capable of tracing and comprehending the investigations of Euclid; and that imagination they are dull, tasteless and anomolous .... some have been liberally educated and all have lived in countries where the arts and sciences are cultivated to a considerable degree .... But never yet could I find that a black had uttered a thought above the level of plain narration; never see an elementary trait of painting or sculpture."

(Thomas Jefferson, Notes on Virginia, p. 139–140; from Jordan, 1969, p. 436–437.)

The contemporary debate on the nature and cause of differences in cognitive ability contains an old refrain with roots deep in the past for the same two issues emerge again and again. Do populations in a society differ on a general intellectual skill or on specified talents? Are the group differences innate or acquired? Jefferson, like J. P. Guilford, believed in a profile of specific abilities, but, like Jensen, believed that the deficiency in reasoning was innate. Benjamin Rush and Samuel Smith, among others, believed the deficiences to be complex but a product of slavery and, therefore, remedial (Jordan, 1969). It is interesting that Jefferson did not suggest that other equally obvious psychological differences between negro slave and free white were innate. The differences in cleanliness and thievery between slave and slave owner were regarded as acquired because 18th century Americans assumed that the creator had to have given all men morality since a sense of right and wrong was necessary for survival. Reasoning and imagination, it was implied, were less essential; presumably some could get along without them. Additionally, grace of phrase and keeness of mind brought a special status to the holder that could not be attained by simple honesty. There is a final reason why the argument for innateness is always easier to propose for intellectual than for other qualities. Morality and character seem to be products of our will. We have the sense that we can be honest and kind if we choose. But insight, an elegant metaphor, or a creative invention seem beyond volition. That is one reason why we award much more respect to Kant, Beethoven or Einstein than we do to the most honest of men. The belief that elegant intellectual products cannot be had through simple persistence, despite Edison's epigram about the ratio of perspiration to inspiration, is based on the faith that forces beyond our control are contributing to mental ability. In a society that respects rational, material explanations that can be confirmed or refuted in empirical observation, it is reasonable to suppose that biological forces emanating from heredity would comprise that special force.

If we believe we can affect change in a personal quality we are likely to award formative power to the environment. If we have the sense that consciousness is insufficient, we are more prepared to award influence either to external forces, like social prejudice, or to biological factors, like heredity. Most societies award a special potency to qualities that cannot simply be willed, like the ability to trance or being born with a cawl. Moreover, rare qualities are more exciting than common ones. A leaf seems less beautiful than a flower; a robin not as lovely as a heron, not because of symmetry of form but, we suggest, because the second instance is less common. (Of course some rarities are devalued, mental retardation, schizophrenia among them, but that is because they violate basic assumptions about proper behavior.) Thus, those valued human qualities that are less frequent and seem beyond our sphere of personal domination have a special power to either awe or frighten us. We are tempted, quite naturally, to attribute their occurrence to forces we cannot alter. In this sense the environmental explanation of cultural deprivation is intuitively more difficult to defend than the biological one. Given the paucity of firm evidence, it is likely that a committed defense of the nurture explanation of differences in cognitive ability derives its strength, in part, from a wish to believe that an egalitarian society can be achieved.

The problem

The problem is to understand why the children of economically disadvantaged minority families attain lower scores on local tests of intellectual ability and master school tasks more slowly. The problem can be simplified by noting that being a member of an ethnic minority adds only a little to the functional relation. Relative poverty is the major predictor of both intelligence test scores and grades. Moreover, the relation between relative poverty and cognitive ability is even found in small isolated subsistence farming villages in Latin America and Africa where the range of wealth between poor and middle class is $50 a year rather than $15 000, and where all families are impoverished by American standards.

The presumed explanations

The candidates for explanation of the relation between poverty and academic progress fall into four complementary, not mutually exclusive, categories. All four presumed etiologies are hypothetical essences which, like Newton's aether, may turn out to be invalid ideas.

Cognitive ability. A unified intelligence versus an orchestration of talents
One presumed cause of failure on academic and IQ tests is "deficient intelligence". That statement might have meaning if the referent for the non-deficient pole could be specified absolutely. The sentence, "John's eyesight is deficient," has meaning, for the diagnosis of impairment is relative to an absolute criterion of 20–20 vision. With operations and corrective lenses, most children could have adequate eyesight, at least theoretically. But deficient intelligence is diagnosed with respect to the ability of other children. Although the scores on IQ tests seem to imply an absolute criterion, because 100 is claimed to be the average score, all the tests are age graded and based upon a particular norming sample. Hence it is not possible for all children to be of adequate intelligence. Success on a certain set of questions on either the Stanford – Binet or the Wechsler intelligence tests has no meaning apart from the age, nationality, and language of the child taking the test.

But let us ignore this problem and assume for the moment that the IQ score does indeed reflect a biological quality of the child, best defined as "the ability to profit from new experiences and the ability to learn new symbolic information quickly", a definition with which few would quarrel. The difficulty with that definition is that there is often no relation between the child's IQ score, the presumed index of his intelligence, and the ease with which the child learns a new set of symbolic codes (Holtzman et al., 1975). Moreover, investigations of cognitive functioning which sample a very broad set of mental abilities do not always find uniformly high correlations among test scores (Stevenson et al., 1976). This is not only true of modern societies, it is true of children in non-modern communities as well. Rogoff has found no relation between quality of recognition memory for objects and recall of sentences in 8–9 year old children living in an Indian village on Lake Atitlan (Rogoff, unpublished*). The lack of unity in a varied battery of cognitive performances, which

---

* Rogoff, B. R. (1976) A study of Cognition in Indian Villages.

holds at all ages, is inconsistent with a position that assumes all children possess differing amounts of some hypothetical mental competence. The postulation of a general intellectual factor is based on the results of factor analyses of mental test data which typically reveal that the first factor contains more variance than any other. But this is not reason enough to posit a "general intelligence". The first factor could just as well index a generalized factor of motivation, linguistic knowledge, or expectation of success that was common to all the test performances.

The alternative view, promoted most extensively by J. P. Guilford (1967), argues for specificity in intellectual functions. Guilford posits 120 different types of abilities based on cognitive processes, nature of information coded and manipulated, and final products. This view is not popular because of the complexity of the conclusion and the awkwardness of its practical implications. No one wants to contemplate administering 120 different tests to children to discover their talents. We prefer the aesthetic simplicity of a single concept and are willing to distort reality, up to a point, to obtain it. Like most poets, when scientists must choose between a beautiful but slightly less accurate statement and a less beautiful but more accurate one, they are tempted to choose the former if they can get away with it. The cognitive profiles of academically retarded children of poverty are more supportive of Guilford than of Spearman, for these children are not consistently less adept than middle-class, academically competent children on varied aspects of intellectual functioning, including memory, perceptual analysis, reasoning, and evaluation.

We believe that the poor school-performance of lower class children is due to a few very specific cognitive impairments, exacerbated by motivational factors. Use and comprehension of the language of the society is one of these central competences. The correlation between school progress and scores on standard vocabulary tests is consistently high and has the highest correlation with school grades of any cognitive ability. Failure to develop the vocabulary forms and language style of the school environment is usually a correlate of school failure. The academically retarded child typically has a less sophisticated repertoire of the linguistic forms used by the school and by the middle class majority. It is still not clear whether the lower class child has, in an absolute sense, a limited language reservoir and limited ability to process language or just a different set of language forms. High school dropouts who obtain lower scores than middle class academically talented children on the vocabulary scales of the standard intelligence tests obtain higher scores than the middle class when they are asked about the meaning of street argot.

Since reading ability, which is the cornerstone of school success, is dependent on language resouces it is at least reasonable to suppose that the causes of the academic deficiency lie with the language repertoire of the lower class child rather than with his ability to learn the symbolic meaning of visual forms. We recently tried to teach some isolated, illiterate Indian children 9 years of age the semantic meaning of 20 logograms (Kagan et al., unpublished*). Most learned the meaning of the 20 symbols

---

*Kagan, J., Klein, R. E., Finley, G., Rogoff, B. and Nolan, E. (1976) Cognitive development. A cross-cultural study.

in less than a half dozen exposures and were able to read lengthy "sentences" composed of these logograms (see also Gleitman and Rozin, 1973).

Minimal brain damage

A second presumed cause of academic failure among poor children is a subtle anatomical or biochemical lesion in the central nervous system. These children are called "minimally brain damaged" (Wender, 1971). The adjective minimal is used because it has been difficult to locate the site of the lesion. The bases for the diagnosis are hyperactivity, clumsiness and poor performance on tests that require copying designs and perceptual analysis, a syndrome which some believe reflects damage to brain stem areas and, hence, difficulty in concentration and motor coordination. We should note here the paradox that although the main problem in school progress is linguistic, most who believe that academically retarded children are minimally brain damaged do not believe the lesion is in the language hemisphere.

The problem with this explanation of academic retardation is that children diagnosed as minimally brain damaged perform similarly to academically retarded children who are diagnosed as biologically intact (Mattis et al., 1975). Moreover, children diagnosed as brain damaged perform more poorly on subscales of intelligence tests measuring language and acquired knowledge than they do on questions requiring more dynamic cognitive processes like memory and reasoning. The hypothesis of minimal brain damage gains its greatest strength from the established fact that there is more disease and greater reproductive risk accompanying pregnancy and delivery among lower class than among middle class parents. Since toxemia, prematurity and anoxia at delivery can lead to damage to the central nervous system it is logical to assume that the poor child is subject to greater risk for central nervous system trauma during the pre-, peri-, and early postnatal periods.

Developmental retardation

A third candidate for explanation is a slower rate of development of those parts of the brain that are involved in cognitive functions, especially language, or slower development of monitoring cognitive functions as a result of lack of environmental challenge.

One specific form of immaturity is a delay in the normal dominance of that part of the left hemisphere primarily responsible for detecting and comprehending language. Dominance of the left or right hemisphere of the brain with respect to language is often assessed by putting earphones on a child and simultaneously presenting two different words to the two ears, and then asking the child which word he heard. If he consistently reports the word played to his right ear, he is regarded as having left hemisphere dominance for language; if he reports the word played to his left ear he is regarded as having right hemisphere dominance for language. It is believed that this is because there is a stronger neurological connection between each ear and the opposite side of the brain (i.e., the right ear and the left hemisphere, the left ear and the right hemisphere).

The results of experiments comparing normal and reading retarded children are inconclusive. In one study, for example, 5 and 6 year old children with serious delays in speech were compared with normal children. They heard 40 different word pairs, differing in one phonetic element (for example leg versus led). The 40 different word pairs were read to the child as well as 40 pairs or trios of numbers. Although the language-retarded children differed from the normal children in reporting the numbers (they reported more digits heard in the left ear than the right) they did not differ from normals in reporting words. Both normal and language-retarded children reported two-thirds of the words they heard in the right ear, indicating normal left hemisphere dominance for language. But the difference in reporting of numbers implies a possible difference in brain functioning between the two groups (Sommer and Taylor, 1972).

Some believe that a child whose left hemisphere areas were slower to mature (myelination of the areas of the temporal lobe typically occur later in development) would be slower in mastering the competence necessary for reading. The child would eventually develop these skills, but perhaps a year or two late. Presumably if one could identify these children in kindergarten, the schools could either begin some simple tutoring in reading skills or, at the least, refrain from coming to the premature conclusion that the children were permanently unable to master school skills. In one study (Satz et al., unpublished*) diagnostic tests were initially given to a large number of boys entering kindergarten. Two years later the scientists assessed the boys' reading levels at the end of Grade 1. 18 children were diagnosed as being severely retarded in reading at the end of Grade 1 (4% of the entire group) and the kindergarten tests had predicted low levels of mastery for all 18 of these children. The most sensitive tests were (1) knowledge of the alphabet, (2) a test that seemed to measure reflectivity – impulsivity, and (3) a test in which the child first had to learn numbers for each of the fingers on his hands; the examiner then touched one finger or several fingers (the child could not see his own hand) and the child had to say the number of the finger or fingers touched by the examiner. This test required the coordination of both perception and memory. The child had to detect which finger was touched, remember the numbers that corresponded to each of the fingers, and finally coordinate these pieces of information. Eventually all children perform well on these tests, but 5 and 6 year olds who have difficulty with them are likely to become reading problems.

Another argument put forward to support delayed maturity as one explanation for early reading difficulty is the fact that in the United States young girls' scores on reading readiness and primary grade reading achievement tests are typically higher than those of boys (Balow, 1963; Dykstra and Tinney, 1969).

Since girls develop faster than boys physically, it is not unreasonable to assume that their psychological development may also be precocious. Hence girls may be temporarily more prepared for reading instruction than boys. A study of reading achievement scores in Germany, however, revealed that boys' scores were higher than those of girls. Moreover, in the German sample there was no preponderance of boys over

---

*Satz, P., Freil, J. and Rudegair, F. (1974) Some predictive antecedants of specific reading disability, University of Florida.

girls who scored in the lowest 10% on the reading tests. (In the United States, you will remember, more boys than girls generally obtain very low scores on reading tests, see Preston, 1962.)

These results suggest either that the reading superiority of American girls is not due to earlier biological maturation, or else that cultural factors have the power to overcome slight differences in biological maturity between the sexes. In any case, the German data imply that American teachers should not tacitly accept the boys' greater difficulty in mastering reading as inevitable.

We will have to wait for future research to determine how much retardation in the attainment of left hemisphere dominance for language is a major cause of reading and language deficit. At present, the hypothesis that reading disabilities are due to a lag in the development of the normal dominance of the left hemisphere of the brain and associated cognitive functions seems reasonable, although it is certainly not proven beyond dispute.

A second form of the immaturity hypothesis is concerned with the rate of development of cognitive systems involved in complex monitoring functions. It is fairly well established that between the ages of 5–10, a set of cognitive processes emerge which is necessary for school progress. The time of appearance of these functions can vary by as much as 3–5 years. These executive functions include: (1) reflecting on one's thought and the consequences of actions, (2) recognizing a problem and adjusting effort so that it is in accord with the difficulty of the problem, (3) maintaining flexibility; ability to give up initially incorrect solutions, (4) activating strategies of organization, rehearsal and retrieval, (5) controlling anxiety and resisting distraction, (6) faith in the power of thought, (7) relating information to a larger structure or network.

Some of these executive functions facilitate recall memory. We recently found that Guatemalan children growing up in extremely isolated villages were 3 to 4 years late in activating the strategies necessary for remembering a lengthy series of pictures or words. Middle class American children can remember a string of 12 words or 12 pictures by 8 or 9 years of age, while the isolated Indian children did not perform at that level of competence until several years later. One interpretation of the 3 to 4 year lag is that the American child experiences more frequent challenges in school and both earlier and greater encouragement to develop intellectual skills than do the isolated Guatemalan children. These experiences facilitate the development of these executive functions.

It is likely that a larger proportion of lower than middle class children develop some of these executive competences late, due to the family's lack of encouragement and reward of intellectual progress; hence they enter school less well prepared.

Motives, standards and expectations

A final presumed cause of slower academic progress, which is the most difficult to specify, is psycho-dynamic in nature. It is believed that many lower class children care less about academic success and/or are less confident of mastery. This explanation, which is as hypothetical as intelligence, minimal brain damage, or delayed maturation, requires an analysis of what is meant by the terms motive, standard, and expectation, and a statement of how these processes interact. All children and adults possess a hierarchically organized cognitive representation of goals they want to attain. The set of representations is a motive hierarchy. Each of the goals in the hierarchy is associated, to differing degrees, with an evaluative dimension that defines its moral standing (a standard), and a subjective estimate of the probability of attaining the goal. Other things equal, motives that are closely linked to standards take precedence over those minimally linked to standards. But that statement should not be taken to mean that the latter will never ascend the hierarchy and dominate the child's thought and actions, for the child will often play with sand rather than seek affirmation of his worth from his family. Thus the hierarchy of motives is not constant from hour to hour and we need a principle that tells us how and when the hierarchy is altered, if even temporarily.

One process that affects the motive hierarchy is uncertainty. When the child is temporarily uncertain about attainment of a goal that goal will ascend in the hierarchy and remain there until the uncertainty is partially resolved. Uncertainty is synonymous with expectation of goal attainment. Both the subjective belief in easy attainment of a goal as well as a belief that the goal is unattainable are associated with minimal uncertainty. Uncertainty is maximal when the child does not have a firm expectation of either attainment or frustration. The salience of the motive in the hierarchy bears a curvilinear relation to uncertainty of attainment and a linear relation to the strength of the link to the evaluative component. A combination of these two functional relations implies that a motive is most likely to remain high in the hierarchy when the child is uncertain of attaining a goal which is strongly linked to a positive standard. Let us now apply these simple principles to the school progress of lower and middle class children.

We assume first that all children are uncertain about the receipt of parental approval and punishments. They want affirmation of their value and minimal restriction, punishment and signs of disfavour. All children, especially those of school age, are sensitive to the assignments that parents give them, the qualities they should attain in order to keep uncertainty low. Middle class parents are more likely than lower class parents to make intellectual talent and school progress requirements for continued approval. Lower class parents are more likely to make obedience and inhibition of aggression requirements for family acceptance, even though both groups of children are concerned with both school progress and obedience. The motivation to perform well in school is less salient among lower class children than the motive to avoid disapproval and punishment from adults. To volunteer answers or to move ahead in the workbook are a little dangerous, for these behaviors increase the probability one might provoke chastisement or punishment.

The school context adds another ingredient. The child is acutely sensitive to his talents and qualities vis-a-vis other children his age. 7 year olds are remarkably accurate in ranking the abilities of their peers and in placing themselves in that rank order. As early as the second grade, the child perceives how capable he is in school tasks in comparison with others. Since a lower class child enters school both less prepared intellectually and less highly motivated, he quickly falls behind the middle class child. In a year or two he realizes he is not as academically competent as the former and concludes that he can never be. The only standard he has to judge his competence is the performance of the other children. By the fourth and fifth grade the lower class child has become relatively certain he cannot meet the requirements of the school's tasks. Since motivational salience is linked to uncertaintly, the motivation to work at school tasks drops in the hierarchy, for uncertainty over mastery has become resolved. The divergence in talent increases rapidly after that decision and by adolescence the chasm between middle and lower class children becomes enormous.

The child from an economically impoverished family develops a different profile of psychological qualities from infancy. He learns a different vocabulary, perhaps a less rich one, is not socialized in a manner that makes intellectual and academic progress salient in his hierarchy of motives, is at risk for subtle central nervous system insult, and is consistently exposed to children who have more of what the society values. It is a case in which different does not have the connotation of equally valuable.

Class differences in infancy

The class differences in developmental history appear early, usually by the second year of life (McCall, in the press). We have found that day-care versus home-rearing was far less important than ethnicity or class in a group of Chinese and Caucasian infants seen over the period 3–29 months of age. Working-class children, both Chinese and Caucasian, performed less well than middle-class children on tests of linguistic sophistication at 2.5 years of age, although the middle and lower class children were equivalent on tests of memory for location and perceptual analysis.

The early influence of class on young children was also revealed in a follow-up investigation of 75 Caucasian, first-born, 10 years olds who had been seen a decade earlier for extensive assessments at 4, 8, 13 and 27 months. Wechsler IQ scores and reading ability at age 10 were correlated with social class of the child's family ($r = 0.5$), while variation during infancy in attentiveness, activity and quality of play had little or no predictive power to these school-related dependent variables.

The power of social class to predict IQ was seen in most dramatic form in a study of over 25 000 lower and middle class infants who were assessed regularly from birth through age 4 and on whom extensive biological information on child and mother were available from before birth. The correlation between maternal education and the family's social class, on the one hand, and the Stanford-Binet IQ at age 4, on the other, was $+0.42$ for the Caucasian children. When a large and varied set of relevant prenatal and neonatal biological variables was added to the stepwise regression equation, including birth weight, anoxia and mother's health, the correlation increased by only a small amount to $+0.46$. For the black children, the comparable correlations were $+0.26$ for class with IQ and $+0.32$ when all the biological variables were added to the regression equation. This result is not to be interpreted as indicating that toxemia, apnea, birth weight or mother's health are unimportant for intellectual talent, but rather that when IQ is the criterion, social class has most of the variance (Broman et al., 1975).

Why does class predict intellectual ability better than any other psychological dimension psychologists have devised, whether the setting be America, England or a Guatemalan village where intelligence is not the most valued human quality? What is happening in the homes of the less poor that gives their children a cognitive advantage? We suggest that one factor is a belief, held by both parent and child, that each can meet challenges and solve them. In any community, those with more of what is valued, be it land, cattle, money, lineage, form of birth, property or intelligence, feel more potent. They hold the illusion that they are in greater control of each day than those with less of the valued entities. The privileged are more likely to communicate this mood to their children. Wiener has suggested that adults interpret success or failure on tasks as attributable to either internal factors (ability and motivation) or to external factors (task difficulty and luck). The family with grater status in the community is more likely to persuade its children that the internal factor of effort is effective and that they have greater ability than their peers in the community. The middle class parents persuade their children that each is an agent of personal effectance. The family's enhanced status is viewed as a partial validation of that assumption. The less potent families, unwilling to acknowledge they are less able or lazier, are more likely to interpret their disadvantaged position to external forces beyond their control, to the difficulty of tasks set by others and to luck. Such beliefs discourage individual effort. Many observers of lower-class children have suggested that an important difference is in the attitude each adopts toward a new task. The middle-class child is the unrealistic optimist persuaded of the value of persistence and motivation; the poor child doubts his capability to do what is demanded. Of course the prophesy is self-fulfilling and the cycle continues. One of the nicest supports for this suggestion comes from the difference in school progress between first and later-born children of the same sex growing up in middle class families. The first-born typically obtains better IQ scores and grades than the later-born because the latter, exposed daily to the more competent older sibling, develops doubts over his ability to master difficult tasks.

Recommendations

Since part of the problem of the lower-class child is inherent in the inevitable ranking in comparison of self with others, it may be impossible to remove completely class differences in intellectual progress. We can only alleviate them by reducing the range of performance. The presumed causes we have listed imply three remedial actions. First, the lower class family should be exhorted to encourage the development of language skills in their children and to make intellectual talent and school progress a more central value. Since the lower-class child is more at risk for academic failure, a program of early detection instituted around 4 to 5 years of age might be useful. Such a program could diagnose the children most likely to have difficulty and offer them one-to-one tutoring prior to entrance in the first grade. Third, schools with a large number of poor children might be given more of the community's resources than they now receive. Finally, the society might decide to celebrate, in a serious way, a broader array of talents. Suppose the school gave as much status and prestige to artistic, musical and physical skills as it does to reading and mathematics. Such a change in emphasis might help to persuade the lower class child that he has important areas of talent. That realization might buffer the expectation of failure that surrounds the assessment of intellectual skills. Of course this is an ethical issue. The larger community believes that intellectual competences are sacred and is not prepared, at the moment, to alter those priorities to help the less advantaged child. Much of the West is still committed to a modern form of social Darwinism that is not so much prejudiced against the poor as it is convinced that not all can survive. Some must fail; it is nature's way. As long as the West believes its morality should be in accord with natural law and remains convinced that the jungle is a proper metaphor for human society, we will continue to have more culturally deprived children than we need to.

Acknowledgement

The research reported in this paper was supported by grants from the Carnegie Corporation of New York, Spencer Foundation, and the Grant Foundation. This essay was written while the author was a Belding Scholar of the Foundation for Child Development.

Literature cited

Balow, I. H. (1963) Sex differences in first grade reading, *Elem. Engl. 40*, 303–320

Broman, S. H., Nichols, P. L. and Kennedy, W. A. (1975) *Preschool IQ. Prenatal and Early Developmental Correlates*, L. Erlbaum, Hillsdale, N.J.

Dykstra, R. and Tinney, S. (1969) Sex differences in reading readiness. First grade achievement and second grade achievement, *Read. Real. Proc. Internl. Read. Assoc. 13*, 623–628

Flavell, J. H., Friedrichs, E. J. and Hoyt, J. D. (1970) Developmental changes in memorization processes, *Cognitive Psychol. 1*, 324–340

Gleitman, L. R. and Rozin, P. (1973) Teaching reading by use of a syllabary, *Read. Res. Q. 8*, 447–501

Guilford, J. P. (1967) *The Nature of Human Intelligence*, McGraw-Hill, New York

Holtzman, W. H., Diaz-Guerrero, R. and Swartz, J. D. (1975) *Personality Development in Two Cultures*, University of Texas Press, Austin

Jordan, W. D. (1969) *White over Black*, Penguin Books, New York

Kreutzer, M. A., Leonard, S. C. and Flavell, J. H. (1975) An interview study of children's knowledge about memory, *Monogr. Soc. Res. Child Devel. 40*, Serial No. 159

Mattis, S., French, J. H. and Rapin, I. (1975) Dyslexia in children and young adults. Three independent neuropsychological syndromes, *J. Devel. Med. Child Neurol. 17*, 150–163

McCall, R. B. (1977) Development of intellectual functioning in infancy and the prediction of later IQ. In: *Handbook of Infancy* (J. Osofsky, ed.) in the press

Preston, R. (1962) Reading achievement of German and American children, *Sch. Soc. 90*, 350–354

Rogoff, B., Newcombe, N. and Kagan, J. (1974) Planfulness and recognition memory, *Child Devel. 45*, 972–977

Schachter, F. F., Kirshner, K., Klips, B., Friedricks, M. and Sanders, K. (1974) Everyday preschool interpersonal speech usage. Methodological, developmental and sociolinguistic studies, *Monogr. Soc. Res. Child Devel. 39*, Serial No. 156

Sommer, R. K. and Taylor, M. L. (1972) Cerebral speech dominance in language disordered and normal children, *Cortex 8*, 224–232

Stevenson, H. W., Parker, T., Wilkinson, A., Hegion, A. and Fish, E. (1976) Longitudinal study of individual differences in cognitive development and scholastic achievement, *J. Educ. Psychol. 68*, 377–400

Wender, P. H. (1971) *Minimal Brain Dysfunction in Children*, John Wiley, New York

Genetics, environment and intelligence, edited by A. Oliverio
© *Elsevier/North-Holland Biomedical Press, 1977*

Socioeconomic status and its relation to cognitive performance as mediated through the family environment
19

KEVIN MARJORIBANKS

Introduction

Although there have been many investigations of the relations between socioeconomic status, assessments of family environments and measures of children's cognitive performance the interpretations of the research have been extremely equivocal. Many of the studies (e.g., Dave, 1963; Wolf, 1964; Plowden, 1967; Vernon, 1969; Marjoribanks, 1972; Toomey, 1974) suggest: (a) that socioeconomic status is a relatively poor predictor of children's cognitive performance when compared with more sensitive parent interview measures of the family environment, and (b) that the family environment influences children's outcomes to an important extent independently of socioeconomic status. However, such an interpretation of the relation between socioeconomic status, family environment and cognitive performance has been subjected to trenchant criticism (e.g., Bernstein and Davies, 1969; Connell, 1972, 1974; Halsey, 1975). The criticism proposes that in many of the studies the concept of social class has been trivialised to the point where differences of parental attitude are conceived of as separate factors rather than as an integral part of the work and community situation of children. For example, Halsey suggests that "it is essential to insist that the effect of class on educational experience is not to be thought of as one factor from which parental attitudes and motivations to succeed in education are independent" (1975).

Equivocal interpretations have been produced from prior research because the studies have generally been cross-sectional in design and also have tended to rely on the use of restricted statistical techniques. Studies have used product–moment correlations which reveal only bivariate relations or analysis of variance techniques which require the grouping of variables into levels. Also simple additive regression models have been used to examine how much variance in cognitive scores of children is associated with the socioeconomic status of families, when status measures are included in regression equations containing refined assessments of the family environment. However, the results generated from these latter studies have depended on the order in which the socioeconomic status measures are added to the regression equations.

Some of the statistical limitations have been overcome in recent research by the use of path analytic techniques (e.g. Keeves, 1972; Duncan et al., 1972; Williams, 1975; Alexander and Eckland, 1975). A path model which has generated much research relevant to an examination of relations between socioeconomic status, family environment and cognitive performance is the Wisconsin model of status attainment (e.g. see Sewell et al., 1969; Sewell et al., 1970; Woelfel and Haller, 1971; Sewell and Hauser, 1972; Haller and Portes, 1973; Alexander and Eckland, 1974; Alexander et al., 1975). In the model a causal pattern is proposed which links the socioeconomic status background of children and their eventual educational and occupational attainments via a chain of intervening variables. However, the model is limited by its inadequate conceptualization of the family environment. Generally, family influences are assessed in terms of a simple measure of children's perceptions of parental encouragement, which fails to reflect the complexity of the family environment. Alexander and Eckland (1974) suggest another limitation of many of the studies which have used the Wisconsin-type model of educational attainment when they indicate that most of the research has been restricted to samples of males. In their own study, which included males and females, Alexander and Eckland found that "in nearly every comparison between the sexes, female outcomes were somewhat more strongly dependent on social class origins" (1974).

In the present study an attempt is made to overcome some of the conceptual and statistical limitations of much of the previous research which has examined relations between socio-economic status, family environment and the cognitive performance of children. With longitudinal data collected on three age cohorts of English girls and boys, regression surface analysis and path analytic techniques were used to investigate the relations which are shown in the schematic path model, in Fig. 1.

Method

The sample

The data for the study were collected as part of a national survey of schoolchildren in England (Plowden, 1967) and then collected as part of a follow-up study of the same children, four years later (Peaker, 1971). In the initial survey the sampling

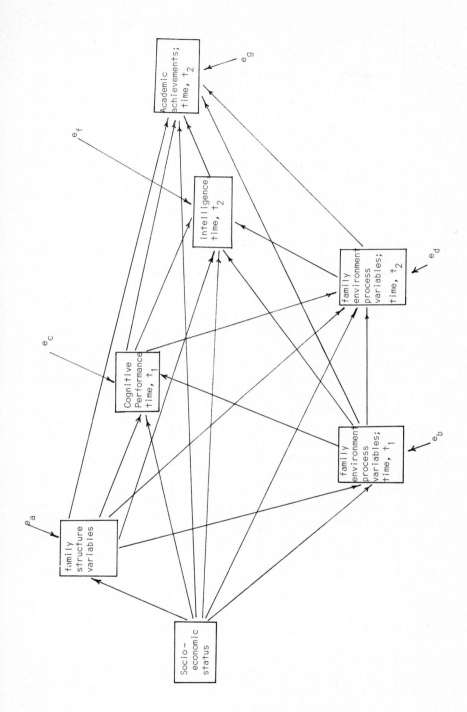

Fig. 1 Schematic path model for relations between socioeconomic status, family environment and cognitive performance.

procedure had two stages. First, a stratified random sample was taken from all types of government supported elementary schools in England which resulted in the selection of 173 schools. In the second stage of the sampling procedure a systematic sample of children was chosen from the schools which produced three age cohorts, each of approximately 1000 children (see Plowden, 1967, Vol. 2, 147–150). The average age of the children in the senior cohort was approximately 11, of the middle cohort, 8, and of the junior group, 7. When the children were surveyed 4 years later, the number in each cohort was: (a) senior group: 397 girls and 382 boys, (b) middle group: 371 girls and 382 boys, (c) junior group: 406 girls and 407 boys. The investigation includes those children who were present during both surveys.

Measures

Socioeconomic status of the families of the children was defined in terms of three indicators: father occupation (8-point scale), father education (5-point scale) and family income (8-point scale). Family structure was measured in terms of the number of children in the family and a crowding ratio index which was an 8-point scale (related to a bedroom deficiency index; a high score indicates a favourable crowding ratio).

Family environment

In both the Plowden survey and in the follow-up study, a structured interview schedule was used to gather information about the family environments of the children. Parents were interviewed in their homes by government social survey interviewers. For the present study, factor scaling (Armor, 1974) was used to construct environment measures from the indices which had been assessed in the national surveys. For each cohort, data on approximately 20 environment indices were available for both time periods. Because it is often suggested that parents structure different educational environments for girls and boys (e.g. see Lee and Gropper, 1974) the analysis of the environment indices was conducted separately for each sex group within the three cohorts.

In the factor scaling process, scores on the environment indices were factor analyzed using principal component analysis. After eliminating indices with small factor loadings (≤ 0.40) the remaining indices were refactored. From the different analyses within the cohorts, 6 environment process variables were identified. These variables were labeled: press for achievement, parental aspirations for child, knowledge of child's school environment, press for intellectuality, parent–teacher interaction and parent–child activeness. Items which were used to assess the environmental process variables are shown in Table I. The table also indicates in which cohorts and sex groups the environmental variables were identified.

Cognitive performance

In the follow-up survey the children in the three age groups were tested using the Alice Heim non-verbal intelligence test, the Vernon graded mathematics test and the Watts–Vernon English comprehension test. During the first survey the senior children

Table I Environmental process variables and their related environment items

Environment process variables	Environment items
Press for achievement (senior girls t_2 and senior boys t_2)	Whether parents want child: to stay on at school, have a professional occupation, to take university entrance examinations, to have a tertiary education. Parents support the raising of the age at which children can leave school and approve of girls staying on at school. Mother and father belong to a library, mother reads, father reads, the child has library books at home, and the number of books in the home.
Educational aspirations for child (senior boys t_1, senior girls t_1; middle boys t_1, t_2, middle girls t_1, t_2; junior boys t_1, t_2, junior girls, t_2)	Whether parents want child: to attend an academic secondary school, stay at school as long as possible, have tertiary education, take university entrance examinations, and to have a professional occupation.
Knowledge of child's school environment (senior girls t_1; middle girls t_1, middle boys t_1; junior girls, t_1)	Whether child talks to parents about school-work, child brings home school books to read, parents are happy about teaching methods, parents would like to have more information about the school, parents have visited the school; and whether parents considered that: teachers were interested in what they thought about their child's education, teachers would like to keep parents out of school, teachers seem interested in all children, teachers only told them what they thought parents wanted to know, teachers were pleased to see them at school.
Press for intellectuality (senior boys t_1; middle girls t_2, middle boys t_2; junior girls t_1, t_2 junior boys t_1, t_2)	Whether the parents played with the child in the evenings, did things with the child at weekends, take an interest in how the child is progressing at school, had visited the school; whether the husband helped with caring for the child; whether parents talked to class teachers, discussed educational matters with principal or teachers, attended school functions.
Parent–teacher interaction (senior girls t_2, senior boys t_2)	Whether it is easy to see teachers whenever parents want to, teachers seem pleased when parents visit school, feel that teachers would like to keep parents out of school. Teachers are interested in what parents think about child's education, parents feel they would be interfering if they visited the school, parents would like teachers to visit homes, parents would like to be consulted by teachers, parents are satisfied with present school.
Parent–child activeness (senior girls t_1; middle girls t_1)	Whether parents have time to do things with their children, and how much time; whether parents: help child with schoolwork, play with child in the evenings and at weekends.

t_1 and t_2 indicate that data were collected on the environment variables in the first and second surveys, respectively.

Table II Relationship between cognitive scores and measures of socioeconomic status and family environment

Environment variable	Cognitive scores: senior cohort			
	Reading, t_1	Intelligence, t_2	English, t_2	Mathematics, t_2
Father occupation	09 [a](23)	21 (22)	26 (30)	23 (37)
Family income	08[a] (22)	10 (23)	16 (26)	17 (29)
Father education	13 (21)	19 (17)	25 (23)	28 (31)
Sibsize	−13 (−25)	−17 (−08[a])	−23 (−25)	−17 (−22)
Crowding ratio	14 (15)	14 (09[a])	16 (17)	14 (14)
Educational aspirations, t_1	27 (48)	25 (38)	43 (48)	44 (54)
Knowledge of child's school, t_1	b (21)	b (20)	b (27)	b (34)
Parent–child activeness, t_1	b (21)	b (13)	b (25)	b (27)
Press for intellectuality, t_1	26 (b)	30 (b)	41 (b)	38 (b)
Press for achievement, t_2	49 (35)	38 (34)	61 (61)	54 (56)
Parent–teacher interaction, t_2	17 (06)	16 (19)	19 (19)	24 (27)
Multiple r	0.33 (0.54)	0.42 (0.45)	0.64 (0.66)	0.60 (0.69)
100 r^2	11.06 (29.3)	17.9 (20.45)	41.19 (44.07)	36.0 (48.0)

Environment variable	Cognitive scores: middle cohort				
	Sentence reading, t_2	N.S. 45 reading, t_1	Intelligence, t_2	English, t_2	Mathematics, t_2
Father occupation	12 (13)	13 (11)	25 (16)	33 (20)	32 (20)
Family income	18 (25)	16 (19)	24 (27)	33 (34)	29 (27)
Father education	18 (21)	16 (18)	27 (22)	36 (30)	33 (27)
Sibsize	−15 (−08[a])	−07[a] (−07[a])	−18 (−16)	−19 (−17)	−19 (−16)
Crowding ratio	07[a] (12)	06[a] (12)	16 (17)	22 (19)	19 (20)
Educational aspirations, t_1	23 (11)	18 (11)	26 (16)	33 (23)	38 (19)
Knowledge of child's school, t_1	08[a] (19)	16 (18)	12 (19)	17 (18)	20 (16)
Parent–child activeness, t_1	b (08[a])	b (07[a])	b (14)	b (09[a])	b (08[a])
Educational aspirations, t_2	38 (27)	29 (26)	32 (35)	50 (38)	44 (35)
Press for intellectuality, t_2	10 (06[a])	09[a] (11)	13 (18)	21 (21)	20 (19)
Multiple r	0.31 (0.33)	0.28 (0.29)	0.41 (0.44)	0.57 (0.51)	0.55 (0.46)
100 r^2	9.80 (10.88)	7.60 (8.43)	17.16 (19.63)	32.57 (26.31)	29.89 (20.80)

Cognitive scores: junior cohort

	Intelligence, t_1	Reading, t_1	Intelligence, t_2	English, t_2	Mathematics, t_2
Father occupation	14 (13)	14 (20)	20 (20)	31 (26)	26 (21)
Family income	13 (08[a])	15 (10)	16 (05[a])	27 (15)	24 (12)
Father education	17 (07[a])	21 (13)	14 (09)	19 (17)	22 (19)
Sibsize	−10 (−14)	−08[a] (−17)	−04[a] (−14)	−18 (−21)	−08 (−23)
Crowding ratio	11 (09)	13 (11)	18 (20)	29 (19)	19 (17)
Educational aspirations, t_1	15 (b)	10 (b)	20 (b)	16 (b)	27 (b)
Knowledge of child's school, t_1	b (17)	b (14)	b (19)	b (15)	b (20)
Press for intellectuality, t_1	21 (18)	21 (17)	22 (21)	32 (28)	27 (23)
Educational aspirations, t_2	23 (26)	22 (30)	33 (26)	36 (36)	38 (39)
Press for intellectuality, t_2	24 (23)	19 (24)	24 (27)	34 (27)	32 (29)
Multiple r	0.26 (0.25)	0.27 (0.29)	0.38 (0.39)	0.47 (0.45)	0.46 (0.48)
100 r^2	6.64 (6.50)	7.14 (8.17)	14.45 (15.35)	22.35 (20.47)	21.03 (22.93)

Decimals for the zero-order correlations have been omitted. Figures for girls are in parentheses. An a indicates that the relationship is not significant beyond the 0.05 level. A b indicates that the environment variable was not identified for the particular sex group. t_1 and t_2 indicate that the variables were measured at time 1 and time 2, respectively. For the cognitive scores measured at time 1, only the early environment variables were included in the multiple regression models to determine multiple r.

were assessed on the Watts–Vernon reading test, the middle group on the N.F.E.R. Sentence Reading test and the N.F.E.R., N.S. 45 Reading test, while the junior group was assessed using the N.F.E.R., N.S. 45 Reading test and the N.F.E.R. Picture Intelligence test. All of the tests have acceptable reliability estimates.

Results

The first investigation of the relations between socioeconomic status, family environment and cognitive performance involved an analysis of zero-order correlations. In Table II, the results show a set of moderate relations between the environment variables and the performance scores. Generally, the environment variables have stronger relations with the English and mathematics scores than with the intelligence test scores, which supports previous research (e.g., see Dave, 1963; Fraser, 1959; Vernon, 1969; Jensen, 1973a, 1973b). Sibsize and crowding ratio have low to moderate relations with the cognitive scores which again replicates much prior research (e.g., see Nisbet, 1953; Anastasi, 1956; Fraser, 1959; Maxwell, 1969; Record et al., 1969; Vernon, 1969; Marjoribanks and Walberg, 1975; Marjoribanks et al., 1975; Zajonc and Markus, 1975). When the environment variables were combined into a predictor set they accounted for a low to moderate percentage of the variance in the intelligence scores and a moderate to high percentage of the variance in the academic achievement scores. For the achievement scores the amount of variance associated with the environment measures increased from the junior to the senior cohorts. For example, for junior and middle girls the environment accounted for approximately 20% of the variance in mathematics scores, while in the senior cohort approximately 48% of the variance was associated with the environment variables. However, for intelligence the relation with the environment appears to be much more stable. In the junior cohort the environment accounted for approximately 15% of the variance in those intelligence test scores which were measured during the second survey, while in the senior cohort the amount of variance increased only to approximately 20%. The greater stability of the relation between the environment variables and intelligence provides support for propositions made by Bloom (1964) and Jensen (1973a, 1973b).

In general, within each cohort, the press for achievement and educational aspiration measures have the strongest predictive validities in relation to the performance scores while the status indicators and remaining process variables have somewhat similar relations with the cognitive measures. Relationships between the environment variables and cognitive performance were investigated further by using regression surface analysis and path analytic techniques.

Regression surface analysis

Regression surfaces were plotted using raw regression weights generated from regression models of the form: $Z = aX + bY + \text{constant}$, where Z, X and Y represent measures of cognitive performance measured at time t_2, socioeconomic status and family environment, respectively. For the analysis socioeconomic status was defined in terms of an equally weighted composite of father occupation, father education and family income. The environmental process variables which were isolated for each time period, within each cohort and sex group (see Table I), were combined to provide a measure of the cumulative environment between the two time periods. It was found that the two-term equations accounted for as much variance in the cognitive scores as complex many-term equations which contained quadratic terms (to test for non-linearity) and product terms (to test for interactions). In the more complex models the raw regression weights between the cognitive scores and the quadratic and product predictor terms were not significant. The results of the regression analysis are shown in Table III and they indicate that for both sexes and within each cohort there are strong relationships between family environment and each cognitive measure. The most significant group differences occur between the senior girls and senior boys. At different family environment levels, the socio-economic status of boys' families is not related directly to the performance scores while for the senior girls, socioeconomic status continues to have direct influences on the cognitive measures. This latter finding provides tentative support for Alexander and Eckland, who in a longitudinal study of the educational attainment of American students found that "status background influences were a double liability for women in that such influences were found to be considerably more determinant of high school process and outcome variables for females" (1974).

As it is not possible in the space available to present all the regression surfaces

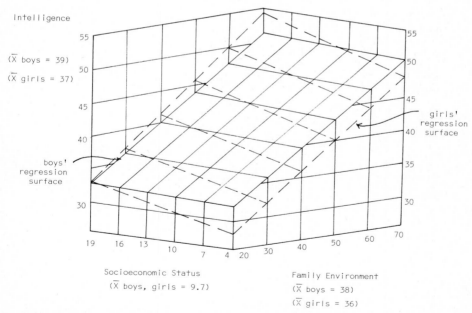

Fig. 2   Fitted-intelligence scores in relation to socioeconomic status, and family environment: senior group girls and boys.

Table III   Raw regression weights for multiple regression of cognitive performance, measured at time t_2, on socioeconomic status and family environment

Predictor variable	Senior girls			Middle girls			Junior girls		
	Intelligence	English	Mathematics	Intelligence	English	Mathematics	Intelligence	English	Mathematics
Socioeconomic status	0.4959**	0.4145**	0.8148**	0.6849**	0.6814**	0.7695**	0.0334*	0.2806*	0.3267*
Family environment	0.4099**	0.4801**	0.7045**	0.4297**	0.2699**	0.3246**	0.0100*	0.1621**	0.2654**
Multiple r	0.4169	0.5858	0.6530	0.3893	0.4545	0.4022	0.2270	0.3627	0.3600
$100\,r^2$	17.38	34.31	42.64	15.13	20.66	16.18	5.13	13.16	12.96

Predictor variable	Senior boys			Middle boys			Junior boys		
	Intelligence	English	Mathematics	Intelligence	English	Mathematics	Intelligence	English	Mathematics
Socioeconomic status	0.0931	0.0278	0.1102	0.7479**	0.6506**	0.7180**	0.0399*	0.3766**	0.5084*
Family environment	0.3687**	0.4401**	0.6735**	0.3904**	0.4375**	0.5976**	0.0107**	0.2006**	0.3349**
Multiple r	0.4000	0.5881	0.5653	0.3751	0.5262	0.5092	0.2630	0.4260	0.4124
$100\,r^2$	16.0	34.59	31.95	14.07	27.69	25.93	6.91	18.15	17.01

*Value of raw regression weight exceeds twice its standard error.
**Value of raw regression weight exceeds three times its standard error.

that were generated from the data, only four surfaces have been plotted in two figures. The surfaces show the differential socioeconomic status relations with the cognitive scores, at different levels of family environment. In Fig. 2, the surfaces reflect the regression-fitted relationship between socioeconomic status and the intelligence scores of senior girls and senior boys at different levels of family environment. At each socioeconomic status level, increases in family environment are associated with sizable increments in intelligence scores. For example, in the boys' sample, as the family environment scores increase from 30 to 60, the regression-estimated intelligence scores change by approximately 10 points at each status level. At each environment level the shapes of the surfaces show that for girls, increases in status are related to increments in intelligence while for boys, changes in status are not associated with changes in the intelligence scores.

In Fig. 3, the surfaces show the regression-fitted relation between socioeconomic status and the English achievement of junior group children, at different environment levels. The figures reflect the shapes of most of the regression surfaces, in which there are significant relations between the cognitive scores and measures of socioeconomic status and environmental process variables. Thus the regression surface analysis suggests support for Halsey's proposition that "the effect of class on educational experience is not to be thought of as one factor from which parental attitudes and motivations to succeed in education are independent" (1975).

While the regression surface analysis provides a means of examining relations

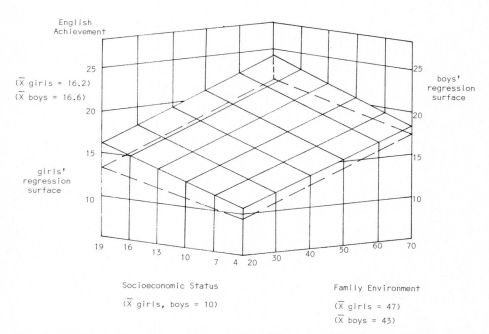

Fig. 3   Fitted-English scores in relation to socioeconomic status and family environment: junior group girls and boys.

Table IV Regression coefficients in standard form for analysis of path model

Dependent variables	Predetermined variables: senior boys											r^2
	A	B	C	D	E	F	G	J	K	L	M	
D	099[a]	062[a]	-021[a]									0.010[a]
E	131	026[a]	135									0.057
F	149	144	115									0.099
F	137	157	117	-184	-048[a]							0.126
G	234	147	164									0.179
G	206	159	152	-205	054[a]							0.235
J	035[a]	030[a]	101[a]									0.019[a]
J	018[a]	033[a]	091[a]	-095[a]	059[a]							0.037
J	-046[a]	-025[a]	-041[a]	-023[a]	060[a]	207	169					0.111
K	273	123	196									0.219
K	256	133	192	-165	009[a]							0.247
K	134	022[a]	096	-027[a]	005[a]	338	366					0.503
K	140	026[a]	090	-023[a]	-004[a]	308	341	149				0.523
L	124	-036[a]	032[a]		-004[a]							0.017[a]
L	128	-038[a]	033[a]	034[a]	-004[a]							0.018[a]

	C1	C2	C3	C4	C5	C6	C7	C8	C9	C10	C11	
L	106[a]	−052[a]	018[a]	054[a]	−013[a]	−039	129					0.030[a]
L	108[a]	−051[a]	016[a]	055[a]	−016[a]	−048[a]	121					0.033[a]
M	153	007[a]	112[a]	−149	007[a]	136	188					0.053
M	137	017[a]	108[a]	−085[a]	003	106[a]	164					0.076
M	080[a]	−034[a]	064[a]	−082[a]	−005[a]	041[a]	072[a]	047[a]				0.130
M	086[a]	−030[a]	058[a]	−082[a]	−003[a]							0.149
M	042[a]	−030[a]	035[a]									0.189
N	174	045[a]	154	−226	−026[a]	296	230					0.091
N	155	060[a]	153	−124	−024[a]	228	174					0.136
N	067[a]	−023[a]	−083[a]	−116	−045[a]	111	024[a]	145				0.282
N	082[a]	−014[a]	070[a]	−114	−041[a]	098	b	106	228	112		0.380
N	013[a]	−019[a]	032[a]	−086	−040[a]						329	0.472
N	b	−009[a]	020[a]									0.560
O	123	057[a]	197	−167	−016[a]	319	197	330	396	119		0.093
O	109[a]	068[a]	195	−067[a]	−011[a]	264	153	266	321	082		0.118
O	024[a]	−013[a]	128	−061[a]	−027[a]	180	029[a]	231	300	181		0.263
O	037[a]	−006[a]	117	−064[a]	−023[a]	165	001[a]	262	211	138		0.324
O	−025[a]	−005[a]	087[a]	−032[a]	−022[a]			209				0.403
O	−041[a]	007[a]	073[a]					168			387	0.525

Table IV (continued)

Dependent variables	Predetermined variables: senior girls												
	A	B	C	D	E	F	H	I	J	K	L	M	r^2
D	−122	010ᵃ	−009ᵃ										0.015ᵃ
E	096ᵃ	167	182										0.123
F	165	126	184										0.136
F	159	148	204	−146	−120								0.154
H	077ᵃ	088ᵃ	−012ᵃ										0.018ᵃ
H	078ᵃ	110ᵃ	009ᵃ	−088ᵃ	−119								0.029
I	108	136	150										0.094
I	075ᵃ	130	139	−230	049ᵃ								0.158
J	132	116	115										0.080
J	108	132	128	−267	−080ᵃ								0.136
J	035ᵃ	060ᵃ	046ᵃ	−198	−018ᵃ	394	124	002ᵃ					0.293
K	159	165	268										0.214
K	137	173	273	−209	−034ᵃ								0.252
K	057ᵃ	087ᵃ	175	−116	022ᵃ	396	121	109					0.434
K	049ᵃ	074ᵃ	166	−073ᵃ	026ᵃ	313	095	109	212				0.465
L	209	−032ᵃ	−087ᵃ	014ᵃ	−012ᵃ								0.035
L	212	−030ᵃ	−085ᵃ	062ᵃ	029ᵃ								0.035
L	175	−080ᵃ	−106ᵃ			050ᵃ	316	056ᵃ					0.149

L	171	-086[a]	-111	084[a]	031[a]	007[a]	303	056[a]	111				0.158
M	133	145	063[a]	-070[a]	-037[a]	313	135	-030[a]	242	079[a]	087[a]		0.073
M	128	153	069[a]	-019[a]	018[a]	218	105	-030[a]	216				0.077
M	070[a]	095[a]	008[a]	029[a]	022[a]	192	071[a]	-044[a]					0.184
M	062[a]	081[a]	-003[a]	027[a]	017[a]								0.225
M	043[a]	083[a]	-007[a]										0.235
N	194	140	102[a]	-248	-062[a]	364	176	022[a]	507	324	025[a]	230	0.118
N	170	153	111	-174	002[a]	164	113	021[a]	435	306	005[a]		0.168
N	096	077[a]	032[a]	-074[a]	010[a]	063[a]	075	-016[a]	386				0.327
N	079[a]	046[a]	009[a]	-052[a]	001[a]	019[a]	059[a]	-006[a]					0.509
N	058[a]	025[a]	-041[a]	-048[a]	-003[a]								0.567
N	049[a]	006[a]	-040[a]										0.607
O	248	120	170	-234	-123	394	241	011[a]	365	156	103	333	0.179
O	231	143	190	-153	-048[a]	250	196	010[a]	321	130	074		0.220
O	149	057[a]	106	-080[a]	-041[a]	200	150	-012[a]	249				0.430
O	136	035[a]	089	-077[a]	-049[a]	137	126	002[a]					0.525
O	111	033[a]	075[a]	-086	-054[a]								0.548
O	097	005[a]	077										0.633

[a] indicates that coefficients are not significant at the 0.05 level. Decimal points for the coefficients have been omitted. Variables are A, father occupation; B, family income; C, father education; D, sibsize; E, crowding ratio; F, educational aspirations t_1; G, press for intellectuality t_1; H, knowledge of child's school environment t_1; I, parent–child activeness t_1; J, early reading achievement t_1; K, press for achievement t_2; L, parent–teacher interaction t_2; M, intelligence t_2; N, English achievement t_2; O, mathematics achievement t_2.

between socioeconomic status, environment and cognitive performance it does not permit an analysis of all the relations shown between the variables in Fig. 1. Therefore path analytic techniques were used to examine the path model.

Path analysis

Because of the large number of findings and the limitations of space, only the path results for the senior group are presented in detail. In Table IV, the results show that press for achievement (t_2), parent–teacher interaction (t_2) and early reading scores (t_1) have significant direct relations with intelligence. Press for achievement (t_2) is related directly to educational aspirations (t_1), press for intellectuality (t_1) early reading performance (t_1) and father occupation while parent–teacher interaction (t_2) is related to press for intellectuality (t_1). Early reading performance is influenced directly by the two environment process variables measured at time, t_1. The regression coefficients also show that the socioeconomic status measures and sibsize have direct effects on the early process variables and that they account for a moderate percentage of the variance in the process scores. Thus the results, for the senior boys, suggest that the early learning environment created by parents is, in part, determined by the family structure and the socioeconomic status of the family and that later learning environments, reading achievement (t_1), and intelligence (t_2) are influenced by the earlier environment.

In the senior girls, a slightly different pattern of direct effects emerges in relation to intelligence. Reading achievement (t_1) and educational aspirations (t_1) have direct effects on intelligence but the later process variables do not add significantly to an explanation of the differences in the intelligence scores of the girls. That is, intelligence may become more stable, in relation to environmental influences, at an earlier age for girls than for boys.

For both senior girls and boys, reading (t_1), press for achievement (t_2) and intelligence (t_2) have the strongest direct effects on English achievement. However for mathematics the pattern of relations is quite different as performance is related directly to environment variables measured at time, t_1 with father occupation, father education and sibsize continuing to influence directly the mathematics scores of girls.

The findings for the senior children suggest the proposition that socioeconomic status may have two separate influences on the cognitive performance of children. First, a "contextual effect" in which socioeconomic status effects the learning environment that parents provide for their children. The contextual effect of socioeconomic status on cognitive performance is transmitted via the different learning environments which are created by families. A second influence of socioeconomic status may be labeled the "individual effect", which is assessed by the remaining direct effect on children's cognitive performances after accounting for the influence of the intervening environment process variables. It is possible that the "individual effect" reflects an interpretation by children of the socioeconomic status of their family which results in children adapting their behaviors. The path analysis and the regression surface analysis suggest that by adolescence, the cognitive performances of boys are related to the "contextual effect" of socioeconomic status but not directly to the "individual effect" while girls are influenced by both the contextual and individual effects.

In the middle boys' group, reading (t_1) was the only variable to have a direct effect on intelligence (t_2). Reading (t_1) was related directly to sibsize, crowding ratio and educational aspirations (t_1), and these latter measures were related to the status indicators. The English performance (t_2) of the boys was influenced directly by intelligence (t_2), educational aspirations (t_2) and reading (t_1) while their mathematics scores were related directly to the early environment process measures, intelligence (t_2) and later process variables. For middle group girls, the two reading measures (t_1), educational aspirations (t_2) and knowledge of child's school environment (t_1) had direct effects on intelligence (t_2), with the reading measures being influenced by family income. English achievement for the girls was related directly to the earlier reading scores (t_1), intelligence (t_2), and educational aspirations (t_2) as well as family income. Mathematics performance was influenced directly by intelligence (t_2) and early reading scores (t_1).

In the junior group, the intelligence scores (t_2) of the boys was influenced directly by intelligence (t_1), educational aspirations (t_2), as well as sibsize and crowding ratio. Educational aspirations (t_2) also had direct relations with the family structure variables. Father occupation had a direct effect on the English achievement of the junior boys as did intelligence (t_2) educational aspirations (t_2) and early reading achievement (t_1) while in mathematics, the main direct effects were in relation to intelligence (t_2), educational aspirations (t_1) and reading (t_1). In junior girls, father occupation, crowding ratio, intelligence (t_1) and educational aspirations (t_2) had direct effects on intelligence (t_2) while the English and mathematics scores were influenced directly by early reading performance (t_1), educational aspirations (t_2) and intelligence (t_2).

The path analysis indicates the complexity of the relations between environment variables and cognitive performance for different age groups and between girls and boys. There is an indication in the results that girls are influenced more than boys by the "individual effects" of socioeconomic status. However, critics of the proposition that socioeconomic status may have dual effects, "contextual and individual", on the cognitive performances of children might suggest that the inclusion of other environmental measures into the model will mediate all the effects of socioeconomic status on the performance measures. For example, the work by Walberg (1971, 1972) and Trickett and Moos (1973) has stressed the importance of classroom and school environments on learning outcomes. Also, Haller and Portes (1973) have examined the importance of the relationship between socioeconomic status and the neighborhood or peer group environment. They suggest that the socioeconomic status of the family "sets limits on the pool of significant others confronted by the individual and the nature of their orientations. It affects, for example, the class and general background of possible friends and hence the likelihood of their having and conveying college plans" (1973).

Hopefully, the present study indicates the need for analyses which involve detailed assessments of the family, school and neighborhood environments and also assessments of how children interpret and react to the socioeconomic status of their families. Although the research has shown, through regression surface analysis and path analysis, the powerful influence of the family environment on the cognitive outcomes of children, it has shown also the presence of a set of moderate unmediated relations between socioeconomic status and cognitive performance. It may be found that even if more refined and more inclusive environment measures were considered, that socioeconomic status continues to have a direct effect on cognitive performance. It is possible that even when the ceiling of the "contexual effects" of socioeconomic status on cognitive performance is reached that there will remain an "individual effect". Because of this possibility and because of the strong interrelationships that have been shown to be present between socioeconomic status, family environment and cognitive performance the study supports Halsey's contention (1975) that "a theory which explains educational achievement as the outcome of a set of individual attributes has lost the meaning of those structural forces which we know as class".

Literature cited

Alexander, K. L. and Eckland, B. K. (1974) Sex differences in the educational attainment process, *Am. Sociol. Rev. 39*, 668–682

Alexander, K. L. and Eckland, B. K. (1975) Contextual effects in the high school attainment process, *Am. Sociol. Rev. 40*, 402–416

Alexander, K. L., Eckland, B. K. and Griffin, L. J. (1975) The Wisconsin model of socioeconomic achievement: a replication, *Am. J. Sociol. 81*, 324–342

Anastasi, A. (1956) Intelligence and family size, *Psychol. Bull. 53*, 187–209

Armor, D. J. (1974) Theta reliability and factor scaling. In: *Sociological Methodology, 1973–1974* (H. L. Costner, ed.) pp. 17–50, Jossey-Bass, San Francisco

Bernstein, B. and Davies, B. (1969) Some sociological comments on Plowden. In: *Perspectives on Plowden* (R. Peters, ed.) pp. 55–83, Routledge and Kegan Paul, London

Bloom, B. S. (1964) *Stability and Change in Human Characteristics*, Wiley, London

Connell, R. W. (1972) Class structure and personal socialisation. In: *Socialisation in Australia* (F. J. Hunt, ed.) pp. 38–66, Angus and Robertson, Sydney

Connell, R. W. (1974) The causes of educational inequality: further observations, *Aust. N.Z. J. Sociol. 10*, 186–189

Dave, R. H. (1963) *The Identification and Measurement of Environmental Process Variables that are Related to Educational Attainment*, Ph.D. thesis, University of Chicago

Duncan, O. D., Featherman, D. L. and Duncan, B. (1972) *Socioeconomic Background and Achievement*, Seminar Press, New York

Fraser, E. (1959) *Home Environment and the School*, University of London Press, London

Haller, A. O. and Portes, A. (1973) Status attainment processes, *Sociol. Educ. 46*, 51–91

Halsey, A. H. (1975) Sociology and the equality debate, *Oxford Rev. Educ. 1*, 9–23

Jensen, A. R. (1973a) *Educational Differences*, Methuen, London

Jensen, A. R. (1973b) *Educability and Group Differences*, Methuen, London

Keeves, J. P. (1972) *Educational Environment and Student Achievement*, Almquist and Wiksell, Stockholm

Lee, P. C. and Gropper, N. B. (1974) Sex-role culture and educational practice, *Harv. Educ. Rev. 44*, 369–410

Marjoribanks, K. (1972) Environment, social class and mental abilities, *J. Educ. Psychol. 63*, 103–109

Marjoribanks, K. and Walberg, H. J. (1975) Birth order , family size, social class and intelligence, *Soc. Biol. 22*, 261–268

Marjoribanks, K., Walberg, H. J. and Bargen, M. (1975) Mental abilities: sibling constellation and social class correlates, *Br. J. Soc. Clin. Psychol. 14*, 109–116

Maxwell, J. (1969) Intelligence, education and fertility: a comparison between the 1932 and 1947 Scottish surveys, *J. Biosoc. Sci. 1*, 247–271

Nisbet, J. D. (1953) Family environment and intelligence, *Eugen. Rev. 45*, 31–42

Peaker, G. F. (1971) *The Plowden Children Four Years Later*, National Foundation for Educational Research, London

Plowden, B. (1967) *Children and their Primary Schools*, H. M. Stationery Office, London

Record, R. G., McKeown, T. and Edwards, J. H. (1969) The relation of measured intelligence to birth order and maternal age, *Ann. Hum. Genet. Lond. 33*, 61–69

Sewell, W. H., Haller, A. O. and Ohlendorf, G. W. (1970) The educational and early occupational attainment process: replication and revision, *Am. Sociol. Rev. 35*, 1014–1027

Sewell, W. H., Haller, A. O. and Portes, A. (1969) The educational and early occupational attainment process, *Am. Sociol. Rev. 34*, 82–92

Sewell, W. H. and Hauser, R. M. (1972) Causes and consequences of higher education: models of the status attainment process, *Am. J. Agr. Econ. 54*, 851–861

Toomey, D. (1974) What causes educational disadvantage? *Aust. N.Z. J. Sociol. 10*, 31–37

Trickett, E. M. and Moos, R. H. (1973) Social environment of junior high and high school classrooms, *J. Educ. Psychol. 65*, 93–102

Vernon, P. E. (1969) *Intelligence and Cultural Environment*, Methuen, London

Walberg, H. J. (1971) Models for optimizing and individualizing school learning, *Interchange 3*, 15–27

Walberg, H. J. (1972) Social environment and individual learning: a test of the Bloom model, *J. Educ. Psychol. 63*, 69–73

Williams, T. (1975) Educational ambition: teachers and students, *Sociol. Educ. 48*, 107–133

Woelfel, J. and Haller, A. O. (1971) Significant others, the self-reflexive act and the attitude formation process, *Am. Sociol. Rev. 36*, 74–87

Wolf, R. M. (1964) *The Identification and Measurement of Environmental Process Variables Related to Intelligence*, Ph.D. Thesis, University of Chicago

Zajonc, R. B. and Markus, G. B. (1975) Birth order and intellectual development, *Psychol. Rev. 82*, 74–88

Genetics, environment and intelligence, edited by A. Oliverio
© *Elsevier/North-Holland Biomedical Press, 1977*

Ethnic differences and behavioural development in children

20

PHILIP R. DE LACEY

Introduction

Man is the pinnacle of the universe. Or so he asserts in most impressive arguments: he holds sway over other creatures most of the time; his societies are usually more complex and efficient than are seen among other social animals; and he has fewer young, and frequently nurtures them better than do other animals, even other mammals. His effective mastery over the physical environment is clearly demonstrated in his rapacious assimilation of the earth's resources, checked only by his intermittent concern for his future well being, and qualified only by his inescapable mortality. His attitude to his world is inevitably species centred.

The problem of human ranking

It is a short step from what might be termed this species-centricity to the sentiments of ethnocentricity, from a belief in omnipotence over the universe to a conviction that one's own group of people is more valuable than others. The criteria by which such a judgment is made are often not articulated; they may range from technology to tranquility, from reliance on materials to dependence on a god, from skin colour to manual dexterity, from one attribute to a combination of several. Sometimes unconsciously, often uncritically, the criteria employed as the basis of the judgment become accepted, not only by the group considering itself more valuable, but also by other, even subjugated, groups. The judgments, as Pike (1967) puts it, are emic, deriving from a belief system widely upheld in one particular cultural group, rather than representing a common denominator of several such groups.

Ethnocentric attitudes date from antiquity. They generally emerge from a series of military, organisational or fortuitous success experienced by a particular community of people in comparison with neighbouring communities. Nurcombe (1976a) recalls that the ancient Romans, for example, had little regard for the mental competence for the Britons of their time. Cicero warned his contemporaries: "Do not obtain your slaves from Britain, because they are so stupid and so utterly incapable of being taught that they are not fit to form a part of the household of Athens."

Yet, in their astute deference to political pragmatism, the Romans admitted to full citizenship of their empire members of quite a variety of ethnic and cultural groups, learning early a lesson not understood by the dominant Norman–French culture in England until 1381, with the powerful uprising of Watt Tyler. The lesson was clear: ensure sufficient social mobility to cream off potential leaders of lower-ranking rebels and to allow them to develop an investment with the established structure, achieve this, and society is the more stable. This policy has been remarkably successful for centuries: epitomised at the household level by the admirable Crichton, and at the national level by many European colonial administrative structures which have often continued well beyond the independence of former colonies.

At the beginning of the last quarter of the twentieth century, as for long before, white people run the world. As Jencks (1972) remarked, those who possess power tend to believe that they deserve it, rather than that they have acquired it in other ways, for example "by venality, cunning or historical accident" (p. 83). A consequence of the political and economic superiority of white people is the emergence of a rather facile and simplistic scientific racism, whose basic premise is, in the words of Bagley (1975), that "there are major differences between different racial or ethnic groups in terms of intelligence, personality and moral characteristics, and that these differences are biological in nature ... therefore that one racial group is superior to another" (p. 31). Facile because it is so easy to show that non-western people, particularly their children, whose naivete plays into the hands of the testers, do poorly on (western) psychological tests by comparison with (western) white children. Simplistic because the point of view has not taken into account the complex of cumulative environmental impediments described by Jencks and Nurcombe, and including generations of malnutrition, disease, trauma, hostile rejection, inappropriate learning opportunities – in a phrase, physical and mental impoverishment.

Ranking groups of people on some value scale, then, has long been a common pastime among many ethnic or national groups. It is no less common among subethnic groups or social classes. Sometimes, over history, as in heterogeneous Britain or India, intranational groupings are the vestiges of a series of invasions. At other times, as in more homogeneous Polynesia, they have been the consequences of factional competition between groups within the same nation or culture. Often, sub-ethnic groupings are the consequences of a confounding of both processes.

The ultimate example of social ranking occurs among individuals within the family. Each succeeding generation learns, in general, to venerate preceding generations. Early in life, children learn that parents are remarkable in providing basic needs, capability of being threatening, and ability to solve problems better than children. In most societies, which are patriarchal, girls learn also early in their childhood that there are many respects in which they are destined to take second place to men.

The second two thirds of the twentieth century has so far been notable for the substantial rearrangement, even a breaking down, of many examples of rigid social ranking. Most European colonies have gained independence; women and children are becoming more liberated; and students are being represented, sometimes with more than tokenism, on university committees. Yet the phenomenon of social ranking still remains strong, and the perception by individuals and groups of their ranking status continues to be keen.

The development of ranking perception

Recognition of one's own location on a status ranking has long been an early part of socialization. The location perceived can be said to depend mainly upon three criteria. The first of these might be the acquisitive effectiveness of oneself and one's family, manifested in the possession of power over property and people. For example, in developing his Australian occupational prestige scale, Congalton (1963) found he had also developed a rank order of incomes. Both students and citizens at large placed "professors" high on the scale, rather, they said, because professors were supposed to be paid high salaries and to exercise control over others, than because they were likely to make important contributions to society. Some of the aura of old, respectable families is probably based as much on the control they once exercised over people and objects as on their humanitarianism, the social rituals they observed, or their interest in the fine arts.

A second criterion of status location is the transient one of the age of the individual. This criterion may have increased in importance in some parts of the world in recent decades. Fifty years ago, Christopher Robin, while acknowledging some useful attributes in the family gardner, found him something of an oddity, and quite acceptably referred to him by his first names, Johnathan Jo. Though present-day 6-year-olds would be more likely to call him Mr. Smith, his Australian peers might recognise his oddness with his social status in the endemic and not unendearing term "stupid old bastard". Age is not always the prior status determinant, but it can be important in the extended family in cultures as far apart as Greeks and Australian Aboriginals. Among such peoples, grandmothers often exercise considerable control over teenage grandchildren, even after they have been immersed in Anglo-Saxon derived cultures for some years.

A third criterion, and a very old and powerful one, has been a set of attributes valued by influential social groups among European nations, and often referred to by them as intelligence and breeding, which they believed to be largely inherited. Examples cited were the various royal families, and the small number of families which effectively governed Britain from the eighteenth to the twentieth centuries. The set of attributes defining this criterion included learning and observing set social rituals; speed and efficiency of perception, coding and problem solving; recognition of male dominance; a well-developed self concept; an acknowledgement if not an appreciation of the fine arts; and a large measure of ethnocentricity. This criterion, once regarded as crucial, has come under increasing scrutiny and question during the present century, with the rise of environmentalism, and with the improvement in techniques of measuring human attributes and in testing hypotheses concerning them.

Children learn early to recognise these criteria of social ranking, and to hypothesise about their own location on a human ranking scale. In England, Brian Jackson (1966) describes how children in primary school learn to identify, among their peers, a priesthood of able, beautiful people, generally located in A streams of schools still practising streaming. Of all human institutions, schools if they wish to be are as effective as any in perpetuating the notion that social ranking is important. They do this not only through their administrative structures, which are characteristically feudalistic, but also through their continuing emphasis on competition, which serves both as a convenient motivating device for successful pupils and an act of homage to the principle of success. Children who succeed at their school tasks are still often revered by teachers for their good work, while those who do less well are encouraged to feel some guilt about their bad performance. Especially the more able children soon learn that good work is likely to bring a good job in the end, with high social ranking and all the material benefits that result. Rather sadly, this typically European value orientation is tending to extend its influence to many other parts of the world.

A magnificent obsession

How much are human behaviour patterns common to all mankind? How much is there a communality of thought processes from one ethnic or cultural group to another? Is there a psychic unity of Man?

This question, a constant and vexing one for anthropologists and psychologists in modern times, is in essence a restatement of a more general, and more ancient, question posed by Plato, and reiterated by Kant. Their answer has been to the effect that the form is everywhere the same: only the content differs from place to place, and from time to time. It provides at least a working hypothesis for contemporary social scientists.

For several centuries, the relevance of this ancient answer to issues in anthropology and psychology went unappreciated by western explorers and colonists, as their interest in other cultures, often perforce, increased. Since the discovery of the New World, many European scientists and administrators have become preoccupied with points of view and devices for making comparisons between their own and other cultures, almost always in ways which showed European cultures up in a more favourable light. This has been notwithstanding almost constant political and religious turmoil, often with attendant barbarism, in their own home continent. During the last hundred years, under the pressing consequences of colonization, this preoccupation has become, for some students of cultural contrasts, something approaching an obsession.

Among the greatest ethnic and cultural contrasts to be found anywhere in the world is the one between middle-class Europeans and Australian Aboriginals. It has long been customary for European explorers and colonists, with a noticeable lack of discriminatory precision and often the support of the Church, to categorize, almost in pre-operational fashion, virtually all non-Europeans in one or two stereo-typical categories. Thus the term "native" is to be found in official reports, parliamentary enactments and popular literature in references to the inhabitants of regions as widely scattered as Africa, the Americas, the Pacific and Asia. Captain James Cook referred to the indigenous inhabitants of Australia as Indians. Before him, in 1621, the Dutch explorer Janzen remarked of Aboriginals in the north-eastern Cape York area of Australia, after he saw "many human bones in different places", that:

> "It may be safely assumed that (they) are cannibals, and when hungry do not spare one another ... And even the men are more miserable and unsightly than I have ever seen in my age and time"
>
> (Jack, 1921, p. 47).

This statement must stand out as a remarkable example of ethnocentrism and patriarchy; but in this it was not far removed from an observation of Abel Tasman. Twenty years later he described Aboriginals as:

> "naked, beach-roaming wretches, destitute of rice and not possessed of fruits worth mentioning, excessively poor and of a very malignant nature."
>
> (Jack, 1921, p. 64).

Even in the nineteenth century, attitudes by eminent scholars to non-Europeans were often not noticeably different. In 1869, for example, Galton observed that:

> "The number amongst negroes of those who we should call half-witted is very large ... The mistakes the negroes made in their own matters were so childish, stupid and simpleton-like as frequently (to) make me ashamed of my own species."
>
> (Nurcombe, 1976a).

Even more explicit was the anatomist Fiske in 1893:

> "If we take into account the creasing of the cerebral surface, the differences between the brain of a Shakespeare and that of an Australian savage would doubtless be fifty times greater than the difference between the Australian's brain and that of an orang-utang."

But not long after these comments, the ethnocentrism of westerners took a turn for the better with the publication of the report of the Cambridge anthropological expedition of 1899–1901 (Haddon, 1901). This was the first substantial intercultural study of perceptual and cognitive characteristics using scientific methodology, and it happened to take place in northern Australia and New Guinea. The study was carried out at a time when perceptual and motor skills were believed to be closely related to intellectual skills. On many of the perceptual and motor skills investigated, the Aboriginal subjects performed at a similar level to English subjects.

However, the intellectual reputation of Aboriginals and some other ethnic groups again suffered a downturn in the west with the maze studies of Porteus, which began in 1915 and continued for half a century (Porteus, 1965). On the basis of maze performance, generally of the pencil-and-paper variety, Porteus constructed a supposed hierarchy of intellect, with Europeans located, interestingly, on top.

As the century progressed, a few other workers tried various intelligence tests on Aboriginals, always with results which were interpreted to indicate a marked inferiority to Europeans. Aboriginal children were often found to show an early and rapid mental growth rate which asymptoted in late childhood – about the time that Aboriginal children might have perceived their limited life prospects at the hands of the dominant white culture. It did not seem to occur to the white testers that such a perception might have had a bearing on the willingness of older Aboriginal children to respond to them.

The earliest glimmer of a breakdown of ethnocentricity came with the more etic approach of Fowler, Traylen and McElwain, who carried out a survey of desert Aboriginal children in 1939. The following year, Fowler cautioned that:

"the testing of natives by ordinary intelligence tests is extremely difficult and the results very unreliable. Tests satisfactory in one culture are notoriously unreliable in another, and this unreliability is more clearly seen when the cultures are as far apart as those of the Australian white and the native"

(Kearney, de Lacey and Davidson, 1973, p. 39)

This observation was a milestone in the history of cross-cultural psychology, and was made about the time when the culture-fair movement, sponsored by Cattell and others in the United States, was beginning to try to design intelligence tests that would be valid across cultures. The objective of this movement was to eliminate from tests content which was specific to only one or two cultures. The search for universal content, however, did not meet with remarkable success: psychometric theory was unequal to the task.

One mankind or many? An environmental argument

Meanwhile, schools of anthropologists had taken up opposing points of view on the question of psychic unity. In 1911, Boas supported the principle, while Lévy-Bruhl

(1922) proposed that many non-western people possessed a "primitive mentality", employing thought modes that are qualitatively different from western thinking patterns.

The debate was later joined by linguists and learning theorists. Behaviourists like Skinner (1972), on one hand, suggested that the language of the infant is learned by operant conditioning, as parents reinforce the appropriate rather than the inappropriate collections of phonemes he utters. On the other hand, Chomsky (1957) and Lenneberg (1967) argued that language is biologically based, since it shows a high degree of structural communality across cultures, and since children's language forms (e.g. "all-gone sticky" for washing the hands) are not always repetitions of the forms of adult words or phrases.

But is there, then, a psychic unity of mankind? In some degree, undoubtedly there is. Common patterns of neural processes across cultures are associated with universal bipedal locomotion, or the development of stereoscopic vision. Facial expressions of mirth or anger are everywhere recognized for what they are. Why not fundamental cognitive processes, albeit substantially adapted from place to place, to allow the development of locally desirable skills to meet the requirements for successful living? It is this local adaptation of universal processes that is the basis of a major environmentalist position, the useful ecological functionalism hypothesis developed by Berry in Canada.

Berry's ecological hypothesis has been described both in an original simpler form (Berry, 1971) and subsequently in a more elaborated schema (Berry, 1974). In a molar approach to ecological–behavioural interaction, by contrast with molecular or S–R points of view, Berry is concerned with the persisting influences bearing upon organisms from the long-term ecology or physical environment. The model, which reflects a functionalist tradition in the sense that it emphasises interactions, represents both physical and cultural influences bearing upon the individual, as well as the reciprocal influences the individual can exert upon his environment, either through his own responses or with the aid of technological devices. Four universal "intermediate bonds," mediating between the ecology and the individual, are represented by culture, socialization, nutrition and disease, and gene pool, in the original model.

As Berry acknowledges (1974), his ecological functionalism is indebted to the probablistic functionalism of Brunswick (1957). Both Berry and Brunswick avoid any commitment to determinism; Berry is explicit in describing the recent elaboration of his model as probablistic. This elaborated model differs from the original, simpler, static, linear model in incorporating a dynamic structure which provides for feedback loops between variables. The elaborated model includes 6 major components and 19 relationships.

According to the ecological hypothesis, within a given culture, certain behaviours are in ecological demand, and identifiable cultural aids appear, to help individuals develop behaviours appropriate to their ecologies. The crucial bases of the ecologies are physical variables. Where soil fertility and rainfall are low and temperatures are extreme, such as in the sub-arctic or Central Australia, agriculture is not normally possible, so that sparsely-populated societies subsist in a nomadic, hunting (fish or game) or gathering economy. By contrast, where rainfall is abundant and temperatures and soil fertility are kinder, such as in equatorial Africa, greater concentrations of sedentary people engage in agriculture, and can store their food to ensure a reliable supply. From these premises, the hypotheses predicts, there emerge not only molar cultural and life-style characteristics, but also typical molecular patterns of mental life, often consistently manifested across perceptual, cognitive and effective domains and in social behaviour.

Berry admits that his elaborated model has yet to be validated, but he claims that it is based already on some substantial empirical data, some of which he cites, such as the Barry, Child and Bacon (1959) study of child-rearing patterns. In addition to Berry's own studies, other reports have also remarked the correlates of ecology in psychological research, for example those of Whiting (1963), Dawson (1967) and Dasen (1974, 1975).

Though the ecological paradigm of which Berry was a prominent advocate has been probably the most outstanding for viewing cognitive patterns as a correlate of environment, there have been others. All have contributed, in the years since the second world war, to the demise of ethnocentric attitudes to researches into the nature of human mentality. Notable among them are the pronouncements of United Nations agencies, and the observations of Pike (1967), who has articulated a dichotomy of approaches on the question of the relationship between cultural characteristics and human behaviour, implicit in the notion of etic in contrast to emic points of view:

"The etic viewpoint studies behaviour as from outside of a particular system, and as an essential initial approach to an alien system. The emic viewpoint results from studying behaviour from inside the system" (p. 37).

Pike had coined the words "etic" and "emic" from the pair of linguistic terms phonetic (referring to all vocal sounds) and phonemic (referring to units of significant sounds in a given language). Over the last decade, Pike's model has been widely employed as a basis for stating the point of departure for a range of intercultural studies.

Subsequently, issues on the methodology and validity of comparing characteristics of subjects across cultures have been raised (e.g. Berry, 1969) and a range of solutions to inherent problems suggested (e.g. Brislin et al., 1973).

Not surprisingly, the ecological hypothesis is not in accord with all major proposals on the origins of intelligence. Notably, it is at odds with the point of view of Jensen (1969, 1973), which, through its argument that both levels of intelligence (Level I and Level II) are essentially genetically determined. An outstanding refutation of Jensen's position is offered by Nurcombe (1976b), who offers an alternative approach to explaining group or ethnic differences based on a model which relates potential, competence and performance. Nurcombe, unlike Jensen, leaves open the question of whether potential is inherently different between ethnic groups. Potential to Nurcombe is "the aggregate of the genetically determined possibilities that interact with each other and the environment during development to produce competence"

(p. 37). Realization, the interaction referred to, occurs through the complementary processes of differentiation and integration of developing capacities to produce competence, which is expressed as performance. Samples of performance yield scores or stages in test results. Nurcombe's appears to be a sound paradigm, quite compatible with Piagetian theory, as with Berry's ecological functionalism.

A further study supporting the ecological hypothesis was carried out by Dasen, de Lacey and Seagrim (1973). They gave Piagetian and verbal IQ tests to 36 Aboriginal children (all who could be located) who had been fostered or adopted in Adelaide, South Australia, by white families. Despite the problematical case histories of several of these children, resulting in poor health and marked anxiety, they scored about as well, overall, as white children in Canberra, a new city with an environment generally more favourable to most of its inhabitants in terms of living conditions than the older state capitals.

Essentially a hypothesis in the environmentalist tradition, the ecological proposal offers a much-needed direction to intercultural studies. This it does by emphasizing the necessity of taking account of the environments of groups of children under study, in much more than the rather cursory way that has been characteristic of many studies hitherto. Cross-disciplinary studies are beginning to appear, which consider the social and historical interests of the subjects under study more than merely superficially. For example, Twomey (forthcoming) is studying cognitive and schooling characteristics of Aboriginal children in settlements on the far south coast of New South Wales at the same time as he is collaborating in a substantial social and economic history of the area. Twomey is basing the sociological component of his study on the culture-of-poverty notion of Lewis (1966), and is consequently examining how much Aboriginals' life styles provide a design for living and a resource for solving life's problems. The way is thus opening for students of cross-cultural psychology to undertake much more meaningful and more productive studies, than hitherto, of the fascinating diversity of Man's psychic unity, in their quest for universal principles of human psychology.

Ecology and the Piagetian tradition

Some evidence drawn from the Piagetian tradition, since Mead's study of 1932, has also tended to support the ecological hypothesis. This evidence has broadly been of two kinds: first, studies which have shown differences in acquisition of characteristics of operational thinking (usually classification or conservation) accountable in terms of environmental demands; and secondly studies which have shown change in rate of acquisition of operational thinking with changes in environment. The first kind of evidence is illustrated by de Lemos (1969) who found conservation to be slower to develop in Aboriginal children than white children, and Zulu children to trail whites in developing some spatial skills. Presumably, Aboriginals and Zulus had less need to develop these skills in their normal environments. This kind of evidence has also been demonstrated by the present author in the differences found between rural black and city white children in Australia and the United States in classificatory skills (de Lacey 1970, 1976). In Australia, these differences disappeared, however, where the ecology of white and black children was similar.

The second kind of evidence, based on changes in rate of development of operational thinking accompanying changes in ecology, has been reported by Peluffo (1967) in Italy, and by de Lacey (1971b) and de Lacey et al. (1973) as a result of deliberate intervention in the environment in Australia. Peluffo showed that children moving from southern rural Italy to Genoa were initially retarded in concrete-operational thinking, as measured by tests of conservation. Subsequently, however, the rate of development of the migrants changed, to be more like their new city peers'. The Australian intervention example is described later in this chapter.

Piagetian theory has provided the basis for a range of cross-cultural studies, reviewed by Dasen (1972) and Ashton (1975). The Piagetian approach to the comparative measurement of cognition has two major advantages over the psychometric approach, which employs standardized and rather ethnocentric intelligence tests. The first is that mental processes rather than products are being investigated. This means that test content can be changed to suit the experiences of children wherever they are raised, so long as the underlying processes remain constant. This has, in fact been done, for example in a series of studies by the present author (de Lacey, 1970, 1971a, 1971b, 1972, 1976; de Lacey and Smock, 1974b). A second advantage of employing Piagetian theory cross-culturally is the flexibility inherent in Piaget's testing procedure, which he calls the clinical method (Piaget, 1929), having noted its similarity to psychiatric interviews. Although a greater variety of apparatus has been used in testing over the last 20 years, and although rather more emphasis has been placed on correct solutions to test items rather than reasons for solutions than hitherto (Dasen, 1975), the clinical method of studying children's cognition has remained basically intact. The clinical method is essentially a loosely structured interview, in which the experimenter is free to adapt his questioning of the child to the child's age and to the nature of his responses. The experimenter not only takes note of the child's responses, but also of the child's explanations of them; for the goal of the clinical method is to identify the qualitative nature of the mental processes underlying these responses.

As Flavell explains the clinical method, it is a technique which "permits the child to move on his own intellectually, to display cognitive orientation which is natural to him at that period in his development . . . The hope is that in this way the problems posed can really be relevant to the child's ongoing intellectual functioning, and will permit pertinent interpretable behaviour to emerge" (Flavell 1963, p. 28).

Flavell (1963), p. 29) warns of both dangers and difficulties inherent in employing the clinical method. For example, the experimenter may miss the significance of important child behaviours; and in the resulting behaviour protocols he may underestimate or over-estimate the child's intellectual level through a too-hasty interpretation of the child's responses. The skill and ingenuity of the examiner, advises Flavell, must in part compensate for such difficulties of the clinical method. Piaget had earlier made this point when he said:

It is so hard not to talk too much when questioning a child, especially for a pedagogue! It is so hard not to be suggestive! And above all, it is so hard to find the middle course between systematisation due to preconceived ideas and incoherence due to the absence of any directing hypothesis ... The psychologist must, in fact, make up for the uncertainties in the method of interrogation by sharpening the subtleties of his interpretation"

(Piaget, 1929, p. 9).

Perhaps one of the most telling appraisals of the clinical method is that of Claparède. In introducing one of Piaget's earlier books, Claparède commented:

"It is, in fact, that method of observation, which consists in letting the child talk and in noticing the manner in which his thought unfolds itself ... The clinical method ... which is also an art, the art of questioning, does not confine itself to superficial observations, but aims at capturing what is hidden behind the immediate appearance of things. It analyses down to its ultimate constituents the least little remark made by the young subjects. It does not give up the struggle when the child gives incomprehensible or contradictory answers, but only follows closer in chase of ever-receding thought, drives from cover, pursues and tracks it down till it can seize it, dissect it and lay bare the secrets of its composition"

(Claparède, 1926, pp. xiii–xiv).

While it is a highly flexible procedure, the clinical method is structured to the extent that the primary questions are laid down; but it is up to the examiner to repeat, rephrase or explain his questions, according to his own judgement of the child, and of the clues the child gives in his responses regarding the likely nature of his thought processes. It is in this respect, as Wallace (1965, p. 57) has pointed out, that the use of the clinical method demands both imagination and critical sense. But, in allowing discretionary freedom to follow up clues to unexpected, and often crucial, indicators of children's thinking, the clinical method is likely to provide the basis for a truer comparison of children's thought processes than can be obtained by the use of standardised tests in the psychometric tradition, in many cross-cultural situations.

Some Piagetian surveys

If Piagetian tests are going to show up differences in performance (in Nurcombe's sense) between two ethnic groups anywhere, then they should do so in Australia. For here are two coexisting cultures – Anglo-saxon-derived whites and indigenous Aboriginals – which are probably more dissimilar than are to be found anywhere else in the world. On the one hand, the white inhabitants represent an accumulation of, and participation in, slowly developing symbolic systems, technologies and experiences, associated with frequent interactions with many cultural groups over many centuries. On the other hand, the sparse population of Aboriginals has been virtually cut off from the rest of humanity, with minimal technology, in a relatively hostile environment, for about 30 000 years.

During the 1960's, a series of studies of performance of Aboriginal children based on Piagetian tests was carried out. All of the researchers experienced some difficulty in communicating with the more remote Aboriginal children, partly because of the awesomeness of their presence (despite efforts to overcome this) and partly because there was no completely adequate common language. On occasion the psychologists tried to use interpreters, but this ploy had to be abandoned because control of the situation was lost during vernacular dialogues which developed between interpreter and subject. The results must be contaminated by these influences. Nevertheless, these studies provided some new and interesting cross-cultural information.

The first of these studies was an extensive one of conservation performance by de Lemos (1969). Her findings supported Piaget's notion of an invariant sequence of stages of development, though there was some suggestion of a reversal of the weight–volume sequence found by Piaget within the period of concrete operations. She also found that part-whites scored better than full-blood Aboriginals among children sharing identical life ways in the same settlement in Central Australia. Neither of these findings, however, could be replicated by Dasen (1973), who tested children in the same Central Australian settlement, including some of the same subjects. Meanwhile, Jensen (1973) and Eysenck (1971) had used de Lemos' findings to support their notion that intelligence is mainly inherited. Dasen did not claim that his findings were any more valid than de Lemos', but, since the matter is under dispute, her findings cannot properly be used as evidence for the Jensenist point of view until the issue is resolved.

An outstanding examination of Piagetian evidence for the ecological hypothesis has been made by Dasen (1972, 1975). He compared performance on spatial and conservation tasks among groups of subjects well separated on an eco-cultural continuum: low-food-accumulating Eskimos, as well as Aboriginals, and high-food-accumulating Ebrié on the Ivory Coast. He demonstrated clear support for the hypothesis from the spatial test results, and some support from the conservation results. Dasen noted that the differences between samples did not occur in the younger groups as noticeably, and attributed this to the effects of schooling (especially where the teachers were white) and to the possibility that the ecological demands for the development of spatial skills occur over the complete range of development, whereas the presses for the development of conservation occur as a result of more socio-cultural mediation, such as experience at purchasing at food markets. Dasen also draws attention to a distinction between competence and spontaneous performance in conservation, illustrated by 12 to 14 year old Eskimo non-conservers who learnt to conserve liquids quite quickly by comparison with 10 and 11 year olds who apparently lacked the competence possessed by the older children. Dasen concluded that discrepancies in rates of development in different areas of concrete operations might be due to different adaptive values of these areas, and to schooling.

The third study, carried out by the present author (de Lacey, 1970), employed two samples of Aboriginal children, distinguished by their degree of contact with Europeans; and two samples of white children, distinguished by their levels of income. The instruments used were four tests of classificatory ability, based on the work of Inhelder and Piaget (1964). The battery included the some-and-all test; the test of hierarchical classification, a version of the multiple or multiplicative classification test, with some of the content changed to suit local conditions; and the Nixon test, tapping ability to reclassify sets of small wooden rods differing in three attributes—height, diameter and colour. The Piagetian rubic was followed of requiring subjects not only to solve the problems, but also to explain their answers. The procedures have been described elsewhere (de Lacey, 1970, 1974).

On all four tests, the order of performance was the same: the high-income whites did best, followed by the low-income whites, the high-contact Aboriginals, and last the low-contact Aboriginals. Most similar of the two groups were the middle-scoring ones: the low-income whites and the high-contact Aboriginals, some of whom lived in a city and some on an off-shore island. A replication of the study with town-dwelling Aboriginals believed to have little or no white parentage showed indistinguishable differences with low-income whites (de Lacey, 1971a). Like Peluffo's study (Peluffo, 1967), this study offered some support for the ecological functionalism hypothesis (which had not yet been published, however, when the studies were carried out) in an ontogenetic rather than a phylogenetic sense. This suggests that individuals and families, within one lifespan, are capable of substantial sociological change, even while maintaining some cohesion as identifiable groups. Wheeler (1942) had earlier produced support for this hypothesis. His low-IQ American mountain children improved their IQ scores after a new motorway suddenly facilitated access to mainstream lifeways.

In commenting upon the present author's study just described, Ashton (1975) refers to the survey design employed and remarks that "this interpretation makes distinct value judgements in favour of western performance patterns" (p. 484). An alternative interpretation, however, is the recognition of a social reality. For better or for worse, there is no doubt that the tentacles of western technology and life styles are still extending into much of the world of non-western peoples. This process is more inexorable where the indigenous population is small, or poor, or both, such as among almost all Australian Aboriginals, right throughout the continent. In a very real way, then, there is as much an etic, as an emic, quality about the value judgement of what accommodations to the dominant culture are worthwhile fostering in children.

To choose or be chosen

How much of an indigenous culture can survive the pervasive intrusions of westernism? For how long? For the thoughtful indigene, in Australia at least, the consequence of these questions is a nice dilemma: how can he retain substantial and valued components of his own life ways, while at the same time accommodating to the apparent western advantages of food, health services, housing, transport and energy? This dilemma is especially acute when he wrestles with deciding upon the most suitable kind of schooling for his children, in whatever light he can cast upon the probable demands the society of the future will make upon them. Some older

Aboriginals in remote areas are more concerned with passing on their cultural heritage to the new generation than adopting westernized schooling; and their sentiments are reinforced by white proponents of a traditional wish to "leave the natives be," free to choose their own life style. Specifically it is often argued that parents, and children, should have a choice in their schooling, as to policies, curricula and control. How can such choices be ensured?

Ultimately, of course, no-one has a clear choice on this kind of issue, unless all the options are both apparent and available, and all the implications are understood. This condition is clear in the management of countries described as democratic, in most of which a representative range of possible philosophies of government are neither apparent nor available, while the possible consequences of electing those that are seem obscure to say the least. Even less available are choices of schooling, except for a minority of parents who can afford private-school fees.

Attention has been drawn to the especial constraints upon choices for Aboriginals by Nurcombe (1971), where these choices concern life styles in a western-dominated society. To ask Aboriginal parents what kind of schooling they would prefer for their children is rather like asking the present author which valley he would prefer to live in on Mars. The answer in both cases could be little more specific, or meaningful, than – a nice one. But most parents, Aboriginal or white, immigrant or native born, would tend, given nominal choice, to opt for a kind of education that would help prepare their children for the life they will need to live 20 or 30 or 40 years on.

What kind of Australian society will children of today find at the end of the century? Around the year 2000 A.D., it is better than an even bet, the popular nursery rhymes will include Humpty Dumpty and Old King Cole, beer will be the most popular adult drink, and most of the current idioms will still be in vogue, spoken with the unmistakable tones of the Australian accent. Despite the influx of around 3 million immigrants from Europe in the last thirty years, compounded with the 150 000 Aboriginals, the anglosaxon-derived culture is likely to remain relatively intransigent.

The basis for the prediction is the recent history of Australia, especially by comparison with other former British colonies of the nineteenth century, such as Canada and New Zealand. Despite a built-in acceptance of public responsibility for communications, railway transport, and major radio and television operations, mediated through government agencies, Australia has shown a remarkable potential conservatism to be the dominant influence of the present century. Compared with its near neighbour, New Zealand, Australia was years later with female franchise, old-age pensions, free places in secondary schools, and accrediting for university entrance. Almost 40 years after New Zealand, Australia introduced a national health insurance scheme in 1975, only to earn the distinction the following year to become the first – and possibly only – western country to begin dismantling one. So effectively had the founding fathers created a constitution resistant to change that it took sixteen years to get all the states to agree to set up a federal civil aviation authority. A further conservative characteristic, though one shared with many less intransigent countries, is the preoccupation by most schools with academic studies leading to university courses. It is now 40 years since the number of high-school pupils going on to university became less than those who were not; yet the curricula are still geared principally to suit the minority who are destined for universities.

It was in this climate that a fresh breeze of change blew across the country after 1972. Greatly increased allocations were made to education and welfare, including substantial grants to Aboriginal groups. Many Aboriginal children reared in make-shift huts with dirt floors found themselves in houses within the town limits. Funds for educational innovations, often for the benefit of immigrant and Aboriginal children, were made available, often paid directly to teacher applicants. But the change of direction was short-lived. Economic pressures and a reversion to conservative government brought about a levelling off of the rate of increase of expenditure on education and welfare, and even some regression. Moreover, even throughout the temporary change of political direction, the prerequisites for access to economic independence, and a share in political and economic power remained the same. Children still had to learn to jump through the hoops set up by the dominant culture to make it.

As much as a recognition of this reality as an attempt to make the choice of future life style more real, an experimental preschool was established in 1969 in Bourke, New South Wales, a town of about 3500 people, a greater proportion of whom have a lower income than the state average. The project was part of the Arid Zone Project, an experiment in community psychiatry sponsored by the medical school of the University of New South Wales. The original directors were Nurcombe and Moffitt (1970), who based the main emphasis of their programme on the language enrichment researches of Bereiter and Engelmann (1966), though this approach was later somewhat modified. During the first full year of operation, 1970, they demonstrated clearly that a language-enrichment programme could raise IQ scores by an average of around 25 points, while matched children in a parallel traditional programme showed little gain. The latter finding was a replication of results reported by Harries (unpublished*) in another New South Wales country town.

Subsequently, follow-up studies (de Lacey et al., 1972; de Lacey and Nurcombe, 1976) showed some erosion of gains, as had already been reported in several North American experiments, but nevertheless no sign of the expected cumulative deficit. On the contrary, there was a maintenance of some of the gains, especially by some of the white children. The evaluators were probably excessively cautious in their reports, for they included in their analysis of results a small number of Aboriginal children who did not proceed to school the year after their preschooling, but spent the year untutored and playing in the bush: their IQ, verbal and concept-development scores all plummetted. Nor did the evaluators take account of the much higher absentee and truancy rates for Aboriginal children at the primary and secondary schools in the town.

---

* Harries, W. (1969). Effects of rural preschooling, Litt. B. Thesis, University of New England Library, Armidale, N.S.W.

Since its inception, the preschool has provided 2 h of preschooling a day for the 48 lowest-scoring black or white children in the town, on a verbal selection test given at age 3.5. Essential ingredients of the programme now include low pupil–teacher ratio, effective teachers and aides, emphasis on language and concept-development training, cars to collect and deliver the children with no transport, daily nutritious snacks, home involvement through home visiting by teachers and aides, and recently a programme of guided play (Cocking and de Lacey, 1975). Each year the average scores on the selection test have tended to rise. It is assumed that the preschool has contributed to this result, but no doubt other events have also played their part. The New South Wales Health Commission has intensified health-care programmes, television – including Sesame Street – arrived in the town in 1972, and vitamin fortification was without advertisement added to the bread flour for a period. This latter factor is believed by Kamien (1975), a research physician, to have contributed to a sharp reduction in the relatively high level of pathological conditions among Aboriginal children. The bread-fortifying programme has, however, been discontinued, apparently for ethical reasons.

The consequences emerging from the Bourke preschool project, which is reported more fully elsewhere (Nurcombe, 1976a; de Lacey, 1974), are that a language-enrichment preschool operation can be correlated with a substantial rise in level of verbal and conceptual performance, and that subsequent erosion of gains made is lessened with closer approximation to the greater participation of the parents and the home in children's cognitive and emotional needs (in line with the findings of Levenstein (1974) in the U.S.), appropriate follow-through into formal schooling, and attention to health, housing and other welfare needs. The end result is likely to be an enhancement of ability to make a real choice, by both children and parents, as to the kind of life style they wish to adopt, in the light of the perceived ecological demands, both social and physical; and as to the aids considered necessary to meet these demands. At a more specific level, greater verbal and number facility appears to be allowing more low-income children in Bourke to begin to meet more of the expectations of primary-school teachers. The first step towards mitigating the continual school failure that children there have hitherto experienced seems to have been taken.

Culture and humanity

From its first weeks, any human infant is learning to adapt, to be compatible with its physical and social environment. This it normally achieves, as Piaget reminds us, by adjusting both itself (accommodation) and the environment (assimilation) in an equilibrated way, at the levels of physical action and mental representations of physical action. Just as he learns early in life the complementary perceptual and cognitive processes of discrimination and generalization, so he learns in middle and later childhood to develop the further complementary processes of differentiation and integration. Whereas formerly there was a widespread tendency to believe that these processes were determined primarily by in-built mechanisms, now there is more reason to suppose that they are susceptible to development and modification in response to environmental stimulation and demands. There is perhaps the most detailed evidence on this point in the area of differentiation.

It was Werner (1948) who applied the biological model of differentiation to psychology, Witkin et al. (1962) who developed the notion of psychological differentiation, and Berry (1966, 1971) who was prominent in transporting the concept across cultural boundaries and especially to the area of his particular concern, ecological functionalism. Recently describing characteristics of psychological differentiation, Witkin and Berry (1975) suggest that an increase in differentiation is typical of development, that greater differentiation implies specialization of function, separation of the self from the environment, and more harmonious integration and at the same time complexity of functioning within the individual. Greater differentiation, moreover, can generally be seen across several domains of mental life, rather than merely discretely in separate domains. A person showing high levels of differentiation in the perceptual domain of functioning may thus also be expected to show high levels of cognitive or affective differentiation. Across cultures, it appears that highly developed differentiation has adaptive value where populations are low and nomadic, in a hunting (fish or game) economy such as the Eskimo's. Here, children are raised permissively, with full rein allowed to let them learn to explore and to become knowledgeable, resourceful, field-independent and adaptable. By contrast, in sedentary cultures, there is less advantage in developing the process of differentiation. Among many African and Asian societies, for example, populations are large, dense, and sedentary, societies are elaborately structured and life is predictable. In this climate, children are raised in a constrained environment, disciplined so that they learn their prescribed niche in society. They become, as adults, less resourceful, less adaptable and field-dependent. As a basis for cross-cultural comparisons, differentiation theory has much to offer, since it appears to be a crucial element in socialization, a universal in all human existence.

Human universals, can we conclude, beginning with the anatomical and biological attributes of the species and its basic perceptual and cognitive mechanisms, extend to the fundamental process of readiness to socialize. Implicit in the process of socialization is the identification by the child of his own status with respect to others in his group, and in turn the status of his own group within a universal hierarchy or network of groups. It is within this area of status learning that the acquisition of deep-seated and permanent sentiments of prejudice or understanding occurs.

As the methodology of enquiry into differences between ethnic and cultural groups becomes more sophisticated and valid, so apparently the considerable adaptability of human beings is revealed. Even within the severe constraints of family and cultural socialization, long-standing defective nutrition, and rampant pathology, enterprises such as the Bourke project seem to be confirming this capacious adaptability. Not the least factor in the matter of adaptation is the growth of Man as a social being, concerned about the welfare of the other members of his species. Indeed, Brameld (1971) regards the development of social concern and sensitivity as a key function of formal schooling. Fortunately, throughout almost all cultures there seems to exist, albeit at various levels of consciousness, concern

422

for the less favoured, the less able, the more vulnerable – in a phrase, for the notion of social justice. If any attribute will do so, this notion seems the most crucial to any claim Man has to being pinnacle of the Universe.

Literature cited

Ashton, P. T. (1975) Cross-cultural Piagetian research: an experimental perspective, *Harv. Educ. Rev. 45*, 475–506

Bagley, C. (1975) On the intellectual equality of races. In: *Race and Education Across Cultures* (G. K. Gadgendra and C. Bagley, eds.) Heinemann, London.

Barry, H., Child, I. and Bacon, M. (1959) The relation of child training to subsistence economy, *Am. Anthropol. 61*, 51–63

Bereiter, C. and Engelmann, S. (1966) *Teaching Disadvantaged Children in the Preschool*, Prentice-Hall, Englewood Cliffs, N. J.

Berry, J. W. (1966) Temne and Eskimo perceptual skills, *Intl. J. Psychol. 1*, 415–518

Berry, J. W. (1969) On cross-cultural comparability, *Intl. J. Psychol. 4*, 119–128

Berry, J. W. (1971) Ecological and cultural factors in spatial-skill development, *Can. J. Behav. Sci. 3*, 324–336

Berry, J. W. (1974) Differentiation across cultures: cognitive style and affective style. In: *Readings in Cross-Cultural Psychology* (J. L. M. Dawson and W. J. Lonner, eds.) Hong Kong University Press, Hong Kong

Boas, F. (1911) *The Mind of Primitive Man*, Macmillan, New York

Brameld, T. (1971) *Patterns of Educational Philosophy: Divergence and Convergence in Culturological Perspective*, Holt, Rinehart and Winston, New York

Brislin, R. W., Lonner, W. J. and Thorndike, R. M. (1973) *Cross-Cultural Research Methods*, Wiley, New York

Bruner, J. S., Greenfield, P. M. and Olver, R. R. (1966) *Studies in Cognitive Growth*, Wiley, New York

Brunswick, E. (1957) Scope and aspects of the cognitive problem. In: *Cognition. The Colorado Symposium* (H. Gruber, ed.) Harvard University Press, Cambridge, Mass.

Chomsky, N. (1957) *Syntactic Structures*, Mouton, The Hague

Claparède, E. (1926) Introduction. In: J. Piaget, (1932) *Language and Thought of the Child*, Routledge and Kegan Paul, London

Cocking, R. D. and de Lacey, P. R. (1975) A theoretical framework for the role of guided play in early learning. In: *Before School Begins* (M. E. Poole, D. F. Davis, F. D. Kielcrup and J. L. Evans, eds.) Wiley, Sydney

Congalton, A. A. (1963) *Occupational Status in Australia* (Studies in Sociology No. 3) University of New South Wales (School of Sociology) Sydney

Dasen, P. R. (1972) Cross-cultural Piatetian research: a summary, *J. Cross-Cul. Psychol. 3*, 23–39

Dasen, P. R. (1973) Piagetian research in Central Australia. In: *The Psychology of Aboriginal Australians* (G. E. Kearney, P. R. de Lacey and G. R. Davidson, eds.) Wiley, Sydney

Dasen, P. R. (1974) The influence of ecology, culture and European contact on cognitive development in Australian Aborigines. In: *Culture and Cognition: Readings in Cross-Cultural Psychology* (J. W. Berry and P. R. Dasen, eds.) Methuen, London

Dasen, P. R. (1975) Concrete-operational development in three cultures, *J. Cross-Cul. Psychol. 6*, 156–172

Dasen, P. R., de Lacey, P. R. and Seagrim, G. N. (1973) An investigation of reasoning ability in adopted and fostered Aboriginal children (The Adelaide Study). In: *The Psychology of Aboriginal Australians* (G. E. Kearney, P. R. de Lacey and G. R. Davidson, eds.) Wiley, Sydney

Dawson, J. L. M. (1967) Cultural and psychological influences upon spatial-perceptual processes in West Africa, Parts I and II. *Intl. J. Psychol. 2*, 115–128 and 171–185

de Lacey, P. R. (1970) A cross-cultural study of classificatory ability, *J. Cross-Cult. Psychol. 1*, 293–304

de Lacey, P. R. (1971a) Classificatory ability and verbal intelligence among high-contact Aboriginal and low-socioeconomic white Australian children, *J. Cross-Cult. Psychol. 2*, 393–396

de Lacey, P. R. (1971b) Verbal intelligence, operational thinking and environment in part-Aboriginal children, *Aust. J. Psychol. 23*, 145–149

de Lacey, P. R. (1972) The relationship between classificatory ability and verbal intelligence, *Intl. J. Psychol. 7*, 243–246

de Lacey, P. R. (1974) *So Many Lessons To Learn*, Penguin, Ringwood, Vic.

de Lacey, P. R. (1976) Lifeways and cognitive performance in Australia and America. In: *Aboriginal Cognition: Retrospect and Prospect* (D. W. McElwain and G. E. Kearney, eds.) Australian Institute of Aboriginal Studies, Canberra

de Lacey, P. R. and Nurcombe, B. (1976) Effects of enrichment preschooling at Bourke: a further follow-up study, University of Wollongong, unpublished report

de Lacey, P. R. Nurcombe, B., Taylor, L. and Moffitt, P. (1973) The duration of the effects of enrichment preschooling: an Australian follow-up study, *Exceptional Child, 40*, 171–176

de Lacey, P. R. and Smock, C. D. (1974a) *A Survey of Children in Different School Programmes*, Follow-Through Research Report, University of Georgia, Athens, Ga.

de Lacey, P. R. and Smock, C. D. (1974b) *Lifeways and Performance in Australia and the United States*, Follow-Through Research Report, University of Georgia, Athens, Ga.

de Lemos, M. M. (1969) The development of conservation in Aboriginal children, *Intl. J. Psychol. 4*, 255–269

Eysenck, J. H. (1971) *Race, Intelligence and Education*, Temple Smith, London

Flavell, J. H. (1963) *The Developmental Psychology of Jean Piaget*, Van Nostrand, Princeton, N.J.

Fowler, H. L. (1940) Report on the psychological tests of natives in the north-west of western Australia. In: *The Psychology of Aboriginal Australians* (G. E. Kearney, P. R. de Lacey and G. R. Davidson, eds.) (1973) Wiley, Sydney

Haddon, A. C. (ed.) (1901) *Reports of the Cambridge Anthropological Expedition to the Torres Strait*, Vol. 2, Physiology and Psychology, Cambridge University Press, London

Harries, W. (1969) *Effects of Rural Preschooling*, unpublished Litt. B. Thesis; University of New England Library, Armidale, N.S.W.

Inhelder, B. and Piaget, J. (1964) *The Early Growth of Logic in the Child*, Routledge and Kegan Paul, London

Jack, R. L. (1921) *Northernmost Australia*, George Robertson, Melbourne

Jackson, B. (1966) *Education and the Working Class*, Penguin, Harmondsworth, Middx.

Jencks, C. (1972) *Inequality. A Reassessment of the Effects of Family and Schooling in America*, Basic Books, New York

Jenson, A. R. (1969) How much can we boost IQ and educational achievement? *Harv. Educ. Rev. 39*, 1–123

Jensen, A. R. (1973) *Educability and Group Differences*, Harper and Row, New York

Kamien, M. (1975) Nutrition and the Australian Aborigines: effects of the fortification of white flour. *Aust. Med. J. 5*, 123–133

Kearney, G. E., de Lacey, P. R. and Davidson, G. R. (eds.) (1973) *The Psychology of Australian Aborigines*, Wiley, Sydney

Klippel, M. D. (1975) Measurement of intelligence among three New Zealand ethnic groups: product versus process approaches, *J. Cross-Cult. Psychol. 6*, 365–376

Lenneburg, E. H. (1964) *New Directions in the Study of Language*, Massachusetts Institute of Technology Press, Cambridge, Mass.

Leonard, C. (1977) *Relationships between Piagetian and Psychometric Tests among Mentally Retarded Children*, University of Wollongong, Wollongong, N.S.W., forthcoming

Levenstein, P. (1974) A message from home. A home-based intervention method for low-income preschoolers. Paper presented at NICHD and Rose F. Kennedy Centre Conference, *The Mentally Retarded and Society*, Albert Einstein College of Medicine, Niles, Mich. (Mimeo)

Lévy-Bruhl, L. (1923) *Primitive Mentality*, Allen and Unwin, London

Lewis, O. (1966) The culture of poverty, *Sci. Am. 215*, 19–25

Mead, M. (1932) An investigation into the thought of primitive children with reference to animism, *J. R. Anthropol. Inst. 62*, 173–190

Nurcombe, B. (1971) *Assimilation or Cultural Pluralism. Whose Choice?* Paper presented at 43rd Conference of the Australian and New Zealand Association for the Advancement of Science. University of Queensland, Brisbane, Qld.

Nurcombe, B. (1976a) *Children of the Dispossessed*, University of Hawaii Press, Honolulu, Hawaii

Nurcombe, B. (1976b) The great debate, *Aust. N. Z. J. Psychiat. 10*, 21–25

Nurcombe, B. and Moffitt, P. (1970) Cultural deprivation and language deficit, *Aust. Psychol. 3*, 249–253

Peluffo, N. (1967) Culture and cognitive problems, *Intl. J. Psychol. 2*, 187–198

Piaget, J. (1929) The child's conception of the world, Routledge and Kegan Paul, London

Pike, K. L. (1967) *Language in Relation to a Unified Theory of the Structures of Human Behaviour*, Mouton, The Hague

Porteus, S. D. (1965) *Porteus Maze Tests. Fifty Years of Application*, Pacific Books, Palo Alto, Cal.

Skinner, B. F. (1972) *Cumulative Record*, Appleton-Century Crofts, New York

Taylor, L. J. and de Lacey, P. R. (1974) Three dimensions of intellectual functioning in Australian Aboriginal and disadvantaged European children, *J. Cross-Cult. Psychol. 5*, 49–58

Twomey, A. (1977) *Cognition in Context: Abilities of Aboriginal Children in Social and Historical Perspectives*, University of Wollongong, Wollongong, N.S.W. in the press

Wallace, J. G. (1965) *Concept Growth and the Education of the child*, National Foundation for Educational Research, Slough, Bucks.

Werner, H. (1948) *A Comparative Psychology of Mental Development*, Follett, Chicago

Wheeler, L. R. (1942) A comparative study of the intelligence of East Tennesse mountain children, *J. Educ. Psychol. 33*, 321–334

Whiting, B. B. (ed.) (1963) *Six Cultures. Studies in Child Rearing*, Wiley, New York

Witkin, H. A. and Berry, J. W. (1975) Psychological differentiation in cross-cultural perspective, *J. Cross-Cult. Psychol. 6*, 4–87

Witkin, H. A., Dyk, R. B., Faterson, A. H., Goodenough, D. R. and Karp, S. A. (1962) *Psychological Differentiation. Studies of Development*, Wiley, New York, (Republished: Potomoe, Md., Lawrence Earlbaum Associates, 1974)

Genetics, environment and intelligence, edited by A. Oliverio
© Elsevier/North-Holland Biomedical Press, 1977

Is child stimulation effective?　　　　21

MAGALI BOVET and JACQUES VONECHE

Introduction

The question put before us could be reformulated in the following terms: what are the effects of positive, planned experience upon children's cognitive growth?

It should be understood that the present authors are not going to deal with early stimulation as usually defined: a study in the role of stimulus deprivation in young disadvantaged children, reared in the absence of parents, in institutions or in the wild. From Victor, the wild child of Aveyron in France (J. Itard, 1801, 1806) Amala and Kamala in India to Yves Chenau from St-Brévin (France) the 7-year old boy discovered on May 24, 1963, about fifty wild children have been discovered and suppositions have been made on the influence of a lack of human stimulation upon these children. They have been inconclusive on the whole by lack of baseline data.

Animal studies, on the other hand, have shown the importance of stimulation (especially tactual manipulations) on the survival and growth of newborn young-sters. Clinical studies on children reared in institutional settings have shown the severe loss that some of these children endure in their cognitive and emotional maturation because of the lack of attachment, poverty of the environment and general dismal conditions of their life experience. All these studies demonstrate the necessity of early stimulation, handling and care required by growing mammals. In addition, overstimulation tends to produce the same effects as understimulation, pretty much as overvitaminosis provokes the same disastrous consequences as undervitaminosis. One could say that child psychologists nowadays are in the position of nutritionists a few decades ago: they know the quantitative differences that make the difference but they do not know yet the qualitative coordinations among determinant factors.

These are the reasons why the present authors have focused their attention upon a problem of stimulation that lends itself better to experimental investigation: the training of the concept of conservation in normal children.

The intention of the present chapter is to consider the major different approaches to the problem of accelerating intellectual development in relation to the work of Jean Piaget. Therefore, it will be necessary (1) to state briefly Piaget's own position and his own view of the place of specific experience; (2) the possible reformulation suggested by the work of Inhelder, Sinclair and Bovet; (3) the discussion of the effectiveness of stimulation procedures developed in different empirical and theoretical contexts; (4) the discussion of the degree to which the training studies meet Piaget's own criteria of cognitive reorganisation as well as any tentative modification of Piagetian theory which may appear to be suggested.

Equilibrium model of cognitive development

The question of stimulating a child's thinking implies a prior question: what is known about the nature of a child's thinking?

Piaget's contribution

Among child psychologists interested in the development of cognition, Piaget takes a special significance for two main reasons: (1) he has offered, over fifty years of intensive research, a uniquely comprehensive view of the developmental process and (2) he has established a whole class of experimental concepts, which were, at the time of their presentation, entirely new: conservation, reversibility, transitivity, etc.

Recently, some doubts have been raised about the validity of Piaget's theory as well as the adequacy of the evidence presented. The importance of theoretical concepts such as conservation has been questioned in the light of studies on the efficacy of training methods in relation to the acquisitions of operational structures.

It is, then, very important to stress once again the basic tenets of Piaget's theory of cognitive development. Piaget's psychology is deeply rooted in philosophy. The starting point of his reflection is the conflict between the classical philosophical schools of empiricism and rationalism. Does man's thinking derive from experience or is it the result of the imposition of universal structures or categories pre-existing to experience? Piaget refuses the alternative as well as the amalgamation nature–nurture. For him, there is a third and more central factor in the development of knowledge, equilibration. Equilibration pertains to the functioning of the system as a whole, and thus encompasses the other two classical factors of development: maturation and experience, which are the biopsychological equivalents of the philosophical alternative between rationalism and empiricism.

In fact, Piaget says three things at once. First, endogenous restructuration is a continuous process. Second, the basic nature of this process is to seek out equilibrium states. Third, the movement toward equilibrium of interest in the study of biology and knowledge is not toward greater and greater passivity, but is an active process tending toward the growth of intelligence, more and more complex, flexible and inclusive structures.

"Life is essentially autoregulation"*, Piaget states, echoing a theme which has been important, at least, since Claude Bernard introduced the concept of homeostasis. In some respects, there may be special regulatory organs, but in some cases, we can only look to the totality of relationships among organs as providing this regulation.

> "Cognitive processes seem, then, to be at one and the same time the outcome of organic autoregulation reflecting its essential mechanisms, and the most highly differentiated organs of this regulation at the core of interactions with the environment so much so that, in the case of man, these processes are being extended to the universe itself"**

Cognitive processes are "organs"? At first reading, this seems like a kind of objective idealism giving material reality status to ideas. In another reading, what Piaget seems to mean is simply that cognition cannot be said to occur in any one of the conventionally defined organ systems of the body, but draws upon them and reorganizes them in a new set of functional relations. Thus "cognitive autoregulation makes use of the general systems of organic regulation such as are found at every genetic, morphogenetic, physiological and nervous level, and forthwith adapts them to their new situation. . . . This situation constitutes the exchanges with environment that form the basis of behaviour"†.

But, for Piaget, there are some crucial differences between cognition and organic functioning: "The outstanding characteristic of cognitive organizations is the progressive dissociation of form and content".†† In at least four ways, then, Piaget's formulations seem to have a ring of philosophical idealism: the teleological note of autoregulation (Piaget would say teleonomical instead of teleological), the assertion that cognitive processes are "organs", the claim of their universality and completeness, and the ultimate separation of form and content. But Piaget strongly believes that modern developments in systems theory and cybernetics provide the conceptual tools for understanding a growing, self-regulating, adaptive system without giving way to teleology.

---

* Piaget, J., *Biology and Knowledge*, p. 26.
** Ibid. p. 34.
† Ibid. p. 36–37.
†† Ibid. p. 153.

The development of the adaptive side of Piaget's theoretical biology appeared recently in a book entitled: "Adaptation vitale et psychologie de l'intelligence: sélection organique et phénocopie"*. His aim in the book was to re-state his critique of neo-Darwinism, to expound his own interactionist position and to elaborate a broad hypothesis about the way in which changes in the gene complex can be viewed as an extension of the self-regulating activities of the organism.

After developing the biological argument, he elaborates its analogues in cognition. Even the reader who remains sceptical of the seemingly neo-Lamarkian tone of the biological part will find the psychological part challenging, especially if the reader is interested in the appearance of novelties.

There are two key-points in neo-Darwinism which provoke Piaget's criticism. First, mutation is considered to be a random process, in the sense that a given mutation, when it occurs has no relation to the adaptive needs of the organism. Second, natural selection is a process in which the organism is essentially passive: it is the environment that responds to the mutation that has happened to the organism.

Piaget raises certain objections to this picture. First, the sheer improbability of the evolution of complex organs on the basis of chance alone. Second, the gene complex is not sealed off from the rest of the body; it is known to control the functioning and the development of the organism. It is implausible to think of this relation as one-way. Third, each individual gene is not simply sitting there waiting for a situation to happen to it, or not, as chance decrees. It is indeed interacting with other genes, influencing their activity and being influenced by them.

Piaget wants a model that presents the organism as perpetually active, taking the initiative of mutation as part of a total process of organized self-regulation. It is with these aims in mind that he advances the phenocopy hypothesis.

He, first, makes the general point of anticipation as a general biological function. Many structural changes occur in an organism at a moment when they are not yet useful. The development of anticipation depends on the past (memory, stored information, etc.). The series of feed-backs by which this is made possible is very similar to Waddington's genetic assimilation**. Thus, there is a continuity from memory to anticipation and a stored scenario can be run either backwards in memory, or forwards in anticipation.

The phenocopy hypothesis proposes that there are both exogenous and endogenous variations in phenotypes. Once the exogenous form is established, the organism re-invents it by changing itself in such a manner that the same phenotypic result is now produced by endogenous means. The endogenous or genotypic form is somehow a copy of the phenotypic form, hence phenocopy.

The endogenous form is eventually substituted for the exogenous form. At each level, from gene complex to cognitive structures, the organism has a system for

---

* Paris, Hermann, 1974, not yet translated.
** Conrad Waddington: The Nature of Life, New York, Harper, 1961.

sensing that something is or is not working properly. If not, a process of variation (mutation, groping) begins, until a response occurs that solves the "problem". Thus in clearly pointing at the central role of exogenous knowledge, in the formulation of re-invention and substitution, and in reducing the role of chance "to proportions which are not negligible but modest, since the essential characteristic of that cardinal function of life, assimilation, is precisely to struggle against chance in such a way as to make use of it"*. Piaget's work on phenocopy represents a change from earlier positions.

Equilibration and cognitive growth

In the present state of affairs, it is apparent that equilibration means the drive for homeostasis or more accurately homeorhesis in an active system that learns from its experiences only to the extent that it can assimilate them to existing structures.

Whenever the exogenous pressure is such as to render assimilation impossible, disequilibrium occurs and the organism begins to grope for a solution by constructing a new structure that will adapt to the demands of both environment and organism.

Thus "the question comes up whether to teach the structure or to present the child with situations where he is active and creates the structure himself"**. From what we have just learned about phenocopy it is clear that the goal of stimulation is not to increase the amount of knowledge in the child but to create the possibilities for the child to invent and discover new cognitive or, more generally, adaptive structures. In other words, the role of stimulation is to provide enough exogenous pressure upon the organism to provoke an imbalance in the homeostatic structure with which the organism was functioning before.

There are two limitations to the production of such imbalances. First, because of structural limitations, they cannot occur at all times, but only in critical periods of development.

Second, the role of experience is limited to the enrichment of the environment, in sharp contrast with the drill approach of demonstrations, exercises and step-by-step learning procedures generally used to reinforce a certain type of response. There is no escape from the invariable, hierarchical order of stages.

But, the invariance in the sequence of development should not be mistaken. Its order rests neither on the nature of the environment, nor on a genetic-nativistic argument concerning a natural hierarchy of dispositions (putative later forms cannot be manifested in the absence or suppression of earlier ones) but on a logical argument showing that putative later forms presuppose "earlier" ones.

---

* Adaptation vitale, loc. cit, p. 108, translated by Gruber and Vonèche.
** Duckworth, E. (1964) In: Piaget Rediscovered, R. E. Ripple, and V. E. Rockcastle, (Eds.), p. 1–5, Cornell University Press, Ithaca, N.Y.

Role of specific experience in Genevan studies of learning

In a book entitled: "Learning and the development of cognition*" B. Inhelder, H. Sinclair and M. Bovet have asked three basic questions about learning: (1) what are the connections among cognitive structures; (2) what is their mode of generation; (3) what dynamic factors make cognitive development possible?

It should be understood that these questions have been posed from a Piagetian viewpoint and not in reference to the current preoccupations of learning theorists in psychology. In this perspective, learning is supposed to be equivalent to inducing a new cognitive level of functioning in the subjects. This means two things: (1) it requires the definition of the cognitive structure to be induced; (2) it supposes that practicing some specific schemata will bring a given child to the required cognitive level. Changes in the cognitive structure of a child are supposed to happen by means of cognitive conflict. There are two aspects to cognitive conflicts: (1) the simultaneous stimulation of schemata hierarchically located at such a distance from one another as to be in opposition; (2) the realization or cognizance by the child of the necessity to supersede this opposition or contradiction in a new cognitive structure coordinating the previously opposed schemata. A simple example of such a coordination is given by the so-called detour behaviour. An animal or a young child is presented with a goal object which, because of a glass partition between the subject and the object, can be reached only in a roundabout way. Lower animals and very young children are unable to coordinate the direct action of going toward the goal with the reverse action of going away from it into one single successful action of reaching the goal by detour.

The results of the Genevan studies on learning show evidence that cognitive changes induced in one domain lead to changes in that domain as well as in other domains. For instance, changes in the grasp of the concept of class inclusion, due to learning, led to changes in the understanding of the notion of quantity and vice-versa. But these changes are not completely symmetrical. There are in any learning some specific and some general characteristics to the connections established by the subjects. Thus, these interconnections among different schemata help understand the filiation of representional schemata operant during training.

From a dynamic viewpoint, the role of training should not, nevertheless, be understood as a mere activation of dormant schemata. Learning is not, for the Genevan school, simply an epiphenomenon of natural cognitive development. Although, it can only take place by following certain cognitive pathways similar for cognition to Waddington's creodes in embryology, learning à la Genevan remains the product of a specific procedure of cognitive conflict resolution. Indeed, learning should neither be identified with any type of drill, nor with a mere recognition of microstages representing the missing links from one stage to the next one. The coordination of schemata taking place during training is not equivalent to a series of close-ups on

---

*Harvard University Press, Cambridge, Mass. U.S.A., 1974.

specific aspects of natural development. The specificity of learning consists in its being an experimental strategy for discovery which is directed by previous actions up to the point that they become organized by internal necessity into a coherent totality, the new structure of equilibrium. This organization by necessity is the mark of equilibrium, since it frees the organism from the historical processes (i.e. specific learning procedures: practice, reinforcement, need reduction or verbal rule learning) through which the new structure has been attained in order to make it more or less permanently reversible, i.e. logical. Consequently, learning is, for the Genevans, a sub-variety of re-equilibration, that is to say: constant re-organisations of cognitive structures into more and more encompassing entities capable of assimilating novelty and conflict. The general function of re-equilibration is then evident: it prevents the increase of entropy in the system. Such an accretion would be inevitable, if any new external stimulation were to leave its indelible mark upon the organism.

Training research

Piaget's concept of conservation has been the most extensively studied and analyzed in training researches on cognitive development. There are many reasons for this centrality of conservation. First, Piaget assigns a pivotal role to the child's attainment of conservation in the development of intelligence. Second, the acquisition of conservation of physical quantities throughout perceptual transformations of their appearances cannot be based upon experience, since the attributes which are conserved cannot be seen to stay constant. Mere observation is not sufficient. In fact, it is misleading.

The problem is that younger children (non-conservers) believe that change in quantity can be brought about by transformations such as deformations and rearrangements, whereas older ones (conservers) hold the opposite to be true. This dramatic change does not seem to be brought about by any sensory experience. The only testable proof of conservation is logical in nature: reversibility, that is to say that a direct operation such as a displacement in one direction can be nullified by a reverse operation such as coming back to the initial place. That means also that a certain arrangement of things can always be returned to whenever rearranged. Without this reversibility, all transformation would always alter irremediably the state of the world and nothing would remain constant in an ever flowing universe, as Heraclitus claimed.

The question is thus: is it possible to train children for logical thinking? The commonest approach to this problem of training seems to be to obtain a sample of groups of children around the age of 6 years who fail to conserve in a particular field, and to subject the various groups to training procedures while one, or more, group serves as control and receives no specific training, and then, to post-test the subjects and assess the effects that training has had in bringing about the particular conservations.

By such a procedure, the researchers expect to discover precisely what kind of procedure facilitates the development of the particular concept.

Many researchers have looked at the importance of the social transmission of necessary information. Others, following Piaget, would see actions and their internalisation into operations as being instrumental in the attainment of conservation. For Piaget, operations are internalized actions which are reversible and belong to a structure. In conservation experiments, two domains of experience are thus delineated: the sensory experience of change: rearrangement, deformation, etc ... and the reflexive experience upon one's own actions infering that changes of a certain sort do not affect the quantities involved in the transformations. The puzzling aspect of this reflexive experience is that it is neither taught nor innate; it needs time and past experience to take place.

In one paradigmatic type of training for conservation, Bruner (1964) and his various associates have tried to reduce the dependence of the child on the immediate stimulus by removing misleading perceptual cues, by encouraging the child to rely on memory, higher mental processes, etc ... But this procedure works only with children who spontaneously start to see that there could be something misleading with complete reliance upon perception.

Braine (1965) and Shanks (1965), in another paradigmatic type of training for conservation, have encouraged children to differentiate neatly between the irrelevant perceptual properties of an object such as shape or height, and rational answers guided by deduction. Once again, this method works only with children in a period of hesitation about conservation.

Smedslund (1961) and Wohlwill (1962) have proposed an experimental paradigm for the teaching of conservation based upon the inference of the absence of addition or subtraction. But, once again, the factor of inference does not solve the problem of finding a basis for conservation, since it is only possible to infer the absence of change in quantity under transformation from the absence of addition and subtraction when it is already assumed that these transformations do not involve addition and subtraction.

Training studies involving the concepts of number and length

In an unpublished master's thesis, E. M. Churchill (1958) sought to train children in the mathematical processes of grouping and seriating, matching and ordering various objects. She claims a remarkable advance in these processes in the children of the experimental group versus those of the control group. Her procedure of training was to pretest the subjects on Piaget's number concept tasks. Then, over a period of a month she gave informal practice in play situations in the specified number skills to the experimental group. The careful examination of the total data demonstrates a clear improvement of the experimental group over the control group.

Phemister (1960) in her doctoral dissertation, made a longitudinal study of children from their entrance to school during a period of 6 months. The experiment involved the total classroom situation. This approach made strict controls difficult.

But it allowed the experimenter to follow individually each subject.

The results are interesting: they support Piaget's 3 sub-stage definition of a development of logical thinking (pre-conservation-transition-conservation) which is invariant; an improvement in performance of statistical significance suggests that experimental training over a long period can accelerate cognitive restructuring.

Wohlwill (1960) traced the development of number concept from the time where a child is beginning to use mathematical language to the age of 7 or 8 years. Instead of doing a classical longitudinal study, Wohlwill used a scalogram analysis to compensate for time, expense and loss of subjects inevitable in direct longitudinal studies. The experiment consisted in presenting each individual subject with cards containing 2, 3 and 4 dots in varying configurations, the aim being to enable the child to establish a set corresponding to the particular number dimension. Post-tests followed which showed the child's ability to transfer this operation to problems in which the correspondence between sample cards and choice cards required symbolic representations in a variety of ways and degrees. A scaling of difficulty was hypothesized by the experimenter who demonstrated that there was a constant developmental process at work in the conceptualization of number. This process observes three phases: the child responds to number in perceptual terms, then, in conceptual ones and, in a final phase, in relational terms where the relationships among the individual numbers are conceptualized fully.

Wohlwill and Lowe (1962) based their training study of the conservation of number upon three hypotheses: reinforcement, differentiation and inference. The method employed was as follows: a verbal pre-test was given to diagnose ability to handle number concept and conservation; it was followed by a non-verbal test of conservation in the form of multiple-choice trials. A series of training tasks were then given to the subjects. Lastly, verbal and non-verbal tests for conservation of number were administered. Four different training conditions were used: reinforced practice, addition and subtraction, dissociation and control. The results of the verbal pre-test showed that subjects had the ability to count and to use numbers symbolically, but they showed a tendency to confuse length with number. The experimenters did not find any transfer from non-verbal conservation training to the verbal post-test. The role of addition and subtraction was considered as important by the authors for the acquisition of non-verbal conservation of number.

Gruen (1965) sought to compare directly the effects of two different training procedures: inducement of cognitive conflict and reinforcement of practice. The subjects were pre-tested for conservation of number, length, and substance. Then half of them were pretrained in the vocabulary used in the experiment ("more", "same", in relation to numbers only). Training for conservation was given to the experimental group. At the post-test, the experimental group did not behave significantly differently from the control one. However, cognitive conflict seemed slightly better at inducing conservation responses than reinforced practice. Training in vocabulary seemed also to affect the end result of subjects, because of the emphasis put upon the relation between two quantities. Lastly, there was little or no evidence of generalization of conservation from number to length and substance. Beilin (1965) sought to investigate a relationship between learning and the unitary nature of cognitive development. He employed verbal and non-verbal training techniques in situations of reinforcement and non-reinforcement, divided into 4 training conditions: (1) non-verbal reinforcement; (2) verbal orientation reinforcement; (3) verbal rule instruction; (4) equilibrium. The results showed little convergence of conservation performance across tasks before and after training. An increase in the number of subjects displaying conservation behaviour was restricted only to the domain in which training was given. The most effective training condition was verbal rule instruction; which Beilin explains in terms of the task requirements themselves. There was no transfer across tasks.

Wallach and Sprott (1964) attempted to develop number conservation by showing children the reversibility inherent in various arrangements. They were very successful in training subjects for conservation, when compared with other experimenters, but their subjects had a mean age of 7.0, in the experimental group, which is the average age of natural attainment of conservation in Western subjects.

Wallach et al. (1967) tested the role of reversibility, addition and subtraction and misleading perceptual cues in number conservation acquisition. The experiment went as follows: firstly, the subjects were given pre-tests on the conservation of number and liquid quantities and were ordered into 4 groups: (1) conservers; (2) non-conservers; (3) conservers of number only; (4) conservers of liquid only. Groups 2 and 4 were then given training in reversibility and addition/subtraction and immediately tested on number conservation. Non-conservers failing to show number conservation were given training on liquid reversibility followed by a post-test. The original non-conservers who had shown conservation of number were post-tested for conservation of liquid. If transfer was not recorded, they were given transfer training in liquid conservation and immediately post-tested on that. If they still failed, they were given liquid reversibility training and then post-tested.

Addition and subtraction was not found to be a necessary experience to accompagny reversibility training for the acquisition of number conservation. There is no transfer from the conservation of number to that of liquid, unless the transition between number conservation tasks and liquid conservation ones is minimised by intermediary tasks.

Gelman (1969) used the standard three-phase design; (a) training was initiated within 2 weeks of pre-testing, (b) post-testing after the last day of training and (c) presenting the subjects with a second post-test 2 or 3 weeks later. Three training conditions were devised: (1) modified learning set with length and number stimuli; (2) a modification of these problems without feed-back; (3) modified learning set with "junk" stimuli. The children were initially trained to choose objects which were the "same" or "different" and rewarded for right answers. They were encouraged to alternate between length and number in order to determine the particular relevance of a given perceptual cue. Learning set training consisted of 16 six-trial problems in both length and number. Each problem consisted of 3 stimulus objects, two containing identical quantities and one different ones. In the second condition, the procedure was identical except that no feedback was given. To the extent that conservation is a matter of attention and discrimination, Gelman has been successful in inducing conservation responses in non-conservers, since all subjects discriminated correctly the same from the different.

Bryant's (1974) assumption is that very young children do not know which methods of estimating "how many" are correct. The role of Bryant's training procedure is to teach very young children strategies to establish such a distinction. The confusion induced by standard Piagetian conservation tests is due, for Bryant, not to a misunderstanding of invariance but to the arbitrary resolution of a conflict between past and present judgments. In several experiments reported in his book, Bryant taught the subjects aged from 3 to 5 years, to rely on one-to-one correspondence instead of using the criterion of length, that is, reduced attention to misleading cues. Thus the subjects were successful in learning conservation.

Training studies mainly involving weight, substance, space and liquid

These studies were started by Smedslund in 1959 in an exploratory study investigating the effects of external reinforcement on the conservation of weight. Three groups of children were involved in the experiment, all of whom were consistent non-conservers. In the first group, the subjects were shown with a pair of scales that weight remains constant during transformation of the shape of the objects. In the second group, some of the demonstrations with object deformations on the scale were replaced by addition and subtraction of matter. Smedslund's hypothesis was that the first group of subjects should do considerably better than the second one if classical learning theory was to be substantiated since there was direct reinforcement of the correct answers in this procedure. If equilibration theory was correct, the subjects who had been trained in addition and subtraction operations should fare better than the subject of the first group. A third group of children acted as control. Smedslund recorded a certain amount of learning in both groups especially in the first one, but he does not immediately translate that as evidence in favour of classical learning theory. Reinforcement might well have led the children to use "pseudo-concepts" that could be extinguishable under proper extinction training. In addition, Smedslund aptly pointed out that the lack of cognitive conflict in the addition/subtraction situation was not conducive to the acquisition of conservation, since no cognitive restructuring was felt necessary in the absence of conflict. This holds true in spite of the fact that, in one of his test items, Smedslund had a situation in which a bit of plasticine was taken away from one of the objects and ostensibly put on the table before the child was asked the question of equality. For the child not to be fooled by this, the child must already have coordinated the schemata for addition/subtraction with those of deformation.

Gréco (1959) looked into the possibility of training subjects in the conceptualization of logical groupings contained in spatial problems. The experiment involved a cardboard cylinder and a wooden rod to which were fastened different color beads. The rod was stuck into the cylinder until it could not be seen and the subjects were asked which color would come out first at the opposite end. The cylinder was then rotated in the horizontal plane through 180° once or twice and the same question was asked again to the subjects. A first group of subjects was trained in the two or one rotations separately. The other group was trained in a mixture of both. Both groups learned to predict the outcome correctly. A post-test for the stability of the acquisition was given as well as a transfer on a rod with a different bead order. The results showed an extended amount of stability and generalization one or three months after. But the subjects trained separately for each rotation (one or two) had forgotten everything about their training, whereas the subjects trained on mixed rotations had reorganized their activity as to understand the structural system behind rotations. Gréco concludes to the superiority of cognitive conflict learning upon rote learning.

Smedslund's attempt at the extinction of conservation behaviour bears on the same point as Gréco's study just mentioned: the distinction between classical learning theory and equilibration theory. Smedslund's hypothesis was as follows: if one can extinguish conservation behaviour, one should recognize that learning theory is correct, if not, one should agree with Piaget. The experimental design included: (1) a pre-test to assess the cognitive level of subjects; (2) a group of 5–7 year-old non-conservers was trained in the same way as usual with scales in the conservation of weight; (3) the successful subjects in the post-test as well as the natural conservers tested in the pre-test became the subjects of the extinction experiment. Quantities of matter were taken away from one of the subjects inconspicuously. The results are striking: none of the trained conservers maintained their conservation answers. They showed little surprise at the inequality of quantities and readily reverted to non-conservation. About half of the natural conservers maintained their answers, (in spite of the evidence before them suggesting that the experimenter had surreptitiously taken away some of the matter). Smedslund's suggestion is that trained conservers learned only an arbitrary empirical law and thus, were ready to change it in the face of evidence contrary to the rule.

In a follow-up study, Smedslund attempted the extinction of the visual components involved in the conceptualization of weight. He sought to by-pass the normal early and unreliable dependence on perceptual data by making such information unreliable and contradictory. It was presumed that thereby subjects would seek more reliable symbolic cues. The results indicated that the children did not change their minds after this training. Conservers kept conserving and non-conservers did not attain conservation.

Obviously, for Smedlund, the next step was to bring about conservation without reinforcement in conflict situation; which would be support for the equilibration theory. Deformation and addition/subtraction controls were used with each pair of items which was clearly stated to be equal in size and volume. No change was observed in the subjects. Some used addition/subtraction schemata to give their answers and gave conservation answers in the post-test. The remaining subjects (the majority) relied on perceptual cues and were unable to reach conservation at the post-test. Of interest is the fact that the passage to conservation in the subjects using addition/subtraction schemata was made possible via a conflict between perceptual evidence and operative certainty that, when nothing is added or subtracted, nothing is changed.

In 1963, Smedslund investigated the role of experience by observation alone in the development of symbolic imagery. He used for that the classical Piagetian observation that children do not, at a certain age, anticipate that water levels remain constantly horizontal, no matter the tilt of the container. After demonstration of the phenomenon during a 360° slow rotation of a jar containing a liquid, the children who, at the pre-test did not anticipate the horizontality of water level, did not report the fact in their post-test drawings. This shows, according to Smedslund, that virtually no observational learning occurs in the acquisition of concrete operations.

What seemed to be a more important factor of learning was practice. In his study on the transitivity of weight, Smedslund (1963) showed that free practice by an experimental group with a material allowing for free seriation of weight by means of a pair of scales was a determinant factor in the acquisition of transitivity of weight. Younger subjects improved better under such conditions than they did when they were allowed to use the material according to a sequence fixed by the experimenter. So frequency of use seems to be more important than the observation that weight A is heavier than weight C.

In the same vein, Beilin et al. (1966) produced evidence seeming to indicate that through verbal and perceptual training on water level representation children's anticipatory imagery could be improved and that perceptual training method was better. The most effective training method was the one in which not only subjects had to verify their guess of the orientation of water surface in a jar tilted behind a screen, but in addition, had the experimenter demonstrate the phenomenon to them afterwards. Subjects trained verbally by means of booklets describing the phenomenon more or less like a crash course in physics were less efficient in the post-test than those trained perceptually.

Beilin and Franklin (1962) looked at the effect of training children of different ages in operational thinking in the fields of length and area measurements. Subjects were instructed in measuring by superposition and unit iteration methods as well as in conservation of length and area. The aim of the experimenters was to generate generalization from specific examples. The training had 4 parts: part one involved the subject determining which of two rectangles was the larger, first by superpositioning one on the other and then by counting out the area of each rectangle by using a common measure (unit interaction). Part two used Piaget's material of barns scattered on fields. Non-conservers believe that a cow has less to eat when the barns are randomly located on the field and more when they are arranged in a row in a corner of the field. Part three involved the experimenter cutting a triangle from the corner of one of two equal rectangles and placing it somewhere on the edge of the same rectangle, and pointing out that the "space" is the same irrespectively of the placement of the triangle. Part four consists of demonstrations of conservation, superposition and iteration on the area and length materials used previously in order to reinforce generalization of the previous experiments. Then a test of transfer was administered.

The results tended to support Lovell's (1965) finding about the considerable variability of the acquisition of an operation at one level. The subjects already in advanced stages of natural development (transitional stage, namely) showed the most progress. Progress was much more marked for length than for area conservation.

Sigel et al. (1966) set out to test the hypothesis that conservation of quantity may be induced by the embodiment of the operations of multiple classification, multiplication of relations and reversibility in the training procedure. The subjects of the training group improved slightly their performance whereas the control subjects did not show any improvement in the post-test. Side observations are interesting here: conservation was not "taught" but discovered by many children during the training; the order of acquisitions followed Piaget's substages and multiple training of this sort gave rise to reorganization of the cognitive structures in training.

Bearison (1969) studied the effect of measurement upon conservation. The aim of the experiment was to demonstrate how children can be trained to conserve liquid quantities via the rational use of measuring and counting, as means for verifying their conservation (or non-conservation) hypotheses. The question that Bearison asked was rather simple and straightforward: do children use certain already established schemata, for instance measuring to solve a more complex problem such as conserving quantities of continuous matter and, if they do not, can we train them to do so and with what effects? The subjects were all non-conservers matched into two equivalent groups out of which one was the experimental group and the other the control. The control received no training at all, whereas the experimental group was trained to measure the quantity of liquid given to them with little measuring bottles and to count the number of measuring bottles that went into each standard glass. The results indicate that children subjected to this training profited from it to a large extent. But, Bearison carefully pointed out that some experimental subjects did not benefit at all from the training. This individual sensitivity to training was subsequently noted by various experimenters (Halford, 1970; Brainerd, 1972). Lefebvre and Pinard (1974) showed that the effect of training directly correlated the child's initial level of sensitivity to cognitive conflict. This initial level was assessed by tests involving mainly three salient aspects: child's conceptual consistency, articulation of functional schemata, ability to accept the "empirical sanction of facts". The more consistent, articulate and hypothetico-deductive the child is, the more he will benefit from training in cognitive conflict.

This raises the more general question of the factors that seem determinant in training. A first potential factor recognized by several authors has been the role of verbal feedback. Does the child learn from an experimenter who tells him or her that he/she is correct or wrong? Overbeck and Schwartz (1970) tried to induce weight conservation through a verbal correction procedure. They found that the older subjects were more influenced by the training procedure than were the younger ones. But the same subjects were also more likely to be concrete operational for some other concepts and thus more sensitive to conflict between one domain of conservation and another.

Figurelli and Keller (1972) in a study which was an extension of Beilin's verbal rule instruction training procedure plus verbal feedback, did not differentiate the effects of verbal feedback versus multiple operations training. Siegler and Liebert (1972) who did differentiate the two factors showed that those subjects who were provided both rules and feedback attained conservation in larger number than those who received either feedback or rule instruction.

Hamel and Riksen (1973) trained subjects for "renversabilité" (i.e. to do an action both ways, like pouring something out of a glass and pouring it back) and showed that those trained performed significantly better only in the specific task for which they had been trained. Roll (1970) trained, during one month, 16 subjects who were administered 44 trials of "renversible" deformations; 11 of them produced conservation judgments on the post-test but only 4 were able to justify their judgment.

Miller and Lipps (1973) tested the resistance of subjects considered as conservers to violations of weight conservation and weight transitivity, both notions being acquired at about the same time by children and presenting strong interrelationships. They found that their subjects showed more resistance to violations of weight transitivity than to violations of weight conservation. This finding is to be compared with two studies by Toniolo and Hooper (1975) who discovered that transitivity precedes conservation in the sequence of acquisition. But Gonchar (1975) showed that class, relation and number concepts were acquired at about the same time. For more than half the subjects the acquisition of these three notions were strictly concomitant, the rest showing no specific pattern of décalage. This structural mix in response patterns is also observed by Bingham–Newman and Saunders (1975) in their 3-year longitudinal assessment of Piagetian cognitive abilities in the preoperational child. Although they found a notable lack of synchrony among the tasks of their test-battery, there was nevertheless a general trend that seriation came before measurement and number and transitivity before conservation.

From these recent studies, one gains the impression that the preoperational period is transitional in many ways. Not only is it the passage between sensori-motor modes of thinking and concrete operational ones, but it seems, in addition, to be a period of considerable reorganization and disorganization; which raises the question of the status of the horizontal décalage. Are all these horizontal differentials or asynchronisms organized in a developmental sequence to which one could apply a weak form of grouping (groupement) i.e. recurrent application of the same grouping to different contents or is the theoretical concept of groupement somewhat inadequate?

Evaluation and conclusion

Evaluation of the effectiveness of specific strategies

The most striking result of these short-term training experiments is their partial lack of effectiveness. When progress from pre- to post-test is reported, it is never clear whether this is attributable to learning only or to a combination of factors (including learning), since, generally, the subjects who benefited the most from training were also variously described as older, more mature, more articulate, etc., in a word, more advanced in the natural process of mastering conservation. Since the bulk of subjects belonged to the transitional substage of conservation acquisition, a period described by Piaget as being made of oscillations about the idea of conservation, and given the experimental procedures employed in the pre-test, it is not improbable that some subjects have been erroneously categorized either in a substage inferior to their competence or superior to it, because of momentary perturbations in performance.

Consequently it becomes difficult to draw the conclusion that stages of cognitive development can be accelerated by training. The most that could be said would be that, during transitional periods of cognitive re-organization, there are some possibilities to make the most out of such critical periods to help the natural dominant process take place by the sort of assistance that a midwife brings to the birth of a baby. Conservation could be induced as a baby could be. This return to Socratic maieutics which seems very reasonable and in line with Piagetian ideas about cognitive development seems too nativistic to be really Piagetian, as we would like to argue now. First, if short-term stimulation has not been very effective so far, this could be due not necessarily to the nature of the beast but to faulty procedures of training. We feel that this possibility should not be excluded a priori. It is possible, if not likely, that researchers so far have not yet reached out for the preconserving child in their attempts at training for conservation. Of course, such a position could easily be taxed of either preformism or empiricism. The very metaphor of reaching our for the preconserver could imply that such a child already possesses all the mental equipment necessary to further development. But, on the other hand, if, in the metaphor of reaching out, the movement of pulling at oneself from the part of the experimenter is read then the growing child becomes a passive wax that can be molded by the hand reaching out.

There is a difference between a note of methodological caution and epistemological positions. As a matter of fact, the acceptance of the critical period hypothesis presents, for us, a double difficulty. It presupposes that stages and substages of cognitive development are not constructed by the observer but form a series of constituting properties of their subject matter; which is a form of a critical substantialism. It weakens considerably the model of equilibration by making it a sort of alternator. The motor of development would be sensitive to external stimulation only during certain phases called critical periods. Its advantages upon a genetic-nativistic model à la Lorenz would then be minimal. Moreover, adopting such a position would be skipping over one of the most interesting issues raised by training studies: the nature of stages.

In effect, the issue of teaching children how to think revolves around two key-points: the determination of a developmental level and the way in which cognitive development takes place. Determining developmental levels is essentially structural in nature. It requires the recognition of the unity of a certain period of development when it is compared to another one: the order of succession of acquisitions must be constant; the structures constructed at a given stage must be integrated in the structure of the following stage, and the unity of the stage must be marked by a structure of the whole ("structure d'ensemble"). This structure of the whole must play the role of final equilibrium whereas the stage itself should include both the preparation of this structure and its completion or state of equilibrium. So whereas the structural aspect insists upon distinct and natural divisions in the course of cognitive growth, the genetic aspect emphasizes continuity and thus the conventional character of any division. Faced with this dialectical opposition between the process of formation and the final form of equilibrium in Piaget's stages, child psychologists have, at first, attempted to accelerate only the process of cognitive change, because the logical superstructure of each stage seemed unnecessary or untrue to them. In a second phase, they grew interested in what could be labelled "the assimilatory speed of cognitive growth", or relationship between the initial developmental level of the child and the time that was needed for cognitive change to take place. This phase was represented by Goustard and Matalon's (1959) study, Smedslund's (1959) ensemble of research as well as Beilin's (1965) experiments. Lefebvre and Pinard (1974) have remarked that the higher the initial developmental level, the better the chances to induce cognitive change in a short time.

The question of the assimilatory speed of cognitive development was also linked with that of the role of cognitive conflict in inducing conservation. Gréco (1959) and Smedslund (1959, 1961) almost at the same time as Berlyne was publishing his book "Conflict Arousal and Curiosity" (1960) carried out the first Piagetian studies on the role of cognitive conflict in teaching conservation. They discovered that it was a very effective method and this was confirmed by Gruen in 1965. Is conflict effective because it arouses the subject or because a contradiction must be overcome for logical reasons? The question cannot be answered directly, since motivational studies are lacking. But, to the extent that motivation can be equated with knowledge of the results, the studies by Phemister (1960), Churchill (1958), Wohlwill and Lowe (1962), Gruen (1965) and Beilin (1965) show a moderate influence of getting feedback about one's own responses upon performances.

Since there was a strong verbal aspect to the explicitation of conservation, a number of authors (Bruner, 1964; Gruen, 1965; Beilin, 1965; Beilin et al., 1966; Figurelli and Keller, 1972; Siegler and Liebert, 1972) have tried to by-pass what they called the misleading perceptual cues by relying almost exclusively on the symbolic strategies illustrated mainly by language. Their results showed that this method of teaching conservation was probably the least effective when compared to frequency of practice and cognitive conflict. The mere removal of misleading perceptual cues was not effective (Bruner, 1964; Smedslund, 1961; Wohlwill and Lowe, 1962; and Wallach et al., 1967). This record of "failure" led researchers into a modification of their strategies. They started to test explicitly the stage hypothesis of intellectual development by dissociating the factors involved in conservation according to the theory itself by training separately for them: (a) reversibility (Hammel et al., 1970); (b) measurement and counting (Bearison, 1969), (c) addition/subtraction schemata (Smedslund, Beilin, Gruen) (d) multiple classification and multiple relationality (Beilin et al., 1966; Beilin and Franklin, 1962; Figurelli and Keller, 1972).

These new strategies led to limited gains only. If addition and subtraction seemed methodologically necessary for attaining conservation, counting, unit iteration, multiple classification and multiple relationality, compensation and identity training were more or less insufficient.

If we now consider the question of authenticity of the acquisitions, three basic criteria must be met: (a) temporal stability of the acquisition, (b) amount of inter-task transfer, (c) construction of more complex structure. All the studies reviewed here have investigated the question of stability over a few months. There is something paradoxical in this respect, since all these studies are short-term training studies for operations that take years to be naturally established. Hence, long-lasting effects should not be expected. Further studies are needed to meet the criterion of durability.

The amount of transfer from one task to another varies: Gréco, Wohlwill, and Wallach, Wall and Anderson reported qualified transfer from the trained task to untrained ones, whereas Wohlwill and Lowe, Gruen, Beilin, Hammel and Ricksen report no transfer at all. The matter is further complicated by the fact that Beilin and Franklin as well as Overbeck and Schwartz reported a limited amount of transfer. It seems that the degree of generalisation depends on the amount of intermediary tasks between the activated schemata and the ones to be activated by transfer. Thus that Inhelder et al. obtain more transference than their American fellow-researchers, should not come as a surprise, since their constant preoccupation was to generate a filiation of schemata by bringing the inter-task distance to a minimum. This concern should explain also why they registered progress from the first post-test to the second one; which was accounted for by reviewers of their work as due to their methodological slovenliness. Nevertheless, in spite of their use of "decalages" (lags) between for example number and length conservation, the Genevans found some limitations to the filiation of schemata, for instance between discontinuous and continuous quantities.

The question of establishing more complex structures remains unsolved, since it is difficult, in the present studies, to distinguish increasing generalization from major structural complexity. Whenever a child generalizes a response to a specific situation to similar ones, does it proceed step by step or is it the sign of emergence of a more complex structure?

If it was the emergence of a new cognitive structure, then the presence of the various lags should be reduced to a minimum. On the other hand, if it was a simple generalization by continuity of schemata, the limits of this generalization should appear almost immediately. This point remains undecided and perhaps undecidable in the studies reviewed here; which raises a basic theoretical question.

Theoretical considerations

If the main results of training studies had been the clear possibility to speed up cognitive development, it would have meant that such a development was under direct social control, with the sorry recognition that the concept of stage was meaningless. In effect, if cognitive development depended only upon social transmission or on properties of the stimuli, there would be no reason for an invariant sequence of development. The growth of knowledge would be characterized by randomness only. Knowledge would come either in toto or in a different order for every individual depending on the variety of encounters with reality.

On the other hand, if there had been no possibility whatsoever to alter the stepwise process of cognitive development, then cognitive development would have been the mere unfolding of genetic competences.

What has been observed is a natural order of acquisition with the possibility of activating the acquisition by a proper stimulation given at the proper moment and in the proper way. This could lead to a concept of cognitive development characterized by three phases: a phase of preparation; one of crisis during which the subjects are most sensitive to conflict; and one of reconstruction marked by closure upon a new logical structure. If such a conception were true, it would mean a return to a sort of cognitive neo-Darwinism in which the developmental (genetic) complex is sometimes sealed off from the environment, sometimes open to it. This form of geneticism is implausible for a number of reasons. First, an individual does not sit listless waiting for something to happen to him or her. Second, any form of behaviour is always in interaction with others. Third, this alternation of sensitivity and insensitivity to the environment relies upon a genetic (nativistic) argument concerning a hierarchy of dispositions according to which putative later forms cannot be manifested in the absence or suppression of earlier ones. Cognitive development would thence ignore the phenomenon of rupture and would boil down to a mere process of advances and delays. This is clearly not demonstrated by the facts at hand in training studies.

Another possibility would have been the emergence of a total structure at any moment during learning. Then, development would be conceived as a dynamic concept in which any new form is simply a metamorphosis of the same archetypical design, pretty much as any new sentence is a variation upon the same structurofunctional archetype in Chomsky's transformational grammar. This would be a return to a fundamentally Darwinian theory of learning with all the theoretical difficulties mentioned above. Once again, this viewpoint has not been verified experimentally.

The only tenable position seems to be a logical one showing that the passage from one form of cognitive behaviour to another is regulated by a double process of internal regulation and external argumentation. The role of external argumentation seems to be, at a theoretical level, one of separating true development from mere chronological unfolding and true development from the Spencer–Darwinian mechanical notion of the descent. In addition, external argumentation seems to play also a role in eliciting the general architecture of schemata by opposition to the accumulative model of the acquisition of schemata. Training studies seem to show that, more than a logical structure, what is important is the dynamic role played by the differences in developmental rates (décalage) of the various schemata at the child's disposal. If this were to be true, it would mean a radical modification of our conception of cognitive development, since the hallmark of a stage would not be its logical structure, but its internal architecture. The necessity of such an architecture, from a logical viewpoint would thus be always an ex post facto explanation, separating past experience (history or evolution) from genesis, giving us a process of ideal ordering of systems of thought.

Instead of being the motor of change, internal regulation is its regulator. It constantly reorganizes the different levels of development within a given individual. This reorganization aims essentially at the functional invariance of the individual by integrating novelty to old schemata and by differentiating them among themselves. So we are back to the old philosophical question of the one and the multiple as stated by Plato or that of invariance and transformation as stated by pre-Socratic philosophers. As Empodocles put it 25 centuries ago, Eros and Conflict are ingredients of all coming-into-being and passing-away.

Literature cited

Bearison, D. J. (1969) Role of measurement operations in the acquisition of conservation, *Devel. Psychol. 1*, 653–660

Beilin, H. and Franklin, I. C. (1962) Logical operations in area and length measurement: age and training effects, *Child Devel. 33*, 607–618

Beilin, H. (1965) Learning and operational convergence in logical thought development, *J. Exp. Child Psychol. 2*, 317–339

Beilin, H., Kagan, J. and Rabinowitz, R. (1966) Effects of verbal and perceptual training on water level representation, *Child Devel. 37*, 317–328

Berlyne, D. (1960) *Conflict Arousal and Curiosity*, McGraw-Hill, New York

Bingham-Newman, A. M. and Saunders, R. A. (1975) *Development of Cognitive Abilities in the Preoperational Period. A Longitudinal Comparison of Two Preschool Settings*, Paper presented at a S.R.C.D. meeting, Denver, Col.

Braine, M. D. S. and Shanks, B. L. (1965) The conservation of shape property and a proposal about the origin of conservation, *Can. J. Psychol. 19*, 197–207

Braine, M. D. S. and Shanks, B. L. (1965) The development of conservation of size, *J. Verb. Learn. Behav. 4*, 227–242

Brainerd, C. J. (1972) The age-stage issue in conservation acquisition, *Psychon. Sci. 29*, 115–117

Bruner, J. S. (1964) The course of cognitive growth, *Am. Psychol. 19*, 1–15

Bryant, P. E. (1974) *Perception and Understanding in Young Children*, pp. 126–152, Methuen, London

Chomsky, N. (1969) *La Linguistique Cartésienne*, p. 189, Seuil, Paris

Churchill, E. M. (1958) Number concepts of the young child, *Res. Stud., Univ. Leeds 17*, 43

Duckworth, E. (1964) *Piaget Rediscovered* (R. E. Ripple and V. N. Rockcastle, eds.) pp. 1–5, Cornell University Press, Ithaca, N.Y.

Figurelli, J. C. and Keller, H. R. (1972) The effects of training and socioeconomic class upon the acquisition of conservation concepts, *Child Devel. 43*, 293–298

Gelman, R. J. (1969) Conservation acquisition. A problem of learning to attend to relevant attributes, *J. Exp. Child Psychol. 9*, 167–187

Gonchar, A. J. (1975) *A Study in the Nature and Development of the Natural Number Concept: Initial and Supplementary Analyses*, Technical Report of the Wisconsin Research and Development Center of Cognitive Learning

Gréco, P. (1959) L'apprentissage dans une situation à structure opératoire concrète: les inversions successives de l'ordre linéaire par des rotations de 180°, *Etud. Épistémol. Génét. 7*, 68–182

Gruen, G. E. (1965) Experiences affecting the development of number conservation in children, *Child Devlop. 36*, 963–979

Halford, G. S. (1970) A theory of the acquisition of conservation, *Psychol. Rev. 77*, 302–316

Hamel, B. R. and Riksen, B. O. M. (1973) Identity reversibility, verbal rule instruction and conservation, *Devel. Psychol. 9*, 66–72

Inhelder, B., Sinclair, H. and Bovet, M. (1974) *Learning and the Development of Cognition*, Harvard University Press, Cambridge, Mass.

Itard, J. (1964) *Les Enfants Sauvages*, L. Malson, p. 249, Paris

Lefebvre, M. and Pinard, A. (1974) Influence du niveau initial de sensibilité au conflit sur l'apprentissage de la conservation des quantités par une méthode de conflit congnitif, *Can. J. Behav. Sci. 6*, 398–413

Lovell, K. (1965) *Second Start: Educational Implications of Piaget's Work*, BBC Broadcast, February 1965

Miller, S. A. and Lipps, L. (1973) Extinction of conservation and transitivity of weight, *J. Exp. Child Psychol. 16*, 388–402

Overbeck, C. and Schwartz, M. (1970) Training in conservation of weight, *J. Exp. Child Psychol. 9*, 253–264

Phemister, A. (1960) *An Investigation into Children's Understanding of Number on School Entry and of the Effectiveness of Infant Classroom Teaching based on Piaget's Theory*, Dissertation, Manchester University

Piaget, J. (1971) *Biology and Knowledge*, p. 384, Chicago University Press

Piaget, J. (1974) *Adaptation Vitale et Psychologie de l'Intelligence. Sélection Organique et Phénocopie*, Hermann, Paris

Roll, S. (1970) Reversibility training and stimulus desiderability as factors in conservation of number, *Child. Devel. 40*, 707–726

Siegler, R. S. and Liebert, R. M. (1972) Effects of presenting relevant rules and complete feedback on the conservation of liquid quantity task, *Devel. Psychol. 7*, 133–138

Sigel, I. E., Roeper, A. and Hooper, F. H. (1966) A training precedure for the acquisition of Piaget's conservation of quantity: a pilot study and its replication, *Br. J. Educ. Psychol. 36*, 301–311

Smedslund, J. (1959) Apprentissage des notions de la conservation et de la transitivité du poids, *Etud. Épistémol. Génét. 9*, 85–124

Smedslund, J. (1961) The acquisition of substance and weight in children, *Scand. J. Psychol. 2*, 11–210

Smedslund, J. (1963a) The effect of observation on children's representation of the spatial orientation of a water surface, *J. Genet. Psychol. 102*, 195–201

Smedslund, J. (1963b) Patterns of experience and the acquisition of the concrete transitivity of weight in 8-year-old children, *Scand. J. Psychol. 4*, 251–256

Strauss, S. (1972) Inducing cognitive development and learning: a review of short-term training experiments. 1. The organismic developmental approach, *Cognition 1*, 324–357

Toniolo, T. and Hooper, F. H. (1975) *Micro-Analyses of Logical Reasoning-Sequential Relationships. Conservation and Transitivity*, Technical Report of the Wisconsin Research and Development Center for Cognitive Learning

Waddington, C. (1961) *The Nature of Life*, Harper, New York

Wallach, L. and Sprott, R. L. (1964) Inducing number conservation in children, *Child Devel. 35*, 1057–1071

Wohlwill, J. F. (1960) A study of the development of the number concept by scalogram analysis, *J. Genet. Psychol. 97*, 345–377

Wohlwill, J. F. and Lowe, R. C. (1962) An experimental analysis of the development of the conservation of number, *Child Devel. 33*, 153–167

Subject index